DATE DUE

GAYLORD   PRINTED IN U.S.A.

love saves the day

a history of american dance music culture, 1970–1979

tim lawrence

duke university press   durham and london   2003

© 2003 Duke University Press

All rights reserved.

Printed in the United States of

America on acid-free paper ⊗

Designed by Amy Ruth Buchanan

Typeset in Scala and Helvetica by

Tseng Information Systems, Inc.

Library of Congress Cataloging-in-

Publication Data appear on the last

printed page of this book.

contents

figures

preface

It's the last day of a summer visit to Caprarola, Italy. We've been staying with Enrica's grandma—*nonna*—and in the afternoon we visit Aunt Adele and her brother, Father Pietro, who has been working as a missionary in the west African state of Burkina Faso for the last thirty years. I sit next to Pietro, and when he asks me what I do I say that I'm writing a book about seventies dance culture. To my surprise his eyes light up and he starts to talk about a new DJing software package he has purchased for his computer. I ask for a demonstration, and as we go upstairs I tell Pietro—who is *extremely* good-humored—that one of the most important clubs in New York in the early seventies was located in a church and that, according to some, DJs are the new priests. He chuckles. We sit down and Pietro opens OtsJuke DJ, which he uses to program Radio Maria. He starts to play Bob Dylan and segues from "Blowing in the Wind" into "Città Vuota" by the Italian vocalist Mina before rounding off the mix with some quick-fire scratching. He laughs out loud and so do I. Priests, it transpires, are the new DJs.

Dance music culture has gone through a remarkable resurrection during the last thirty years. At the end of the 1960s it looked like the American love affair with the French-inspired phenomenon of discotheque had died when the media started to issue obituary notices for a fad that had apparently failed to become a lifestyle. Then, at the beginning of 1970, the Loft and the Sanctuary spawned a new mode of DJing and dancing that went on to become the most distinctive cultural ritual of the decade. Following a roller-coaster ride of adulation and denunciation, club culture has since become a standard feature of the entertainment landscape. Today's dance music infrastructure of mushrooming nightclubs and self-reproducing subgenres enables top-name DJs to charge thousands of dollars for a night's work while international superstars regularly turn to dance producers and remixers for made-to-measure revitalization. Spanning the Americas, Europe, Asia, and Africa—including Burkina Faso—dance culture in its various aesthetic guises has become a global phenomenon.

Even though contemporary practices around DJing techniques, dance floor design, and music aesthetics were largely in place by the end of 1979, the "disco decade" has yet to receive any kind of sustained examination. A flurry of tongue-in-cheek books appeared at the end of the seventies—Albert Goldman's *Disco* was the best of an indifferent bunch—and after a gap of some twenty years the seemingly perpetual seventies revival has produced a handful of additional accounts. Anthony Haden-Guest's four-hundred-page account of Studio 54, *The Last Party*, is typical of this latest wave. Instead of analyzing the dance floor dynamic, Haden-Guest prefers to describe in slobbering detail the designer outfits and drug preferences of *every* celebrity to descend upon the midtown discotheque, and he becomes so absorbed in pointless anecdotes and name-dropping that he can barely stir up the enthusiasm to reference the club's principal DJ (who receives a seventeen-word mention). The book's treacherously misleading title, which suggests that party culture effectively ended with the closure of Studio 54, must also be news to those who experienced the rapturous reverberations of Body & Soul, the Funhouse, the Loft, the Paradise Garage, the Saint, Shelter, the Sound Factory, and a whole series of other venues that flourished long after Studio 54 had said its goodnights. If only Haden-Guest had bothered to jump in a cab and go downtown—which is exactly where *Love Saves the Day* both begins and ends.

At the other end of the publishing market, academic authors have struggled to even acknowledge disco's existence. Jacque Attali's compelling *Noise*, published in 1977, is typical in this respect. Arguing that the combination of specialized training, self-glorifying musicians, and capitalist reproduction was suffocating the music market of the late seventies, the philosopher-economist called for the creation of a "new" type of collective, improvised, and participatory method of making music. Yet while Attali couldn't have theorized the unfolding discotheque dynamic with any more precision, the DJ–dancer alliance did not find its way into his analysis. Timing might have been a factor: Attali, after all, was writing just a couple of years after disco culture had become visible. But such a line of reasoning would be easier to sustain were it not for the fact that Attali's oversight has since become endemic. In Richard Crawford's otherwise excellent *America's Musical Life*, for example, seventies dance music—which, like jazz, had many international influences but largely *happened* in the United States—doesn't merit a single reference in nine hundred pages. Perhaps that is because disco is more readily associated with America's musical death.

That, I must confess, was also my blinkered position before I was introduced to David Mancuso, who at the time was a familiar reference for downtown dance veterans, plus anyone who had come across two distant interviews (one in the *Village Voice* in 1975 and a second in *Collusion* in 1983). I didn't qualify on either count, but Stephan Prescott—who'd danced at the Loft between 1989 and 1992 before opening Dance Tracks in the East Village—was edging his way toward veteran status, and he set up an interview with the reclusive party host, whom I met for the first time in a neighborhood Italian restaurant in April 1997. With his big beard, scraggly hair, piercing eyes, and contented potbelly, Mancuso looked like a cross between a disheveled vagabond, a biblical prophet, and a cuddly bear, and he also talked a mystical talk, speaking excitedly in a scrambled code that I could barely follow. By the end of the meal the history of American dance music was less clear than it had ever been, but I was intrigued by his story of a forgotten underworld that ran at a twisted tangent to disco, and as I continued to meet up with better known figures such as Tony Humphries, Frankie Knuckles, and David Morales, I made a point of asking them if they had ever danced at the Loft. Time and time again they would describe Mancuso as their most important influence, a musical messiah who also happened to resemble Jesus Christ. There was clearly more to the 1970s than I—or any other author—had assumed.

I quickly pieced together an alternative web of house parties and discotheques that could be traced back to the pre-disco era of the Loft and another dance space called the Sanctuary. Yet rather than restrict myself to narrating the evolution of this culture, I decided to trace the lines of influence and interaction that might have flowed between this clandestine party network and the better known celebrity version of disco. What, if any, were the links between the Loft and Studio 54? Did the Sanctuary have anything to do with *Saturday Night Fever*? And how did downtown relate to midtown and the boroughs? As my research into the Brownian movement of airborne sound waves, freelance DJs, itinerant party hosts, mobile neighborhood populations, and reproducible vinyl records deepened, it became increasingly clear that important connections did indeed exist. Continually cutting across hallowed boundaries, this intricate interaction suggested that no meaningful distinction could be made between the mythically separate cultural terrains of the "underground" and the "mainstream," and that my topography should accordingly cover all aspects of the American nightscape.

As a result *Love Saves the Day* is something of an A to Z of seventies dance culture that begins with Abramowitz and ends with Zurawin, drawing in the balloon blowers, club owners, concession stand cooks, dancers, DJs, journalists, label executives, musicians, party hosts, producers, promoters, record shop assistants, remixers, song writers, sound engineers, and vocalists who lie in-between. Their actions are organized not as a dictionary of disco but as an integrated, chronological *audio*biography in which the three pillars of dance music—the venues, the DJs, and the music—are analyzed simultaneously rather than separately within the context of broader economic and social trends. As such this is the first book to be singularly dedicated to the analysis of the most significant, yet least understood, decade in contemporary dance music culture.

Whether it makes sense to try and put all of this into words is another matter. As Jim Feldman, reporting from the dance floor of the Paradise Garage, noted, "Sociological analysis is irrelevant in the face of the obvious: we like to wiggle and bump."[1] Hopefully there won't be too much sociology in what follows, although a little thought-provoking history might appeal to those who weren't there at the time—or to those who were there but still want to place their experience within the broader milieu of the decade. While reading will never be as much fun as wiggling and bumping, it might evoke some fond memories and even instigate some future moves.

Some readers might take a while to get fully warmed up: the chronological history that follows is told at a rate of approximately a year per chapter. All interviews were conducted, unless otherwise footnoted, by myself. The bibliography includes book, film, and journal references; newspaper and magazine citations appear only in the endnotes. For those who are more interested in listening to Harold Melvin & the Blue Notes than in scanning the endnotes, a discography at the back of the book lists all records that are directly referred to in the narrative. That discography also includes additional information on another set of shorter select discographies that are woven into the narrative and catalogue the contemporaneous preferences of various DJS.

acknowledgments

As a Londoner writing about an American decade that began when I was three years old, I inevitably have many people to thank. What is less inevitable is that I should want to thank them for their extraordinary generosity, dedication, perseverance, energy, and even friendship. It would have been easy for the protagonists of this book to block my path, but they didn't. "Even though you weren't around at the time," David Mancuso generously told me, "you seem to be a guide." While "courier" might be a better description, I nevertheless became a conduit for impassioned testimonies of a forgotten past, and I cherished this research process to the extent that I refused to let go of it until the very last day of writing. I hope the conversations will continue.

The archival research that underpins *Love Saves the Day* was very much a collective effort. François Kevorkian took the time to photocopy his pristine set of *Mixmaster* newsletters; Bob Casey allowed me to borrow his cherished *Melting Pot* magazines; and Charlie Grappone dug out several issues of *Vinyl Maniac*. Vince Aletti, Michael Cappello, Kenny Carpenter, Ken Cayre, Jim Feldman, Michael Fesco, Michael Gomes, Jellybean, Laura at the *New York Post*, David Mancuso, Jackie McCloy, Alex Rosner, Nicky Siano and Tim Watson supplied me with an assortment of cuttings, documents, and flyers. The British Library, the Lincoln Center Library, and the New York Public Library provided access to crucial collections of newspapers and magazines, and the librarians at Columbia University, Sussex University, and the University of East London were unswerving in their assistance and patience.

I was also fortunate enough to be introduced to a series of recordings that are so vivid they evoke a dance floor I never experienced. Steve

D'Acquisto and David Mancuso put together a wonderful compilation of personal favorites during a long and lazy afternoon at D'Acquisto's Brooklyn apartment. François Kevorkian recreated a mini-set of Galaxy 21 classics in the early hours of a weekday morning just before one of our red-eye interviews was about to begin. Nicky Siano had the wherewithal to record a number of live sessions at the Gallery, and these tapes offer scintillating shafts of sound from a still murky period. Jim Feldman kindly passed on a series of outrageously expressive recordings from the Paradise Garage that joyfully bear no resemblance to the plastic professionalism of the contemporary market in mix CDS. Stephan Prescott at Dance Tracks on East Third Street and Charlie Grappone at Vinyl Mania on Carmine Street picked out more classics than I thought I could afford.

As for visual evidence, almost no photos were taken on the dance floors of the downtown party network: these were private spaces and cameras were rightly regarded as an unwanted intrusion. I have eked out what is available and am grateful to Vince Aletti, Richard Brezner, Kenny Carpenter, Bob Casey, Steve D'Acquisto, David DePino, Michael Fesco, Michael Gomes, Francis Grasso, François Kevorkian, Jorge La Torre, Joey Llanos, David Mancuso, Tom Moulton, Alex Rosner, and Nicky Siano for supplying material from their private collections. Thanks, also, to Andy Reynolds at West End Records for sending me copies of Nick Baratta's photos from the Paradise Garage, Nick Baratta for allowing me to use them, Stephen Koch at the Peter Hujar Archive for providing me a print of Peter Hujar's photo of David Mancuso, Gordon Munro for giving me permission to use the photos he shot for the launch of Studio 54's brand of jeans, and Eric Weisbard at the Experience Music Project for facilitating the use of the Double Exposure, Trammps, and Barry White photos, as well as the Studio 54 jeans ads. Finally I would like to thank Waring Abbott, whose collection of photos from the seventies is as precious as it is unrivalled.

Interviewing the protagonists of seventies dance culture has been far and away the most important and fulfilling aspect of my research. I ended up completing some three hundred interviews for the book—plus an uncivilized number of e-mail conversations—returning to key players time and time again in an attempt to deepen my understanding, iron out discrepancies, and decipher precise dates. Thank you, then, Vince Aletti, Arthur Baker, John "Jellybean" Benitez, Bruce Berger, Miles Berger, Richard Brezner, Jane Brinton, Jocelyn Brown, Archie Burnett, Nathan Bush, Michael Cappello, Kenny Carpenter, Joey Carvello, Paul Casella,

Bob Casey, Pete Castagne, Ken Cayre, Denise Chapman, Mel Cheren, Brian Chin, Sybil Christopher, Ronald Colez, Alec Costandinos, Frank Crapanzano, Frankie Crocker, Steve D'Acquisto, Carmen D'Alessio, Nick De Krechewo, David DePino, Frederick Dunson, Allan Felder, Jim Feldman, Michael Fesco, Rochelle Fleming, Maria Garbin, Michael Gomes, Charlie Grappone, Francis Grasso, Penny Grill, André Halmon, Alan Harris, Lisa Hazel, Kevin Hedge, Loleatta Holloway, Tony Humphries, François Kevorkian, Frankie Knuckles, Danny Krivit, Jorge La Torre, Manny Lehman, Robbie Leslie, Joey Llanos, Bert Lockett, Robin Lord, David Mancuso, Scott Mandell, Jackie McCloy, Vince Montana, David Morales, Giorgio Moroder, Tom Moulton, Terry Noël, Steve Ostrow, Vince Pellegrino, Danny Pucciarelli, Mark Riley, Ralphie Rosario, Alex Rosner, Judy Russell, Jessie Saunders, Marvin Schlachter, Robin Sciortino, Screamin' Rachel, Bobby Shaw, Nicky Siano, Bunny Sigler, Scott Smokin' Silz, Byron Stingily, Mike Stone, Diane Strafaci, Freddy Taylor, Danny Tenaglia, David Todd, Hippie Torales, Curtis Urbina, Judy Weinstein, Bret Wilcox, Robert Williams, and Earl Young. Your time and energy has made this project possible.

I would also like to thank—and apologize to—a number of interviewees who ultimately don't appear in this book, including Armando, Juan Atkins, Maurice Bernstein, Gail Bruesewitz, Joaquin "Joe" Claussell, Jemal Countess, John Davis, Nick Ditomasso, Leslie Doyle, Chip E., Mark Finkelstein, Bruce Forest, Kenny "Dope" Gonzalez, Paris Grey, Larry Heard, Steve "Silk" Hurley, Hisa Ishioka, Marshall Jefferson, Ian Levine, Lil' Louis, Shep Pettibone, DJ Pierre, Gladys Pizarro, Jamie Principle, Kevin Saunderson, Larry Sherman, Spanky, Elyse Stefanishin, Todd Terry, Ron Trent, Curtis Urbina, Junior Vasquez, "Little" Louie Vega, Donna Ward, and Charles Williams. *Love Saves the Day* was originally going to run from 1970–2000 but ended up surging past any kind of reasonable word limit by 1980. Your stories will be told in the sequel.

Love Saves the Day began life as a book proposal and subsequently disguised itself as a doctorate before it returned to its original status. Through this tangled journey I have benefited from the generous funding of the British Academy as well as the advice, encouragement, and insights of several academics. John Archer told me that it was legitimate to write about dance music in the first place, even in the Department of English at Columbia University. Rob Nixon hatched the idea of writing a "quick book" on dance culture. Edward Said served as a constant reminder that academia is at its most compelling when it looks outward rather than inward. Geoffrey Hempstead had the good sense to encourage me to drop my original doctoral project and replace it with my research on dance culture. Alan Sinfield, who took over from Geoffrey after my first year at Sussex, was a model supervisor. Simon Frith and Andy Medhurst helped me over the final hurdle and supplied me with important insights.

I am also grateful to: Enrica Balestra, Jeremy Gilbert, Charlie Kronengold, and Helen Lane for reading an earlier draft of the manuscript and delivering such incisive suggestions; David Mancuso for the title; Stephan Prescott for the early contacts; Quinton Scott for the late contacts; Brian Chin, Phil Hudson, and Charlie Kronengold for the discographical assistance; Barry Walters for the comments on the dance-rock continuum; Pete Ardkawah at BBE and David Hill at Nuphonic for the music and the commissions; Eric Weisbard at the Experience Music Project for the collaborative crossover; Jane Lerner for the magazines; Will Stern for the technical assistance; Lorenzo and Sara Mengarelli, Adele Cristofari, and Father Pietro Ruzzi for the emergency Internet service; Simon Frith, Alan Sinfield, and Eric Weisbard for the funding assists; Elliott Trice, Tim Watson, and the staff at the University of East London for the ongoing conversations; Lorraine Williams for the loans; Michael Gomes for the excellent meals and for telling me I was "the historian"; the Rhythm Doctor, Evil Olive, Femi B, and Rob Acteson for the unforgettable Feel Real parties at the Gardening Club; Louie Vega for enticing me to move to Manhattan; Joe Claussell, François Kevorkian, Danny Krivit, and David Mancuso for keeping the spirit alive during my final years in New York; Mark Raphael for the late nights; Elliott Trice and Shaun Fletcher for the hospitality and friendship; Jonny Zucker for always asking; Stephen Pevner for the advice; Jim Shapiro for the ongoing guidance; Paul Glantz, Nick Lansman, Robert Lobatto, and Jonny Zucker for brotherhood; and Tessa Lawrence, Helen and David Lane, Rita Balestra, Elide Ruzzi, and Elsa and Giorgio Baron for the emotional and gastronomic sustenance.

At the risk of repeating certain names, I would like to acknowledge Richard Brezner, Bob Casey, Steve D'Acquisto, David DePino, Michael Gomes, François Kevorkian, Jorge La Torre, David Mancuso, and Nicky Siano, whose dedication to this project has been quite remarkable. Many thanks, also, to writers Vince Aletti, Brian Chin, and Michael Gomes, who were there at the time and knew so much more about this culture than I did when I started: your cooperation has been as magnanimous as it has been unexpected. I am also grateful to Leigh Anne Couch, Amy Ruth Buchanan, Christine Dahlin, Patty Van Norman, and the rest of the team at Duke University Press for coordinating the production process with such precision and patience. Finally, I would like to extend a special thanks to my editor, Ken Wissoker, who persuaded me to combine a passion for dance music with the rigors of historical scholarship. Your guidance throughout the six years it has taken to complete *Love Saves the Day* has been exemplary.

This book is written in memory of John Addison, Phil Alexion, Ronnie Baker, Neil Bogart, Joey Bonfiglio, Michael Brody, David Bruie, Jim Burgess, Patrick Cowley, Robert DeSilva, Angelo Di Giuseppe, Bernard Edwards, Jonathan Fearing, Cameron Flowers, Kenn Friedman, Armando Galvez, Noel Garcia, Walter Gibbons, Bobby Guttadaro, James Hamilton, Ron Hardy, Norman Harris, Dan Hartman, Jim Jessup, Richie Kaczor, Larry Levan, Richard Long, Bruce Mailman, Van McCoy, Jacques Morali, Al Murphy, Larry Patterson, Sharon Redd, Eddie Rivera, Richie Rivera, David Rodriguez, Jose Rodriguez, Steve Rubell, Arthur Russell, Tee Scott, Marc Paul Simon, Tony Smith, David Sokoloff, Jimmy Stuard, Sylvester, Roy Thode, Barry White, Ray Yeates, and Karen Young, as well as David Cole and Patrick Jenkins, all of whom are now dancing in a different dimension. It was also a huge blow to learn that Steve D'Acquisto, Allan Felder, and Francis Grasso—influential music makers and enthusiastic interviewees—all passed away during the writing of the book. *Love Saves the Day* is dedicated to my parents, who heartbreakingly aren't around anymore. It is also written for Enrica and Carlotta, who make it all worthwhile. Where I would be without you, I really don't know.

introduction

A couple of hundred revelers make their way toward 674 Broadway, situated just north of Houston. The district is deserted—manufacturers have either closed down or moved out of Manhattan—and its cobbled streets and unlit buildings resemble an abandoned film set. But something is going on outside number 674, and by midnight partygoers have begun to form a queue in front of the imposing warehouse. They are greeted at the entrance to the building and asked to show their invitation, after which they make their way up the stairwell to the first floor landing where another person checks off their name. Then they climb to the second floor and make a two-dollar contribution. Finally they enter the Loft.

The interior—an ex-industrial shell that somehow manages to be both expansive and intimate at the same time—is just as striking as the exterior. There doesn't appear to be a bedroom or a bathroom, and the open plan living area is decorated with hundreds of multicolored balloons that hang from the ceiling, float in midair, and bounce along the timber floor. A yoga shrine runs along one of the walls, a sumptuous buffet of juice, fruit, and nuts along another, and a huge mirror ball is suspended from the center of the ceiling. The rest of the room is empty. Nobody lives like this. Not even New Yorkers. Or at least they didn't until now.

Gentle music drifts out of two sets of Klipschorn speakers, filling the room with possibility, and as the guests acclimatize to their new surroundings bodies begin to sway, arms start to stretch, legs limber up, and feet unconsciously flicker. Note by note, beat by beat, the music becomes more intense and rhythmic until everyone and everything is drawn into a dizzying display of movement. The source of the music, however, remains a mystery: party host David Mancuso is placing records on his AR turntables but his inspiration comes from the dancers, who in turn are inspired by the music. The messages are untraceably complex—no physicist could hope to calculate the unfolding relations of energy, force, and motion—but the communication is unmistakable. This is a new situation, and it will soon become the incubator for the most influential network of club owners and DJs of the 1970s and 1980s.

* * *

Seven years later, in 1977, a different kind of venue opens in a different part of town. Named after its location, Studio 54 is situated at 254 West Fifty-fourth Street in the heart of the Broadway theater district. The entrance door is easy to detect thanks to the fact that several hundred patrons are trying—and for the most part failing—to get in. Celebrities, it transpires, are a crucial part of the unfolding scene. Scores of them have been invited, and an impressive number show up. The chaos is so intense, though, that many—including, reportedly, Frank Sinatra—don't even bother to get out of their limos. Presiding over the pandemonium is Steve Rubell who, along with his partner, Ian Schrager, is the owner of the new discotheque. By all accounts he is rather happy with himself.

Inside the venue, dancers could be forgiven for wondering what they have walked into. Studio 54, after all, is situated in an old theater, and it appears to have more in common with a Broadway show than a discotheque. The impression is fairly accurate. Carmen D'Alessio, ex-PR chief for Valentino and the creative brain behind the Studio concept, wanted to combine stage and dance floor in order to create a revolving multimedia set that functions around the clock, and she employed a phonebook's worth of Broadway luminaries to install the interior decor and lighting, instructing them to create the maximum dramatic effect. The resulting combination of panache and pyrotechnics is both exciting and disorienting.

The dancers dance, although to a broken rhythm. There is so much to look at that the aural experience is strangely muted. Richie Kaczor, one of the best DJs on the circuit, is in charge of the wheels of steel, but few know who he is and even fewer want to find out. There are, finally, far more important things for Studio's clientele to focus on, like the celebrity who may or may not be dancing in their vicinity, or the possibility that somebody will think that *they* are a celebrity, or that Studio will somehow provide them with the big break they have been waiting for. A substantial media presence intensifies the atmosphere: film crews record the spectacle and photographers capture snapshots of glamour in action. Whatever their status, dancers believe they are participating in a new form of democracy with the flashing lights, rather than the ballot box or the street protest, the key to equality. Like the Loft, this is a novel situation, and it will be seen by many to represent the wondrous peak of the disco boom.

* * *

These contrasting scenes are drawn from two of the most influential venues of the decade. One is low-key and secretive, while the other is brazen and publicity-hungry. One embodies downtown, while the other symbolizes midtown. One is focused on the DJ and the dance, while the other is more interested in flashing lights and spectacular sets. The two parties appear to have nothing to do with each other: they come from different traditions and espouse different ideals. Indeed they could even be described as antagonists, battling over the way in which America should dance.

Yet a number of unexpected connections exist between the Loft and Studio 54. The sound system at Studio 54, for example, has been installed by a close acquaintance of David Mancuso. Nicky Siano, one of the two DJs employed by Studio, used to be a Loft regular. Carmen D'Alessio also used to be a Loft head, and she even briefly attempts to introduce a Loft-style invitation system at the new location. And while the owners of Studio haven't actually visited the Loft, one of them—Steve Rubell—has been nabbing ideas from a number of Loft offshoots. These parties clearly have more in common than meets the eye—or the ear.

Love Saves the Day—the coded name of David Mancuso's inaugural Valentine's Day party—tells the story of both the Loft and Studio 54. In the first instance it describes these parties as separate phenomena. One, after all, was the linchpin of the New York underground while the other became the focal point of excessive midtown hedonism. Yet *Love Saves the Day* also explores the connections that existed between these two parties, joining up the dots in order to reveal the way in which dance culture evolved from the reclusive model of the Loft to the extroverted paradigm of Studio 54, as well as the way in which these venues became crucial nodal points on the much wider continuum of "nightworld."

That continuum didn't begin and end in Manhattan but also extended to an assortment of urban centers and suburban satellites that both followed and fed back into dance music's metropolitan hub. Wherever they were located, venues almost invariably attracted and then lost their core crowds, sometimes because a favorite DJ moved on, sometimes because a group of gatecrashers spoiled the party, sometimes because a better alternative opened up in another part of town, and sometimes because city governments decided that enough was enough. These authorities acted according to a series of Byzantine edicts that encompassed questions of alcohol consumption, entrance policies, fire exits, building use, opening hours, noise levels, and sexual preferences, although they were eventually forced to concede that they had only limited control over one particular variety of the private party species. Owners, for their part, had to not only deal with these restless regulators but also keep their eye on what appeared to be a continually expanding sector. Amidst the clamor, some got to have an occasional dance, which helped them remember, fleetingly, why they had entered "clubland" in the first place. Others, though, were more interested in the twists and turns of the discotheque market than anything that could be witnessed on the dance floor, and they ended up paying a different price for their profit-driven passion.

Operating at the vulnerable nexus of this network of dancers and moguls, DJs became the key conduits of dance culture in the 1970s thanks to their ability to pick out hot records, create fresh taste patterns, develop new turntable techniques, and compel people to dance. Their favorite slabs of vinyl carried the spiral grooves of one-hit wonders, anonymous producers, electric remixers, fiery divas, and pop sensations. Some of these music makers worked for independent labels while others were tied to major labels. All, one way or another, operated within a market that originally revolved around dinky forty-fives and ended up worshipping at the altar of the twelve-inch single. In between times, the early chaos of "party music" was displaced by the more obviously marketable terminology of "disco," although all sorts of protagonists had all sorts of problems with this highly politicized genre. Initially indifferent, the media — a complex network of fanzines, magazines, newspapers, radio stations, television channels, and film companies — became exaggeratedly enthusiastic about the disco phenomenon until events conspired to rock and then sink their favorite boat. These and other stories lie at the pulsing heart of this particular journey through the nightscape of the 1970s.

1. beginnings

David Mancuso was born into an unhappy family on 20 October 1944. Ten days later he was whisked away and placed into a children's home in Utica where a nun called Sister Alicia looked after him. Mancuso's memory of the period is hazy, but he recalls one aspect of the orphanage with absolute clarity—Sister Alicia's party room. "It had balloons, crepe paper, a refrigerator, a piano, and a record player with records lying on top," he says. "We would wear party hats and play games around these little tables." Sister Alicia organized a party at every opportunity. "We were kids and we were bubbling with energy so she would get us together and have these parties. She gave parties as often as possible. I wouldn't be surprised if it was every day, or at least every Saturday night."

The orphanage was an unorthodox experiment in social engineering. With twenty children from a variety of social backgrounds cast together under one roof, their original parents a fading memory, domestic life assumed some unusual patterns. The steady flow of arrivals and departures meant that the combination of brothers and sisters changed continuously, and as a result the children grew up with a perception of families as extended, diverse, and precarious rather than nuclear, homogeneous, and stable. "It was a different head," says Mancuso, "another plateau." Bedtime was especially unusual. "What must it have been like at night to get twenty of us to sleep? The crying and the laughing and the noises that we made in that room must have been very interesting, very *tribal*."

Mancuso returned to live with his mother when he was five years old but remained a "runaway from home" and at the age of fourteen went to reform school. "The dormitory where we slept was this old wood building, and the acoustics were incredible," says Mancuso. "The night supervisor

David Mancuso in the orphanage with Sister Alicia in the background. Courtesy of David Mancuso

was a little man, real cool, and he would sit there and listen to WKBW all night. The room was very ambient, and I'd just lie in bed and listen to the radio fading in and fading out. Nobody complained. We were just happy that the supervisor liked R&B." At the age of fifteen Mancuso returned to his family home, although he didn't stay long. "My mother had a lot of problems with the person she was married to so they allowed me to move out. I went to live in a room for $7.50 a week. I got a little financial assistance from the state, which paid for my room and two meals a day, and I earned some extra money by shining shoes." Mancuso quit high school the day he turned sixteen, got a job washing dishes, saved some money, and then traveled to Manhattan for the first time on Labor Day 1962. He returned a month later and rented an apartment on the Upper West Side, embarking on a career that encompassed fast food (sandwich preparation in a Grand Central Station kiosk), Holt, Rinehart and Winston publishers (typist and then head of the Xerox department), Restaurant Associates (personnel manager), and finally freelance antiques (the office routine having become too tedious).

It was during this period that Jimmy Miller, a friend from Brooklyn Heights, introduced Mancuso to the possibilities of "really good" sound reproduction. "He invited me into his living room and there was this beautiful music, but I couldn't see any equipment. I asked him where the sound was coming from and he pointed toward his windows. I said, '*What the hell have you got behind those curtains?*' He drew them back and I saw my first-ever Klipschorns. I said, 'Wow!' I'd never heard anything like it." A fortnight later, Miller told Mancuso that an audio hobbyist called Richard Long was selling two of the speakers. "Richard was working for GE in New Jersey, and he looked like someone who would work for GE. He was replacing his Klipschorns with Bose speakers so I bought his Klipschorns from him. He was a hi-fi guy, and I decided to stay in touch with him. It was a hobby for him, and it was a hobby for me."

Aural inspiration didn't descend only from Brooklyn Heights. In the mid-sixties Mancuso traveled to Trinidad, and, when his stay at the Hilton was "discontinued" after he invited some locals to hang out in the hotel, he went to visit a friend of a friend, who took him on a trek. "We were walking through these really thick woods and all of a sudden I heard this music," says Mancuso. "We came into this opening and there was this steel band practicing for the carnival. It was the first time I had heard this kind of music, and it completely blew my mind. The rhythm was awesome." The experience was a formative one. "It was like being in a jungle and coming across a tribe having their own little party and making music. It was a real rough form of musicianship—very resourceful and very pure.

David Mancuso and friends praying by their bedsides. Courtesy of David Mancuso

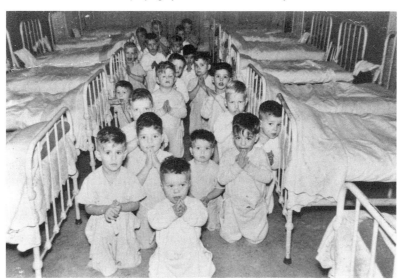

Remember, I had come from Utica to New York and didn't know too much about anything, so this was like discovering Utopia."

Mancuso returned to New York and continued the festivities. "I would go to the Village, I would go to Harlem, I would go to Staten Island, I would go to wherever I heard there was a party going on. I've always had all sorts of friends, which probably has something to do with growing up in the orphanage." Mancuso's favorite form of entertainment was the rent party—a central feature of black nightlife ever since one million African Americans migrated to northern industrial centers between 1900 and 1920 only to face exorbitant housing costs set by greedy absentee landlords. "I used to go to bars that were open to the public, but I preferred rent parties because they were a little more intimate and you would be among your friends. I wanted to get to know people and develop relationships. I wasn't so much into the transient side of things."

Not that the club scene was exactly flourishing, the Peppermint Lounge, home of the Twist craze, having closed in 1966. Nor were the clubs that remained particularly accessible, with Le Club, Le Directoire, L'Interdit, and Il Mio Club unblushingly marketing themselves as chic and sophisticated Parisian nightclubs that enforced elitist door policies. True, Arthur offered some sort of respite, touting itself as a democratic alternative to these phony French funhouses, but entry was restricted to young professional straight couples, and the discotheque's dress code was finally too formal for anyone to build up a serious sweat. Max's Kansas City, a restaurant-discotheque on Union Square, provided live music interspersed with the selections of DJ Claude Purvis and was significantly less conservative, but dancing didn't drive the space.

When it came to public venues, Mancuso preferred to go to the Electric Circus, which opened in June 1967, and the Fillmore East, which opened in the spring of 1968. Both of these psychedelic haunts were situated in the East Village—the Electric Circus was located in an old Polish working-man's club on St. Mark's Place, the Fillmore East, in the words of the *New York Times*, on "freaky Second Avenue"—and both hosted live entertainment.[1] "I went to the Electric Circus at least once a month," says Mancuso. "Everybody was having fun, and they had good sound in there. It was very mixed, very integrated, very intense, very free, very positive." The Fillmore East showcased some of his favorite artists. "I heard Nina Simone perform there. I went with my friend Larry Patterson. The Fillmore East would often be noisy but that night everybody was very focused. She was wonderful."

Mancuso didn't go to the Fillmore East just to listen to music. "That's where I also first heard Timothy Leary. He gave a series of lectures backed by the Joshua Light Show." The ex-Harvard academic was already an important figure for Mancuso, who had first taken Sandoz when he was twenty and the drug was still legal. An early trip coincided with a snowstorm ("each flake was like a universe"), and ten tabs later he came across Leary's *The Psychedelic Experience Based on the Tibetan Book of the Dead*, which argues that psychedelics can provide a shortcut to enlightenment. "The book blew me away. It became my bible and I started getting involved with him." The young acolyte met the acid guru at his LSD (League for Spiritual Discovery) headquarters in the West Village, went to his Technicolor lectures, and became a regular at his private parties. "People were tripping but the parties were more social than serious. There was food and music. I knew we were on a journey."

Mancuso's personal voyage took a vital turn in 1965 when he moved into 647 Broadway, just north of Houston, and started to pay a monthly rent of $175. Like SoHo, NoHo (as the north of Houston area was nicknamed) had historically functioned as a manufacturing district, drawing on New York's immigrant population as its low-wage workforce, and, when industry relocated to the cheaper terrain of New Jersey and beyond, New York's artists moved in, delighted to exchange their cramped Upper East Side apartments for a range of stunningly expansive lofts. The influx triggered a sophisticated experiment into the relationship between art, space, and living that might have seemed to exclude the likes of Utica-born Mancuso. Nevertheless, he quickly established himself as a key player within this creative population, intent as he was on reintroducing *art* back into the *party*. "Everyone loved my space," says Mancuso. "There might have been a hundred people living like this so it was very new. A lot of people would just come and hang out there. There were all sorts of activities going on."

Some of the activities were influenced by Leary. "I would organize these intimate gatherings where we would experiment with acid," says Mancuso. "There were never more than five of us when we did this. One person would take nothing, another would take half a tab, and the rest would take a whole tab. It was all very new, and we took it very seriously.

We used *The Psychedelic Experience* as our guide." Leary also had a bearing on the decoration of the loft space. "I built a yoga shrine, which I used for yoga and tripping. In the beginning it was three feet by five feet, and it eventually grew to fifteen feet by thirty feet. As you walked into the loft you were immediately drawn to this area. It was gorgeous." Music—which, like LSD, can function as a therapeutic potion that "deprograms" the mind before opening up a mystical trail to spiritual transcendence—was also introduced into the equation. "Leary played music at his lectures and parties, and I went in the same direction. I bought a Tandberg tape recorder so that I could play tapes. The Buddha was always positioned between my two speakers." That was the perfect position from which to hear the homemade compilations, which drew on a diverse range of sources and were structured to complement the hallucinogenic experience. "I made these journey tapes that would last for five hours. They drew on everything from classical music to the Moody Blues. They would start off very peacefully, and the reentry would be more about movement, more jazz-oriented. Somebody might get up and start dancing around the room at some point, although they weren't dance sessions."

The dancing became more sustained when Mancuso started to hold "mixed-media" parties in which different activities would go on in different parts of his loft at the same time, and when the boogying intensified the host decided to reorganize his space in order to maximize the dance floor. "At the end of 1966, I decided to throw a really big dance party," he says. "I took down this three-foot wall to open up the main part of the loft, and I rearranged the shrine. The Buddha stayed in the same place but the rest of it became more wall-based. In the end the dance area measured nineteen feet by forty-three feet." Having already added a McIntosh amplifier and an AR turntable to his system, Mancuso now went out and bought a couple of Cornwalls (Klipschorns that could fit into the corner of a wall) especially for the dance fest. "The sound was very intense. It was the best thing out there for dancing. My whole space was configured for the party." Invitations were sent out, about a hundred revelers showed up, and the dancing ran from around ten until two. "My tapes followed the same geography as before, but this time the trip was different. They started off slow but then progressed into something that was more dance-oriented than psychedelic. The purpose of the party was hardcore dancing."

The bimonthly bashes came to an abrupt halt when Mancuso gave away his stereo, stopped throwing parties, and went on an inward journey at the beginning of 1969. "I wanted to find myself so I gave up all material possessions. I went on a monk trip." In an attempt to peel away the various layers that had come to make up his personality, Mancuso quit drugs, smoking, and cooked food. Having disposed of his money, the ascetic started to shoplift his minimal diet from the local grocery store, and as part of his protest against the world of property he took his apartment door off its hinges (when Mancuso returned one night to discover a homeless person on the sofa he just "went with the flow"). As the journey into essence intensified he stopped wearing clothes in the home that was no longer his own, passing the day in various states of yogic meditation. "I kept asking myself, 'Who am I?' I wanted to see where this journey was going to take me."

The next stop was a psychiatric ward in Bellevue Hospital, visiting doctors having determined that Mancuso was catatonic—in a state of inertia or apparent stupor often associated with schizophrenia and characterized by purposeless excitement and abnormal posturing. The treatment got off to a slow start: when a doctor asked the new arrival his name he said nothing, unable to confirm that he *was* David Mancuso, and at medicine time he would slip his pills under his tongue and spit them out in the bathroom in order to maintain his strict drug-free diet. For the rest of the day the silent and now bearded patient was happy to take up the lotus position in the TV room and watch the world drift by on the flickering screen, and this routine only came to an end when a nurse uncovered his tongue ruse and forced him to swallow twenty-five milligrams of Thorazine. "I went to bed and stayed there. I felt like I was lying at the bottom of the ocean. It was then that something finally snapped, and I told myself that this was not where I wanted to go."

Having side-stepped the various day trips organized by the hospital, Mancuso went on the next outing and, when an opportunity presented itself, slipped away and headed to St. Mark's Place, where he stayed with a close friend called Haryuro and reflected on his experience. "During this whole episode I knew exactly what I *didn't* want to do," he says. "I could have pulled back at any moment, but I waited for as long as I could because I thought that something would present itself. When they took me to the hospital I wasn't worried because I thought it could be the key."

Progressive and experimental as it might have been, downtown New York wasn't ready for Mancuso. "The problem was that I tried to shed my ego in the center of the capitalistic world where any kind of deviation looks weird. If I had gone to a monastery in the mountains they would have welcomed me with open arms. They would have considered me to be *normal.*"

It was during his stay with Haryuro that Mancuso learned that another friend, anticipating his return to the corporeal world, had sold the key to his abandoned loft for $1,800. The cash enabled the otherwise penniless escapee to buy back his beloved apartment and, drawn to the idea of dancing his way out of debt, he retrieved his sound system and decided to start holding regular rent parties. In keeping with the dissident philosophy of the era, the NoHo resident invited Long (general collaborator) and Purvis (featured DJ) to participate in a special organizing collective that was dubbed Coalition, and the two of them agreed, confident that the Broadway gatherings would take off. After all, regular rent parties relied on a common console and were normally held in cramped apartments, whereas the Coalition evenings were going to be built around a high quality sound system and a spacious loft in which the bedroom and kitchen were conveniently hidden from view (the landlord having ensured that a visiting inspector wouldn't be able to see that the industrial property was being illegally put to residential use). Yet the parties failed to generate any momentum—in part because Purvis didn't adapt his DJing style to the Broadway venue, which required a different rhythm than the one that motored the bar scene at Max's Kansas City—and, faced with dwindling numbers, Long and Purvis joined forces and voted to start selling alcohol in order to convert Coalition into a full-fledged after-hours venue. Mancuso, however, vehemently opposed the plan on the grounds that he would be the one who went to prison in the event of a police raid, and, unwilling to accept that his partners should finally be able to decide what went on in his own home, he disbanded the collective, which "was a little too idealistic from the business point of view."

With Valentine's Day approaching, the irrepressible reveler decided to rekindle the intimacy that had attracted him to the rent party scene in the first place. Out went the open-house policy and in came the time-honored method of individual homemade invitations, which Mancuso embellished with Salvador Dali's "The Persistence of Memory" and the words *Love Saves the Day* (you didn't need to be an army intelligence officer to spot the reference to acid). The personalized invites worked out perfectly, with about a hundred people turning up, and as the party slipped into gear Mancuso's only regret was that he might not be able to speak to his guests, given that he had reluctantly decided to take control of the music. "No way did I want to be a disc jockey," he says. "I only did it because I used to hang out with these people all the time so I knew what kind of music we liked." However, as the dance floor began to respond to his selections Mancuso realized that he could communicate with his guests after all—through music—and as his apartment started to steam up he ripped off his t-shirt, abandoning himself to the psychic stream of the party. "We were on the same wavelength," he says.

In Mancuso's terms, a "third ear"—the aural equivalent of the all-seeing "third eye"—had started to beat, directing the path of both the music selector and the crowd according to sonic trajectories that had acquired a supernatural momentum. "There was neither the DJ nor the dancer. Someone would approach me to play a record and I would already have it in my hand or it would already be on the turntable. We would look at each other in recognition. It got very psychic because we knew we were following a sonic trail." The path manifested itself with a bewildering kinetic energy. "When a plane takes off there's a moment when the pilot decides that the speed is right, he pulls back and—boom!—you leave the ground. The party was like that. There was a point at which it just went up. It didn't happen right away. It took time. But it happened." The experience was enlightening. "*Om* is the source of all sound—it's a Buddhist chant where voices gel together and vibrate—and I felt as though we had returned h-*om*-e. It was very childlike, very peaceful, very liberating. It seemed to be correct. It reflected what I thought the world was supposed to be about. Everybody was there and we were like a family. There didn't seem to be any conflicts. Music helped us reach that place. Music was the key to get back h-*om*-e." The musical journey had begun.

* * *

In an uncanny act of synchronicity, a discotheque on West Forty-third Street called the Sanctuary matched the evolution of the Broadway parties beat for beat, opening as a straight venue around the time that Mancuso initiated his ill-fated Coalition nights before reinventing itself as Manhattan's first explicitly gay-run discotheque within a week or two of the foundational Love Saves the Day party. Yet, while the life cycles of the two dance venues were perfectly coordinated, they descended from contrasting families, for whereas the Loft emerged from the long lineage of rent parties, the Sanctuary came out of the relatively recent phenomenon of the discotheque.

A French invention, the discotheque was imported to New York when Oliver Coquelin opened a members-only venue called Le Club on New Year's Eve 1962. By February 1965 the *New York Times* was declaring that the city's fifteen discotheques—or discothèques, as the word was still being written—constituted a "trend." "The common denominator of the discothèque is darkness, a small dance floor and the beat," noted the *Times*. "After that, they vary from the propriety of L'Interdit, a private club in the Gotham Hotel, to Shepheard's, correct down to the wine steward in red vest and chain, to the fairly new Discothèque-au-Go-Go, at 44 West 56th Street, which plays frug music only, has waitresses with low necklines and slit skirts, and scantily clad dance demonstrators behind glass." Whatever the venue, the figure of the DJ—who had been no more than an afterthought when Coquelin opened Le Club and hired his bandleader's African American butler, Slim Hyatt, to put on the records at the very last minute—was becoming increasingly central, with Hyatt himself now "one of the most revered names" on the circuit. "From a closetlike room with three turntables, Mr. Hyatt views the dance floor through a pillbox slit," added the *Times*. "It is his function, and experts agree that it is a vital one, to gauge the mood of the dancers and, by his selection of the disks, to keep them dancing."[2]

Hyatt was now playing at Shepheard's, having risen to prominence at the expense of the nine musicians who had been employed to accompany his selections when the venue opened in December 1963. By July 1964 the musicians had left, although the cause of their departure remained murky: the American Federation of Musicians claimed that Shepheard's was simply trying to save money, whereas the discotheque's management asserted that the "union forbids their members to play simultaneously with what they refer to as 'canned music'." With no resolution forthcoming, the union, maintaining that its members should be hired to play alternately with the DJ's selections, started to picket Shepheard's and two other discotheques—the Ginza (which had sent its five musicians packing a fortnight after it opened in September 1964) and the Hob Nob (which had bypassed the AFM altogether)—at the beginning of March 1965. "We are in direct competition with the discothèque recordings that are used publicly for profit," a union official told the *New York Times*. "Therefore, we have a right to place pickets wherever those recordings are played. The managements of places depending on live music also feel that the discothèque is giving them unfair competition." Hob Nob owner Al Lang stood his ground. "We don't intend to employ musicians because we don't need them."[3]

DJs were also displacing jukeboxes, which had begun to burst into bars, restaurants, and taverns following the repeal of Prohibition at the beginning of 1933, even if, as dance historian Katrina Hazzard-Gordon comments, they "were not fully accepted until the late 1940s or early 1950s."[4] Some ten years later the jukebox faced the challenge of the discotheque DJ, an altogether more flexible transmitter of technologically mediated music, and in the middle of 1965 *Billboard* reported that DJs were beginning to gain the upper hand. "The 'spinner,' with his turntable, speakers and specialized record library, sets up shop in a neighborhood bar (usually on weekends), 'gives with the cool jive,' dedicates records to patrons and silences the juke box during prime play hours."[5] In August, however, the jukebox industry took its finger off the panic button and started to welcome the unprecedented media attention that the discotheque craze had brought to the "new coin-operated Go-Go craze."[6] Discotheques, argued *Billboard* journalist Aaron Sternfield, were giving "the music machine industry a shot in the arm" and helping to "create a breed of music listeners who will be a factor in the industry long after the discotheque infatuation has cooled off."[7]

The AFM also managed to snatch victory out of the jaws of defeat when Sybil Burton, having just split up with the Elizabeth-Taylor-bound Richard Burton, opened Arthur on the site of the old El Morocco—a stuffy private discotheque that had closed when its jet-set clientele got bored—and employed an in-house band, the Wild Ones, to supply the musical entertainment. Burton had come up with the idea of opening Arthur following a visit to London's Ad Lib in the winter of 1964 and, in an act that was characteristic of what historian Arthur Marwick identifies as an "outburst of entrepreneurialism" in the sixties, raised the necessary $88,000 by selling eighty-eight shares at $1,000 a piece.[8] Burton then poached the Wild Ones from the Peppermint Lounge, appointed the band's Armenian American drummer Jordan Christopher as her musical director and, in deciding to open on 5 May, became the first discotheque entrepreneur to aggressively target the new urban class of hairdressers, models, and shop assistants. "People said that we were crazy because everybody would be leaving for the summer," she says. "Our response was, 'Who leaves for the summer? Not the people who *work* in New York.'"

Nor the people who act, dance, sing, and write if the opening night roll call is anything to go by. As the *New York Times* reported, "By midnight on Wednesday, even the 'in' people were having trouble getting in—they were being barred by velvet ropes in the lobby or milling around outside where Republican Senator Jacob K. Javits's limousine was parked. Jake and Marion (Mrs. Javits) did get in, also Truman Capote and Tennessee Williams and Baby Jane Holzer and Liza Minnelli and Sophie Tucker, and a lot of people who were dressed and acting as if they were 'in.'"⁹ When another high-profile guest, the Beatle-suited Rudolf Nureyev, started to dance with Burton, an AP photographer snapped up the moment, and the widely circulated image sealed Arthur's birth as not only a discotheque but also a media phenomenon. New York's first *mediatheque* had come into being.

In a kind of AFM dream sequence come true, however, the inaugural DJ failed to maintain the energy when the Wild Ones took a break and ended up killing the musical flow in a matter of seconds. Christopher responded by contacting Terry Noël, an old colleague who had been born Terry Noël Pichoske on 25 December and dropped his surname when he was hired to dance at the Peppermint Lounge. Noël visited Arthur on the second night and wasn't impressed. "The DJing was sporadic," he says. "The DJ would play some slow song and then he would go into some wild, fast song. It just made no sense at all. I took Sybil out on the dance floor and said, 'The music *stinks!*'"

Noël was given a chance to try his hand behind the turntables and, thanks to his spiky blond hair, fuck-you attitude, and unprecedented ability to manipulate vinyl forty-fives, seized the musical center stage. "I would start off slow and then I would build up," he says. "Sinatra and the Mamas and the Papas were slow records. I would always start that way because there were a lot of people who would only dance to slow records. Then I would take the rhythm a little bit higher, then a little bit higher, and before they knew it they would be dancing to the Stones." Noël was so good he went on to supplant the Wild Ones, suggesting that the AFM's belief that live musicians would always win a head-to-head contest with a DJ was misplaced. "Terry would suss out the crowd," says Burton. "He'd see what they responded to, and after an hour he would have them in the palm of his hand. It was quite extraordinary." Less conservative than Hyatt—in part because he was playing at a less conservative venue—Noël had uncovered the potential power of the DJ.

Arthur's more dance-conscious clientele were nevertheless frustrated. "Arthur was a very glamorous club where you sat in big booths and drank huge drinks, but the music was secondary," says Michael Fesco, a Broadway singer/dancer. "The DJ would put on a Frank Sinatra song, and then he would put on the Beatles. You wouldn't be terribly interested in dancing to more than one or two of those things before he would put on something that you didn't like." Unfortunately strutting took precedence over sweating. "People were always trying to make a show of themselves," adds Fesco. "There could never be any serious dancing because everyone was so dressed up." That didn't stop Arthur from becoming an apparently unstoppable profit machine that recouped its investment within twelve months, and Sybil Christopher (who had married Jordan Christopher) and her associates, capitalizing on the coming-of-age of the postwar baby boom and the rise of "youth culture," attempted to maximize their profits by opening franchise venues in several cities.

Within a couple of years, however, a customer reported the New York flagship to the Human Rights Commission following a door incident in which he and his African American date were allegedly humiliated by staff, and in November 1968 the Los Angeles branch was stripped of its name and association with the parent club. The increasingly unsavory atmosphere culminated in a shooting that left Sybil Christopher disillusioned and keen to move on, and the majority of her patrons seemed to be of the same mind. The hostess held a final party on 22 June 1969 and then sold the venue to nightworld impresario Bradley Pierce for $100,000. "It's had its day and there's no use going on," commented Eli Ellentuch, manager of the nightspot, which was subsequently converted into a supper club. "The novelty has faded. People are going to other places, doing other things."[10]

"Other places" included the less clean-cut, less smiley Sanctuary, which was located on the Hell's Kitchen end of West Forty-third Street between Ninth and Tenth Avenues. Owned by Arnie Lord, the discotheque had originally been christened the Church until New York's Roman Catholic representatives—who were upset about the appropriation of their name as well as a gigantic mural that depicted a devil surrounded by angels engaging in various forms of sexual intercourse—served an injunction against the venue a couple of days after it opened. The Church would have probably survived in its original incarnation if Lord's first name had been *The* rather than *Arnie*, but it wasn't, and so the proprietor reluctantly renamed his discotheque and, in a compromise move, placed clusters of plastic fruit over the more explicit parts of the mural. The injunction was lifted within a week, the less inflammatory yet grander gesture of converting a church into a discotheque having passed unchallenged.

The transition was virtually seamless, in part because religious ceremonies that combined sacred worship with ecstatic communal transcendence were remarkably close to the future shape of dance culture. Critic Kai Fikentscher has pointed to the way in which both the African American church and the nightclub "feature ritualized activities centered around music, dance, and worship, in which there are no set boundaries between secular and sacred domains," and while the Sanctuary didn't come out of the gospel tradition the space was still fervor-friendly.[11] Downstairs the catacombs were turned into a lounge area that functioned as a chill-out zone for anybody who was dead on their feet. Upstairs the pews were rearranged so that they lined the circumference of the dance floor, facing the new congregants of the night. And—in the most ingenious metamorphosis of all—the altar was converted into a DJ booth, which implied that the focal point of religious worship wasn't going to have to change. The fledgling culture of the discotheque was beginning to exploit its neo-spiritual potential.

Yet despite its innovative interior, the Sanctuary wasn't a particularly happening venue. Frequented by managers and their secretaries who were looking for a discreet date in an unfashionable locale, the club was comatose during the week and rarely attracted more than a couple of hundred punters over the weekend. Lord attempted to make ends meet by renting out the space for fashion shows, and when that failed to pay the bills he decided to hire a new DJ. "I only took eight records to the audition," says Francis Grasso, a young Italian American mixer whose slot coincided with a catwalk spectacle. "I said to myself, 'If I can't do it in eight songs then I might as well go home.' I started to play, and all of a sudden these models started bopping to my music and smiling at me. After six records the guy said, 'You're hired!' I walked out of there higher than a kite."

Grasso's journey to the Sanctuary had begun at a set of traffic lights on Avenue X in Brooklyn. "I was riding my brand new BSA Mark IV motorbike," he says. "This driver went through a red light and knocked me over. I flew a hundred feet and a chunk came out of my helmet. The driver cursed me and called me a longhaired motorcycle freak. All of this while I was lying in the road." Grasso was whisked to the hospital. "The injury resulted in a very pretty color scheme. My leg was yellow, red, purple, and blue. That was when I lost my ability to move my feet." The sensation repeated itself in a less acute form several months later when Grasso visited Arthur, a doctor having advised him to go dancing as part of his rehabilitation. "It was boring," he says. "It was couples only. You couldn't go in as a stag. The people were boring, and the decor was boring." That was more than could be said for the DJ. "Terry Noël was the first DJ I ever heard, and I thought he was terrible. He was into power stuff with the crowd. He would go for two or three records and just when you would want the build-up to keep going he would sink you in a hole with something like 'Love Me Tender' by Elvis Presley. The whole dance floor would clear, and everybody would go back to what they were doing before it all started. It was like, 'Dance phase is over! Everybody sit down! You will be told when you can stand up again!' It was all about his *superiority*."

Something of a straight queen with his pretty face, big hair, tasseled shirts, and tight leopard-skin tops, Grasso preferred the scene at Salvation, which had been opened by Pierce and was located in the heart of the Village at 1 Sheridan Square, the site of the legendary jazz club Café Society. "Bradley Pierce had a good formula," says Grasso. "There was free soda, and people experimented with drugs. He catered to a mixture of models, rock and roll groups, and people on the fringe of the press." The atmosphere was markedly more relaxed than it had been at Arthur. "Freaky people were let in and you didn't have to wear the perfunctory suit or have a nine-to-five job. It was more happening in the Village, and Salvation swept everything before it. That was where I got my feel for nightclubs and nightclub people."

Grasso's recuperation was symbolically consummated when a nearby club called Trude Heller's offered him work as a professional dancer. He spent his first night shuffling along a narrow ledge for twenty dollars and quit the following morning. "I was exhausted," he says, "and my feet were killing me." Grasso found a new job at a fashion outlet on Central Park South, where an early customer identified himself as the bar manager from the newly reincarnated Salvation, which was known as Salvation II. The client offered Grasso an open invitation and, disguising his age via a fake driving license, the biker-turned-bopper established himself as a nimble-footed and popular regular. The only person who didn't like Grasso was the discotheque's DJ. "I knew Francis from Arthur," says Noël, who was hired to spin records at the new venue. "He was just a groupie." Noël didn't have much time for such people, who were filed, along with just about everyone else, under the expansive category of "susceptible mass." "I manipulated dancers to the point that I could make them stand up, sit down, have a drink, come up, dance again, and then sit down again. *I fucked with their minds.*" The puppeteer DJ, however, also fucked with his own mind, and one extended LSD binge too many prompted the discotheque's owner to invite Grasso to fill in for the evening. "Within half an hour I was having a great time," he says. "When Terry showed up they told him he had been replaced. I don't think he was very happy."

Grasso held onto his position until Salvation II closed a couple of months later under the cloud of a financial scandal. Refusing to get downbeat, the dancing DJ landed himself a twenty-five-dollar-a-night slot in a restaurant-discotheque called Tarot in the summer of 1969, although he soon began to wonder if he had moved into the discotheque business just as it was about to fizzle out, the entertainment cosmos having taken a sharp turn northward when the party population of New York abandoned the city for Woodstock. Tarot's cards forecast an uncertain future—discotheques appeared to be horribly out-of-sync with the political, demonstrative times—but Grasso's qualms were eased in the autumn when he auditioned at the Sanctuary and doubled his wage packet overnight. Then another business brouhaha persuaded Lord to sell his venue to Seymour and Shelley, a middle-aged Jewish double act who ran a series of gay bars in the West Village and were known just by their first names. "The Sanctuary was still straight over New Year's Eve 1970," says Grasso. "We put on a New Year's Day breakfast for the dancers, and I remember having to buy the bagels from Brooklyn on my way to the club. The management didn't want to part with any more cash. The Sanctuary must have reopened four or five weeks into the new year."

Lurking in the shadowy corners of the discotheque was the Mafia, whose notorious control of just about every gay bar owner in the West Village hit the headlines on 23 March 1970 when law enforcement officials received a series of "letters from the grave" from the attorney of Robert Wood, who had taken control of Salvation before succumbing to Mafia intimidation. The discovery of Wood's bullet-ridden body in Queens on

18 February prompted the police to intensify their campaign to clamp down on the Mob's pervasive hold over gay haunts. "Several of the Mafia 'families' are in the act," declared a police official, "and they're spreading their infiltration so fast and so far that sometimes they don't even know whose joint is whose." An investigator added: "A Mob guy will spot a place that's making it rich. He goes in and smashes a glass on the bar or he spits in the barman's face. Then he waits a couple of days to see if his boss gets a message from another 'family' telling him, 'Pull your punk off that joint—it's mine.' In that case, they lay off. But if the message doesn't come they know it's fair game and they start moving in."[12]

The police were in the perfect position to know what was going on—they, after all, received regular payoffs in exchange for a dose of makeshift freedom—and this pattern would have recurred in the West Forty-third Street discotheque. "Seymour and Shelley probably came up with the idea of buying the Sanctuary," says Grasso, "but you couldn't open up without a connection." Having followed unofficial protocol and made regular payments to the Mafia and the local district office in exchange for non-interference in their West Village bars, Seymour and Shelley knew that they could make the new project work on a financial level. "They traveled in rich circles, walked around in full-length mink coats, and went to well-known restaurants," says Grasso, the only employee to survive the takeover. "Shelley lived in Gramercy Park, and he was so into money that he would leave the price tag on his antiques. They were creaming money off from their venues in the Village, and there was so much money to be made the Mob didn't care."

Having established the business framework for their operation, Seymour and Shelley started to publicize the venue in their West Village hangouts and hired a well-known gay maître d'hôtel to spread the word and man the door. "The maître d' knew a lot of the fashion artsy-fartsy crowd, and he told them to come," says Grasso. "There were a lot of designers and Broadway chorus dancers." Approximately five hundred dancers showed up, of whom "60 percent were white, 25 percent were Spanish, 15 percent were black." Grasso was particularly impressed by the energy of the gay contingent. "The opening night was a bang. I'd never seen a crowd party like that before. I said to myself, 'This is going to be fun!'"

* * *

Back on Broadway, David Mancuso soon established his parties as a weekly affair, although this time he avoided creating a formal framework. "I didn't want to run a club or an after-hours spot," he says. "I didn't want to be categorized. I just wanted to have a house party." The gatherings ran from midnight until six in the morning, making Mancuso's home one of the few Manhattan nightspots to stay open after 4 A.M.—which was when the Sanctuary closed—and almost certainly the only one that wasn't selling liquor. The Broadway events were also probably the cheapest: complimentary invitation cards were sent out by mail four times a year on the equinoxes and the solstices, and admission was just two dollars, after which the party operated as a strictly commerce-free zone, with Mancuso maintaining that drugs (which were widely used in the absence of alcohol) should not be peddled on the dance floor. "I never sold anything on the premises and I never allowed anything to be sold on the premises. Everything was covered by the contribution." That included the food, which was a positive, even ideological, combination of assorted organic dishes, delicious breads, and freshly squeezed fruit punch that functioned as the perfect fuel for people who wanted to dance until dawn. "I tried to create a situation in which there was no economic inequality. If someone couldn't afford to pay the contribution at the door then they could write me an IOU."

Finding the door in the first place remained a formidable obstacle. "These were the first parties where you had to know somebody to get in," says David DePino, who went to the Broadway spot several times. "You couldn't find out about them by asking around because nobody knew and they were never advertised. You had to be invited. It was very underground." It was also very mixed, with Mancuso's invitees—who could bring along a guest—cutting across the boundaries of class, color, sex, and sexuality. "There was no one checking your sexuality or racial identity at the door," says Mancuso. "I just knew different people." Economically the congregation spanned rich and poor; racially it was United Nations leaning toward black and Latino/a; sex-wise, women were always central to the setup (even if men were dominant); and sexually it was as wide as the ocean (although fish that swam in the same direction were in the majority). "It wasn't a black party or a gay party. There'd be a mixture of people. Divine used to go. Now how do you categorize her?"

The new system was an out-and-out success. Gatekeepers Steve Abramowitz and Maria Garbin gave unfamiliar visitors a serious grill-

Loft invitation: Spanky and the Gang. David Mancuso: "Claude Purvis turned me onto Spanky and the Gang. He said, 'Always use this picture.'" Courtesy of David Mancuso

ing to stop the uninvited from hitching a lift with an easygoing member, people got to know each other, and the parties settled into a social groove, functioning as an all-too-rare example of New York's much-talked-about-but-rarely-witnessed melting pot. "By the end of 1970 you couldn't squeeze anyone else in, and it stayed like that for four and a half years, regardless," says Mancuso. "I remember when we had the first blizzard, and people walked from over the bridge. They actually found a way to come." By the middle of 1971 the parties had acquired a name. "I wasn't looking for a name. I wasn't into promoting or advertising. It wasn't necessary. I was just inviting people to my house. I wanted a party, not attention." The revelers, however, persisted in asking Mancuso what his space was called. "I said to people, 'Call it whatever you want to call it!' I figured either the right name would attach itself or it wouldn't." The right name attached itself. "Because I lived in a loft building, people started to say that they were going to the Loft. It's a given name and is sacred."

In every other department Mancuso maintained a careful control over the organization and execution of his parties. "Mondays and Tuesdays were rest days, and I would go upstate," he says. "Then I would return to Manhattan and start to prepare for the next party. I found out that if I started working on Thursday I would be in too much of a rush so I began to get ready from high noon on Wednesday." The host was rigorously disciplined. "My diet, my sleep, the sound, the balloons, the menu, the floor, the theme—everything built up to Saturday night. I knew that at some point the party would take off, and everyone would go into Musicland, and I wanted to get there too."

DePino remembers the destination well. "There were these two black boys dancing, and I think they must have been on acid because they were so lost in the music," he says. "One of the boys was reaching up to touch a balloon but instead of jumping he used his mind to make his body bigger. He was moving his body and stretching *exactly* to the beat of the music, and as the song peaked and everybody was screaming for it this kid actually *touched* the balloon, even though his feet were still on the floor, and it *freaked me out*." The effect was almost supernatural. "David entranced these people. I said to myself, 'There must be a subliminal message in his music!' Nobody had inhibitions. Nobody was insecure. There were no mirrors—because if you were dancing wild and caught a glimpse of yourself and saw how ridiculous you looked you would maintain yourself—and there were no clocks to tell the time. You went through the looking glass."

The absence of clocks contributed to the dance dynamic. In the everyday world the clock signifies the unstoppable forward movement of teleological time, but party time unfolds in a different dimension—thus Mancuso's decision to print Salvador Dali's melting watches on the Love Saves the Day invitation. When clocks are nowhere to be seen, time starts to dissolve, and this provided the dancers at the Loft with an opportunity to forget their socialized selves—the person who has to get up at a certain time, go to work at a certain time, take lunch at a certain time, leave work at a certain time, etc.—and experiment with a different cycle. "Once you walked into the Loft you were cut off from the outside world," says Mancuso. "You got into a timeless, mindless state. There was actually a clock in the back room but it only had one hand. It was made out of wood and after a short while it stopped working."

Time, though, didn't simply stand still, but went into symbolic reverse thanks to Mancuso's practice of decorating the Loft with hundreds and hundreds of balloons. "Everybody loves balloons and they don't cost a million dollars," he says. "There were always lots and lots of balloons." The decor created a reassuringly familiar setting, drawing guests into the therapeutic and nostalgic domain of their childhood and the set-piece birthday party. "It was a childlike experience, not childish. You could let yourself go." Inflated with just the right amount of air and/or helium, the multicolored balloons either drifted just below the ceiling or bobbled along at chest height, encouraging dancers to participate in the creation of a bewildering display of Brownian motion. "It was a very safe environment. People could regain what might have been lost."

The Loft—which was dark, warm, and, at 1,850 square feet, really quite cozy—also symbolically recreated the irretrievable scene of the womb, where the most constant and memorable sound is that of the mother's beating heart, which pulses along at, roughly speaking, the rate of a dance record. The secure and cocoon-like contours of the dance space created the perfect milieu for experimental regression—there was always lots of screaming and growling and whooping—and the sheer density of bodies accelerated the transformation from autonomous adult to childlike dancer. Unable to avoid body contact on all sides, individual dancers had little choice but to dissolve into the amorphous whole, and, as the distinctions between self and other collapsed, they relinquished their socialized desire for independence and separation. "You could be on the dance floor and the most beautiful woman that you had ever seen in your life would come and dance right on top of you," says Loft regular Frankie Knuckles, a young design student and club kid from the Bronx. "Then the minute you turned around a man who looked just as good would do the same thing. Or you would be sandwiched between the two of them, or between two women, or between two men, and you would feel completely comfortable."

Whereas social dancing traditionally functioned as a rite of seduction, at least in the Western world, Mancuso introduced an alternative set of priorities. "The Loft chipped away at the ritual of sex as the driving force behind parties," says Mark Riley, one of Mancuso's devoted followers. "Dance was not a means to sex but drove the space." Revelers refigured the dance floor as a site not of foreplay but of spiritual communion where, thanks to the unique combination of decor, space, music, drugs, lighting, and dance, as well as Mancuso's guiding party ethos, sensation wasn't confined to the genitals but was *everywhere*—in every new touch, sound, sight, and smell. Freud defined the sexuality of an infant in similar terms—he called it the polymorphous perverse—and while the Loft didn't enable a literal return to an irretrievable childhood it nevertheless functioned as the affective medium through which dancers invented new possibilities of bodily pleasure that didn't revolve around genital sex. "There was an exchange of passion," says Lisa Hazel, who first went to the Loft when she was sixteen. "We would get off on each other's movements." The resulting combination of grace and stamina was exceptional. "The dancing was very jazz-spirited," says Danny Krivit, an early regular whose father ran a popular gay bar in the Village called the Ninth Circle. "It was just free. Before the Loft people thought they were free but they were just jerking around and jumping up and down."

A new musical matrix—in which music played the dancers, percolating into their bloodstream—contributed to this sense of freedom. Writing in 1964, Claude Lévi-Strauss commented on the unique corporeality of the musical experience, noting that music is as much a function of "visceral rhythms" as the brain, and this trait was magnified at the Loft, where music was played for an extended period of time and for an explicitly physical purpose: to hail the dancer and drive the dance.[13] Loft dancers, however, weren't simply permeated by sound but also used their bodies to produce their own waves. Percussion instruments—whistles, tambourines, maracas—functioned as prosthetic extensions that enabled dancers to generate sound and rhythm. Boots, shoes, and sneakers flickered across the wooden floorboards as if they were a continuation of the sound system. Vocal cries combined with the vinyl to produce a hybrid mantra. And inaudible physical gestures—arm movements, facial expressions, sweat—sent signals to the ever-watchful Mancuso. Dancers, in other words, didn't just embody the music in their dance. They also produced music as part of a vibrant circuit.

A mirror ball—the size of which was magnified by the smallness of the room—both reflected and shaped the movement on the dance floor. At the start of the party the sphere would be static as it waited for the gathered night crawlers to forget about the outside world and acclimatize to their new habitat. Then, as the mood became more focused, it would begin to hesitatingly rotate and gather momentum until, when the party hit full flow, it would switch into autopilot, triggering shrieks of excitement as it sent out its crisp, bright, laser-like beams into the otherwise dark environment. "At some point I would just let the mirror ball spin," says Mancuso. "But I would also slow it down if we were about to go into another phase. The mirror ball would always reflect the energy of the room."

That energy was never individualistic. Rather, it was social, and contained the possibility of collective politics. Rooted in the party, this new form of *social*ism echoed Mancuso's experience in the children's home, with the Broadway crowd revolving around a cross-section of New York's grown-up orphans—people who for one reason or another were not part of the idealized white, Anglo-Saxon, Protestant nuclear family. Overseeing this close but chaotic community was the "bearded Sister Alicia" who, in a multileveled gesture, kept control of his restless children by throwing parties and in so doing reenacted a powerful and symbolic scene from his own history while simultaneously giving to others that which he had received himself. Evidence of the connection emerged when Mancuso was finally reunited with his adopted mother, who showed him some old photos of the orphanage. One picture grabbed his attention. It was a snapshot of the party room. "That's a carbon copy of the Loft," he told her. Alicia nodded and told Mancuso to flip the photo over. "She had made a note of the date the photo was taken. It was Valentine's Day, 1949."

* * *

"In the postwar period," writes historian Charles Kaiser, "New York City became the literal gay metropolis for hundreds of thousands of immigrants from within and without the United States: the place they chose to learn how to live openly, honestly and without shame."[14] That was certainly the experience of the Peruvian-born Jorge La Torre who, having spent some time trying out Paris, arrived in New York on 2 February 1968 and decided within twenty-four hours that he was going to stay. "I was searching for a freedom," he says. "I didn't know exactly what that freedom involved but as soon as I arrived I just felt comfortable. I went to the Stonewall on my first night, and that cemented my decision to live in New York. The energy and the freedom that people were expressing was more than I had ever imagined. I felt extremely comfortable. It felt like home." Over the coming weeks La Torre explored every nook and cranny of the burgeoning gay bar scene, but the Stonewall remained his favorite hangout. "There were other bars in which you sometimes squeezed in a little dancing, assuming that the circumstances were ok, but dancing was the *central activity* at the Stonewall. The Stonewall was the biggest and the most fun."

While gay men had historically used a variety of public spaces to meet friends, find partners, and have sex, this intricate network had only tentatively included the relatively new institution of the discotheque. "If you were gay and attractive then you could get into places like Arthur and Cheetah," says Richard Brezner, who moved from Shaker Heights, Ohio, to New York in order to go to the School of Visual Arts in 1966. "There were always gay people there and I never felt uncomfortable, but they weren't gay clubs. They just let in a certain number, a kind of quota, to give the place more of a party atmosphere." Brezner preferred Salvation, even though the venue was more of an after-hours joint than a discotheque. "It was definitely leaning toward gay, and it was definitely a bit sleazy," he says. "There were women there, although they had to be either fag hags—forgive my language, because I hate that word—or club kids. It was a very sensual club." La Torre remembers Salvation as being more mixed than anything else. "It was a really fabulous venue, although it wasn't specifically gay. We blended in with everyone else who went there. Your sexual preference didn't matter in a place like that. It was more important that everybody was having a good time, and that was what brought all these people together."

Sexual preference did matter at the Stonewall Inn, however, and this made it an easy target for the NYPD, which would turn a blind eye to the illegal gatherings in exchange for a reputed two thousand dollars a week. Reprisals were inevitable if the Mob-controlled management forgot to hand a bulging brown envelope to the man from the local precinct, and this is exactly what happened on 17 June 1969 when eight police officers raided the Christopher Street location and served the manager with a warrant for selling liquor without a license. Drag queens were arrested and the rest of the patrons were ordered to leave the bar, but, instead of dispersing, the irate revelers—many of whom were on edge following the funeral of Judy Garland some twelve hours earlier—hung around outside the venue as the more extravagant queens were bundled into a police truck. "The next person to come out was a dyke, and she put up a struggle—from car to door to car again," reported the *Village Voice*. "It was at that moment that the scene became explosive. Limp wrists were forgotten. Beer cans and bottles were heaved at the windows, and a rain of coins descended on the cops."[15] The police soon faced a full-scale riot that went on for several nights.

Stonewall should have never happened in the first place given that the Appellate Division had overruled the State Liquor Authority's regulation that prohibited bars and restaurants from selling drinks to homosexuals in 1967. But while the "the ruling was well worth having," historian Martin Duberman points out that "it hardly put an end to police harassment of gay bars or to the police practice of sending out comely young cops, carefully attired in up-to-date chinos and tennis shoes, to entrap gay men on the street."[16] Counter to popular history, this harassment *continued* in the post-Stonewall era, and the arrest of 167 people in a predawn raid on the Snake Pit (a bar that police said "was frequented by homosexuals") at the beginning of March 1970 confirmed that the new dawn was in many respects an optical illusion.[17] Being gay still meant that you were legally gray.

Stonewall has nevertheless come to symbolize the birth of not only the Western gay liberation movement but also, as an effect of this, discotheques such as the Sanctuary, which are regularly said to have "reflected" and "endorsed" this "outpouring of repressed energy" and "mood of defiant hedonism."[18] Yet while the chronological connection is powerful, Stonewall's impact on the dance culture was not immediately apparent. There was, after all, an eight-month gap between the uprising and the reopening of the Sanctuary, so the rush of post-Stonewall gay adrenaline was less than overpowering, and Stonewall remained something of a minor event for the Sanctuary's predominantly middle-class fashion/dance/design crowd, relatively few of whom would have ever visited the street-oriented bar in order to drink and dance. "We were familiar with the Stonewall," says Michael Fesco, who first went to the Sanctuary in the spring of 1970. "It was only three blocks away from where I lived, but I never went before the riot and I never went afterward." A number of Stonewall regulars who subsequently transferred their loyalties to the Sanctuary were also untouched by the action. "The Stonewall rebellion wasn't significant for me politically," says La Torre. "I wasn't politically enlightened at the time. All I was interested in was having fun, going out dancing, and getting high."

Indeed the Stonewall rebellion didn't permeate gay consciousness as the-decisive-turning-point-in-the-history-of-gay-liberation for some time. "I heard about it on the television or something like that," says Fesco, "but I paid very little attention to it." Brezner—who moved into the West Village in 1969—had a similar experience. "Even though I lived in New York I don't remember Stonewall being a big deal, and when I see archival footage of it on TV I go, 'Oh, God, where *was* I?'" Echoing Duberman's argument that the rebellion helped to focus various strands of protest that were already in motion, Sanctuary habitué Vince Aletti notes that the uprising was first and foremost a symbolic occasion. "Stonewall was more mythological than real," he says. "The sense that we were entering a new era had been building up for a while."

The Sanctuary didn't so much grow out of the Stonewall as parallel it. Few of the discotheque's dancers would have been engaged in activist-style politics, just as few of the activists would have spent much time in the West Forty-third Street club. "I really don't think the activists went to the discotheques, and I don't think that many of the people going to discotheques were into the political thing," says Bob Casey, who arrived in New York in August 1969 after a year and a half in Vietnam and was part of the emerging gay scene. "A few activists did the dirty work while the throngs enjoyed the benefits." How important was the Greenwich Village riot to dance culture? "Stonewall was but a footnote in the evolution of disco." Just like gay liberation, however, the Sanctuary reinforced the movement toward a more jubilant way of life. "It was inevitable that gay activity would move into something a little bigger and a little more celebratory," says Aletti, "and it didn't surprise me that discos followed."

Seymour and Shelley were the first entrepreneurs to realize this potential. "I went to the opening night, and it was certainly the first place where gay men could congregate in such a large crowd," says Brezner, who was a close friend of the discotheque's manager, Alan Litke. "The Sanctuary's dance floor was big and when it was crowded, which it generally was, it was really exciting. The lines outside were massive. The Sanctuary was definitely the scene in town." La Torre, who "heard about the Sanctuary the minute it opened," was similarly dazzled. "I thought it was the most glamorous place I had ever seen, and it was always packed to the rafters. The whole setup was very decadent and the experience of seeing Francis on what had once been the altar with his long hair, muscular body, and skin-tight t-shirts was just amazing. He looked like a Minotaur to me—a creature of sorts. Of course the fact that we were on acid enhanced the visual aspect of it all."

A "hairdresser to the stars," Litke was able to prepare his core clientele in advance of the opening, and Brezner became part of a group of models and associated professionals that the manager would wave in for free. "The designer Steven Burrows was part of our entourage," he says. "Steve used to throw his tight little designer tank tops at us, and we would go to the Sanctuary every night. We went there to dance and have a good time, and we were the type of people they wanted around. Once the Sanctuary opened I don't think the word needed spreading. It was just the place people wanted to be." The West Forty-third Street discotheque was quite unlike any other environment. "The Sanctuary was really spectacular, really beautiful. It was just a place to go and have a really good time. I literally stayed until closing every night." Festive and expressive, dancers were energized by their new surroundings. "The Sanctuary was the first place that I ever saw a drag queen perform. She was dressed in sequins and sang along to 'Ain't No Mountain High Enough' by Diana Ross. I remember being bowled over. It was really something."

It would, however, be a mistake to describe the Sanctuary as Manhattan's first gay discotheque (the Stonewall having already been "disqualified" due to its reliance on a jukebox). "It had an incredible mixture of people," says La Torre. "There were people dressed in furs and diamonds, and there were the funkiest kids from the East Village. A lot of straight people thought that it was the coolest place in town and there were definitely a lot of women because that was part of what was going on at the time. I would say that women made up 25 percent of the crowd from the very beginning, probably more. People came from all cultural backgrounds, from all walks of life, and it was the mixture of people that made the place happen. That was the thing that most impressed me."

That this should have been so is in many respects obvious. New York State law, which asserted that all-male dancing was illegal and that discotheques should contain at least one woman for every three men, dictated that the Sanctuary could never function as a homogeneous gay discotheque, and even if the restrictions had been fully lifted there probably weren't enough self-realized gay dancers to fill the floor at this early stage in the culture's evolution. Repression and discretion were also key factors, with closeted gay men regularly going out with women in order to pass as straight, and then there were the motivating considerations of fashion, companionship, and sex, with women functioning as style gurus, best friends, and even bed partners for many gay men.

None of this should undermine the importance of the Sanctuary's gay contingent. "I don't know if I was aware of going to a gay discotheque so much as a discotheque that I thought was ours," says Brezner. La Torre shared this sense of inclusive ownership. "The guys at the front door were gay and that was absolutely crucial. If you were gay they made you feel very welcome, and that was important to us. They were in charge, and their policy was to have a mixed crowd. That was fine by us as long as we were able to behave like we wanted to. The Sanctuary was certainly more gay than some of the other places I had been to."

Realizing that the converted church could become the next profitable culture club for gay men (and their friends), Seymour and Shelley introduced their West Village clientele to a pulsing paradise in which conversation was optional, free-flowing bodily contact inevitable, and the rhythmic beat more exhilarating than anything that was going on in the bars or the bathhouses. The subsequent influx of gay men transformed the club from an insignificant and ephemeral straight space into a flourishing business. Triggering a profound shift in the wider demographics of the discotheque, gay consumers—lacking not only meeting places but also (to their financial advantage) dependents—now promised to inject a new and more sustained current into what had become a struggling entertainment institution. Straights were on their way out, and, coming out in increasing numbers, gay men were on their way in.

2. consolidation

A virtuoso of West African percussion, Babatunde Olatunji traveled from Nigeria to the United States in 1950 in order to study at Morehouse College in Atlanta on a Rotary International scholarship. He applied to take a Ph.D. at New York University in the hope that this would enable him to pursue a diplomatic career but quickly ran out of money and turned to music in order to earn a living. It proved to be an auspicious U-turn: in 1958 he was invited to appear as a featured soloist at a Radio City Symphony Orchestra concert at Radio City Music Hall, and he was subsequently offered a record deal by Columbia. Featuring four drummers and nine female singers, *Drums of Passion* was released the following year and became a national hit, effectively introducing African percussion to the American listener.

Francis Grasso purchased the mesmerizing slab of vinyl in a record store on Flatbush Avenue. "I was a wee teenager," he says. "I had always wanted to be a drummer and was fascinated with African beats. The album had this outrageous cover of all these men playing drums. It was a favorite of mine way before I became a disc jockey." *Drums of Passion* lived up to its name. "I took it with me whenever I wanted to get laid. All of the women said that it was so rhythmically sexual. When I went to a girl's house I took Olatunji and Johnny Mathis. I would start off with Olatunji and end up with Johnny Mathis." Grasso started to play the polyrhythmic sounds of the African artist only once Seymour and Shelley had taken control of the Sanctuary, and "Jin-Go-Lo-Ba (Drums of Passion)" became his most radical statement—older music for a bolder dance floor. "You needed a crowd that was limber enough. Straight people were clumsy and had no rhythm, whereas gay men were right on. They moved their hips, their bodies, and their arms, and the faster the music got the crazier they reacted. I didn't want to play Olatunji until I had an audience for it." Santana had coincidentally just come out with a cover version of "Jin-Go-Lo-Ba," renamed "Jingo," and the Sanctuary DJ used this popular remake as his cue. "I said to myself, 'If Santana works then the real shit is going to kill them!' I was good at mixing one record into another so I played the Santana and brought in 'Jin-Go-Lo-Ba.' The crowd preferred the Olatunji, where there's no screaming guitar. They got into it straight away."

Francis Grasso

Select Discography (Sanctuary 1970)

Abaco Dream, "Life and Death in G & A"

James Brown, "Cold Sweat," from *Live at the Apollo, Volume 2*

James Brown, "Get Up I Feel Like Being a Sex Machine"

James Brown, "Mother Popcorn (You Got to Have a Mother for Me)"

Chicago, "I'm a Man"

The Four Tops, "Still Waters"

Jimi Hendrix, *Band of Gypsys*

The Jackson 5, "ABC"

King Crimson, *In the Court of the Crimson King*

Led Zeppelin, "Immigrant Song"

Led Zeppelin, "Whole Lotta Love"

Little Sister, "You're the One"

The Marketts, "Out of Limits"

Olatunji, "Jin-Go-Lo-Ba (Drums of Passion)"

Osibisa, *Osibisa*

Rare Earth, "Get Ready"

Mitch Ryder & the Detroit Wheels, *The Detroit-Memphis Experiment*

Sam and Dave, "Hold On! I'm a Coming"

The Temptations, "I Can't Get Next To You"

Within the framework of the public discotheque circuit, Grasso's range of music was unique. In addition to Olatunji and Santana he would play the raw funk of James Brown, the rock-like reverberations of the Doobie

Brothers, the sweet sounds of boyhood hero Johnny Mathis, and the African-rock fusion of Osibisa, as well as Motown staples such as the Supremes and the Jackson 5. "Terry Noël was on a different wavelength," says Grasso. "He would play the Beatles, he would play the Stones, he would play Elvis, and he would play bubble gum. He wasn't very big on black. I played more soul, more R&B, more African, and more rock. I played things nobody would dream of playing. I gave you the full bag." David DePino, who was working behind the bar, found himself shuffling to a new beat. "Francis got heavy. He played all kinds of music—things that you wouldn't expect to hear."

Grasso's method of mixing was initially less radical than his actual selections. Leaning heavily on radio protocol as well as the practice of other discotheque DJs, he would segue from one record to the next by using his fingertip to grip the non-playing record as the turntable spun underneath. When the outgoing track recited its final phrases he would release his hold, and the two records would overlap for a couple of seconds, bleeding into each other and establishing a temporary bridge—or "blend," as it was more frequently described—that maintained the musical flow and helped to generate a hypnotic groove. That groove became virtually seamless if the DJ "slip-cued" between two copies of an extended single in which the recording was pressed up in "two halves" on the A- and B-sides of a forty-five.

These were standard tricks of a nascent trade, but, as the reaction from the dance floor became progressively more intense, Grasso set about inventing a technique that would dramatically extend the effect. Using his headphones to their full potential, the DJ started to use his left ear to listen to the incoming selection and his right ear to hear the amplified sound in order to forge an imaginary amalgam that, if everything was in place, could be transformed into sonic reality. "Somewhere in the middle of my head," says Grasso, "I would make the mix." The DJ's most famous permutation layered the Latin beats of Chicago's "I'm a Man" over the erotic groans of the vocal break in Led Zeppelin's "Whole Lotta Love." "You really couldn't dance to the Zeppelin once it went into that orgasmic tripping stuff, but if you mixed it with the Chicago then you could. Amazingly, the entire break of 'Whole Lotta Love' lasted exactly the same time as 'I'm a Man,' so as the 'I'm a Man' finished the full song of 'A Whole Lotta Love' would come back." Unstable and exciting, the vinyl compound emerged as a heightened moment of DJ musicianship, with Grasso casting aside entrenched notions of artistic integrity—that these were *separate records*—in favor of exploratory combinations that became longer and longer. "Nobody mixed like me. Nobody was willing to hang out that long. Because if you hang out that long the chances of mistakes are that much greater."

The problem of combining two records that were in all likelihood running at different tempos, and whose live drummers were prone to rhythmic shifts, was compounded by inflexible mixing technology. "Back then you couldn't adjust speeds," says Grasso. "You had to catch it at the right moment. There was no room for error, and you couldn't play catch up. I had Thorens turntables and you couldn't do that on Thorens." If the DJ wanted to increase the tempo he would simply bring in a record that ran half a beat faster. "I would build it up slowly. I was dealing with people who were high. The idea was to make them enjoy their head, not fuck with their head. I took care of the people who paid to hear me."

Unfavorable conditions made Grasso's feats all the more remarkable. The average forty-five lasted little more than two minutes, in which time the DJ would have to find his next record, cue it up, make the mix, and work the lights. "The lights were on my right-hand side on a switchboard, but to work the main room lights I had to go out of my booth, run past the service bar and go into this little room where there were these heavy-duty switches. I would flip the switches to the beat of the music, and then I'd run back to my booth. I earned my pay." Grasso also operated the discotheque's state-of-the-art strobes, which generated a profoundly disorienting environment. "When the strobe lights went on they really *strobed*," says DePino. "They made it look like people were dancing in slow motion. It was intense, surreal." Frank Crapanzano was similarly spellbound. "The Sanctuary was the first place I ever saw a strobe light. The effect was so overwhelming I had to stop dancing—*and I'm a dancer.* Everyone looked ominous and satanic. It was just beyond."

Timesaving strategies were crucial for Grasso. When he needed to go for a pee, he visited the sink in the utility room, which was a short walk from the altar. (The men's toilet was deemed out-of-bounds because he was worried the Sanctuary's gay contingent would get the wrong idea about his sexuality, and the women's bathroom on the other side of the discotheque was far away.) The discovery that records could be "read" also helped Grasso streamline the mixing process. "If you look at an album carefully you can see which parts of the album are vocal and which parts are musical so you've already got a head start. The dark black grooves are instrumental sections and the lighter black is the vocal." Ultimately, however, Grasso was more interested in reading the mood on the dance floor. "I always played according to what I got from the crowd. If I saw them maintain the level of intensity then I'd bring in a quicker record. It always depended on the vibe."

Inspired by the fresh combination of space, light, and sound, the sheer density of bodies, the expansive danceability of Grasso's selections, the feeling of commonality forged by their wider repression, and the sense of security that came with a gay-controlled door, the crowd danced to a new dynamic that was quite unique within the short history of the disco-theque. "I loved to go out on the floor," says Sanctuary regular Richard Brezner. "There was nothing better than grabbing someone you knew or someone you had just met and dancing with them." In a break with estab-lished etiquette, dancing wasn't necessarily partnered. "If a song came on that I really loved I thought nothing of going out onto the dance floor by myself and just dancing." When partnerships formed they did so sponta-neously. "Ninety-nine percent of the time somebody would start to dance with you or a group of people would grab your arm and pull you in to join them. You always gravitated toward holding someone."

The nascent dance ritual enabled gay men, ethnic groups, and women to experiment with a new way of being that revolved around commu-nal hedonism, ecstatic release, stylish yet functional clothing, and bodily rather than verbal communication. Yet just as the dance ritual recast the identity of the crowd, so the shifting identity of the crowd revolutionized the dance ritual, and this interaction enabled—or even required—Grasso to perform not only longer and longer mixes but also longer and longer sets. "I saw people dance three hours straight," says the DJ. "*I couldn't be-lieve it.*" Grasso was compelled to revise his habit of sprinkling his sets with occasional slow records. "I learned the importance of playing slow records from being in the straight clubs. They didn't charge at the door so you had to encourage people to drink more. I would play music that people could dance slow to, and if they wanted to drink then they could drink." The tactic, though, was now defunct. "When the Sanctuary went gay, I didn't play that many slow records because they were drinkers and they knew how to party. Just the sheer heat and numbers made them drink. The energy level was *phenomenal*. At one point I used to feel that if I brought the tempo down they would boo me because they were having so much fun."

Grasso moved onto a different musical plane. "The straight crowd really didn't want to get too sweaty, but when it went gay I could do things that the straights couldn't have handled. I was ready to play, and they were ready to dance. We met." A self-declared stud who talks of sleeping with some five hundred women during his DJing years, Grasso developed his most intimate relationship with Seymour and Shelley's gay clientele. "Musically my creative juices were stirred up. I had this burning desire to do better all the time, and the people came expecting me to perform. It was like kismet, a state of nirvana where everything meets together." As befitted this gayest of mixed discotheques, power was being exercised from the bottom up.

What had emerged in the Sanctuary—and simultaneously in the Loft—was a social and egalitarian model of making music in which the DJ played in relation to the crowd, leading and following in roughly equal measure. In order to lead, the DJ would buy records, rehearse certain mixes, and make live selections, the combination of which suggested a dominant position in relationship to the crowd. But the role of following, in which the DJ would improvise in order to take account of the energy and desires of the dance floor, was equally important given that no amount of preparation could fully anticipate the mood of the dance floor. With improvisation came discovery (rather than familiarity), freedom (as opposed to control), and chaos (instead of order). As a result the relationship between the DJ and the crowd resembled a dynamic conversation between separate agents that, when combined, had a greater total effect than the sum of their individual parts.

This synergistic alliance amounted to an intensified version of the participatory and democratic form of making music known as call-and-response, or antiphony, which features reciprocal conversations between participants in styles as varied as folk, gospel, and jazz. The synergy of the discotheque, however, was unique inasmuch as the music was never separable from its various authors. Of course, the individual units of vinyl that comprised the DJ set might have been for sale, but the blended and mixed combination wasn't. Nor could it be either recreated in a recording studio (the dancers wouldn't fit) or effectively taped within the discotheque (the screams of the crowd would be either lost or too disruptive for home listening, plus no format could fully reproduce the entire length of the nightclub nuptial). DJs were spearheading a turntable revolution.

* * *

A makeshift imitation of the Sanctuary was shipped out to Fire Island when Michael Fesco opened the Ice Palace on Memorial Day weekend 1970, roughly three months after his first visit to the converted church on Forty-third Street. "After going to the Sanctuary I said, 'I've just got to do something like *this!*'" says Fesco. "I sat there in the rafters mesmerized by the people on the dance floor. I said, 'Look at them! They're just having the most *fantaaastic* time! This is what I'm going to do in the Boom Boom Room!'"

Situated on Cherry Grove, a gay Fire Island community that dates back to the 1920s, the Boom Boom Room had been handed over to Fesco in the summer of 1969. "I was invited to help manage the Beach Hotel and Club, and I turned up for the interview in a black mohair suit and tie. The friend who gave me the job turned out to be a heavy drinker, and after a month I found myself running the entire complex." That included the hotel itself, the Sea Shack restaurant, and the hotel bar. "There was a jukebox in the bar, and the neighbors would complain about the music. The only thing they could hear was this 'boom, boom, boom,' so it was referred to as the Boom Boom Room." At the beginning of 1970 it became the Doom Doom Room. "As soon as I went to the Sanctuary I knew its days were over."

Fesco opted for a wholesale revamp. "There was a novel called *The Ice Palace*, and I thought the name would be perfect for the Boom Boom Room. It was always so damn hot in there that I thought a nice cool name would be psychologically appreciated." In line with the new concept, Fesco covered the walls with a mass of cut-price industrial tinfoil purchased on Canal Street, and, in an attempt to emulate Seymour and Shelley's discotheque, the ungainly jukebox was replaced with a sound system and a DJ. "We rented the equipment for the summer—that's how unfamiliar we were with the possibilities." The Ice Palace opened on 30 May 1970. "We had a line outside that ran all the way to the beach. I believe 1,800 people came to the opening. We charged five dollars admission, and my rent for the season was assured."

Fortunately for Fesco, the opening coincided with a marked relaxation in state surveillance. "The police were *severe* in Cherry Grove before 1970,

Michael Fesco at
the Ice Palace,
September 1970.
Courtesy of
Michael Fesco

and if you were caught dancing with another man you were arrested," he says. "You had to have one woman for every three men on the dance floor, which was hysterical. We had a corral that you had to pass through in order to get onto the dance floor. That was where we would count heads: one girl, three boys, one girl, three boys. The lesbians who lived on the island made up the numbers." The situation eased considerably at the turn of the decade, and roughly one thousand patrons decided to make the most of the looser environment every Saturday night. "In 1970 we did not have to use a checkpoint, although all of the old-timers still danced with women just to be on the safe side."

The world of protest politics fleetingly came into focus on 28 June, the anniversary of the Stonewall uprising. "There was a small rally in Washington Square Park," says Fesco. "The only reason I was aware of it was because some of the entertainers I was hiring for the Ice Palace were also performing on the march." Yet while the "Gay-In" attracted the media attention, the party lifestyle that Fesco was importing to Fire Island signaled a more profound, if less publicly visible, shift in gay culture. "The

Stonewall organization was a very small group. The nightclub world was where people wanted to go because that was where boys could take off their shirts and sweat and dance. That was where you met your boyfriends and that is what it was all about. Sex. You know it was very hard to *pull* while you were on a street protest."

Inasmuch as Fesco faced any competition, it came from the Sandpiper, a fancy seafood restaurant that owners Ron Malcolm and Gene Smith converted into a dine-and-dance facility that same summer. Based half a mile down the beach in the Pines, the Sandpiper served food to a demographically mixed clientele, yet relatively few straights—who made up roughly half of the neighborhood at the time—would hang around for the dance ritual, which usually began at around 11:30 P.M. and continued until 2 A.M. The fact that the Sandpiper was first and foremost a restaurant put it at something of a disadvantage to the Ice Palace, which was never compromised by anything as functional as food, and the lack of an integrated DJ setup meant that the dancers had to make do with prerecorded tapes. But what the Sandpiper lacked in infrastructure it made up for in attitude, with its dancers convinced of their superiority. The Pines was, after all, a relatively recent gay community that had been, in the words of Martin Duberman, "developed as an alternative for upscale homosexuals disenchanted with the 'plebeian' atmosphere of Cherry Grove," and by the summer of 1970 the class divide was unmistakable.[1]

Nevertheless, many Pines partygoers still had to dig deep in order to pay for their holiday. "Only the select few owned and lived in their own houses," says Richard Brezner, who made his first trip to the Pines some six months before he became a Sanctuary habitué, paying twenty-five dollars for a residential share over a holiday weekend. "The majority of people scrimped and saved during the year so that they could rent a house with eight or ten other guys, who either became your friends or your enemies. A lot of the people who stayed in the Pines couldn't really afford to be there." Relative poverty, however, failed to puncture the pervasive atmosphere of snootiness. "I felt that a lot of the Fire Island Pines mentality was elitist and that resulted in a form of exclusion," adds Brezner. "Sometimes it was wonderful being with other people of the same sexual persuasion in an environment where there was no prejudice or judgment, but that was only on the surface. For the most part you had to be rich, socially connected, well endowed sexually or have a perfect gym body to be popular." If you made the cut, a version of gay utopia lay in wait. "There was no place on earth like Fire Island Pines. The first time I went the whole scene awed me. I remember getting off the boat in the Pines harbor and seeing all of these beautiful yachts, a low row of shops, and men holding hands. It was like paradise. In the early seventies I couldn't wait to get there, and once I was there I didn't want to come home." Social critique wasn't high on anyone's list of priorities. "I was always tuned into what was going on and much of it disturbed me. But, hey, we were all young!"

The Sandpiper embodied these patterns and impressions. "It was the focal point of our social life in the Pines," says Jorge La Torre, who visited the resort for the first time in the summer of 1970 when Richard Orbach, who had designed the multiuse building, invited him to stay at his house. "There was nowhere else to go. The crowd was very stylish and good-looking." Alan Harris, the president of Yves St. Laurent and a more seasoned visitor to the island, also gravitated toward the venue. "My lover had a house on Cherry Grove, and when I stayed with him we partied at the Ice Palace, but I was unhappy in the relationship and tried to escape from the Grove as much as possible. There is no doubt that the Sandpiper had an elitist edge. That particular group thought they were invulnerable and immortal at that point."

Music and sex became part of the same exploratory continuum. "You would know people in the Sandpiper, but for the most part you were just looking at attractive people who were wearing next to nothing and who were out to dance and have a good time," says Brezner. "People were brought together by music. We danced *all* night, *every* night. Everything was very free. The environment literally took over your soul." Flexible glass walls further blurred the sex/dance boundary. "If the weather was warm they would open the doors, which led onto a deck. You could walk outside and be in one of the most beautiful places on earth. People were having sex everywhere—on the boardwalk, under the boardwalk, I mean everywhere. Even *I* was guilty." Police officers blushed and looked away. "Laws that would be enforced in New York City didn't really hold true on Fire Island."

Of course, the law wasn't strictly enforced in New York when officers received the right kind of payoff. That was certainly the case with the Continental Baths, a miniature out-of-season Fire Island that, along with a handful of other bathhouses, operated as a public sex space for gay men in the city. Situated on Seventy-fourth Street and Broadway, the Baths had been opened by Steve Ostrow on 16 September 1968, and a month later

La Torre visited the venue for the first time. "I had just moved into an apartment on West End Avenue and Seventy-first, a few blocks from the Baths," says La Torre. "I saw this peculiar ad in the *Village Voice* which read: 'Continental Baths: for sophisticated males only.' You had to read between the lines back then. I went along with a friend of mine, and we fell in love with the place." La Torre started to work at the establishment a few weeks later, and soon after that he became Ostrow's lover. "Steve was very closeted. He was married with two kids, and I think he opened the Baths as a place where he could have his affairs and screw around without the world having to know. I am sure that he never thought that it would turn into such a big thing."

The Baths was raided for the first time in March 1969. "One of our customers touched a detective," says Ostrow. "He brought out these hand-cuffs from under his towel and sent out a radio signal, at which point dozens of uniformed police officers raced in and arrested everyone in sight. Our customers were hustled off to the detention center and charged with 'being on the premises of a bawdy house' under an archaic law dating back to the 1800s." From that point on the Baths was raided at least twice a week. "The police always used the same 'enticement and entrapment' scheme to justify the raids. To the credit of the judicial system, the charges were always dismissed when the accused came up for hearings. The raids were basically a degrading and punishing harassment tactic."

That tactic was used more sparingly after Ostrow agreed to comply with the local precinct's payment proposal. "The police department esti-mated we were grossing about forty thousand dollars a week in revenue," says the bathhouse entrepreneur. "They asked if we would like to buy forty tickets to the Policeman's Ball. It turned out that the tickets cost a hundred dollars each, and that there was a Policeman's Ball *every* week!" The police did indeed rent a cheap hall and run a dance every Friday night—in order to cover themselves. "Of course no one ever showed up ex-cept the cops. All of them shared in the take according to their place in the hierarchy." From that point on the police launched occasional token raids, which they were obliged to carry out in order to keep up appearances. "They always tipped us off in advance," says Ostrow. "I would empty the club except for one or two employees, who would be detained overnight by the police and then released the following morning. I rewarded the employees with a hundred-dollar cash bonus."

The Baths took off in 1970 when La Torre suggested that Ostrow alter the content of the shows. "The entertainment was organized by Steve," says La Torre. "He was an opera fanatic so he would invite opera singers to perform. That was the real passion in his life, and he even performed there himself, but to me it was kind of ludicrous. I said, 'Why don't you have other types of music?'" Ostrow decided to launch a regular Saturday night show that featured up-and-coming performers, and the new slot soon became a huge success. "We gave Bette Midler her break," says La Torre. "Steve and I went to this place where they showcased talent, and I said, 'We have to get her!'" The Baths became a catalyst in the vocalist's career. "Her timing couldn't have been more perfect," says Brezner, a good friend of La Torre and a regular at the Baths. "It was a time of gay abandon, and the crowd went *wild*. Bette was absolutely electrifying, although the enthusiasm of the crowd certainly spurred her on."

The introduction of the discotheque followed. "Some people arrived early for the show so we determined that we needed a bar," says La Torre. "But after the show we had three hundred people bottled in with nothing to do so we had to figure out how we could entertain them. I suggested that we bring dance music into the picture. It was a natural progression because in an unconscious way we were looking for an outlet, and we wanted to have our own way of life. We had gone to mixed places like the Sanctuary, and now we wanted our own place." When the dance floor was inaugurated in 1970, the Continental Baths became America's first gay male discotheque, for while the Salvation, the Sanctuary, the Ice Palace, and the Sandpiper had all entertained heavily gay populations, they also admitted significant numbers of women—and, to varying degrees, straight men. The Baths, in contrast, attracted gay men.

Ostrow's operation was far from flawless. The sound system was perfunctory, and the discotheque was secondary to the bathhouse, which meant that dancing didn't dominate the menu but instead operated as something saucy that happened to go well with meat. "I don't think dancing is what was on most people's minds when they went there," says Brezner. "It was dark, sexually charged, and clandestine." Yet the unique environment, which literally stripped away the class signifiers of designer clothes and ocean houses, encouraged gay sex to take on new meanings. "If you were naked in a towel you could be anything," says La Torre. "There were no outward signs of class or wealth or profession, and people dropped their barriers. It was very liberating, and people began to see the whole gay experience with totally different eyes." Gay sex also helped the dance floor take on new meanings. "There was a certain code of behavior you had to observe at the Pines," adds La Torre. "You really couldn't be totally open about your sexuality because it was still a public venue. But you didn't have that barrier at the Baths. At the Baths you could just walk out of your room and go straight onto the dance floor. The environment allowed people that extra freedom." In return, the dance floor embellished the experience of gay sex and gay community. "There is no question that sex was the reason for them being there, but the dancing became increasingly important. More than anything else, dancing was the activity that brought these people together."

* * *

" 'Look, I'd like to take you to this place, but do you have a problem with gay people?' " Mark Riley—black and straight—was on the verge of being offered an invite to David Mancuso's Loft, save for this one proviso. "I said, 'No, of course not,' because I really wasn't raised to have a problem with people being gay," says Riley. "So my friend said, 'OK, fine, because you're going to see gay people there. It's not going to be totally gay but you're going to see guys dancing with guys. If that bothers you, *don't go!*' " Riley knew what the warning was all about: the Loft might have opened on the cusp of the black civil rights and gay liberation demonstrations, but the two movements were far from united in their goals. Straight blacks accused white gays of being racist, and white gays regularly pointed to straight black homophobia. "Blacks and gays didn't have the world's greatest relationship, certainly not black straight people and gays. It took a while before people realized that you could come together around music."

Caught in the crossfire stood the barely acknowledged constituency of black gay men who, combining necessity with desire, had begun to organize their own events. "In the late sixties there were very few places where black gay people were welcome," says Riley. "The exception was a quarter in East Harlem along Second Avenue and Third Avenue between 116th Street and 125th Street where black and Puerto Rican gays used to give parties in these abandoned loft spaces. The landlords would rent out the lofts for a nominal fee, and the organizers would bring in a small sound system. There weren't many people living in the area, so the gay crowds that went to these parties could dance in relative anonymity."

The practice dated back to the Harlem Renaissance of the 1920s and 1930s, when African American lesbians and gay men socialized in cabarets, speakeasies, and drag balls, or buffet flats (private apartments that could be hired for the night) and rent parties when they wanted a little more privacy. The black poet Langston Hughes became a central figure, describing the balls as "spectacles in color," and although, as historian Eric Garber notes, the network declined following the stock market crash of 1929 and the repeal of Prohibition, a number of venues and social networks survived, of which the Second and Third Avenue lofts were the most recent manifestation.[2] "This was a scene unto itself," says Riley, "and it was a scene that David eventually got into."

In a parallel development, black transvestites began to form tightknit groups whose raison d'être was to "throw shade"—or give attitude. "It was just a little underground scene that emerged in the sixties, more of a gang than anything else," says David DePino, one of the subculture's narrator-promoters. "These little groups of fairies named themselves after fashion designers and formed these 'houses.' They tried to turn each other out on the dance floor. Queens would stop and scream as they tried to outperform other queens, and these little competitions began to develop." Adverse conditions helped cement the emergent culture. "Drag queens weren't so accepted back then so they started to organize their own parties. The queens would organize competitions, and they began to develop these different categories, such as best dress. People heard they were fun and they caught on. The scene spiraled when black drag queens who hated each other set up their own houses."

The House of Dupree was the product of one such rivalry. "Paris Dupree was Duchess's best friend, and Duchess was the head of the House of Wong," says DePino. "Duchess was always the one walking the balls [parading down an imaginary catwalk in a costume prepared by the rest of the house], and I guess it created a little rift. Instead of beading Duchess's gowns and getting Duchess ready, Paris wanted to walk herself. Paris and Duchess had a falling out, and Paris started her own house." It soon became clear that Paris could indeed do no *wong* when she transformed the act of throwing shade into a distinctive dance in the early seventies. "It all started at an after-hours club called Footsteps on Second Avenue and Fourteenth Street," says DePino. "Paris Dupree was there, and a bunch of these black queens were throwing shade at each other. Paris had a *Vogue* magazine in her bag, and while she was dancing she took it out, opened it up to a page where a model was posing, and then stopped in that pose on the beat. Then she turned to the next page and stopped in the new pose, again on the beat." A bodily version of call-and-response ensued. "Another queen came up and did another pose in front of Paris, and then Paris went in front of her and did another pose. This was all shade—they were trying to make a prettier pose than each other—and it soon caught on at the balls. At first they called it posing, and then, because it started from *Vogue* magazine, they called it vogueing."

Slowly but surely, a black gay bar scene began to emerge. "Most of the black gay kids would hang out in Tabletops, Vosco, Andrés, Jay's, and the Crystal Ballroom," says Frankie Knuckles. "These places didn't have DJs. They all had jukeboxes." Knuckles had been introduced to the Manhattan scene by Larry Levan, a fifteen-year-old dance enthusiast from Brooklyn. "Larry and I pretty much grew up together," adds Knuckles, who was a year younger than his friend. "A drag queen called Gerald introduced me to Larry. Gerald lived a couple of blocks away from me in the South Bronx, and he told me that Larry was his boyfriend. Larry and I just clicked immediately. We were best friends."

Christened Laurence Philpot, Levan had adopted his mother's maiden name in the absence of his father, and he subsequently took on Duchess's name in order to join a new family. "Larry was in the House of Wong," says DePino. "He had a relationship with Duchess, and then they became just friends. Duchess was a part-time drag queen at the time—she was really a boy that went in drag—and Larry used to hang out with Paris and help Duchess bead her dresses. They all grew up in Brooklyn together. It was a whole crowd." Knuckles, whose drag name was Setter, was also drawn into this expressive scene. "Kids were wearing outfits that they made at home," he says. "They looked like Las Vegas showgirls. They wore these beaded gowns from head to toe and headdresses that went all the way up to the ceiling. They *worked* on these outfits." Within a year Knuckles and Levan were established night owls. "Larry was the first person to take me down into Manhattan and show me these different clubs," says Knuckles. "It wasn't long before we were recognized as clubbers. If a club was opening they would invite us because we were always first on the dance floor. We were club kids before the term was invented."

The duo's entry onto the discotheque scene was timed to perfection. While Fire Island remained de facto out-of-bounds for black gay men, the Sanctuary and the Continental Baths were thoroughly mixed, and a number of other venues even began to target this pariah group specifically. One of the first was the Planetarium, an after-hours joint on Second

Avenue between Eleventh and Twelfth Streets that was painted black and had little stars hanging from the ceiling. Another forerunner was Jungle, a small club located on Second Avenue and Fifty-ninth Street that developed its motif via amplified "jungle noises" and paintings of foliage and trees. And Shaft, opened by Richard Long following the disbandment of the Coalition party collective, was also a popular option.

None of these venues, however, prepared Knuckles for the Loft. "I was at the Planetarium one night with some friends, and Larry came by. I hadn't seen him for a couple of months so we were playing catch up, laughing and giggling on the dance floor, and he asked me, 'Have you been to the Loft yet?' I said, 'No-ooo, I heard about it but I haven't been there,' and he said, 'Let's go!' " They arrived to discover a line of some fifty people. "We walked past them, and at the top of the steps there was this girl at the door named Yvonne. She knew Larry, who was a member at this point—Larry had met David, and they were becoming close—and Larry introduced me to her. We just walked right in, and I tell you it was unlike anything I'd ever seen before in my life. It was a trip. And the music was the absolute best."

The significant black gay presence at 674 Broadway meant that the likes of Knuckles and Levan never felt as if they were a token element brought in to add an exotic flavor (indeed if any group carried a curiosity value it was the straight whites). Ultimately, though, the Loft's appeal lay in its definitively mixed crowd and its quest to explore, rather than fix, identity. "The first time I went to the Loft I couldn't make out what the identity of the crowd was," says Knuckles. "At points it seemed like it was straight, at others it looked gay. In the end sexuality didn't mean a thing." Nathan Bush, who arrived from another part of town, was also won over by the multifarious makeup of the dance floor. "I was raised in Queens, so I mainly went to house parties, but the Loft was a completely different world. Instead of partying with people from your neighborhood, you met all types of people—artists, musicians, fashion designers, bankers, lawyers, doctors. Male, female, straight, gay, it didn't matter. The Loft was like a microcosm of New York. It was well mixed."

Bush had gone to school at St. Philip's Episcopal Church—with Levan. "I knew Larry when I was only ten years old," he says. "We were altar boys together. We all used to call him egghead because of the shape of his head. Larry was always getting into trouble. He couldn't remember what to do at the altar and stuff like that." Identities were already coming into focus. "I

guess you could say Larry was definitely gay at that point because he used to say, 'My cassock's not long enough! It's not dragging on the ground!' "
The two friends drifted apart when Levan switched schools, and Bush's reluctance to dance in gay-identified public spaces made it unlikely that they would meet again. "I didn't go to Stonewall and places like that because you didn't know who you were going to run into," he says. "I was still at high school and living at home, and I didn't want to run the risk of being seen in a gay club or a gay bar. But being in the Loft felt very safe because most of the people I met there were *not* from my immediate world, and once I got in I realized there were people I already knew. It was just that no one had told anyone else that they were going to these parties. That was when I ran into Larry again."

Bush and Levan started to hang out with a clique from the Fashion Institute of Technology whose main purposes in life were to sew and to dance. "The group included Shamako, Donald Woods, Raymond Gills, Larry, and myself," says Bush. "We used to dress to go out. We didn't wear suits, but we were always dressed. We didn't wear sneakers. That was unheard of. We wore shoes." Shamako became the key figure. "He used to sew for us, and we would wear all of these clothes that were a step ahead of fashion. They were club clothes, and eventually straight men started to wear the same kind of thing." Microcircuits were beginning to form within the Loft network, and one of the most influential revolved around Bush, Knuckles, and Levan, as well as figures such as Larry Patterson (one of Mancuso's closest friends) and Mike Stone (an intimate of Richard Long). A new alliance of black gay men was connecting, coming into consciousness, and getting excited about the future.

* * *

The Loft was necessarily private and discreet, but did this make it elitist? After all, venues such as Le Club were also closed to the public and depended on their exclusivity in order to function. Yet, while the entrance doors of these uptown venues were carefully regulated in order to protect the social preferences of the wealthy and the well connected from the hoi polloi, David Mancuso's selectiveness was organized around the defense of groups that wielded significantly less power. The admission policy revealed all: whereas participants in the European-inspired private clubs bought their elitism in the form of membership cards, Mancuso issued his invitations for free. Cultural influence, however, didn't have a price tag, for while Le Clubbers were driven by faddish, hedonistic fashion, Lofters were forging a radical lifestyle that, thanks to its underground (as it was referred to internally) status, would survive the fleeting present.

Radical and surreptitious, the term *underground* had forged its identity in entirely different circumstances when some one hundred thousand African Americans escaped enslavement on the Underground Railroad, a vast yet clandestine network of paths and roads that was established between the American Revolution and the Civil War. The term was subsequently used to describe the indigenous warriors who resisted the Nazi occupation of Paris before retiring to the Left Bank for a late-night glass of wine and a dose of "nigger" jazz music. Historian Arthur Marwick traces the contemporary American underground back to 1955 and the formation of the *Village Voice*, "the world's first underground newspaper," although activist, poet, and chronicler Jeff Nutall notes in his 1968 book *Bomb Culture* that the "word Underground was still, in the early sixties, not yet in common use," adding that the term probably began to circulate in New York around 1964.[3] A wide range of antiestablishment films, newspapers, poems, and plays began to circulate over the next couple of years and, together with the hippies and the yippies, formed a movement that was, in the words of Nutall, "concerned with world unity, world peace, current conflagrations, over-authoritarian government, nuclear disarmament and, above all, the appropriation of the maximum freedom for the individual, whereby he could strike and appropriate those levels of ecstasy that would provide him with a reason for living—thence to offer that ecstasy to other people in the hope that they too might start to want to live, might not wreck the whole boat through their own distaste for the voyage."[4]

Rock music, nature, love, drugs, and togetherness were the order of the day, and Mancuso considered himself to be part of this transitional coalition. "To me the underground began in the early sixties with the 'psychedelic,' 'hippie' movement," he says. "That was when I started to hear about an underground that didn't simply refer to politics. If you went to a provocative lecture that wasn't advertised, that was underground. It would be very private. It had to be word-of-mouth. It was kept very under. The underground was where it was safe. It was where you wanted to be." The Loft, according to Mancuso, occupied a similar space. "I didn't want to get involved in the entertainment business of the status quo. The Loft wasn't about that at all, and if somebody suggested that I should do something that would bring the Loft into visibility in some sort of way I would say, 'No, I want to keep it underground.'" Guests were asked to cooperate. "When you walked out of the door you didn't discuss what had gone on inside. You wouldn't say where you went or what you did. Going to an underground function meant that nobody knew about it except a few people and that whatever happened there was kept private. That's what kept it underground."

In many respects the sixties represented the coming out of the underground. The civil rights demonstrations, the antiwar movement, the Stonewall rebellion, and the burgeoning feminist movement were all explicitly public campaigns, and the countercultural practices that evolved around the consumption of rock and drugs also became increasingly public thanks to the emergence of the open-air music festival. Monterey, situated on the Californian coast south of San Francisco, marked the culmination of the Summer of Love of 1967, and, in August 1969, 250,000 revelers converged on Woodstock in upstate New York to listen to Janis Joplin, Jimi Hendrix, and the Who. Described by *Time* magazine as "history's largest happening" and "one of the most significant political and social events of the age," Woodstock embodied the newfound confidence of supposedly marginal groups that were now prepared to flaunt their beliefs and practices in the open air.[5] The countercultural movement was on the verge of seizing the political center—and inevitably shed the chrysalis of its clandestine identity in the process.

The social and political rebellions of the sixties underpinned the Loft's radical blend. "A lot of people were bonding and making relationships because of the Vietnam War and Martin Luther King," says Mancuso. "There were all the ingredients for a really good soup." The demos and the dance floor were part of the same continuum. "I was on the streets and in the party. Dancing and politics were on the same wavelength, and the Loft created a little social progress in tune with the times." Yet despite his long hair, flowing beard, passion for yoga, communitarian outlook, dedication to nature, and interest in psychedelics, Mancuso didn't identify himself as a hippie. "I wouldn't say I lived my life as a hippie. Real hippies lived in the woods or on communes. But I didn't think of *hippie* as a negative term." Nor did Mancuso align himself with the yippies—members of Jerry Rubin's Youth International Party—who were more overtly political than the hippies. "Yippie, hippie, jippie! I was like, 'We're *human!*' I didn't want to get into a categorized group." He was, however, prepared to describe himself as countercultural. "I was antiestablishment. I didn't like what was going on and I tried to do whatever I could to change what was happening in a positive way."

The term *countercultural* is a useful one, for while new leftists focused on political demonstrations, counterculturalists were more interested in lifestyle and leisure. Of course there wasn't a clear-cut distinction between the two, but Mancuso was finally less bothered about conventional politics than—to quote Theodore Roszak's 1968 definition of counterculture—"the effort to discover new types of community, new family patterns, new sexual mores, new kinds of livelihood, new aesthetic forms, new personal identities on the far side of power politics, the bourgeois home, and the Protestant work ethic."[6] Bringing together the diverse components of the often-segregated rainbow coalition into an egalitarian, tolerant, and positive space, the *social*ist party host contributed to what one cultural critic describes as "the moment of rupture against the consensual 'center.'"[7] And at the Loft rupture was realized through rapture.

For those who believe the sixties were part of an irrepressible wave of public protest, it might appear to be something of a misnomer to describe the private, cocoon-like phenomenon of the Loft as being representative of the times. However, a series of setbacks for the countercultural coalition at the turn of the decade provided Mancuso's parties with a new significance. Those setbacks ostensibly began in December 1969 at the free Altamont pop festival in San Francisco, which turned sour when Hell's Angels bouncers, supposedly high on LSD, beat up members of the audience during a Rolling Stones concert and finally stabbed one man to death. Two more violent deaths ensued, plus one drug-related drowning, and hundreds were injured. "Is this the new community?" one participant asked *Rolling Stone*. "Is this what Woodstock promised? Gathered together as a tribe, what happened? Brutality, murder, despoliation, you name it . . ."[8]

A wide-ranging critique of the countercultural movement followed. "*What went wrong?*" asked the twenty-seven-year-old rock critic Ellen Willis in an article for the *New York Review of Books*. "*We blew it—how?*"[9] Albert Goldman, analyzing the rock establishment, agreed. "'Grab the money and run' is their basic philosophy," he argued in the *New York Times*.[10] None of this, however, anticipated the shock waves that followed the brutal repression of a student protest against the Vietnam War at Kent State University on 4 May 1970 when, without provocation, the Ohio National Guard opened fire, killing four students and wounding another nine. History more or less repeated itself eleven days later when police gunned down demonstrators at Jackson State University, killing two and injuring nine. Suddenly the idea of a safe indoor party made perfect sense. "In the sixties people really thought that they would change the world," says Michael Gomes, an early devotee of the New York night network. "But after things like Kent State and the repression of the Black Panthers, the next youth wave realized that they couldn't change the world." Not that Mancuso's mixed crowd had necessarily been overly optimistic in the first place. As Gomes adds, black gay men and other marginalized groups "couldn't tune in and drop out because they had *nothing to drop out from.*" So, instead of creating a new world, these disenfranchised groups "created their own world, their own little artificial paradise, in which the clubs became these sanctuaries."

The countercultural movement hastily crawled back inside its cocoon. Having come out of the sixties, Mancuso formed a perfect bridge into the seventies by providing the disenfranchised and backpedaling rainbow coalition with a space in which to explore its sameness and difference— like glowworms coming out in the night to produce flashes of light in an otherwise gloomy terrain. Yet the subterranean status of the Loft didn't simply rest on the subordinate identity of the crowd, nor was it confined to the music-dance aesthetic being developed on Mancuso's dance floor. The Loft was also necessarily clandestine because Mancuso's guests were *trance*gressors who tripped out to music in a gray legal space. The drugs were, of course, illegal, but dancing was arguably the greater crime given that the Loft was situated in a building that had been set aside for industrial use in which Mancuso organized ostensibly commercial parties without a certificate of occupancy, a cabaret license, or officially sanctioned fire exits. Going to the Loft and keeping quiet about it wasn't a pose. It was a pragmatic practice.

3. pollination

The Haven opened on the site of the old Salvation in May 1970, the Salvation having lost its liquor license in December 1969 and its operator a couple of months later. Avant-gardism arrived in the form of Francis Grasso, who, just as Mancuso was settling into a groove, got itchy feet and left the Sanctuary to become the resident DJ at the revamped venue. It was, on the surface, a strange move, for, while the Sanctuary could hold over a thousand people, the Haven was chock-a-block with just three hundred. However, the DJ was unhappy with Seymour and Shelley, whom he found "obtrusive, rude, and notoriously cheap," and, when the new owner of the Haven, Nick Di Martino, offered him a quasi-managerial role plus a way into CBS-FM radio, he jumped at the opportunity. "At the time the profession was really open," says Grasso. "I realized there was money to be made."

Di Martino—the stepson of Paul Di Bella, a soldier in the Mafia family of Carlo Gambino, the reputed "boss of bosses" according to law enforcement officials—initially marketed the Haven as "the ultimate teen-age club," but by the end of the summer it had become a cliquish after-hours spot that attracted a mixed crowd of street people, gay men, and high society speed freaks.[1] "I didn't have to dress up anymore," says Grasso. "At the Sanctuary I wore slacks, at the Haven I wore jeans. You let it all hang out in the Village." The hours were also more relaxed—"The place wouldn't get moving until midnight, and it finished at seven in the morning"—and, thanks to Grasso, few left early in order to hunt down an alternative club. "It was *the* spot," says Steve D'Acquisto, a twenty-six-year-old cabbie who heard about the venue from a succession of passenger-revelers. "Francis was playing primitive funk and percussive soul long before anybody else. He was the integrator. Nobody stood there and thought, 'This isn't the Beatles.' They just dug his selections and were opened up to the world of dance. His mixing ability enabled him to integrate music."

An established record fanatic, D'Acquisto quickly befriended the DJ, and the duo became a trio when the driver invited a beautiful and not especially innocent sixteen-year-old called Michael Cappello to visit the club. "I went to the Haven with Steve and fell in love with Francis Grasso," says Cappello, who had previously hung out at the Electric Circus. "I had never heard music being blended before. Every change was on beat. There were no collisions. Everything flowed." That was until the awestruck newcomer dropped an enormous glass tumbler onto one of the turntables. "I was so amazed at what he was doing, it just came out of my hand. Francis wanted to *kill me!*"

Friendship prevailed and then flourished when D'Acquisto and Cappello became Grasso's trainee-alternates. "I told mystical stories and political stories, stories about love and stories about freedom," says D'Acquisto. "Life was a trip, and I wanted everyone to be high on music." Cappello listened carefully—and occasionally winced. "Steve had a different style to Francis and myself. He wasn't as smooth, and he wasn't as adventurous. He was more top ten. But he would do clever things with words. He liked to talk to people." Cappello, for his part, was technically closer to Grasso. "I spent so much time in the booth with Francis that I ended up playing like him. I was crisp. I would never miss a beat." Like a proud older brother, D'Acquisto looked on in admiration. "Michael was extremely creative with his mixes. He would do extraordinary things with records. He was a prodigy, a really great DJ." Cappello also demonstrated a talent for spotting a killer record when he started to rotate "Give It Up or Turnit a Loose" from the live album *Sex Machine.* "Michael found it first," says D'Acquisto. "We were all playing the eleven-minute version of 'Sex Machine' until Michael discovered 'Give It Up'."

Grasso, however, never really believed in the teenager's dedication or the taxi driver's ability. "Michael spent more time with me in the booth, and he was more in my mold, but he ruined a great many records on me," says the mentor-DJ. "He taught me to take speed in order to stay awake, but unfortunately he didn't follow his own advice. He used to take downs and fall on top of the record while it was playing. Michael tried his best, but he never really cared. People liked him because he was easygoing, but he could never really get a crowd to scream and yell." And D'Acquisto?

"Steve was a methodical player. He was more of an automaton than a DJ. Whereas Michael was a natural, Steve actually needed to be taught."

D'Acquisto was finally more reliable and more enthusiastic, and he got his first solo spot when Di Martino made an emergency phone call to Grasso. "Someone was supposed to fill in for Francis but failed to show up," says D'Acquisto. "Francis had just played for fourteen consecutive nights, and we were hanging out together. He was really wiped so he looked at me and said, 'Do you want to go and play records?' I said, 'What do *I* know about playing records?' Francis replied, 'Just make believe you're me!'" A few hours later, Grasso went to check up on his protégé and found him sitting outside the club. "Steve had dropped a tab of acid. He'd left an LP on the turntable and he just sat there saying, 'I can't do it! I can't do it!' This was the first night he was solo and he takes a trip!"

Michael Cappello, Steve D'Acquisto, Francis Grasso

Select Discography (Haven 1970)

James Brown, "Get Up I Feel Like Being Like a Sex Machine," from *Sex Machine*

James Brown, "Give It Up or Turnit a Loose," from *Sex Machine*

James Brown, "It's a New Day"

The Doors, "Roadhouse Blues"

The Four Tops, "I Can't Help Myself (Sugar Pie Honey Bunch)"

Aretha Franklin, "Respect"

Marvin Gaye, "I Heard It through the Grapevine"

Isaac Hayes, "By the Time I Get to Phoenix"

Gladys Knight & the Pips, "Got Myself a Good Man"

Wilson Pickett, "I'm a Midnight Mover"

Diana Ross, "Ain't No Mountain High Enough"

The Supremes, "Stoned Love"

Marva Whitney, "It's My Thing (You Can't Tell Me Who to Sock It to)"

Stevie Wonder, "Signed, Sealed, Delivered, I'm Yours"

So was formed the most influential DJing bloc of the period, with Cappello, D'Acquisto, and Grasso combining to make the new generation of club DJs—which also included Mancuso and would soon count Bobby Guttadaro and Nicky Siano among its number—a thoroughly Italian American one. Some sort of logic underpinned the ethnic pattern, for here was a hip, new profession of low to middling status that suited Cappello and company's second-generation aspirations. As the children of immigrant parents, they were already familiar with insecurity and up-heaval, and they used this know-how in order to negotiate the unstable terrain of nightworld. They also understood that flexibility and movement were integral to the process of finding a better job, which was just as well because few vocations were as insecure as that of the DJ. Having heard how their families had lugged around their prize possessions in order to survive, they now symbolically repeated the cycle with their cherished records, which they carried from venue to venue. Crucially, jobs were also relatively easy to come by, thanks to the fact that Italian Americans *ran* a high proportion of New York discotheques, and many of them were linked to the Mafia. Best, then, not to pay too much homage to the history of the French discotheque. New York *disco* ended in an *o* because it was Italian Americano.

At the same time, ethnic affinity hardly served as any kind of guarantee when it came to fair employment practices. Grasso was "let down" by Di Martino, who rapidly reneged on the promise of handing his DJ a mana-gerial stake in the operation, and things also didn't work out at CBS-FM, where he came up with the idea of 101 continuous minutes of music only to have the idea pinched from him by a producer. "I told them that the advertisements broke the mood of the radio station," says Grasso. "If they kept the music flowing they would hold on to their audience, and they could group all of the commercials together at the end. I even prepared a tape in their studio on Fifty-first Street. Unfortunately they forgot to tell me that they were going to steal my idea."

Di Martino received his comeuppance on 18 July 1971 when he was ar-rested for his involvement in the New Showplace, one of nine after-hours bars to be shut down as part of a wider federal and city police action that was aimed at the Mafia. "We hope that the underworld will think twice now about getting into this business," the chief of the New York Joint Strike Force told the *New York Times*.[2] As it happens, Di Martino's par-ticipation in the New Showplace wasn't clear-cut—he was believed to be part-owner of the building that housed the club—and law enforcement officials dismissively described him as being "unimportant."[3] There was, however, no ambiguity about his involvement in the Haven, which had been a high profile target ever since police raided the club in the summer of 1970 and arrested several people on charges of drug possession. These charges continued to plague the club and its clients, who were subsequently depicted by Assistant Attorney James Burke as being "a virtual congregation of narcotic addicts who roam the streets at will, threatening the residents."[4] Then, at the end of July, the state supreme court ordered the Haven to close.

Grasso had long since moved on—long at least in nightworld time, where nights seem like weeks and weeks seem like months—having left the Haven to return to the Sanctuary until a better offer arrived from the manager of a discotheque in the Empire Hotel called Machine. "They would cram two or three thousand people in there," says Cappello, who worked as Grasso's alternate. "That place was a *zoo*. People were all over the lobby. It must have scared the shit out of the people who were staying there." Fear, according to Grasso, also began to permeate the club itself when bouncers started to beat up clients for drug dealing before selling the seized contraband themselves, so when Di Martino offered him another deal he negotiated hard and became the joint owner of Café Francis—the first nightspot to be named after its mixer. "I became a commodity," says Grasso. "I became something nobody wanted to lose. 'You got hold of Francis, you made a lot of money.' That's exactly how it was put to me." The same sentiment was expressed in nonverbal terms when, on the opening night of the new venue, a Mafia man linked to the Machine approached Grasso, led him outside and gave him a severe beating. "Francis had twelve bodyguards and we didn't even see him leave," says Cappello, who was also Grasso's alternate at the new venue. "All of a sudden Steve came over and said, 'They've got Francis!' They broke his nose."

Grasso believes he was the victim of an overzealous foot soldier. "The guy was supposed to scare me into coming back to Machine but he got carried away. It's really nice to find out that you weren't supposed to be hit after you've been hit." However, Cappello reckons that both the foot soldier and Grasso knew exactly what was about to happen. "There might have been a few things going on at Machine but I didn't see any violence. The owners were paying him a lot of money so that he wouldn't play anywhere else, and he was treated like a king. He left because he had an ego like you wouldn't believe and when Nicky dangled this carrot in front of him he couldn't resist." Guilt, maintains Cappello, was written all over the DJ's decision to leave the protected zone of his booth. "If a guy walks into a beating he has got to be a moron and he has got to know he was wrong." D'Acquisto viewed events with a mixture of sadness and scorn. "If Francis felt he was a star, at the time it was valid. He had a huge following, and he was the first to perfect the art of DJing. But he got arrogant."

Grasso returned to Café Francis several months and a trip to the emergency ward later but hated everything about it. "The idea was sold to me as a brand new Rolls Royce but when reality intervened I found myself walking into a dungeon." The discotheque's design certainly lacked taste: *Francis* was spelled out in alternating red and yellow neon lights above the club's MacDougal Street entrance, and thousands of "I saw Francis" and "Francis Forever" button badges were scattered around the venue. "It was all Nicky Di Martino. I had nothing to do with it. It was so depressing I couldn't even play there." For the first time in the short history of the discotheque, it had become clear that no DJ, however skilled, could overcome a badly designed space, and that was a humbling lesson for a young professional who had come to believe in his own invincibility. Grasso's "fan base," it emerged, was more interested in the Sanctuary as an integrated complex than Grasso himself. "Francis was a great disc jockey, but I don't know if he was so different from the others," says Brezner. "The Sanctuary just made everything sound grand, and it was such an early stage that people were just happy to be there in that environment." La Torre agrees. "I don't know why we liked Francis so much. His music was definitely very good, and he kept us going on the dance floor, but I think it was the visuals and the space that made the experience so special."

D'Acquisto, meanwhile, had briefly played at the Sanctuary and Year 2000 before moving to Tamburlaine, a Chinese restaurant at 148 East Forty-eighth Street that metamorphosed into a nightclub at ten o'clock. Opened by Robert Chiu in October 1966, the eatery had featured music and dancing from the very beginning, with the Herb Waters quartet playing, in the words of the *New York Post*, "smooth music for dancing."[5] Some four years later, Nick Falco, a budding nightworld impresario, offered to create a post-dinner discotheque and set about hiring first Grasso (who was otherwise employed) and then D'Acquisto (who was recommended by Grasso) as his DJ. "It was a fabulous space," says D'Acquisto. "The decor was mock Oriental. There was a bridge, a pool, and these two trees. At ten o'clock, they would serve this wonderful buffet of free Chinese food. Jackie Onassis, Peter Max, and Keith Moon all came. It was the first time high society mixed with street people." D'Acquisto—whose biggest record was Marvin Gaye's "What's Going On"—proved to be a more than

Francis Grasso at Café Francis. Courtesy of Steve D'Acquisto

Michael Cappello at Café Francis. Courtesy of Steve D'Acquisto

adequate DJ, even though he had to work inside an enclosed booth. "Steve was the first DJ I heard," says Frankie Knuckles, who was studying at the nearby High School of Art and Design and would walk down to the club on Wednesday nights to hang out with the transvestites on the dance floor. "He wasn't a mixer, but back then mixing wasn't that important. His selection of music was excellent, and he kept the energy going."

Steve D'Acquisto

Select Discography (Tamburlaine 1971)

Booker T. and the MG's, "Melting Pot"

Bobby Byrd, "Hot Pants—I'm Coming, Coming, I'm Coming"

The Equals, "Black Skinned Blue Eyed Boys"

Marvin Gaye, "What's Going On"

Al Green, "Let's Stay Together"

The Isley Brothers, "Get Into Something"

Curtis Mayfield, "Move On Up"

Osmond Brothers, "One Bad Apple"

Wilson Pickett, "Don't Knock My Love"

Diana Ross, "Ain't No Mountain High Enough"

Titanic, "Sultana"

Tamburlaine rapidly established itself as a serious alternative to the Sanctuary for New York's evolving gay club crowd. "For a while it became *the* club to go to," says Jorge La Torre. "It was a fun place, and it was easier to get to know people because it was a lot smaller than the Sanctuary." David DePino, who had grown up with Falco on Mulberry Street in Little Italy and whose sister worked in the venue's cloakroom, also loved the new space. "Sanctuary was gay and straight, whereas Tamburlaine was gay, gay, gay. Tamburlaine was over-the-top gay." Few believed that D'Acquisto was the catalyst that drove the Tamburlaine (even though the DJ says that Tamburlaine was his "greatest club"). "I don't remember Steve D'Acquisto so much," says La Torre. "He certainly wasn't as important as Francis Grasso. The in-group went along, and that's what made it relevant." DePino concurs. "Steve D'Acquisto was good, but Tamburlaine was the star. It was all drag queens, rhinestones, and mink coats. Tamburlaine was so flamboyant, so wild, and it was right there, bang in the middle of everything on Forty-eighth and Lexington. It was such a scandal."

The scandal was nevertheless about to be officially—if quietly—tolerated, thanks in no small part to the negotiating skills of the Gay Activist Alliance and, less predictably, Steve Ostrow. "We were central to the campaign," says the owner of the Continental Baths. "We set up tables on Broadway and organized a petition on the need to change the laws on enticement and entrapment as well as legalize homosexuality. We collected 250,000 signatures and took them to the government." A mixture of idealism and entrepreneurship drove Ostrow. "Steve was very involved in negotiating away the restrictions on men dancing with each other," says La Torre. "It was in his interest to bring about these legal changes, and he made it his business to know the people who were working in city hall."

In October 1971, Mayor John Lindsay's administration went public on the need for reform. "The laws are impossible to enforce and have simply been a vehicle for corruption and oppression," announced the deputy commissioner from the Department of Consumer Affairs. "Homosexuals have a right to congregate in places of public accommodation. They have a right to a drink." Lindsay's spokesperson added his voice to the decision to relax regulations governing the admission of gay men to cabarets, dance halls, and restaurants, announcing that the changes "appear to be consistent with administration policy of broadening safeguards for citizens against all forms of arbitrary victimization."[6] In December the landmark proposals were adopted. "We can rightfully take 30 percent of the credit," says Ostrow. "The other 70 percent came from the Gay Activist Alliance." The Tamburlaine, however, would only be a brief beneficiary.

* * *

Francis Grasso packed up his records and left the discotheque that carried his name after just a couple of months. Broken-hearted and broken-faced, he thought that he would probably never DJ again, but then came a timely call from the Sanctuary. "I was the prodigal son," he says. "No matter how many times I left, I would always return. It's very important to be able to relax where you work, and of all the clubs I worked in I was never more at home than when I was playing at the Sanctuary." By now the Sanctuary needed Grasso as much as Grasso needed the Sanctuary. The venue had lost its liquor license following a series of raids, numbers were down, and co-owner Shelley had been shot dead. "Shelley was into Puerto Rican hustle boys," says Grasso. "He went to hang out at Port Authority, and the story goes that he was killed by a male prostitute. He took the kid home and got his head cracked open. Seymour had always told Shelley that he went round with too rough a crowd, but Shelley's attitude was 'the rougher the better.'"

Grasso and the Sanctuary once again worked their magic on each other. The DJ was reenergized by the dramatic space on West Forty-third Street, and the discotheque entered into a period of bustling popularity. "There was an intense rivalry between Steve and Francis," says David DePino. "Tamburlaine became *the* biggest club to go to in the gay world, and Sanctuary was *the* biggest after-hours venue, so you always went from one to the other. Francis's name was out there, and Steve became a real diva. You couldn't go into the booth with Steve, and you couldn't talk to him. It was like, 'Steve, would you play this for me?' *'Leave me alone!'"* Tamburlaine had the higher public profile. "Sanctuary was underground," says DePino. "People didn't know where the Sanctuary was, and it opened at 5 A.M. so there was never a line to get in. But Tamburlaine was in a very busy neighborhood. Directoire, Hippopotamus, and Le Club were on the same block so it attracted a lot of attention, and nobody had ever seen a six-foot-five drag queen with two tons of hair and fourteen feather boas walk out of a limousine before." The Catholic Church responded in a familiar manner. "The Arch Diocese submitted a forty-eight page subpoena to have Tamburlaine closed."

The action was rendered meaningless when Tamburlaine burned down in mysterious circumstances on Christmas Eve 1971.[7] "Nicky Falco had a torch job done on the place because Mr. Chiu was fed up with him," says D'Acquisto. "It was a vindictive measure. Nicky Falco was a thug. He was sponsored by the Mafia." DePino disagrees. "I know Nicky didn't start the fire because the club was in its heyday. Some people think it might have been the landlord, some people think it might have been a neighbor, and some people think it might have been natural." Whatever the cause, Falco responded by shifting his energies to another venue, Tambourine, a bar-discotheque with a deliberately similar name that was situated at 350 East Eighty-first Street, near First Avenue. D'Acquisto was asked to play, word began to spread, and David Mancuso became an early visitor. "I had been to Tamburlaine," says the Loft host. "I heard it had moved, and I wanted to see the new location." Mancuso enjoyed D'Acquisto's selections and decided to invite him to one of his parties. "David came up to me and

I said, 'You're beautiful!'" says D'Acquisto. "We were like brothers at first sight. He said, 'Would you like to come to a party?' and he gave me an invitation to the Loft."

D'Acquisto took Cappello as his guest, and by the end of the night the two of them—who up until that point had never entertained any serious doubts that they, along with Grasso, had nightworld under their thumb—were converts to the cause of the house party. "I thought David looked like Jesus Christ," says Cappello, who was self-confessedly high at the time. "He had the best sound, and the music was excellent. I loved the Loft." D'Acquisto was equally impressed. "I walked in, and the whole place was just shimmering. It was like a cross between outer space and a big playhouse. I'd never seen anything like it. I was blown away." Excited about their discovery, the two Brooklynites took Grasso to the Broadway party. "I said to myself, 'This guy is great,'" remembers the Sanctuary DJ. "That was the one and only time—I swear to God—I ever walked into another venue and said, 'This is incredible.' That night I said to myself, 'Wait a minute, I don't think I'm the best in New York anymore!'"

Less senior than Grasso, less driven than D'Acquisto, and less mystical than Mancuso, Cappello hadn't given a moment's thought to whether he was the best or not, but that didn't stop him from landing work as the resident at the Haven and the Sanctuary before Seymour invited him to take over at a new venue called the Limelight, which was situated in the heart of Greenwich Village on Seventh Avenue and Sheridan Square. "Limelight was very quaint," says Cappello. "There were these old brick walls, and it had this magnificent stained glass ceiling over the dance floor. The crowd was very diverse—gay, straight, and racially mixed. Limelight was a real dance place. People danced all night. Limelight was my turning point."

A not-so-private fan club soon began to form. "Michael was hot," says future girlfriend Lisa Hazel. "He had a swagger. He was incredible looking, Italian Roman, a lot of sex appeal. There were lots of boyfriends and girlfriends. Everybody wanted Michael." Nicky Siano, then a sixteen-year-old self-described "wisp of a queen" who wore "nutty professor" big glasses, was equally mesmerized. "The first time I saw Michael I was in awe. He was moving in time to the music, and his long hair was swaying back and forth." Diehard Grasso fans, however, kept their cool. "Michael Cappello was just some cute kid who played records," say Richard Brezner. "There was no comparison whatsoever with Francis. Francis broke new ground. I never thought of Michael as being serious." Jorge La Torre also managed to retain his composure in the DJ's presence. "Michael Cappello was good rather than great. He was popular because he was personable and good-looking." Cappello nevertheless did know how to play. "Of all the DJs back then, my favorite was Michael Cappello," says DePino. "He had a way of making you dance and not wearing you out. He used to say, 'Watch the room! If you see a certain number of people dancing to four or five records you should change your style, let them go drink, and get the people that are drinking to come and dance. Move your room around!'" Siano was also impressed by the DJ's technique. "Michael was just so smooth. He just plopped the needle down, and it sounded great. I thought Michael was a great DJ."

Mancuso aside—and to a certain extent Mancuso always was aside—the Brooklyn troika were the most accomplished and in-demand DJs. "The DJs made the club, and there weren't enough of us," says Cappello. "Francis, Steve, and me were it in the early seventies. We had it sewn up." The line between success and catastrophe, however, remained unnervingly thin, even for the Limelight idol. "Nicky Falco walked into the club one night with seven guys," recalls the mixer. "They came up to me and said, 'You're coming to work for us!' I said, 'No way! I'm not getting into a Francis thing!'" Cappello pointed to the front door where the owner was standing. "I said, 'Listen to me! You go and see him! I'll work for whoever's standing at the end!' I was in demand, and it got scary."

Grasso also found himself back on the tightrope that ran between triumph and tragedy. "When the Sanctuary went after-hours it became a lot more straight, and toward the end Seymour was just cashing in on demand," says the DJ. "I rocked the house, and it got out of control." The decision to hire out the discotheque as a location for Alan Pakula's 1971 film *Klute* typified and accelerated this shifting profile. "The crowd ended up spilling out onto the street. The whole block became the Sanctuary. Oh, please, it was so *pervasive*! Those kids trashed the block. People were sucking and fucking all over the place. I pitied those poor people that paid rent. It was like Mardi Gras every Friday, and we were open until twelve o'clock midday."

Drugs rather than sexuality now drove the space, and, with Shelley no longer around to broker deals with the police, raids were increasingly frequent. "One night I went to work and there were cops at the door," says

Grasso. "They asked me, 'What are you carrying in that bag?' I said, 'I work here! These are my records!' We now had New York City policemen as our doormen!" That didn't stop drug consumption shifting from LSD and poppers to speed and quaaludes. "The management was paying five cents a piece for the quaaludes before selling them on for three dollars. That's when people started dancing by themselves. They were in a world of their own." Mark Riley, who had heard about the venue from some gay friends, was part of the newly enlightened throng. "The booth was directly in front of a stained glass window, so early in the morning, when the first rays of the sun would come through, you would think that Francis was a priest and we were his congregation—because it used to get like that."

The situation was unsustainable. Toward the end of March 1972 the state attorney general described the discotheque as "a menace to the community" and "a supermarket for drugs." Seeking a state supreme court order to close the club, he said, "The lure of the Sanctuary has attracted numerous youths to the neighborhood who have made life miserable for the residents by threatening, abusing, molesting, and intimidating them."[8] Permission was swiftly granted, and Riley, still spinning, witnessed the last rites unfold. "The fire department walked in at about six-thirty in the morning wearing gas masks. We all thought they were part of the club and were wearing these terrific outfits. I said, 'Jesus, this is a great place!' Turned out they closed the space down."

D'Acquisto's fortunes also plummeted. "Tambourine was a much smaller place than Tamburlaine," he says. "It was seedier. Drugs started playing a bigger part, and it attracted all of these cocaine addicts. None of the nice people from Tamburlaine would go there." The absentees included La Torre ("Tambourine was much less important than Tamburlaine") and DePino ("Tambourine was a shadow of Tamburlaine"), and when violence became endemic D'Acquisto decided that it was time to move on. "One of the bouncers got shot. They took his body and laid it across my feet in the DJ booth. I put on James Brown, *Live at the Apollo*, took my records and left. I said, 'I'm out of here! I don't do shootings!'" Shell-shocked, D'Acquisto left New York and traveled to Montreal at the end of July, and the following month the media reported that police were being "summoned with depressing regularity to clear the street, investigate shootings, stabbings or beatings, and to arrest drug violators" at the venue.[9] When Tambourine was closed at the beginning of September, residents strung colored lights on their balconies and organized an Eighty-first Street block party.[10]

* * *

Back on Fire Island, the competition between the Sandpiper and the Ice Palace was building up. Malcolm—who took care of the discotheque side of the business—installed Don Finley behind the turntables, and the DJ established a dedicated following that included a proportion of Michael Fesco's crowd from the Grove. "It was the beginning of learning," says Alan Harris. "I would have to say that Don Finley was God for that period. There was nothing better than seeing everyone sing along to 'What's Going On' and 'Ain't No Mountain High Enough.' He knew when to interject those records to create the maximum sensual effect, and people began to feel comfortable dancing in one another's arms." Richard Brezner was part of the throng. " 'What's Going On' was *the* song. I remember hearing those first two words—'Mother, mother'—and those gorgeous string arrangements. When it was played in the Sandpiper everyone would hug and sway. The warmth of the music, the romantic sounds—it all embodied Fire Island Pines."

It also embodied Cherry Grove, where the Philadelphia-born David Todd had replaced stand-in DJ Bob Casey. "I was hired to do the electrics and the sound, but the guy who was spinning came down with hepatitis," says Casey. "I took over, but I wasn't prepared for it. I had no records and no history of hanging out in clubs. Nor did I really want to do it. My thing was sound." Fesco soon found a replacement. "I was working at a record shop on Thirty-fourth Street, opposite Macy's, and Michael Fesco happened to be one of my customers," says Todd. "I'd never DJed before, but Michael liked my selections and wanted to know if I'd give it a try. That's how I got started. Marvin Gaye's 'What's Going On' was the big record that summer."

Todd, however, struggled to match his Pines counterpart. "By the spring of 1971, Don Finley had a following that kept the crowd all season," says Casey. "People would swarm to the Sandpiper to hear him. It was Fesco's worst year." It could, however, have been a whole lot worse. "The Sandpiper was small in comparison to the Ice Palace, and we still held our own," says Fesco. "Saturday nights were always full. It was just the weekdays that suffered." Sundays were also sluggish, but then Fesco, drawing on an earlier visit to London in which he had participated in the custom of going to a gay bar at teatime on a Sunday afternoon, introduced high tea. "I had to do something to pay the rent so I hired this huge silver service, and we actually served tea and crumpets at 4 P.M. I got our DJ to play records and persuaded one of Cherry Grove's famous drag queens to dress up in his finest ball gown and serve tea."

Fesco's Sunday afternoon monopoly was short-lived—"Everybody picked up on the idea within three or four months"—but nobody could copy his decision to hire a young Italian American (what else?) DJ called Bobby Guttadaro as the season drew to a close. With his neat brown hair, trimmed mustache, heavy black glasses, and freshly signed graduation certificate from the Brooklyn College of Pharmacy, Guttadaro appeared to be too clean-cut to be a DJ, but that didn't worry Casey, who auditioned the DJ, or Fesco, who wasn't being picky. "Bobby Guttadaro had a bunch of records," says the Ice Palace boss, "and in those days if you had the records I would hire you!" Guttadaro immediately dispelled any doubts about his ability when he became the first spinner to home in on "Theme from Shaft" by Isaac Hayes, although his colleagues were still left with the problem of what to call him given that there were already three other Bobbys at the Ice Palace. "In the end I was the only one to hold onto my real name," says Casey. "We had Bobby Bartender, Bobby Doorman, Bobby DJ, and Bob Casey."

In the winter Fesco decided to embark on a grand redesign. Casey was hired to install a new sound system, the DJ booth was moved onto the dance floor, and the discotheque area was divided into two. "The main floor was actually a very small area," says Casey. "It made the Ice Palace a much warmer and cozier place. They knew that it would take a much smaller crowd to fill the place and create a very hot night." Fesco also came up with the idea of setting up a small system in the Sea Shack restaurant so that Bobby DJ could start to generate a pre–Memorial Day buzz. "I remember helping Bobby bring his records up from the ferry in early April," says Casey. "It was so cold that the boardwalks were covered in ice, and the only way we could move the hand truck was to walk in the sand, pushing and sliding the cart on the icy wood." The nights showcased Bobby DJ as a new talent. "By 1972 Bobby had a few thousand forty-fives and thirty-threes. Every week he would make a trip to his home in Brooklyn and spend hours picking out stuff for that weekend, including some surprises." Guttadaro pushed gospel songs like "Rain" by Dorothy Morrison, and he would also regularly drop in a Carmen Miranda number from the

1940s. "That was Bobby's music—real up, real happy, party time. Bobby had fun when he played. His humor always shone through. He was far more spontaneous than Don Finley."

Word had spread by the time the Ice Palace finally opened. "Saturday night was jammed," says Casey. "Just when you couldn't fit another sweaty body onto the dance floor the staff pulled back the portable partition, and the crowd poured into the big room. It was an instantaneous success. With all credit to Mike Fesco it worked flawlessly." The trend of the previous year was reversed in a single night: now it was the Pines partygoers who were making the half-mile trek along the beach. "You could take a water taxi, which took five minutes, or you could walk through an area known as the meat rack, in which case you would pass through the section where everyone was having sex in the bushes," says Richard Brezner. "Sometimes you made it to the Grove, and sometimes you didn't." Those who made it witnessed Fesco's most successful season to date. "The Ice Palace was the *only* place to be on a Saturday night," says Casey. "Nineteen seventy-two was a pivotal year."

Fesco strengthened his dominance by starting a movie night (followed by dancing) and holding special shows that would feature live acts such as fifties songster-turned-actress Della Reese and jazz singer Carmen McCrea (again followed by dancing). In addition, Casey started to organize a "demented American Bandstand" on Sunday afternoons where he would play oldies from the fifties and early sixties, interspersing his selections with gossipy banter and spoof commercials. "Say, is the riding getting rough, chafed, irritable?" ran a favorite. "Then get into life smoother, deeper, and faster with KY sterile lubricant. Forget that old-fashioned method. Spit spreads germs, anyway. So remember. If you want to fly, buy KY!" The sessions were a hit. "As the crowd began to show up, Mike rushed a few bartenders into position, and those gay dollars came pouring in," says Casey. "By 3:45 the Ice Palace would be jammed with people doing the Lindy Hop, the Slop, the Bop, the Stroll, and, of course, the Twist. In 1972 the Pines didn't have a chance."

Inasmuch as the Sandpiper had a reply, it came in the form of soul aficionado Tom Moulton, who made his first trip to Fire Island that summer. "I had been working in the music business, but I started to get very turned off by the politics," remembers Moulton. "I kept saying, 'This is lousy! Why do I have to subject myself to this kind of crap?'" Moulton quit the music industry at the end of 1969, and, falling back on his chis-

Bob Casey in
the DJ booth at
the Ice Palace.
Courtesy of
Bob Casey

eled looks, began to model for an agency called Bookings International where John Whyte, the owner of the Boatel, a hotel complex situated in the Fire Island Pines, was also putting his handsome profile to profitable use. When the owner of the agency told Moulton that he should visit Whyte's establishment, his response was brusque. "I heard about Fire Island. It's just a haven of sin and drugs!" He went out all the same and ended up going to Whyte's Sunday Tea Dance. "I was amazed that all of these white people were dancing to black music. The rose-tinted glasses came out and I thought, 'Oh, isn't this wonderful! The music is bringing everybody together!'" The only problem lay in the organization of the music, which lacked continuity. "I was so frustrated listening to this guy try to play. People would start to dance, and two minutes later you would hear this other song come in. It sounded terrible, and most people would leave the floor."

Moulton came up with the idea of compiling a tape of nonstop music, put together a forty-five minute mix, and handed his work to Whyte. "It took me eighty hours to make that tape," says Moulton. "It was so tight and so right, and all he could say was, 'Don't give up your day job!'" The next morning Moulton made his way to the ferry, entered a nearby café to kill time, and started talking to the manager, Gene Smith, who was in charge of running the restaurant end of the Sandpiper. "He asked me why I was looking so gloomy and I told him the whole story. He said that he didn't know anything about music but would pass the tape on to his partner, who ran the discotheque." Ron Malcolm phoned Moulton a couple of Saturdays later to say that his compilation had flopped, but in less than twenty-four hours Moulton received a surprise 2 A.M. call. "I picked up the phone and said, 'Hello, who's this?' *Is this Tom? Is this Tom?*' I said, 'Yeah, but turn down the music, I can hardly hear you!' *'Listen to the screaming!'* 'Who is this?' *'Ron!'* I didn't know who Ron was so I said, 'Call me tomorrow!'" Malcolm had wanted to tell Moulton that his tape had filled in for an absent DJ and had been a huge success. "We spoke the following day, and he said that on Fridays the crowd was tired and wanted something familiar, but by Saturday night they were ready for something fresh."

Malcolm requested more of the same—much more—and eventually Moulton agreed to produce recordings for the Sandpiper's three peak events: Memorial Day, the Fourth of July, and Labor Day. According to the compiler, the tapes were more effective than any DJ. "Don't forget, humans make mistakes, whereas my tapes were perfect." The tapes were also well behaved and reliable, unlike the increasingly temperamental Finley, but as far as Casey was concerned they did nothing to chip away at Bobby DJ's summer supremacy. "I don't remember ever seeing or hearing a 'good' night at any club that was playing tapes. It doesn't work that way. The DJ has to be able to feel the crowd and vice versa." Alan Harris was also unmoved. "The tapes worked at the Boatel at Tea Time because there was a less chemically oriented society in the afternoon, but they didn't work at the Sandpiper." The ability of the DJ to improvise remained central to the dance floor dynamic.

Back at the Ice Palace, Guttadaro was winding down. In the middle of September he played at the Miss Fire Island contest, and the following week he took to the turntables at the Art Festival Ball, the last big event of the season. "After that we moved some equipment to the Sea Shack restaurant, and we put Bobby in a little square space," says Casey. "We called it the Ice Cube." By this point Guttadaro was playing for time as much as anything else, and a more durable position emerged when Continental Baths owner Steve Ostrow invited him to replace Jorge La Torre, who had in turn replaced Don Finley. "Don Finley started to play at the Baths at the end of his first season at the Sandpiper in the fall of 1971," says La Torre. "Richard Orbach knew him and made the introduction." Finley soon established a name for himself on the Manhattan circuit. "Don was

Steve Ostrow (right) and Richard Orbach at the Continental Baths. Courtesy of Jorge La Torre

one of the best," says Michael Cappello. "He couldn't mix, but he played incredible music. He was into really good soul. He took chances." However, he also walked out of the Baths after a few months, at which point Ostrow turned to La Torre. "I DJed for six or seven months," says La Torre. "I did it because I had to. I loved being a DJ, but I loved being on the dance floor even more. I realized that I had to decide between one and the other, and I chose the dance floor. That was when we asked Bobby Guttadaro to play."

Guttadaro didn't need much persuading. The Baths had become the hottest gay discotheque in the city following the demise of Tamburlaine and, thanks to its nightly shows and the rising reputation of Bette Midler, the venue was the focus of a double-page spread in *Women's Wear Daily* in February 1972. "It's the steamiest spot in town," declared the fashion industry newspaper. "Nicknamed the Tubs by the regulars, the Continental Bath & Health Club is making a big splash with the Firsties, those young New Yorkers who are the first anywhere. Just to be first."[11] The feature was pivotal. "We were already a fully formed club, but the article made people aware that the Continental Baths was a fashionable place to go," says La Torre. "We hit full stride at that point. It became terribly chic to go to the Baths—to this *steam box*. All sorts of celebrities came along." The unofficial in-house celebrity, though, was La Torre. "Jorge had incredible style," says Ostrow. "Everyone followed him when it came to fashion. Jorge became a gay icon, and a lot of important people came to the Baths because of him."

Guttadaro blended in perfectly. "I was much more impressed with the kind of music he played than I had been with Don Finley and even Francis Grasso," says La Torre. "It was more high energy, and his mixing was a little more creative than some of the other DJs. Plus he was a nice guy." Within a couple of weeks it was clear that hundreds of other dancers were of a similar opinion. "Bobby called me up and said, 'You're not going to believe this!'" says the ubiquitous Casey, who lived just a few blocks away on Sixty-ninth Street. "We walked down the stairs, and the entire crowd from the Grove was there. It was like a bus from Fire Island had dumped everybody at the Baths. The crowd came back looking for a place to go and—bam! Bobby was probably the first DJ to 'bring his crowd with him.'" La Torre maintains that the Ice Palace crowd had in fact been visiting the Tubs all along. "The Cherry Grove element had been coming already because they are the kind of people that like going to places like the Baths. We were a public venue, and anyone who could afford the entrance fee was entitled to get in." Yet there was no doubting the crowd's delight when they realized that Guttadaro was the new DJ. "In the middle of the night Bobby repeated his favorite mix of the summer—'Date With the Rain' into 'Zing Went the Strings of My Heart'—and you could hardly hear the music the cheer was so loud," remembers Casey. "It was like saying, 'One more time!' Bobby just burst out laughing."

The Baths was starting to function as a social beehive for New York's gay male population. "All sorts of possibilities stemmed from the experience," says La Torre. "It gave gay men a great deal of confidence, and people started to think, 'We can take this one step further.'" The relaxation of restrictions on gay male dancing at the end of 1971 contributed to the gathering momentum. "The gay community had been involved in the clubs from the very beginning, and once the police backed off it took on more of a gay tone. The scene had already been ignited, and now it began to take shape."

The discotheque's infrastructure, however, was beginning to fall apart. "Bobby and I saw Bette Midler in her last performance at the Baths, and the sound system broke down, the air conditioning broke down, everything broke down," says Casey. "The DJ booth was tiny. There was no place to put records, and the door to the dressing room was behind the booth.

That was how Bobby got to meet Bette Midler." And that was also how Casey, who had launched his own sound company, Virgo Sound, in August 1972, got to install another system. "Bob Casey was fun, and he was very talented at what he did," says La Torre. "He could be a little obnoxious at times, but he was the man to talk to when you wanted a new system." The setup made its debut at the Thanksgiving party in the last week of November—just in time to meet head on the opening of Tenth Floor.

* * *

David Bruie, Jim Jessup, and David Sokoloff weren't nightworld's most likely club coordinators—Bruie was a charming and popular party boy with a great build, Jessup was a crazy, older self-designated "man of the world" who came from Montreal and worked as an architect, and Sokoloff was an intelligent yet hazardously insecure and enigmatic outsider who ran his family's construction company—but that didn't stop them from dreaming. "They were one of a series of elite groups on Fire Island," says Richard Brezner, a close friend of Sokoloff. "David Sokoloff and David Bruie used to stay at Jim Jessup's house in the Pines." Jorge La Torre also knew the threesome from the holiday destination. "They all came to parties at my house at the Pines. The Sandpiper closed really early so we would invite people over to keep the party going." The circle subsequently regrouped at the Continental Baths before they decided to open their own venue. "It was kind of like Judy Garland and Mickey Rooney—'I know, let's get a group together and have a show!'" says Brezner. "They just wanted to get a group of people together, open a club, and make some money. I don't think there was anything deep going on."

David Mancuso's Loft provided the impresarios with an up-and-running party template. "Jim Jessup used to come to the Loft, and I got along with him very well," says Mancuso. "One day he said he and a couple of friends wanted to open a Loft-style party that would be strictly gay and white. They wanted a private club atmosphere so that it would be more discreet, and they said they would only proceed if I said it was OK." Fortunately Mancuso was on a *trance*mission: the dance was political, the music contained the message, and he wanted the combination to spread—as long as the process of reproduction remained organic and discreet. "I told them, 'Please, go right ahead!' I gave them all the help I could. It was like a good joint. You passed it. I said we were like bees and could pollinate." With the waiting list for the Loft parties heartbreakingly long, Bruie, Jes-

David Sokoloff. Photo
by Richard Brezner

sup, and Sokoloff promised to provide a much-needed release valve. "It was all leading to a common goal," says Mancuso. "We didn't try to define it because it would have become like an organized religion. It was just a feeling."

Named after its location—the tenth floor of an ex–sewing machine factory in an unused manufacturing block at 151 West Twenty-fifth Street by Fifth Avenue—the Tenth Floor opened on Wednesday 6 December 1972 with a party that started at ten and wound up at three. Minimalism ruled the night: the decor was sparse in the extreme, the slender sound system consisted of six Bose speakers, and the capacity was limited to a couple of hundred people. "It wasn't a beautiful, expansive place," says Brezner. "It was a tiny loft, a thousand square feet at the most. There was nothing impressive about it, and I'm sure it didn't cost them much. They just painted it and installed a sound system. There was nothing special about the space except that it afforded people a private place to go."

Ray Yeates, a light-skinned black DJ with piercing light blue eyes, provided the music and homed in on records such as Area Code 615's "Stone Fox Chase," "I'll Take You There" by the Staple Singers, the Glass House's "I Can't Be You (You Can't Be Me)," and the quasi-autobiographical "Black

Skinned Blue Eyed Boys" by the Equals. "He was one of the first DJs to go techno," says Bob Casey, who installed the sound system. "He believed he had to educate the dancers so he played avant-garde, spaced-out stuff, and in the process of sticking his neck out he had both good and bad nights." Alan Harris remembers the bad. "The age of quaaludes hit very heavily, and Ray would collapse on the turntables." Brezner recalls the good. "Ray certainly got people moving, and he became *very* popular." According to Brezner, Yeates was both pragmatic and progressive. "He played music that no one else played, and he also used this feature called 'sound-on-sound.' He would take the record he was playing to one channel and bring in the next record on the other channel. Then he would flip a switch and the new record would be playing through both channels. It was a very primitive way of mixing, but it *worked at the time.*"

The quality of Yeates's performance, however, didn't finally make a huge amount of difference. "There was as much if not more nondancing space as dancing space," says Brezner. "The dance floor might have held

Ray Yeates. Photo by
Richard Brezner

a hundred people at the very most." Inasmuch as there was a dance floor, it didn't drive the parties, ostensibly because of the excruciating climb to the entrance—the elevator was famous for being out of order—although more probably because of the networking tendencies of the venue's upwardly mobile, strictly gay crowd. "There was more looking than dancing," says the shaven-headed, black-mustachioed Frank Crapanzano. "It was very sociable, lots of conversation. It was the Sanctuary with a face." Vince Aletti agrees. "It was fun, but less intense than the Loft."

Thanks to the intimacy of the invitation system, the Tenth Floor became the first dance venue to meld together the emerging yet nevertheless fragmented constellation of gay individuals and cliques into a fugitive clan. "At the Tenth Floor people would say, 'Oh, you know *my* group of friends wants to meet *your* group of friends,'" says Crapanzano. "People were identified with certain families, and these families came together and got to know each other. Then our peripheral friends would say, 'Oh, take me with you because that way we'll meet lots of people!' So the family grew." The emergence of an unofficial uniform reinforced the clan's sense of identity, for, whereas the dancers at the Sanctuary had simply dressed up in their Saturday night best, Tenth Floor regulars donned Levi's jeans, construction boots, a hooded zippered sweatshirt, and a waist-length flight jacket that was silver on the outside and orange on the inside, with the hood of the sweatshirt invariably flipped outside the jacket. "The Tenth Floor's neighbor made the flight jackets," says Casey. "First the owners and staff wore them, then their friends wore them, and before you could mix two records together it was a trend. Bloomingdale's was selling them within a year."

The outfit augmented the bonding process, as did the perception that the members of the Tenth Floor constituted an emerging elite. "The Tenth Floor crowd had begun to form at the Pines and the Baths," says La Torre who, despite his affiliations, was a big fan of the new venue, "but this was one step up." Regulars were referred to as "the five hundred"—the five hundred people you apparently always wanted to be with—and Mancuso's invitation template inadvertently contributed to the atmosphere of superior chic. "The Tenth Floor was the first disco where all of the gay 'stars' would go," says Crapanzano. "Egon von Furstenberg would be there. Famous models would be there. It was very exclusive and very glamorous." Yet while class was deemed to be crucial, it was also impenetrable. "It had more to do with what you looked like, how you dressed, and possibly what you did for a living than how much money you had," says Brezner. "I'm not sure anybody knew about other people's financial situation, and everybody tried to masquerade as being more than they were, which is a gay thing *and* a New York thing."

If you were black, however, it was usually difficult to masquerade as white and that appeared to matter at the Tenth Floor where the crowd was overwhelmingly Caucasian. "There were just high-level blacks—fashion models and designers," says Crapanzano. "Like everything else in our society, that's the way it was." Others, such as Loft devotee Nathan Bush, detected an element of design. "It was obvious you weren't welcome. Even though I went with friends, and I knew some of the people who were dancing, I felt uneasy." Bush had grown up in a predominantly white school system and had always felt comfortable in any crowd so he kept telling himself that there was no reason why he shouldn't be able to communicate in this new environment, but it didn't work. "If you tried to dance or socialize people gave you this look like, 'Jesus, what are you doing here?' They might not have felt that way, but a lot of white people are insensitive to people of color. The cultures are slightly different so sometimes the person might not want to be insulting, but it comes across that way. I said to one of my friends, 'I don't think we're meant to be here.'"

Others dismiss the charge of latent racism. "I don't think there was anything like that going on," says Brezner. "Ray Yeates was black, and David Sokoloff was just like me—the color of your skin just wasn't a factor. Jim Jessup only liked black boys." The Peruvian La Torre even detects an element of self-sabotage. "People didn't go out of their way to exclude blacks," he says. "It just sort of happened. They didn't want to be a part of the Tenth Floor because they didn't feel comfortable, and I think that had something to do with there not being very many black people around. It was the blacks who more or less alienated themselves." According to Bush, though, the handful of African American and Latino men who did fit in usually did so as boyfriends and sex objects rather than full-fledged cardholders. "There was a group of Spanish men and black men that some of us called 'snow queens.' They were very small in number, and they didn't like black men or Hispanic men. They only liked white men. So we called them 'snow queens.' That's a very strong term, but—what can I say?—you label people."

Sex was more overt than it had ever been at the Sanctuary. "I always saw the Tenth Floor as a little on the foreboding side," says Brezner. "Sex was very incestuous, and that wasn't my cup of tea. I come from a middle-to upper-middle class Jewish family in Ohio, and no matter how much pot I smoked that wasn't my intention. My brain wouldn't let me do it." As far as Brezner was concerned, the claustrophobic atmosphere was pervasive and invasive. "I didn't feel I could go there and get lost and have a good time. There were too many people around that I knew and didn't care for because they thought they were hot stuff, which was pretty much what that place was about." The gay scene was changing, and Brezner felt nostalgic. "There was nothing similar about the Tenth Floor and the Sanctuary, and I preferred the Sanctuary. The Sanctuary was a party palace, whereas at the Tenth Floor people took themselves very seriously. It was a snotty, gay social thing. If you weren't a member then the big thing was, 'Can they get me in?' That always made me nauseous. To me it turned into *the* pretentious party of all times. I'm biting my tongue saying that, but that is the way I saw it. I didn't like my best friend's club."

Other Tenth Floor patrons felt more comfortable with the free-for-all atmosphere of Mancuso's Broadway parties. "I went to the Tenth Floor and I went to the Loft, and there was a big difference between the two," says Harris, who went to Mancuso's party as the guest of his lover, Cary Finkelstein. "There was no attitude at the Loft. David was a *really nice man*, he played the type of music I liked, and he had a very crossover crowd. The Loft was, 'Let's embrace everybody who can get in.' The Tenth Floor, on the other hand, was much more attitudinal. It was about who's in and who's out." There was also a different sexual agenda at the Chelsea venue. "The Loft was about dancing, whereas the Tenth Floor was about dancing and getting laid," adds Harris. "At David's, the group was too diverse for that. You would dance with a three-hundred-pound black lady and have the most fabulous time. That wouldn't happen at the Tenth Floor—they would screen that person out at the door. The Loft was warm and loving, whereas the Tenth Floor was sensual and sexual. There was definitely a feeling of, 'Let's go out and get laid,' and the Tenth Floor met that demand. It was certainly needed at the time."

Mancuso visited the offshoot and was left unmoved. "I went to the parties once or twice. They were OK, but it wasn't my scene. They only took a part of the party. It was a white male gay thing." While the Tenth Floor revealed the dispiriting ease with which the communal and protective Loft invite system could be restyled effortlessly into a socially elitist door policy, the Loft host wasn't unduly distressed. "The Tenth Floor was fine. I didn't have a problem with it. I had seen places like that before, only they weren't in loft spaces or organized around cards. But I had my own parties to be getting on with." And even though the first bees to leave his hive had carried an uncomfortable sting in their tail, Mancuso's influence was beginning to extend beyond his own parties. The Loft had become a transferable template that could be applied to alternative groups and spaces, and this now included the scene that had traveled from the Sanctuary to Fire Island to the Continental Baths to the Tenth Floor. The dance was developing, and Mancuso had devised the framework through which it could spread.

4. recognition

Fronted by a plainclothes policeman, officers made their first raid on the Loft in 1972. "We asked to see this guy's invite and he didn't have one so he had to go away," says David Mancuso. "However, he was good-looking, and he persuaded someone to take him in as a guest." Having done what he had to do, the cop left the party and returned with re-inforcements, at which point Mancuso and Abramowitz were arrested and charged with running an unlicensed cabaret. "They thought we were a fly-by-night after-hours joint who wouldn't fight the case, but they were wrong." Mancuso's position was surprisingly strong: his events were not open to the public, and there was no alcohol for sale, which meant that he and Abramowitz were not guilty of running an illegal cabaret. "We were able to prove that the cop was a guest and not a member of the public. They targeted us because nobody else was open at half past four in the morning without drugs, gambling, drink, or cash, but they found *nothing*. The judge said we were a private party, not a cabaret."

The threat of closure continued to hang over the Loft, however, for while the space was safe—there were sufficient fire exits and so on—the paperwork was missing, and the judge hadn't gone as far as the Loft host would have liked. "The case was thrown out of court but no prece-dents were established," he says. "The police could still come along and do the same thing two weeks later." Operating in gray legal territory, the parties attracted raids like flypaper, and as a result Mancuso decided to introduce an elaborate warning system that was already in use in a number of West Village bars. "If the cops were coming then we would flip a switch, and a warning light would go on in David's booth," says Steve D'Acquisto, who returned to Manhattan in February 1973. "Yellow was caution, they're driving by. Flashing yellow indicated they're slowing down. Flashing red was they're coming up the steps. You had to take the music off, turn up the lights, and everybody would just hang around and sit on the floor."

When the sirens weren't ringing Mancuso could play whatever he wanted, safe in the knowledge that there was no club proprietor threatening to impose a playlist, and his selections revolved around heavily percussive tracks such as Exuma's "Exuma, the Obeah Man," jazz and soul-influenced cuts like "City, Country, City" by War and powerful peace songs such as Willie Hutch's "Brother's Gonna Work It Out," as well as epic recordings like "Girl You Need a Change of Mind" by Eddie Kendricks. "All of these records had balls. People said what they wanted to say, and the music drew everybody in. It was in sync with the times."

David Mancuso

Select Discography (Loft 1970–73)

Brian Auger & the Trinity, "Listen Here"

Babe Ruth, "The Mexican"

Barrabas, "Wild Safari"

Barrabas, "Woman"

The Beatles, "Here Comes the Sun"

Beginning of the End, "Funky Nassau"

Booker T. and the MG's, "Melting Pot"

James Brown, "Get Up I Feel Like Being a Sex Machine (Parts 1 and 2)"

James Brown, "Give It Up or Turnit a Loose," from *Sex Machine*

Chakachas, "Jungle Fever"

Cymande, "Bra"

Manu Dibango, "Soul Makossa"

The Equals, "Black Skinned Blue Eyed Boys"

Exuma, "Exuma, the Obeah Man"

Aretha Franklin, "Ain't No Way"

Al Green, "Love and Happiness"

Willie Hutch, "Brother's Gonna Work It Out"

The Intruders, "I'll Always Love My Mama"

The J.B.'s, "Gimme Some More"

Eddie Kendricks, "Girl You Need a Change of Mind"

Morgana King, "A Taste of Honey"

Gladys Knight & the Pips, "It's Time to Go Now"

Little Sister, "You're the One"

Curtis Mayfield, "Move On Up"

Dorothy Morrison, "Rain"

Van Morrison, *Astral Weeks*

The O'Jays, "Love Train"

Olatunji, "Drums of Passion"

Osibisa, "Survival"

Edwin Starr, "War"

Traffic, "Glad"

Tribe, "Koke"

Troubadours du Roi Baudouin, "Missa Luba"

War, "City, Country, City"

War, "The World Is a Ghetto"

Epic in their scope, panoramic in their field of vision, and finely variegated in their structure, "Girl You Need a Change of Mind" and "City, Country, City" were the standout tracks, microcosmic representatives of a programming philosophy that had germinated in the countryside before it was transplanted to NoHo. "Girl," which was organized around an intense series of peaks and troughs, distilled the rhythms of life into a concentrated eight-minute chronicle, and "City, Country, City" described Mancuso's biographical map, with the record's journey from city to country to city operating as a dual metaphor for the different tempos of rural and urban life plus the Loft reveler's split existence between Woodstock and Manhattan. Crucially, both records contained the kind of ebb and flow that Mancuso had first recognized in the countryside—the way in which the day would begin quietly at sunrise, intensify in the afternoon, and then become soft at sunset—and, drawing on *The Psychedelic Experience Based on the Tibetan Book of the Dead* and its theory of spiritual enlightenment, he began to program his music around this "natural rhythm" in order to sustain his guests over an entire night. "Leary wrote that there were three stages, or three Bardos, in a trip, and I found myself using the same structure. The first Bardo would be very smooth, perfect, calm. The second Bardo would be like a circus. And the third Bardo was about re-entry, so people would go back into the outside world relatively smoothly."

Like a weaver, Mancuso would gather different fibers, knitting them together to produce an intricate musical tapestry. Records were integrated according to their instrumental or verbal meaning, and, as the connections unfurled, a story would evolve that always exceeded the confines of the musical format. In isolation the vinyl tracks were limited and autonomous, but the elaborate juxtaposition of different records over a period of six to eight hours would extend the narrative from a short tale to an intricate epic. Yet, just like the framework mapped out in *The Psychedelic Experience*, the musical Bardos rarely surfaced as separate experiences but instead intersected with each other. While Mancuso's extended set usually opened with a range of esoteric selections that slowly built into a fully charged session of African and Latin rhythms, driving R&B, and danceable rock before ending on a calmer note, the "musical host" (as Mancuso preferred to think of himself) was never afraid to mix things up, throwing in an expected Nina Simone song here and a sound effect there. "David would get very atmospheric," says Frankie Knuckles. "He could have the most incredible energy going on in the room, and then all of a sudden he would create a tropical rainstorm. The room would be completely blacked out, and you would hear this crackling of thunder and rain, which became louder and louder. It was *hot*, and everybody would be standing there, some half-naked, whistling and screaming. Then you heard this wind blowing, and after a short while you would also start to feel it because he turned these fans on." Dancers pinched themselves to check where they were standing. "It was as big as life, and if you were on acid it wasn't your imagination—this shit was real."

Initially Mancuso didn't have a mixer—the piece of equipment that enables a DJ to play two records simultaneously, with separate volume controls for each channel—and as a result he would move between phono one and phono two in order to maintain the musical flow. "He would just keep bringing the needle back, and when it was time he would just turn this switch," says Danny Krivit. "Sometimes the records would be right on, sometimes not, but there was always a feeling going on." After about a year he got hold of a rudimentary mixer and started basic blending, although within the context of the wider drama the concept of mixing simply wasn't an issue. "David was never about the mix, and everybody knew that," says Knuckles. "It wasn't a problem. The best thing about

David was that he had such an incredible taste for music, and he knew how to *play* that music. He wasn't trying to be technically sharp in terms of mixing or overlaying or blending. He just put on the record and let it play. You enjoyed it, and then it was time for the next one."

Mancuso rarely obtained his music from exclusive sources. He didn't set foot in a record company until the late 1970s, so relatively few promotional packages came his way, and he generally went to the same record shops as other DJs (first Colony Records, then Downstairs Records). Indeed, Mancuso was a less fanatical buyer than most and more often than not obtained records not by purchasing them but by receiving them from friends. Mancuso's most important skill, however, was to unearth a diamond from a heap of dirt, and to most ears his selections were radically new. "When I met David I didn't know who he was," says Ronnie Coles—originally and subsequently Ronald Cesario Colez—a one-time Broadway dancer who now worked as a sales assistant at Colony, specializing in pop, R&B, and musical scores. "He was buying all of these odd records that nobody else was asking for. He invited me to go to the Loft, and that was my introduction to this whole dance scene. His music was incredible, and the majority of what he played was on import." Seasoned night owl David DePino was also swept away by Mancuso's sound. "The music was very different. I didn't recognize anything." And Loft devotee Aletti was similarly dazzled. "It was exciting, a whole new group of records. Eventually I realized that I had some of the same records but I hadn't heard them in the same way, or else he would play different cuts off the same album."

Mancuso's superior audio system, which now included two Philips turntables, provided the foundation for this expansive repertoire. "David was able to play songs that were inherently underground and bring them to your attention right away," says Krivit. "If I played an obscure song like 'City, Country, City' on a crummy system the crowd would be bored in two minutes, but at the Loft you would really get lost in it. Nobody could touch David's sound for the longest time." A series of concerts, including a Ravi Shankar performance at Lincoln Center, had encouraged the party host to try and make his audio system sound as real or as live as possible ("I tried to improve my sound system so that it would take me back to the live moment"), and a transcendental experience at the Blue Hole near Mount Tremper, some twelve miles outside of Woodstock, intensified the mission.

"There was this little stream that went into a quarry," says Mancuso.

"It was maybe a few feet wide, and there were these little whirlpools that looked like speakers, so I leaned over and got as close to them as possible without getting wet. The sound was incredible. It was the cleanest sound I had ever heard, and there was all this information. It was almost as if I could hear the history of life, not in words but in music." The experience raised Mancuso's life energy. "It made me happy. I knew it was correct. It was constantly giving birth. It wasn't repetitive. It was as organic as you could get. It was coming directly from the source. And I thought to myself, wouldn't it be wonderful if you could record this correctly so that when you played it back it would be accurate enough for you to empathize with the original moment? I wanted to be able to hear the spirit of the babbling brook in my room."

In 1972 Mancuso came up with an idea that would revolutionize his sound system: an additional array of tweeters. Industry-standard loudspeakers contained a single tweeter for the transmission of high-end treble frequencies, but Mancuso wanted to introduce eight JBL tweeters for his two speakers, with each cluster arranged like flowers so that they would face north, south, east, and west. "I wanted to get as close as possible to pure sound, and I thought the tweeter arrays would help with the high hats, which weren't as sharp as I thought they could have been in some recordings. I was trying to create stereo vision so that you could see the whole sonic painting, and I wanted to find out if the tweeters would help me do this."

Unable to turn his sonic fantasy into reality, Mancuso turned to sound system specialist Alex Rosner, who had developed an unbreakable bond with music ever since a joint performance with his father at Auschwitz had saved his life. "The commandant recognized the two of us from the concert, and he winked at my father as he pulled all the other kids away," says Rosner, who played the accordion alongside his father's violin. "All of the other children were killed." Once in America, Rosner studied electrical engineering, but a sideline in installing hi-fis became so successful that he ended up building the stereophonic discotheques at the Canada-A-Go-Go and the Carnival-A-Go-Go stands at the World's Fair 1964–65. Rosner also sold Mancuso the Cornwalls that coincided with the conversion of the Broadway loft into a dedicated dance space, and the soundman was eventually invited to one of the Broadway parties. "I had only been involved in discotheques as an extension of my high fidelity hobby, but when I walked into the Loft and saw what was going on there I just tore

Alex Rosner landing in the United States with his accordion. Courtesy of Alex Rosner

my shirt off and started to dance. David was very idealistic, and that idealism caught me. From that point on when someone wanted a club I bent over backwards to give them the lowest possible price."

Over the next couple of years, Rosner established himself as New York City's premier discotheque sound specialist. He provided Mancuso with his homemade stereo mixer, the "Rosie," and he also installed systems at a series of high-profile venues, including Directoire, the Ginza, the Limelight, Max's Kansas City, Shepheard's, Tambourine, and Tamburlaine, as well as the Haven, where he worked on the system alongside Richard Long. "Richard and I were going to be partners, but that didn't last very long," says Rosner. "There was a turntable problem on the first Saturday night after opening, and since Richard lived around the corner from the Haven and I lived in Queens I called Richard to see if he would handle it. He said he was in the middle of a party at his house and couldn't leave so I went, took care of the problem, and dissolved our partnership the next day. We never worked together again after that."

For all of his experience, however, Rosner was skeptical when Mancuso told him about his idea of creating an array of tweeters. "I poohpoohed the idea and said that it was too much. David replied, 'Never mind what you think. Just make them for me!'" Along with his technician, Angelo Di Giuseppe, Rosner mounted the tweeters onto two fourteen-inch wooden plates and hung them from the ceiling so that the end product resembled a cross between a chandelier and a miniature flying saucer. "The sound was magnificent," remembers Rosner, who quickly switched into ironic mode. "So I said, 'Gee, it's a great idea! I'm glad you listened to me!'" The fizzing energy of the new tweeters resuscitated the sound system. Flat records could now be sharpened, enabling dancers to hear high-end frequencies that were being drowned out by the hullabaloo of the party, and the placement of the arrays above the dance floor produced a new geography of listening in which the treble emanated from the center of the room and moved outwards rather than downwards. "It was like a ripple in the water," says Rosner. "The illusion was that the entire sound was coming right from the dance floor, even though only the highs were coming from there."

The only problem was that the sound was now top-heavy, so Mancuso decided to try and bolster the bass. "Some recordings needed a little more bottom," he says. "There is hardly any bass on 'Girl You Need a Change of Mind,' and I wanted to be able to make it fuller. I thought I could season the sound without messing up the frequencies." As with the tweeter arrays, these low-end reinforcements—later dubbed "subwoofers" or "basshorns"—didn't require the invention of a new technological concept but rather the strategic redeployment of an already existing component. "I asked Richard Long to go out and buy me some Vega bass bottom speakers," says Mancuso. "Richard was on the verge of setting up a sound company at this point, and I wanted to give both him and Alex business. Alex was good for the whole sound, but Richard liked bass, and I wanted bass reinforcements." Long, however, insisted that Mancuso try out his custom-designed equipment instead of the Vegas. "He built these speakers, and they blew out the first night. He came back, repaired them, and then they blew out again. I didn't like them and they didn't work so at that point I went out and bought the Vegas. I was quite content with the result. I had Richard build me the crossover for the bass bottoms, just as Alex had built the crossover for the tweeters."

The result was startlingly impressive, with the bass receiving such a boost that, in the words of Rosner, "it vibrated in your *loins*." The competition was left way behind. "David showed me this tremendous setup," says Bob Casey, who received a personal tour in 1972. "He wasn't at all comfortable because he wanted better this and better that. He was hoping I might come up with some ideas, but he knew more about it than I did. From this point on all systems were judged against Mancuso's. The Loft put a new demand on high-quality systems." The sound of nightworld was beginning to crystallize, and Mancuso was its most influential innovator.

* * *

Gay men might have been central to the revival of dance culture in Manhattan, but gay dance floors were few and far between. If you wanted to dance at the Ice Palace or the Sandpiper, then you had to leave the city, and if you went to the Continental Baths or the Tenth Floor then you would have to put up with two of the tiniest dance floors around. Most other venues were mixed, which meant they included an important contingent of gay men but were not restricted according to sexuality—or anything else for that matter. "Who or what a person was sexually was not that big an issue at the time," says Michael Gomes, who moved from Toronto to New York in 1973. "Race, color, belief, and sex were minor details in the dance. What was important was *can you get down?* There was no gay or straight, just the joy of the music. This was what made the period so special." DJs appeared to embody this fluid situation. "Many of them indulged or were indulged in the male-male sexual act, but orientation is a different thing," adds Gomes. "You definitely would not have pronounced them gay according to the standards of the time. Many of them had girlfriends, and others had been married." That, however, didn't stop them from doubling up as girls. "We all used to call each other 'Mary,' even if you were straight. It was, 'Mary, where are you going tonight?' 'Mary, who's she sleeping with?' The original reference was Jimi Hendrix's 'And the Wind Cries Mary.' We were all experimenting with new means of communication and used any tools that worked."

When female friends managed to charm their way into this inner circle they usually did so as mother figures, surrogate sisters, essential confidants, fashion stylists, and dance partners, with the wheels of steel a no-go zone. The exclusion was historical. Figures such as Regine, one of the French "originals," and Sybil Christopher, one of the proprietors at Arthur, successfully played the role of hostess, but their female contemporaries rarely found their way into the DJ booth, and when they did they were usually required to go topless and dance to their selections.[1] Even though that particular ritual was relatively short-lived, openings were ostensibly even harder to come by for female jocks in the expanding ecosystem of the early 1970s. "The club owners were male, white, and straight," says Gomes. "They knew that a lot of the dancers were gay, so they probably figured that a woman DJ wouldn't be able to draw in a gay crowd. It was all about who had a following and who could fill a room." Not that sex and gender were easily demarcated categories. "Most of the women who did break through were lesbians. The female DJs were the real male DJs because in the underworld everything is reversed, right?"

The relatively short list of butch femme mixers included Bert Lockett, who had trained as a radio DJ in the mid-sixties before she landed a spot at Ernie's Bar on Seventh Avenue between 136th and 137th Streets in 1970. "Bert was technically a male DJ," says Gomes, who met the Buffalo-born jock during an outdoor performance in Bryant Park. "She didn't play gay. She was the 'dyke on the mike.' That was one of her monikers." Not that it was necessarily an advantage to be a lesbian. "Some of the men didn't know I was a woman," says Lockett, who had short hair and would regularly wear a jacket and tie. "They would get very angry if they found out I was a girl. I looked like a fella, and they had a problem with that." Inasmuch as Lockett had a problem, it lay with her co-DJ. "He worked six nights a week, and he was so jealous of my ass he started to tell me what records to play. The audience was saying, 'They need to get rid of him and let *her* play!' In the end I had to leave that place because he was getting out of hand."

Lockett set herself up as a mobile and attempted to break into the lesbian scene. "Bonnie and Clyde was a gay women's club where the customers would just come in, have a drink, and then leave. I went up to the owner, who was called Elaine, and I told her that I was a disc jockey and asked for a chance. I had a trial and she said, 'I want you Friday, Saturday, *and* Sunday!' I got those people to buy drinks. It was phenomenal." Lockett was forging new ground. "I was the only woman who was top stuff, by which I mean I was known in the city." Even the lesbian scene had its downside, though. "Women disc jockeys weren't respected, not even by women. It turned out to be very evil in Bonnie and Clyde, and I ended up leaving."

Lockett's next break arrived in early 1972 when she became the inaugural DJ at a newly established gay male club called Better Days, which was situated on Forty-ninth Street and Eighth Avenue. "I had gay men try to touch me," she says, "because they thought I was a cute guy." The crowd, however, proved to be harder than usual to win over. "The gay male audience took their parties *seriously* because that was all they did. They were more critical." That still made them easy customers in comparison to the proprietor's wife. "She kept requesting some record, and I told her, 'I can't get to it. When I get to it I'll play it.' She kept on asking for this record, and in the end I had a big blow-up with her. The owner fired me for talking to her like that."

Lockett was replaced by Toraino "Tee" Scott, a black gay dance fanatic who got his break at the Candy Store on Fifty-sixth Street between Fifth and Sixth Avenues when he complained that a newly installed DJ couldn't play as well as his predecessor. "There was this rumor that they were trying to oust the other guy on some stupid technicality," Scott told Daniel Wang in an interview. "So I went up to the manager and told him, 'You know, I don't want to say anything bad about this guy's playing, but I'm sorry, he's just not the same as the guy that you had before.'" Scott's complaint won him the opportunity to audition at the club, and after three weeks of propping up the bar he was offered a fifteen-minute slot. "I had a handful of albums and three or four forty-fives with me, and when I started playing it caused such a reaction downstairs that people came running upstairs to the DJ booth to find out who I was. I ended up playing forty-five minutes that night instead of fifteen. The manager said, 'I'll be in touch with you!'" [2]

Scott started playing regularly three weeks later, and two months after that a Candy Store regular told him that Better Days was looking for a new DJ. "Bert Lockett did a real no-no with the boss's wife," Scott told Wang. "The boss's wife had asked her to play a request, and Bert told her, 'I don't play requests!' and the woman said, 'Do you know who I am?' And Bert said, 'I don't give a fuck who you are, I don't play requests!' That was the end of her job." Scott auditioned, seized the residency, and set about putting Better Days on the map, which was no easy task given that the booth didn't have a cueing system, the lightboard didn't work, and the sound system was Neanderthal. The new resident initiated a major renovation. First, he designed an amplifier with a headphone so that he could pre-cue his records; next he bought hundreds of feet of AC line cord in order to control the lighting system; and finally he persuaded Alex Rosner to wire up some tweeters and bass reinforcements. "Better Days was a bar-club, and I had to compete with the underground clubs," says Scott, who had started to hang out at the Loft and took his sound system prompts from Mancuso. "I had to diligently start improving my sound system and my music. I made it so that when you came to Better Days you started dancing from the time you got in there until you left."[3]

As new names began to emerge, older ones, including Francis Grasso, continued to fade. "Earlier crowds were in awe of what they were listening to," says Michael Cappello, who hired the ex-Sanctuary resident as his alternate at the Limelight, "but Francis would hang out in the mix, and it could be rough for the dancer, whereas my mixes were short and I never lost a beat." Grasso was also out of sync with important shifts in dance floor taste. "Limelight was a gay bar, and Francis wasn't into girl stuff. I didn't employ him for long." A boisterous Puerto Rican called David Rodriguez, who *was* into girl stuff and called himself the Contessa to prove it, took Grasso's place in February 1972. "David's ear was not in the mainstream, and he would play these very off-the-wall female vocalists," says Limelight regular Nicky Siano. "They weren't always that great, but once in a while he would find a really amazing record." The DJ's discoveries included Brenda Holloway's "Just Look What You've Done," "I've Got to Use My Imagination" by Gladys Knight & the Pips, Betty Wright's "If You Love Me Like You Say You Love Me," "Dirty Ol' Man" by the Three Degrees, "Up the Ladder to the Roof" by the Supremes, and, most influentially, "Yes We Can Can" by the Pointer Sisters.

Rodriguez would link these and other records together in an utterly distinctive style. "David was the queen of storytelling," says Siano. "A lot of people did that, but no one did it like Rodriguez. With him it was *all about the words*, and he would actually match up the words between one song and another song so that they would form a complete sentence. It was really quite interesting sometimes. Rodriguez was more of a risktaker than any of us." A uniquely extreme performer, the Contessa was also renowned for turning on the PA in order to announce his mood so that dancers who felt differently could find another club ("You're only a bunch of ants on my mound!" was a signature phrase). Friends attest that Rodriguez didn't know when to stop with the drugs and that he was "not a happy drunk," yet he also possessed the sharpest wit on the circuit—Siano remembers Rodriguez saying "I'm more of a man than you'll ever be and more of a woman than you'll ever get" long before anyone else had come up with the line—and some of the scene's toughest critics were admirers. "Rodriguez was very, very good," says Jorge La Torre. "He was extremely expressive." That was enough to make Rodriguez a key player.

David Rodriguez (center right) at the Limelight. Michael Gomes: "A disc jockey at work. The guy on the right selects the records, the guy on the left provides the gossip." Photo by Waring Abbott

"He was more of a star than Steve D'Acquisto," says Siano. "He developed a following and that was what made a DJ a star."

Grasso, meanwhile, finally realized that his own star status had been effectively extinguished when his old boss Seymour opened a spot called Hollywood at 128 West Forty-fifth Street and overlooked him in favor of not one but five other DJs: Joey Palminteri, Frank Strivelli, Tony Gioe, Paul Casella, and Richie Kaczor. "I knew Richie Kaczor when he had thoughts of becoming a disc jockey," says Grasso. "He was a regular at the Sanctuary, and later on I found out that he was a friend of Irene, one of my ex-fiancées. He used to get Irene to put these questions to me. When I asked her why she wanted to know she said, 'My friend wants to become a disc jockey.' Richie Kaczor's style was similar to my own, but he was more syncopated, less wham-bam."

Situated on the site of the old Peppermint Lounge, Hollywood entertained a shifting clientele. On weekends the club—which was fitted out with an Alex Rosner sound system—would attract a low-key straight crowd, but, as one of the only nightspots that opened every night, it also became *the* major hangout for DJS and dance aficionados who needed a midweek music fix, and the young, mustachioed Kaczor—whose specialty involved manipulating the variable speed controls so that the playing record and the incoming record would run at the same beats per minute—was quickly recognized as an important talent. "I was mixing, but I don't think I was as good as Richie," says Paul Casella, who played weekends at the Monastery, the most important discotheque in Queens. "He was one of the first guys to overlay records and play them back-to-back. He would take two copies of 'Girl You Need a Change of Mind' and play one behind the other for the entire record, and then he would get out of it and bring in the next record, which would be perfectly in sync even though he only had two turntables. It just drove people insane. He was so good and his mixing was flawless. I told him, 'I'm using that!' He said, 'No problem, don't worry!'"

Thanks to the resilience of entrepreneurs such as Seymour combined with the unquenchable demand of dancers such as La Torre, clubs continued to open more quickly than they closed, and this momentum was boosted by John Addison's entry onto the scene. A closeted horticulture student from South Africa, Addison had earned his first American dollars as a model with Ford before he decided to enter the transitional world of clubland. "I've always loved throwing parties," he later explained to the *National Observer.* "Even as a kid growing up, I'd have my friends dress up in togas and come over for Roman parties—with slaves and everything. That was in South Africa, and they were always elaborate productions. So when I came to the States it was natural for me to get into discos."[4]

Having unsuccessfully applied for a job at Arthur, Addison teamed up with Fifi Nicolas, set up the Fi-Jo Disco Corporation, and launched Superstar at 420 East Seventy-first Street. The venue was forced to close in May 1972 when the state attorney general charged that it had become "a notorious public nuisance," but by then Addison and Nicolas had launched Together, an all-night juice bar with a jukebox that was situated next to the Fifty-ninth Street Bridge. "There was no advertising," Addison told the *National Observer.* "It was a completely underground club. But everybody knew about it, and everybody came."[5] The sleek South African, however, was ultimately interested in the kind of money garnered from bar takings, and he accordingly turned his attention to Le Jardin, which he

Bobby DJ at
Le Jardin. Photo
by Waring Abbott

opened in the basement of the Diplomat Hotel on West Forty-third Street. On the surface, the new venue promised to replicate the Euro sophistication of discotheques such as Le Club through its art deco roof garden, silver palms, and high-tech lighting. Yet Addison, whose roughed-up fur coat symbolized his refined-but-streetwise persona, was also keen to draw in the dance-crazy downtown crowd, and so he accordingly established an open-door policy and headhunted Bobby DJ from the Continental Baths. "John had money and knew people who had money," says Steve D'Acquisto. "He was smart, sophisticated, and classy. He was in a different sphere to the pseudo-Mafia world of the other club owners." The class of Le Club was about to meet the synergy of the Sanctuary.

Le Jardin opened for business in the middle of June 1973, and while the new venue didn't receive—or indeed seek—the same kind of press coverage as the launch of Arthur, the right kind of celebrities nevertheless made an appearance. "John Addison told me the next day that Diana Ross and her group showed up for about an hour or so," says Bob Casey, who installed the club's sound system. "She was escorted to the roof garden, which Addison had created for the 'in' crowd. He was excited because he felt that the word would really get around." The presence of key dancers from the Grove and the Pines also boosted the discotheque's prospects. "Le Jardin was a quite fabulous place," says La Torre. "I loved it. The music was great, and I knew a lot of people there. We were just partying very hard at that point. The place was packed." While Addison had marketed his venue as "a club for gentlemen," it ended up attracting a crowd that was mixed leaning toward gay. "Of all the discos, Le Jardin was one of the most mixed," adds La Torre. "John Addison got the gay crowd, but there were also a lot of celebrities. I don't think it was ever John Addison's intention to create a gay club." Once again, boundaries were being blurred. "Le Jardin's target group was upscale avant-garde, fashionable, and trendsetting," says Casey. "All of these characteristics were compatible with its very large gay following, as well as the straights who ran in those circles."

Yet for all of the continuities between the dancers at Le Jardin and other club crowds, Addison's venue generated a qualitatively different impression. "Up until Le Jardin dancing had been a more or less underground thing," says La Torre. "Clubs were in basements or places that nobody ever

John Addison, urbane myth, at Le Jardin. Photo by Waring Abbott

Dancers at Le Jardin. Photo by Waring Abbott

went to. But Le Jardin was extremely visible, smack bang in the middle of Times Square and Sixth Avenue." That, combined with Addison's chic-on-the-cheap furnishings, left a number of purists somewhat discontented. "Le Jardin was bigger than the Limelight, prettier, less cozy," says Michael Cappello. "The people were nice enough, but it was definitely more commercial." Michael Gomes was also left with an empty feeling. "Le Jardin was supposed to be the height of New York glamour, but it was just a basement with some wicker chairs," he says. "People went there to be seen rather than to dance. Boy was it a disappointment. *Toronto* had better clubs than New York!" Fortunately, however, Gomes was about to discover a party space that would make him change his mind.

* * *

Nicky Siano and Robin Lord didn't do what American high school seniors were supposed to do. They ate in the West Village, made love within earshot of Siano's parents, dealt drugs, and danced at the Firehouse, which was situated in the home of the Gay Activist Alliance and featured Richie Rivera behind the turntables. "The Firehouse was your basic hangout," says Lord. "There weren't a lot of drugs. There was maybe some pot but no acid or downs. It was the kind of hangout that my mother really didn't mind me going to all that much." Synergistic levels were comparatively low. "There was dancing, but it was secondary, and it never had the rhythm. They didn't have a disc jockey that could work the crowd, and the sound system was just a blaring noise."

Siano and Lord were introduced to the more radical end of New York's nascent night network by Dale Zotos, third-grade teacher by day and dancing queen by night. "Dale was the ex-girlfriend of my older brother, Joe," says Siano. "She wanted to take us to these clubs." The first was Tamburlaine, which they visited the night it burned down. Next came Tambourine, where they bought quaaludes from the six-foot-six Judy Gemini and threw up all over the dance floor. Then Zotos took the duo to the Loft. "It was *pulsating!*" says Lord. "It was instantaneous, and it was contact high." Mancuso made his usual impression. "David was ethereal, not of this world. He had all these people who were worshipping him. Nicky thought he was the perfect DJ."

In fact, Siano maintained that Mancuso *surpassed* any meaningful definition of the DJ. "There were these white lights, these six-hundred-watt floods, and these floods were *so bright* and they would *flash*," says Siano. "Your pupils would dilate, and then—boom!—the next second David would throw you into total darkness so you would go totally blind for a moment. Then he would turn on the air conditioner, and all of a sudden you would feel this cold chill. Then there would be a couple of people sitting next to this table lamp, and the lamp would just go out. It would be just so-ooo freaky-deaky you would just have to *scream!*" Mancuso had complete control over the environment. "I thought he understood what people were going through on the dance floor psychologically, and he would send out different stimuli to make the dance floor react. Every record was an experience. Never, *ever*, did he play records. He created an environment for each record. He was so much more than a DJ."

In contrast, Siano regarded the porn-star-cum-mixer Tony Mansfield—who played at the Round Table, a cabaret club that featured the La Fleur sisters and attracted a crowd of mainly white but also Latino gay men—as being much *less* than a DJ. "I kept asking Mansfield for a song," says Siano, "and he didn't know what it was." Sensing an opening for her music-mad boyfriend, Lord—who says that Siano was "already collecting records and knew all the titles, artists, and labels by heart"—approached Freddy, the club's mobster manager, and told him that Mansfield was an "asshole" who needed to be sacked. "The Mafia guy didn't like Mansfield, who was a prima donna, and he was also after Robin," says Siano. "She looked good. She had a thin waist, a big chest, and she was all of sixteen." So when the manager made a pass Lord proposed a trade. "I got Nicky the job at the Round Table," she says. "Nicky had a gift, I recognized his gift, and I was the kind of friend who would use my influence to help him get a foot in the door. I was experimenting with my own powers and quickly learned that I didn't have to do much to wrap an old guy like Freddy around my finger." An exchange of favors took place. "Had it not been for me being the type of sixteen-year-old girl that dirty old men were very attracted to Nicky would not have got his start at the Round Table. However, I believe that the outcome would have ultimately been the same, as if it was pre-destined. Nicky would have landed another DJing job via a different path."

The Round Table paid Siano—who had come out as gay while continuing to be heavily involved with Lord—twenty dollars for the 9 P.M. to 4 A.M. shift. "I got my first taste," says the DJ, who made his debut around the middle of 1972. "They were really into the music, and I could manipulate the crowd, but they had no fucking headphones and I hated that. The mixing was really hit and miss." Nothing, though, was missing when it came to the music. "We were dealing drugs so we had money, and I had all the records. I was already possessed." There was a downside to the drugs, however, and it had nothing to do with the intended effect of the Tuinals. "We caught Nicky selling drugs in the Loft on three separate occasions," says Mancuso. "We were freaked out because everything was shared and here was this kid trying to push downs. He didn't know what he was doing. It was the first time I ever had to kick somebody out." Lord and Siano were operating on a different wavelength. "David was adamant that drugs shouldn't be sold at the Loft, and part of our problem was that we didn't see the harm in it," says Lord. "We supported ourselves through high school selling drugs. There wasn't the same culture of fear back then."

Fluttering around like a couple of carefree butterflies, Siano and Lord —who were always more of a team than a couple, even if they continued to occasionally sleep with each other—decided to open their own venue. "We thought, 'Fine,'" says Lord. "'You won't let us in? We'll open our own club!'" Their concept—to open a heterosexual version of the Loft—was potentially brilliant. "The only club we had been to for straight people was incredibly lame," says Siano. "So we went to my brother, pitched him the idea, and he was really into it." The timing of their business proposal was perfect. A close friend of Joe Siano had just received a substantial payment for injuries sustained in Vietnam, and the veteran agreed to lend the entrepreneurs sixteen thousand dollars. Lord and Siano subsequently found a three-thousand-square-foot space on Twenty-second Street between Sixth and Seventh Avenues and, blissfully unaware of the legal machinations of the outside world, opened the Gallery in February 1973. "We didn't look into licensing or anything like that," says Siano. "We just wanted to dance. It was as simple as that."

Alex Rosner was hired to install the sound system and determined that while several features of the Loft's benchmark system were simple to transfer—most notably the tweeter arrays, the bass reinforcements, and the crossovers—the speakers weren't, largely because the room was too big to take Klipschorns (even after Siano came up with the idea of building an interior wall around the dance floor). "We used several two-way ALTEC Lansing Voice of the Theatre horn-type speakers for the midrange," says Rosner. "The space was larger than the Loft so there was more reverberation, but the sound was quite clear." So, too, were Siano's sonic expectations. "Nicky wasn't as obsessed about the sound as David. I was never totally sure that I understood what David was after, and he would sometimes doubt the results, which would lead me to also doubt the results, even if I didn't think there was a problem. I never had that problem with Nicky. He knew what he wanted, trusted my judgments, and we never had a difference of opinion."

Mancuso's house party setup also wound its way into the Gallery. An invite system regulated who could get in and who couldn't, refreshments were given out for free, and a cozy "Welcome Home" sign was suspended above the DJ booth. Yet while the first night was a success, with 150 of Joe's friends showing up, that turned out to be a comparatively busy party, and numbers soon dwindled to 75. "I didn't feel that those *breeders* appreciated the gay music I was playing," says Siano, who turned eighteen in March. "The bills were being paid, but we weren't making any money." With little else to do, Siano intermittently attempted to feign his way into Mancuso's bustling parties when the Gallery wound up for the night. "I was so possessed that I used to wear this big Afro wig and these glasses so that I could sneak in as another person. An *Afro wig* on this *white boy* and I got in a couple of times, I swear to God!"

The crowd at the Gallery began to take on a hipper hue when Frankie Knuckles and Larry Levan started to hang out at the club. "Frankie could never afford the three-dollar fee, and he was always let in for free, partly in the hope that he would bring his friends with him," says Lord. "Then Joe suggested that Frankie work for his entry so he started to show up early and help us set up the party. We just kind of adopted him, and he was the *best* at blowing up balloons!" Knuckles knew what kind of look to go for. "We definitely followed a lot of the same recipes as the Loft," he says. "We decorated the place with balloons and streamers and all the rest of it." Before long a friend started to help out. "Frankie came up to me," remembers Siano. "He said, 'I know this really sweet kid. He's a little flaky sometimes, but he's a hard worker. Would you be interested in hiring him?' I said, 'You know, Frankie, if he's a friend of yours let's try him out.' And it was Larry Levan."

The Gallery received a timely boost when David Mancuso announced that he was going to close the Loft for the summer. "It was serendipitous," says Siano. "We were there already, and David was meant to share his wealth." As Mancuso geared up for his goodbye party, the Gallery team penciled in a second opening for the following weekend. "We stood outside the Loft and handed out about five hundred flyers," says Lord. "We had actually given out some invitations right before we first opened Gallery but had only received a lukewarm response. But when we found out David was closing we repeated the exercise." The leaving party itself was a frenzied affair. "Larry climbed up the fire escape and sneaked through the window because we weren't letting anybody else in," says Mancuso. "The last record I played that night was 'September Song,' which contains the line, 'I'll see you in September.'" Then, according to Siano, who heard the following anecdote secondhand, a particularly distraught dancer approached Mancuso at the end of the night and said, "David, man, what am I going to do now?" The party host bent down and picked up a flyer that read, "What are you doing this summer? Come to the Gallery!" Mancuso reputedly told the desperate night crawler, "Why don't you go here?" The eyewitness observed the unfolding scene and reported back to Siano. "David was hanging around with Michael, and they were laughing like it was a big joke," says the Gallery DJ, "but it wasn't."

Joe remained skeptical. "Robin and I had been telling my brother that this was going to be big," says Siano, "but he didn't take any notice and ended up buying the regular supplies." They were nowhere near enough.

Loft regulars began to queue before the party had even begun, and by the end of the evening five hundred people had filed through the entrance. "I signed them all up," says Lord. "It was a big night to add to our membership list!" Ditto the following week when an additional hundred partygoers decided to try the Gallery, and ditto the week after that when another hundred faces appeared. In the time it took David Mancuso to fly to London and find his way to Ronnie Scott's, the Gallery had become the most happening party in Manhattan.

The identity of the crowd was far from uniform. "The Gallery was 60 percent gay and 40 percent straight or confused," says Michael Gomes, who was introduced to the venue in 1973 by ex–Loft regular Patrick Willoughby and soon became one of Siano's closest friends. "As David Rodriguez would say, 'Straight to the next man!' or 'He's bisexual: he likes men and boys!' " Identities were in flux. "It was never clearly defined along black gay lines," says Siano. "There were so many people who were just *sexual*. A lot of black men would have sex with other men but didn't consider it gay sex. Puerto Rican men, who would never have been caught dead in a gay club, were 'Just hanging out, man, getting blow jobs, fucking some ass.' It wasn't about gay or straight. It was about, 'Hey, let's party!' "

The dance floor acquired a quasi-religious aura. "People used to say it was like coming to church," says Siano. "They definitely used the Gallery to forget their troubles. When you scream as loud as you want to and dance for six hours and just let go of your inhibitions it's an incredibly powerful experience. The endorphins start flowing, whether you're on drugs or not, and you get a natural high." As with the Loft, talk of childhood was also irrepressible. "Jesus said, 'Come as a child,' and I think of that line when I think of the Gallery. We all became children who just wanted to freely express ourselves. People would become really expressive on that dance floor."

The revelers soon included some of Manhattan's best-known DJs, and two of them—Michael Cappello and David Rodriguez—were curious enough to scrutinize Siano from inside the DJ booth. "The first thing David Rodriguez said to me was, 'Mary, do you have 'Stoned Out of My Mind' by the Chi-Lites?' " remembers Siano. "He and Michael had heard of me, and they knew I played at the Round Table, but they didn't know that the skinny queen on the dance floor at the Limelight with that big-breasted chick was me. Then they came to the Gallery and realized that I was this Nicky Siano guy people were talking about." Pudgy and pushy,

Frankie Knuckles blowing up balloons at the Gallery. Courtesy of Nicky Siano

The Gallery dance floor. Courtesy of Nicky Siano

Rodriguez moved the lightman to one side and started talking to Siano, initiating a friendship that would be crucial to the young mixer's development. "David became my mentor, and for a while I felt like I couldn't play without him being there. He encouraged me, he molded me, and he gave me the basic tools." Every Saturday the Puerto Rican DJ would arrive early and whisper the following words of advice in Siano's ear: "Mary, don't ever cut off the words. If you've got to cut off the words, wait until they've finished the sentence. And it's got to blend. You really want to hear the first note of the next record and the last note of the last record. If you can't hear that last note, you want to hear the first note, and if you can't hear either one, then make sure that you're not chopping through any words. And you can tell a story: you can link all your love records together . . ."

Yet if Rodriguez supplied Siano with the dos and don'ts of how to DJ, it was Cappello who provided him with a sense of the craft's potential. "Nicky hung out a lot at the Limelight," says Cappello, "and every once in a while his head would pop up over the booth and he would ask questions." More often than not, Siano wanted to know what was going on in a specific mix. "When Michael played you didn't know the record was changing sometimes, but that wasn't because the beat was matching," says Siano. "It was because the records blended so well musically." Siano's favorite mix involved James Brown's "Give It Up" and "Law of the Land" by the Temptations. "Michael would wait for the break in 'Give It Up,' when James Brown claps his hands and chants 'Clap your hands now, stomp your feet now, clap your hands now, stomp your feet now, in the jungle brother' and then he would bring in 'Law of the Land,' which opens with these handclaps. It was more like a musician creating a composition than a DJ stringing records together. He was phenomenally, instinctually talented, and he had a tremendous influence on me."

Siano, though, was far more than an amalgamation of the best bits of Cappello, Rodriguez, and company. As a dynamic, innovative, and inspiring artist in his own right, the Gallery DJ developed a uniquely progressive style that was all about heightening the intensity of the dance floor experience. "Rodriguez believed that it was more important to train the dancers than for them to have a good time," says Siano. "We sometimes had fights over this because I thought that you couldn't make them like something they didn't like. He would say, 'You have the power!' and I would reply, 'I've got the power because I please them!' " That notion of pleasure was fundamental to Siano's ethos, and it was most forcefully articulated in his attempt to extend the duration of the peak for as long as possible. "Other DJs would play three records to peak a crowd," he says. "I'd play ten! I'd play peak records until they were screaming so loud that I couldn't hear the music. I was doing that because if I was on the dance floor that's what I would have wanted."

Siano's programming strategy heightened the drama still further. Whereas other DJs would alter the tempo gradually over the course of a set, the Gallery mixer juxtaposed wildly different records and, contrary to the general practice of letting a record end before making the blend, would also interrupt a track in mid-flow, riding roughshod over the precious boundaries of authorship. "There were a lot of records that I cut off, some of them pretty abruptly. If the mix was fabulous, right then, right there, I would go for it." Part magician, part entertainer, Siano played tricks of the now-you-hear-it, now-you-don't variety to the extent that even the most knowledgeable dancer could no longer predict when one record would end and the next would begin. "David was cool and laid back, whereas Nicky was frantic and intense," says Gomes. "If David would flow through the night, Nicky would build between the most extreme tempos. David was gradual, whereas Nicky would drive people crazy, up and down and up and down."

Siano didn't so much play records as make music. If the DJ liked one particular section of a record he would buy an extra copy so that he could extend it. Grasso had been the first to develop the technique, and Cappello and Rodriguez had also enjoyed playing with two copies, but it was Siano who, bathing in the fierce applause that dancers would send his way, took the concept to new levels of artistic ingenuity. "I used two copies with 'I Got It' by Gloria Spencer," says Siano. "It starts, 'Dnn dnn, yeah yeah, dnn dnn, yeah yeah, dnn dnn, yeah yeah,' and then she goes, 'I got it.' I would play the beginning part over and over and over and over, and then finally bring in the rest of the song. I built my own records."

Siano also played with the sound to an unprecedented degree. "David Mancuso was into the vinyl as pure sound," says Siano. "I was into making it what I wanted it to be, and I always wanted something more *sensational*." The DJ generated treble-driven peaks and bass-heavy valleys by altering the output of the basshorns and the tweeter arrays (which were serviced by a separate amp), tweaking the treble and bass on the mixer (which would calibrate the sound coming out of the ALTEC Lansing speakers), switching off the ALTECs altogether (which would cut everything except the basshorns and tweeter arrays), and turning the Acousta set on and off (which would also change the output of the main speakers). "I would turn everything off except the tweeter arrays and have them dancing to tss, tss, tss, tss, tss, tss, tss, tss for a while," says Siano. "Then I would turn on the bass, and then I'd turn on the main speakers. When I did that the room would just *explode*."

Other DJs had already toyed with the sound. Mancuso would turn the tweeter arrays and bass reinforcements on and off, and Cappello and Rodriguez fooled around with the treble on their Bozak mixer (which had been designed by Rudy Bozak, with the assistance of Rosner, back in 1971). Yet Siano transformed this marginal practice into a DJing art, spontaneously remixing each record according to its own accents while simultaneously reading the mood of the dance floor. "The record had to have a break," he says. "I loved the break because that was where I got to work the sound. I always used to ask, 'Does the song have a break?' I remember Rodriguez saying, 'Mary, stop saying that! It doesn't always have to have a break!' and I'd say, 'But I *like* the break!' I played with it *all*. The sound would change five zillion times during the evening."

Siano also developed a reputation for his ability to maintain the musical flow via a series of smooth blends. Grasso had been the first to develop the art, combining records that ran at similar speeds, and Cappello carried on where Grasso left off, developing a quicker and cleaner technique. The practice, however, remained a hazardous one. "Michael would put the needle down and hope for the best," says Siano. "Seventy percent of the time he would get there but 30 percent of the time it just didn't work out. I started doing it scientifically so I was there 90 percent of the time." Richie Kaczor inspired Siano to find that extra 20 percent. "Richie was a phenomenal disc jockey," says Siano. "I heard him at Hollywood for the first time on my eighteenth birthday in March 1973. After that I told Alex that I needed turntables with variable speeds, and I started blending beat for beat. Other people didn't make that transition. Michael didn't make that transition." Knuckles watched in awe. "It was like discovering the wheel," he says. "Nicky would constantly play with the speed, and I had never heard anybody do that before. He got it right, and everybody knew he got it right. It became difficult listening to other guys play in the old style after that."

Some of the other guys who were still playing in the old style didn't agree. "Raising and lowering speeds didn't happen until some people decided they wanted to get fancy," says Francis Grasso. "Well, since almost everything innovative had been done by then, they tried that shit, and for the most part it really sucked." The ex–Sanctuary DJ believed that the speed controls were not only redundant but also damaging. "If you have people that are music savvy they will notice that you've speeded up the records, and it will bother them. If you're a good disc jockey and you're playing a record that's 100 beats per minute you should have the knowledge to pick out a record that runs at 101 or 102 beats per minute. You don't take a record that plays at 105 beats per minute and slow it down. You're using equipment to alter the actual record." That, according to Grasso, didn't simply harm the integrity of the vinyl. "Why would you want to fuck around with a live crowd when that's who's paying you? Why would somebody want to go from one to bang-zoom like you were in Star Trek and you went into warp phase? And why would you want to shut the sound off? I never knocked Nicky Siano. He did his thing. I just never understood it. I never thought he took care of his audience. He'd get so high he thought he was the emperor of the room."

Siano *was* ruling, however, and the fact that dancers were flocking to hear him rather than Grasso suggested that, despite the misgivings of the ex–Sanctuary mixer, he was taking the art of DJing to a new and electrifying plane. "Nicky Siano was the king of the DJs," says Gallery devotee Kenny Carpenter. "He was so fierce he could put on a record and people would just scream. There was no other DJ like Nicky Siano. He was the best DJ I ever heard." It was clear, as connoisseurs of the emerging downtown party network acknowledged, that Siano's rise couldn't be straightforwardly explained by Mancuso's temporary absence. The Gallery DJ had his own style, and in musical terms this difference was manifested in his devotion to vocalists, especially of the diva variety. "The Gallery was gayer than the Loft," says Gomes. "It was women singing songs." This divergence reflected the contrasting personalities of the two party engineers, for whereas Mancuso was quiet, calm, and reclusive, Siano was the happy-go-lucky extrovert. "I'd play a record like 'Just Look What You've Done' by Brenda Holloway," says the DJ. "It was a very up-tempo Motown song: *Just look what you've done, you've turned my heart to stone!*' David would never play something like that, but I did, and people got a little more excited on my dance floor."

Nicky Siano

Select Discography (Gallery 1972–73)

Barrabas, "Woman"

Booker T. and the MG's, "Melting Pot"

Genie Brown, "Can't Stop Talking"

James Brown, "Give It Up or Turnit a Loose"

Lynn Collins, "Think (About It)"

Creative Source, "Who Is He and What Is He to You?"

Manu Dibango, "Soul Makossa"

The Doobie Brothers, "Long Train Running"

First Choice, "Love and Happiness"

First Choice, "Newsy Neighbours"

First Choice, "The Player"

Brenda Holloway, "Just Look What You've Done"

The Intruders, "I'll Always Love My Mama"

The Isley Brothers, "Get into Something"

Eddie Kendricks, "Girl You Need a Change of Mind"

Eddie Kendricks, "Keep on Truckin'"

Little Sister, "You're the One"

Love Unlimited Orchestra, "Love's Theme"

Harold Melvin & the Blue Notes, "The Love I Lost"

MFSB, "Love Is the Message"

MFSB featuring The Three Degrees, "TSOP (The Sound of Philadelphia)"

The O'Jays, "For the Love of Money"

The O'Jays, "Love Train"

Wilson Pickett, "Don't Knock My Love"

The Pointer Sisters, "Yes We Can Can"

Gloria Spencer, "I Got It"

The Temptations, "Law of the Land"

The Three Degrees, "Dirty Ol' Man"

The Trammps, "Love Epidemic"

The Trammps, "Zing Went the Strings in My Heart"

Ultra High Frequency, "We're On the Right Track"

War, "City, Country, City"

The dancers from the Loft and the Gallery discovered different sub-jectivities in the two venues, with contrasting DJ personalities and musi-cal agendas producing distinctive party scenarios. Whereas the atmo-spheric and mysterious Loft created the conditions for the emergence of the tripped-out amorphous dancer, the gayer Gallery established an in-stitutional framework in which the dancing queen could flourish. "Nicky brought the sissy out in the butch boys," says DePino, who worked along-side Knuckles and Levan. "He made you want to put on a skirt and spin." Bob Casey was left with a similar sensation. "It was smoky, it was mobbed, it was great!" says the soundman. "Nicky's Gallery was the first place I saw dancers jump up and spin the mirror ball. There was a real party atmo-sphere. The energy was so up and so happy that I thought to myself, 'This is the way it should be!' The Gallery became my benchmark 'club.'"

John Addison, whose unrivaled cash flow meant that he could hand-pick the hottest DJs on the circuit, apparently felt the same way. Having installed Bobby DJ on the weekends, the owner of Le Jardin went in search of the perfect weekday spinner and found his answer at the Gallery, where Robin Lord persuaded him to pay fifty dollars a night for Siano's services. "Le Jardin was up and down," says Siano, who started playing Wednesdays, Thursdays, and Sundays in the summer of 1973. "Sometimes it wasn't crowded at all, but then it would be packed. There were a lot of celebrities. I remember having an autograph book that was full. Paul Lynde, Bobby Short, Pierre Cardin, Mick Jagger, Bianca, and many others signed it."

Yet the most important signature was that of Siano, who was now im-printing his musical vision on midtown Manhattan. That was something that Mancuso was never going to do—the Loft host had decided that it was safest if he stayed at home after he accidentally played records from the scratch pile at the Planetarium while the resident went on a bathroom break—and while Michael Cappello, Bobby Guttadaro, Richie Kaczor, and Tee Scott were also performing in midtown discotheques, none of them could quite match Siano's combination of DJing brilliance, prophetic fer-vor, and sheer lovability. "Nicky didn't have any airs about him," says Casey. "He was just a very cool, confident guy who knew what he wanted.

He worked the dance floor like no other DJ, and at the end of a successful night he just wanted to go somewhere and fuck his brains out. He
deserved it!"

* * *

Like the engineers of collage, DJs communicated through found objects,
speaking a language that was not their own, integrating records that had
entered the world as separate entities but were now part of a variable
whole. While mixing techniques were becoming an increasingly important feature of this ever more complex equation, *juxtaposition* was as important as *transition*, and *what* you played was still as important as *how*
you played. To some extent, that was because vinyl was surprisingly difficult to come by—dance remained an uncultivated market, and DJs had
to rummage around record shops for their raw material. Joe Maimone
at Capitol Records had championed an alternative promotional strategy
to the traditional avenue of radio when he supplied Le Club's Slim Hyatt
with a copy of Bobbie Gentry's "Ode To Billie Joe" in 1967, but for the most
part DJs had no contact with the promotional arm of the music industry
and were left to fend for themselves.[6] "That is what it was all about—the
quest to find new records," says Steve D'Acquisto. "We had this thing, and
we had to keep moving it along."

Every DJ worth his salt could cite a record that they were credited with
spinning before everyone else—"Give It Up or Turnit a Loose" went to
Michael Cappello, "Black Skinned Blue Eyed Boys" to Steve D'Acquisto
and/or Ray Yeates, "Rain" to Francis Grasso, "Theme From Shaft" to
Bobby Guttadaro, "Yes We Can Can" to David Rodriguez, "Giving Up" to
Nicky Siano, and "Girl You Need a Change of Mind" to David Mancuso—
and in next to no time "Girl" established itself as the most important of
them all. Recorded for the second Eddie Kendricks album, *People . . . Hold
On*, the track contained the kind of earthy energy that was perfect for
peaking the dance floor thanks to producer Frank Wilson's decision to
employ Kendricks's road band, the Young Senators, for the recording. "I
wanted to move away from the 'Motown Sound' and get closer to what
people were hearing when Eddie played live," Wilson told veteran music
executive, producer, and writer Harry Weinger. "We got that live feel with
'Girl You Need a Change of Mind.'" The recording also stood out because
of Wilson's ingenious redeployment of the break—a gospel technique
that introduces a sweeping and apparently decisive end to a song that is

instantaneously followed by the piecemeal reintroduction of the instrumental and vocal parts. "My background is the church," added Wilson. "It's not unusual in a church song to have a breakdown like that. Here, the idea was spontaneous. I stood out in the studio with the musicians, giving instructions as we were cutting for them to break it down to nothing, then gradually come in one by one and rebuild to the original fervor of the song."[7]

Wilson wasn't exactly pioneering new ground when it came to secularizing the break. Jazz artists had made good use of the technique for many decades, and the call to "give the drummer some"—some space for a solo—revolved around the practice of cutting all instrumentation save for the drums. Nevertheless, the break was rarely taken into the recording studio, in part because it could be properly deployed only within the relatively expansive framework of a long-playing album and in part because its aesthetic qualities weren't always appropriate: rock musicians were hardly interested in the kind of celebratory energy that was intrinsic to the break, and funk artists were more interested in generating a concentrated and constant rhythmic riff than a variable and undulating emotional journey. "Give It Up," a live recording that only existed in LP format, was the most significant funk exception, and it is no coincidence that this auxiliary track, which contains a minute-long break, became Brown's biggest club hit to date.

"Girl," however, remained the most influential and enduring dance record of the period, for whereas "Give It Up" (which came a close second) revolved around a frantic energy that broke and then returned with a sudden vengeance, the Motown release communicated the organic ecstasy of the gospel mass onto vinyl, with Wilson using the method to flawless effect not once but twice. The result was a dizzying dance floor sensation that lasted for almost eight minutes—even if Wilson didn't know what to make of it all. "When I began hearing reports about what was happening with the record in the New York disco clubs, I was shocked. That was not what we were going for. We were after radio."[8]

Going after radio, of course, was normal practice, and the popularity of "Girl" on the dance floor didn't do anything to alter the status quo. After all, it was still far from evident that the clubs were generating the kind of sales that Kendricks and his colleagues wanted, and when "Girl" was finally released as a single in January 1973 its chart performance was unremarkable considering that Kendricks was an established artist who had already made a name for himself as the lead singer of the Temptations. "Girl" peaked at number thirteen on the R&B chart and eighty-seven on pop, and it is unlikely that many of New York's night crawlers would have gone out of their way to invest in the truncated and, quite frankly, decimated forty-five version. The taste of the DJ and the sales performance of a record remained ostensibly separate phenomena.

Perceptions began to shift following the release of Manu Dibango's "Soul Makossa," an African jazz sensation that combined a driving beat with echoed vocals and Dibango's frenzied soprano sax. Originally a French pressing on Fiesta, the record made its way into the United States via an African import company in Brooklyn. Alfie Davison (once of Jungle) and David Mancuso were the first spinners to get hold of the record, and within weeks DJs and dancers alike were hunting for a slab of vinyl that didn't exist. "David went to this little Jamaican shop and found 'Soul Makossa,'" says Nicky Siano. "David gave it to David Rodriguez and Michael Cappello, and David Rodriguez told me where to get it. I bought five copies." Within days the rare import was retailing at an inflated price, and by the middle of May *Billboard* was moved to run a special item on the import, which was "fetching a record price of between $2 and $3 in New York record shops because of its unprecedented popularity in the black community."⁹ Siano remembers the ensuing of panic. "People went *wild* trying to find that record. *No one* had 'Soul Makossa.'" Bootlegs and cover versions poured out until Ahmet Ertegun and Jerry Wexler of Atlantic licensed the original track for the American market. As it happens, Wexler had already dipped his toes into the discotheque market when he signed Killer Joe Piro to produce a series of "authentic discotheque albums" in March 1965 — *Billboard* described Piro as "the darling of the discotheques and the jet set's favorite teacher" — and the label's renewed interest in dance was rewarded when Dibango entered the charts on 23 June 1973.¹⁰

New York's DJs had inspired their first verifiable hit, for, while records such as "Theme From Shaft" by Isaac Hayes and "Papa Was a Rolling Stone" by the Temptations had received intense play in the clubs, their subsequent commercial success could not be attributed to the DJs in any straightforward way ("Theme" was clearly lifted by the popularity of the accompanying blaxploitation film and "Papa" benefited from the fact that the Temptations already had an established following). "Soul Makossa," though, was different. "It was hard to say disc jockeys had power when a record like 'Papa Was a Rolling Stone' was a hit," says Vince Aletti. "All those records were really big club records, but they were also big radio records, and it was difficult to tell which happened first. 'Soul Makossa,' though, definitely took off in the clubs." DJs could hardly contain their joy. "It was like you were about to have a baby and watch it be born," says Mancuso. "It was wonderful."

New York's night priests had become, if not the biological parents, then at least the midwives of the music industry, delivering other people's children in a matter of weeks rather than months. "A group of us used to go to this omelet house called David's Pot Belly when we finished playing at four in the morning," says Siano. "David Rodriguez and Michael Cappello would go down from the Limelight, and I would go straight from Le Jardin. John Addison had employed Robin to run the coatroom at Le Jardin, and she paid Larry and this friend of ours called Rique Spencer to help her, so all four of us would go together. Other DJs would also come along." Food ostensibly drove the space. "They had everything omelet—cherries, apple, bananas, cream cheese, hamburger, asparagus, broccoli. Robin and I fell in love with the cream cheese omelets, and they also made these round potato pancakes that were *so* good." Music, though, always found its way to the top of the menu. "It was a really important place for us to discuss what was going on. We compared notes on everything. We talked about 'Soul Makossa' at that table."

Dibango's chart success represented a significant turning point in the cultural economy of Entertainment America, and its importance was formally recognized when "Soul Makossa" became the paradigmatic focal point of the first dedicated piece of journalism to be written about night-world since the demise of Arthur. "*Paar-ty! Paar-ty!*" wrote Aletti in "Discotheque Rock," which appeared in *Rolling Stone* in September 1973. "You hear the chant at concerts, rising like a tribal rallying cry on a shrill wave of whistles and hard-beaten tambourines. It's at once a call to get down and party, a statement that there's a party going on and an indication that discotheques, where the chant originated, are back in force after their virtual disappearance with the flashbulb pop of the Sixties."[11] Aletti added, "Actually, discotheques never died; they just went back underground where the hardcore dance crowd—blacks, Latins, gays—was. But in the last year they've returned not only as a rapidly spreading social phenomenon (via juice bars, after-hours clubs, private lofts open on weekends to members only, floating groups of party-givers who take over the ballrooms of old hotels from midnight to dawn) but as a strong influence on the music people listen to and buy." Dibango's surprise chart hit was "one of the most spectacular discotheque records of recent months" as well as "a perfect example of the genre," which was characterized as being "Afro-Latin in sound or instrumentation, heavy on the drums, with minimal lyrics, sometimes in a foreign language, and a repetitious chorus," with the most popular cuts "usually the longest and the most instrumental, performed by black groups who are, frequently, not American."[12] Underpinning the trend lay the DJ, who had a uniquely mobile position within the music market. "Because these DJs are much closer to the minute-to-minute changes in people's listening/dancing taste, they are the first to reflect these changes in the music they play, months ahead of trade magazine charts and all but a few radio station playlists."[13] *Billboard*, an implied culprit, took just three weeks to come up with an abridged version of Aletti's groundbreaking article, which it ran under the headline "Discotheques Break Singles."[14] The message was clear: records no longer had to suffocate for lack of radio airplay.

Aletti's article marked the moment when the nascent New York dance network materialized into a recognizable scene—something that extended beyond a discreet party here and an isolated record there. Previously unidentifiable, the loose, unstable, almost volatile assortment of DJs, clubs, and records had crystallized to such an extent that by the autumn of 1973 they now contained an internal pattern. Quasi-invisible to the common eye, this crystalline culture was beginning to reflect light in such brilliant flashes that it became more and more discernible, and it was at this moment that an inherent (though veiled) characteristic of the downtown party network—which internally referred to itself as the "underground"—became evident. That is, it could never be entirely distinguished from the so-called mainstream because there was always a degree of overlap between the two. The purpose of the underground, in all of its various historical formations, had been to effect wider change, and this contradictory and irresolvable tension between protecting oneself from overexposure while simultaneously transforming the world also permeated the downtown party network. The new wave of DJs formed a popular avant-garde that, in contrast to more insular cultural revolutionaries, wanted to spread their radical message rather than bask in their unpopularity. "I didn't get the feeling that I was violating the underground," says Aletti. "People didn't want to remain underground. They were ready to be recognized."

5. visibility

Kenny Gamble, the singer-songwriter of R&B band Kenny Gamble and the Romeos, and Leon Huff, a talented pianist, met in the lobby of Philadelphia's Schubert Building in 1964. Within a year they were making music together, and, unable to break into the inner circle at Cameo-Parkway, the happening Philadelphia label, they formed their own independent production company, Gamble. "(We'll Be) United" by the Intruders, which featured Vince Montana on vibes and a string arrangement by Bobby Martin, reached number fourteen on the R&B charts, and subsequent collaborations with the Intruders, as well as productions with Jerry Butler (on Mercury) and Wilson Pickett (on Atlantic), raised the profile of the recording team. They lacked, however, the kind of backing that could transform them into key players in the music market, and, by the time their distribution agreement with Chess Records came apart at the seams, they were ready for the kind of financial stability that could ostensibly be guaranteed by a major record company.

That company materialized in 1971 when Clive Davis, the president of Columbia Records, a division of the Columbia Broadcasting Systems (CBS) parent company, realized that he was being left behind in the fast-emerging black music market. "*Billboard* lists the Top Two Hundred albums each week, and as I read this and other trade papers, I noticed that more and more of the top-selling albums featured rhythm and blues music," Davis wrote in his autobiography. "There suddenly seemed to be a greater receptivity to R&B crossovers." According to internal Columbia research, black audiences were beginning to buy more albums and white audiences were starting to tune into black music, the result of which was unprecedented album sales for artists such as Isaac Hayes, Curtis Mayfield, Diana Ross and the Supremes, and the Temptations. "Until now, the area had been dominated by Atlantic, Motown and Stax Records," concluded Davis. "Columbia had barely scratched the surface."[1]

The executive responded by hiring Columbia's first tranche of black promoters, but he still needed to give them something to promote, and when Columbia's own internal black A&R managers failed to come up with any significant findings he started to pray for "outside help."[2] That help arrived when Gamble and Huff knocked on his door. "We began talking immediately about building careers. Earlier, they had made plenty of *single* hits but had never really produced artists with album appeal. They wanted this badly, and they also wanted the kind of merchandising and promotional efforts that could build careers for their people." The final deal promised seventy-five thousand dollars for fifteen singles as well as a smaller number of albums at twenty-five thousand dollars apiece. "By every yardstick of independent producing deals, this was modest," commented Davis. "But from Gamble and Huff's viewpoint, money mattered considerably less at the time than the chance to be associated with a quality record operation which would give maximum exposure to their productions."[3]

Philadelphia International Records was set up in 1971, and in May of the following year Davis's strategy was validated when a special CBS-commissioned report, conducted by the Harvard University Business School, urged the company to enter into the soul market. "The fact that 30 percent of the top 40 is composed of records which have 'crossed over' from soul stations underscores the strategic importance of soul stations as one of the most effective vehicles for getting on to the top 40," noted the report. "What this means is that the competition among promoters for soul airplay involves far more than simply the prospect of record sales to black consumers."[4] The report warned CBS against attempting to acquire any of the big three specialized national companies—Atlantic, Motown, and Stax—and suggested instead that it could outmaneuver equally negligent majors such as Capitol, MCA, and RCA by developing a "well-planned and well-financed initiative aimed at long-term market penetration" as well as raiding smaller independent companies.[5] The creation of Philadelphia International constituted one such raid, and, just two months after the publication of what came to be known as the Harvard Report, Davis was able to bask in the glory of PIR's first hit, "Back Stabbers" by the O'Jays, which reached number one on the R&B chart and number three on the pop chart.

A streetwise cautionary tale about the hypocrisy of modern life, "Back Stabbers" provided a forceful example of Gamble and Huff's "message music." The first song to be penned by the team of Gene McFadden and John Whitehead (with some assistance from Huff), "Back Stabbers" evoked the shifting sands of black masculinity in its story about a man whose friends want to steal his woman as well as the wider national crisis that had been created by political backstabbers such as President Nixon, whose treacherous Watergate shenanigans were coming to light, and Senator Daniel Moynihan, who insisted that African American men were responsible for the continuing cycle of black poverty. Yet despite its heavy message, "Back Stabbers" didn't come across as a preachy record because its socially aware lyrics were positioned within a sound that was both soulful and complex. Featuring Huff on piano, Montana on vibes, and Norman Harris on guitar, plus a groundbreaking arrangement by the pivotal figure of Thom Bell (who began life as a pianist in Kenny Gamble and the Romeos before becoming the guiding force behind the Delfonics, the Spinners, and the Stylistics), the record marked the introduction of a new pop complexity in which the instrumental intricacies of jazz were combined with the swooping orchestral grandeur of classical music. "The Philly sound was a take-off of Motown, only more sophisticated," says Montana.

In contrast to bebop and progressive rock, Philly Soul didn't sacrifice danceability on the altar of sophistication. Yet while Gamble and Huff had produced foot-tapping hits for the O'Jays, Jerry Butler, and Wilson Pickett, the duo were apparently determined to steer Harold Melvin & the Blue Notes away from the dance floor. The band's first single, "If You Don't Know Me by Now," a quiet ballad featuring high harmonies and a delicate beat, had sparked a gold album, and Gamble and Huff, deliberately shelving the band's electrifying 1972 recording of "Bad Luck," wrote "The Love I Lost" as another slow number. That, however, wasn't how their session musicians wanted to play it. "The song was written and rehearsed as a ballad, and Gamble and Huff came into the studio with the intention of cutting it as a ballad," says Philadelphia producer Bunny Sigler. "They played all day, and it wasn't working. But then the musicians picked up the groove."

The musicians in question were Ronnie Baker (bass), Norman Harris (guitar), and Earl Young (drums)—or Baker-Harris-Young, as they were alphabetically known. "We met playing in nightclubs in the early sixties," says Young. "That's where you learned how to play. You were paid nothing—just a couple of dollars. We played around the streets for a long time before we got into the studio." Harris was the first to get work, and he brought in Baker before Young completed the trio. "I happened to be in the studio one day, and the drummer didn't show up," says Young. "They asked me if I could fill in, and I just played what I knew. After that, when people called one guy they would get all of us. It meant they didn't have to search around for musicians." The trio quickly established themselves as the tightest and most prolific rhythm section in the city, and Young— whose heroes included Bernard Purdy and Clyde Stubblefield—emerged as a particularly influential figure when he inadvertently created a new rhythm for the dance floor. "I thought the Detroit sound was unique," he says. "Motown used four-four on the snare—khh, khh, khh, khh—and the heartbeat on the bass—dmm-dmm, dmm-dmm, dmm-dmm, dmm-dmm—and they also used four-four on the tambourines." Young, though, wanted to switch things around. "I would use cymbals more than the average drummer, and I realized that if I played the four-four [all four beats of the measure] on the bass I could work different patterns on the cymbals." The yet-to-be named disco beat was about to be born.

Young says that he started to up the tempo with the recording of Wilson Pickett's "Don't Let the Green Grass Fool You," released on Atlantic in 1970, but it wasn't until "Zing Went the Strings of My Heart," the first single released by Young's Philadelphia-based band the Trammps, that nightworld began to take note. "I told Norman and Ronnie it was time for us to try something on our own," says Young. "We put our money together and got a deal with Buddah Records. Neil Bogart put out 'Zing,' and it was a big hit." Four-on-the-floor soon spread: Frank Wilson inverted Holland-Dozier-Holland's four-on-the-top during the recording session of "Girl You Need a Change of Mind"—even though the result still sounded largely snare-oriented—and Norman Whitfield created a tougher, more disciplined, bass-driven four-on-the-floor for the rumbling, apocalyptic "Law of the Land" by the Temptations. Yet, while Detroit was apparently nodding its head in the direction of Philadelphia's nascent beat, Gamble and Huff kept the shackles on Young until the recording session for "The Love I Lost" hit an interminable rut and the drummer decided to let loose.

The Trammps. Courtesy of the Vince Aletti Collection

Young's shuffling rhythm and shifting percussive accents ended up setting off the entire song, which was recorded as a six-minute-twenty-four-
second album cut, and when the record was tested at Columbia's summer
sales conference it became obvious that the label had a hit on its hands. "It
was clearly the most exciting soul record at the convention," commented
Columbia's marketing director. "Everybody kept requesting it at the hospitality suite."[6]

Columbia held back other singles in order to concentrate on the Harold
Melvin track, which was released as a three-minute-thirty-five-second
single in September, and "The Love I Lost" subsequently reached the top
of the soul charts before peaking at number seven on the Hot 100. The
clubs, however, were more interested in the long album version, which
was released in October. "Originally it was part one and part two on a
single," says Nicky Siano, "but when the album came out, and they connected the record together, it took on a whole new dimension." Whereas
Motown's standard snare drum had tended to make for a somewhat
monotonous experience on the dance floor, Young's thumping bass and
flashing polyrhythmic cymbals simply compelled dancers to move their
bodies. " 'The Love I Lost' was *huge* at the Gallery," adds Siano. "Earl
Young was responsible for the disco sound more than anyone else. It

really caught on, and Philadelphia International produced hit after hit after hit."

Gamble and Huff were initially unaware of the excitement. "As a musician, you're in the trenches working hard," says fellow musician Montana. "You don't get to see what's going on until someone tells you." That someone turned out to be Don Cornelius, head of the nationally syndicated dance program *Soul Train*, who asked the Philadelphia producers to come up with an up-tempo theme song for his show. The result was "TSOP (The Sound of Philadelphia)" by MFSB—which stood for Mother, Father, Sister, Brother. Engineered by Joe Tarsia (in many respects the unheralded architect of the Philadelphia Sound) and arranged by Bobby Martin (another quiet but crucial operator within the empire at Sigma Sound), "TSOP" combined a pounding Baker-Harris-Young rhythm track with the melodic patterns of Huff's organ and the Philadelphia Symphony Orchestra. The Philadelphia focus was shifting from black domestic and public life to the communal space of the dance floor, and while this new formula was still a kind of "message music," the message was now firmly situated within the music and not the lyrics (or rather clipped slogans from the Three Degrees). "It's getting hard, it's time to get down"—one of the lines from "TSOP"—might have referred to the appeal of the dance floor in difficult times but it had other connotations as well, and Gamble and Huff weren't about to tell anyone their intended meaning.

"TSOP" reached number one on the R&B and pop charts in the spring of 1974, but by then an alternative club anthem had already emerged in the form of "Love Is the Message," which appeared alongside the *Soul Train* theme on MFSB's debut album, *TSOP (The Sound of Philadelphia)*. In contrast to the catchy pop refrains that underpinned the theme-song appeal of "TSOP," "Love Is the Message" represented a deeper jazz-dance sophistication. Everything revolved around Young's drums (which veered between two basic grooves, with intermittent fills signaling each change of section), and Martin's moody strings (which, after a busy opening, glided between two eerily beautiful notes like a seagull swooping across an ocean at shifting altitudes). "There had been nothing like it previously on Philadelphia," says Michael Gomes. "The O'Jays had a more R&B feel." More than any other release, "Love Is the Message" defined the artistic and emotional potential of the *textured* disco aesthetic in which various layers of instrumental sounds could shift gradually or dramatically between different moods. "All of a sudden there was this lush fluidity that had nothing to do with Motown," says Gomes. "'Love Is the Message' represented what disco would become."

* * *

David Mancuso had been in a happy-go-lucky mood when he traveled to Europe in the summer of 1973. With his parties packed to capacity, the only problem was how to satisfy demand, and a seemingly simple solution presented itself when a rent-shy neighbor was kicked out of the Broadway building. Mancuso made an offer on the vacant space, expanded his apartment to 3,500 square feet, arranged for the original archways (which had been filled in with bricks) to be opened up, and flew off to Europe, overjoyed that there would be room for an additional 150 guests on his return. Delight turned to dismay, however, when Mancuso, flipping through the *International Herald Tribune* in the lobby of the Lancaster Gate Hotel in London, read about the collapse of the Broadway Central Hotel, which was just a stone's throw away from the Loft. Initially the debacle, which occurred on 3 August and injured at least a dozen people, was put down to the Broadway Central's age and the "weakening of its structure by decades of vibrations from subways and heavy traffic."[7] However, a subsequent inquiry revealed that the owners had removed one of the building's supporting columns without permission, and the exposé triggered a series of inspections by New York City's Building Department. "Everyone was asking if the block was safe," says Mancuso, who became a target. "That's when we became visible."

The inspectors weren't the only ones waiting for Mancuso's return. So was the team at the Gallery, which had seamlessly supplanted the Loft as the best party in Manhattan in just three months. "I felt bad," says Nicky Siano. "I loved David, I respected him, I thought his place was cool as shit, and I felt guilty about being in competition." If Mancuso was concerned, it didn't show. "David didn't seem to care about the competition," says Robin Lord. "I don't think he thought of it in that way. I definitely didn't sense that David had much, if any, of the competitive nature that Nicky thrived on." When the Loft host reopened in the autumn it quickly became clear that he had nothing to worry about (even though the cost of the contribution had by this time risen to four dollars). Mancuso recaptured a significant proportion of his crowd, and the extensive waiting list for invitation cards enabled him to fill any gaps within a matter of weeks. "Most of the people who were Loft members definitely went back to the Loft on Saturdays," says Nathan Bush, who had spent the summer on Siano's dance floor. "The Loft was home base." When Mancuso visited the neighboring venue, he even approved of what he saw. "The Gallery was the only place that stuck to my formula," he says. "Nicky came closer to the Loft than anybody."

Mancuso's latest musical offering came in the form of *Barrabas*, an album by a Spanish rock group of the same name that was released by RCA in Spain in 1972 and had disappeared without a trace in America following a brief promotional push in May 1973. "I found the record in a flea market in Amsterdam. I didn't even listen to it. I just liked the cover and the titles. I used to do that with a lot of records." The Loft host ended up rotating two tracks, "Wild Safari" and "Woman," both of which combined Afro-rock with a dash of electric Latin percussion, and as word got around he did his best to spread the manna. "When people got into it, I bought as many copies as possible. In the end I had to call RCA in Spain. First I ordered one box, and when those went I ordered another three boxes." One of the copies became a gesture of solidarity toward Siano. "We were speaking," says the Gallery DJ. "I looked up to David and was in awe of him. When I heard the Barrabas I said, 'I have to have that!' and he gave me a copy."

Mancuso's successful relaunch persuaded Siano and Lord to open on Fridays as well as Saturdays and the fact that Friday became the venue's busiest night indicates that a substantial number of Loft devotees were beginning their weekend at the Gallery before heading to Broadway on Saturday. "We were all basically going out both nights if possible so some of David's crowd would go to Gallery on Fridays," says Bush. "Eventually people who couldn't get into the Loft went to the Gallery, and they brought their friends and told other people, so Gallery's membership kept growing." Lord, for one, didn't notice any kind of sustained slump. "We lost some people when the Loft reopened, especially the first party after David returned, but we never really felt it," she says. "More people started joining the whole after-hours scene that summer, and it turned out that there were more than enough guests to go around." The Gallery added to its membership when a group of Siano's friends who had spent the summer on Fire Island started to go to the party in the autumn, and designers such as Steven Burrows and Willy Smith followed in tow. Having made up about 10 percent of the crowd at the June take-off, whites now comprised some 30 percent. "The crowd just sort of grew and divided naturally," says Lord. "We started to get more Fire Islanders. Some folk became more regular at one party than the other, but a lot were doing both places on a regular basis."

A new anthem for the Gallery's shifting population emerged when PIR released "TSOP," which Siano managed to secure during a visit to Columbia's offices on 23 December 1973. "David Rodriguez took me to all the record companies and got me connections," he says. "They all knew us, and *we got records*, honey. We would go every week to different companies, and we would come home with thirty, forty, fifty records. *Nobody* was getting more free records than David Rodriguez and me. Michael Cappello was too stoned, and David Mancuso was too proud. We were the pioneers for getting free records." The Philadelphia International coup soon followed. "David Rodriguez and I heard it in Laverne Perry's office. Everybody was after Gamble and Huff productions at this point and 'TSOP' was really smooth, really exciting." The only problem lay in Perry's limited supply. "She had two copies. She gave us one, and David stole the other. We were the only ones with copies that holiday, and we played 'TSOP' to death over Christmas and New Year's. It wasn't in the stores until after the holiday."

"Love Is the Message" only emerged as an alternative anthem a couple of months later. "I heard some cute kid play it in Le Jardin," says Siano, who was waiting to start his midweek set at John Addison's discotheque when the would-be DJ asked if he could play a couple of records. "He had the album, and he turned over 'TSOP' and put on 'Love Is the Message,' and who was there that night? David Mancuso. David came to the booth and said, 'What *is* that record?' I took a look and told him. The following weekend I started playing that record, working it back and forth, putting in sound effects, and it became *my* record. It was my theme song."

The emergence of "Love Is the Message" coincided with Siano's decision to act on a longstanding dream—to play a sound effect on a third turntable while he mixed two records—so at the beginning of 1974 the DJ unplugged the record player in his apartment, took it to the Gallery, and lined up the mix to end all mixes. "I was playing 'Love Is the Message,' and I was going into 'Girl You Need a Change of Mind,'" says Siano. "In the background I had this sound effect of an airplane blasting, and the two records were playing and blending together." The crowd couldn't believe its ears. "They were just looking in the booth and going, 'Aagghh! Aaaagggghhhh!' They were jumping and screaming so loud that the floor started to move and the paint from the ceiling chipped onto Robin's desk, which was downstairs on the first floor."

Yet while the Gallery's infrastructure wobbled away, it was Mancuso's walls that were coming under scrutiny. "The police knew I didn't have a Certificate of Occupancy and the fire department knew I didn't have a Certificate of Public Assembly, but they hadn't bothered me because I had sprinklers and emergency lights," says the Loft host. "But when the hotel fell down it was a big scene, and if anything was incorrect in any of those buildings they were going to correct it." The inspections culminated in a front-page article in the *New York Times* on 21 May 1974 in which an angry neighbor argued that Mancuso's extension had undermined the safety of the old warehouse. "That wall holds the building up," the resident declared, adding that he was worried the building would collapse as a result of what the newspaper described as "Mr. Mancuso's masonry handiwork, the vibrations from his neighbor's massive stereo system and the stomping of '500 frenzied dancers.'"[8]

Mancuso maintained that he had simply knocked through a hollow wall—the supporting arches remained intact—but his situation was weakened by his lack of legal paperwork. "I had done my research. In no way did the work compromise the existing bearing wall. However, the buildings department said that the situation was too sensitive and that I had to vacate. Everyone was panicking. I could have fought a battle, but the easiest thing was to leave." On 2 June 1974 the Sunday edition of the *New York Times* ran another front-page article on the Loft, this time reporting that Mancuso had been told to vacate his premises by the buildings department. "The order," ran the report, "which was posted on Friday and took effect immediately, was described by Cornelius Dennis, the department's Manhattan borough superintendent, as a rare and unusually severe response to an 'extreme situation.'"[9] Appropriately the last record to be played at the Broadway Loft was "Law of the Land" by the Temptations—and this before Mancuso knew that he was about to be evicted.

The Loft wasn't the only casualty. "When they hit me, they hit everyone," says Mancuso, "including the Gallery." With no prior warning, the fire department entered Siano's venue a couple of months later and announced its immediate closure, citing inadequate fire exits as the causal factor. "I remember going downstairs having very little on," says Siano, who still had the wherewithal to grab a box of prelaced strawberries on his way out. "There were at least three hundred people on the street, and

Bobby DJ and Michael Cappello at Le Jardin. Photo by Waring Abbott

I went around saying, 'Have the strawberries, darling, they're *fabulous!*' "
The gathering knew exactly what Siano meant and started to eat the fruit,
which the DJ had placed on top of the police car. Then, in a final gesture
of defiance, the mixer reentered the building, opened the windows, and
played his favorite record.

But if love was still the message coming out of the Gallery, it was
about to fall on deaf ears at Le Jardin. "John Addison would come into my
booth," says Siano, "and he would say, 'Nicky, you are blowing me away
tonight! Your lights, your sounds are simply amazing! I just cannot get
over it! You are the best, the greatest!' And I would say, 'No, Michael Cappello's the greatest. I'm the second greatest.'" A couple of months later
Siano heard that Addison had pinned a poster of Cappello to his bedside
wall, and soon after that the Gallery spinner received a phone call from
his Le Jardin employer in which he was told that he had been replaced by
the Limelight idol. "I set myself up for that one," says Siano. "We had this
code of ethics that if a DJ was fired you could go in there and work, but
you couldn't go in there and solicit his job. That soon went asunder."

The episode would have hurt more had it not been for the fact that
it was around this time that Siano began to generate the kind of public
profile that other DJs could only dream about. The seedlings of celeb-

rity status sprouted in July 1974 when *New York* magazine published an article on the impact of the DJ on nightworld that featured Siano, a "great changer," as its carefree case study.

> "Bad changes hurt my ears," Nicky says, swaying his rear end in time to the motion of the needle on his v.u. meter, part of his $20,000 sound system. He flips 45's across his body like dwarf Frisbees, landing them perfectly on one of his three turntables. Most D.J.'s use only two, but Nicky needs the extra record player for his "jet plane and boat sounds." His feet are operating a lighting system that will snap down limp irises. The tweeters are divorced from the woofers and hang overhead so any tune with a lot of highs is sure to go right to your heart. "When they get off . . . I get off," Nicky says, "and I want to make them scream."[10]

The new wave of discotheques and lofts—which, according to the article, could be set up for $50,000 and maintained for $2,500 a week, plus $1,000 a month "to help with city authorities"—had undercut and wrong-footed the wider club industry. "These figures are eye-opening, considering that choice groups like Gladys Knight and the Pips are asking up to $25,000 weekly to entertain a similar number of people at a cabaret," concluded *New York*. "Why spring for the $25-to-$30 a couple it costs to see Gladys at a club when you can watch her for free on TV and then go out and dance to only her best stuff, eat as much fresh fruit as you want, and wash it down with wickedly flavored punch . . . all for about $10?"[11]

Not for the first time, musical practices were running ahead of history, and on this occasion they were anticipating the broader labor market revolution of the eighties and nineties. It all boiled down to *deck*onomics—the cost of the DJ and a couple of decks versus the expense of an entire band. As flexible, nonunionized, low-wage workers earning a top rate of fifty dollars a night, DJs were able to significantly undercut the terms and conditions of the bands, and their rising popularity coincided with a growing hostility toward performing groups. "I felt that live musicians had forfeited their right to perform in nightclubs," says soundman Alex Rosner. "They were costly, they would get stoned, and they were unreliable. There was no stopping the discos, and as far as I was concerned the musicians could go into the recording studio."

* * *

Nicky Siano was beginning to influence other wannabe mixers. "Larry and I would blow up balloons, set up the food bar, prepare the punch, and give out acid, but we also spent a lot of time hanging out in the booth, watching Nicky's every move," says Frankie Knuckles. "He pretty much taught us what he was doing." Larry Levan charmed his way one step further, becoming Siano's lieutenant and lover, fulfilling the DJ's most urgent instructions—" 'Larry, check the speakers! Larry, put this acid in the punch! Larry, go get *me* some punch!' "—as well as doubling as Siano's lightman on Saturdays. The relationship also resulted in Levan receiving private tutorials from the fastest rising star on the New York circuit. "Larry wanted to play records," says Siano. "We used to go into the Gallery when it was closed and fool around in the booth. I gave him the list of rules." He also inadvertently gave Levan his first DJing break. "One night I was like, 'Oh, I just can't play!' I lived around the corner, and my friend Rique came to my house and said, 'Mary! Larry Levan's playing records, and you know *she* can't play records. You *have* to come to work!' "

Levan didn't only hover around the booth at the Gallery where, like the Loft, opportunities to play were inevitably restricted. He also began to gravitate toward the DJ enclosure at the Continental Baths. "We had just installed an entire new system, and we built another booth in the middle of the dance floor," says Jorge La Torre. "Larry was totally mesmerized by the setup. He kept pestering me to let him play." Permission wasn't forthcoming. "I remember feeling nervous. We knew Larry because he had started to hang out at the Baths, but he had no demonstrable skills of any sort, and I don't remember him telling me that he had played anywhere else. I was very skeptical because I knew how strongly Steve felt about the new equipment."

Biding his time, Levan eventually persuaded Knuckles to hang out with him at the Tubs. "He was always trying to get me to come down, and I refused to go," says Knuckles. "I finally decided to go for the Fourth of July weekend and ended up staying for what I thought was three or four days." With no natural light, the bathhouse had played tricks with time. "It was only when I went outside that I realized I'd been there for two weeks." During this and subsequent stays the duo created quite an impression. "Larry was hanging out on a regular basis as a customer, and then Frankie started to come along, too," says La Torre. "I remember them sharing a room and sleeping there. In fact they practically lived in the Baths, to be honest. I don't know if they didn't have a place to live or what but they would come for days on end."

The aspiring DJs created a good impression. "They were very nice and very friendly, and I had gotten to like them because they spent so much time at the Baths as customers," adds La Torre. "I just thought they were people who loved to party, and I liked the way in which they were into music." Eventually the de facto dance floor manager gave Levan and Knuckles a chance to play. "The Baths was open twenty-four hours a day, and it was usually quiet in the afternoon. The people who had stayed over-night usually checked out in the morning, and the people who were going to come in the evening didn't usually arrive until four or five, so there was a period during the day when there was hardly anyone around, and that was when I let Larry and Frankie practice on the sound system."

Around the same time an extended game of musical chairs produced a series of DJing vacancies that eventually ricocheted their way down to the young enthusiasts. The sequence began when David Rodriguez was hired by the Baths to replace the Le Jardin-bound Guttadaro in the summer of 1973, and Joey Bonfiglio, who had helped Bob Casey install the new sound system, was employed to organize the microphones for the shows, work the lights, and fill in as the alternate. Rodriguez, though, wasn't as reliable as he might have been—"He wasn't always showing up, and he destroyed the equipment," says Casey—and Ostrow finally dismissed the fiery DJ in the early spring of 1974. Bonfiglio was then invited to step behind the wheels of steel, and the new resident asked Levan to work as his alternate and lightman. "I think Joey kind of pulled Larry," says Knuckles, "and Larry ended up playing Mondays and Tuesdays." The new team settled into a groove until Bonfiglio put in an unsuccessful request for a raise on the eve of Memorial Day weekend 1974. "Steve Ostrow refused to pay him what he wanted—and was worth—so he just upped and walked," says Casey. Ever the maid-in-waiting, Levan was now in the right place at the right time. "Larry was there, and he was familiar with the sound system," says La Torre. "When the opportunity came we let him take over." It was a pragmatic appointment. "Steve and I were fairly good at spotting talent. When I saw Bette I said, 'We've got to have her!' I don't remember having that kind of experience with Larry. I don't remember thinking he was spectacular. We just needed a DJ, and he was there."

Levan didn't have any records, however, and he remembers being told that he had five hours to get something together in time for the looming holiday party. "I went back to Brooklyn and borrowed records from my friend Ronnie Roberts, who had everything," Levan told Steven Harvey in 1983. "I went back and worked three straight days."[12] Siano, whose relationship with Levan had petered out some time earlier, wasn't impressed. "I felt kind of used by Larry," he says. "I'd introduced him to my record company contacts, and when he got the job at the Continental Baths he went behind my back and used my name in order to put together a collection. He never came to me for help. I would have helped him, but he obviously had other ideas. Frankie never did that. Frankie was the exact opposite in that respect."

Knuckles got his break behind the turntables thanks to Levan. "It was just Larry at the beginning, but sometimes he would play part of the night, and then he would give Frankie a chance," says La Torre. "He would ask us if it would be ok to let Frankie play, and we would say, 'Yes.' Larry had proven himself, and it made us feel more comfortable about letting Frankie have a go." Knuckles was subsequently offered a start-of-the-week slot at Better Days. "I kind of knew Frankie through various channels, but we became friends during this club boom, and Frankie was trying to play at the Continental Baths," Tee Scott told Daniel Wang. "So one night I saw him sitting there with his head in his hands, and I said, 'I'm overworked with seven nights a week over at Better Days, so why don't you have two of my nights there?' "[13] Knuckles told Scott that he wouldn't—*couldn't*— play, but he was persuading nobody. "Tee told me, 'Look, you're in this booth with Nicky every week, what do you mean you can't do it?' He let me use his records, and I gradually built up a clientele of about four or five hundred." The run was short-lived. "Six months into the job I was told that they were shutting the night down because they weren't making any money. I thought it was doing well, but that's what I was told."

Luckily for Knuckles, Levan handed him his start-of-the-week nights. "I played Mondays and Tuesdays," says Knuckles. "Larry played Wednesday through to Sunday." The slow afternoons, however, remained the most important slot of all. "For the most part nobody was paying any attention to the dance floor so we would turn off the main system and just use the monitors in the booth. We'd be in there smoking a joint and playing records, just feeding off each other." Influences began to materialize. "Larry's style was more David, and I was more Nicky. I was into the mix, just like Nicky, whereas Larry went for the atmosphere and the feeling, which was more like David. Larry's main focus was creating moods."

Frankie Knuckles and Larry Levan at the Continental Baths. Courtesy of Bob Casey

Having learned their trade from the Italian American pioneers of the early seventies, African American DJs were beginning to make an impact. "We were like a brethren back then," says Knuckles. "There weren't that many black DJs playing in New York City, let alone black gay ones, and you could pretty well count us on one hand. There was me, Larry, Tee Scott, and David Todd. I guess we were like the second generation. We were the next wave."

As it happens they had yet to make a significant splash in the Baths, at least in La Torre's expert eyes. "I couldn't say that Larry particularly added anything to the place," he comments. "Larry might have played more soulful music, and he was good at doing tricks with the turntables, but overall he was just one more good DJ." Ditto Knuckles. "I thought he was almost as good as Larry. They were so close. I saw the two of them as one, and the same went for their playing." According to their peers, however, Levan was the more exciting talent—"Larry was the man," notes Siano. "Frankie wasn't really anyone"—and by the fall it had become clear that the nineteen-year-old DJ was riding the crest of this second generational wave when he was invited to become the resident at downtown's latest and (following the closure of the Loft and the Gallery) only functioning loft party, the SoHo Place, which was situated in Richard Long's apartment on 452 Broadway, just a couple of blocks from Mancuso's old haunt. "The idea was to do another Loft," says Mike Stone, who had been a regular at the Broadway parties and was now living with Long as the soundman's occasional lover. "The SoHo Place had started as a series of dinner parties in 1973, and when the Loft closed I told Richard that it was the perfect time to start a regular party. Richard had started his own audio company, and he wanted to showcase his sound equipment so we went ahead with the idea. David Mancuso was the inspiration."

Readily admitting that he wanted to *be* Mancuso, Stone began the trial party in poll position behind the DJ booth, and Alfie Davison stood in as his alternate, but the promoter-cum-DJ gave himself the sack when he heard Levan, who had been invited to the test-run by Long following a tip-off from Mancuso. "I was so embarrassed," says Stone. "Larry left me floored. He knew how to handle a sound system. He was a genius right from the beginning. It was clear he would be number one." When the young DJ was offered the SoHo job, he accepted without hesitation, leaving Knuckles in control at the Baths. "By this time Continental was jam-packed, and I had outgrown it," Levan told Harvey.[14] SoHo Place opened in time for Halloween 1974, and soon after Long decided that the parties would benefit from the assistance of an old hand—Robin Lord. "Richard was interested in having me work at the door of the club because I knew all the right people to admit," she says. "He also needed administrative help with his business, and I could type and set up files. I ended up moving into the room behind his DJ booth, and I worked for him instead of paying rent." Lord helped the parties generate business. "Richard was getting the rough crowd along to the SoHo, which is what he liked sexually, but he also wanted dancey people at the parties. I helped get the word out and gave Richard some legitimacy with the crowd he was hoping to attract."

Long was every inch the geeky soundman. "He was tall, white, wore glasses, and dressed in polyester," says Lord. "He always looked like he needed to wash his hair, which was long and maintained a sort of stringy, greasy look. He was educated and intelligent and didn't seem to be close with anyone. He also didn't seem to care much about his surroundings." What he did care about was his burgeoning sound system business. "Richard wasn't into competing with David or Nicky," adds Lord. "He just wanted to create a little success and help his sound business grow. He invited prospective customers to hear the sound system in the atmosphere of a real club." Stone maintains that Long leapfrogged the competition in next to no time. "The SoHo was where Richard began to really develop his sound. He changed it each week. It became the biggest thing and by the mid-seventies Richard was *the* man." Lord, though, wasn't particularly impressed with the result. "Gallery's sound system always sounded better to me. I always felt that Alex Rosner did a better job."

The SoHo Place quickly settled into a groove, and, keen to appear at the only up-and-running loft venue in town, Knuckles, Scott, and Siano all made guest appearances. "They were all mixing by this point," says Stone. "Nicky was the first ingenious mixer and mixing became everything. It was the most exciting part of the record." Featuring Manhattan's hottest DJs, the SoHo Place started to attract two to three hundred guests every Friday night. "The club went from being empty to being so crowded you couldn't walk," Levan told Harvey.[15] Lord, though, remained detached ("The parties never developed the atmosphere or mystique of either the Loft or the Gallery"), and David DePino was also unmoved ("SoHo Place was a bad imitation of the Loft"). That, though, was nothing compared to the reaction of Long's neighbors. "There were big problems with the people upstairs," says Lord. "Richard told them that he was showcasing the sound systems that he built and offered them money to go and stay in hotels. They weren't very happy." Stone concedes that the problem was exacerbated by Long's penchant for booming bass. "At first the neighbors accepted us, but then they started to complain. It was also unheard of to have blacks living in SoHo at the time."

Yet while the neighbors had officialdom on their side—the City Planning Commission had initiated a campaign against SoHo dance venues in August 1974, declaring that they exploit "the energy of the art center" while contributing "nothing to its growth"—the downtown night network kept on rebounding like a colony of ants, and the Gallery became the latest nightspot to confound the city's regulatory bodies when it reopened on Mercer and Houston in November 1974.[16] "Second Gallery was newish-looking," says Siano. "It was more like a club, except that it went beyond the clubs of the time. Clubs had a homey, underground feel, whereas the second Gallery was high-tech and innovative." The centerpiece was a new three-tier lighting system, which was designed by Siano and Robert De-Silva, a friend from the Round Table era. "I introduced Robert to the Loft, and he made me see things about the lighting that I took for granted. He was really into the lighting, and he not only worked the lights at the Gallery but also installed and designed many of them." The effect was groundbreaking. "If you were on the dance floor the lights looked as if they went into the ceiling. Traditional club systems would flash and move around, but this actually gave you a unique spatial effect."

Opening night drew in 1,600 dancers, with Siano treating his packed dance floor to a special edition of LaBelle's "What Can I Do For You?" from the album *Nightbirds*. "That was the first time that I turned off the sound in the middle of a record," he says. " 'What Can I Do For You?' was *the* big song, and they sang the entire thing." The party was a runaway success. "It was like an 'Open House' in a small town," reported *Melting Pot*, the magazine of the National Association of Discotheque Disc Jockeys (NADD), which had been launched by Bob Casey in August. "The atmosphere started out warm and congenial and went up hill from there. Nicky Siano was in his prime and the croud [sic]—well, the croud [sic] was the epitomy [sic] of the word 'TOGETHER.' If there was a way of recording the people along with the music,—oh, what a tape it would be."[17] Combined with the punch, it was enough to send anyone dizzy, so when Gomes told Siano that he could hear a thumping sound from upstairs the DJ replied, "You're high, child." Ever inquisitive, Gomes decided to investigate, and after two flights of stairs he discovered the source: another DJ, some speakers, and several hundred dancers. Gomes returned to the Gallery, and Siano asked him what the crowd was like. "White and gay," Gomes replied. "Oh, that's alright then," said Siano. "There's nothing to worry about."

Gomes had walked into the Manhattan version of the Boom Boom Room, although this time Michael Fesco's inspiration had come not from the Sanctuary but the Tenth Floor. "The Tenth Floor was the beginning of the concept of the A-list," says Fesco, who had been introduced to the party by his Venezuelan lover, a friend of Armando Galvez, one of the DJs at the venue. "It was mostly Pines people and a few of us from the Grove. It was a wonderfully charming little club and it certainly gave me something to think about." Fesco gave it some thought and decided to produce an expanded version of the private party. "Going to the Tenth Floor gave me the idea to do a private club in a loft space."

Fesco was in need of a new direction, having resigned from the Ice Palace at the end of a difficult summer in 1973. The season had begun

badly when the Boatel and the Sandpiper hired Bob Casey to revamp their sound systems, and it got worse when the Sandpiper started to gnaw away at Fesco's Friday and Saturday night crowd at the Ice Palace. "It was a much bigger battle in 1973," says Casey. "People really had to make a decision about whether they wanted to go to the Pines or the Grove." As if that wasn't enough, the appearance of a rogue pyromaniac halfway through the season convinced Fesco that it was time to move on. "I was so stressed out," he says. "By the time the police finally caught him I couldn't deal with it anymore."

The party promoter started looking for a space in Manhattan the following summer and eventually stumbled into an old (and future) sweatshop on the second-floor of 599 Broadway, situated on the corner of Houston Street—and directly above the site of the soon-to-open new Gallery. "Back then it was a deserted part of town," says Fesco. "The space was fifty feet wide and two hundred feet long, and the ceilings were fourteen feet high. One of the great things about the room was it had no support columns, which made it feel very spacious. Everyone said it was too big, but I thought it was perfect." Fesco began to reconstruct the space in September, hiring Frankie Montaguto to install the sound and lights, and soon after he received an unexpected fillip when it emerged that the Tenth Floor, an inevitable if pint-sized rival, wasn't going to reopen. "It was all terribly illegal," says Fesco. "They had no fire escapes. I think they closed of their own volition. It started as a fun little hobby and when the newness wore off and it became a financial responsibility they decided to get out."

Richard Brezner confirms that the owners had become sick and tired of the pretentious monster they had inadvertently created. "The funny thing is both David Sokoloff and Jim Jessup were about as unpretentious as you could get, and while David Bruie was very status conscious he already had his social standing." Sokoloff became a particularly miserable figure. "Within a couple of months of its opening David dreaded going to the Tenth Floor. He used to call me and beg me to go with him so he would have a friend there. He didn't find it fun, and that's not a good place to be for a club owner." The popularity of the venue combined with the general lack of space had also turned the door policy into a nightmare. "David was always having problems with members abusing their privileges and not calling ahead with the names of their guests. They would just show up

---

opposite: Dance floor at the new Gallery. Courtesy of Nicky Siano

with all these people, and the club would become overcrowded. People would have to wait in line to get in, and there wouldn't be enough room for members." Eventually the tension pervaded the entire infrastructure of the club. "They used to have meetings, and they always used to disagree on things. It started out as a social place for a specific group of members and their friends, and I don't think that's what it wound up being."

Fesco launched his new venue in December 1974. "We called it Flamingo," says the party host. "The designer Getty Miller came up with the name, and I thought it had a very musical sound. The word 'flamingo' just rippled off your tongue." However, it initially looked like the venue was going to struggle to take off. "The opening was like every opening. Everything was piled up in the corner. Getty showed up with a truckload of gladiolas, and that was the decor for the night." The door policy was equally chaotic. "I closed the door at five hundred and refused to let anyone else in. I didn't have a clue about the capacity. I eventually found out we could admit twenty-five hundred." Nevertheless the party was a tremendous success, running as it did until 6 A.M., and Vince Aletti gave the venue a glowing review. "Even with the rugs rolled and stacked at one end and a ladder still standing at the other it looked like the best space in town," he wrote. "Armando Galvez, who has done occasional parties and some incredible tapes, was the opening night deejay, so the place was, in his word, 'hectic.' Wonderfully hectic."[18]

Armando Galvez

Select Discography (Flamingo) [Source: Record World, *28 December 1974]*

Biddu Orchestra, "Blue Eyed Soul"

Disco Tex & the Sex-O-Lettes, "Get Dancin' "

Gloria Gaynor, "Never Can Say Goodbye"

LaBelle, "What Can I Do for You?"

Laura Lee, "(If You Want to Try Love Again) Remember Me"

Gene Page, "Satin Soul"

Sister Sledge, "Love Don't You Go through No Changes on Me"

The Stylistics, "Hey Girl, Come and Get It"

The Temptations, "Happy People"

Universal Mind, "Something Fishy Going On"

Making the most of early demand and drawing on the entertainment paradigm established at the Ice Palace, Fesco started to open Flamingo four nights a week. Thursday became movie night, Friday and Saturday were regular party nights, and by Sunday it was time for Tea Dance. The much-hyped social scene at the Tenth Floor started to look positively meek, as did the Chelsea venue's bare bones infrastructure, which had never incorporated anything as futuristic as Montaguto's enormous beat-sensitive light board. "Flamingo was the first gymnasium disco," says Tenth-Floor-turned-Flamingo-regular Frank Crapanzano. "It was the granddaddy of the discos, the diamond on the tiara." Indeed, Fesco even started to attract the up-market gay crowd—something that he had failed to achieve at the Ice Palace—and he consolidated their patronage by borrowing the Tenth Floor's private membership system. "My lover at the time was friendly with the Pines people so the conceited crowd became the Flamingo crowd," says Fesco, who charged thirty-five dollars for the membership cards, although some were reportedly sold on for an extraordinary six hundred dollars. "They were known as the A-list. Everyone was very beautiful. Gorgeous boys would go home with gorgeous guys."

The boys and the guys were also overwhelmingly white, all of which contributed to good neighborly relations. "The Gallery wasn't completely gay, and it certainly wasn't completely white," says Fesco, "so there was never a rivalry there." But while the racial split might have suited the respective parties, others felt uneasy. "Flamingo only had a smattering of blacks," says Mark Riley, who visited the venue on industry-related business. "They were very conscious of not wanting to drive away their gay white crowd by admitting a large number of gay blacks." Fesco confirms the existence of a racial divide but rejects the charge of premeditated exclusion. "We were 99 percent gay and 99 percent white, but there was no conscious membership policy. Some people just happened to like the kind of music that we played, and others preferred the music that was being played at places like the Gallery. We attracted very distinct crowds. None of my friends knew the Nicky Siano crowd and vice versa."

Flamingo introduced a new, sexually charged atmosphere into the still-formative culture of the gay discotheque, although as with other gay clubs there was more promise than fulfillment. "Sex was not the reason the boys went to Flamingo," says Fesco. "Sex happened after leaving the club when great numbers would go to the Saint Marks Baths." Club copulation simply wasn't viable. "Most of the clubs had bathrooms that were so small

View of Flamingo from the turntables. Courtesy of Michael Fesco

and so crowded that sex would have been somewhat difficult," says Casey. "With one or two urinals and one commode for a crowd of two hundred plus, most patrons would not have put up with it." On-the-spot sex accordingly happened elsewhere. "Anybody could get their dick sucked in any number of places. A busy disco would not have been anyone's first choice."

You could, however, cruise, and Flamingo, above all other gay venues, offered the ideal environment for the kind of casual interaction that could lead to something else. The sheer density of bodies made contact inevitable, and the more expansive dance floor situation nurtured an erotic exchange of transient glances and brushing torsos in which anonymous men could experience scores of fleeting, non-orgasmic sexual encounters in a single evening. "At discos like Flamingo you cruised, you met, you got a name and a number, or you left together," says Casey. "If you were hanging around as the evening wound down, you were either waiting to go home with a bartender or a waiter, or you were so wasted you had to be thrown out. People like that ended up at a tea room, the train station, or the back of a truck."

* * *

Barry White formed Love Unlimited—a girl group that featured Diane Taylor, Linda James, and Glodean James plus a forty-piece backing orches-

Decorating Flamingo exterior. Courtesy of Michael Fesco

Billy Smith, promoter,
20th Century. Photo
by Waring Abbott

tra—in 1969, and the band recorded its first chart hit in the spring of
1972 with "Walkin' in the Rain with the One I Love." The following summer, the Texas-born White released the group's second album, *Under the
Influence of . . .* , deploying a lush, orchestrated aesthetic that suggests
that, in tandem with the material emerging from Philadelphia International, the sonic symphonic had become a national phenomenon. Even
though it was recorded as an album filler, "Love's Theme" provided a
particularly stunning example of the new aesthetic, but 20th Century
had other promotional priorities for the six-foot-three-inch, 270-pound
White, who was simultaneously establishing himself as a major independent recording artist in his own right, having notched up hits with "I'm
Gonna Love You Just a Little More Baby," "I've Got So Much to Give,"
and "Never, Never Gonna Give You Up." Then, however, David Rodriguez and Nicky Siano paid a visit to Billy Smith, the label's East Coast
promotion under-assistant. "We went down into the basement and saw
the Love Unlimited album on the shelf," says Siano. "Billy said, 'These
are dead albums waiting to be trashed,' and David replied, 'They've got

black people on the cover—give them to us!' David and I started playing 'Love's Theme' and it took off from there." Realizing he had nothing to lose, Smith distributed free copies of the LP to New York's leading DJs, and, when demand spiraled, "Love's Theme" was released as a single by the renamed Love Unlimited Orchestra. By February 1974 it had reached number one. " 'Love's Theme' was in the top twenty before it even got any airplay," says Siano. "The power we had was phenomenal!"

Aside from a pocket-sized piece in *Billboard*, however, that power had yet to be recognized by the music industry, and few radio jocks were ready to accept that their monopoly over the hit parade was being broken up. That included the African American Frankie Crocker, who had hopped from New York's rising WWRL to the poppier WMCA before settling at the one-time militant WBLS, which subsequently became a vehicle for his slick, hip, upwardly mobile style. "The building block was Crocker's drive-time program (from 4 to 7 P.M.) and a programming concept called the 'Total Black Experience in Sound,' " notes music critic Nelson George. "The pop-jazz of Grover Washington, Jr., Miles Davis's fusion, the expansive R&B sound of Stevie Wonder, Donny Hathaway, Marvin Gaye, and Isaac Hayes—all found a home in the WBLS format."[19] So did the Love Unlimited Orchestra. "I was the first guy to play Barry White," says Crocker. "I was the only person in the city playing Barry White, and the rest of it was from there."

Siano was in the back of a cab with Rodriguez when he heard the WBLS DJ announce that he was premiering "Love's Theme." "I started screaming, 'This queen isn't premiering anything!' Billy Smith gave the record to me and David and then Michael, and it was just the three of us playing it. I used to get really irate when radio tried to take the credit for what we did." The balance sheet was amended in July, however, when 20th Century decided to award a gold record not only to Crocker but also to Guttadaro, who was also playing the track. Engineered by Smith, the award marked a significant shift in power from the radio DJs, who had received stacks of gold records, to the discotheque DJs, for whom this was a first. "Most of the promotion guys from the record companies today have something to work on other than the radio stations, where it's quite difficult to break a new record," the promoter told *Melting Pot*. "Today they also have the discotheques." Smith was careful to give WBLS its due ("They sell the most R&B records"), but he provocatively added that even radio's finest could barely keep pace with the club DJs ("Frankie Crocker of WBLS goes to the discos

Barry White. Courtesy of the Vince Aletti Collection

to stay up on things").[20] Any lingering doubt over who should take credit was effectively resolved when White went to Le Jardin to thank Bobby DJ and his peers for turning "Love's Theme" into a hit.

Siano was kept out of the equation. "I think it was a political thing," says the Gallery mixer. "Billy was mad at me because I put acid in his water one day." Yet while that may well have been a factor, a deeper politics was also at work. "Bobby wasn't necessarily the first one to play the record," Smith told *Melting Pot*, "but he received the gold record for—and I'll quote from the press release; 'In recognition for his efforts in helping to break LOVE'S THEME.'" So why did Guttadaro receive the trophy? "The whole thing was to break the disco deejay in the record world."[21] And Bobby DJ, the friendly pharmacist who played in America's highest profile club, was more "breakable" than Siano, the impulsive mixer from the depths of the downtown party network.

Radio's hit-making monopoly came under further pressure after "Rock the Boat," an RCA single by the unknown Hues Corporation that discotheque DJs had been spinning some eight months in advance of their radio counterparts, hit the top of the charts in July and eventually went gold. When the similar-sounding "Rock Your Baby" by George McCrae on TK went to number one later in the same month, it became clear that club DJs were collectively generating a new style of music that was selling like crazy. "We were dealing with the same crowds every week, and we programmed them," says Siano. "We heavily rotated records, just like radio, and the next week that record would be a hit." New York's night priests had become the self-conscious lightning conductors of the fledgling dance music industry.

They also became aware of the value of not just their ability to hear but their capacity to construct when patrons began to offer them between thirty and seventy-five dollars for the reel-to-reel tapes that they regularly made for emergency situations. By October this trade had become a front-page story in Billboard, which highlighted the illegitimate nature of the practice before pointing out that "non-disco spots such as beauty parlors, cafes or other locations desiring hip background music" were buying the prerecorded selections as a "cool alternative to Muzak or other wired music services."[22] Yet while the record companies were no doubt miffed at the way in which their music was being sold without permission, they demonstrated the marketing acumen of a tortoise when it came to pushing this promising product. Bob Casey, in his capacity as the head of the National Association of Discotheque Disc Jockeys, contacted licensing organizations and record companies to explore what kind of fee would be required to legitimately market the tapes only to hit a wall of bureaucracy. Red tape was blocking the potential sale of audiotape.

The sense of an emerging dance genre nevertheless accelerated when Billboard ran a front-page story on the emergence of the "disco mix" at the beginning of November. "Specially mixed versions of commercial singles are being offered to discotheques here by a number of labels looking to capitalize on the clubs' growing reputation as record 'breakout' points," ran the report. "At such labels as Scepter, Chess/Janus and Roulette, executives say that the clubs are a definite influence in breaking records and that they consider it well worth the time and effort to reach the disco audience. Notably, several of these special mixes have generated local market reaction which, they say, has eclipsed that of the original commercial copy."[23]

Don Downing's "Dream World" was a case in point. The record was mixed by Tom Moulton who, having traveled around New York's labels in

order to complain about the brevity of their dance records, eventually received his reward when Scepter executive-cum-clubber Mel Cheren gave
him the opportunity to put some of his ideas into practice. Cheren was
obviously of a similar mind, having come up with the superficially penny-
pinching yet fundamentally DJ-friendly idea of putting an instrumental
mix of "We're On the Right Track" by Ultra High Frequency on the B-side
of the record, and he inventively ran Moulton's work with Downing as an
A-side "commercial mix" that ran at two minutes thirty-six seconds and a
B-side "disco mix" that lasted for four minutes thirteen seconds. " 'Dream
World' started out in one key and modulated up," says Moulton. "There
was no way I could have extended the record by looping it back to the
beginning. It would have sounded horrible. So at the end of the record I
took out the strings, horns, and guitar, and I brought up the congas and
the bass. I let the groove run and then took it back to the original modu-
lation." Moulton had deployed the first studio-designed break in order to
get out of a corner, and the result, which went on to sell ten thousand
copies without radio play, became a headline.

Dance music's impressive run continued when "Kung Fu Fighting" by
Carl Douglas reached number one in November and helped 20th Century
record its first two-million-dollar month—general manager Tom Rodden
said in the December issue of *Melting Pot* that the release had taken off
in the discos, and the company awarded gold records to Bobby DJ, David
Rodriguez, and Frank Strivelli for their efforts—and the momentum was
maintained when Midland International released "Doctor's Orders" by
Carol Douglas and sold one hundred thousand copies before radio caught
on.[24] Spinning music and spinning from their extraordinary surge onto
the music scene, DJs provided further confirmation of the power of their
taste when they propelled "Do It ('Til You're Satisfied)" to the top of
the charts in that same month. The Brothers Truckin' record was also
mixed by Moulton, who completed the job before he laid his hands on
"Dream World," even though Downing's song was released first. Moulton
transformed the three-minute excursion of "Do It" into a five-and-a-half-
minute exploration, and when it became clear that the extended playing
time meant that the booming low-end frequencies wouldn't fit on the
cramped seven-inch format, Moulton killed the bass drum to a dull thud
and raised the hi-hats as well as the cymbal crashes. "The group hated
it," he remembers. "They said that it wasn't the way they recorded it, and
that it was unnatural. They were particularly upset about the way I used

the organ." However, in October *Billboard* ran a story on the emerging hit, which Scepter owner Florence Greenberg credited to New York's club crowds, and all remaining arguments were set to one side when "Do It" by the astutely renamed B. T. Express topped the charts and went gold.[25]

Even though he was based in Los Angeles, *Billboard* chart editor Bill Wardlow couldn't help but take note—he was, after all, dating Greenberg at the time—and he subsequently asked the label mogul to arrange for him to be shown around New York's clubs. Greenberg asked Cheren to lead the tour, and when he was forced to back out Moulton stepped in. "I asked Bill Wardlow, 'Where would you like to go?'" says Moulton. "'Do you want to go to the big high-profile clubs or do you want to go to a couple of underground spots that are progressive and don't give a damn what everybody else thinks?' He said, 'I want to go to the underground clubs!'" Moulton took Wardlow to the Limelight and arrived to discover Rodriguez in full flow. "Everybody was calling out for 'Date with the Rain,'" says Moulton. "So what did Rodriguez do? He played this up-tempo ballad by Gladys Knight & the Pips called 'Make Yours a Happy Home.'" The crowd refused to dance, only to discover that the Limelight DJ wasn't in the mood to compromise. "He grabbed the PA and announced, 'Unless you get up and dance I'm going to play this record all night!' Eventually the owner started to bang on the booth and screamed, 'You're *fired*!' Rodriguez carried on playing the Gladys Knight and declared, 'This is all you're going to hear unless you dance so if you're not going to dance you might as well leave!'" Demoralized and exhausted, the Limelight clientele slowly started to move, but that wasn't good enough for the DJ, who then told them that he wanted to see a little more enthusiasm. "Finally Rodriguez said, 'Is it rain you want? I'll give you rain!' He proceeded to play these thunder sound effects, and after about twenty minutes you could start to hear *'Got a date with the rain'* through this storm. It was the Kendricks, and the crowd went crazy." Wardlow was stupefied. "He told me, 'I can't believe people react to music like this, and it isn't even being played on the radio!' I said, 'Thaaat's riiight!'"

Billboard had launched its first discotheque chart back in February 1965, and now, almost ten years later, Wardlow decided to revive the idea in light of the fact that discotheques were proliferating, their DJs were generating sales, studio hands were creating special "disco mixes," and even sound system companies were using the word "disco" to market their wares. "He wanted to create this regular column called 'Disco Action,' and he asked me if I would be interested in writing it," says Moulton. "I said, 'Well, I obviously couldn't review my own mixes because that would be a conflict of interest.' Bill replied, 'There's one thing I'd say about you, Tom. You're honest, and I don't think you'd ever let it get in your way.'"

Moulton used his very first column to highlight the case of Gloria Gaynor's "Never Can Say Goodbye." Produced at the end of 1973 by Tony Bongiovi, Meco Monardo, and Jay Ellis at Mediasound Studios, the record had gone on to become a major club hit. "Heavy heavy play and audience response on the new Gloria Gaynor 'Never Can Say Goodbye,'" reported *Melting Pot* in September 1974. "It's the kind of reaction that forces a disco record above ground and wins it airplay in other key markets."[26] No support, however, was forthcoming. "MGM said it was a dance record, and they couldn't care less," says Moulton. "They thought, 'Big deal, so it's a fast version of a Michael Jackson song.'" Radio proved to be equally unenthusiastic, even when the song sneaked into the lower echelons of the chart, and so Moulton decided to use his debut column to highlight the scandal. "With large numbers of discos reportedly opening around the country," he wrote, "four questions most asked of discos by their customers are: (1) The name of the record being played and the artist. (2) Is it new? (3) Where can it be purchased? (4) If Gloria Gaynor is so popular at discos, why isn't she being played on radio?"[27] Instead of flinching, Wardlow backed his columnist with a provocative full-page ad that asked how a record could sell so many copies without the support of a single radio station. "MGM was so mad at *Billboard* they threatened to pull their ads," says Moulton. "It was rough."

"Never Can Say" eventually peaked at number nine in the charts and stayed in the hit parade for a total of seventeen weeks, yet the low-profile Moulton, who produced an innovative mix for Gaynor's ensuing album, remained the more influential figure. "There were three songs on side one, and I turned them into a continuous eighteen-minute mix," says the studio whiz who didn't receive a credit for his work. "Nobody had done that before, and Gloria wasn't very happy. When she heard it she said, 'I don't sing much! What am I supposed to do when we perform the song?' I said, 'You learn to *dance!*'" Having practiced her steps, Gaynor sent out a batch of autographed LPs to New York's DJs "to show her appreciation for all the help they have given her," and two of the recipients, Michael Cappello and David Rodriguez, confirmed that Moulton had done the right thing for the dance floor.[28] "Both report a predictably knock-out response," Vince Aletti reported in a new column for *Record World*, "especially when the pressing is playing straight through ('It gives me a chance to take a break, too,' Rodriguez adds)."[29]

Moulton was rebuilding records according to a new set of priorities. "I started making drastic changes right from the beginning," he says. "People called me the doctor. They would bring me their sick record, and I would fix it. They all thought I was crazy in terms of the way I changed everything around." The mixer would start off by studying the recording at home, after which he would take it into the studio and ask for certain tracks to be taken out so that he could "hear what's hidden." Although the vocals were usually left alone, the instrumentation was almost always changed, and when the engineers said that Moulton was requesting the impossible he would reply, "Well, how can we create that illusion?"

Whereas MFSB and Barry White had introduced the orchestra into dance music, Moulton was now introducing dance music to symphonic structures. "I always wanted to make songs sound like a suite. Each record would go through different movements to produce a mini musical masterpiece." The mixer's opus would unfold around a foundation of constant beats, and the innovative technique of looping back provided him with much of his additional material. "He would stretch the instrumen-

Michael Cappello at Le Jardin. Photo by Waring Abbott

tal so that by the end of the song people would be that much more excited about it," says music critic Brian Chin. "To think that producers used to curse him for what he did!" A self-declared quality freak, Moulton regularly added upper-midrange to the bass and vocals to make sure they were clearly audible, and he also organized the tracks so that the horns and the strings came out of different channels in order to create a visual quality. "I wanted my work to sound good in the discotheques. I didn't like muddy. I wanted crystal clear."

Exploiting the full potential of his column, Moulton also became an important chronicler of the way in which club culture was spreading throughout the States. Miami—home of TK Records, which was proactively servicing local DJs—was ostensibly the most important center outside of New York. "Barry Lederer reports from Miami that the disco scene there has been going strong for some two-and-a-half years now," Moulton wrote in December 1974.[30] Los Angeles followed closely behind, even if the city's DJs were less progressive than their New York counterparts (clubs weren't receiving promotional copies, and audiences preferred to dance to familiar music). "There is a feeling that the disco club scene here is starting to get established," reported Moulton. "Not as a fad but as a legitimate entertainment outlet."[31]

That entertainment outlet was firmly establishing itself in Boston, where Joey Carvello (Yesterdays), Danae Jacaividis (Chaps), John Luongo (Rhinoceros), and Jimmy Stuard (1270) were generating the most progressive scene outside of Manhattan. Luongo ostensibly led the way. "John was this Italian guy who was playing at the number one black club in Boston, and he was great," says Arthur Baker, a rock 'n' roll head who worked at a record store in downtown Boston before he went to college in nearby Amherst in 1973. "He would take two seven-inch singles, and he would extend the break by going back and forth between these two records." Carvello, however, rated Stuard more highly. "John was a mentor figure. He was a quick-cut artist, not a blender. Jimmy was the first Boston DJ to do overlays and real mixing."

Another major talent was also emerging at the Monastery in Queens. "Paul Casella was so artistically intense," says David Todd, who became friendly with the Monastery DJ while the two of them were visiting record companies in order to pick up complimentary copies. "He overlapped records and made them talk to each other. The beats were so in sync it just took you on a trip. Paul seemed to be in a league of his own." Casella, who also played a midweek slot at Hollywood, had to work out ways of carrying his suburban crowd with him. "It was a lot easier to program if you were playing in Manhattan," he says. "The crowds were more open, and you could be a lot more creative. At the Monastery you couldn't be too new, but I tried to get them into interesting things. I would play less conventional records at the beginning of the night to get them used to the sound. Then I would try them again in the middle of the night, and if I didn't get the reaction I wanted I would bring them back with a safer record. At least they would have heard what I wanted to play."

With Atlanta, Chicago, Long Island, New Jersey, San Francisco, and Washington, D.C. also producing noteworthy scenes, clubs were beginning to generate a national profile beyond the specialist music publications, and at the end of 1974 the *New York Times* ran its first major analysis of the budding culture. "The new urban clubs attract a clientele led by a polyglot coalition of young white, black and Latino gays and straights," wrote the newspaper's music critic Henry Edwards. "What this group has shared in common for the past two years is the notion that an evening out can best be spent in a non-stop, dusk-to-dawn onslaught of thumping rhythmic activity. They are captivated by rhythm-and-blues tunes possessing diabolically intense rhythm tracks and mesmeric melodic patterns." Airwaves were also "popularizing the fad" with the knock-on effect that "the public at large suddenly appeared to be as eager for a rhythm fix as the most flamboyant urban trendy." Discotheque culture was consequently providing the wider recording sector with a new focus. "The industry has marshaled its production and merchandising apparatus and given full-scale support to disco-soul not only because it wants to sell records, but also because a new trend always gives the illusion of renewed vitality."[32]

Yet while discotheques and what was now being referred to as disco music (which simply referred to music that worked well in the discotheques, whether it was soul or funk or something else) were becoming more and more visible, the DJs who had largely developed and sustained this phenomenon remained inconspicuous, the Cinderellas of a market that refused to acknowledge the labor on which it was built. "Some of us were dealing drugs to make money," says one (who wishes to remain anonymous). "That was the only way we could afford to buy records. We weren't getting paid anything, and the clubs weren't about to buy us any records, so how else could we afford to keep up? We weren't into getting rich. We were starving artists who did what we had to do to maintain our art." Aletti provided a rare moment of recognition when he started to invite a rotating roster of DJs to publish their current playlists in his "Disco File" column and mixers—Richie Kaczor, Tee Scott, Tom Savarese, and Wayne Thorberg were the first—leapt at this opportunity to heighten their profile and increase their chances of getting free records.

Richie Kaczor

Select Discography (Hollywood) [Source: Record World, 16 November 1974]

B. T. Express, "Express"

Disco Tex & the Sex-O-Lettes, "Get Dancin' "

Carol Douglas, "Doctor's Orders"

First Choice, "Guilty"

Gloria Gaynor, "Never Can Say Goodbye"

The Hues Corporation, "Rockin' Soul"

B.B. King, "Philadelphia"

The Modulations, "I Can't Fight Your Love"

Jimmy Ruffin, "Tell Me What You Want"

Barry White, "You're the First, the Last, My Everything"

Although record companies for the most part continued to make life difficult for their unofficial promoters, some began to emulate Billy Smith's successful strategy at 20th Century and Atlantic and RCA went one step further when they appointed Doug Riddick—the DJ at Opus 1— and David Todd—who was now DJing at Adam's Apple—to their promotion departments. "I was going round from label to label picking up promos," says Todd, who was developing a reputation for his expert beat mixes. "Tom Draper was working at RCA records during the 'Rock the Boat' era, and he happened to enjoy my feedback. I didn't bullshit him just to get promos. If a record worked I would tell him why, and if a record didn't work I would tell him why." Overall, however, the situation was chaotic. Some companies opened their doors, others didn't. Some records were sent out, others weren't. There was no system, no democracy, and no equality, just the random acts of imperious executives who, at least as far as the DJs were concerned, rarely appreciated the artistry and power of their licensed music.

Realizing that communication between the companies, clubs, and DJs had become damagingly dysfunctional, Wardlow decided to organize an end-of-year survey of approximately thirty club owners and sixty DJs, the results of which were unambiguous. Club owners maintained that business was overwhelmingly "good" if not "excellent," even though other areas of the entertainment industry were suffering in line with the turndown in the U.S. economy, and DJs argued that record companies would "enhance their chances of success by releasing disks with extended playing times, preferably in the area of five minutes." Aware of their role in breaking records, the jocks also demanded "more consideration" on the part of manufacturers when it came to servicing product.[33] Conflict was imminent.

6. expansion

Whereas radio DJs operated as the representatives of modernity, discotheque DJs were rapidly establishing themselves as the prophets of postmodernity. After all, the vast majority of radio jocks played top-forty music in order to boost growth within a corporate-driven economy, whereas discotheque DJs usually played less familiar artists whose defining criteria was their functionality, not their profitability. Radio jocks performed in time-constricted shows and usually played records that lasted for three minutes, whereas discotheque DJs developed seemingly endless sets, combining records of varying lengths into an endlessly shifting mix of blended compositions. Radio jocks were determined generalists who played familiar records that would increase ratings, whereas discotheque DJs were flexible specialists who would sift through a spiraling quantity of musical information in order to satisfy a niche group of dancers. Radio jocks were permanent employees, whereas discotheque DJs were peripheral freelancers.

Unfortunately for the protagonists of the downtown party network and beyond, America Inc. was still geared up for the kind of tightly defined market that prioritized radio above the discotheques. By the beginning of 1975, ABC, CBS, EMI, PolyGram, RCA, and Warner Communications controlled just over 80 percent of the music market, and their mutual objective was to develop a selection of superstars who would sell albums en masse. "If an artist can only sell 100,000 records . . . then this company is not interested in pursuing that artist," declared a CBS executive. "We're looking for the major, major breakthroughs."[1] Radio DJs remained the key vehicle for generating these kind of sales, and as a result they, and not their discotheque counterparts, continued to receive most of the attention, as well as the vast majority of free records.

Unnerved by the haphazard nature of this distribution system, discotheque and private party DJs started to besiege record companies in an attempt to get free product. Some, such as RCA, welcomed the onrush and took advantage of the situation. "I had RCA order me two Technics turntables and a mixer for the office," says David Todd. "I would show DJs how a record could work if they were having problems with it, and if they had some ideas they could show me. RCA became a pretty big hangout." Most companies, though, felt overwhelmed. "It's getting to be too much," one PR man told *Melting Pot* in January 1975. "We want to service the disco deejays, but *who's* a disco deejay?"[2] The DJs were equally disgruntled. "It was getting to be crazy," says Jackie McCloy, who played at Penrod's in East Meadow, New York. "You would walk into any record label, and you would see maybe a hundred guys in the lobby. They would all be waiting to see the promotions director, and he would only meet up with one or two DJs at a time."

New York's mixers intensified their invasion of the executive suites following the publication of a list of record company addresses by *Melting Pot*, and the labels, in an attempt to bring the situation under control, subsequently established a strict mid-morning visiting window that provocatively paid no heed to the fact that when DJs worked a nine-to-five shift it was P.M. to A.M., not A.M. to P.M. "They would set the most ridiculous pick-up times that were totally out-of-sync with our lifestyles," says Steve D'Acquisto. "Remember we ate dinner at four o' clock in the morning and would end up passing out some time around seven, yet the companies wanted us at their Manhattan offices by eleven, even though we all lived in Brooklyn. Nine would have been more humane because then we could have stayed up all night and gone to bed once we'd collected our records, but eleven was *just impossible*. They couldn't have picked a worse time if they had tried."

As it happens New York's most prominent DJs were generally getting what they wanted when they wanted, but second-tier spinners were less fortunate, and that unhappy band included D'Acquisto, who was denied a copy of Esther Phillips's "What a Diff'rence a Day Makes" by Terry Serafino, head of promotions at CTI, soon after the companies introduced their new visiting hours. "Terry Serafino wouldn't give me a test pressing," says

D'Acquisto, who might have expected better considering that Tom Moulton had just commended him "for turning a number of DJs and disco stores" onto a string of fast-breaking records.[3] "He told me that it was only for the top DJs, which really irritated me. A caste system was emerging. Instead of us all sharing this music, ten DJs would get a record, and forty wouldn't." The mixer, who knew his rights even when he didn't have any, told his best friend about the incident. "I was very upset," says David Mancuso. "I had never wanted to be on anybody's special list because that implied that I was better than someone else. I thought it was all bullshit so I never went to visit record companies in order to get records. When Steve told me what had happened, I thought it sounded like the discrimination was getting worse."

Realizing that it was time to talk, Sharon Heyward and Bob Casey teamed up to organize an open forum between the companies and the DJs for the beginning of May. The duo's credentials were strong: Heyward, of Curtom Records, had thrown a popular three-hour party for New York's DJs on the Circle Line cruise following the success of "Rock the Boat," and Casey, following a conversation with his colleague Joey Bonfiglio during that very same party, had founded the National Association of Discotheque Disc Jockeys (NADD), a loosely structured trade organization that hoped to emulate the Audio Engineering Society by turning DJs into a sensible white-collar profession. However, the meeting itself, which was held on the dance floor at Hollywood, struggled to contain the tensions that had been emerging between the haves and the have-nots of the discotheque divide. "I saw it crumbling apart," says Francis Grasso. "I finally spoke up at the end of the meeting, and I said, 'I'd like to see more of us get along!' Steve stood up and said, 'That's Francis!' and I got a round of applause." D'Acquisto, who had been sitting on the floor at the back of the room alongside Mancuso, was also beginning to despair. "It was the record companies versus the DJs. We felt that we were at the mercy of the record companies, and it turned into a shouting match. At one point Nicky Siano walked in all fucked up. It was turning into a catastrophe, and we had to do something."

As the meeting edged its way to a close, Mancuso turned to D'Acquisto and said that they should try and form a record pool. "I thought the DJs were very disorganized and unprofessional during the meeting," remembers Mancuso. "We really needed to get our act together if we wanted to work with the record companies, so I told Steve it might be a good idea if we got together by ourselves and came up with a proposal. I said we could form a pool or something." D'Acquisto didn't know what he was talking about. "I said, 'What do you mean?' David said, 'Like a car pool, where everybody jumps in and gets organized. Every DJ would be treated equally.' We decided we needed to have a DJ-only meeting." All of this happened inside a couple of minutes, at which point Mancuso urged D'Acquisto to make an announcement. "I went to the microphone and proposed that the DJs have a separate meeting," says D'Acquisto. "At that point the record companies freaked out. They said, 'You don't need to do that!' I told them that it had nothing to do with them."

The Record Pool was officially inaugurated on 2 June 1975 at 99 Prince Street, where Mancuso was preparing to reopen the Loft, and as the membership roll records, sixty-five of the heftiest names on the DJ circuit turned up. Michael Cappello (Le Jardin), Paul Casella (Monastery/Sound Machine), Steve D'Acquisto (Broadway), Walter Gibbons (Limelight/Galaxy 21), Tony Gioe (Hollywood), Frank Knuckles (Continental Baths), Larry Levan (SoHo), Joey Madonia (Disco I), David Mancuso (the Loft), Bacho Manoval (Talk of the Town/Revelation), Larry Patterson (Le Jock), Eddie Rivera (Cork & Bottle), David Rodriguez (Make-Believe Ballroom), Toraino "Tee" Scott (Better Days) and Thomas A. Savarese (12 West), plus mobiles Bert Lockett and Flowers, were just some of the names—as signed by the DJs themselves—that made up the numbers.

All agreed, as the minutes recorded, that the Record Pool would "serve as a central point to exchange information about up-coming releases, present releases, and who's playing what and where." Somewhat improbably, the gathering also resolved "that anyone of us who receives a record or information pertaining to a record will immediately inform the Record Pool of its existence, and begin the process of making the record available to all members of the Pool." Finally, and most powerfully, came the Record Pool's "Declaration of Intent," which ran:

> We the undersigned have agreed to become associated in the RECORD POOL which has been established for the mutual benefit of discotheque DJs and record companies. The RECORD POOL will be a self-service, self-regulated, independent calm center which will act as a point of exchange between record companies and discotheque DJs.

The POOL will take responsibility for establishing the absolute legitimacy of the DJS involved. The POOL will be a place to receive and distribute recordings and information pertaining to recordings.

The RECORD POOL will enhance rapport among the participants. The benefits to the record companies would be a direct and efficient means of distributing their product to the discotheque DJS. In turn, we as a group and individually will inform the record companies about the progress of their products. This will result in our being able to devote more time and energy to the creative aspects of listening and presenting music.[4]

Coauthored by Paul Casella (the clean-cut suburban club jock), Steve D'Acquisto (the rabblerousing disenfranchised alternate), and David Mancuso (the purist, idealistic musical host), the declaration marked the maturation of a collection of workers who now viewed themselves as a cohesive group—even a profession—with common interests, skills, and, ostensibly, values. Formed to generate greater equality in the music industry by channeling money from the owners (the record companies) to the nonowners (the DJS) while simultaneously guaranteeing that the nonowners, some of whom were more equal than others, now received level treatment, the Pool saw itself as a kind of liberation movement. African Americans, gays, lesbians, and women had all, to varying degrees, been emancipated in the sixties, and now it was the turn of music to be set free. "We spent days getting the wording right," says D'Acquisto, who quickly became the organization's unofficial spokesman. "It was very exciting. We believed that utopia was in our reach. It was our Declaration of Independence."

As with every self-respecting artisan association, there was also an elected president, David Mancuso, plus a series of accompanying officers—Vincent L. Aletti (vice president), Stefano D'Acquisto (secretary), and Dwight Thompson (treasurer)—who were also elected. "The Record Pool was an amazing concept, and I wanted to help it along," says Mancuso, who donated his new space free of charge. "The record companies were making millions, and DJS were lucky to make twenty dollars a night, so we decided to redress the balance. A pool of thought already existed between the DJS, and the Record Pool was all about teamwork. It was like a drop of water going into the ocean and merging with all of the other drops of water. We were much stronger when we acted together."

Record Pool meeting, 13 June 1975. Photo by Waring Abbott

Michael Cappello at the Record Pool. Photo by Waring Abbott

Record Pool party at Prince Street, 30 June 1975. Photo by Waring Abbott

Having cued up everything except for the vinyl, the DJs invited the music magnates to a summit at the Prince Street Loft on 30 June. It turned out to be a spectacular event: more than 25 companies showed up, several from outside New York, and they were joined by an additional 150 DJs. As the ever-present Aletti reported in *Record World*, "Before the meeting was over, in a kind of charged, fund-raising benefit atmosphere, the Pool had gotten verbal commitments for participation from nearly all the record companies present, including Capitol, Polydor, RCA, Arista, Avco, Fania, London, Mercury, MCA, Scepter, Roulette, Private Stock, Curtom, Midland International, and Fantasy." Each pledge to use the Pool as a central distribution point brought cheers from the crowd, "turning what already felt like a party—there were balloons floating all over, plates of cold cuts and cheese, a huge bowl of punch and a decorated cake—into a celebration."[5]

Record companies flocked to make the most of this self-regulating, self-financing promotion machine that allowed them to work alongside DJs without actually having to meet in person. Writing to the new organization on 4 June, Billy Smith of 20th Century declared, "The Record Pool establishes what has been needed in the record industry for some time now." Within a week United Artists, Warner Brothers, Elektra/Asylum, and Motown had also signed up with the organization, and Mel Cheren of Scepter Records contributed to the momentum by digging into his discotheque-lined pockets in order to donate two hundred dollars toward the construction of shelving units and bins.

Their decision to collaborate was validated at the end of July when the *Village Voice*, in the most comprehensive analysis of the disco industry to date, argued that it was the DJs, and not the stars or the record companies, who were driving the disco market. Focusing on Le Jardin, reporters Richard Szathmary and Lucian Trustcott IV noted that "there was nary a whisper from the crowd" when Barry White—the "undisputed king of discos"—failed to show up at John Addison's venue. Instead "Bobby DJ and his partner Michael 'Michael DJ' Cappello stood at the dual Thorens turntables and expertly spun the *real* reason they were there, the disco sound." The Record Pool held the key to the new market. Each week, the reporters guesstimated, its members played approximately fifty new releases to some 240,000 dancers, who then left the discotheques to buy their favorite records, which were subsequently pushed by radio. Like the disco experience, "the whole thing seems to feed on itself, pushing disco sales higher and higher and higher." Nobody doubted that the Record Pool had "rapidly amassed a great deal of power in the disco record business" and the record companies were taking it "very seriously."[6]

The Pool—or at least D'Acquisto, who the *Voice* reporters homed in on—was also apparently taking *itself* very seriously. "'Give me those two membership cards,'" D'Acquisto reportedly told an assistant. "'I'm going to mark these guys 'reprimand.' Who do they think they are, coming in here for records when they haven't been properly certified. Here. I'll spell it out clearly. Liars. How do you spell liars, somebody? L-Y-E-R-S? L-Y-A-R-S? Oh, hell. They're liars, no matter how you spell it. We'll reprimand them at the next meeting, in front of everybody. Then we'll let the people deal with them.'"[7] Szathmary and Trustcott's perception was clear: while the Record Pool had to be beyond suspicion, it was beginning to sound more like a military training camp than an "independent calm center."

By the end of the month, 183 DJs had joined the New York Record Pool, and the resulting pressure on D'Acquisto and Mancuso was so intense they couldn't even begin to think about expanding to meet popular demand. "There was an unbelievable amount of work," says Mancuso. "It was taking up 110 percent of my time." Others quickly picked up the slack.

"I was very tight with Paul Casella," remembers McCloy. "I said, 'Hey, we would like to set up a Long Island subchapter of the New York Record Pool,' and Paul replied, 'Talk to Steve and David. Whatever they say is cool with me. I'll put in a good word for you.'" Casella's good word wasn't enough. "Steve told me, 'I don't know, we've already got our hands full.' David said, 'Listen, whatever you guys want to do, go ahead and do it. We'll do everything we can to help you set up your own pool.'" Teaming up with Long Island DJ Vince Michaels, McCloy formed the Long Island Record Pool—the second pool in the country—a short while after Szathmary and Trustcott had gone to press.

Yet while the music was beginning to spread, some DJs were heavily invested in preserving the status quo, and that band included Michael Cappello. "At that time I was like *the guy*," says the Le Jardin DJ. "The record companies would hand me shit like you wouldn't believe. I couldn't even *listen* to all the fucking records that I was getting. Billy Smith used to let me go in the warehouse. 'Go ahead, take what you want!' I would get boxes full of records, and I'd sell the albums for two dollars a piece." Cappello was wary of the Pool from the very start. "All I could see was 'Oh, love,' because David had that aura about him. Well, David had what David had and Nicky had what Nicky had, but I was freelance, and I knew for a fact that as soon as the Record Pool started there were going to be tons of DJs out there, and we were going to be scratching for it."

To make matters worse, Cappello felt that D'Acquisto and Mancuso were unnecessarily officious. "I was the top dog, and they were looking to put me down. They gave me attitude because they knew I was getting all the records first. It was like going back to school. You give somebody a little bit of power, and then they start to tell you when to wait, where to wait, you've got to do this, you've got to do that, you're not getting this, you've got to get a letter from your boss. It was aggravation." According to Cappello, the organization was chaotic from the very beginning. "Steve and David were not equipped to handle it. Steve was angry because he wasn't getting records, and David didn't even *want* records. They had no idea what they were dealing with, and as soon as people got those records and started yelling and screaming at each other they said, 'What the fuck did we do?' The politics and the people turned ugly. After three visits I stopped going."

Mancuso maintains that the "aggravation" was a necessary prerequisite to the organization's success. "The record companies wanted to know that they were servicing working DJS, and they said that it was our responsibility to guarantee their legitimacy. This presented us with a real problem because almost every DJ was working off the books, which made it very difficult to verify that they were actively employed." It looked like the procedural impasse might sink the Pool until Mancuso approached his attorney, Mel Katz. "Mel said we should ask the clubs to write a letter saying that such and such a DJ was working for them and to sign it with a corporate seal. The club owners went for it, so all the DJS had to get was this one letter. I thought the idea was a stroke of genius because it allowed the DJS to continue working off the books *and* to start to pick up free records. It wasn't like we were asking for an arm and a leg, and it also meant that we could keep our independence from the record companies." Leading DJS were given as much leeway as possible. "DJS like Michael could still maintain their rapport with the record companies if they wanted to. We said, 'Keep your contacts but also be a member of the Pool in order to strengthen the organization!' Michael helped out a lot in the beginning, and he was a very sweet person, but finally he wanted to be treated like a superstar."

Cappello wasn't the only malcontent. So was Bob Casey, who vehemently opposed every aspect of what he calls the "hippie yippie" organization. "Sorry folks but I'm not quite ready for Communism, Socialism or Record Pools," he wrote in the June/July issue of *Melting Pot*. "I believe in good old American free enterprise, freedom of speech, press [sic] and I believe in the right of the individual."[8] Casey disliked the "caustic" D'Acquisto, who had been thrown out of a record company office and was therefore an inappropriate representative. He opposed the compulsory two-dollar fee charged by the Pool to subsidize the administrative costs. He disapproved of the way in which the Pool "treated DJS like cattle rather than talent." He believed that the music business should not be forced to service DJS en masse. And he continued to argue that the Pool should follow NADD's broader agenda: to organize, promote, and advance DJS rather than focus solely on the distribution of records.

The representatives of the New York and Long Island Record Pools disagreed. "Through the Record Pool we were legitimized and unified," says D'Acquisto. "We understood that we were a force. The record companies had no choice but to go along with us." They also found Casey—who ran D'Acquisto a close race when it came to belligerence—intrusive and insufferable. "He used to walk in and try to throw all of this shit at us," says

Mancuso. "He kept going on about us wanting to start a union. It was bullshit." What's more, Casey wasn't supplying DJS with what they really wanted. "NADD was just an organization that would verify which DJS were legitimate and which DJS weren't legitimate," says McCloy. "They issued legitimate DJS with a card so they could go and get product from a label, but they never actually serviced product themselves." Finally, Casey came from neither side of the DJ/industry divide and that wasn't good enough for the jocks. "For whatever reason, Bob Casey just didn't click with the guys," says D'Acquisto. "Plus he was a soundman, and all of us felt that this had to come from the DJS."

D'Acquisto maintains that his clash with Casey was no big thing. "I just didn't want to be a part of his organization. I wrote an article for his magazine once, but I didn't really look up to him." Casey, however, begs to differ. "I can't even begin to remember the rumors that D'Acquisto started and the damage he tried to do. He didn't just want to form the Record Pool. He wanted to destroy NADD, and he discussed this with Bobby Guttadaro, David Rodriguez, and a few others. They all thought it stunk pretty bad, and Richie Kaczor was the first one to actively come to my aid." Kaczor's assistance came in the form of an article, which he submitted to *Melting Pot* on the strict condition that Casey didn't "edit a single word." When the Virgo Sound boss agreed, the Hollywood DJ sat down with Bonfiglio and started to type up his article.

"Well, it was bound to happen," wrote Kaczor. "Take some moranic [sic] jerk-offs, add some greed and a little bit of foolish pride and a heaping amount of pseudo-ego—What do you have?—A discotheque disc jockey! Not saying all are like this, because they're not. But why must a few *has-beens* who are too stubborn to give way to newer things, ruin it for the rest of the 'jocks' . . . It seems that the big thing to do nowadays is either start your own organization or see how many people you can rip-off, or rip apart . . . whichever your fetish might be." The divisions ran deep. "Being a disco dj, I've come across many real people as well as many phony ones. Unfortunately the phony ones—outweigh the real ones and what is happening now is distrust, contempt and real hate among people who are suppose [sic] to bring some sort of happiness to people." D'Acquisto was all but mentioned by name. "Big Deal—so you don't have an original copy of a record—or a test-pressing on a multicolor disc. SO WHAT!!! Do you have to rob innocent people who have probably helped you more than you ever thought. One thought—If you can't do it by yourself—GIVE UP."[9]

Kaczor and Bonfiglio were still in the office when Casey arrived the next morning. "On the coffee table were the first drafts of the next issue all typed up, cut and pasted, and ready to go," says Casey. "They had worked all night on the paper. Then Richie jumped up with a big smile and said, 'Bob, don't give up! You mean too much to us! Don't let the scumbags get to you!'" New York's DJs had never been so simultaneously united and disunited.

* * *

Robin Lord relished the power that came with policing the door at the Gallery. If you didn't have an invite and you weren't a guest you couldn't get in, end of story, goodnight, next. So when an unfamiliar, accented voice asked if he could pay to enter the party on an especially busy evening an impatient Lord asked to see his card. "I was very frazzled because it had been nonstop since we opened, so by this point I was barely looking up," remembers Lord. "I just kept on saying, 'Members only! If you do not have a membership card I *cannot* let you in tonight! Invitation? May I see it please!' Of course all of the queens were saying, 'C'mon Robin! You know me! Please let me in! Just *me*!' or 'Nicky invited me *personally*! You've *got* to let me in!'" The new arrival tried a different tactic. "He said, 'We're not members, but John Addison referred us,' and I told him, 'Sorry, I don't care *who* you were sent by, we're only admitting members for the remainder of the night!'" At this point one of the gatekeeper's assistants intervened. "He said, 'Robin, it's Mick Jagger and David Bowie!' I said, 'Yeah, right!' and looked up. At first I didn't recognize Mick Jagger, who was dressed in a suit and was way too normal for our crowd, but behind him, to his right, was *unmistakably* David Bowie. He was also wearing a suit but was far less normal-looking." Lord zipped into reverse and threw out the welcome mat. "I wrote up two comp admittance cards, the crowd parted, and they were absorbed into the Gallery. My sisters were both working the refreshment table, and they told me that Bowie and Jagger were holding hands. They also gave them a five-dollar tip, which was *unheard of*!"

Authoritative and charismatic, Lord had become a dance world celebrity in her own right. "She was just as famous as me," says Nicky Siano. "She was known as the doorwoman at the Gallery." That, for the most part, was where she remained. "I was never much of a dancer and was totally inhibited when I did dance unless I was at a place where everyone was *the worst dancer who ever lived,* and I knew that even *I* could look good, like at my cousin Barry's bar mitzvah." But every now and again Lord would take to the dance floor, and these appearances became more frequent with the release of "Fly, Robin, Fly" by German dance act Silver Convention in the summer of 1975. "'Fly, Robin, Fly' was very big at the Gallery," says Siano. "Of course Robin loved the song and was on the dance floor every time I played it."

"Fly, Robin, Fly" was produced by German duo Michael Kunze and Silvester Levay as the follow-up to "Save Me," which had caused a reasonable ripple back in March 1975. An insistent four-on-the-floor beat dominated both records, which featured a sparse arrangement that hovered around a foundational rhythm and minimal vocals. A cross between "Love's Theme," a Volkswagen robot, and a sacred mantra, the raw and somewhat repetitive aesthetic of the releases had more to do with dubious logistics than inspirational foresight. "They had recorded the music and the background vocals for 'Save Me,' but had some kind of problem with the singer or the melody," says Giorgio Moroder, a Munich-based producer-musician-songwriter who was friendly with Kunze and Levay. "Then they realized that they already had a song with just the background vocals. It sounded very interesting." Power was beginning to shift in the recording studio: with B. T. Express, the group hadn't liked the mix, but now it was the mixer who didn't like the group.

Disco was about to move onto a different plain. Following a tip-off from David Todd, R&B producer Van McCoy recorded "The Hustle," which topped the charts and popularized a new dance in its slipstream. Warner Brothers issued a pilot program of discotheque singles in the form of a "Disco Survival Pack" that included twenty dance-oriented singles. Motown launched three compilation albums that were specially aimed at what was now being referred to as the "disco market." Flagging folk-rock group the Bee Gees released a disco track called "Jive Talkin'." David Bowie, who was "nuts about the Three Degrees," recorded his *Young Americans* album at PIR's Sigma Sound Studios in an attempt to recreate the Philadelphia feeling.[10] And Mick Jagger declared an interest in recording a cover version of Shirley & Company's "Shame, Shame, Shame," seemingly unembarrassed that the song had been written as a taunt from black disco singers to white rock 'n' rollers who had forgotten how to write danceable rhythms. International rock stars were moving in on the scene, much to the chagrin of downtown purists. "It's gotten out of control," Colony Records sales assistant Ronnie Coles, who had become *the* key supplier of dance music to New York's ravenous DJs, told the *Village Voice*. "Everybody's going disco, rock and rollers, old soul people, jazz people on obscure little jazz labels. They know that *anybody* can hit. Anybody."[11]

The onrush didn't damage Tom Moulton, who was beginning to receive the kind of critical acclaim that would secure his position as the progenitor of the new sound. "He has gone beyond that of a trend-setter and can truly be called an innovator in establishing the 'disco mix' on record tracks," declared *Melting Pot* in June 1975.[12] A month later, Aletti also sang Moulton's praises in a review of Scepter's *Disco Gold*, which he described as "the best of the disco repackages yet released because it contains the most hard-to-get material in specially re-mixed, re-edited and, in most cases, lengthened versions whipped up by Tom Moulton, who seems to have single-handedly invented the profession of disco mixer."[13]

Back in Philadelphia, however, Gamble and Huff—ostensibly basking in the knowledge that Moulton had noted that "Love Is the Message" was "already considered a 'classic' " at the end of 1974—were beginning to discover that it was as easy to miss as it was to hit.[14] For sure, the PIR producers were still producing some of the finest dance hits of the year: the belatedly released "Bad Luck" by Harold Melvin & the Blue Notes, which ran at six minutes twenty-nine seconds and appeared on the group's new album *To Be True*, and the freshly recorded "I Love Music" by the O'Jays both stirred up a storm on dance floors. But "Let's Go Disco," recorded for the latest MFSB album, *Universal Love*, was a genuine stinker. "That was the only song they wrote for disco, and it was horrid," says Michael Gomes. "It was nothing compared to 'Love Is the Message.' " Worse still, some of their most important talents were beginning to take flight. Bunny Sigler started to stretch his wings by producing South Shore Commission's "Free Man," which was released on Wand, Scepter's subsidiary label, at the end of April, and Ronnie Baker, Norman Harris, and Earl Young began to record for a new Manhattan label called Salsoul Records around the same time. The Philadelphia empire was about to implode.

Salsoul was the unlikely creation of Joe, Ken, and Stan Cayre, three Jewish Syrian American brothers who, having grown up in the family's lingerie business, were more familiar with all-cotton panties than all-night parties. Their reeducation had begun in 1966 when an opportunity emerged to distribute Mexican music in the United States. Caytronics, the company formed to manage the operation, tapped into a supposedly nonexistent market, and it was soon granted exclusive rights to the Latin catalogues of Columbia and RCA. The leap into production followed when Joe Bataan, an established Fania artist immersed in bugalu—a musical style that combined R&B with Latin instrumentation and bilingual vocals —approached Caytronics in 1973. "Joe Bataan went up to my brother with a master of an LP and said it was for sale," remembers Ken Cayre. "He wanted five thousand dollars." A deal was struck with the African Filipino artist, and while *Salsoul*—which referred to the recording's combination of salsa and soul—didn't get air play on the Spanish stations, Bataan had a handy contact in the form of WBLS DJ Frankie Crocker, who gave heavy rotation to "Latin Strut" and "Aftershower Funk." Fifty thousand albums and one hundred thousand singles later, Columbia bought the distribution rights to "Latin Strut" as well as first option on any future Mericana (the name of the Caytronics subsidiary label on which Bataan was released) production for $100,000. "They proceeded to immediately lose airplay," says Cayre. "But we had their money."

The brothers used the Columbia windfall to open Salsoul Records, and Ken Cayre, who had been entrusted with the job of reinvesting the capital, decided to enter the dance market. "Kenny and I had been going to the posh uptown clubs," says Denise Chapman, who worked alongside Cayre and accompanied him on his nocturnal adventures. "They were no big deal." But then an office worker suggested that the two of them go to Le Jardin and "a whole new world" was opened up. "We heard 'The Love I Lost,' 'Newsy Neighbors,' and 'Love Is the Message' all on the same night," says Chapman. "I saw a look come over Kenny's eyes while we were dancing, and I knew he was feeling the same thing that I was. When we were sitting on the couches, he said, 'This is the kind of music I want to make! I want to make the kind of music that makes me feel the way this does!' " That night Chapman stayed until Bobby DJ played his last record, went straight to work without changing, and, when Salsoul closed for the day, headed back to the club. "I ended up wearing the same dress for three consecutive days," she says.

Back in his new Tenth Avenue headquarters, Cayre hatched a plan of action. "I decided to find some musicians and call them the Salsoul Orchestra, which would promote the label if we had a hit. The first single would also be called 'Salsoul' and it would be an instrumental." Now all Cayre had to do was find the right musicians. "I looked at what I was buying, and I kept turning to Philadelphia International records. I noticed that my favorite albums featured Earl Young on drums, Ronnie Baker on bass, Norman Harris on guitar, and Vince Montana on vibes, so I asked Joe Bataan to set up a meeting with one of these musicians." Bataan made some calls and came back with a number. "He put me in touch with Vince."

Montana was a second generation Italian American who had attempted to escape the poverty of his South Philadelphia home through jazz. "I played with Charlie Parker and Clifford Brown, but it wasn't a great living, and when I got married I had to have money coming in." After a stint in Las Vegas, Montana returned to Philadelphia and started to work at Sigma Sound, pursuing a lifelong love of Latin, jazz, and classical music in his spare time, and when Bataan called Montana decided that a demo tape of a Latin band would match the taste of the Salsoul boss. "I played Kenny this Latin thing," Montana recalls, "and he said, 'Oh, God, I'm sick and tired of Latin music! I want something different!'" Montana was about to leave when Bataan intervened and told Cayre that the Philadelphia musician could provide Salsoul with the sound he was looking for. Montana paused while Cayre outlined his agenda. "I told him we were looking for an R&B rhythm and Latin percussion with a pretty melody on top," says Cayre. "It was a new kind of music. I wanted to do what Philadelphia International was doing but with a twist of disco."

Montana said that he could deliver and was promptly ushered into Joe Cayre's office, where he was given a check for ten thousand dollars—enough to bring in a string of Latin-oriented musicians, including Roy Armando, Andy Gonzalez, Manny Oquendo, Peter "Choki" Quintero, and Larry Washington. In the spring of 1975, Montana recorded "Nice Vibes," and the "Salsoul Hustle," which astutely referenced Van McCoy's smash hit and was released as the first single. "I emphasized the Latino rhythm sections," says Montana. "MFSB only used one conga player, Larry Washington, and he would play timbales once in a while, but they never went too Latin, whereas I went *very* Latin."

Even though CBS turned down the "Salsoul Hustle," Cayre's foothold in the New York market helped the record become a club hit and a "world premiere" on Crocker's show, and in an attempt to maintain the momentum the Salsoul boss commissioned Montana to produce a Salsoul Orchestra album, handing him the remainder of the CBS capital. There was just one condition: Montana had to employ the so-far unused Baker-Harris-Young rhythm section. "I insisted that Vince bring me all three," says Cayre. "It was critical for me to get that sound. I always felt there was something unusual between Ron Baker's bass and Earl Young's drums that no one could come close to recreating. Somehow the bass made the drums sound fatter." A reluctant Montana eventually agreed, and "Tangerine" became the first Salsoul track to feature the hipster street musicians. "Things didn't go well at the session," says Cayre. "Vince felt they were not playing well. We were there for about three hours on this one song. Finally Norman calmed everything down, and we recorded 'Tangerine' at about four 'o clock in the morning. It turned out to be the first major hit on the album."

Cayre's coup was astonishing. A close-knit group of the most sought-after session musicians in the United States had switched allegiance from Gamble and Huff's high-profile production line to a small-time label run by three Sephardic nobodies. "I went to Philadelphia with both my pockets filled with cash," explains Cayre. "I bought them champagne, I bought them Chinese food, and I bought them the kind of cigarettes that they liked to smoke. Instead of getting paid six weeks later through the union, with dues taken out, they walked out of the session with money. I paid these guys three times the union rate." Fortuitously for the Salsoul boss, the Philadelphia session musicians were a rebellion in search of an outlet. "We were working our butts off and made $135 for three hours—before tax," says Young. "I was hardly making enough money to take care of my family. I don't know how many gold records I cut in Philadelphia, and all I got was a thank you and a paycheck and 'goodbye.' Salsoul was the first to give the little guy a chance, and that made us really want to come up to New York."

Not that the rhythm section's first appearance on Salsoul made any difference to CBS, which once again turned down the final product. "My brothers were very upset," says Cayre. "They felt that I'd blown the hundred thousand dollars." When the other majors also passed on the album, Cayre took matters into his own hands and pressed up fifteen thousand copies, plus another five hundred for the DJs. "The album sold out over the weekend. All the stores called us up on Monday morning to put in reorders." And this was just in New York. "As the album started to get national airplay, word spread that Salsoul featured some of the best musicians from Philadelphia. We ended up selling over half a million LPs. A label was born."

* * *

Neil Bogart—born Bogatz—created Casablanca Records out of nothing. Having worked as a promoter at MGM and as a general manager at Buddah, he approached Warner Brothers in 1973 and proposed that the music giant bankroll and distribute a new Los Angeles label that would be titled after the movie that starred his namesake. Warners agreed, but Bogart got off to a shaky start with his first single, "Virginia" by Bill Amesbury, which was released in January 1974, and things deteriorated when the parent company refused to promote Bogart's first major signing, the rock band Kiss. After a year, the self-made mogul asked Warners to release Casablanca from its distribution deal, and the entertainment giant, which had yet to see any return on its investment, willingly agreed. Bogart's major breakthrough followed when he was introduced to "Love to Love You Baby," which featured the tantalizing vocals of Donna Summer and the extraordinary production of Giorgio Moroder. "Neil hated disco before he got to Casablanca," says Tom Moulton. "I remember him saying that disco was going nowhere. But, boy, did he start to sing a different tune after Donna Summer. *Instant turnaround.*"

Raised in Ortisei, northern Italy, Moroder had studied architecture at college before dropping out after just one year in order to pursue an alternative form of design and construction—music. Having lived the life of a poor artist in Berlin, he moved to Munich, where he played the bass in a covers band and crooned the night away in various discotheques. In the early 1970s, Moroder teamed up with producer-lyricist Pete Bellotte, and the two of them recorded a string of domestic hits, including "Nachts Scheint die Sonne," which featured a cameo appearance by one of Robert Moog's rudimentary and still rare synthesizers. The producers subsequently discovered Sommer [sic], née Donna Gaines, who had married an Austrian actor called Helmut Sommer and was working as a backing vocalist in Munich. Moroder and Bellotte initially employed her as a background vocalist on an English-language song that was supposed to catapult the duo into the Anglo-American market. It didn't, but Sommer's voice and looks convinced them that they had found a future star, and the new team recorded two pop records—"Hostage" and "Lady of the Night"—on their Oasis label. Accidentally issued under the name Donna

Summer rather than Donna Sommer, both records went gold in Europe but failed to get a release in America.

Inspired by Jane Birkin and Serge Gainsbourg's moderately successful reissue of the 1969 international hit "Je T'Aime . . . Moi Non Plus," "Love to Love You Baby" came next, Moroder having asked Summer if she would be prepared to play the part of Birkin. "I always wanted to do a sexy song, just for the fun of it," says Moroder. "Donna was really interested in the idea." Summer came up with the title, and the producer headed straight into the studio, where he composed the song in a couple of hours and recorded the track a few days later, using a Side Man as a "rhythm director" in order to maintain a steady tempo. "It was a little cheap Japanese machine that went 'dung, dung.' You couldn't use it on the actual record—the real bass drum still sounded much better—but it helped with the edits." Then came the Jane Birkin bit, at which point Summer said auf Wiedersehen to her husband, snuggled up to the microphone, and . . . what? What did Summer do in the darkened studio? Nothing, insists the born-again Christian, who to this day maintains that the carnal cries were those of another woman, which Moroder dubbed onto the track once she had gone home for the day. The producer, however, remembers the session differently. "Donna sang it as soon as I had recorded the track with the musicians," he says. "I remember the husband was there in the studio. She didn't loosen up at all, so I just threw everybody out of the studio and dimmed the lights. She couldn't see into the control booth so she felt as if she was by herself and safe. I think it was done in one take."

"Love to Love You Baby," which featured four minutes worth of orgasmic groaning, offered a radically alternative recording of sexuality: that of female pleasure and fantasy. America, after all, had only just come to terms with Mick Jagger's risqué "(I Can't Get No) Satisfaction" and "Let's Spend the Night Together," which were centered around straight male desire, and while "Je T'Aime" stood as something of a precedent, the transformation of the English Birkin into a sultry French lover was a slightly embarrassing ploy to seduce an Anglo-American straight male market that, thanks to Gainsbourg's presence, was secure in the knowledge that men remained the necessary agent to the female orgasm. Of course, it wasn't easy to limit the interpretation of Summer's ooohs and aaahs to the liberation of female sexuality, open as they were to heterosexual men in search of a pornographic soundtrack, yet lesbians and autoerotic female fantasists could also enjoy the recording, largely because the absence of an instructing male voice gave the record a polyvalent potential. A man (or woman for that matter) could have been servicing Summer, but it is just as likely that her ecstasy was self-induced. Unlike Jagger, she could get "satisfaction"—all by herself.

Then again, maybe Summer—just like the gay boys and the straight girls on the dance floor—found a male sexual partner in the form of Moroder's music, in which, dismantling rock music's prioritization of the voice and the lead guitar, the four-on-the-floor beat of the bass drum was elevated to the center of the mix, providing an unmistakably phallic counterpoint to Summer's groans. "I just felt the bass drum was so important," says Moroder. "The thought was, 'Why not help the dancers to dance even better by making the drum into more of a stomping sound?'" Significantly more rigid than Young's rhythm, the steady thud of a bass beat was dominant, with the lyrics subjected to this all-consuming rhythm. "Michael Kunze found a great formula so I decided to do 'Love to Love You Baby' in the same way."

The single created a stir at MIDEM—the annual music trade show held in Cannes—at the beginning of 1975 and was quickly licensed to Casablanca, but the American release of "Love to Love You Baby" turned out to be an anticlimax, failing to even generate the flawed thrill of a premature orgasm (known in the music market as a "one-hit wonder"). Bogart nevertheless continued to play "Love to Love You Baby" at his private house parties, and it was there that the record, as legend has it, took off in unanticipated ways, prompting the Casablanca chief to telephone Moroder the following evening. "He was very excited," says the producer. "He told me that people had kept on requesting the record at this party, and he came up with the idea of doing a long version that would last the whole side of an album."

Moroder used a simple yet ingenious device to extend the record, bringing in a fresh bass line twenty seconds from the end of the original recording. As the seven-inch version faded, the bass continued, forming a bridge to the newly recorded material, which accentuated the layered approach of the original and transformed the track from a four-minute masturbatory gimmick into a seventeen-minute orgasmic symphony that welled up and relaxed and welled up yet again as if it was designed for extended sex—or the dance floor. Cramped and unexceptional in its origi-

Donna Summer with Neil Bogart (left) entering 12 West for an *After Dark* party, 24 October 1975. Photo by Waring Abbott

nal version, Moroder's mobile and flowing Autobahn aesthetic found its most meaningful expression in the expansive album remix. The template for what would later be dubbed *Eurodisco* had been established.

The album version of "Love to Love You Baby" caused an immediate stir when it arrived at DJ headquarters, Prince Street, in the middle of September 1975. "Thanks to Phil Gill, who brought the Donna Summer album down to the last Record Pool meeting and had everyone racing to the booth asking, 'What *is* that?'" reported Vince Aletti.[15] New York's collectivized DJs jumped on the song, and, as a Casablanca executive later revealed, the album sold one hundred thousand copies "overnight" before receiving "airplay at any radio station."[16] Frankie Crocker, who received an early copy from Bogart, a personal friend, was probably the first radio jock to play the naughty number. "Even when other jocks caught on," says Crocker, "WBLS was the only radio station playing Donna Summer during the day." Sales received an additional boost when the Reverend Jesse Jackson denounced its sexually explicit content, and the record subsequently established itself as Casablanca's breakthrough album. "Donna Summer came to the Record Pool," remembers Mancuso. "She walked around a bit. It was her way of saying thank you to the DJs. It was no big to-do. She seemed very shy."

"Love to Love You Baby" provided a glimpse into the studio-oriented future of dance music, for while Summer had a genuinely great voice, and her high-pitched whimpers had given the world of pop a seizure, Moroder and Bellotte were equally influential figures, anonymous alchemists who knew how to turn base vinyl into a gold record. Nor were the Munich-based producers acting in isolation. Michael Kunze and Silvester Levay could be found a stone's throw away, and French producers Jacques Morali and Henri Belolo were also beginning to develop a reputation as a serious production team following their work on the Ritchie Family's debut album, *Brazil*, which was recorded at Sigma Sound and hailed as an instant disco classic. Kenny Gamble and Leon Huff, operating behind the façade of MSFB, had also demonstrated that producers didn't need a star in order to produce a smash hit, and musicians such as Vince Montana, eyeing the bulging pockets of their Philadelphia proprietors, were starting to try their hand in the studio. Faceless bands were dominating the dance floor.

The development fortified an industry that had spent the first six months of the year wiping its brow, fearful that the countrywide recession was responsible for lethargic music sales. As *Business Week* reported in December 1975, "the year suddenly came to life in late summer, and companies everywhere began reporting record sales of records for single months and for the entire third quarter."[17] CBS chalked up yearly sales of $402 million, Warner Communications recorded an all-time high in September, and RCA experienced what President Kenneth Glancy described as "the most successful third quarter ever."[18] The recovery couldn't simply be attributed to disco—CBS, for instance, was beginning to enjoy the fruits of the sophisticated six-month marketing campaign that had launched Bruce Springsteen as a rock superstar. Disco, however, was definitely playing its part. "We know the people in clubs are interested in music, and we can gauge their reactions to test pressings of new acts of songs," commented Mel Ilberman, vice president for operations at RCA. "If they like them, we can increase production accordingly." The laws of gravity, it appeared, didn't apply to music. As *Business Week* concluded, "There is a certain amount of incredulity among record men that the business again seems bent on proving what they claimed all along: that it is recession-proof."[19]

A question mark nonetheless hung over the long-term viability of dance producers and disco artists, whose inconspicuous personas contradicted everything the music industry believed about the business of selling records. For sure, high-profile rock artists were beginning to edge their way into dance music but, as Ken Emerson pointed out in an end-of-year critique in the *New York Times*, these artists usually lacked the necessary humility to make a successful dance record. "An untheatrical anonymity . . . is extremely important to successful dance music, and the biggest disco hits of the past couple of years have been scored not by stars but by relatively obscure performers." Noting that some disco bands were shunning celebrity altogether by assuming nondescript monikers, Emerson astutely added, "This lack of personal identity on the part of disco performers allows unawed dancers to assert their own identities—through their dress, through their partners and through the steps they execute. Such a dance-floor democracy has been alien to white rock, which promotes a superstar elite and generally subordinates the music to the mystiques of its makers."[20]

Yet label owners, aiming for megaprofits, were determined to bypass these shadowy producers in their search for identifiable performers, and that is what Bogart got with Donna Summer, whose X-rated rise to fame suggested that the disco market was maturing in more ways than one. "Neil always talked about signing or buying a major act—and he saw in Donna a major act," says Cecil Holmes, Bogart's principal partner at Casablanca. "'All we have to do is develop her,' he'd say."[21] Unaware of the meaning of excess, the Casablanca chief launched a campaign that introduced a whole new meaning to the verb *develop*. As Frederic Dannen records in *Hit Men*, "When Bogart brought Donna Summer from Germany to New York to promote her first hit album, *Love to Love You Baby*, he had Hansen's of Los Angeles sculpt a life-size cake in her image. The cake was flown to New York in two first-class airline seats, met by a freezer ambulance, and taken to the Penta discotheque for Summer's performance there."[22] Unbounded extravagance, incalculable sugar, and a waiting ambulance—the cake was nothing less than the perfect metaphor for what disco was about to become.

* * *

Le Jardin may have established itself as the king of New York's clubs, but it wasn't until 3 March 1975—some three months before the formation of the New York Record Pool—that it found a suitable partner in the form of Gloria Gaynor, who was crowned the "Queen of Discos" in a special ceremony at John Addison's venue. "Gloria Gaynor's manager came up with the idea," says Bob Casey. "It was a promotional publicity stunt. He wanted NADD to do the crowning, and so I called around the members asking if they wanted her to be crowned 'Queen.' They all said yes. It was a cool idea." Casey agreed to organize the event on the condition that Addison let in NADD members for free. "It really pissed him off when over a hundred members showed up from as far north as Boston to as far south as Washington D.C." No detail was spared during a ceremony in which the singer was dressed in a thirty-pound cape, whisked along a red carpet, lowered onto a thrown, decorated with a crown, and handed a trophy. "Joey Bonfiglio read out the proclamation," says Casey. "It went, 'On behalf of the members of NADD as well as discotheque disc jockeys around the world, I hereby crown Gloria Gaynor queen of the disco. God save the Queen!' The music blasted out, and the crowd went wild."

Michael Cappello

Select Discography (Le Jardin) [Source: Record World, *4 January 1975]*

B. T. Express, "Do It ('Til You're Satisfied)"

B. T. Express, "Express"

Disco Tex & the Sex-O-Lettes "Get Dancin' "

Carol Douglas, "Doctor's Orders"

Ecstasy, Passion & Pain, "Ask Me"

Gloria Gaynor, "Never Can Say Goodbye"

LaBelle, "Lady Marmalade"

LaBelle, "What Can I Do for You?"

Jimmy Ruffin, "Tell Me What You Want"

Shirley & Company, "Shame, Shame, Shame"

The crowd in question, however, was beginning to change. While Le Jardin had never operated as a strictly gay club, its high proportion of gay regulars combined with a cast of visiting celebrities that included Andy

Gloria Gaynor at Le Jardin, 24 June 1975, during a pilot for *Discomania*. Photo by Waring Abbott

Warhol, David Bowie, Rudolf Nureyev, Pierre Cardin, Truman Capote, Warren Beatty, and Elton John had helped it generate something of a cutting-edge reputation, and this core group now moved on because Addison had spent more time skimming off profits than reinvesting in his venue. "A club's success depended on the way in which it maintained or reinvented itself," says Casey. "A successful gay club turned straight when it fell out of fashion with the gays. Once a club started letting in straights—and one could usually spot them by dress or cologne—it was because it needed to keep making money. An owner of a club had to do what he had to do. Rarely has there ever been a club that started out straight and turned gay. It is usually the other way around. The gays get bored or want to find a better place."

In March the gay-interest magazine *After Dark* described Le Jardin's patrons as being "bisexual chic," but by July the *Village Voice* noted that dancers "from the outlying boroughs, from Jersey and the Island, and even Westchester" had taken over the venue, helping it become "a million-dollar-plus operation."[23] Business had never been better. "The place was

The new crowd at
Le Jardin. Photo by
Waring Abbott

almost constantly packed," says Steve D'Acquisto, who worked as an alternate DJ at the discotheque. "There would be a couple of thousand on Fridays and Saturdays, with five hundred to six hundred on Mondays." Whatever the night, the coated figure of Addison would carefully regulate who got in and who was turned away, with around twenty-five people rejected on a weekday night and approximately one hundred on a Friday or a Saturday. "It has to do with the aura you give off, in dress and personality," Addison told Sheila Weller of the *New York Sunday News*, denying that bridge-and-tunnel geek had come to replace cosmopolitan chic. "Our people here are pretty and with-it. If someone is starchy-looking, they wouldn't add anything to the place. They'd be uncomfortable. There are a lot of stockbrokers I wouldn't let in."[24] The demographics, however, had irrefutably changed. "Now loyal regulars avoid weekends," the *New York Post* reported in August. "Recently, says one visitor, 'it all seemed to be secretaries and young men without jobs.'"[25]

An incredulous Jorge La Torre watched on. "We had Le Jardin to ourselves for about a year and a half," he remembers. "It was amazing that in such a short period of time discotheques had become so much more acceptable to the general public. At the time of the Sanctuary, it was a novelty but with Le Jardin it was the thing to do. It took those first five years of the seventies for it to get across to the mainstream, and Le Jardin played a big part in that because celebrities went there, and it was open to the general public." The process by which the pejoratively named bridge-and-tunnel crowd found out about Addison's discotheque was no great mystery. Having set off on the dance trail, suburbanites were keen to sample the energy of the most notorious venues, and Le Jardin, situated in the middle of Times Square and the focus of just about every article written about the discotheque phenomenon, was hardly difficult to track down. "Once it started reaching the papers it acquired a different tone altogether," says La Torre. "The cat was out of the bag at that point, and the masses had to do it. Le Jardin was the next step. There were lines to get in, and they had to hold back the crowd."

The talk was of growth, growth, growth, with Manhattan at the dynamic center of what had now established itself as a national—and to a certain extent international—phenomenon. According to the Department of Consumer Affairs, which was responsible for issuing licenses for cabarets, clubs, and public dance halls in the city, forty-five new permits were issued in 1975, "pushing discotheque dancing," in the words of the *Times*, "to the top of the New York late-night entertainment scene."[26] Riding on the back of a profound shift from the production of goods to the production of events in the American economy of the 1970s, the exponential growth in discotheques took everyone by surprise. "The longest line in New York, next to those for disaster movies, is to get into discotheques," Steven Gaines wrote in the *New York Sunday News*. "Nobody, not even the owners of these non-stop dancing emporiums, can explain why their popularity has soared in the past year."[27]

That wasn't strictly true. "We're doin' good business because it's much cheaper for them to come in here and have fun than to go and sit in a movie," Mario Mannino, manager of the newly opened Sound Machine, told Weller. Casey, who was busy installing sound systems all over the place, concurred. "People have always lost themselves in dancing when the economy's been bad," he told the *New York Sunday News* journalist. "The discos now are doing exactly the same thing that the big dance halls with the crystal chandeliers did during the Depression. Everyone's out to spend their unemployment check, their welfare: to lose themselves." Addison, counting his dollars, added his voice to the theory of escape. "They're in *fantasyland* here," he explained. "The worse things get economically, the more it'll crowd up." An alternative population was now tapping into the gay-oriented practice of dancing as a form of release. "Straight, middle-class people never learned how to party," noted a gay Puerto Rican partygoer. "To them, a party is where you get all dressed up just to stand around with a drink in your hand, talking business. But for us, partying is release, celebration. The more hostile the vibes in your life, the better you learn how to party, 'cause that's your salvation. Now that things aren't going so well for the stockbroker in Westchester and his wife, they come down here, where it doesn't matter how much money you make, or what the label in your coat says."[28]

The combination of America's withdrawal from Vietnam, the taming of the Black Power movement, the pardoning of Richard Nixon, the oil crisis, and the onset of stagflation marked the end of the sixties, the "long decade" in which, as Arthur Marwick notes, a radical political agenda that revolved around civil rights, feminism, gay liberation, and antiwar protests had emerged within a broader environment of economic prosperity, governmental liberalism, and unnecessary governmental repression.[29] Yet while street protests dwindled as the downturn set in, the agendas that had emerged during the sixties didn't simply disappear but rather wove their way into other forms of cultural organization. The kind of unity that had characterized the demographics of rainbow alliance politics and the kind of expressive bodily politics that was immanent within the rebellions around gender and sexuality had discovered their earliest dance-oriented articulation in the Loft, the Sanctuary, and the discotheques on Fire Island, and by the mid-seventies these potentially progressive practices had found their way into the multiplying phenomenon of the discotheque, which was now attracting previously sheltered middle-class WASPs who, less sure of their philosophical footing now that the economy was turning sour, had begun to discover the value of the dance floor as a space of cathartic escape and communal expression. "Dance Your Troubles Away," Archie Bell & the Drells commanded their listeners in an end-of-year release, and Michael Gomes, ears pricked, noted that the six-minute-twenty-second single and the eponymous album "is perfect for dancing your troubles away."[30]

Yet while pleasure was unambiguously central to seventies dance practices, it is far from clear that disco culture amounted to a clear-cut renunciation of puritanism, if only because notions of labor remained so central to its ethos. The work of the marathon dance session combined with the ex-industrial location of so many parties suggested a strange continuity between the old manufacturing warehouse (a site of manual labor) and the newly converted warehouse (a site of bodily workout). Unemployment may have been spiraling, but an alternative mode of work continued within nightworld, where the increasingly mechanical nature of dance music added to the impression that the dancers were being propelled forward like obedient machines. The factory, argued Karl Marx, turns human beings into mere appendages of flesh attached to machinery. Now, however, the only visible product at the end of a ten-hour shift was a sweating body and a smiling face. This was nonreproductive, pleasurable work.

The emergence of this new night shift coincided with the conversion of industrial-based economies into neo-liberal markets, and dance culture was at its most prolific in countries that were at the forefront of this epochal transformation. While America might have led the discotheque boom, Britain, France, and Germany also boasted sizable scenes, as did Japan, which became the world's second-largest economic power during the 1970s. These countries weren't simply the forerunners of the new global economic order: they were also the representatives of a relentless work ethic that was now being displaced onto the leisure space of the all-night party. "Work hard, play hard" was about to become the new mantra of consumer capitalism, and disco in many respects complemented this new lifestyle.

* * *

The new times became associated with a new Latin social dance called the Hustle that, like the Twist, had grown out of tough economic conditions. Drawn from the mambo, the dance required partners to hold hands while one led the other in a series of learned step-and-spin sequences and, popularized by Van McCoy's hit single, it subsequently emerged as a conspicuous ingredient of the discotheque revival. The critical response to the routine was mixed. Writing in the *New York Times*, William Safire welcomed it as a conservative return to self-discipline, responsibility, and communication after a fifteen-year period of "frantic self-expression" and "personal isolationism" on the dance floor, while Vince Aletti maintained that it offered the possibility of "more inventiveness and excitement on the dance floor."[31] Indeed, the *Record World* columnist even predicted that dance contests could become the next big form of entertainment. "Watching good dancers in competition was more fun than most of the concerts I've been to over the past year and as a contest it certainly beats the dreary routine of the Miss America shows," he declared. "Wouldn't it be great to have star dancers with the sort of pop cultural status we now give football players and rock stars?"[32]

By the autumn other dance styles were beginning to emerge. The Walk, in which dancers interspersed regular paces with occasional 360-degree spot-turns, and the L.A. Hustle, in which dancers moved in coordinated lines across the floor, were two of the most important, and both were on display when Richard Nader cordoned off Madison Square Garden on 28 November to hold what he described as "the world's largest discotheque."[33] The four-hour "Disco Dance Party" attempted to merge the concept of the discotheque with the profit-potential of a large concert, and fourteen thousand dancers paid to hear a roster of entertainers that included Crown Heights Affair, Ecstasy, Passion & Pain, Gloria Gaynor, and the Trammps. Evoking comparisons with Woodstock, the party-festival proclaimed that disco culture was now a major trend.

In a sense, "Disco Dance Party" represented the culmination of everything that the downtown party network had ever dreamed of: the wholesale adoption of their countercultural practices by a broader population that had previously been antagonistic to dance. What's more, the speed with which discotheque culture had seeped into the mainstream suggested that, for all of Stonewall's symbolic resonance, the gay trendsetters who were so central to the discotheque revival were having a significantly greater influence on American society than the activists of the Gay Liberation Front. While there were dance converts who, hustling and walking to their heart's content, remained oblivious of the culture's tendencies, significant sections of straight America were undeniably drawn to the racial and sexual strains that lay at the heart of the new wave of discotheques.

As the message began to spread, however, the pioneers also started to lose control of the script—and something was lost in translation. "It's hard to give a firm number on how many discotheques there are in New York because every Joe's Pizzeria in town is now hooking up a couple of turntables and calling itself a 'discotheque,'" Bob Casey told the *New York Sunday News*. "I've heard reports there are as many as 175 in the five boroughs now, but I'd say there are only 20 good, genuine ones."[34] Richie

Kaczor said much the same in a piece for *Melting Pot*. "Now it seems every 'Joe's Bar & Grill' has been turned into a disco," he wrote, "which is all well and good for Joe, who is cashing in on all of this popularity."[35] The discotheque had, it appeared, become a disco check.

For veteran insiders it was easy to spot a fake. There would be a lack of energy on the dance floor, the sound system would be second-rate, the drug of choice would be alcohol, and the atmosphere would be cagey. "We're trying to have the kind of place where a guy isn't afraid to leave his girl alone while he goes to the bathroom," said Frank Ricci, manager at Factoria on East Fifty-eighth Street, providing a perfect description of one such pit. "We're trying to—oh how can I put this tactfully? We're trying to discourage *certain elements*. We don't discourage blacks, as long as they're in couples. But we do . . . well, let me put it this way: Have you ever been down to Le Jardin, to the Limelight? They're such *fag joints*!"[36]

Restaurateurs, who usually owned licensed venues and could create a makeshift dance floor by shifting a few tables, were both the most predictable converts to and the most predictable abusers of the flourishing entertainment sector. Where, though, were they going to get their DJs, for spinning remained an undeveloped profession and qualified practitioners were in short supply? The drought was all too much for the owner of the Emerson Steakhouse chain of restaurants based in Rockville, Maryland, who, having converted twelve eateries into Dimples discotheques by the spring of 1975, decided to set up his own school of DJing. Graduates were issued regulated playlists in which they were required to play a specified roster of records, programming the top thirty, two or three times a night.

New York's aficionados recoiled in horror. "Clearly, disco DJing is the glamour, no-experience-necessary profession of the year, but is this what it's coming to?" asked Vince Aletti. "The best DJs—a number of whom were making record-to-record collages and brilliant musical connections years before the media discovered the disco phenomenon, years before many of us were ready to hear them—are artists, tastemakers, shaping the immediate environment with their music. God knows all those people out there at their double turntables are not cruising the same heights of creativity but, until now, they haven't been reduced to playlist automatons."[37] The fledgling practice of the DJ was being turned into the musical equivalent of a hamburger chef, mindlessly serving up a menu of processed meat.

When Maurice Brahms opened Infinity on 5 November 1975, it became clear that even the downtown party network wasn't insulated from the march of the moneymen. A cousin of Addison, Brahms had visited Flamingo and was stunned by both the club's theatricality and what he perceived to be the untapped potential of the gay discotheque market. Another restaurateur, Brahms decided to open a club along similar lines, found a factory space on lower Broadway and offered to better the rent of the resident Hare Krishna group. "The landlord asked me for a thousand dollars a month," Brahms recalled in an interview with writer Anthony Haden-Guest. "I told him, 'I'll give you twelve or thirteen hundred, but I want a lease of fifteen years. Where I can do whatever I want.' He gave me everything I wanted. He thought I was crazy."[38]

Brahms spent fifty thousand dollars opening the club, although he made an astute saving on the money it would have cost to paint a name across the entrance. "I felt the whole mystique of the place was to make a person struggle to find it." The secrecy, however, only went so far. "We advertised in *Michael's Thing*, a gay magazine, and we did a membership, and I said, 'COMING SOON! COMING SOON! with a penis sign . . . and then IT'S FINALLY COME! . . .'"[39] The membership system more or less replicated Michael Fesco's model—one thousand members were to pay annual dues of thirty-five dollars plus six dollars a visit—and the interior design was the most elaborate (and most offensive) to date, with Brahms deploying a lighting system that included fifty-four spinning laser beams and seventy neon sculpture lights, plus a one-hundred-foot-long dance floor surrounded by giant mirrors. It was these mirrors rather than the seemingly endless construction costs that provided Infinity with its name. "If you looked in the mirror, the neon balls just went on forever."[40]

Yet, while Infinity was supposed to be a gay club—and anyone who wasn't in the know would soon get the idea when they bumped into its towering six-foot pink neon penis—Brahms decided to stagger the all-important first night, inviting the straight uptown crowd for eight o'clock and the gay downtown crowd for ten, by which point the straights would be starting to go home. Except that, come the anointed hour, the straights were going nowhere, and by ten-thirty there were approximately two thousand people in the converted warehouse, dancing to the sweet and distinctly bumpy selections of Bobby DJ, who had left Le Jardin prior to spending the summer season at the Ice Palace and now found work at Infinity. "The opening night was a disaster," recalls Casey. "The DJ booth was built right on the dance floor, and when the crowd got big and the dancing became intense the stylus simply jumped across the record. Bobby performed the old trick of placing a coin on the tone arm, but it didn't help much and permanently damaged some records." A distressed Guttadaro called Casey in the middle of the night and pleaded with him to come to the converted warehouse. "He played tapes for the rest of the night, and the next day I invented the 'infinite suspension' of the turntables by using pieces of wood, teak hooks, and number ninety-four rubber bands."

Brahms wasn't troubled by the opening night chaos. "My policy was: Everybody pays!" he told Haden-Guest. "I wasn't there to become famous. I was there to make as much money as I possibly could."[41] Which is exactly what he did. "On a normal week," Forbes reported, "Infinity will turn over some 5,000 customers, for a weekly admission gross of around $30,000. Membership and bar revenues are gravy." Swooning at the math, the business magazine noted that the discotheque had "earned back its start-up costs in less than seven weeks."[42] Brahms maintains his crowd was thoroughly mixed—"you would see gays, straights, transvestites, bisexuals, movie stars, paupers, everything"—even though, with the money in the bank, he didn't really care.[43] Yet while the cast list might have included Giorgio Sant'Angelo, Franco Rossellini, and Calvin Klein, the club's members were unknowing and unfashionable, according to aficionados of the downtown night network. "It was a bridge-and-tunnel crowd," says Steve D'Acquisto. "There were only a few New Yorkers." Casey agrees. "Infinity was the first club to use neon lighting and mirrors all over the place, and it was as tacky then as it is today. Gays never took the place seriously."

Whereas the Gallery had failed to draw in the straight crowd when it first opened, Infinity succeeded without even trying, confirming the full extent of a demographic shift in New York's dancing population. "I was two years ahead of wanting these kind of people to hear this music," reflects Nicky Siano. "But it was naturally evolving and everyone was getting the message. People wanted to do this." A once-marginal counterculture had become an *everynight* pastime.

* * *

By the autumn of 1975, the Continental Baths had, like Le Jardin, lost a high proportion of its gay clientele. "We've done such a good job liberating the city, we've almost hurt our own business," Steve Ostrow told Sheila Weller of the *New York Sunday News* in August. "We *used* to be the only ball game in town."[44] But some felt the decline of the venue had more to do with Ostrow's drifting focus. "He simply lost his vision and control," says Bob Casey. "He opened the Baths to regular-clothed outsiders for the Saturday night shows and some dancing, and they had to leave by 2 A.M. Before long, women were sneaking into the backrooms and then became a local part of the Baths." Casey says that while the "egomaniac" Ostrow had lost the "serious bath crowd" to other bathhouses by the end of 1974, its decline had nothing to do with the emergence of rival gay venues. "My God, this is New York!" says the Virgo Sound boss. "There were always more than enough faggots to go around and still have three hundred fucking in the bushes of Central Park at midnight. The gays did not want a 'bi' baths and took their business elsewhere."

Ostrow acknowledges that the shows finally undermined his core crowd. "For the first year, they were only open to men, but as soon as the raids stopped I started to admit the general public. In the long run that led to the downfall of the Baths. The shows were an expression of who I was—I'm an entertainment person—but they were resented by the hard-core gay crowd that was just interested in sex. In the end they went to other sex places that didn't have our overheads. After that we were in a rough financial shape." As Ostrow's income began to dry up, the Baths went down the drain. "The place became a dump," says Casey. "By 1975 he could no longer afford to pay me to maintain the system, and I took a large fifty-five gallon fish tank with fish in trade."

Despite his commitment to the Baths, La Torre went with the flow. "It happens with almost every club," he says. "You become bored, you stop going, and you move on. I wasn't disappointed because the whole male club thing had already arrived. I wanted to go out dancing and be stimulated in as many ways as possible, and there were more variations of the same thing. The Tenth Floor was a must-do venue for a while—it was a place where you wouldn't think of *not* going—and with Flamingo this kind of religious attendance became even more accentuated. Flamingo was the *only* place to go."

At the same time, La Torre was going through a series of personal changes that were connected to the wider development and consolidation of the gay discotheque. "I always knew that I was gay since I first became aware of my sexuality, so I never had a conflict about it, but being with women was the thing to do, and I experimented with girls when I was growing up," he says. "Women were always part of my entourage when I went out in New York, and I would fool around with them, even though

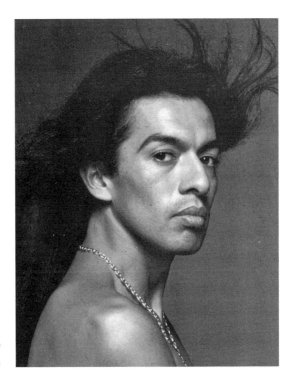

Jorge La Torre.
Courtesy of
Jorge La Torre

I identified as being gay. All of this probably developed because if you wanted to go dancing you had to have a girl with you. Women were very much a part of the picture, whether you wanted them or not." La Torre continued to date women until the mid-seventies. "There was this girl that I liked who was a model. We had sex, we went to clubs, and we had a great time together, but when she started to talk about marriage I realized that this was not what I wanted to do, and I began to let it go. I just didn't feel the same way as she did, and I was drifting more and more into men." Changes in New York state law facilitated the shift. "This will sound terrible, but by this point you didn't need women to go to dance. Men and women had been equally attractive to me at the Sanctuary, but that changed with Flamingo. I became much more adventurous with men, and women began to lose their attraction. I was having different kinds of experiences with men, and they seemed to be more fulfilling to me. Nobody pushed me. I just went in that direction. I was obviously looking for it."

Social spaces were influencing the identity of gay men. Initially the likes of La Torre had taken on some of the characteristics of the sixties clubber, who would dress up for the occasion, dance with a partner, spend liberal amounts of money on alcohol, and even sleep with a woman. Yet these gay men didn't just assimilate into discotheque culture but also reshaped it, revising the relationship between the dancer and the dance floor as well as the rapport between the dancers themselves at the Continental Baths, the Ice Palace, the Sanctuary, the Sandpiper, Tamburlaine, and the Tenth Floor. For sure, these venues were limited in various ways: the Continental Baths was first and foremost a bathhouse, not a discotheque; the Ice Palace and the Sandpiper were always engaged in a race against closing time; the Sanctuary was mixed; the Tamburlaine was a restaurant-bar; and the Tenth Floor was tiny. But Flamingo was designed to overcome these drawbacks, and, functioning as a cross between a finishing school and an incubator, Michael Fesco's venue became the space in which these shifting articulations of gay identity solidified into a distinct culture.

New rituals around dress (and undress) emerged on the dance floor. "Serious dancing began with Flamingo," says Fesco, "and it soon got to the point where you would take your shirt off." Lean, small, and uninhibited, La Torre had started to shed excess clothing at an earlier stage. "I was at Tamburlaine the first time I took my top off," he says. "I was just so hot, and I was tripping my brains out on acid, and I just wanted to get rid of my shirt. A handful of people did it." Similar states of undress were emerging at one end of Fire Island. "It was happening to a degree at Cherry Grove, but the Sandpiper people were *slightly proper* when they went out, and they were also a more fashion-conscious crowd," adds La Torre. "If you wore a fabulous shirt to the Sandpiper you weren't about to take it off!" It wasn't until Flamingo that the practice became institutionalized. "In a sense it was engineered," says Fesco. "There was no air conditioning, and I made sure the windows were closed so it would heat up. They *had* to take off their shirts."

An identifiable look also began to take shape in Fesco's venue. Facial hair came in the form of long sideburns and mustaches (not goatees). Clothing centered on construction boots and jeans (t-shirts were tucked into the back pocket). And bodies were increasingly toned and muscular (although "walking refrigerators" were few and far between). Again, Flamingo didn't invent this look: mustaches had been sprouting for some time, construction boots had kicked in at the Tenth Floor, and working out was already beginning to find a fairly regular window in the gay diary. "We had a small but fabulously equipped gym at the Baths which not too many people used because once they got there they had other things in mind," says La Torre. "But people became more aware of their bodies at the Baths because everyone was walking around in a towel, and the people who had been working out began to inspire other people to try and develop the same physique." Fire Island's beaches had a similar effect, but going to the gym only became *the* thing to do when men started to take their shirts off at Flamingo. "Michael was very tall and very good-looking," says La Torre. "He dressed in a certain kind of way, and he became very influential. The macho look became the style to emulate."

Dancing simultaneously became a form of expression and release that required individuals to lose themselves in the crowd, relinquishing their ego to the wider group. "The dance was the purpose," says La Torre. "You would spend the whole night there. That was what brought people together, and it got really intense. The sexual energy in the place was just incredible, and it was exacerbated by the amount of drugs everybody was consuming. There was a kind of pure, male, testosterone-driven male bonding, and that was what Flamingo was all about." The Continental Baths hadn't clicked in the same way. "The environment was ideal, but it didn't happen. People were definitely running around half-naked with just a towel, and people were definitely getting high all the time, but people weren't quite ready for it and the bonding hadn't occurred. People would drift on and off the dance floor for whatever reason. I would like to say it happened at the Baths, but it didn't." Things changed at Michael Fesco's venue. "It was just very charged. It was really tribal, and it began to acquire a spiritual edge."

Not for the first time, the factory warehouse was figured as a site of bodily passion. As Marcel Jean commented in 1960, "Different writers have described 'the sexual frenzy of factories,' obsessive rhythms, exhalations, cries, panting sounds, shining dart-pointed instruments, articulated rods dripping with sweat, simulacra of inexhaustible loves. Could not man himself become a machine in his amorous activity and make love indefinitely, like a machine?"[45] Now, however, sexual energies were being sublimated into a different kind of work, and gay men were especially drawn to channeling their desires into all-night dancing. Subjecting themselves to the discipline of the beat, the dancers at Flamingo assumed the identity of not so much workers as slaves to the rhythm.

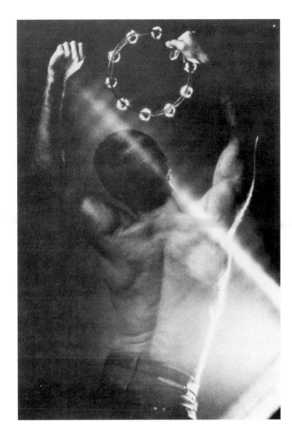

Flamingo flyer.
Courtesy of
Michael Fesco

Special theme parties became the ultimate setting for the new, self-styled Flamingettes. "Michael was the first person to introduce theme parties," says La Torre, who became a close friend of Fesco and, according to the owner, "was a tremendous source of information" with regard to what was happening on the dance floor. "There was the White Party, the Red Party, and the Black Party, which was in essence a leather party. Everybody would dress up in black, and there would be all sorts of performance artists carrying out sexual acts, animals, tattooists, and so on. Michael was very creative." Even though he had been working in the Baths for five years, the black parties, the first of which was held in March 1975, had a significant impact on La Torre. "I was very young at the time, and I wasn't particularly out there sexually speaking so it was all rather mesmerizing. Michael brought these more explicit practices out of the closet, and it liberated a lot of people."

An anthem for this coalescing identity emerged in the spring of 1975 when Mel Cheren handed Armando Galvez a copy of South Shore Commission's "Free Man," a Bunny Sigler production for Wand that had been reworked by Tom Moulton. The New York mixer hadn't enjoyed the Philadelphia producer's effort—"the record was way too fast"—and accordingly slowed down the tempo to such an extent that the sexual negotiations between vocalists Frank McCurry and Sheryl Henry (he's available and "braggin' 'bout it" but she "don't need no part-time lover") ended up sounding like a male-male exchange, prompting critics and dancers to interpret "Free Man" as a tribute to gay liberation. Moulton is dismissive of the mistake. "Hell, no! She's the one who sings, 'Are you free, man?' It had nothing to do with gay rights."

Of course the intended meaning of the lyrics didn't really matter—what counted was the way in which the song was interpreted. Yet it was also becoming clear that, for all the ecstatic unity that was being generated on Fesco's dance floor, some gay men were freer than others. "It was really the onset of starting to dance at midnight and encoring at six o'clock in the morning," says Alan Harris. "During that period there were very intense moments, there were very social moments, and there were moments of passion and drive and camaraderie. But it was very cliquish and although there may have been ten different cliques, with twenty to thirty people in each clique, it was still a very select group of people. Michael was going after a very affluent crowd and you really needed to know a whole group of people—Michael Fesco, Armando Galvez, Calvin Klein—if you were going to get in." A high proportion of gay men didn't fit the mold. "The economy was very depressed, and there were many unemployed gay people who couldn't afford to go partying with these people on a Saturday night. They needed an alternative."

A powerful executive who was accustomed to analyzing markets, making strategic decisions, and, in his own words, "getting his own way," Harris sat down with his lover Cary Finkelstein and devised a more accessible party space for gay men. "The concept was to create a completely safe and nonelitist environment for a larger group of people," he says. "That meant we needed to create a membership system in which members could bring along a guest, and we also needed to provide high-energy foods and service, plus no alcohol. It had to have the elements that were required to put you into sensory overload so it had to have the music, the environment, the lighting, the airflow, and the right location. The sound also had to be close to perfect so that when you left in the morning your ears didn't ring." Save for the all-gay makeup of the crowd, the Loft permeated every level of this vision. "I would certainly pay respect to David Mancuso for educating me in that type of environment as well as that type of sound and experience. He was a master."

Teaming up with Vincent Sorrentino, Geoffrey Tonkel, and Louis Cataldo—all of whom were straight—Finkelstein and Harris set about enacting their plan. "We all sat down and brainstormed, and the idea just sounded better than we could believe," says Harris. "There was a lot of faith and a lot of goodwill." Yet as the project began to take shape, Harris received a warning from one of the Tenth Floor's ex-operators. "David Sokoloff took me aside and said, 'The last thing you want to do is get involved in gay nightlife in New York City.' I asked him why, and he said, 'Because it will kill you!' I said, 'That's an interesting statement coming from someone who has operated a very successful establishment!' He said, 'You don't understand what success can take out of you and how you need to keep working on that!' " Undeterred, Harris and his partners discovered an ideal building for their project in a notorious cruising zone underneath the West Side Highway on West Street at the foot of the abandoned piers on the Hudson River. "The dance floor had to be two, two-and-a-half times the size of the dance floor at Flamingo, if not bigger, and then there was a wood-slatted ceiling, so the room held the sound beautifully. It was like a drum. The bass floated on the top as opposed to the bottom." The club itself, however, was in danger of sinking. "We all put in an initial sum, the total of which came to around twenty-five thousand dollars," says Harris. "Cary managed to quadruple the initial investment in expenditures, and we found ourselves about one hundred thousand dollars in debt. My background says that that's a lot of money to be responsible for."

Named after its location, 12 West opened in March 1975 to the characterless sounds of Roger Gyhra. "Roger was originally slated to be a partner, but he couldn't come up with the financing," says Harris. "We gave him the opening night because of his involvement, and he must have played Van McCoy's 'The Hustle' six times. He couldn't hold the crowd." The turnout, however, was strong, and when Tom Savarese—who had made a name for himself at the Ice Palace the previous summer—was employed to take over the wheels of steel the venue rapidly established itself as an important addition to Manhattan's night network. "It was completely mind-boggling from the night it opened," says Harris. "Never in my wildest dreams did I anticipate that it would be such a success." By May, Vince Aletti was referring to 12 West as "the new private club everyone's talking about," and in July the *Village Voice* commented that "12 West is *the* place right now."[46] One thousand two hundred and fifty members agreed, enabling the management team to devise new ways of expanding the business. "Within the year," the *New York Post* reported in August, "12 West expects to add a restaurant, to present cabaret, sponsor charter flights, market teeshirts and, in December, it's said, Bloomingdale's is planning to open a Disco Shop wherein will be sold, among other items, bathrobes and toothbrushes bearing the 12 West logo."[47]

Tom Savarese

Select Discography (12 West) [Source: Record World, *17 May 1975]*

Bimbo Jet, "El Bimbo"

Hamilton Bohannon, "Foot Stompin Music/Disco Stomp"

Consumer Rapport, "Ease On Down the Road"

Ramsey Lewis, "Sun Goddess"

Harold Melvin & the Blue Notes, "Bad Luck"

Moment of Truth, "Helplessly"

Rockin' Horse, "Love Do Me Right"

South Shore Commission, "Free Man"

Dionne Warwick, "Take It from Me"

Betty Wright, "Where Is the Love"

While the planned spin-offs might have been very un-Loft-like, 12 West nevertheless offered the kind of mix that would have made Mancuso smile. "You found people who were overweight, people who were short, people who weren't muscular, people who danced by themselves, people who just strolled around the dance floor, and people who were older," says Harris. "There were women, as well, including a group from the New York Ballet, although I wouldn't say there was an overabundance of women because it wasn't really designed for them." The dancers (and strollers) were also more multiethnic than their Flamingo counterparts. "The crowd was white, Latino, and Asian, although the Asian community wasn't as large back then. Plus there was definitely a black element."

Flamingo's upscale clan couldn't help but feel a certain sense of superiority. "Twelve West was very neighborhood and downscale," says Frank Crapanzano, "whereas Flamingo was more upper-eastside fashion." Fesco, too, was aware of a divide. "I was very strict about membership, and Flamingo was full to capacity, whereas 12 West was more or less open to the public. The crowd that went to 12 West would have come to Flamingo if they had the chance, but they couldn't get in. They had no place else to go, and because of that 12 West became a kind of secondary club." Twelve West regulars, however, were content with their position in the gay cosmos. "Flamingo was a hot club, and for the most part the men were extraordinarily attractive, but I never liked it there," says Richard Brezner, who adopted 12 West as a second home. "I probably went to Flamingo a dozen times, and in my mind it always had a very dark, evil feeling to it." Twelve West generated a different atmosphere. "It was more of a 'normal' person's club. You didn't go there to be judged. You went there to dance and have a good time. Twelve West was a real party scene, and I thought the people there were much nicer. A lot of people thought of 12 West as the place for Flamingo rejects. All of us knew that's what was going on and none of us cared." Nor, finally, did Fesco. "Personally I never thought of Flamingo as a status symbol, but the public did. I was like, 'Whaaat?' It was hardly my attitude. Twelve West was a charming club. It had a nice feel about it. However, in those days we could afford to be condescending to each other because there were so many of us running around."

* * *

As the white gay scene gathered momentum the black gay network suffered a setback when Richard Long was forced to close the SoHo Place toward the end of 1975 after angry (and tired) neighbors set aside their bohemian credentials and took the host to court, forcing him to rein in his party-cum-workshop. "There were threats from the Mafia, and we had to go to court because of the noise," says Mike Stone. "Eventually Richard closed the club, and after a while we started to do special parties once a month, once a year, with Larry Levan as DJ."

Levan didn't have to wait long for another job offer. "While the SoHo was getting ready to close I got a call from a Michael Brody," the mixer told Manny Lehman. "I said, 'Who the hell is Michael Brody?' I called him back, and he asked me to come to his office. He told me he had a club downtown that I should come look at. I said, 'Great, I could use the job.'"[48] According to Stone, Brody first spotted Levan at the SoHo. "He would come along and watch our every move, hoping that we would close. When he knew we were going to shut down he told Larry that he had a raw space." Levan visited the nascent venue at 143 Reade Street, eyed Alex Rosner's sound system—which was built around a McIntosh amplifier, a Bozak mixer, and Klipschorn speakers—and said yes. "It reminded me a lot of the old Loft," he told Lehman.[49]

That was the intended effect. "Michael Brody and I met in 1963," says Mel Cheren. "We were together for ten years, and during that time we went to the Loft. Michael was obviously impressed because he fashioned Reade Street after it." Even though they had just broken up, Brody used five thousand dollars from the joint account he still held with Cheren to start up Reade Street, which was situated in an old egg and butter storage plant in TriBeCa. Yet while the space was promising—the first floor was converted into a concession area and lounge, and the second floor contained another lounge that led onto the dance floor, which was positioned in the old refrigerator—the parties took a while to build. "They struggled to get the thing started," says Cheren. "Then one day Michael said to me, 'Mel, I've found the guy that's going to make it happen for me!'"

Levan didn't yet have the drawing power of David Mancuso or Nicky Siano, but he had become enough of a name to attract a following, and the job of building the crowd at Reade Street was made easier by the fact that, with the SoHo Place closed and the Loft yet to reopen, the Gallery— itself only open on Saturdays after Fridays failed to take off—provided the only direct competition. "Some of the Loft crowd had followed Larry to SoHo, and when he moved to Reade Street they followed him there," says Nathan Bush, who had been asked by Brody to organize the food for a surprise birthday party for Cheren and was subsequently invited to run the weekly concession stand. "Larry took off at SoHo, but he made more of a name for himself at Reade Street. He was really in control at Reade Street. He would give Michael ideas about all sorts of things." Levan also toyed with the temperature as if the seasons were his own invention. "He would turn on the fridge if he thought it was getting too hot. It was like air conditioning."

Certain downtown devotees weren't convinced. "Music was no longer the main thrust," says Rosner. "It was more about cruising and sex. The emphasis at the Loft and the Gallery was on dancing, whereas at Reade

Street it was on hormones." Mancuso was another reluctant visitor, although for different reasons. "I worked the lights for Larry one night, and they shorted. Smoke started coming out, and something told me that it would be better to stay at home." Richard Brezner was even more nervous. "Reade Street was such a death trap. It was in a freezer, so if someone closed the door and struck a match you would burn. It wasn't very appetizing." Siano—who by this point had made up with Levan—also had his reservations. "The space was very tight and very enclosed. It was great for the sound and controlling the room, but I felt very claustrophobic in there."

Other night network aficionados, however, were more enthusiastic. "Reade Street had a lot of the same characteristics as the Loft," says Cheren, whose first loyalty was to Flamingo but who was nevertheless impressed by his ex-partner's venture. "It was a club where the main element was the party." Bush agreed. "The parties at Reade Street were very intense. They were heavy drug parties. That was when people started doing MDA [similar to Ecstasy]." Gallery loyalist Michael Gomes was also won over. "When we got there at 4:30 in the morning, the party was still jumping, and lollipops were still dangling from the balloons," he wrote in *Mixmaster*, a deliberately low-tech newsletter that, in contrast to the glossy trade publications, focused on the figure of the DJ. "I found out why *Larry* was voted Best Disk Jockey of the Year at the Turn-It-Out Awards: his audience really loves him. It was all, 'Promise you'll call me tomorrow Larry.'"[50] Levan made a similar impression on Robin Lord. "I remember Reade Street being a nice place. It felt 'lighter' somehow. Larry himself was far less serious than either David or Nicky. He did not have the 'mystery' of David or the 'persona' of Nicky. He was just Larry—always a smile."

Mancuso, meanwhile, was desperately trying to reopen the Loft. Penny Grill, a Broadway regular and a resident at 99 Prince Street, had introduced him to the all-but-vacant block, and the landlord, Raymond Zurawin, agreed to rent out his space to the party practitioner on the condition that he brought the building up to code. However, the fact that the new location took Mancuso four blocks southwest of his old NoHo haunt meant that he now officially lived on the upper edge of SoHo, and it quickly became clear that local residents were nervous about the impact the Loft might have on real estate values.

SoHo Weekly News editor Michael Goldstein—who had attempted to

Nicky Siano and Larry Levan at the Gallery. Photo by Michael Gomes

move into the Prince Street premises but was turned down by the landlord on a number of counts that ranged from the financial to the personal — spearheaded the campaign against Mancuso, aware that the Loft could provide his journal with a popular community rallying point. "Michael's preconceived notion," ex–*News* writer Henry Post told Aletti, who covered the dispute for the *Village Voice*, "was that the Loft — not that he'd ever been there — was a drug haven, with people out in the street, muggings, blacks." Before long, Charles Leslie of the SoHo Artists Association was announcing, "This is the beginning of an invasion."[51]

Mancuso, who could hardly be said to be invading an area he had lived in for the best part of a decade, responded by preparing a "Declaration of Intent," which he issued shortly before the formation of the New York Record Pool. "Our presence at 99 Prince Street is legitimate and we intend to stay," it began.

> We intend to continue what we started four years ago. We hurt no one in the process; on the contrary, we feel we fill a need. We give good value. We give employment to deserving young people. We have always acted decently. We did not have a happy childhood, but it has not soured us on life. We seek to impart to our weekly affairs a joy we

missed in our growing years. We intend to continue our work in the same decent, orderly, law-abiding manner. To those who do not know us, do not be misled by gossip. Give us the opportunity to prove what we say in our own humble way.

Mancuso simultaneously started to fight for his right to party on a second, legalistic front. Prince Street, after all, represented a major investment, and he needed to be protected from the kind of regulatory assaults that he had faced at Broadway. "The fact that we were illegal bothered me," he says. "I knew I was vulnerable, and I did whatever I could to minimize the risk. I didn't want anything to happen to the parties, and finally it did." Acquiring a Certificate of Occupancy and of Public Assembly proved to be relatively straightforward, but Mancuso was keenly aware that these weren't enough to dispel the ambiguous licensing laws that had cast such a long shadow over his previous home. As a result he ingeniously set himself up as an entertainment association—99 Prince Street Gallery, Inc.— and applied for a cabaret license that he desperately didn't want. "I was out to establish something. I wanted my freedom. This was my revolution. I wanted to protect our privacy and establish our right to do our own thing. I had the longest hearing in the history of consumer affairs to determine whether or not I was running a cabaret. I drove them crazy."

Case #CAB 553475 was occasionally vicious. "The SoHo organizations said that there were undisclosed partners behind the Loft, but when they came to testify there was nothing there." Mancuso's detractors also tried to swing Zurawin against his new tenant, but the landlord was having none of it. "This was an area for people with new ideas, but it's turned into something else," he told Vince Aletti. "I don't see many struggling young artists—just lofts for the rich who are concerned about dog leashes and the crime rate."[52] Somewhat improbably, Yves St. Laurent became another important player in Mancuso's campaign when he hired 99 Prince Street to celebrate the launch of his spring menswear line. "The place they had booked fell through," says Mancuso. "They offered me $850, and on the day there were diamonds, minks, limos, everything. I was like, '*Now let's see them complain!*'"

Mancuso sealed his victory in the autumn when a letter dated 2 September 1975 slipped into his mailbox. "Dear Sirs," wrote Commissioner Guggenheimer on behalf of the Department of Consumer Affairs. "Please take notice that your application has been denied for the reason(s) indi-

David Mancuso
inside the Prince
Street Loft. Courtesy
Matthew Marks
Gallery. © The Estate
of Peter Hujar.

cated below." A check had been entered in the following box: "Other Applicant is not a Cabaret as defined by the Administrative Code, in that the applicant does not sell food or drink to the public, either directly or indirectly." The rejection was a double victory for Mancuso, who had not only won his case, but had simultaneously established a legal precedent that would underpin New York's nightlife for years to come: run an invitation-only party, don't sell alcohol, and you would be beyond state interference. "The ruling benefited everybody because consumer affairs was a terrible department to deal with," says Mancuso. "They wanted to see your finances for the last five years, who you were married to, who your relatives were. They looked up your ass."

The Loft officially reopened on 20 October 1975, some seventeen months after the last party at Broadway. "It was very crowded," remembers Grill. "There were maybe a thousand people that night. Everyone wanted to come and see what the Loft was about." An unusually nervous Mancuso was reasonably pleased with the outcome. "The party was ok from my point of view, but I was still exploring." It was clear that a number of adjustments still needed to be made. "The place wasn't really developed, and the sound wasn't where I wanted it to be. I had a lot of new speakers, and I realized I would need some time to get the sound properly adjusted." It was, however, a good start. "Broadway had been shut down very suddenly, and as soon as that happened my goal was to just have another party. I had achieved that."

The achievement was symbolically important. When Mancuso had opened in 1970, he was one. Now, following the resurrection of the Loft, the mushrooming private party network—which also included Flamingo, the Gallery, Reade Street, and 12 West—numbered five. Stretching from the corner of Houston to TriBeCa to West Twelfth Street to SoHo, the parties had expanded their geographical reach, and, running from the strictly gay to the dedicatedly mixed, there was pretty well something for everyone. By dint of being a shallow community with an elastic philosophy, the night network had managed to maintain a certain mobility and flexibility and, following Case #CAB 553475, there was also the prospect of legal stability.

At the same time, boundaries that had always been unstable were beginning to dissolve, with key figures such as Mancuso and Siano exerting considerable influence over the music market. The Loft guru was now hosting a DJ association that enabled spinners to get hold of free music that, if they liked it enough, they could turn into a smash hit, and Siano had established himself as the DJ's DJ, a human barometer who could forecast climactic shifts in musical taste. "When you play a record and it goes to number one on the national pop charts and you were the person responsible for turning everyone onto that record how could you ever consider that underground?" asks Siano, who had received a thank-you letter from Barbra Streisand in the fall of 1975 for "all the excitement" he had "helped cause" by playing "Shake Me, Wake Me," an album cut that the vocalist's record company subsequently decided to release as a single.

Media interest ensued, with journalists shifting the spotlight from midtown to downtown. "This is not where it's at," Richie Kaczor, nodding disdainfully at the singles-bar-turned-disco scene, told Sheila Weller of the *New York Sunday News* during their tour of nightworld at the end of August 1975. "'Come on. I want to take you to a club I'm in love with.'" The Hollywood DJ headed straight to the Gallery. "The wildness is exquisitely wholesome," reported Weller. "Furious dancing. Gentle laughter. Crepe paper and tinsel. Body energy shakes the room, yet sex is the *last* thing it calls to mind." The "frenetic holiness" of the dance ritual swept Weller away. "The floor is a drum to the dancers—many of them gay, most of them black—whose upsprung fists and tambourines lob the balloons and streamers above at what seem to be collectively-chosen intervals. 'Get ready for a *rush*!' Richie whispers, and the song smoothly melts into 'Love Is the Message' over which deejay Nicky Siano—one of the city's best—blares jet-plane sound effects."[53]

Visible yet invisible, central yet peripheral, inside yet outside, the downtown party network was of yet not of this world, a ghostly presence that operated outside the core institutions of the entertainment industry yet influenced their direction. And while it was also becoming clear that the proliferation of disco meant that downtown DJs inevitably began to lose control over the culture's practical deployment, they continued to go about their business in much the same way as they had always done, hoping that their dance floors would jump and that others would, over time, learn how to join in. "This is the party spirit at its peak, but a lot of New York clubs aren't ready for it yet," concluded Weller. "The prejudices that kept the scene underground for so long are still operative, and the minorities that pioneered the new disco boom are being discouraged from a spate of snazzy new clubs that disco purists think of as rip-offs."[54] Who would prevail?

7. prominence

Competition between the trade magazines that were covering disco was heating up. *Melting Pot* came out with its first cut-and-paste issue in August 1974, *Billboard* launched Tom Moulton's "Disco Action" column at the beginning of November 1974, and *Record World* responded by inviting Vince Aletti to write a weekly piece in the middle of the same month. Aletti quickly established himself as a particularly influential voice, for while he lacked the musical know-how, studio experience, and first-hand insider knowledge of Moulton, he was a dedicated full-time writer who had an excellent ear, a silky pen, and an impressive network of DJ contacts. "Steve D'Acquisto, Michael Cappello, David Rodriguez, and I would go to Vince's house every couple of weeks in the beginning," says David Mancuso. "He would ask us what we thought about certain records, and they would end up in his column. It was basically inside information. He knew what horses were coming in."

If *Billboard* wanted to establish itself as the most authoritative chronicle of the disco scene, it should have clearly picked a fight with *Record World*. Instead, Bill Wardlow, the magazine's tall and distinguished associate publisher, aimed his armory at *Melting Pot*, initiating a paranoid and ultimately futile dispute when he claimed that *Billboard* was the first trade magazine to cover the discotheque industry by dint of the fact that *Melting Pot* couldn't be classified as a trade magazine. Wardlow received a mouthful in return. "The MELTING POT *is* a TRADE publication," replied the journal of the National Association of Discotheque Disc Jockeys in February 1975. "In fact, it *is* a TRADE MAGAZINE, and in essence is more of a TRADE magazine in the DISCO industry, than your so-called TRADE GIANTS!"[1]

In June, Bob Casey's struggle to secure his right to self-determination spread to a second front when the establishment of the Record Pool challenged (and superseded) NADD's status as the most important organization for spinners. Then, in the autumn, the soundman decided that it was time to spend more time focusing on his sound company and accordingly appointed Richie Kaczor as the DJ organization's administrative director and Alex Kabbaz as the editor of *Melting Pot*. Civil war soon broke out. "After one issue, Kabbaz demanded 51 percent ownership of the paper," says Casey. "I refused, and he stole the entire NADD and *Melting Pot* mailing list." According to the Virgo Sound boss, Kabbaz created his own magazine, *Discothekin'* and pressed it up under Casey's name. In January 1976, *Billboard* ran a short item on the inauguration of the new magazine, but the first issue didn't generate any significant revenue, and Casey was left with "a staggering printing bill that literally broke the bank of *Melting Pot*."

As all of this was unfolding, *Billboard* successfully positioned itself at the center of the budding discotheque industry by organizing a three-day conference at the Roosevelt Hotel in New York. The brainchild of Wardlow, the First Annual International Disco Forum opened on 21 January with a speech by Lee Zhito, the magazine's publisher/editor, who declared, "The time is right for disco."[2] The *New York Times*, eyeing the way in which the exhibition rooms of the normally sedate hotel were now jam-packed with flashing lights, equipment displays, record executives, music journalists, DJs, and technical specialists, was compelled to agree. "What it all amounts to is the most tangible sign yet of the packaging and dissemination of a disco craze that can legitimately count New York as its center," noted the newspaper. "The Roosevelt convention shows us the way the American entertainment industry moved in to market it all to the masses."[3]

Attended by some five hundred registrants, the panels drove home the message that, as *Billboard* reported, "disco is rapidly becoming the universal pop music, and that the industry now has another viable tool to tap additional consumer dollars."[4] Yet the conference wasn't simply an exercise in public relations and self-congratulation, with participants expressing a desire for a greater A&R emphasis on orchestrated music as well as better access to promotional records. Reassurances were forthcoming. "The word from such labels as Buddah, Scepter, Salsoul, TK, Private Stock, Phonogram, Midland International and Atlantic, among others," noted *Billboard*, "was that manufacturer-disco ties will be greatly enhanced during 1976, mainly in the area of providing promotional product, and that the industry at-large will benefit."[5]

Some of the livelier discussions went unreported, however, and that included the exchange that revolved around Casey's non-invitation to the forum's closing "hot seat" session, which was to include performers Van McCoy and the members of LaBelle, as well as notables such as Jane Brinton (Aristocrat Mobile Disco), Joe Cayre (Caytronics/Mericana/Salsoul), Diane Hyatt (Epic), Richard Long (Disco Sound), Michael O'Harro (freelance disco consultant), Sonny Taylor (wwRL), Johnny Walker (BBC Radio), and one Alex Kabbaz (*Discothekin'*). "I was told that the shit hit the fan on the second day of the conference with regard to why I wasn't on the panel," says Casey. "When Wardlow tried to change the subject, many—some say half—of the DJs got up and walked out. Wardlow's secretary called me later on in the afternoon and 'invited' me to attend the next morning's panel." The session was a bad-tempered affair. "Wardlow interrupted my opening comments by saying that he didn't want any confrontational remarks and that the forum was for sharing views on the industry. I said, 'What about the concerns of the DJs?' Wardlow said something like, 'Don't push me!' The crowd cheered. But it was very clear to me that the forum was not a 'forum' but a big publicity show for *Billboard*." The spectacle culminated later on that evening with a special ceremony in which Atlantic Records, KC & the Sunshine Band, LaBelle, Richard Long, Van McCoy, Richard Nader, Michael O'Harro, the Salsoul Orchestra, Donna Summer, and Earl Young all received formal awards, after which Wardlow extended a special thanks to Casey's nemesis, Kabbaz, for his "assistance in pulling the Forum together."[6]

The following day, Casey sat alone in his darkened office (Steve Ostrow's glowing fish tank provided the only light). He had just received a letter from an insurance company that accepted NADD as an accredited group and offered its DJs a low rate for health coverage. "I felt very depressed and alone. I was broke and had two pending lawsuits from creditors. I asked the question, 'Why am I doing this to myself?' I no longer had the stomach to fight—and I had the basic human instinct to survive." Casey folded NADD and *Melting Pot*, spent the next eight months paying off his debts, and then moved on. "Everybody was taking advantage of the DJs. It was who you knew, who you blew. I wanted to legitimize the profession, but nobody gave a fuck. The DJs didn't want health insurance. They just wanted records."

The New York Record Pool, meanwhile, was flourishing, and bands soon started to perform at the Prince Street headquarters for free. "I said to the companies, 'If the DJs are playing this record, it would be nice if the artist could come down and play it for them,'" says David Mancuso. "The DJs were never going to fill up the space by themselves, so I asked the record companies if Loft people could also come along. They said, 'Fine.' There would be eight or nine hundred people there. *Free party*." Guest acts included Brass Construction, B. T. Express, Benny Digs of Revelation, and T-Connection. "They did it as a way of saying thank you, and it was also good promotion. I didn't charge the record companies rent so they were getting a free space. All they had to do was pay for the food and the salaries of about eight people. It was very cheap for them. They had the artist perform in front of the people who were playing their records and the people who were buying their records."

Replica organizations began to open throughout the country. Long Island led the way and Philadelphia soon followed, after which Atlanta, Boston, Southern California, Chicago, and Florida got in on the act. "I came to New York for the *Billboard* convention," says Jane Brinton, who had been running mobile parties in California since the early seventies and had been invited to the forum to describe her experience. "I went to the Loft and heard all of these tracks that had never made it out to the West Coast, so I went back to California and started the Southern California Disco DJs Association with A. J. Miller." Brinton and Miller spread the word, called up the record companies, and held an inaugural meeting. "Neil Bogart came, along with Donna Summer, and record companies started sending us a hundred copies of new records. The pool was really influential in bringing a lot of New York underground music to the West Coast."

Back at Prince Street, however, Steve D'Acquisto and David Mancuso were beginning to have "differences of opinion" with a number of record companies. "At one point they wanted to get royalties for the songs they were playing, and a lot of the labels became concerned," says RCA dance promoter David Todd. "It was never going to work because there was no way of properly tracking who was playing what." In a parallel development, Atlantic's Doug Riddick started to express concerns that DJs were offloading free vinyl in order to make some quick cash. "He thought that we were dishonest and that we were padding the list in order to get extra records," says D'Acquisto. "We decided that if we didn't receive the full quota then we would return the records to the company. How were we supposed to choose who would get the records and who wouldn't?"

Riddick began to relax when, following further "differences of opinion," he finally persuaded the New York Record Pool to introduce feedback sheets in September 1975. From that point on, response forms were issued with the promotional records, and DJs were required to answer a series of questions in order to qualify for the next batch. Once collated, the information amounted to a sophisticated marketing operation through which companies could forecast a record's potential long before its national release—all of which was very handy in the disco market, where artists were relatively unknown and the dominant format was still the ephemeral single rather than the stable album. DJs, however, had to fill in the forms accurately, and it wasn't long before Ronnie Coles—who was headhunted to replace Riddick—asserted that the pool's members were foundering in this respect. "We weren't getting proper feedback on the records we were giving them," says Coles. "I cut our supply until the New York Record Pool agreed to start filling out detailed feedback sheets. After that I was very proud of the organization."

Yet while relations between the record companies and the Record Pool were being ironed out, tensions within the organization were beginning to escalate. "David and Steve had too much control in terms of verification and dispensing records," says Francis Grasso, who had slipped into relative anonymity at Villa Nova Part II. "They didn't give me trouble, but I gave Steve trouble. I was drinking a Heineken in the office and he said something that upset me. I threw my empty bottle into this metal garbage pail, and that shut him up. He had become a more-righteous-than-thou person, and I didn't agree with the way he was throwing his weight around."

Tensions continued to mount when Mancuso and D'Acquisto stopped arguing with their peers and began to lock horns with each other. Mancuso had become increasingly anxious about D'Acquisto's overbearing presence in the day-to-day running of the Pool, and D'Acquisto was struggling to maintain a generous disposition in his dealings with the Loft host. "David was unique among disc jockeys in New York in that he ran his space, and the competitive thing between David and Steve started because of that," says Mark Riley, a mutual friend. "At the height of the Loft, if David wanted to sit on his ass and sleep six days a week he could have done that. David had really defined the true meaning of freedom for himself, at least in the environment of the mid-1970s, and to an extent everybody wanted that. Steve wasn't the only person that envied that. Hell, *I* envied that. But Steve wanted it more than most, and he could never figure out how come David had it and he didn't."

The first major clash occurred around the issue of the feedback forms. "That was the point when I realized the Record Pool was going wrong," says D'Acquisto. "We became the pawns of the record companies. It had never even occurred to me that *we* should provide *them* with information. I thought they should be paying *us* for our work and supporting *us* with monthly dues!" More of a mediator, Mancuso disagreed. "Steve hated the idea—he wanted to be the mother of all information—but I thought it was a fair and meaningful exchange. When Doug mentioned the idea my reaction was, 'Well, you know, it makes sense.' I thought that we needed to give something back to the record companies, and I also thought that it was *right* that we should give them this information because it would help get better music out there." D'Acquisto refused to compromise. "I kept saying, 'We should think about it!'" remembers Mancuso. "Steve would say, 'No, no, no!'"

The two friends managed to agree to disagree until United Artists, intent on making the most of the disco market, sent advance copies of War's "Low Rider" to not only the Pool but also to Manhattan's best-known discotheques in mid-September. That included Le Jardin, where D'Acquisto was handed a hundred copies to give away as part of a mid-week dance contest, and, while every entrant turned out to be a winner, the combination of a sluggish evening and the excessive allocation meant that the alternate failed to offload his entire batch. Turning a blind eye to the "Not For Sale" notice that had been attached to every copy, D'Acquisto took the surplus promos to a friendly record store and did a little business, but the DJ's scam backfired when United Artists uncovered the misdemeanor. While the underhand deal was hardly an unprecedented instance of DJ opportunism, that didn't deter the record company from threatening to strike the New York Record Pool off the delivery list if Mancuso didn't make an example of the hapless culprit. "United Artists had said, 'Fuck radio, we're going to break the record without them!'" comments Mancuso. "They wanted to break the record exclusively through the Record Pool, and it was a major decision, our finest moment. What happened with Steve was the worst thing that could have happened."

The pressure was unendurable for the already strained friendship. D'Acquisto protested that the records, which were sent to him in his capacity as a Le Jardin DJ, had nothing to do with the Record Pool, but nobody was willing to buy his story. "Steve had a knack of just saying, 'Oh, not me, I didn't do that!'" says Michael Cappello, who kept a close eye on the unfolding row. Mancuso, in his capacity as Pool president, maintained that the organization's representatives had to be beyond suspicion and that, as far as the record companies were concerned, D'Acquisto now had a tarnished reputation. In an attempt to resolve the conflict, Mancuso told D'Acquisto that he should resign as secretary of the Pool and stay on as a consultant, after which he could, if the members of the Pool voted for him, be reelected once things had cooled down. Incensed and combustible, D'Acquisto wasn't interested. "The whole thing was a setup!" he declared and stormed out of Prince Street.

Eddie Rivera, DJ at the Cork & Bottle, was appointed to fill D'Acquisto's position as secretary, even though Mancuso had been riled by the mixer's decision to convene a separate Latin Music Department within the Pool that aimed to broaden the exposure of Latin music. "I opposed the idea," says Mancuso. "I said, 'Why can't we all stay together?'" According to the Loft host, Rivera used his new status to carry out favors for the Latin DJs in order to win their allegiance, and as tension between the parties mounted an argument broke out. "I missed a meeting, and Eddie said, 'We voted on this and that,'" remembers Mancuso. "I asked to see the minutes, and they were missing. He was up to something. I started to see the game he was playing, and I was very upset. The situation was out of control. I might have asked him to resign."

Rivera complied and took the Latin DJs with him, forming the International Disco Record Center in association with Kabbaz. "Our main goal is to provide a direct communication vehicle between the record industry and their audience," Rivera told *Discothekin'* in March 1976.[7] Riley, however, detected other objectives. "Eddie believed that the Pool should be a for-profit entity, whereas David was always very vigorous in maintaining that since the Pool was getting music for free there should be no charge over and above administrative costs. Eddie saw many opportunities to make money through the Pool, and that's exactly what he did with IDRC. They clashed fundamentally over this."

* * *

Vinyl, which had been spinning round and round for years, was about to undergo a real revolution. "The twelve-inch happened by accident," says Tom Moulton. "I was cutting a reference disc for Al Downing's 'I'll Be Holding On,' and Jose Rodriguez ran out of seven-inch blanks." Rodriguez suggested that they put the material onto a twelve-inch blank. "I said, 'Oh, it's a shame, the single only uses up a little bit of space.'" To which Rodriguez replied, "We'll just open it up and spread out the grooves." The result? "I almost died because the level was so loud." Steve D'Acquisto, Walter Gibbons, Bobby Guttadaro, Richie Kaczor, and David Rodriguez were the first DJs to hear the result. "They used to come over to my apartment every Friday to hear my week's work," says Moulton. "I played them the twelve-inch, and they loved it." Yet while the increase in volume was revelatory, the Al Downing acetate hadn't exploited the format's potential to accommodate longer recordings, and even the improvement in sound quality was lost when Chess records eventually released Moulton's five-and-a-half-minute "disco mix" on a forty-five toward the end of 1974.

A flurry of extended recordings ensued. At the beginning of May 1975, Atlantic Records released a DJ-only "Disco Disc" series of long-playing seven-inch singles that included album cuts of "Mad Love" by Barrabas and "Disco Queen" by Hot Chocolate, and a week later the same label released special versions of "Ease On Down the Road" by Consumer Rapport and "Tornado" from *The Wiz* original cast recording—again as noncommercial long-playing seven-inch singles. Warners simultaneously announced that it was going to issue an extended version of "Dance, Dance, Dance" by Calhoon on a ten-inch format at $33\frac{1}{3}$ RPM, although a series of delays resulted in the record being released at the beginning of July on a one-sided twelve-inch disco disc that ran at six minutes nineteen seconds.[8]

By that time, Mel Cheren had stepped in to transform Moulton's fortuitous mistake into every DJ's dream when he released Bobby Moore's "Call Me Your Anything Man" as a twelve-inch single—the *first* twelve-inch single—in the middle of June. "Scepter Records is launching a policy of servicing discos with 12-inch 45s to keep the recording level at a maximum as often as possible," *Billboard* reported. "According to Stanley Greenberg of the label, Scepter has found that to produce a single of more than five minutes in length, the recording level requires lowering. With the new, larger singles, the problem is hopefully remedied."[9] Even if the record's George McCrae–style production values were unexceptional, the format amounted to a major breakthrough. As Vince Aletti reported in his Disco File column, Moore's "long disco mix runs just over six minutes and will be shipped to DJs on special 12-inch records at 33¹/₃ to give it its best, hottest sound—something other record companies have been talking about doing for the disco market but that Scepter is the first to carry out."[10]

Yet, while extended recordings could now be generated specifically for the dance floor without having to squeeze onto the constricted grooves of a forty-five or experience life alongside a collection of inferior album cuts, the newborn format suffered a symbolic setback when the following month Scepter released *Disco Gold*. Containing some of Moulton's finest work to date, including a mesmerizing six-and-a-half minute version of Patti Jo's "Make Me Believe in You" (a Curtis Mayfield production that was originally released on Wand in 1973), *Disco Gold* was a long-playing album rather than a series of twelve-inch singles. DJs were more than mollified by Cheren's decision to pay them a special tribute on the back cover—"Thanks. For without your help this album would not be possible"—but it wasn't until the spring of 1976 that the twelve-inch single became a for-sale commodity when Ken Cayre attempted to consolidate the success of the faceless Salsoul Orchestra by signing a string of recognizable stars and bands, one of which he decided to promote via the new format.

Once again, Philadelphia proved to be a rich source of talent for Cayre when Norman Harris introduced him to Double Exposure, one of his own discoveries. Determined to make the most of the new signing, the label mogul decided to push Double Exposure's first release—"Ten Percent," arranged and produced by Harris, and featuring the Salsoul Orchestra—on both the traditional seven-inch and the nascent twelve-inch formats. This was the first time that any record company had attempted to sell the "giant single," and the Salsoul head compounded the risk by employing a DJ, who had never set foot in a studio, to mastermind the reediting process. "I asked the boss of Atlantic the key to success. He said, 'Walk slowly and hope you bump into a genius.'" Cayre followed his advice and bumped into Walter Gibbons who, true to his profession, was visiting record labels like a believer visits a house of prayer. "Walter was a big fan of Salsoul," says Cayre. "He would regularly come to the office for records." Denise Chapman, now head of promotions at the label, became the DJ's point of contact, and the two of them hit it off. "A lot of the girls got into a Bette Davis bitchiness, but not Walter," says Chapman. "He

Walter Gibbons.
Courtesy of
Kenny Carpenter

just loved the music and went to his own beat." Crucially, Gibbons "took everything seriously" and "would show up on time," and these qualities—which weren't exactly common in your average DJ—persuaded Cayre and Chapman to give him the "Ten Percent" assignment. "At the time no other studio had allowed a nonproducer to mix a record," says Cayre, "but we had confidence in Walter, and it was clear that the DJs understood how dance crowds responded to records."

A tiny, shy twenty-two-year-old from Brooklyn, Gibbons didn't have the charismatic pulling power of Cappello, Guttadaro, Levan, Mancuso, Savarese, or Siano, and he'd spent most of his short DJing career bouncing around a series of unremarkable commercial clubs including the Outside Inn in Queens and Galaxy 21 on Twenty-third Street. "David Todd was Walter's DJ hero," says Kenny Carpenter, who got a job working the lights at Galaxy 21 on his first visit to the club. "Walter used to visit David in Philadelphia. He always said that David could hold the beat of a mix longer than anybody else." Gibbons didn't attract much attention until he started to push "2 Pigs and a Hog" from the *Cooley High* soundtrack, which he introduced to Hector LeBron (Limelight), Tony Smith (Barefoot Boy), and Tony Gioe (Hollywood). "The cut is only 1:46, but the DJs play it two or three times in a row, making it longer," reported Moulton in October 1975. "The LP has been around for several months and Walter believed in the record enough to try and convince others."[11] Gibbons also believed in the percussion-heavy "Happy Song" by Rare Earth and Jermaine Jackson's "Erucu," and by the end of the year his technique of taking two records and working them back and forth in order to extend the drum breaks beyond the horizon of New York's tribal imaginary had earned him the reputation of being a highly skilled original. "Walter was so innovative," says Carpenter. "He would buy two copies of a record like 'Happy Song,' and he would loop the thirty-second conga section."

Walter Gibbons

Select Discography (Outside Inn, Queens) [Source: Record World,

   13 September 1975]

Blue Magic, "Magic of the Blue/We're On the Right Track"

B. T. Express, "Peace Pipe"

Cooley High Original Soundtrack, "2 Pigs and a Hog"

Gloria Gaynor, "Casanova Brown/(If You Want It) Do It Yourself/How High the Moon"

Jimmy "Bo" Horne, "Gimme Some"

LaBelle, "Messin' with My Mind"

The Ritchie Family, "Brazil"

Silver Convention, "Fly, Robin, Fly"

Sound Experience, "He's Looking Good, and Moving Fast"

Tavares, "It Only Takes a Minute"

The rhythmic crescendo at Galaxy 21 intensified in February 1976 when the club's owner, George Freeman, hired François Kevorkian, a young French drummer who had traveled to Manhattan the previous September, to play alongside the DJ. "I was very enamored with Hendrix, Santana, Jeff Beck, Miles Davis, and Herbie Hancock, and I came to the conclusion that I was wasting my time in France," says Kevorkian. "I came to New York to establish a sort of beachhead for the rest of my band. My bass player came three or four months later with his girlfriend, and she decided that they were going to live in California. The guitar player never made it." Life picked up when Kevorkian began to fine-tune his technique with the Miles Davis drummer Tony Williams—"He traded drum lessons for French lessons"—and the new arrival landed his first serious job when he stumbled into Freeman. "I didn't really have anywhere to live so I decided to search through the ads in the *Village Voice*. Instead of looking for a reasonable apartment to share, I decided to look for the most expensive apartment to share. I didn't have any money and figured that if somebody had a big apartment and was looking for a roommate then they could probably afford to hire somebody to help them look after the place." Kevorkian called the owner of the priciest apartment. "I explained my situation to this person called George Freeman, and he said, 'Listen, I'm not into sharing my apartment, but I've got this club, and if you want to come down I'll hire you to play the drums.'" Kevorkian agreed, much to the irritation of Gibbons. "Walter got terribly upset. He kept saying that I was throwing him off and that he couldn't mix the way he wanted to, but I kept going. He tried to trip me up by playing all of the drum solos of all the records, although I managed to stay with it most of the time. It seems people liked what I was doing because if they hadn't I would have been thrown out after the first night."

Kevorkian was in a perfect position to witness the DJ's percussive-expressive agenda. "Walter's DJing was very emotional, based on crescendos and drumming. His style was fiery and flamboyant. Walter's thing was drums for days. I guess he preferred them when they were on vinyl." Rare Earth's "Happy Song" remained his trademark record. "You would never hear the actual song. You just heard the drums. It seemed like he kept them going forever, although I would imagine it was actually about ten minutes." Gibbons was the first Manhattan DJ to cultivate such a purist, percussive aesthetic, and his mixing technique was precision personified. "The break in 'Happy Song' is only thirty seconds long, and he knew exactly how to make it click because to me it sounded like one record. I was playing along with the drums, and it was always the same pattern, always the same number of bars. He had this uncanny sense of mixing that was so accurate it was *unbelievable*." The Galaxy DJ's technical perfection disguised the difficulty of the mix. "When you listened to the record it was like, 'Wait a minute, where do I cue up to know exactly where I am?' It's not easy. The record doesn't just start. It fades up. You really have to have a very keen ear to pick it out through the headphones."

A version of this method was also going on in the Bronx, where the Jamaican-born DJ Kool Herc had started to play back-to-back breaks around the same time as Gibbons. Initially Herc had pushed reggae at his parties but, according to music critic David Toop, his selections "failed to cut the ice," and in 1974 "he switched to Latin-tinged funk, just playing the fragments that were popular with the dancers and ignoring the rest of the track. The most popular part was usually the percussion break."[12] Afrika Bambaataa remembers that Herc began to turn to "certain disco records that had funky percussion breaks like the Incredible Bongo Band when they came out with 'Apache' and he just kept that beat *going*."[13] Cymande's "Bra," "Give It Up or Turnit a Loose" by James Brown, the Dynamic Corvettes's "Funky Music Is the Thing" and "Get into Something" by the Isley Brothers provided other percussive nuggets for Herc's venture into breakbeat eternity, and the crowd's crazed response persuaded him to make the technique a part of his nightly repertoire.

While Herc wasn't mixing with anything like the same degree of precision as Gibbons—the Bronx DJ notoriously faded from one record to the next without lining up the beats—the similarity between their styles was striking. "I grew up on Davidson Avenue in the South Bronx, so I experienced the whole hip-hop scene before it even became hip-hop, with DJs scratching records and quick-cuts," says John "Jellybean" Benitez, the petite, cute son of Puerto Rican immigrants. "I heard Bambaataa and all those guys." Benitez also ventured into Manhattan. "Me and my friend Tony Carrasco would listen to all these DJs. We were two straight guys going to all of these gay clubs. We would buy all the records and go home and practice." Benitez soon started praying to the deity called Gibbons. "I thought I was the greatest DJ in the world until I heard Walter. He would cut up records creatively, he would play two together, he did double beats, he worked the sound system, and he made pressings of his own edits. I said, 'I've got to practice!'" Benitez was drawn to the way Gibbons bridged the ostensibly disconnected worlds of Manhattan and the Bronx. "Walter played a lot of beats and breaks, and I had never heard a disco DJ playing those kinds of records before. His style appealed to my Bronx sensibilities. He just blew me away." The arrival of Kevorkian added a touch of humor to the proceedings. "I never got the impression that Walter really wanted François there so he would do things to totally fuck him up."

Gibbons set the drummer a new test within a week or two of his

debut: how to keep up with his remix of "Ten Percent" by Double Exposure. The diminutive DJ had transformed the final studio production of
the four-minute song into a nine-minute-forty-five-second cut-and-paste
roller coaster at the Frankford/Wayne Mastering Labs and was paid $185
for his efforts ($85 to cover a night's work at Galaxy, plus $100 for the
blend). Having tested his work-in-progress on a reel-to-reel over a period
of months, Gibbons started to play an acetate of the remix—effectively
a ready-made version of the quick-fire collages he had already been con-
cocting at Galaxy—in late February/early March, and at the end of April
Salsoul sent out 2,500 copies of the recording to club DJs. Breaking new
ground, "Ten Percent" was commercially released in May 1976, much to
the chagrin of songwriter Allan Felder. "The mixer cut up the lyrics and
changed the music," he says. "It was as if the writers and producers were
nothing." Cayre, though, stood his ground. "We broke our first record
via the discos, and that's where our strength still is," he told *Billboard*,
which ran a front-page story on the release. "We feel that disco spinners
are better equipped to judge the public's response to disco product."[14]

The public's response was everything Salsoul could have hoped for.
"I went to hear Walter at Galaxy with David Todd and Larry Patterson,"
says Arthur Baker, who was DJing in his college town of Amherst, Mas-
sachusetts, and making midweek trips to New York in order to visit Todd
at his RCA office. "It wasn't an influential club, and there were only a few
people there, but when Walter started playing this track I was blown away.
I thought he was using two records because I had heard John Luongo
going back and forth between two forty-fives. I thought, 'Hey, he must be
really quick!' Then I went up to the booth to take a look and saw that it was
just one record. I was like, 'Wow! This is fucking amazing!' " The reedit
embodied the dexterity and imagination of one of New York's most inventive night priests. "I heard it on an acetate in the Gallery," says Michael
Gomes. "It sounded so new, going backwards and forwards. It built and
built like it would never stop. The dance floor just exploded."

Salsoul made sure that their new commodity had a different feel from
the regular twelve-inch album by packaging "Ten Percent" in a universal four-color album jacket that contained a center cut-out, which enabled buyers to read information about the title and artist on the record's
inner label. There was also a new price of $2.98, which retailers generally
knocked down to $2.29, and a new speed of forty-five RPM, rather than the
standard album tempo of thirty-three. "There are two reasons for the 45

Double Exposure. Courtesy of the Vince Aletti Collection

RPM speed," Salsoul marketing chief Chuck Gregory told *Billboard.* "One is practical and the other is psychological. On the practical side is the fact that the wider groove allows you to turn it up and play it real hot without popping the needle out of the groove. The psychological reason for the 45 RPM speed is the fact that even a 9-minute version at 33¹/₃ would still only take up a relatively small portion of the vinyl in a 12-inch pancake and the customer would see this and think he is being cheated. The faster speed takes up more space and doesn't call the customer's attention to a lot of unused vinyl space."[15]

The twelve-inch provided Double Exposure with a double exposure, prompting *Billboard* and *Record World* to run simultaneous front-page stories on Salsoul's marketing strategy. Joe Cayre, the president of Cayre Industries, noted that sales of the twelve-inch had been excellent "all over the country," with the "giant forty-five" selling 110,000 copies in a single week.[16] "Radio plus discos has really created a market," added Gregory. "The twelve inch is outselling the other size by two-to-one."[17] Some retailers went further. "The big record is selling very well," reported Albert Dakins of the Record Museum chain in Philadelphia. "As a matter of fact it's outselling the standard single by 10 to one. It's not only the R&B and club people who are buying it. We're even getting people who are into rock 'n' roll asking for the record."[18] Sales were also strong in Disco Central. "It's the hottest item I have had in years in the store," noted Dave

Rothfeld of Korvette's on Thirty-fourth Street. "It looks like Joe Cayre has got a winner with this idea."[19]

That was certainly what Cheren appeared to be thinking when he rush-released Jesse Green's "Nice & Slow" on the new format. The record had begun life as a noncommissioned remix by Howard Metz, the DJ at Circus Maximus in Los Angeles, who received a promotional copy of the seven-inch and decided to reinvent and extend the three-minute-five-second vocal version and the four-minute-forty-second instrumental flip side (both of which had been mixed by Cheren). Metz sent his five-minute-forty-five-second remix to Scepter, and Cheren was sufficiently impressed to go back into the studio and use it as a guideline for a new commercial twelve-inch. "We saw how the Salsoul record was selling," says Cheren, "and decided to do the same."

By the end of June it had become clear that the "giant single" was about to consolidate its position. "A greater market impact from the new commercial 12-inch disco single is expected shortly, as a number of labels here have given the go-ahead on releasing retail versions of disks previously used for promotional purposes only," reported Billboard. "The goods will come from Roulette, CTI, Scepter, RCA-distributed Midland International and possibly Amherst."[20] Yet, with the music industry absorbed by the commercial potential of the twelve-inch, an equally seismic development passed by virtually unnoticed: the DJ was about to challenge the producer as the key player in the creation of dance music. For sure, mixers had already edged their way into the recording industry, but Gibbons was the first to get his hands dirty on the cutting-room floor, and his triumphant intervention meant that he and his comrades could now do more than tell record companies which songs were likely to make it in the clubs. "These DJs had extraordinary talent," says Cayre. "They knew firsthand from their booth what the dancers reacted to. The producers might make a good song, but they might not get the right sound or extend the best parts." Gibbons and his contemporaries knew what to do. "The DJs understood how to turn a good song into a great song. They were experts in reconstructive surgery."

* * *

White versus black, straight versus gay, male versus female, brain versus body—all of these age-old contests were finding their freshest articulation within the increasingly trenchant conflict between rock and disco.

"Death to disco shit!" raged John Holmstrom in *Punk* magazine. "Long live the rock! Kill Yourself. Jump off a fuckin' cliff. Drive nails into your head. Become a robot and join the staff at Disneyland. OD. Anything. Just don't listen to disco shit. I've seen that canned crap take real live people and turn them into dogs! And vice versa. The epitome of all that's wrong with Western civilization is disco."[21]

Sensing an easy target in the rising number of disco remakes, imitations, and gimmick records, rock critics began to round up on the new dance genre. Disco, the charge ran, subjugated harmony, melody, and vocals to its all-consuming beat and the resulting music—*if it could be called that*—was mindless, formula-ridden, mechanical, predictable, anonymous, and superficial. Having wallowed in a pit of accusation and counteraccusation for the best part of the last five years over who was to blame for rock's descent from countercultural movement to money-making depoliticized careerism, rock's ambassadors were rediscovering the sense of external struggle that had provided them with so much power in the 1960s. Whereas the earlier movement had rallied around peace and freedom, the aim of the new campaign was death to disco.

The attack was in many respects absurd. Yes, some dud disco records were being released, but this was hardly a novel experience within the history of music production. For sure, the disco formula, which finally didn't refer to much more than danceable music that contained a four-on-the-floor beat, had become more familiar and more predictable, but again this was hardly a new development within the genre-driven music industry. Absolutely, the beat and the bass were more prominent in disco than other genres, but even the most radical examples of this new aesthetic were still packed with strings, keyboards, and, often, vocals. The "mindless" break, if there was one, might last for a long thirty seconds.

Rock 'n' roll and rock had of course been attacked in precisely the same terms, but relativity reigned supreme in the partisan universe of the music business, and rock's proponents now understood their favorite genre to be serious thinking music rather than brainless body music. The fact that disco was foregrounding rhythm to such an extent that it was sidelining the key symbols of rock's authority—the lead vocalist and the lead guitarist—constituted a significant challenge, and the ideological nature of this conflict was reflected in the contrasting identities of the two constituencies. Whereas white heterosexual men dominated rock, disco was teeming with African Americans, gays, and women.

On the ground, however, the two camps couldn't always be seamlessly divided—and not just because both genres refused to slip neatly into their respective half of this binary divide. Internal loyalties were also fracturing to the extent that Vince Aletti and Michael Gomes had become, at least on the surface, as sick of disco as the *Punk* editorialist. "This Sound is everywhere," Gomes declared in *Mixmaster* in February 1976. "I even heard a Muzak version of Gloria Gaynor's hit 'Never Can Say Goodbye' in an elevator."[22] Aletti—who had described *Mixmaster* as his "favorite disco newsletter . . . the only one with both style and gossip" in December 1975—was also growing weary. "Disco, the only major pop trend to hit the music business in years, has been treated like a sell-out line on Seventh Avenue," he complained. "Cheap knock-offs—'disco versions' often just a step above elevator Muzak—are everywhere."[23] While Holmstrom was opposed to the new genre per se, however, dance music's most discerning commentators were simply frustrated at the way in which a new music had so quickly become old.

Billboard remained optimistic. "While disco may be a formula style music," argued reporter Bob Kirsch, "creative producers, arrangers, writers and artists are making quality product from that formula."[24] The subsequent release in the first half of the year of "For the Love of Money" by the Disco Dub Band, Ecstasy, Passion & Pain's "Touch and Go," "Turn the Beat Around" by Vicky Sue Robinson, Diana Ross's "Love Hangover," and "That's Where the Happy People Go" by the Trammps certainly suggested that disco still had plenty of potential to both move and surprise, and any remaining doubts about the genre's potential were apparently resolved by the release of Double Exposure's "Ten Percent."

By the summer, however, record executives, acting "for the love of money," were starting to talk of a "disco hangover" in which sales were running at "fifty percent" of their recent volume, suggesting that the future of disco was "touch and go" unless its makers managed to "turn the beat around." "I think disco has dropped in importance with regard to the record business," lamented Bob Reno, president of Midland International, which had enjoyed hits with "Doctor's Orders" and "Fly, Robin, Fly." "It's not nearly as big as it was a year ago, due either to the fact that the market has less volume or that the glut of disco material has diluted everybody's sales."[25] It was now a long two years since disco had enjoyed the double success of "Rock the Boat" and "Rock Your Baby." "That's the American way," Reno told *Billboard.* "You get a new car and two years later, no matter how nice it is, you're bored with it. Everything in this business is transitory."[26]

Record companies began to take out their frustration on the DJs. "We were *giving away* hundreds of records a week only to hear some kid say 'Yeh, it's nice' or 'I'm playing it,'" an unnamed representative told the increasingly influential *Mixmaster* in July 1976. "But when all reports were in they could be playing the record all night long and their audience still wouldn't know who the artist was, plus we weren't receiving any revenue from it. That's when we lost interest. Then you wouldn't believe their attitudes."[27] At the end of the month DJ-turned-executive David Todd added his voice to the chorus of criticism by questioning the commercial viability of every DJ's favorite new plaything, the twelve-inch single. "Beyond an occasional case of curiosity," RCA's head of disco promotions told *Billboard*, "the average consumer who can get a regular, current two-sided 45 RPM for as little as 95 cents is unlikely to shell out an extra $2 for the privilege of slighter better fidelity, and longer versions of the same song."[28] The intervention didn't quite add up to a betrayal, but the fact that Todd had effectively used his DJ sensibility to climb into his current position, only to rebuff the prevailing instincts of his old colleagues, would have hurt.

Yet, while the first six months of 1976 had yet to produce a disco track that could match the retail success of "The Hustle," the genre was nevertheless producing more top ten hits than it had two years before, and in October *Billboard* was moved to declare that disco was as significant as the Beatles-led "British invasion" of the mid-sixties. "Since late January, in fact, only five non-disco records have been able to make No. 1 on Billboard's Hot 100," noted the magazine. "The other 15 singles to hit the top of the chart in this nine-month period range from the geared-to-radio pop disco of Wings' 'Silly Love Songs' or Elton John and Kiki Dee's 'Don't Go Breaking My Heart' to the Manhattans' disco-tinged soul ballad 'Kiss and Say Goodbye' to a dozen more hits that actually drew heavy play in the nation's discos."[29]

Billboard's definition of disco might have found some opposition in America's more discriminating urban nightspots, but the word was now being bandied about without any sustained regard for its supposed point of reference, and the fact that "Disco Duck" by Rick Dees and His Cast of Idiots and "A Fifth of Beethoven" by the Walter Murphy Band were two of the more recent disco-oriented singles to reach the top of the Hot 100 demonstrated the genre's treacherously imperial potential. Here was a formulaic sound that could artlessly gobble up almost anything within its four-four pulse, from the "low" (quacking) to the "high" (the opening bars of the Fifth Symphony). What's more, disco's tendency to subject its lyrics to the all-consuming beat meant that it was tailor-made for an increasingly global economy. Made in America and displaying near-universal signs and emptied-out phrases, no translation was necessary. The international marketing potential of disco was coming into focus.

At the same time, plenty of good music hit the dance floor over the summer. *Arabian Nights* by the Ritchie Family included the celebratory "The Best Disco in Town." Tom Moulton released a mix of the steamily autobiographical "More, More, More" by the Andrea True Connection, featuring adult-movie actress Andrea True. Undisputed Truth came out with a radically improved eleven-minute-ten-second twelve-inch version of their song "You + Me = Love." And Dr. Buzzard's Original Savannah Band eponymous album, which included the hugely popular "Sour and Sweet," "Cherchez la Femme" and "I'll Play the Fool," rapidly established itself as the most important and eclectic dance release of the summer. "RCA didn't know how big a record they had on their hands," says Todd. "They were going to give it to adult contemporary until I passed it on to every DJ on the mailing list. I pointed out which cuts to focus on, and it went gold. That was when RCA really started to take the disco department seriously."

The run of strong records continued in September. "Message in Our Music" by the O'Jays included a beautifully contrived break that began with sharp handclaps and moved into a more contemplative mode before building to a rousing crescendo. The infectiously sweet yet ultimately pessimistic "Goin' Up in Smoke" by Eddie Kendricks, recorded with Norman Harris, constituted one of the Motown vocalist's most exciting releases since "Girl You Need a Change of Mind." The second Salsoul Orchestra album, *Nice 'n' Naasty*, confirmed Vince Montana's position as one of the most versatile and inventive disco producers of the period. Walter Gibbons's twelve-inch mix of the LP's title track, in which the DJ seized a fleeting percussive break that appeared at the top of the album version and looped it into a tenacious thirty-second workout, became a treasured mini-replica of the DJ's mixing technique. And this was backed with a revamp of another cut from *Nice 'n' Naasty*, "Salsoul 2001," now renamed "Salsoul 3001," which opened with jet engines, bird calls, congas, and timbales before soaring into a powerful combination of orchestral re-frains and sound effects that were played out against a backdrop of relent-less Latin rhythms. "This has got to be one of the year's most extraordi-nary products and although it may be too overwhelming and bizarre for some clubs, others, like New York's Loft, turn to pandemonium when the record comes on," commented Aletti. "Experiment with it if you haven't already."[30]

Combined with the simultaneous release of Stevie Wonder's epic *Songs in the Key of Life* and Donna Summer's concept-driven *Four Seasons of Love*, the effect of these records was enough to persuade *Billboard*—which was busy gearing up for its second forum and needed a positive head-line—that disco had rapidly learned how to preserve its integrity while simultaneously retaining its commercial appeal. "Disco music, which in two short years has revolutionized the entertainment styles of a vast cross-section of America, is undergoing subtle but distinct changes in lyric and rhythm content," wrote Radcliffe Joe. "Record labels, their producers and artists, stung by recurring criticisms that original disco music forms with emphasis on basic rhythms and marginal lyric content were mindless and insulting to the intelligence of audiences, are banding themselves together to mesh sophistication with sound in their pursuit of a new and more widely acceptable disco beat."[31] Tom Moulton added his authorita-tive voice to the argument. "Rhythm patterns are changing," he noted. "The disco record is no longer all rhythms and a bunch of drums."[32] Joe Cayre of Salsoul Records agreed. "A label, producer or artist short-sighted enough to depend exclusively on a beat for success is doomed to failure. There are a number of important elements that must mesh. They are lyric, melody and production, and all must be great. The consumer is de-manding greater intelligence in disco records and we have a responsibility to give it to them."[33]

Sensuous, earthy rhythms still provided the foundation for a suc-cessful club record, however, and Moulton's mixes of "My Love Is Free" by Double Exposure, "Don't Leave Me This Way" by Thelma Houston, and "Disco Inferno" by the Trammps extended the run of made-for-disco records that managed to combine powerful vocals with cleverly constructed rhythm tracks. "I watched and felt the tension of people's bodies waiting for the next record and saw how their bodies reacted to changes and break on the records," Moulton explained. "People react to cymbals like an electric shock. When you bring them down by just playing a drum or a conga, it's like hanging them over a cliff. Then, with the tension of instruments, you take them up the mountain and into a landslide until they're free-floating and safe again. People don't realize it but they love it."[34]

Moulton's mixes handed Aletti additional ammunition with which to round off the year in a confident mood. "Remember, it wasn't until 1974, with the success of 'Love's Theme,' 'Rock Your Baby' and 'Rock the Boat,' that the music business began to acknowledge the existence of disco music as a style and a force," argued the *Record World* columnist. "The popular question then—'Disco is just a fad, isn't it?'—has been replaced with the slightly more enlightened, 'How much longer do you think this thing will last?'" Aletti maintained that the sound was here to stay, if only because it couldn't afford to die. "But the fact that disco music has developed its own prosperous, self-sustaining market wouldn't matter much if the music itself hadn't grown and prospered artistically as well. And disco music did more than survive its own success in 1976. It had one of its most creative years."[35]

Vince Aletti

Top Twenty-five Disco Records of 1976, Record World, 25 December 1976

1. Dr. Buzzard's Original Savannah Band, *Dr. Buzzard's Original Savannah Band*
2. Double Exposure, "Ten Percent"
3. The Trammps, *Where the Happy People Go*
4. Donna Summer, *Four Seasons of Love* and *A Love Trilogy*
5. Vicki Sue Robinson, "Turn the Beat Around"
6. Diana Ross, "Love Hangover"
7. The Ritchie Family, *Arabian Nights*
8. The Salsoul Orchestra. *Nice 'n' Naasty*
9. Brass Construction, *Brass Construction*
10. Lou Rawls, "You'll Never Find Another Love Like Mine"
11. Undisputed Truth "You + Me = Love"
12. Tavares, "Heaven Must Be Missing an Angel" and "Don't Take Away the Music"
13. The Originals, "Down to Love Town"
14. Roberta Kelly, "Trouble Maker"

15. The Emotions, "I Don't Wanna Lose Your Love"

16. D. C. LaRue, "Cathedrals"

17. The Bee Gees, "You Should Be Dancing"

18. Stevie Wonder, "Another Star"/ "I Wish"/ "Sir Duke"

19. Ralph MacDonald, "Calypso Breakdown"

20. Candi Staton, "Young Hearts Run Free"/ "Run to Me"

21. Carol Douglas, "Midnight Love Affair"

22. El Coco, "Let's Get It Together"

23. Thelma Houston, "Don't Leave Me This Way"

24. Love Unlimited Orchestra, "My Sweet Summer Suite"

25. Andrea True Connection, "More, More, More"

Aletti added that disco was selling a surprising number of albums, although singles were deemed to be suffering—the columnist's list of "essential disco singles" was reduced from seventy-five at the end of 1975 to a mere thirty in the current roundup. Their cause hadn't been helped by the commercial launch of the twelve-inch. "The impact on the marketplace hasn't been sufficiently assessed, but disco discs, being the first new record format in years, are being packaged and sold with more creativity and verve than singles and, at least in big disco cities like New York, Boston and San Francisco, are demanding and getting the kind of open display space singles rarely have."[36] There was still hope that civilization would back disco—as long as the math worked.

* * *

Every profession has its hierarchies, and DJing, which was barely seen as a profession at all, was no exception. Women occupied the lowest rung on this denigrated ladder, and, while spin sisters such as Bert Lockett circled around the club and bar scene, it wasn't until 1976 that the Sahara opened as Manhattan's first full-fledged lesbian discotheque and Sharon White, the club's resident, became the first recognizable female DJ of the disco era. "Sharon White played high tempo music for gay girls, but generally it was very difficult for a girl to break through," comments night owl Freddy Taylor. "The club owners wouldn't take a girl seriously, and there was also a lot of chauvinism amongst the male DJs."

The second-lowest rung on the ladder was occupied by the mobiles, a disparate group of DJ vagabonds who had to supply their own equipment, endure regular bouts of backache, and suffer the social humiliation of operating outside the already-frowned-on discotheque circuit. Yet being low was also one of the best places from which to *get down*, and mobiles such as Big John Ashby, Grandmaster Flowers, Bert Lockett, Ras Maboya, and Ronald Plummer personified an open-mindedness that came from the experience of playing to a wide variety of audiences. Bar mitzvahs, gay haunts, singles bars, sweet sixteens, weddings, you name it, the mobile DJ would show up and select the appropriate music. "I understand permanence, and that's why I want to be mobile," Maboya told *Discothekin'* in June 1976. "I could never be a house d.j. Moving around keeps me up with the styles. I can't get stale that way." The maverick mobiles also maintained a healthy distance from club managers. "A house jock is confined," Big John told *Discothekin'*. "He has to deliver the same thing night after night. It's too hard to be creative. A club owner has a formula that makes his place a success. He doesn't want any variety. Being mobile, I don't have to worry about that."[37]

Mobiles faced a different constraint—they had to sell liquor. "If you were a mobile DJ then you couldn't just make them dance," says Michael Gomes. "If they were all on the floor then they weren't at the bar." That, though, didn't worry Lockett. "I would say, 'If you don't want to buy yourself a drink buy me one! I want one with a green bottle and a straw!' The owners loved me." So did her dancers. "In a club you had to keep on mixing, and to me it sounded like the same damn record all night. With a club DJ you almost knew what he was going to do—he would take you up and then he would slowly bring you down—but I never wanted the crowd to know what I was going to do next. I liked to just change the whole thing—boom! I liked to just *flatten them*!" Gomes watched on, admiringly. "Bert would mix it up, and she used to talk over records. It wasn't this beat-on-beat seamless mix. She just threw on anything that she thought would work."

New York's muscle-bound mobiles got most of their work in the boroughs, where they provided a cheap and flexible alternative for bar, pizzeria, and restaurant owners who were reluctant to invest in a permanent sound system. However, as disco took off in the suburbs, and proprietors found themselves opening their makeshift nightclubs more and more regularly, it began to make good financial sense to invest in a cheap audio system, and the emerging suburban discotheque scene became an official story in July 1976 when *New York* magazine published an article by Nik Cohn titled "The Rituals of the New Saturday Night." Keen to introduce an ethnographic angle, Cohn had enlisted a black Hustle virtuoso to take him on a tour of the hottest suburban nightspots, and the highlight turned out to be 2001 Odyssey, a cabaret-turned-discotheque in Bay Ridge, Brooklyn, which attracted a crowd of up to 750 Italian Americans on a weekend night. Cohn's eyewitness account centered on Vincent, an eighteen-year-old Al Pacino look-alike who escaped the tedium of his job in a local hardware store by heading down to 2001 Odyssey. "All day, every day he stood behind a counter and grinned," wrote Cohn, who later confessed that Vincent was a fictional composite character. "He climbed up and down ladders, he made the coffee, he obeyed. Then came the weekend and he was cut loose."[38]

Vincent's gang, the Faces, combined mock mafia with teenage rebellion. "To qualify as an Odyssey Face, an aspirant need only be Italian, between the ages of eighteen and twenty-one, with a minimum stock of six floral shirts, four pairs of tight trousers, two pairs of Gucci-style loafers, two pairs of platforms, either a pendant or a ring, and one item in gold," wrote Cohn. "In addition, he must know how to dance, how to drive, how to handle himself in a fight. He must have respect, even reverence, for Facehood, and contempt for everything else. He must also be fluent in obscenity, offhand in sex. Most important of all, he must play tough."[39] Once inside 2001 Odyssey, Vincent and his macho cohorts would lounge around and intimidate anyone who threatened their territory before marching across the dance floor in a militaristic version of the Bus Stop with a flock of supposedly helpless women in tow. "In general, the female function was simply to be available. To decorate the doorways and booths, to fill up the dance floor. Speak when spoken to, put out as required, and then go away. In short, to obey, and not to fuss."[40] Far from representing, as its name suggested, a journey into the liberated future, 2001 Odyssey embodied—at least according to Cohn—a return journey to the gender hierarchies of the past.

While Cohn's Vincent didn't venture into Manhattan, plenty of his Italian American peers did, and their outlook suggested that the journalist's antihero wasn't wholly representative of suburban sexuality. Take the significantly less clichéd Le Jardin regular Tony Pagano, from Dongan Hills, Staten Island, who was interviewed by Ed McCormack for *Dancing Madness* in 1976. "What my old man doesn't understand is that you don't have to be a fag to be into this scene," Pagano told McCormack. "My old man doesn't understand that dancing is not a tight-assed, up-tight sex role scene. It's just a way of communicating with people you might not have anything to say to if you sat down to talk. It doesn't mean you want to fuck a broad or a guy if you dance with them. You're just doing what comes natural."[41] Then there was the self-described "fag hag" Hollywood DiRusso, who had arrived from Texas and hardly cor-responded to Cohn's speak-when-spoken-to caricature. "Every Eyetalian princess who goes dancing as much as I do—we all see ourselves as the Disco Queen—we're all out there to be noticed, to be . . . discovered! I'm such a severe case that I'm about to take a second job as a cigarette girl at Twelve West." What, asked McCormack, were the drawbacks to being a Disco Queen? "One of the problems is that you have to master the art of looking bored," replied DiRusso. "And that's pretty hard to do when you're really dancing and it's just building and building like an unend-ing multiple orgasm."[42] DiRusso and Pagano might have been no more representative than Vincent, but they did suggest that there was nothing inevitable about the "suburban mindset."

There was also nothing inevitable about the kind of clubs that sub-urbanites preferred to go to, and proof of this was demonstrated by their evacuation of Le Jardin in favor of Infinity. The shift in power became a media subplot when the *Wall Street Journal*, which wasn't exactly known for its coverage of nightworld, ran a front-page feature on the rise of the discotheque industry at the beginning of May 1976. Once again Bobby Guttadaro provided the DJ quotes and color, only now he was playing for Maurice Brahms and not John Addison. "As the throbbing bass tones of 'La Vita' fill the cavernous Infinity discotheque, Bobby DJ looks down from his disc-jockey booth upon a swarm of a thousand dancers," reported the newspaper. "Some are flawlessly executing the fancy steps of the Hustle or the Latin Hustle. Others are spinning, twisting, and jumping mind-lessly under the glare of flashing neon lights. 'Now I'm going to hit them with "There's No Business Like Show Business," ' Bobby DJ screams above the roar. 'This is really going to freak them out!' "[43]

Infinity's ascendancy had a good deal to do with arrival of social starlet Carmen D'Alessio. Born in Lima, D'Alessio had traveled to Manhattan in 1965 and, fluent in several languages, got a job working for the United Nations. Seymour was a friend, and so she naturally went to dance at the Sanctuary, but it was the Loft that really caught her imagination. "I was a regular at the Loft. It was very, very, very cool. It was a great, great party, and I really enjoyed the music. It was completely different from everything else. The music had such a great beat, and the fact that they served food meant that you could hang around all night long." D'Alessio subsequently worked for Yves St. Laurent and then Valentino before she became the Italian designer's Rome-based PR chief. "That's when I came into contact with the international crowd and became part of this glamorous group," she says. In 1975, D'Alessio returned to New York, and the following year she promoted her first party at a club called Tropicalia on Second Avenue, which was owned by a Brazilian friend. "I was very well connected with the South American group, and they asked me to promote the venue because they saw me running around with the so-called jet set." Having read about D'Alessio in the social newspapers, Brahms made his move. "He visited the club and saw the type of crowd I was attracting. He stole me away by offering me double the money I was making at Tropicalia. I did the bicentennial party at Infinity in 1976, which went very well, and I also did Carmen's Carnival. The club was so successful we made the front page of the *Wall Street Journal*."

John Addison and Maurice Brahms didn't fall out over their contrasting fortunes but instead decided to forge an alliance with steak restaurateur Steve Rubell and lawyer Ian Schrager, who had started to hang out at Hippopotamus, Le Jardin, and then Infinity. The contrasting duo—Rubell was effervescent and short, Schrager serious and tall—convinced Brahms and then Addison to enter into a partnership. They decided to open five clubs, starting with one in Boston, a second in Queens, and a third in Washington D.C. The Boston venture was in an old rock venue at 15 Lansdowne Street, which became the name of the new nightspot, and the Queens club, called Enchanted Garden, was in a house next to the Douglaston golf course. Rubell and Schrager gleaned what they needed to glean about setting up a nightclub before the alliance collapsed. Addison took 15 Lansdowne, Rubell and Schrager acquired the yet-to-open Enchanted Garden, and Brahms dropped out of the equation altogether, although an Infinity connection was maintained when Rubell and Schrager, having attended Carmen's Carnival at Infinity, attempted to persuade D'Alessio to work for them on a part-time basis. "I was dancing on top of the shoulders of Sterling St. Jacques when Steve Rubell and Ian Schrager saw me for the first time," says D'Alessio. "That was the moment when they realized that I was responsible for this successful party."

Rubell and Schrager decided to try and employ D'Alessio to promote the Enchanted Garden. "They started calling me and pursuing me," she remembers, "but I didn't want to get involved with anything that was not in New York." Eventually the duo managed to meet D'Alessio over coffee with a mutual friend (the sculptor Ron Ferry, who had installed some of his work in the Queens club) and they managed to persuade her to go out for dinner. "They wined and dined me and my husband. We drank a lot and then they said they wanted to give us a tour of the Enchanted Garden. I said, 'OK, why not?'" D'Alessio was impressed by the space but continued to resist the lure of Queens. "I said there was no way that I could get involved because I wouldn't take my crowd all the way to Queens, plus I didn't know any press out there. I said the only thing I could do was suggest some themes for parties that they could develop with their own crowd. I quoted a very large amount of money thinking that they were going to turn me down, but they didn't. I went ahead and suggested the theme of the first event, which was 1001 Nights, and I told them they should bring in elephants, camels and tents, and that all the men should dress up as sultans. Those parties made the place famous."

D'Alessio's impact was immediate. When *Newsweek* ran a front-page story on "The Disco Whirl" at the beginning of November 1976, reporter Maureen Orth didn't begin her report by focusing on the recently convened *Billboard* Disco Forum II, which opened on 29 September and attracted more than seven hundred participants. Nor did she focus on the names that were driving the disco phenomenon. Instead she opened with a scene from D'Alessio's "Island of Paradise" night at the Enchanted Garden, which included hula girls, palm trees, a seventy-pound roasted pig, a fire dancer, and plenty of bathroom gossip. "In the ladies' room, 21-year-old Yolanda Cimino, a book-keeper, and her girlfriend, a typist, are using one of the seven blow driers and hairbrushes thoughtfully provided by the management," wrote Orth. "The girls come to the Enchanted Garden two or three times a week, but neither one has ever met a boy she has dated for any period of time. 'What I like about dancing here is that you don't have to talk to the guy,' says Yolanda, who spent three hours getting dressed for the evening." The action in the men's room was equally intriguing. "Johnny Boy Musto, 18, an attendant at Shea Stadium, and his buddy, Ray Muccio, a packer for a hamburger franchise, are blow-drying their hair after spending an hour and a half on their toilette at home. Johnny Boy is wearing a black body shirt, half-unbuttoned, several gold chains around his neck and tight-fitting beige pants. 'It's very important you don't wear the same thing for at least four weeks,' he says, earnestly checking himself in the mirror one last time."[44]

The Enchanted Garden, according to *Newsweek*, was part of the "new disco-mania": discotheques had become "one of the biggest entertainment phenomena of the '70s" thanks to their ability to attract "the Beautiful People, the bourgeoisie and the blue-collar worker alike," and numbers had surged from 1,500 two years ago to a current total of ten thousand. Yet despite the upbeat nature of the magazine's survey, there was also a lingering sense of unease. "There is a whiff of scary futurism in the current craze," noted Orth. "Discos have popularized totally programmed environments—and the result is canned sensuality. A contemporary disco is not only a place to let go, to be seen and to watch, it is also an environment where technology throws a cloak of nonthreatening anonymity over insecurities and hangups." While sex was everywhere implied, she added, discos were often curiously asexual. "There is no stigma attached to girls dancing with girls or boys with boys—and no compulsion to find a mate. For some, discos are an Antonioni film on noncommunication come to life. For others, they are a harbinger of the Somazonked masses of 1984."[45]

For others still, however, they provided an environment in which alternative sexual and bodily identities could be explored. Orth's "Somazonked masses" were *trance*-sexuals who, having submerged themselves in the destabilizing sound-light-space environment of the nightclub, tripped out for hours at a time, slipping into a state of semi-forgetting that did not simply represent an act of political abandonment but also provided a potential platform for experimentation. Women dumping their gender-determined preference for conversation? Fine. Men going into the bathroom in couples and spending more time on their hair than the women? OK. Women and men choosing the primeval tremors, vibrations, and pulsations of the collective dance above getting it on? Makes a change. Men and women dancing in same-sex couples? No problem. A denaturalized sexual environment? Perfect. Throw a "cloak of nonthreatening anonymity" over someone and shock, horror, look what happens. S/he starts to behave differently.

* * *

Back in the Village, the owners of 12 West were discovering that they were having their own problems maintaining the "cloak of nonthreatening anonymity" that was so important to gay men who were in the club but not quite out of the closet. "We couldn't stay open too early because we had light coming through skylights," says owner Alan Harris. "People would also begin to look very *gray* at eight in the morning." Consequently the club started to close its doors at five, with Tom Savarese winding up an hour later. "Tom would stop promptly at six o' clock and go into a set of encores that would begin to bring the crowd down. That was when the sound of sleaze started to come into play. People just hung over one another, and then they would put on their sunglasses, stroll out of the club, and go for breakfast or additional acts."

Savarese, however, wasn't happy. He told *Billboard* at the beginning of 1976 that he had reached his goal of becoming "the biggest and the best DJ around," yet he found himself playing at a club that had developed a reputation of being, in contrast to Flamingo, an ugly duckling.[46] Savarese responded by landing himself a summer spot at the Sandpiper, which was playing catch-up with a resuscitated Ice Palace that had doubled its numbers following a major renovation and the introduction of a hot young mixer called Roy Thode. "We had been mainly playing tapes by Tom Moulton," remembers Robbie Leslie, who worked as a waiter/bartender in the Pines restaurant-discotheque. "Then in 1976 we started to have DJs like Tom Savarese, Larry Saunders, and Ricky Ybarra playing every weekend." Savarese attempted to negotiate a more flexible arrangement with 12 West but failed. "Tom gave us an ultimatum," says Harris. "He wanted us to hire him for alternate Saturday nights because he had been offered the opportunity to play at the Sandpiper, and he wanted exposure to that crowd. We pretty much knew that that was the end of Tom's tenure with us." Harris didn't battle to hold onto the DJ. "Tom Savarese was a fabulous technician, but he was too dark for our crowd. When the crowd wanted some level of sweetness his style didn't work."

Savarese was made New York DJ of the year by *Billboard* at the second Disco Forum, and toward the end of October he gave an interview to the magazine that solidified his reputation for being an ambitious business operator. DJs, Savarese declared, had to begin to understand that they were as integral as recording artists to the success of the discotheque industry. "The problem is that too many of them are star-struck," he told Radcliffe Joe. "They see their gig only as a springboard to free drugs or popularity with women; and club owners, aware of this lack of profession-alism, are taking advantage of the jocks." Savarese made it clear that he had no intention of relinquishing his $200-to-$250-a-night fee and wound up the interview by declaring that professional DJs were so integral to a club's operation that, should they move on, the venue in question would undergo "an environmental shock" and a subsequent loss of patronage.[47]

That, though, was hardly the experience at 12 West, which thrived in the wake of Savarese's departure thanks to the arrival of Jimmy Stuard (who had been named Boston DJ of the year at the Disco Forum for his work at 1270). Stuard debuted on Memorial Day weekend, was invited to return for the Bicentennial party, and replaced Savarese within a fort-night. "Jimmy was the most wonderful human being in the world," says Harris. "He wasn't a handsome man. He was just a beautiful man inter-nally, and this gave him an external glow. He was my best friend for a year." Stuard was also an impressive DJ. "It was pure blending and great overlays. He also did lots of echoing and phasing, which was in vogue at the time." Like all good DJs, he also knew how to carry a crowd. "He would play to a peak around three and then bring it down at about three thirty. He would do another peak at about four thirty, and then he would get into a lot of the late-night pleasers. He would end with a production number, which would have overlays from old movies and current films, at around seven in the morning." Fellow Bostonians were thrilled at their incursion into Manhattan. "Jimmy had amazing control of the room," says Joey Car-vello of Yesterdays and the Mirage. "He turned music into a five-act play. When he played it seemed like the records lasted for two to three years."

Jimmy Stuard

Select Discography (12 West) [Source: Record World, *20 November 1976]*

Double Exposure, "My Love Is Free"

Carol Douglas, "Midnight Love Affair"

The Emotions "I Don't Wanna Lose Your Love"

Ralph MacDonald, "Calypso Breakdown"

Van McCoy, "Soul Cha Cha"/ "Rhythms of the World"/ "Indian Warpath"

The Salsoul Orchestra, "It's Good for the Soul"/ "Standing and Waiting on Love"/
 "Ritzy Mambo"/ "Nice 'n' Naasty"

Donna Summer, "Spring Affair"/ "Summer Fever"/ "Autumn Changes"

The Supremes, "Love I Never Knew You Could Feel So Good"/ "Let Yourself Go"/
"You're My Driving Wheel"
Undisputed Truth, "You + Me = Love"
Stevie Wonder, "Another Star"

That was certainly the impression Stuard created when he played an unofficial remix of "Disco Inferno," which had been originally recorded as a four-minute-twenty-second production. "My first mix of 'Disco Inferno' lasted for nineteen minutes, and 12 West was the only place that it ever got played," says Tom Moulton. "I gave an acetate to Jimmy, and he used it at a special party. I never turned it over to Atlantic because I knew they would have had a fit. In the end I cut it down to ten fifty-four." Moulton always knew that he would give the mix to Stuard. "Jimmy and I were really good friends. Jimmy really cared about music, and that was the reason I like him so much. He was the first person I gave my mixes to. I always had a lot of respect for him as a DJ, and I always respected his opinions."

Mancuso, meanwhile, was battling to claw his way up from a six-year low, for while the Loft had reopened in November 1975, dance floor regulars weren't instantaneously enamored with the new setup, and by the third week numbers had fallen dramatically. Mancuso reduced the admission charge from $6.99 to $4.99—the .99 was introduced when the parties moved to 99 Prince Street—and his crowd initially edged back, but the revival proved to be transitory; business soon ebbed away again. The problem was simple: Prince Street wasn't Broadway. At least twice the size of its low-ceilinged, cozy predecessor, the new ten-thousand-square-foot party space was spread over two floors, with the downstairs lounge alone covering more square feet than the original Loft, all of which signaled larger crowds, less intimacy, and greater visibility. "I didn't want a big place, but the rent at the beginning wasn't too bad," says Mancuso. "I moved in because I wanted to continue these parties." Something, though, was missing. "When the Loft on Prince Street opened it was a little cold," says Nicky Siano. "It didn't have the warmth of a house party." Nor was the sound quite right. "The sound system at the Broadway Loft was so far advanced nobody else caught up for five or six years," adds Siano. "The room was so small and the sound was so close it felt like you were *inside* the music. But that impression was much harder to replicate at Prince Street. The sound didn't really work for a while."

The whole operation came under serious threat when the rent bill shot up from $1,800 a month to $6,000 a month, although that didn't stop Mancuso from investing $250,000 in a new sound system. On one level the work had to be done: the larger space required more equipment. Yet, while the eighteen speakers didn't come for free, the real drain had little to do with quantity and everything to do with quality, with the Loft guru determined to take his setup to new levels of flawlessness. "When I first moved into Prince I continued to buy my equipment from Alex, but after a while I started to move in a different direction," he says. "A friend called Harry Muntz made me aware of real sound—he played me reel-to-reel at his house and it blew me away—and after that I only wanted to buy class A equipment." Alex Rosner couldn't supply Mancuso with such high-end merchandise, and so he started to shop at Lyric Hi-Fi. "I started buying really esoteric stuff and spent a lot of money. I was the only one that went out there and spent the *max* on the best possible sound so that there was no question about the quality. I went from A to Z with Lyric, from altering the position of the speakers to changing the turntables, the amplifier, and the wiring. The very last thing was the cartridge."

The repositioning of the speakers created stereo throughout the whole room. "It was like being in a concert hall," says Mancuso. "It didn't matter if you were sitting in the orchestra section or in the last row—you still got stereo." The "wall of sound" revolved around a network of intricately calculated digital delays in which the speakers that ran along the main wall went off fractionally ahead of the other speakers. "I was already on the right path at Broadway," notes Mancuso. "I bought two Klipsch La Scala speakers at the end of my time there and positioned them in the middle of the wall in order to fill the center of the room. I didn't know about time delays, but the layout was the same." The effect was groundbreaking. The new setup made it seem as though the sound was coming from a single point of origin, even though speakers still surrounded the dance floor. "By this time the traditional club sound had been bastardized in so many different ways that when David introduced the wall of sound it came across as a really fabulous thing," says Siano. "It was so fresh and new."

Mancuso also switched from a Philips to a Thorens to a Mitch Cotter turntable, and simultaneously deployed a state-of-the-art Technics di-

rect drive and a Fidelity Research arm. Assembled in the Prince Street Loft by Cotter himself, the system was stretched to its limit when Mancuso played Tchaikovsky's *1812 Overture*, real cannon and all. "They warn you on the label that the record is unlikely to play without jumping because the grooves are so intense. It'll break windows, glasses, everything." When the new configuration successfully played the virtually unplayable, an elated Mancuso phoned his friend and fellow boffin Richard Long. "He said he didn't believe me. He came over, I turned it up, and he was amazed."

The quest for sonic perfection continued with the purchase of a Mark Levinson amp and pre-amp. A musician and an electronics wizard, Levinson had wanted to build an amp and a pre-amp that would enable him to hear every nuance of his own recordings, and the irrepressible quality of his creation meant that friends soon started to request their own models. Before long a hobby turned into a small business. "You couldn't purchase Levinson from anybody but Lyric," says Mancuso. "I was delighted to buy the equipment. Mark is the Walt Disney of audio. I later found out that he had his own amp on Klipschorn speakers."

Mancuso's cartridges also faced a rigorous examination—and were discarded in favor of a Koetsus, which cost three thousand dollars apiece. Artist, musician, swordsman, calligrapher, and hi-fi enthusiast Yosiaki Sugano had designed the state-of-the-art cartridge, which he named after his hero, the celebrated seventeenth-century Japanese artist Honami Koetsu. "You could hear the difference immediately, especially with high quality recordings, so the Koetsus were really worth it," says Mancuso. No profit-conscious party entrepreneur would have given a moment's thought to shelling out so much money for such a vulnerable piece of equipment, but for Mancuso the combination of pure sound and skilled artisanship was irresistible. "Yosiaki Sugano didn't go from the sword to the ploughshare. He went from the sword to the stylus."

Mancuso, however, didn't just buy equipment: he also designed it. "I wanted to create a mixer that was clean and flat with no treble controls and no interference," he says. "There was nothing out there on the market that met these specifications so I decided to design one myself." Work began at Broadway, and Muntz—who acoustically treated the whole of

---

opposite: David Mancuso outside the Prince Street Loft. Courtesy of Steve D'Acquisto

the Prince Street Loft—was employed as an engineer. When Muntz asked Mancuso whether he wanted slides or knobs for the controls the party practitioner chose the latter. "Slides just go up and down whereas knobs are like a dance. I went for the dance." Long was subsequently employed to assemble the piece of equipment. "That's what Richard was good at— building things. He wasn't inventive, but he was incredibly good at building things. I had Harry oversee it to make sure I got what I wanted. Harry was the brain behind Richard." The final product was perfect. "There was no coloration and it sounded better than the Bozak. After that, Richard started to build and manufacture his own mixers, although his version was a step or two down because my design was too high end and too expensive for the average club."

The Loft was not an average club—indeed it wasn't a club at all—and Mancuso was not an average host. In an earlier life he had rid himself of material possessions in an attempt to tap into his inner soul. Now, in his second incarnation as a musical host, he began to dismantle his sound system, only retaining the equipment that contributed to the quest for transparency. "I started to take apart my sound system and removed the components I didn't need. I went slowly because this was a big transition." The rationale was compelling. "The more components you have the more you hurt the original sound, so the system should contain the least amount of electronics possible. You want the music in your brain and in your heart. The purer the sound, the more you will remember it." The tweeter arrays and the sub-woofers, deemed redundant because of the quality of the Klipschorns, were the first items to go. "I had the tweeters installed to put highs into records that were too muddy but they turned into a monster. In the beginning I used them for coloration, but then I started getting carried away. I had an on-off switch for the subwoofers and an on-off switch for the tweeters, and when a record like 'Girl You Need a Change of Mind' reached its climax I would throw on the two switches to create a crescendo. It was done out of ignorance. I wasn't aware of Class A sound, where the sound is more open and everything comes out." Countless other bits of superfluous electronic gadgetry, including the two monitors that helped Mancuso blend, were also disassembled. "I gave up the speakers and made the blend in the 'air.' The quality of the sound was more important than the precision of the blend."

As the sound system evolved, Mancuso began to play different kinds of records. "More and more songs presented themselves to be played. The more that the sound system allows music to be heard, the more music will present itself." The main shift occurred at the beginning of the party, where the host brought in a new layer of early, pre-intro records, which he defined as the "prelude." "The prelude was softer and more delicate than the intro. I would start with a note, and then there would be a couple more notes and then a couple more. It was very important to me that the start was very soft, very gentle." Mancuso was drawn to records that contained a single instrument and were relatively simple. "It would be something like Sandy Bull, who plays the sixteen-string guitar, or Japanese Koto music. The *Nutcracker* was a really long prelude record. I also played Ravi Shankar, Vivaldi, Pink Floyd, Morgana King. It was like a feather floating in the air."

David Mancuso

Select Discography (Loft 1975–76)

Archie Bell & the Drells, "Let's Groove"

The Blackbyrds, "Happy Music"

The Blackbyrds, "Walking in Rhythm"

Double Exposure, "My Love Is Free"

Johnny Hammond, "Los Conquistadores Chocolatés"

Juggy Murray Jones, "Inside America"

The Main Ingredient, "Happiness Is Just around the Bend"

Chuck Mangione with the Hamilton Philharmonic Orchestra, "Land of Make Believe"

Harold Melvin & the Blue Notes, "Wake Up Everybody"

MFSB, "Love Is the Message"

The O'Jays, "Message in Our Music"

Ozo, "Anambra"

Resonance, "Yellow Train"

Demis Roussos, "L.O.V.E. Got a Hold of Me"

Lonnie Liston Smith, "Expansions"

Miroslav Vitous, "New York City"

As the prelude took shape, the intro developed a sharper focus, and the perfect record for this part of the evening materialized when a friend handed Mancuso a copy of "Land of Make Believe" by Chuck Mangione with the Hamilton Philharmonic Orchestra. Featuring Esther Satterfield on vocals, the twelve-minute jazz-inflected epic tapped into an ethereal, artsy sensibility and conjured up an excursion into the unknown—a metaphor for the journey that was about to begin. "I thought 'Land of Make Believe' was a description of the Loft, except that in the Loft your dreams would come true. Everything about the song is absolutely gorgeous. It's up there with 'Love Is the Message.'" Around the same time, Mancuso also stumbled into an ideal reentry record, "Anambra" by Ozo, which worked so well it could have been made for the Loft and almost certainly couldn't be heard in any other dance venue. "If I played it then it was always as the last record. It was very spiritual, very moving. It was like a Buddhist chant. You had to have a really good situation to play it."

Mancuso's revival didn't encroach on the Gallery, where Siano's torch was burning as fiercely as ever. "I remember when David reopened on Prince Street people said he would get a big crowd but it didn't seem to affect us," says the DJ. "We both survived together." As the Gallery went from strength to strength, Siano's performances became more assured and more expressive. "At the end of the evening he would sit down, take off his shoes and socks, and start to mix with his toes," says *Mixmaster* scribe Michael Gomes. "As Nietzsche said, 'Light feet are a sign of genius.' Everybody loved Nicky. Nicky was the first DJ star." Mixers made a point of hearing him. "Lots of DJs used to come to the Gallery at three or four in the morning once they had finished playing," says Robin Lord. "It was a real focal point."

Invitations started to flow in. One call came from Florida: would Siano play the opening night of a new discotheque called Tangerine? The DJ agreed and, carrying an entourage of ten friends, trashed the hotel room for good measure. Another request came from John Whyte at the Boatel: would Siano play for the summer 1975 season? Siano said yes and bonded with the Fire Island crowd until he was dismissed. "One weekend I took Rique and Larry and they fired me. Too many blacks." Yet another invitation came from Steve Rubell: would he be interested in playing at the Enchanted Garden? "Billy Smith introduced us," says Siano. "Stevie was like, 'Oh, oh, I've heard so much about you! Maybe you should play records here!' I was like, 'Huh?' He said, 'Oh, would you, would you?'" Siano agreed to play Tuesday nights in exchange for a weekly fee of $125 plus a limousine to and from the club.

The following Saturday, Rubell went to the Gallery for the first time. "I remember him just staring up at the lights," says Siano. "For a while he would come every single week. He really loved the club." Rubell also had a thing for Siano, even though he had arrived at the SoHo venue with his fiancée. "He sat under my booth. I asked him what was going on, and he just touched me. Then I kissed him on the mouth, and we went home together. I have to say I was responsible for bringing Stevie out of the closet. He was certainly getting married before I met him." However, sex with Stevie failed to persuade Siano to stay at the Enchanted Garden. "After about a year I told Ian, 'I'm really not into this anymore. It's an hour to get here, and it's an hour to go home. I feel like I spend my life in taxicabs. If you ever open a club in the city, call me.'"

If Siano was becoming a bit of a diva, it was because he could afford the costumes. On 4 July 1976 he dressed up as Miss Libby and paraded around in a big crown and draping robes while the Gallery's Declaration of Independence was read out ("We the people of the Gallery . . ."). After a short ceremony, which included the unfurling of Mrs. Siano's home-made Gallery flag, the lights were switched off, and Miss Libby's crown lit up. "My friend Monica was stoned on acid, and she started screaming, 'They're electrocuting him! They're electrocuting him!'" says Siano. "We had to drag her off the dance floor because she was ruining my act." Other impersonations ensued over the coming months. Judy Garland looked exquisite in her $750 outfit, Barbra Streisand's fake putty nose disintegrated in mid-song, and Diana Ross stole the show away from Grace Jones.

Jones had just come out with her first singles, "That's the Trouble" and "Sorry," both of which were produced by Tom Moulton and released on Beam Junction in 1976. "Michael Gomes was good friends with her promoters, Sy and Eileen Berlin and then John Carmen," says Siano. "John Carmen said he wanted me to meet this singer, and I finally said 'OK.' We went to meet her at Sy and Eileen's place, and after a couple of minutes she walked into the room wearing this headdress. We sat there, and they put on 'That's the Trouble' and 'Sorry' and she sang to me. I was bazooted out of my mind and was very entranced by her because she was so exotic. I said, 'You have to come to Gallery Saturday night and do this!' She hadn't appeared in New York, and I guess she saw it as a great opportunity." Jones debuted at the Gallery's Halloween party. "She got on

Nicky Siano as Miss Libby. Courtesy of Nicky Siano

the stage with a chair, which she used as a prop, and she did 'Sorry' and 'That's the Trouble.' People were receptive to Grace, but they didn't go out of their minds because nobody knew who she was. After she finished, I dressed up as Diana Ross, and they went crazy. Afterwards Grace came up to me and said, 'Darling, I didn't know you did things like that!'"

Siano was also doing drugs. Initially his consumption was recreational —at the Round Table he remembers taking a little pot, half a tab of acid, and perhaps some speed—but at the Gallery the pharmaceuticals got heavier. Ups would keep him going, downs would make him happy, and in March 1976 his new friends from the Boatel introduced him to heroin. "I took heroin for the first time on my twenty-first birthday. It made me throw up eight or nine times, but I loved it. It took away the pain." Siano, it transpired, didn't know how to handle success, even within the relative anonymity of New York's night network. "I felt that I had to say the funniest things everywhere I went. I felt very insecure." Heroin provided him

Bottom up: Nicky Siano, Robert DeSilva, Louis Aquilone, Terry Consologio, Billy Cocrin, Rique Spencer, and Kenny Motley on the roof of Siano's apartment. Courtesy of Nicky Siano

with an anesthetic, and his earnings of six to seven hundred dollars a week meant that he could easily finance an intake that rarely cost more than fifty dollars a day. Here was a high priest who really lived up to his name.

Siano's cabinet chest also included angel dust and Tuinals, both of which left him extremely stoned and, every now and again, barely able to perform. Sometimes the DJ would accidentally remove the needle from the wrong record, creating a sharp screeching sound. On other occasions he would pass out and grab hold of the turntable counter on his descent, generating an ear-splitting blitz as the needle skimmed across the vinyl. Yet somehow or other he would usually stage a miraculous recovery. "Nicky Siano would be in the booth, and you would see him going into one of these deep, deep nods," says Kenny Carpenter. "Then you would hear a little crash on the floor, which was the sound of Nicky falling. The record would be down to the last grooves, and somehow or other he would force himself up, reach for a record, and mix it in *flawlessly*. It would be a real anthem like 'Love Hangover' or 'The Love I Lost.' Then he'd manipulate the treble and bass controls and the whole crowd would go, 'Aaagggghhhh!' Larry Levan, Larry Patterson, Walter Gibbons, and Tee Scott would all sit in the booth taking notes, waiting for Nicky to pass out so they could jump over him to get to those turntables. They were like eager wolves."

Nicky Siano

Select Discography (Gallery 1974–76)

B. T. Express, "Express"

B. T. Express, "Peace Pipe"

Double Exposure, "My Love Is Free"

Double Exposure, "Ten Percent"

Dr. Buzzard's Original Savannah Band, "Cherchez la Femme"

Dr. Buzzard's Original Savannah Band, "I'll Play the Fool"

Ecstasy, Passion & Pain featuring Barbara Roy, "Touch and Go"

Executive Suite, "When the Fuel Runs Out"

Loleatta Holloway, "Dreamin' "

Thelma Houston, "Don't Leave Me This Way"

Willie Hutch, "Love Power"

The Joneses, "Love Inflation"

The Joneses, "Sugar Pie Guy"

Margie Joseph, "Prophecy"

LaBelle, "Lady Marmalade"

LaBelle, "Messing with My Mind"

LaBelle, "What Can I Do for You?"

Ramsey Lewis, "Sun Goddess"

George McCrae, "Rock Your Baby"

Harold Melvin & the Blue Notes, "Bad Luck"

Mighty Clouds of Joy, "Mighty High"

The O'Jays, "I Love Music"

The Originals, "Down to Love Town"

Minnie Riperton, "Stick Together"

The Ritchie Family, "Brazil"

Vicky Sue Robinson, "Turn the Beat Around"

Diana Ross, "Love Hangover"

The Salsoul Orchestra, "You're Just the Right Size"

Gil Scott-Heron, "The Bottle"

Silver Convention, "Fly, Robin, Fly"

Candi Staton, "Young Hearts Run Free"

Donna Summer, "Love to Love You Baby"

The Trammps, "Disco Party"

The Trammps, "Hooked for Life"

Undisputed Truth, "You + Me = Love"

Another variety of wolf also happened to be waiting for Siano at Disco Forum II, where the Gallery DJ was invited to participate in a panel on club ownership. "I felt very honored to be asked to speak, but when I got there it was all so serious," he says. "I remember the whole club scene being about laughing and partying, but the panel was so *somber*." His attempt to lighten up the proceedings whenever he could get a word in edgeways turned out to be futile. "No one was talking about how to create a fun atmosphere. They were talking about how to run a moneymaking business. They looked at everything with dollar signs in their eyes."

Money turned out to be the recurring theme of the *Billboard* conference, the tone of which was set by the decision to invite *Forbes* reporter Laury Minard, who was hardly an established connoisseur of the club scene, to deliver the keynote speech. "I think you can expect a hoard of greedy get-rich-quick artists to descend upon discotheques," warned Minard, diplomatically sidestepping the fact that this process was already well underway. "These fellows will likely emblazon their run-down bars and massage parlors with neon lights saying 'discotheque,' meaning, of course, that they have a couple of tired 45s and an old record player to get their customers from their ninth to 10th gin."[48]

Although hardly critical of the development, *Newsweek* also detected a rampant commercialism within the discotheque economy. "Discos are opening—and closing—in everything from Holiday Inns and Hilton hotels to rural potato barns and Bloomingdale's basement," reported the magazine. "There are kiddie discos, senior-citizen discos, rollerskating discos, and discos on wheels, which carry their canned music and lights to suburbia. Disco franchisers talk about becoming 'the McDonald's of the entertainment business.'"[49] As if the paradigm of the multinational hamburger corporation wasn't sufficiently profit-driven, a high proportion of these new venues were also attempting to guarantee financial success by submerging the discotheque into a more general entertainment complex. "In Las Vegas, Paul Anka is building a million-dollar, multileveled disco-gourmet restaurant complex. The Tennessee Gin and Cotton Co. in Los Angeles has a cozy front room with live acts, a side room for billiards, a back Patio for backgammon and an antique bar in addition to the disco. In New York, the famed Copacabana has reopened as a discotheque-cabaret while Regine's, which features luxurious décor and $100 dinners, relies on the most durable concept of all—snob appeal."[50]

The New York Record Pool watched on, effectively helpless, for while it had successfully persuaded the vast majority of DJs to form a united alliance in their confrontation with the record companies, it wasn't able to organize them in the same way when it came to liberating dance spaces. D'Acquisto, Mancuso, and company had won their battle for free records largely because the arrangement suited the companies, but no equivalent deal could be struck with the club owners. What, after all, was in it for them? Organized groups were always going to be tricky to control, and, given that DJs had actually begun life by breaking the picket lines of the musicians' unions, discotheque moguls were only too happy to collaborate with a string of individualized workers who were inevitably fragmented and weak when it came to organizing demands. The obvious solution would have been for DJs to form a union, but that kind of collective action didn't come naturally to a group of flexible freelancers who were aware of the fundamentally transient and precarious nature of their profession, as well as the likelihood that a nonunionized DJ would willingly take their job if they ever went on strike. Tom Savarese was fairly typical. Having willingly joined the New York Record Pool, he told *Billboard* that he viewed the idea of a DJ association as the "first devious beginnings of organized labor" and declared his preference for an alternative "solution" of "a strong individual approach to professionalism" that implored DJs to draw up contracts with employers, be punctual, be consistent, practice, and so on.[51] Nightworld was welcoming in the work template of the 1980s ahead of time.

The organizers of the downtown party network also looked on in dismay at the disfigurement of a culture they had once claimed as their own. Like the Record Pool, they were effectively powerless to intervene, lacking the infinite finances and the critical mass that would have been required to shape these new venues in their own image. Not that a massive amount of money and a captive audience of millions would have made much difference given that their organizing principles—which included a discreet private invite system, a carefully selected dance space, a high quality sound system, and a refined DJ—meant that they would always spread more slowly than their less discerning competitors. Then there was the obscure yet persistent problem of political isolation, for whereas the new breed of discotheque owners easily slipped into a broader, self-affirming, and self-perpetuating alliance of business chiefs and politicians who talked the same kind of serious moneymaking talk, New York's most radical and visionary party people were operating in an ideological vacuum, thanks to the fact that politicians and union leaders were not exactly open to the field of progressive pleasure. Even the *Billboard* conference turned out to be a hostile terrain. "It really got to me," says Siano. "I was very put off by it and, looking back, rightfully so. That particular forum and its moneymaking attitude contributed to the demise of disco."

8. ascendancy

As Vince Aletti mulled over the highs and lows of the outgoing year in his final column for 1976, the future made a surreptitious appearance on the bottom right-hand corner of his "Disco File" page where David Mancuso had listed a track called "Love in 'C' Minor" by an obscure artist called Cerrone as one of the records on his current playlist. Originally issued on a French label called Malligator, the record had entered the Loft and other New York venues via the New York Record Pool. "It was a good production," says Mancuso. "I played it a lot. I liked the record very much, although I wouldn't say that I *loved* it." Aletti, in a review of the record three weeks later, expressed no such reservations. "I first heard 'Love in 'C' Minor' at David Mancuso's Loft in New York where it caused an immediate sensation," he noted before adding that it had "become the hottest record in the club."[1]

Clocking in at sixteen minutes, "Love in 'C' Minor" was a minor epic that exploited time as a platform for drama, with the record reproducing the swoops and surges of "Love to Love You Baby," explicit sexuality and all. Yet while "Love to Love You Baby" and "Love in 'C' Minor" both contained recordings of female sexual arousal, the implications couldn't have been more different. "Love in 'C' Minor" opens with three women talking about cruising and sharing a man, all of which might have been interpreted as a sign of emerging female sexual power were it not for the fact that the *homme* in question is Cerrone, and the fantasy is manifestly his own. When the Frenchman turns toward them one of the women exclaims, "Money ain't all he's got—look at the front of him. That ain't no banana!" and as the rhythmic pulse intensifies the trio reach their simultaneous climax, screaming "Don't stop!" "Right there! Right there!" "Do it! Do it! Do it! Do it!" and "Oh, Cerrohhhne!" This was Donna Summer times three—plus one.

The track itself was cowritten by the definitively multicultural Alec Costandinos, an Egyptian-born Armenian who had lived in Australia, was residing in France, and recorded his music in England. "Cerrone was working in a record store, and he knew that disco was selling," says Costandinos, who had already collaborated with a number of artists, including Demis Roussos. "I agreed to work on the record with him." Like Cerrone, Costandinos had been invigorated by the new sound of dance, and when it emerged that the would-be artist couldn't sing, Costandinos suggested that they sacrifice the vocals in the quest for driving rhythm. "I had heard the kick drum in 'Living in a Glass House' by the Four Tops, which really excited me, and then I heard it again in 'Love to Love You Baby.' I thought the vibe was fabulous. It made me want to record music day and night so I put it in 'Love in 'C' Minor.'" Having pilfered the pulse, the duo squeezed the accelerator: whereas the previous landmarks of European disco had hovered around the 100-beats-per-minute barrier, "Love in 'C' Minor" pumped along at 128, making it the definitive expression of the yet-to-be-named subgenre of Eurodisco. "We had a different purpose than Philadelphia," says Costandinos. "Philadelphia recorded songs with beautiful arrangements and fabulous singers whereas we recorded songs that were going onto the dance floor. We were disco-oriented and raw."

European obedience to stereotype was maintained when German machinery joined French sex in the form of Kraftwerk's *Trans-Europe Express*, which included a travel-as-flowing-art-form title track that simulated a rail journey through its reproduction of a train whistle, electrified wheels, locomotive rhythm, and screeching brakes ("Metal on Metal" was the run-on track). Kraftwerk had already established their experimental credentials by deploying Robert Moog's portable modular synthesizer in *Autobahn*, although their ensuing tour of America suggested that their brand of avant-garde futurism wouldn't translate onto the dance floor. "This is highly cerebral music," wrote one commentator in the spring of 1975, "definitely not for boogeying."[2] However *Trans-Europe Express*, which was released in April 1977, rapidly established itself as an important club hit thanks to its mesmerizing marriage of funky drum beats with automation, repetition, and facelessness. Tom Savarese, who had started to work at Harrah, a new discotheque situated on Broadway and Sixty-second

Street, homed in on "Endless," and David Rodriguez, who had started to work behind the counter at Downstairs Records, told Vince Aletti that he was pushing "Trans-Europe Express" and "Metal on Metal." "Not exactly light entertainment, but quite incredible, especially on a powerful system," concluded the *Record World* columnist. "Highly recommended for freaky crowds, otherwise a little too off-the-wall."[3]

Kraftwerk's members soon found out about their rising dance floor popularity. "I remember somebody took me to a club in about 1976 or 1977, when *Trans-Europe Express* was out," Ralf Hütter told journalist Mark Sinker. "It was some loft club in New York—after hours—just as DJ culture was beginning; when DJ's [*sic*] began making their own records, their own grooves. They took sections from 'Metal On Metal' on *Trans-Europe Express*, and when I went in it was going 'boom-crash-boom-crash,' so I thought 'oh, they're playing the new album.' But it went on for ten minutes! And I thought 'what's happening?' That track is only something like two or three minutes. And later I went to ask the DJ, and he had two copies of the record and he was mixing the two."[4]

Europe's techno invasion gathered pace with the release of Donna Summer's *I Remember Yesterday*, a concept album that journeyed through the decades. The title track, as it happens, was a glossy nostalgia number backed by a big band, and the LP as a whole represented the "maturation" of the sensual starlet into a more conventional artist, indicating that she had in fact *forgotten* all her yesterdays (i.e. the dance scene that had provided Summer with her breakthrough). But if Manhattan's DJs— who, following the rise and rise of Michael Gomes's single-paged newsletter, were now being referred to as "mixmasters"—flipping through the album, were poised to renounce their domesticated diva, the final track on side two reminded them why they had fallen for her in the first place. A brilliant combination of whipped-up synthesizer and dreamy, ecstatic vocals, "I Feel Love" was quite unlike anything else on the album. "The pace is fierce and utterly gripping with the synthesizer effects particularly aggressive and emotionally charged," wrote an enthralled Aletti, who predicted that the track "should easily equal if not surpass" the success of "Love to Love You Baby" in the clubs.[5]

Moroder had started to experiment with the synthesizer several years earlier, intrigued by its seemingly vast array of sounds. "I used a big old Moog to record 'Son of My Father,' " he says. "I borrowed it from a classical composer I knew in Munich. I think he got the second-ever Moog." The trial was short-lived. "I used it as a source of gimmicky sounds in the early seventies but then gave it up because the audience response wasn't really there, and I was always a commercial composer-producer." Moroder re-engaged with the Moog during the recording of "I Feel Love," which he started to work on in his Musicland studio in Munich. "I wanted to conclude with a futuristic song," he says, "and I decided that it had to be done with a synthesizer." In a break with protocol, the producer composed the backing track in advance of the melody, developing a bass line that, due to the technological limits of the Moog, comprised a short sequence of notes. "It was very difficult to work because the oscillators didn't have a quartz to keep the frequency steady, and so it was always out of tune." Moroder introduced a degree of variety by altering the key at regular intervals, although finding a synthesized sound that resembled a drum was only partially achievable. "We managed to create a snare and a hi-hat, but we couldn't find a punchy enough bass drum. Eventually we just did an overdub."

Moroder's melody acquired an eerie, off-key resonance when Summer—almost but not quite echoing the gospel technique whereby vocal repetition empties out language in order to open the self to divine inspiration—submitted herself to the record's synthesized textures. "Sometimes Donna would do crazy things just for the fun of it. Most of the time we would take no notice, but the way she sang 'I Feel Love' was kind of OK." In a final act of twiddling, Moroder decided to double the bass line via a delay in order to generate a fuller effect. The result, though, was imperfect: the delay was entered by ear, and the bass lines were split between the left and right channels. "If you were dancing in a discotheque next to the left speaker then it was alright because you heard the down beat, but if you were next to the right speaker then you only heard the delay. I remember Donna came back from a club and said, 'You know, something is wrong with this recording!' I told her, 'I know what's wrong!' It did quite well all the same." Gloria Gaynor might have been the first queen of disco, but Summer, blending with Moroder's technology, had become its first cyborg princess.

Keen to cash in on a winning formula, Neil Bogart went in search of more Eurodisco talent and inadvertently struck gold when Casablanca's Heart and Soul Orchestra (formerly known as Frankie Crocker's Heart and Soul Orchestra) covered "Love in 'C' Minor" without permission. "Casablanca had acted without my authorization, and when I called them

Henri Belolo (left), Jacques Morali (center), and Richard Rome outside Sigma Sound Studios, Philadelphia. Photo by Waring Abbott

from Paris they knew they had a lawsuit on their hands," remembers Costandinos. "They said, 'Come on over, let's talk!' and they signed me as a producer." In June, Bogart snapped up the rights to the producer's latest project, *Love and Kisses* by Love and Kisses, and the single "I Found Love (Now That I Found You)" became a major chart hit. In a bizarre geo-cultural shift, a West Coast American record company was rapidly establishing itself as the unchallenged epicenter of Eurodisco.

Empowered by the sale of half of his company to PolyGram for a reported ten million dollars, Bogart also signed Jacques Morali and Henri Belolo, and in July 1977 the duo delivered their first recording to the West Coast mogul, *Village People* by the Village People. Appropriately, the group had been dreamt up on the East Coast after Morali took a walk through Greenwich Village and stumbled into a gay bar where a group of boys decked out in butch drag were dancing around a man called Felipé Rose, who was wearing a Native American outfit. The producer was apparently struck by the realization that gay men didn't yet have a disco act they could call their own—Valentino had recorded "I Was Born This Way," ostensibly the first self-consciously gay anthem, in 1975 but there were no gay-identified groups—and so he decided to write and produce a gay concept album that featured Rose plus a group of stand-in models on its cover.

However, the fact that the Village People was in fact a Village Person proved to be a problem when venues started to put in bids for live performances. Morali improvised as best he could, cobbling together a group of freelance singers and dancers, but a more permanent solution was required, and playing Moses, the French producer revisited a string of West Village haunts in order to bring together a People. Two hundred auditions later, the reconstituted group featured six singer-dancers, each of whom donned the costume of a uniformed macho clone: Alex Briley dressed up as a sailor; David Hodo took on the appearance of a construction worker; Glen Hughes played the leather biker; Randy Jones was reincarnated as a cowboy; Victor Willis slipped into a police officer's uniform; and Felipé Rose retained his Native American outfit.

A four-cut concept album, *Village People* featured a combination of pounding rhythms and high-gloss pop that came straight out of the Moroder-Costandinos school of production. Morali and Belolo, working with the Ritchie Family, had already shifted from the polished Philadelphia sound of *Brazil* and *Arabian Nights* to a powerhouse aesthetic for the recording of *African Queens*, which featured Olatunji and six other percussionists, and they retained the new sound on their Casablanca debut. The tracks themselves were cleverly titled after gay urban centers and referenced hot spots such as Folsom Street, Polk Street, Studio One, the Ice Palace, and the Sandpiper along the way. That guaranteed strong early play in the clubs that mattered, and if straight critics didn't always know how to respond to lyrics like "Don't go near the bushes/Somethin' might grab ya," the unambiguous references to an increasingly confident gay culture didn't stop the record from going gold.

More European-oriented disco soon followed. Moroder launched himself as a solo artist with the release of *From Here to Eternity* by Giorgio, a techno-funk collection. Summer continued her prolific run when she and Moroder came out with the double-album *Once Upon a Time*, a reinterpretation of the Cinderella story that included drug highs and urban lows before reaching its happy conclusion. And Cerrone consolidated his reputation as one of Eurodisco's most influential figures when he released *Supernature*, a fable about good and evil that was infused with H. G. Wells's *The Island of Doctor Moreau* and which introduced a Moroder-style synthesizer into its dark impersonation of ecological contortion and sci-fi doom.

By the end of 1977, Eurodisco had established itself as a force to be reckoned with. Built around a thudding four-four beat, futuristic synthesizers, and a penchant for grandiose conceptual themes, the genre had its own aesthetic, and it also looked like it was selling more records than any other strand of disco. "Within the past year, imported disco record products have literally taken the country by storm, resulting in fierce rivalry among local record labels, which are reportedly bidding record prices for licensing rights to these viable new products," *Billboard* reported in September. "Although some record company executives are still reluctant to recognize the impact imports are making on the U.S. market by stating that this country has the best rhythm players in the world, and will always be the center of dance music, successes of such foreign groups as Silver Convention, Cerrone, Love & Kisses, Munich Machine and Georgio [*sic*] Moroder cannot be ignored."[6]

East Coasters were ambivalent. "I liked the Eurodisco sound," says Moulton. "It was light, fluffy, happy music. But it was geared more for the whites." Moulton's skin might have been white, but his heart was black. "My biggest complaint about Eurodisco was that it lacked soul. The records sounded like machines. They would always use black singers to try to put the soul back into the music, but they couldn't do it on a consistent basis. 'Love to Love You Baby' was the only song they ever did that was soulful, and it had that feel because Giorgio took the bass line from 'Money' by the O'Jays. Every record after that didn't have the R&B bass line. Eurodisco developed more of a poppy, classical sound."

* * *

While disco was selling, some companies were beginning to wonder whether it was selling enough to justify the number of free records they were sending to the record pools. Columbia was the first to reexamine the math and reduce its service, and West End—which was formed by Mel Cheren (ex-Scepter promotions manager) and Ed Kushins (ex-Scepter sales manager) in 1976—began to doubt the efficacy of the organization soon after. "It was a great idea because DJs kept coming up to the office, and we didn't know who was legitimate and who wasn't, but it got out of hand," says Mel Cheren. "Companies were giving away more records than they were selling. It became a cancer in the industry." Salsoul, which was generally considered to be the most influential disco label after Atlantic and which also serviced more pools than any other label, also started to recoil, slashing its quota of complimentary promos from three thousand to just four hundred. "It costs too much money," Salsoul head of promotions Denise "Sunshine" Chapman told *Billboard* at the end of April 1977. "It costs us about $8,000 per release to service 3,000 disco DJs. Eight thousand dollars is a lot of money to spend when you can use that money for marketing, distribution and promotion."[7] For all of the play Salsoul had been generating in the clubs, the label had yet to record a major hit. "We're big as far as disco is concerned and we're happy that the DJs love our product, but we have yet to realize a gold record."[8]

Ken Cayre's first signings had failed to provide the breakthrough he was looking for. Double Exposure's album failed to make an impact, and the Salsoul Orchestra's second LP, *Nice 'n' Naasty*, ended up selling less than the first. True, Vince Montana set the cash registers clinking when *Christmas Jollies*, which he produced in just thirty days, went on to fill a couple of hundred thousand Christmas stockings. But Carey wasn't interested in Christmas. He was dreaming about Summer. And if Donna was already taken then he wanted his own superstar diva.

Candidate number one was Loleatta Holloway, a Chicago-born R&B singer who was introduced to Salsoul by her manager and husband Floyd Smith, an occasional recording artist in his own right. "Loleatta had an incredible voice so I took her down to Philadelphia for a couple of sessions," says Cayre. "She met Norman Harris, Allan Felder, and Ron Tyson, and we produced an album." The Salsoul boss put Harris in charge of production and simultaneously handed him a subsidiary label, Gold Mind, as well as the rights to the Holloway project—a controversial move given that "Vince wanted everything to go through him." Cayre, however, regarded Harris as an invaluable asset. "I saw that Norman had a songwriting ability that Vince didn't have, and he could also work as a producer *and* an arranger."

Holloway's album, *Loleatta*, was released to enthusiastic reviews in January 1977, and a month later the vocalist made her nightclub debut at the Gallery's Valentine's Day Massacre party. "Of course my brothers dressed up like hoodlums with machine guns," says Nicky Siano. "I was too stoned to worry about it." By the time Holloway arrived the party was already in full flow, and, barely hesitating to take in her new surroundings, the would-be diva climbed onto the stage, walked up to the microphone, and started to improvise around the freshly imported sounds of "Love in 'C' Minor," which Siano was playing at the time. "I turned the mike up, and she sang along to the Cerrone, going 'Yeah, yeah! Yeah, yeah!' The crowd went bananas, and I just let it happen." Holloway ended up performing just about every track from her album. "She was so excited by the crowd that she just started singing these songs that weren't really popular like 'We're Getting Stronger (The Longer We Stay Together)' and 'Is It Just a Man's Way?' and after that they became real anthems. She tore the place down." Holloway was lost for words. "I was really surprised that the gay crowd was so into me," she says. "I didn't have to build them up. They were already there." Music seismologists, however, barely bothered to catalogue this spot of downtown rumbling. For sure, eventual sales of three hundred thousand copies represented a respectable debut but, in comparison to the earthquake of *Love to Love You Baby*, Loleatta barely registered on the Richter scale.

Not content to pin all of his hopes on Holloway's next release, Cayre began to plug First Choice, a girl group who had been rejected by Scepter before going on to record a string of important club hits on Philly Groove, including "Armed and Extremely Dangerous," "Guilty," "Love and Happiness," "Newsy Neighbors," "The Player," and "Smarty Pants." Warner Brothers subsequently signed and then dropped the group after a brutally brief stint. "The president of Warners had seen us perform in New York alongside George Benson, Dionne Warwick, and Chaka Khan," says lead singer Rochelle Fleming. "When we heard that he wanted to sign us from Philly Groove, we were so excited. We really liked the Warner Brothers name, the publicity was fabulous, and they bought all our clothes for us!" Within a couple of months, however, the Philadelphia trio had plummeted to Last Choice. "We recorded *So Let Us Entertain You*, which was a good album. It looked like the company was going to get behind it, but then they pulled back. Later on we discovered that our manager, Stan Watson, had been trying to push other bands on them. There were some discrepancies, Warners couldn't be bothered, and in the end they let us go."

To the dismay of Fleming, Watson took the group to Norman Harris. "We'd never heard of Gold Mind. All we knew was we weren't getting limos any more!" Then came "Doctor Love" and a chance encounter with the heavyweight-boxing champion of the world. "My eyes were shut tight, and I was singing 'Doctor Love, Doctor Love, he can cure my every pain.' As I opened my eyes there was this *big man* standing in the control room, and it was Cassius Clay! He was friendly with our manager at the time, and we were like, 'Oh my God!' I stopped the recording—I couldn't finish it—and I remember him saying, 'It's going to be a hit record!'"

Harris wasn't so sure. He had missed the session due to a longstanding heart condition, and when cowriters Allan Felder and Ron Tyson supplied him with a tape he immediately summoned Fleming to visit him in hospital. "He said, " 'Chelle, you know you can do better than that!'" remembers the vocalist. "He knew my voice better than any producer, and he said I had to do it again. I was so angry with him. I said, 'You're kidding!' He said, 'No, it sounds lazy!' I had to redo it." The effort was worthwhile. " 'Doctor Love' was our biggest hit to date," says Cayre of the April 1977 release. "It went top forty pop and top ten R&B. It got a lot of recognition, and we thought we were on the verge of breaking a major artist. All of this went through to Norman. He was the catalyst that put Salsoul on the map. He gave us the visibility of a label with recorded artists."

Thanks to Tom Moulton, the song also became one of the year's most popular club hits, although the remixer paid an ominous price for a hard night's work. "The song kept speeding up and slowing down, and I was *so* frustrated," he says. "I constantly had to speed up and slow down the multitrack, and I finally got to the point where I said, 'Oh my God, I can't stand this!' I raised my hands, and I felt these electric jolts. Everything was shutting off and going back on. I sat down and said, 'Let's try to get this thing wrapped up!'" Moulton finished the mix and then asked if somebody could drive him to the hospital. "I went to the emergency room, and the doctor said, 'How long ago did this start?' I said, 'About four hours.' He said, 'Where did you come from?' I said, 'A studio on Twelfth Street.' He said, 'What's more important than your life?' I said, 'Finishing 'Doctor Love!" He thought I was crazy. As it turned out I saw him almost a year later. He recognized me and said, 'You know you were right. 'Doctor Love' is a great record!'"

Moulton was soon up on his feet, but Harris never quite recovered, and the ensuing First Choice album contained the telltale signs of an increasingly fractured life. "The album would have been better if he had produced and written more of it," says Cayre. "Instead he signed a string of young producers and writers who came out with some good songs but nothing that was of the caliber of 'Doctor Love.' Norman should have been up there with producers such as Norman Whitfield, Kenny Gamble, and Leon Huff, but he wasn't focusing 100 percent, and a lot of people took advantage of him." The arrival of Tyson also drove a wedge between Felder and Harris, who had penned the group's hits for Philly Groove. "Allan didn't like sharing the writing spotlight. He became very unhappy and after that the magic went. Subsequent songs weren't as good."

Holloway, meanwhile, was struggling to break through, and her sense of frustration was compounded when she performed as a guest vocalist on "Runaway" for the third Salsoul Orchestra album, *Magic Journey.* "She didn't like the way Vince was behaving," says Cayre, who had agreed to drive the artist to Philadelphia. "He was treating her like it was his song and he was doing her a favor by letting her sing. He should have made her feel important, not just say, 'It's a great song! Just go out and put a vocal on it!'" Holloway's misery was compounded by a nasty cold. "Her voice was a little nasal, but she still had the power and the knowledge to pull it off." Indeed by the end of the session Holloway was even beginning to enjoy herself. "She had to do an ad lib before Vince played the vibes, which had already been laid down. At the end of the ad lib she said, 'C'mon Vince, play your vibes!' She really captured the feeling of the song." Yet while Holloway's lung-busting contribution turned a promising song into a huge club hit, the Salsoul Orchestra received a far more significant boost than the discontented diva, who as the featured vocalist found her name submerged in the minutiae of recording credits.

The slanted scales of musical justice were somewhat rebalanced when Walter Gibbons remixed "Hit and Run," which had appeared on the fast-fading *Loleatta* album. Gibbons was now playing at Better Days on Mondays and Tuesdays, having left Galaxy 21 in acrimonious circumstances. "George Freeman was unhappy about how loud Walter played, and he asked me to install a secret volume control so that he could lower the volume when Walter got too excited," says Alex Rosner. "I told George that it was a bad idea, but he insisted. It didn't take Walter long to figure out what was happening, so on a busy night he just walked out, and most of the crowd followed him." In an attempt to mollify the distraught Freeman, the soundman arranged for a three-way meeting. "We all made up, but Walter was hurt, and I sensed that the relationship between him and George was never the same after that."

Loleatta Holloway. Photo by Waring Abbott

Luckily the rapport between Gibbons and Salsoul was a good deal healthier, with the DJ asking Cayre if he could rework "Hit and Run" just a few days after the release of the LP. The Salsoul chief agreed and decided to entrust Gibbons with the multitrack, thereby allowing him far more flexibility than had been possible with the half-inch master copies that had been handed over for the remix of "Ten Percent." Instead of resorting to a cut-and-paste reedit, the remixer could now listen to each individual track, after which he could dissect and reconstruct the record as he pleased. " 'Hit and Run' was the first time that a studio let a DJ completely rework the song," says Cayre, "and Walter, the genius that he was, turned it into a twelve-minute, unconventional smash."

Gibbons completely restructured the six-minute album version, highlighting Baker, Harris, and Young's exquisite rhythm track by slicing out a swathe of strings, almost all of the horns, and, in an act of consummate bravery, the *first two minutes of Holloway's vocal* as well as *all of her verses*. The remixer's motives were clear: any song that began "Now I might be an old-fashioned country girl, but when it comes to loving you, honey, I know what to do" was never going to inspire the urban dance floor (even Holloway says that "it was the worst song" she had "ever heard"). However, the act nevertheless implied that the artistic integrity of the remixer—and a DJ at that—was becoming more important than that of the writer, the producer, and the vocalist, and nobody in the music industry was ready for that bombshell.

Chapman, who was hanging out with Gibbons during the remix, says that the idea to emphasize the rhythm section and erase Holloway's early vocal was her own, and she made her case by playing Gibbons a copy of "By the Time I Get to Phoenix," an eighteen-minute epic from the album *Hot Buttered Soul* in which Isaac Hayes talks over an unchanging, minimalist rhythm track for the opening eight minutes. "It was my ambition to make 'Hit and Run' more interesting than the album version," she remembers. "I said, 'Listen to this!' Walter loved it. That was the inspiration that we discussed that night in the studio."

In order to retain part of the vocal, Gibbons turned to the second, improvised half of Holloway's performance, which consisted of an extended series of repetitions, screams, tremors, and sighs. "It was the longest song I had ever had to sing, and I ended up doing a lot of vamping," says the vocalist. "Those vamps weren't written for me. They came from my heart

Walter Gibbons at Blank Tapes Studios, New York. Courtesy of François Kevorkian

and my soul." Having filled up three minutes on the album, Holloway's vamps now ran on for a long five minutes on the twelve-inch remix. "She was always wailing or moaning or singing, and we just reintroduced the stuff that had been cut or buried," says Chapman. "Walter just took the multitrack and said, 'Ooh, did you hear her do that!' He was like a child in a candy store. There were so many choices. He wanted all of them, and it just became long." Eleven minutes seven seconds long, to be precise. "This version is really so different from the original," Moulton wrote in his *Billboard* review, "that it must be classified as a new record."[9]

While the twelve-inch translation was far superior to the album version, Salsoul's bigwigs were aghast. "When Walter played me his mix, I initially wanted to choke him," says Cayre. "Loleatta wasn't there anymore. Walter just told me that I had to get used to it." Always up for a party, the mogul went to listen to Gibbons play the twelve-inch in its intended setting, and "after hearing it a couple of times" he knew that Gibbons "had done the right thing." The Salsoul boss wasn't the only convert. "Norman also objected to Walter's remix, and in the beginning he said it was inferior," says Cayre, "but he came round." According to Cayre, Harris also wanted the royalties, which were not inconsiderable given that the release, which notched the three-hundred-thousand mark, outsold both the "Ten Percent" twelve-inch and the "Hit and Run" seven-inch.

Aesthetics aside, "Hit and Run" also confirmed that the twelve-inch had become an important commercial marketing phenomenon, and the format's reputation was further enhanced when the remix of Peter Brown's "Do Ya Wanna Get Funky with Me" on TK—which was released in the same week as the Holloway twelve-inch and was described by Moulton as "something exceptional"—became the first "giant single" to sell more than five hundred thousand copies.[10] "The disco disc field has endured more than its share of skepticism and resistance from both record companies and retailers, and the fact that nearly everyone in the business has approached the disco disc as a fad rather than a true commercial phenomenon has certainly kept the format from realizing its full potential," commented Vince Aletti. "But now that the field has its first gold record, maybe some attitudes will change."[11]

The Brown bonanza confirmed TK (and its subsidiary, Marlin) as one of the most influential independents in the United States, with Henry Stone's Miami-based label displaying a fondness for funky dance records. Following the success of George McCrae's "Rock Your Baby," TK notched up dance floor hits with the Ritchie Family's "The Best Disco in Town" and "African Queens," KC & the Sunshine Band's "Get Down Tonight," "That's the Way (I Like It)" and "(Shake, Shake, Shake) Shake Your Booty," Funk Machine's "Funk Machine," and T-Connection's "Do What You Wanna Do." "TK," says Vince Pellegrino, who started to work for CBS as a sales representative in May 1977, "was owning the marketplace." When Stone released a disco compilation toward the end of the year, his sales manager Howard Smiley was unable to resist taking a backhanded swipe at Cayre's more fashionable yet less profitable label (which had issued its own anthology, *Disco Boogie: Super Hits for Non-Stop Dancing*, segued and looped together by Gibbons, in the summer). "We want this to attract more than just the disco freaks, so we're including legitimate hits and not just obscure disco records."[12]

Somewhere between TK's flourishing office in Florida and Salsoul's humming headquarters in New York lay Gamble and Huff's Philadelphia studios, once the unknowing nerve center of nightworld's evolving soundtrack, now a fading empire. At the end of 1975, Philadelphia International recorded a gross income of more than twenty-five million dollars, making it the second-largest black-owned company in the United States, but there on after Gamble and Huff began to fall out of synch with the club aesthetic. Having alienated the irreplaceable Baker-Harris-Young rhythm section, and having failed to stem an equally damaging exodus of influential songwriters and arrangers, Gamble and Huff were unable to maintain their earlier dance floor momentum—even if "TSOP" had demonstrated an unexpected flair for substituting the message with music and melody with rhythm.

Still, the rise of the twelve-inch provided the producers with an alternative route into the disco market, and they commissioned Tom Moulton—who was still an integral part of the Salsoul setup—to reinvent a selection of their most successful dance hits. Titled *Philadelphia Classics* and released in November 1977, the double pack included a spectacular reworking of "Love Is the Message" that featured an additional keyboard solo by Huff. The producer-cum-keyboard-player had initially told Moulton that he didn't want to add any additional takes to the original session, but the remixer persuaded him to give it a go and unscrewed the recording light before he arrived in the studio. "I played the track from the middle part out, and Huff started fooling around," says Moulton. "He just let it flow because he thought he wasn't being recorded and after two-and-a-half minutes he said, 'I don't think it's going to work!'" Huff got up and left, after which Moulton added the surreptitiously recorded solo to the remix, telling anyone who asked that he had found the extra material on the original tapes. "It's sacrilegious adding something to a song like that, but I felt that it was needed."

Moulton's remix of "Love Is the Message" came at the end of a busy year that had begun with his radically stripped-down mix of "We've Got Our Own Thing" by C. J. & Co., which was released on Westbound. "I kept it very naked because that to me was the magic of the song. That was the first time I had ever done anything so repetitious. I wanted it to build gradually, to creep up on people." Moulton's mix of the group's follow-up, "Devil's Gun," was designed to scare people. "I put all these sound effects in the beginning. It was ahead of its time." Then, in the autumn, he reinvented the role of the remixer and encroached still further into the jealously marked territory of the producer by adding new instruments to the original tapes of Michele's album *Magic Love* (released on West End) and Chocolat's *Kings of Clubs* (released on Salsoul). "I had always added instruments, but the Michele was the first time I changed *everything*," says Moulton, who received a coproducer credit for his efforts. "I liked the vocals, but the sound didn't work. The instruments bounced together."

Moulton continued to edge his way into production when Beam Junc-

Mel Cheren (center), Tom Moulton (right), and Armen Boladian of Westbound Records at "An evening honoring Tom Moulton." Courtesy of Tom Moulton

tion asked him to deliver a sequel to his work with Grace Jones. "They gave me a tape of this song, and when I heard it I said, 'Oh boy, could I make *this* an anthem!'" The song was called "I Need a Man," and that man turned out to be Moulton. "It was really crappy so I went into the studio and changed a lot of things about it. The only trouble was I didn't have a vocal, and Grace was on tour in Europe." Moulton handed an acetate of the instrumental track to Jimmy Stuard, and a couple of weeks later Jones made a surprise appearance. "I let Jimmy play the track a number of times before they knew who it was, and when Grace got back I snuck her into 12 West. Jimmy played the song, and all of a sudden Grace started singing. People went absolutely crazy. They had heard the track but didn't know there were any words to it. They were screaming and yelling, and when she finished singing she said, '*I don't know about you, honey, but I need a fucking man!*' I said, 'She just made a lot of points here!' Grace was determined to become a star, and she became one."

Moulton produced "I Need a Man" and then, to his great displeasure, *Portfolio*, both of which were recorded in Philadelphia. "Grace became very grand when it was time to do the album," he says. "I guess the success went to her head. I finally got so mad I said, 'Grace, it's amazing that with so little talent you can please so many!'" Jones responded by refusing to sing another note until Moulton apologized, at which point the remixer-turned-producer left the studio and caught the train back to New York. "Several hours later I got a call from Sy Berlin. He said, 'Tom, you're home! We're still in Philadelphia!' I said, 'So?' He said, 'What about Grace's album?' I said, 'What about it? You said she isn't going to sing until I apologize, and there's no way I'm apologizing!' I said, 'I'm trying to help her, and *she's* giving *me* crap. You *know* it's not worth it!'" Eventually Jones climbed down, and an unapologetic Moulton finished off the album, which was released in September 1977. "I realized that I preferred dealing with the tape because you didn't have to take any crap from the tape, and you didn't have to play politics with the tape. I figured, hey, I'm in a niche all by myself."

That was true to the extent that Moulton and Gibbons had markedly different approaches to their profession. "I tried to make music for everyone," says Moulton, whose outlook had been influenced by his background in retail and promotion. "I didn't produce dance records—I produced records you could dance to." Whenever Moulton conjured up a remix, he always included a solid seven-inch mix with an intro that lasted no more than ten seconds so that the record would get radio play. "I wanted my work to be a hit, but Walter never thought that way. Walter was the first person to do remixes for the underground. He didn't think in commercial terms. He thought of himself as a jazz musician who didn't want to sacrifice his craft to the system. I always thought that attitude was bullshit." The two remixers were also driven by different aesthetic preferences. "I wanted stuff to sound real, like a live performance," says Moulton. "The more live it was, the more your body could react. Walter came from a different direction. He was into drugs and developed weird sounds. I couldn't understand his sounds."

Moulton didn't like drugs—this, he says, is the main reason he rarely set foot in a discotheque—and according to Chapman the mindset shaped his work. "People who didn't do drugs were afraid they would be out of control, and this was reflected in Tom's mixes," says the Salsoul promoter, who had a bird's-eye view of both Moulton and Gibbons. "He never reached his potential." Gibbons, on the other hand, was transfixed by the dance floor and introduced a drug aesthetic into his remixes that hypnotized his crowd, even if the sound made less sense outside of the club environment. "The 'Hit and Run' mix was off the wall, and that was Walter's personality. He wanted to make music for drugs because he knew it would invoke a better trip. That kind of feeling wasn't in 'Love Is the Message.' Walter understood that the music needed to complement the high."

* * *

Bored of being a catwalk model? Why not become a discotheque mogul? John Addison had made the transition, so had John Whyte, and now Uva Harden wanted to have a go. Blond, blue-eyed, and thoroughly Teutonic, Harden had plenty in the looks department but little in the way of money, and that was exactly what he needed if he was going to convert the abandoned opera-turned-theater-turned-television-studio he had discovered at 254 West Fifty-fourth Street into a fully functioning club. Harden approached real estate developer Yoram Polany to stump up the necessary cash, and Polany persuaded his partner Frank Lloyd, who owned the Marlborough Gallery, to join the team. Lloyd, however, was being sued for defrauding the estate of Mark Rothko, and when he was found guilty to the tune of nine million dollars Harden began to doubt the veracity of his backers. The subsequent indictment of Lloyd for tampering with evidence meant that the art dealer had to either sit it out at his family retreat in the Bahamas or serve an eight-year jail sentence in New York. Lloyd chose the Bahamas, leaving Polany to work on Studio 54—as the club was provisionally titled—but when Harden set up a lunch between Polany and a Mafia representative who demanded 10 percent of future gross takings Polany decided to get out.

As all of this was unfolding, Harden persuaded Carmen D'Alessio to work as the club's promoter. "The idea of having a discotheque in a theater was completely new and completely revolutionary and completely different," she says. "I saw that the space could be used in a very creative and artistic way. I envisioned movie shootings, television programs, and fashion shows. I saw it working twenty-four hours over twenty-four. It could go beyond a club." As Lloyd's legal problems began to deepen, D'Alessio decided to introduce Harden to Steve Rubell and Ian Schrager. "Rothko's wife lived in poverty," says D'Alessio. "She sued the gallery and won the case so we lost our backers. That was the historic moment in which I brought Steve Rubell and Ian Schrager to the Big Apple. I told them that I was going to create a marvelous club and that if they were smart they had better invest." The duo needed some convincing. "They were a little bit skeptical in the beginning because it was so big. I told them that if they trusted me and did things the way I was planning to do them it was going to be a success."

Success is exactly what Rubell and Schrager were enjoying at the Enchanted Garden, thanks in no small part to the installment of local hero Paul Casella as the resident DJ. "Steve and Ian were in a quandary because they had this beautiful club, but it wasn't doing as well as they thought it would do," says Casella. "They were looking for somebody who had a following in the Queens area so my name came up. I kind of built the place up." Rubell left Casella to his own devices. "Steve saw that I was getting a good response and the place was crowded so he more or less left me alone. The only thing he used to like to do was come upstairs at the end of the night, at two-thirty or three o'clock, when all the money was in and all the receipts were covered. He would be a little bit tipsy, and he would want to hear something he liked. He used to ask me to play 'Love Hangover,' and he used to go and sit in the bass speaker."

The Enchanted Garden was, however, facing serious problems off the dance floor. Protective of its precious golf course and tranquil surroundings, the Douglaston neighborhood had launched a sustained campaign to have the club closed down and, following a series of demonstrations, the City Parks Department agreed to evict Rubell and Schrager. The threat was enough to persuade the duo to pursue their dreams in a not-too-distant land. "Steve always planned to develop a club in Manhattan," says Casella. "He came to me one day and said they had two choices—the CBS Studio, which they were looking at, and Tavern on the Green. I guess the lease at Tavern on the Green was more expensive, and he ended up making Studio 54 his New York club."

Having been introduced to the Studio 54 project, Rubell and Schrager rapidly outmaneuvered Harden, who had little to offer now that his backers had disappeared. When his option on the lease lapsed, the Enchanted Garden moguls handed him a belittling finder's fee check for one thousand dollars in the knowledge that they could bring in Jack Dushey, a real estate developer and associate, to finance the venture and D'Alessio to attract the right crowd. "I was supposed to be one of the partners, but when my lawyer and my accountant realized that they were going to speculate with the books they told me that I should change my deal," says D'Alessio. "I ended up making a very high monthly fee and a percentage on the banquets and the membership cards."

In keeping with his background as a restaurateur, Rubell knew how to steal a recipe or two. "He was always coming down to Flamingo with an entourage of nice-looking boys," says Michael Fesco. "He would show up at least twice a month." The plea for advice soon followed. "He called me from the construction site and asked me if I would take a look. In other words, he wanted to pick my brain. I went down and made a few suggestions. My first reaction was envy and my second was *look at all the work!*" Nicky Siano and Maurice Brahms also inadvertently educated Studio's owners in the ways of nightworld, as did John Addison, who introduced Rubell and Schrager to the concept—if not the refined practice—of discotheque chic.

However it was D'Alessio (rather than Rubell and Schrager) who masterminded the extraordinarily elaborate design and character of Studio 54. "I was literally the consultant on everything," says the party promoter, who bypassed established industry experts and hired a series of theater industry virtuosos and design specialists—including Broadway lighting specialists Paul Marantz and Jules Fisher, leading minimalist interior designer Ron Doud, architect Scott Bromley, environmental lighting expert Brian Thompson, and florist Renny Reynolds—to carry out the work. "Everything was conceived and directed by me. I knew all the designers." So what did Steve Rubell and Ian Schrager do? "Nothing much. They were just a couple of guys from Rhode Island who were not very glamorous. They just knew they were doing the right thing, and they raised the money, but other than that it had definitely the taste of a woman who had been involved in fashion."

Rubell and Schrager did, however, take control of the music and the operation of the lights. Richard Long—who was now "controlling the dance market" according to friendly competitor Bob Casey—was employed to install the sound system, Robert DeSilva was brought in to work the lights, and Richie Kaczor was hired as the club's DJ, much to the disappointment of Casella. "I was supposed to open Studio, but it didn't work out," says the Enchanted Garden DJ. "Steve might have felt that there was a difference between playing in Manhattan and playing in Queens. He had these guys that were really successful in New York who couldn't cut it in Queens that well, so maybe he thought I wouldn't do so well in the city." Of course Casella had already cut it in Manhattan at Hollywood, but so had Kaczor, whose sexuality might have given him an important edge. "A couple of things happened between me and Steve," says a deliberately vague Casella. "I'm basically straight, and I think he wanted a gay DJ."

Rubell then called Siano—who was still playing weekends at the Gallery—and asked him if he would play Wednesdays, Thursdays, and Sundays. "I walked into the building a week before opening night, and it was a fucking mess," remembers Siano. "I said, 'Stevie, you're never going to be ready!' He replied, 'Oh, we're going to be ready, don't worry about it!'" The mogul then repeated his request. "Of course I'll play," Siano replied. "I'd love to!" As far as the Gallery mixmaster was concerned, Studio 54 represented the climax of the downtown dance network continuum. "At that time we needed to expand. Bigger clubs were opening, and Studio encapsulated the whole thing. They cashed in on the biggest, the best, the flashiest. It was the culmination of seven years of nightclubs. Studio was just a large version of that little lamp in the corner of the Loft that was turned on and off."

Music, though, was hardly the top priority for Rubell and Schrager as they prepared to open on the evening of Tuesday 26 April 1977. After all, the newspapers, magazines, and TV stations that they had courted so energetically were interested in interior fittings and certifiable stars rather than mustachioed DJs and state-of-the-art sound systems. Kaczor and Long were accordingly left to their own devices as the discotheque operators focused their energies on installing the final items of furniture, repairing their leaking waterfall, and finding an opportune position for the camera crew from *Vogue* to set up its lights and illuminate the scores of celebrities that were *going* to help fill the two-thousand-capacity nightspot. When the doors finally opened, Bianca Jagger, Brooke Shields, Cher, Margaux Hemingway, and Donald Trump paraded onto the dance floor and posed, dutifully and beautifully, for the media as confetti rained down from the heavens. Several key stars, including Mick Jagger, didn't manage to find a way into the club—such was the chaos outside. Even D'Alessio had trouble entering her own special party, which she had organized around a Kenzo fashion show. "I was wearing a fabulous dress by Antonio Lopez that was full of ribbons, and by the time I got through the doors the ribbons were all torn. My mother had to be carried by a bouncer to the other side of the rope in order to get through the mob. It was impossible, unprecedented. Even Frank Sinatra couldn't get in!" Larry Levan and David DePino, both of whom were on DeSilva's guest list, were also denied entry. "I guess it was getting so packed and crazy they didn't pay attention to the list anymore," says DePino. "Robert tried to get us in through the backdoor, but the doorman Marc Benecke found out what was going on, and we were sent away." Similarly denied, a thousand other revelers alleviated their frustration by consuming a secret supply of quaaludes and enjoying an impromptu street orgy.

Yet, for all of the fanfare, the next couple of nights were slow, and Rubell, believing that his core crowd was about to swan off to Fire Island and the Hamptons for the summer, began to brace himself until D'Alessio came up with the idea of throwing a party for her friend Bianca Jagger, whose birthday fell on 2 May. Rubell snapped into action, decorating Studio 54 with thousands of white balloons and hiring a white horse from the Claremont Stables before he telephoned Siano. "Steve called me that afternoon and told me that I was going to play for her birthday party," says the DJ. "The only record I had by the Stones was 'Sympathy for the Devil,' and I remember looking for it and making a point to take it with me." The private party, which was held before the doors officially opened, was a quiet affair. "There was absolutely no one on the dance floor," says Siano. "There were just fifty or a hundred of Bianca's friends, and about four of them were dancing. Liza, Halston, and Mick were on the banquet below the balcony and they were drinking champagne and giggling." After a while Rubell entered the booth. "He asked me, 'Do you have any Stones?' I said, 'Yeah, 'Sympathy for the Devil,'" and he said, 'Put it on!' I put it on, and then he opened the screen that they used to make Studio smaller when it wasn't full, and it revealed the back wall, which was lit up with fifteen-foot letters that said 'Bianca.'" The pièce de résistance followed. "Bianca then rode out on a white stallion bareback, and all the paparazzi ran to the dance floor and started snapping pictures. She was wearing this red chiffon flowing gown by Halston, and she looked terrific. But she didn't look comfortable. She didn't smile. I don't know if at that moment she really appreciated what was going on. Of course, Steve had this big grin on his face."

D'Alessio might have wanted to throw her friend the party of a life-time, but she also needed to raise Studio's profile—which is exactly what she did. The *New York Daily News* ran Jagger on its center pages, and the striking images circulated through the bloodstream of the international media at speed. "Bianca was a very big turning point," says D'Alessio. "She was still married to Mick Jagger, and we got all the press." Exploit-ing the metaphorical potential of their Broadway location for all it was worth, Rubell and Schrager were taking disco's theatricality to previously unimagined levels. "That was the night that Studio really exploded," says

Siano. "From that point on the club was open six days a week, and every night was packed."

D'Alessio began to organize theme parties for fashion friends such as Giorgio Armani, Yves St. Laurent, Valentino, and Gianni Versace on a regular basis, and star performers were wheeled in to add to the sense of occasion (Grace Jones, who appeared from the mouth of a giant cobra lip-synching the words to "I Need a Man" alongside a line of twelve buffed-up boy dancers, delivered a particularly memorable show). New sets were installed with breathless regularity, and even when the stars were missing—or simply hanging out in the VIP basement—confetti guns would unload barrel after barrel of sparkling glitter so that by the end of the evening the floor was a sea of shimmering light. "We would spend about forty thousand dollars on a special party," says D'Alessio. "We knew they were going to give us a big return in publicity and that more people would want to see what was going on. Steve and Ian never had any problems when it came to paying for the special events. They believed in my ideas, and they understood that if you are going to do something for a celebrity of a certain caliber you really have to go all of the way. This is what made the club so spectacular."

As the nightly hostess-cum-special-events-organizer, D'Alessio was initially Studio 54's most visible face—its body as well as its brain—but it wasn't long before the live wire Rubell, aided by an industrial quantity of drugs and the unquenchable desire of a shameless autograph hunter, began to establish himself as the club's charming, madcap host. "Steve thrived on the idea that he had been no one, and suddenly he was famous and rich and arm-in-arm with the top celebrities," says D'Alessio. "He learned very fast, and he loved the role of participating in hosting these fabulous crowds that I had introduced him to." Barely able to contain himself, Rubell also developed the knack of telling everyone about the new friends he was making. "He just *adored* being on the phone talking to all the press and getting publicity."

Rubell also adored drugs—thus the projection on the back wall of a mock Man-in-the-Moon, who would regularly enjoy the benefits of an additional coke-filled spoon in the middle of the night—and he made sure that his special guests were supplied with the pill or powder of their choice. "He was extremely charismatic," says D'Alessio, "and he thrived on providing the stars with goodies so they would be happy." The service came into its own when police raided Studio 54 on 21 May and revoked the club's liquor license, which Rubell and Schrager had been renewing on a day-to-day basis following their failure to secure a full permit in time for the grand opening. "At that point we were just serving nonalcoholic beverages," says D'Alessio. "Of course, Steve was making sure that the regulars still got the amount of alcohol that they wanted."

Rubell also played an active role when it came to, in his own words, "tossing a salad," which had nothing to do with his time as a restaurateur and everything to do with the way in which he (and not the behind-the-scenes Schrager) would execute Studio's fastidious door policy, dictating who could enter and who couldn't. Celebrities—who were courted and publicized far more vigorously than they ever had been at Le Jardin—formed the symbolic heart of Studio's crowd, and a mix of beautiful people, dancers, journalists, wise guys, limo drivers, and other appropriate "types" were waved in to provide character, class, and variety. Money also mattered, although it didn't guarantee admission. "Because the clientele is part of the show here, we have to control the people who get in," Rubell, stealing lines from John Addison, told journalist Steven Gaines in September. "I like people to get loose and not have any inhibitions, so I don't care if a guy who comes to the door is a multimillionaire during the day. But if he looks like he'll be deadwood inside the club, we don't want him."[13] Rollerena, who worked on Wall Street by day and showed up in a wedding dress and roller skates at night, was never turned away. Nor was Disco Sally, Studio's septuagenarian party girl. But when two women showed up for a Halloween party dressed as dual Lady Godivas and riding a horse, Rubell said yes to the horse and no to the women. Breeding still counted for something.

Inasmuch as they could be easily identified, gay men were also given preferential treatment, and an early rumor had it that Studio was going to open as a white gay venue. "Rubell and Schrager wanted it to be a glamorous gay club with a private membership scheme," says Fesco. "Just like Flamingo." Casella was under a similar impression. "Steve was planning a white gay crowd with movie stars, and that's what he got when the place first opened. It was a mixed crowd opening night, but after that it was 75 percent gay." D'Alessio, however, maintains that attracting an exclusively gay clientele had never been on the agenda. "I never, ever envisioned Studio as a gay club. I opened it as a completely straight club. My influences were very European, very international, and very fashion-oriented. Those ingredients came because of my background in fash-

Steve Rubell outside Studio 54 (with Bill Wardlow, in the white suit, trying to get in). Photo by Waring Abbott

ion, not because it was gay-oriented." It was hard, however, to tell which came first. Fashion and gay men had become inextricably intertwined, and, while Studio didn't operate as an exclusively white gay space, it was heavily dependent on this group. "I believe Steve planned to make Studio a white gay club," says Siano. "There was a white gay contingency there, and Thursday night was the white gay boy night. There were always white gay boys there. Lots of them." Combining the queer, the cultured, and the charismatic, Studio evoked and surpassed the early incarnation of John Addison's now defunct discotheque (which closed when his lease with the Hotel Diplomat ended). "Studio was what Le Jardin tried to be," says Siano. "John Addison would do things half-assed, whereas Stevie and Ian just got the best people. They believed in sparing no expense. They really had a flare for doing this. They understood that in order to make money you had to spend money. They didn't hold any bars."

D'Alessio made sure that she secured the right kind of crowd on the dance floor by introducing a modified version of David Mancuso's invitation system. "Carmen D'Alessio was one of the original twelve women at the Loft," recalls Mark Riley. "For a while, any woman you saw at the Loft was either part of that group or one of their friends. The Studio 54 membership policy came directly from Carmen D'Alessio. Steve took her best ideas and ran with them." Like Mancuso, D'Alessio wanted to make sure that her best friends could get into her parties, although unlike Mancuso she wasn't particularly interested in equality. "We knew it was going to be a difficult door," she says. "I knew so many VIPs, and we didn't want them to have a problem getting in. I remember giving out a hundred complimentary cards to our hardcore group that we wanted to see frequently at the club." Preferential treatment was quickly put up for sale. "When Steve realized how much money could be made, he started to sell membership cards," says Riley. "Studio perverted the Loft system."

Those without a membership card had to negotiate Studio 54's velvet rope that, in its echo of opera house pomp and elitism, perfectly symbolized the venue's exclusionary door policy. Schrager initially defended this makeshift yet powerful threshold as a necessary device that had been deployed to shut out neighborhood prostitutes and pimps, but in truth the real threat came from the boroughs, which were officially boring. Rubell didn't exactly waste much time when it came to telling the bridge-and-tunnel crowd that they weren't welcome (even if he could only judge patrons by their dress code and not their zip code). Yet while the extensively reported combination of sex, drugs, and general outrageousness suggested that Studio was going to be unacceptable to the wider population, it quickly became clear that scores upon scores of suburbanites were only too happy to stand and wait outside Manhattan's most prolific source of limousine sightings and tabloid gossip on a nightly basis. Of course, the borough hopefuls knew that in all likelihood they wouldn't be admitted, but the experience still enabled them to enter into the celebrity script, albeit in a subjugated role, and being told that you were a nobody outside of Studio 54 would have still represented some kind of social elevation for a significant number of aspirational enthusiasts. Snotty Manhattan might have said no to the suburbs, but in so doing it was at least required to acknowledge their existence, and Rubell was only too happy to play along, fully aware that each curbside humiliation fed the carefully nurtured myth that Studio catered to an elite clientele. (In reality, it was overwhelmingly attended by ordinary, successful people who liked to think that they were too good to mingle with the bridge-and-tunnel contingent.) The velvet rope no longer barred the way to theater. It had become theater.

Mancuso went to the new nightclub for the first time in order to attend a Record Pool event and left insisting that he would never return. "I didn't like the policy at the door at all. 'You can get in, you can't!' The people had to stand there and hope they would be picked. It was really dehumanizing." As far as the Loft host was concerned, the antagonistic atmosphere seeped into the club itself. "Studio 54 wasn't a place where I wanted to socialize. I didn't care who was famous and not famous. I wanted to go to a place where things were free and relaxed—a place where you could be without becoming." With their emphasis on stars and sets, that was never likely to happen at Rubell and Schrager's discotheque. "Studio 54 was very contrived. There were a lot of distractions. They had a big sound system, but it wasn't musical. It was set up more for an effect than for people to feel relaxed and connect with each other."

Yet while Mancuso saw Studio as the inversion of everything he believed in, others thought that the relationship between the West Fifty-fourth Street club and the downtown party network was becoming increasingly blurred. "I was in both worlds," says Siano. "At the Gallery I emulated elements of David's Loft, but there was another part of it that was much more commercial." The journey between the Gallery and

Studio was consequently a relatively smooth one. "There wasn't any tension when I started playing at Studio. Not for a minute. I remember my brother and my close friends being very supportive because it was a very touted nightclub. People were excited and wishing me the best." Nor were the two crowds entirely distinct. "I had friends at Studio, I had friends at the Gallery, and some of them overlapped. Michael Gomes, Michael Cappello, and all of the designer people came to Studio. It was a big club for them. I didn't have a feeling that that was there and this was here." Nor could anybody deny the professionalism of the midtown venue's spectacular sets. "There was never a club like it, and there will never be a club like it. Everything you loved about theater was in Studio 54. *Phantom of the Opera* had *no* effects compared to Studio 54."

Finally, however, there was relatively little drama, at least of the music-dance variety, for while the performers were everywhere there wasn't a great deal of perspiration, and while the props were ubiquitous the DJs were no longer controlling the action. Instead, it was Rubell and Schrager who directed the show, and both of them were more interested in the bright lights of Broadway than the unfolding and unpredictable communication between the DJ and the dancing crowd. It was all Fellini and no funk. "The atmosphere didn't allow you to focus on the music," says Siano, whose initial euphoria was fairly short-lived. "You didn't need to use your audio as much. At the Loft the lights went out, and you had nothing but that audio working. The experience was just the pureness of the sound and the excitement of the music. At Studio it was the flashing lights, it was the drugs you were taking, it was the celebrity dancing next to you, it was the paparazzi, it was a million other things beside the audio experience." The equation had shifted. "Studio 54 took that experience of a relationship between the disc jockey, the music, and the people on the dance floor and turned it into a relationship between you, a drug, and the club." The differences, finally, were both real and irreconcilable. "A lot of people felt that taking the focus from the audio experience to the club sort of soured the whole experience, and it really did."

Siano lasted for four months before he was given the sack. "It was probably a combination of the drugs I was taking and the music I was playing," he says. "The night they fired me I played 'Trans-Europe Express' from the very beginning, and it was all very dramatic. Steve was up on the banquets with Ritchie, and later on Ritchie told me that Steve had said, 'What the fuck is this record?' 'Trans-Europe Express' was not a big hit right then,

Richie Kaczor
holding Nicky
Siano with David
Rodriguez.
Courtesy of
Nicky Siano

but four weeks later it became a number one record, *excuse me*. I still had that very underground thing about me, and Studio was not the underground." Siano's pharmaceutical intake might have also been a factor. "By this point I was totally strung out on drugs, and I would take these long breaks from the booth, but Steve didn't find me in the bathroom the night I got fired." Given that Rubell was using heavily himself, drugs were an unlikely pretext. "I played the Kraftwerk, and at the end of that night Steve said, 'I don't think you're right for Studio anymore.' Basically I was playing alternative music in an alternative manner, and they weren't down for that. It was the disco era, honey, and they wanted a smooth, seamless night. Everything matched, everything was clean, everything was high-tech, and that fucking ruined it."

That left Richie Kaczor, who confirmed his status as one of New York's top spinners during his Studio residency. "Richie called me the first night he played at Studio," remembers Bob Casey. "He said, 'Bob, I made it! Just thought you'd want to know. I *made* it!'" When Siano was asked to leave, Kaczor found himself in a stronger position than ever, although that didn't stop Rubell from interfering with his work, and one demand too many prompted the DJ to blow the sound system. Rubell hired a re-placement only to immediately regret his decision and rapidly reinstate the former resident, whose wage packet eventually rose to an estimated fifty thousand dollars a year. "I love Richie," Rubell later told the *SoHo Weekly News*. "I'd do anything to keep him."[14]

Rubell had come to appreciate that Kaczor was the perfect DJ for Studio. The ex–Hollywood resident's carefully modulated style, in which he would play sets of different styles of disco, meant that the crowd was always rotating, the key requisite for a successful bar, and as a model professional Kaczor was more reliable than the increasingly stoned Siano. Kaczor's nice-guy personality also guaranteed that he would never try to steal the limelight from the club itself, and the fact that he didn't think of himself as an avant-garde artist meant that he was more than happy to supply Studio's musically unsophisticated clientele with the run-of-the-mill hits that made them happy. "Richie was the perfect DJ for Studio,"

Richie Kaczor
and Steve Rubell
in the DJ booth at
Studio 54. Photo
by Waring Abbott

says Michael Gomes. "The club wanted elevator music as a backdrop for its stars and celebrities. Nicky was too frenetic and raw for that kind of ritzy scene." The Gallery DJ nevertheless continued to hold the utmost respect for Kaczor. "Richie was a great DJ when he was at Studio. A great DJ taps into the vibe of the crowd to help them program the night, and Richie was a master at that. His music was seamless, and that was perfect for Studio. He played to the audience, and I didn't, and that was part of why Steve said I wasn't right for Studio anymore."

Patrons who weren't right for Studio were offered a potential reprieve when cousins Maurice Brahms and John Addison (of Infinity and Le Jardin fame) combined their brains and pockets to launch New York, New York. Situated on Thirty-three West Fifty-second Street, the new discotheque opened on 18 May 1977, just a couple of weeks after Studio 54, against which it was pitched as a high-class rival. "New York, New York has the chicness and elegance of the thirties, with all the excitement of the eighties," Brahms told *After Dark*. "No detail was left untouched, no money spared. We wanted the perfect environment. More money was put into refurbishing the bathrooms than most discotheques spend on the whole club."[15]

Yet while a whipped-up media pronounced the opening night to be a success, the venue was never going to challenge the West Fifty-fourth Street discotheque's supremacy in the star wars, and the decisive blow to the new venue's pretensions came when it failed to secure the after-premiere party of Martin Scorsese's film, *New York, New York*, which starred Liza Minnelli and Robert De Niro. As if to intensify the humiliation, Minnelli spent the night at Studio, and the following day's papers didn't let Brahms and Addison forget it. "Within months New York, New York was catering to just the sort of working-class night-on-the-town clientele who would never get past Benecke's beady eye a few blocks north," wrote an unimpressed Anthony Haden-Guest.[16] Others, though, were drawn to the club's comparatively relaxed door policy. "The club is full of middle and upper middle class New Yorkers, Long Islanders, people from all over the metropolitan area, tourists, out of town businessmen, Orientals, Europeans and South Americans," commented writer Vita Miezitis. "The interracial mix of mainly heterosexual people from various countries makes the inside at times resemble the United Nations Plaza around lunchtime." Miezitis had gone to New York, New York after she had failed to get into Studio 54, and she found that "many people come here for similar reasons—because either they can't get into Studio 54 or they chicken out when they get to Studio 54 and decide they don't want to expose themselves to the 'You're-good-enough-but-you're-not' scrutiny of Steve Rubell."[17]

But if the door policy was different from that of Studio, the lack of any sustained relationship between the DJ and the crowd was effectively the same. "I had been playing for a fickle, sophisticated downtown crowd, so it was easy to play for a commercial venue," says François Kevorkian, who was invited by New York, New York light- and soundman Joey Bonfiglio to become the club's resident DJ in the autumn of 1977. "Unfortunately everyone wanted to hear the top forty hits. Donna Summer and the Bee Gees were major. The *Star Wars* record was also very big. I had to play the Trammps 'Disco Inferno' so many times I became ill."

Having left Galaxy 21 toward the end of the summer in 1976—"Heavy stuff was going on, and maybe after a while the novelty of what I was doing wore off"—Kevorkian started to house-sit for Art Garfunkel while moonlighting in the coatroom at an uptown club called Experiment 4, the first Manhattan residency of John "Jellybean" Benitez, who had hustled his way into the city. "I called all of the clubs and said, 'Hey, I hear you need a DJ!'" says the Bronx mixer. "When they said no, I asked, 'What do you do when the DJ's ill?' Experiment 4 offered me a spot. I got an ovation at the end of my first night, and after that I never wanted to leave Manhattan." Kevorkian made the most of his situation: he used Garfunkel's equipment to reedit his favorite dance tracks, including "Happy Song" by Rare Earth, and passed on the results to an increasingly enthusiastic Benitez. "The Rare Earth edit was inspired by Walter. I did it in 1977. I just copied his mix. I knew the pattern, and I just reproduced it. The drums and bongos looped forever. I didn't know about editing blocks so I just took scissors and scotch tape and stuck everything together. It was just an acetate." When Benitez called in sick, Kevorkian took to the turntables and other gigs ensued, including a stint at Sesame Street, a transient black-run venue that operated out of Flamingo while Fesco spent the summer season on Fire Island. Then came the offer from Bonfiglio—and the frustration of having to play for a comparatively conservative audience.

The experience wasn't a total letdown. "The energy level was unreal," says Kevorkian. "I've never seen a straight crowd respond in the same way." But, as one of the club's core dancers told Miezitis, the vibrant atmosphere was carefully manufactured. "Sometimes, I feel like I'm showing

François Kevorkian (left) at New York, New York with Stuart Bartsky (lightman) and Beth Einsen (DJ). Photo by Bob Popper. Courtesy of François Kevorkian

people what's permitted here when I dance, how crazy they are allowed to get themselves," he explained. "The deejay and I have signals for each other. When he wants more people on the floor or wants me to dance, he'll put on one of my favorite songs, one that he knows I can't resist. At that point, I'll jump on top of the speaker box and just move."[18] It wasn't always fun down below. "People would just stare, and it made me feel very uncomfortable," says Archie Burnett, a lithe twenty-year-old student in search of a dance home. "People would also bump into you and shit like that."

The purists were beginning to protest, but that didn't stop the crowds from clamoring to get in, and demand surged even further when a killer nicknamed "Son of Sam" went on the rampage in the summer of 1977, gunning down four victims as they emerged from neighborhood discotheques. Terrorized dancers from Brooklyn, the Bronx, and Queens reacted by either boycotting local discotheques or catching the subway to Manhattan, which was good news for midtown's venues and bad news for the Enchanted Garden. "The kids have just stopped patronizing the local discos," Schrager told *Billboard* in August, lamenting an 80 to 90 percent decline in the club's business. "They are either staying at home or going to clubs outside the danger zones, in Manhattan, or in Nassau and Suffolk counties on Long Island."[19]

Overall, though, business within the broader discotheque economy was deemed to be extremely good. *Billboard*'s Disco Forum III—held in the Americana Hotel in New York in September—declared clubland was on the verge of becoming America's most financially lucrative sector within the field of entertainment. "More revenue goes through the disco scene than the record business and the motion picture industry," Larry Harris, vice president of Casablanca Records, told the nine hundred registrants. "In fact, disco's $4 billion annually is second only to organized sports in the field of entertainment."[20] Yet, while the delegates repeated their earlier mantra of transforming disco from a "trendy fad" to a "sophisticated business industry," it was also clear that venues such as Studio 54 and New York, New York were never going to satisfy the kind of nationwide demand that disco entrepreneurs believed was there for the taking. As innovative and effectively irreproducible spectacles, the midtown discotheques didn't represent the stabilization of disco into the new status quo. Instead, they intensified the cultural mayhem that had been set in motion at the turn of the decade—the shifting ground that is so often referred to as the underground. Studio could never be reproduced in order to satisfy demand—there was only one Carmen D'Alessio, one Bianca Jagger, and one Steve Rubell, and they were all busy on West Fifty-fourth Street—so if entrepreneurs were going to exploit the dance market to its full potential, then someone needed to promote a more modest version of the discotheque concept to potential bridge-and-tunnel dancers who were more interested in doing than queuing.

* * *

Jimmy Stuard had started to follow a new postset routine. Having played his last record of the night, he would leave 12 West and go to the "cheapest hotel in town," the Everard Baths, which had replaced the Continental Baths as the choice bathhouse-discotheque. "He told me that if you went really late it was a good place to sleep," says Tom Moulton. "He said that it was dark, he could lock the door, and there were never any problems. I said, 'Lots of luck!'" One night in early June, however, Stuard's luck ran out. Someone left a cigarette smoldering on a mattress, and a fire spread throughout the building, which lacked a sprinkler system and proper safety exits. Stuard died of smoke inhalation. He was thirty-two years old and part of a circle of immortal men who weren't supposed to die.

Jimmy Stuard

Select Discography (12 West) [Source: Record World, *2 April 1977]*

Cerrone, "Love in 'C' Minor"/ "Black Is Black"/ "Midnight Lady"

Heart and Soul Orchestra, "Love in C' Minor"

Loleatta Holloway, "Hit and Run"/ "Dreamin' "

Denise LaSalle, "Freedom to Express Yourself"

Carrie Lucas,"I Gotta Keep Dancin' "

Teddy Pendergrass, "I Don't Love You Anymore"/ "The More I Get, the More I
    Want"/ "You Can't Hide from Yourself"

Barbara Pennington, 'Twenty-four Hours a Day"

Shalamar, "Uptown Festival"

T-Connection, "Do What You Wanna Do"

The Trammps, "Body Contact Contract"/ "Disco Inferno"/ "Starvin' "

Tributes flowed in. "To people outside the disco milieu, the idea that someone spinning records is thought of as performing 'his music'— creating his own particular sound out of other people's music—may seem rather presumptuous," wrote Vince Aletti. "But there's no question that a real DJ can shape a night of music with his personality, style and spirit, magically turning a string of records into a spontaneous symphony. Jimmy Stuard, the 1270-to-12 West DJ who died in a fire at New York's Everard Baths last week, was one of the best of these new dance masters and his music will be greatly missed."[21] Moulton took out a page in *Billboard* for his own personal memorial. "A good friend and a man who loved and lived music. Through his artistic creativeness he was able to share his love for music with others. His spirit will live on forever."[22]

Back at 12 West, Jonathan Fearing filled the vacuum left by Stuard. Paul Poulos then replaced Fearing before the residency finally shifted to Jim Burgess—all within the space of a couple of months. "I cannot begin to describe Jim's talent," says owner Alan Harris. "He was an unbelievable DJ." A classically trained opera singer, Burgess established himself as one of the most technically gifted mixers of his generation. "He could do things with beats that no one else could ever accomplish. He could take a four-beat and mix it with a five-beat, and it would come in perfect. He could overlay an entire seven-minute record on a fourteen-minute record, and it would sound like spun gold. He was just phenomenal."

Not to be outdone, Flamingo's Michael Fesco employed the good-cop, bad-cop duo of Howard Merritt and Richie Rivera to play alternate Saturdays (by now the only night the club was open). A slender Puerto Rican, Rivera had started DJing in 1971 when he volunteered to play at the Firehouse. Spots at the Sandpiper and the Anvil ensued, and in the autumn of 1977 he moved to Flamingo, where his penchant for the unfamiliar and the difficult made him a favorite target for industry promoters. "I think that my music should always have a little something more to make it different," he told *Village Voice* reporter Andrew Kopkind. "We have to progress. The music is getting much more sophisticated all the time."[23] Richard Brezner, who received his first DJing lessons as well as a constant supply of acetates and duplicates from Rivera, was a committed fan. "Richie played a great deal of sensual, instrumental, synthesized space music. His music was *so* moody and druggy it took you right out of your body. No one really knew where he got hold of it. He was accepted by a very trendy crowd, and to me his mixing was perfection. He was one of the best DJs that ever lived."

Merritt, a bearded country boy from the Catskills, had caught the discotheque bug when he went to Fire Island "without stopping in the city" in the summer of 1973. At the end of the season he went home and made tapes with a dinky little mixer before hitting the big time when he played Christmas Eve at Flamingo in 1977. Renowned for playing "pretty" music—songs like Barry White's "It's Ecstasy When You Lay Down Next to Me" and Odyssey's "Native New Yorker"—Merritt was the sensitive type. "I realize I have thousands of people in the palm of my hand," he told Kopkind. "I know how seriously they take the music. It means their whole weekend, maybe their whole week. I have to think when they're peaking on drugs and when they're coming down, what their mood shifts are, what is happening on the floor. The music makes it a very emotional experience."[24]

The music also contributed to a subtle yet seismic shift on the dance floor. That, at least, was the experience of Jorge La Torre, who now began to lock into a new level of dance consciousness. "Steve Ostrow and I were

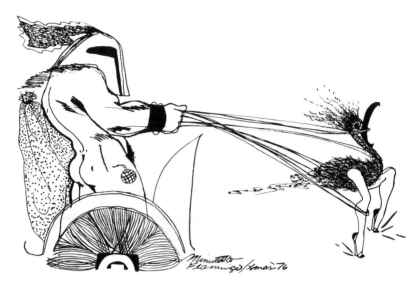

Flamingo flyer, Christmas 1976. Courtesy of Michael Fesco

having a difficult time personally, and our affair came to an end," he says. "I stopped working full-time at the Continental Baths and started to work as a consultant. The club went on for another year or so, but Steve felt the place wouldn't be the same without me. When it closed, he basically blamed me." La Torre's life subsequently opened up in unforeseeable ways. "I had been involved in the Baths, but the thing I was really interested in was the ultimate experience on the dance floor. How high can we go? How far can we take this? I was looking for the ultimate spiritual experience. What form that was going to take, when it was going to happen, and how we were going to go about it, I didn't have a clue."

La Torre first glimpsed the boundless essence of this transcendent experience in 1977. "I distinctly remember experiencing it for the very first time at a Black Party," he says. "All of a sudden it just manifested itself. We all came as one, and I said, 'This is it!' In my mind I literally had to stop myself. I said, 'What is this higher source of energy that I am able to tap into now?' It was a very powerful experience." La Torre says the most important aspect of the experience was its spirituality. "I was so liberated I just let go of myself, but it was very fleeting, almost like an introduction. It made its presence felt for a moment, and that was enough for me to be *completely* intrigued by it. I was totally mesmerized by the experience of this higher force. It was friendly, it was loving, it was great, and it wanted to help. It was a welcoming but overwhelming experience. From then on I said, 'Oh my God!' Literally."

Of course, La Torre had already danced in the Sanctuary, nightworld's most obviously spiritual venue. But, while Seymour and Shelley's discotheque was situated in a church, the mood on the dance floor didn't come close to tapping into the kind of cosmic spirituality that was beginning to surface at Flamingo. "In the early seventies I wasn't really aware that this was what I was looking for," says La Torre. "I just wanted to get high all the time on the dance floor. I remember it being more decadent than spiritual. I don't think it had entered my consciousness that this could be a spiritual experience. I guess these were baby steps that you had to take before you could walk." The new experience was polymorphous rather than genital. "Sexuality dissolved. It just became energy. It wasn't particularly male or female."

Evolving conditions underpinned the new experience—new, at least, for La Torre—and one of these involved the male, gay environment at Flamingo. On one level, men didn't matter. "Dancing had always been the most important thing, and once that part of myself was satisfied I would allow myself to think about meeting somebody and sex." Yet, on another level, men were everything. "It was an all-male environment, and I'm sure that had a lot to do with it. I had been looking for that tribal feeling that we experienced at Flamingo for a very long time without really knowing it, and that was why I loved the place so much."

The novel concentration of gay men, however, couldn't singlehandedly account for the new spirituality. "There wasn't just one single factor," says La Torre. "It was a combination of things. It could have been my mood that night, it could have been the friend that I was with, it could have been the space, it could have been the drugs, and it could have been the music. It could have been any number of things, or just a handful of them." The music, though, did appear to be causal. "The music was becoming more electronic, more beat-driven, and more tribal. That definitely had something to do with the change. It allowed your mind to travel. If you don't have vocals to anchor you to the dance floor it's easier for your mind to go to a different place."

Drugs facilitated the experience. "It was definitely related to drugs," says La Torre. "Drugs made it easier for you to lose your inhibitions and to become less aware of your immediate surroundings." There was no straightforward chemical route. "Some people did one single drug, some

Nicky Siano with Michael Gomes (right) and Miss Millie, 1977. Courtesy of Nicky Siano

people took several drugs together, some people did very little, and some people did a lot. I don't think it had much to do with what drug you had done or how much of it you had done. The main thing was that you had done something—maybe just a joint—to remove yourself from everyday reality and travel to a different realm, or at least to be open to that possibility. If other people were high then you could tap into this source and make it a shared experience. It could be enjoyed as much by someone who did very few drugs or a lot of drugs."

Just as Flamingo began to fly, the neighboring Gallery started to sink, thanks in no small part to Nicky Siano's heroin habit. Yet even when the alarm bells were as shrill as those that rang following his dismissal from Studio 54 in the summer of 1977, the DJ wasn't ready to listen. "When Stevie told me I was like, 'Fuck you! I don't care about you! I'll do something else!' I always had this really grand attitude. My brother was like, 'This was a great opportunity for you and you blew it!'" Around the same time Siano's music began to suffer, and while he maintains that his "half ass was still better than someone else's full throttle" a couple of hundred dancers disagreed and drifted away from the Gallery. "Nicky wanted to produce records, and the commitment was no longer there," says Michael Gomes. "Musically he was just playing regular commercial stuff. He was too tired and too high." Robin Lord had also grown weary of playing the role of partner-cum-promoter-cum-protector. "Nicky had become unpredictable and irresponsible. He was on a downward spiral that no one could stop. Nicky and I had many falling-outs, and at some point I just stopped going to the Gallery."

Nicky Siano

Select Discography (Gallery 1977)

Cerrone, "Love in 'C' Minor"

C. J. & Co., "Devil's Gun"

Lamont Dozier, "Going Back to My Roots"

First Choice, "Doctor Love"

First Choice, "Let No Man Put Asunder"

Loleatta Holloway, "Hit and Run"

Kraftwerk, "Trans-Europe Express"

Love and Kisses, "I Found Love (Now That I Found You)"

Carrie Lucas, "I Gotta Keep Dancin'"

Odyssey, "Native New Yorker"

Teddy Pendergrass, "The More I Get, the More I Want"

Teddy Pendergrass, "You Can't Hide from Yourself"

Barbara Pennington, "Twenty-four Hours a Day"

The Salsoul Orchestra, "Runaway"

Donna Summer, "I Feel Love"

T-Connection, "Do What You Wanna Do"

THP Orchestra, "Two Hot for Love"

The Trammps, "Body Contact Contract"

The Trammps, "Disco Inferno"

Retta Young, "My Man Is on His Way"

Joe Siano, who ran the club's finances and was generally considered to be the power behind the throne, delivered an ultimatum to his younger brother in the autumn of 1977: either the drugs end or the party closes. "He said he wasn't going to continue and watch me kill myself," says Siano. "I said, 'Just close it, see if I care!' I was stoned and arrogant as hell. I was the diva." Joe Siano closed the club. "We sent out a letter saying that the club was going to close in six weeks. At the time we were getting four to six hundred people a week. When the letter went out it was six hundred, the next week it was seven hundred, then it was eight hundred, then it was a thousand, then it was twelve hundred, and closing night was like eighteen hundred people. I remember it being very, very, *very* crowded—like five hundred people too many." If that kind of turnout made everybody wonder why the club was closing, an uncanny incident revealed the timeliness of the decision. "I played 'Turn the Beat Around,' and I turned off the sound when Vicky Sue Robinson went, 'Rat-tat-tat-tat-tat-tat on the drum.' I always turned the sound off at that point, and everybody would scream the line. But that night they didn't sing the line, so I shut the music off and I said on the mike, 'Sing it for me one laaast tiiiiime' in a really out-of-it voice. It was so eerie. It was one last time. It was the end of an era, and it was sad."

Yet, as one epoch drew to a close, another began to come to life when the closure of Michael Brody's fridge-cum-loft venue inadvertently catapulted Siano acolytes Larry Levan and Frankie Knuckles to the clubbing center stage in New York and Chicago respectively. "Reade Street was short-lived," says Mike Stone. "There were landlord problems. The venue was a fire trap, and it was shut after eighteen months." Not content with the modest returns provided by his Reade Street parties, Brody started to look for another, larger venue, and, aware of the need for a crowd-pulling DJ, he set about securing Levan's future involvement. "Michael was so satisfied that when the club had to close because of overcrowding he asked me not to play anywhere else until the new club opened," Levan told Steven Harvey.[25] Happy to wait on developments, he did some casual DJing at a club called Broadway in Brooklyn on Fridays, where his boyfriend, Mario Deserio, was spinning records, and on Saturdays he worked the lights at the Prince Street Loft. "I really didn't require anybody, but I wanted Larry and his friends to stay close to the music," says Mancuso. "Nathan was close to Larry so I got him on to help out in the kitchen." Levan's stint at the Loft only lasted for a few months. "Larry and his friends were hanging out in the booth, and a couple of times they passed me a joint with dust, even though they knew I was allergic to it.

I don't like downtown ["downs" such as angel dust] at all. So when they started bringing that dust around I had to get rid of them."

Mancuso was indirectly responsible for shuttling Levan into his next venue, having introduced Brody to Mel Katz, the Loft's attorney. It was Katz who took Brody to a sprawling garage space on King Street, a desolate industrial block south of Greenwich Village and near the Hudson River, where one of his clients, a struggling club called the Chameleon, which had opened to the sounds of Joey Palminteri playing on top of a mirrored pyramid at the beginning of 1976, was defaulting on the lease to number eighty-four. "We went to look at the space," says David DePino. "I remember walking up this huge ramp and looking at this big abandoned garage. At that point there were no walls so you saw all the windows, and it was all dusty. It looked like a scene out of Dracula with the sun coming through the windows. Larry said, 'This is going to be the new club,' and I gagged because I'd never seen something so big."

Mel Cheren, still a close friend of the club operator, was less fazed. "Michael had a good eye," he says. "He was looking for a bigger venue and reasoned that the Chameleon had failed because it was a big open space. He realized that you had to section it off." Having sold his joint property interests to Cheren, Brody had a significant chunk of capital to pay for the deposit on the building and augment the old sound system from Reade Street, and he set about borrowing additional money from a long list of friends and family members to make up the difference and clinch a ten-year lease. "We wanted to call it the Garage because it was a garage, but we didn't want such an industrial name," says DePino. "Michael said, 'One day we'll make this place pretty.' I replied, 'Yeah, like paradise!' And then Michael said, 'That's it! The Paradise Garage!' They used to pick up on my sarcasm and turn it around on me."

DePino had met Levan through Deserio. "I used to help decorate at Broadway and was close friends with Mario, who was this white Italian boy from Brooklyn. Larry remembers the first time he ever set eyes on me. He was with Mario in the DJ booth, and I was in the middle of the dance floor. The lights were cut except for the spot on the mirror ball so I spun it and went 'aaaaaahhhhhh' in this loud operatic voice. The whole dance floor screamed, and Larry was like, '*Who the hell was that?*' When the lights went on he saw me and told Mario, 'He looks just like you!' Larry came down and introduced himself."

New York's latest club had grown out of another Broadway party. "The

Loft," says Cheren, "was where the seed was planted for the Garage." Alex Rosner was accordingly employed to install the sound system—"I purchased some large JBL midrange horns and drivers," he remembers—and Brody and Levan even attempted to emulate Mancuso's practice of living in his party space. "They both had bedrooms," says DePino, "and they were both living there when Studio 54 opened." But whereas other party operators had simply hoped to emulate the Loft, Brody was determined to take the downtown party network to a different level. "When I first saw the club I said, 'Oh my God!'" says Nathan Bush. "It was this open space, and it went from one end of the block to the other end of the block. Michael showed me a sketch of his ideas, and I said, 'This is going to put the Loft to *shame!*'" Unlike Mancuso, who never really cared about investment strategies and accounting processes, Brody was a levelheaded businessman with a plan. "I didn't think it would put the Loft out of business," adds Bush. "But it was this huge, raw space, so Michael could do anything he wanted with it. It was a step above Gallery and the Loft on Prince Street."

The sheer scale of the project resulted in the development kitty being exhausted long before the club was ready to open. Brody's response was twofold: he moved out of his costly King Street bedroom and provided Levan with the means to do the same, and he also started to organize a series of Friday night "construction parties" in order to raise extra capital. Beginning in January 1977, the parties made the most of the building theme. The membership card came in the form of a little wrench, orange cones and police barriers were placed around the room, sawdust was scattered on the floor, and dancers were told to dress up in worker outfits. "They were held to make money," says DePino. "Then they caught on and became the theme." All in all there were five official construction parties, each of which showcased a new stage in the club's development. "At the last construction party you were able to look through the doorway and see the dance floor."

The Paradise Garage, however, didn't lie dormant between these events. Instead, Brody began to organize other parties that kept the space ticking and continued to raise extra cash along the way. "There were parties every week, regardless," says Bush, who ran the concession stand. "We never went without a party. They called them construction parties, but they weren't official construction parties. They were just parties to keep the place going, to pay the rent, and to try to get the rest of the equipment in there. We had sawdust parties in the Garage for the longest time."

Official or unofficial, these transitional preopening events contained the promise of a new downtown experience. "It was a completely raw, concrete space," says Danny Krivit, who had been friends with Levan since the days of the Broadway Loft. "There were a couple lights in the ceiling, and there was a *serious* sound system, but it was all in the smallest room in the club. It was tight." Krivit was struck by the intensity of the parties. "There were a few hundred people, and it was hot and sweaty. I was a bit stoned, and I kept getting dripped on, so eventually I looked at the ceiling and it was covered with water. I remember thinking this was a new situation. It was similar to the Loft, but it was a little less esoteric. There was a little less of the jazz-style dancing. It was a little more discoey, although this was the funkier side of disco."

Mancuso's mothership had also inspired venues outside of Manhattan. The first satellite, Le Jock, appeared in New Jersey, and the second, US Studio, was opened by an African American social worker turned entrepreneur called Robert Williams in Chicago. "I first met David in the East Village," says Williams. "I was wearing this t-shirt from the Tamburlaine, and David asked me if I wanted to go to one of his parties. He gave me this invite." Williams was blown away by the private venue. "I thought it was extremely wild. I had never been to a party in a loft space, and the energy level was so much higher than anywhere else. It was very intense." Williams and Mancuso became good friends. "I would visit David during nonparty hours, and we hung out together a lot. I used to go to his parties every week, and I always invited a guest. The Loft was the only place I would go on a Saturday night."

Williams reluctantly moved to Chicago in the mid-seventies—he couldn't keep up with the cost of living in New York—and was immediately bored. "There was nothing going on," he says. "The first place I went to was this midwestern gay bar called Bistro. It was very commercial and possibly a little racist. They asked me for all sorts of ID and after a while I managed to get in, but I was like, 'What the hell is this in comparison to New York?'" The newcomer responded by starting up his own parties. "I had studied at the University of Iowa, and my college fraternity brothers used to visit me in New York. I would take them out, and we would have a fantastic time, so when I arrived in Chicago they were really excited. They said, 'It's dull as hell here! Why don't you help us put on a New York–style party?' "

The first event took place on East Belmont Street. "We held it at the house of this guy called Michael Matthews, and he DJed," says Williams. "We rented these huge ALTEC Lansing Voice of the Theatre speakers, and we put up a lot of balloons. I think we might have also put a little acid in the punch." If anything the party went too well: the neighbors called the police, and Williams was forced to seek out an alternative space. "I found this warehouse next to Union Station," he says. "This was the first experience Chicagoans had of going to a party in a loft. We sent out invitations to people who had come to the first party because we wanted to keep it private, but word got around and the numbers ended up tripling. There must have been fifteen hundred people there. The police tried to close it down, but they couldn't get in because it was so packed." The mixed-leaning-toward-gay crowd went on to enjoy two more parties at the venue before it—and Williams's sound system—burned to the ground. "After that we rented a studio on South Michigan Avenue. Unfortunately the fire department was situated right across the street from us, and they didn't like the noise. It also became so packed that during the winter steam would come out of the windows, and the first time that happened they thought the place was on fire. They were like, 'Uh-uh. We can't have this!' They came up with some building code violations and threw us out."

The indefatigable Williams proceeded to uncover a ten-thousand-square-foot floor in an old loft building at 555 West Adams and decided that it was time to get serious. "Up until this point I had been going along for the social ride, but now the parties became more business-oriented," he says. "This German guy called Siegfried Schuh, who was a master violin maker, helped with the finances, and we also introduced an invite system. As the parties developed they became more and more like the Loft." US Studio was registered as a private social club in order to bypass Chicago's cabaret laws, and the parties began to attract a largely homogeneous black gay crowd. "US Studio was an after-hours juice bar," says Frederick Dunson. "I went there out of need. The gay discos in Chicago such as Alfie's, Le Pub, and Dugan's Bistro discriminated against blacks, and the premise of US Studio was that you wouldn't get the hassle of other clubs. You could go and be yourself." Michael Matthews and Benny Winfield DJed, and the parties—which dancers dubbed the Warehouse thanks to the postindustrial design of the venue—began to run until the crack of dawn. "Most clubs closed at three or four, but the kids wanted to dance longer," says Dunson, who eventually took on a variety of jobs at US Studio, from running the fruit bar to managing the office. "The parties at West Adams would start at midnight and end at seven or eight the next morning."

The nocturnal rhythms continued until Williams, who had been elected president of the social club, donned his entrepreneurial cap and proceeded to alienate a key segment of his core crowd. "A number of people weren't paying their dues so I dismissed them," he says. "They ended up opening their own club called the Bowery, which became our first real rival. The Bowery was basically a copy of the Warehouse because that was all they had experienced. Michael Matthews ended up playing there—I guess he didn't like the way I excluded some people from the club—and our crowd followed him." Williams filled in for the absent DJ but failed to stop the drift. "People were promising to come, but they would end up going to the Bowery. We were getting around fifty people a week."

Realizing that he needed to come up with something fresh in order to win back his crowd, Williams moved to an old office building at 206 South Jefferson and set about reinventing his parties. "We happened to look out of the back window of West Adams and saw this cute little building," he says. "It was two stories high and spread across nine thousand square feet. I talked to the broker, and he told me I could lease it so I closed down the Warehouse for a while and hired Richard Long to install a sound system." The party organizer also decided he needed to hire a new DJ. "The crowd hadn't responded to either me or Benny—they were just having a ball going to hear Michael at the Bowery—so I decided to try and lure them back by inviting Larry Levan to DJ." Levan—who had by this point been promised the world by Michael Brody—wasn't interested. "I asked Larry, and he said, 'Are you *crazy*? I'm not going to the *Midwest*!' I said, 'Well, what about Frankie?' and Larry replied, 'You can ask him yourself!'"

Williams knew Knuckles and Levan from way back when. "Larry and I got into some trouble when we were really young," says Knuckles. "We had just come out of this club called Charades at about five in the morning, and we walked past this bread truck parked outside Dunkin' Donuts. Larry was like, 'Keep an eye on me!' and he went inside the truck and came out with these doughnuts. Eventually we were caught by the police and taken to this camp." Williams oversaw the duo's rehabilitation before he bumped into them outside Tamburlaine. "Frankie and Larry were too young to get in, and they were breaking New York's curfew on juveniles so I told them to report to my office the next day. They came and we talked. They weren't bad kids. They were just so in love with the night scene it was hard to contain them." Another chance encounter ensued a year or so later. "Robert was hanging out at the Loft, which was really funny," says Knuckles. "He was still working at the juvenile council and was just part of the scene." Levan and Knuckles had turned their pastime into a profession by the time of their next reunion. "I went to the Continental Baths for one of the shows, and I was kind of in shock because Larry was the DJ and Frankie was doing lights," says Williams. "As it happens I wasn't really into Larry's music that night, but by the time he got to Reade Street I thought he was really good."

Williams attempted to entice Levan to Chicago some three years later, and when that failed, the faltering club entrepreneur turned to Knuckles, who had lost his job at the Continental Baths when the venue went bankrupt toward the end of 1976 ("Steve Ostrow was taking out more money than he put back in") and was now playing at an East Side spot called the Stargate Ballroom. "At first Frankie was a little apprehensive about coming, although he wasn't as blunt as Larry," says Williams. "I proposed that he come out and look at the club. I told him I would pay his way and let him check it out. I said, 'You've got nothing to lose!'" Even though the new Warehouse had yet to open, Knuckles liked what he saw. "The Warehouse," he says, "was structured on the concept of the Loft."

Knuckles was hired to play at the March 1977 opening night that, co-inciding as it did with the release of Odyssey's "Native New Yorker," provided Williams with a made-to-measure promotional slogan. "Invitations were sent out by mail or word-of-mouth," says Dunson. "It was very exclusive. People were begging to be let in. New York was the mecca, and Chicagoans wanted to hear what it was all about." The party went so well that the following morning Williams asked Knuckles if he would move to Chicago. "I said I had to think about it," remembers the DJ. "I had worked at the Continental for three years, and the last thing that ever crossed my mind was that it would close, so I thought, 'What if I move to Chicago and then the club shuts down?'" Knuckles considered the offer for a month before coming up with an alternative proposal. "I thought if I owned a piece of the business then that would give me three times the incentive

Frankie Knuckles (right) and Siegried Schuh in the Warehouse. Courtesy of Robert Williams

to make sure it stayed open. If it's yours you're going to work like crazy to make sure it stays there, so that's what I hit them with." Knuckles says that Williams thought he was kidding. "I was like, 'What happens if you guys shut down? That just leaves me hanging on the line!' So we came to an agreement." Williams maintains that the "agreement" still left him in charge of the Warehouse. "Frankie was an adviser, a kind of silent partner, and he helped me get things off the ground. He was extremely creative. But I owned the business, not Frankie."

Knuckles returned to Chicago in July to discover an all-but-empty venue. "Nobody was coming," he says. "Different DJs were trying to play, and some people involved in the partnership had pulled out. There was a lot of animosity." The kids (as Chicago's black gay men referred to them-selves) had returned to the Bowery, and switching into reconnaissance mode, Knuckles decided to pay a visit to the rival venue, which turned out to be inferior in terms of space, sound, and lighting. "It was just one of those situations where the people that opened the Bowery were better-connected than Robert." The DJ let it be known that he had returned, hoping to entice the crowd back to the Warehouse, but while business picked up it was nowhere near enough. "The Warehouse took a while to

After the party, outside the Warehouse on South Jefferson. Courtesy of Robert Williams

catch on," says Dunson. "There were evenings when I prepared food for five hundred and only ten people showed up." Williams, who had DJed while Knuckles prepared to move to Chicago, even began to wonder if his new recruit would make any kind of difference. "It wasn't going too well because Frankie was playing all of this new stuff. The crowd was used to hearing Michael, not Frankie, and being Midwesterners they were a bit suspicious of his style. They were like, 'He's coming here with all that New York stuff!'"

When the Warehouse closed for restructuring for a month, Knuckles returned to the Bowery. "I went every Saturday, and each week they said, 'Why don't you play records for a bit?' The first night I had to use the records that were already there, but it went well and at the end of that night they said, 'Why don't you come back and play next week?'" Knuckles agreed and ended up playing three weeks on the trot. "Then on the fourth week I was just hanging out, and they said, 'Are you playing?' I said, 'No.' They were like, 'Come on!' I was like, 'No-ooo, if you want to hear me play I'll see you at the Warehouse next week!' Next week at the Warehouse it was packed!" The Bowery closed soon after. "Everyone wanted to hear Frankie," says Williams. "Let's just say that people are a little *fickle.*"

The parties quickly settled into a groove, with three to five hundred kids turning up each week. "It was a community," says Knuckles. "A lot of kids came out at the Warehouse. They found themselves there, and they met their lovers there. Saturday night is what they lived for. They knew they were going to have a good time because that was all they ever had. Nothing else mattered. When you're young these things leave an indelible impression." Knuckles became a pivotal attraction. "Frankie would get really creative," says Dunson. "Other Chicago DJs would play records you heard on the radio and pitch them so they were danceable, whereas Frankie would knock people off their feet." Dunson acknowledges that Artie Feldman, a regular Chicago-based contributor to Vince Aletti's "Disco File" page, was playing a similar set of records at Our Den, a commercial discotheque that had opened in the mid-seventies, "but Frankie's mixing was a lot more elaborate and there was a lot more bass, a lot more strings."

The Warehouse parties also acquired their own distinctive rhythm, shifting into an invisible gear in which the psychic energy emanating from the dance floor and the DJ booth would meet and meld. "I'd be in the booth from eleven o'clock at night until twelve noon, but usually I'd come out and dance around at about eight or nine o'clock," says Knuckles. "It was like we were going on a journey. I was the train conductor, and I had to make sure that everything was working and moving in the same rhythm. By eight or nine o'clock in the morning everybody would be locked into the beat, and the records would be pretty much playing themselves, so it would be easy for me to just slide out, dance around, and check that everybody's head was still in the right place." Knuckles would circle the entire room. "I'd just bounce around the dance floor and come back before the record was done. The crowd got off on that. It wasn't like them and me. I've never liked that mentality. I liked being on the same level." The downtown party network had seized Chicago—although its failure to establish a broader national foothold was about to be exposed.

9. dominance

The future of Nik Cohn's *New York* story on suburban discotheque culture in Brooklyn lay at the bottom of several thousand wastepaper baskets until Robert Stigwood, the head of RSO, read about Vincent's rituals and spotted a commercial opportunity. Stigwood decided to turn the article into a film, even though his company had yet to show any sustained interest in the disco trend beyond welcoming in the unanticipated revenue from the born-again Bee Gees—as well as releasing the unashamedly vulgar "Disco Duck" by Rick Dees and His Cast of Idiots. Screenwriter Norman Wexler was hired to deliver a script based on Cohn's article, Emmy Award nominee John Badham was brought in to direct, and a preproduction party featuring a special dance demonstration by lead actor John Travolta was held on 10 March 1977. Filming began four days later and was completed by the middle of August.

The three-month marketing campaign to promote *Saturday Night Fever* revolved around a symbiotic movie/soundtrack cross-plugging strategy that Stigwood had developed for the promotion of *Jesus Christ Superstar* in 1973. However, a potentially major obstacle to the film's success soon emerged in the form of the Sex Pistols, who had topped the British charts in June 1977 and stolen the front-page headlines of the music media ever since. Still unconvinced that disco was worthy of serious investment, a number of America's most powerful record companies suddenly started to battle each other for Malcolm McLaren's signature, all of which suggested that disco might be about to become passé even before RSO's film hit the screens. Seeing off Arista and Columbia, Warner Brothers won the scramble for the punk sensation, and *Never Mind the Bollocks*, released in early November, hit the stores at exactly the same

John Travolta at the *Saturday Night Fever* preproduction party, 1977. Photo by Waring Abbott

time as the *Saturday Night Fever* soundtrack (which was released in advance of the film). It was punk versus disco, and the critics backed punk. "In terms of publicity and notoriety, the Sex Pistols looked set to repeat their English experience in America," writes Sex Pistols chronicler Jon Savage. "The media were immediately won over: the general consensus—with a few hostile exceptions—was that America was ready for it, whatever 'it' was."[1] The ensuing tour, however, was a disaster, and the album peaked at 106 in the charts. As far as Warner Brothers was concerned, punk was a flunk.

Released in December, *Saturday Night Fever* was first and foremost a film about the all-too-familiar theme of adolescent angst that just happened to be organized around a Brooklyn disco. Tony Manero, the movie's protagonist, is frustrated—he has a going-nowhere job, his typecast Italian American family drives him crazy, and he doesn't even have a girlfriend with whom he can discharge some of his raging hormones. The local discotheque provides him with his only effective outlet, and the first appearance of Stephanie on the flashing floor persuades him that she would be the perfect partner for a forthcoming dance contest. Although their subsequent coffee date is a nightmare, with class snobbery pouring forth from Stephanie's teapot, she agrees to work with him. The social strife subsides as the dance partners work on their steps, and they go on to win the contest, but the celebrations are cut short when Tony gives the trophy to the "real winners," a Latino/a team whose ethnicity had led to their elimination. Stephanie isn't impressed, and any chance of a full-on romance is apparently foreclosed when Manero molests her, although a resolution of sorts emerges when the suicide of a drunken gang member persuades Manero to travel to the heroine's new Manhattan apartment and seek her forgiveness. Attempting to emulate Stephanie's upward mobility, Tony pronounces that he has had enough of Brooklyn.

The introduction of a female love interest had been Wexler's most significant revision to Cohn's unerringly homosocial story, and while this Hollywood-driven change resulted in a more credible representation of the suburban discotheque than that of "The Rituals of the New Saturday Night," it also paved the way for *Saturday Night Fever* to be a film not so much about dance culture as about escaping dance culture. The point of going to a discotheque, it turned out, wasn't really to dance but to meet someone of the opposite sex and then stop dancing. At the end of the film Tony doesn't want to go to Manhattan in order to find a hipper club. What he really wants to do is get an apartment in New York City and quit wasting his life on the dance floor. "I ain't going back," he tells Stephanie, " 'cause it's all bull." It's almost as if he wants to go to the club capital of America *in order to escape the world of the discotheque*. As such the film ends with a sober condemnation of the lifestyle that it supposedly celebrates.

Local DJs nevertheless were generally satisfied with the veracity of RSO's depiction of the Brooklyn scene, which wasn't bad considering that the movie was an imaginative interpretation of an imaginative interpretation. "The way you saw people dressed in *Saturday Night Fever* is the way we dressed," says Dan Pucciarelli, a Bay Ridge DJ. "The guys wore nice pants, a nice shirt, a leather jacket, collar over, collar up. The girls always wore heels, always wore a dress, always put on makeup, always had their hair done." In terms of the music, the film got it half right. "The movie's DJ, Monty Rock, gave the image that DJs were gay pot smokers. Back then there wasn't one DJ in Brooklyn who was gay. Everybody was straight, hardcore, Italian, liked girls. But it was a fair representation of the records we played." The depiction of the local gang culture was more dubious. "The incident when Travolta and his boys went to fight the Spanish boys—that never happened in our neighborhood. You stayed in your own area. Everybody had certain places where they went, and that was that." As for the portrayal of Brooklyn's dance style, that was also wide of the mark. "The dancing was ridiculous. Sure, there were times when people would gather on the floor and do the Hollywood Walk, but nobody danced liked Travolta." The sex, though, was spot on. "The drinking age was eighteen, so there was more stamina, more energy, more people going out. Sex was everywhere. If you went to a dark corner in a club you were bound to find two people getting it on."

The soundtrack received rave reviews. Featuring six tracks by the Bee Gees (the previously released number-one hits "Jive Talking'" and "You Should Be Dancing" plus "How Deep Is Your Love," "More Than a Woman," "Night Fever," and "Stayin' Alive"), as well as contributions from the Trammps ("Disco Inferno"), Kool and the Gang ("Open Sesame"), and MFSB ("K-Jee"), the album captured, in the words of Vince Aletti, "the broad scope of pop disco: not the expansive, complex Eurodisco sound that has dominated the clubs for the past year but a solid, even intelligent introduction to the most accessible music coming up from the dance underground."[2] Aletti believed that the Bee Gees had more than earned their place at the center of the soundtrack. " 'You Should Be Dancing,' released in 1976 but included in this collection, is flawless: loud, dense, wonderfully echoed to create a shimmering intensity," he wrote in the *Village Voice*. "But 'Stayin' Alive' tops it with its deep emotional tug, the wailing voices shifting between helpless cries and frantic, defiant boasts."[3] A demo of the soundtrack, it later emerged, even shaped the film. "The songs were so strong that they actually affected the way we shot the movie," commented RSO Vice President Bill Oakes. "The demos were used on location. For example, the spectacular opening shot of John Travolta walking down the street with the 'Stayin' Alive' music was shot to match the extraordinary composition that the Bee Gees had given us."[4]

The dual impact of *Saturday Night Fever* was far-reaching. By June, the film had topped the one-hundred-million-dollar mark—a figure surpassed only by *The Godfather*—and by the end of the year the soundtrack had sold a record thirty million copies, establishing itself as the largest grossing and most popular album of all time. Music, according to executive producer Kevin McCormick, was the key: the Bee Gees, who notched up another three number-one records along the way, were credited with saving the film from suffering the same fate as *Mean Streets*, which was a "well respected, well-crafted vehicle for a star" that lacked "a hook to make it accessible" to a wider audience. "The Bee Gees provided us with the means to break 'Saturday Night Fever' out," McCormick told *Billboard*, "and to make it available and interesting to millions in America."[5] All in all, it amounted to a quantum leap for the disco industry. "Travolta and the Gibbs [*sic*] boys have inaugurated phase two of the disco boom," declared Aletti, "giving the genre its first chart-topping album and trailing some of the music's best performers in their wake."[6]

Above all else, *Saturday Night Fever* established an imaginative framework for the stabilization of discotheque culture. The film evidently came out of an already-functioning suburban culture whose popularity had inspired Stigwood in the first place, yet in its choice and depiction of that scene *Saturday Night Fever* created a lens through which a discotheque mainstream could come into focus. First, the film deleted any trace of the downtown night network: out went Manhattan's ethnic gays, black funk, drugs, and freeform dancing, and in came suburban straights, shrill white pop, alcohol, and the Hustle. Second, *Saturday Night Fever* tapped into deeply resonant themes, such as the desire of working-class youths to escape the tedium of nine-to-five jobs and the fantasy of imagining oneself as a star under the dazzling lights of the discotheque. Third, the film was set in the kind of discotheque that was easy to access and relatively simple to create: as much as Studio 54 was elitist and impossible to copy, 2001 Odyssey was populist and easy to reproduce. Fourth, the marketing campaign and box-office success of the film meant that a mass-market template for disco was established in the United States for the first time. And, fifth, an impassioned audience left the cinemas, headed toward their local discotheque, and did their best to imitate Stephanie and Tony, blissfully unaware that their moves had been choreographed in fantasyland. Decontextualized and dehistoricized, disco culture was presented as a monolithic and acceptable dating agency for straights, and for the consumers of *Saturd(e-g)ay Night Fever* who knew no better, or who perhaps didn't want to know any better, the dance floor in Bay Ridge became the founding moment of "discomania."

Disco's prospective dominance received a further fillip when Casablanca released a West Coast version of RSO's distinctly East Coast portrayal of the dance phenomenon. Designed by Neil Bogart and produced in association with Motown, *Thank God It's Friday* told the story of a night in the life of a Los Angeles disco, sustaining several narrative plots and giving a cameo role to in-house starlet Donna Summer. On an ideological level, the release represented some sort of progress, for while the light-hearted script brimmed with nightlife clichés, it also avoided the moralizing conclusions of Wexler's screenplay. The critics, however, were unimpressed, and the movie eventually generated a disappointing (now that everything was being measured against the inflated performance of *Saturday Night Fever*) twenty million dollars at the box office.

An increasingly voracious Bogart could at least console himself with the thought that *Thank God It's Friday* had helped to entrench Casablanca's position as the disco industry's most prolific and visible record company, and this was formally recognized when Bill Wardlow invited the mogul to deliver the keynote speech at *Billboard*'s Disco Forum IV, which was held at the New York Hilton Hotel and received an early endorsement from, of all people, Edward Koch. "The disco and its lifestyle has helped to contribute to a more harmonious fellowship toward all creeds and races," announced the New York mayor, proclaiming that 19 to 25 June would be an official "Disco Week." "The beat of the disco is the heartbeat of what makes New York City a special kind of place—vitality, individuality and creativity. People all across America made the disco popular—New York City made it a phenomenon."[7] Barely able to contain his dancing feet, Bogart maintained the remorseless rhythm. "In the three years since 'Love To Love You Baby' the disco wave has swept across the world with a force not seen since the early days of rock'n'roll," trumpeted the executive. "It's a spectacular new wave and the crest is yet to come."[8] As forum performances by Chic, Andy Gibb, Loleatta Holloway, Donna Summer, Tavares, and the Trammps testified, life was about to become a seemingly endless disco party.

Any thoughts that Bogart was dancing in the land of hyperbole were dispelled the following month when *Record World* released statistics showing that music industry sales had shot through the roof during the last year. "Since 1975 there has been a veritable explosion in records, an explosion that has brought the industry unprecedented sales and unprecedented prosperity," proclaimed the journal. "Last year, 1977, was the best year ever in records, setting new highs in sales and revenues. And 1978, only six months old, has already surpassed the first six months of last year."[9] Yet whereas the previous year's sales had been fuelled by the death of Elvis Presley, 1978 was all about *Saturday Night Fever* and disco.

Clubs were also doing good business, and New York's beacon venue,

Neil Bogart and Donna Summer at the *Billboard* Disco Forum 1978 (with Bill Wardlow, center, clapping). Photo by Waring Abbott

the big and brash Studio 54, celebrated its first birthday party in April in typical style, opening with an Issey Miyake fashion show before moving into the usual bacchanalian celebration. Outside the club, Steve Rubell orchestrated the increasingly frantic scene of rejection and admission while inside Truman Capote told the *New York Times* why the wait was worthwhile. "I've been to an awful lot of nightclubs, and this is the best I've ever *seen*," he told reporter Leslie Bennetts. "This is the nightclub of the future. It's very democratic. Boys with boys, girls with girls, girls with boys, blacks with whites, capitalists and Marxists, Chinese and every-thing else—all one big mix!"[10] Accompanied by Halston, Bianca Jagger, and Andy Warhol, Liza Minnelli subsequently made her way to a grand piano and serenaded Rubell with the line "Now it's your birthday, I can't give you anything but love, baby!" Love, somewhat disconcertingly, was once again the message.

The perception that discotheque culture had become unstoppable was reinforced by the launch of a third major discotheque in Manhattan's mid-town district in June 1978. A two-million-dollar operation whose address at 124 West Forty-third Street inevitably prompted talk of rivalry with

Studio, Xenon was owned by Howard Stein, who had been a leading rock concert producer in the sixties, and Peppo Vanini, a former European restaurateur, and while the opening night cast was less glittering than Studio's much publicized lineup, the sight of Rollerena deserting West Fifty-fourth Street for West Forty-third Street would have given Rubell—whose hairline was already receding—pause for thought. Folklore, however, has it that guests immediately nicknamed Xenon "Studio 27" because the dance floor was half the size of its midtown competitor. The launch went from bad to worse when, at one in the morning, Stein and Vanini's $100,000, 8,300 lb. spaceship (designed by special effects whiz Doug Trumbull, who had worked on 2001 and Close Encounters of the Third Kind) reportedly descended into ignominy, with only a couple of its vaunted thirty thousand variations spluttering into action. It was worse outside, where thousands of invitees were turned away in what might have been the worst-planned guest list in clubbing history. "Dozens of limousines, carrying the rich and famous to the opening, passed the place by once their occupants got a look at the mob scene in front of the disco," reported the New York Times. "Many of them went, instead, to Xenon's longer established rival in assaulting the senses, Studio 54."[11] As the infidels returned, Rubell took to the public address system and issued his thanks.

A dodo of a discotheque that, like its so-called "mother ship," had manifestly failed to take off, Xenon closed the following day, with Stein and Vanini telling anyone who could be bothered to listen that they intended to reopen in a couple of weeks. Although few held their breath, the club was up and running by July and, with Jonathan Fearing newly installed as the DJ, Xenon began to steal high profile events from under Studio's nose, staging parties for the likes of Mick Jagger and Pele as well as the Superman premiere. Those who were tired of the brash and flamboyant atmosphere at Studio flocked to the sophisticated—or, as some euphemistically put it, more European—ambience of the West Forty-third Street club. Even Disco Sally joined the exodus, declaring that Xenon was now her "favorite discotheque."[12]

Studio was also beginning to face problems of its own making that could be traced back to Rubell's decision to give an interview to Dan Dorfman of New York magazine in November 1977. Not for the first time, the mogul said things that went way beyond the call of duty, and on this occasion they were noted by one of the city's most keenly read financial reporters. "Profits are astronomical," boasted Rubell. "Only the Mafia does better." He continued, "It's a cash business and you have to worry about the IRS. I don't want them to know everything." When Dorfman asked Rubell if Studio's prospective annual volume was going to top three million dollars, "with an unbelievably high 80 percent filtering down to the bottom line," the mogul replied, "I wouldn't say that's bullshit."[13]

The trouble surrounding the club thickened in March when commodities broker Leslie Duverglas and disco owner Georgio Penco were convicted for supplying forty ounces of "fantastic flake" coke to Dennis Solovay, a Studio regular who also happened to be a federal informant. The story barely made the national press, but that had little effect on the club's internal rumor mill. "The fear spreading among the nose and 'lude set is that Studio 54 has been packed with undercover agents and that the feds are preparing for a massive coke witchhunt," reported the *Village Voice*. "And court observers believe a grand jury may be convened based on these undercover activities."[14] Carefree dancers began to wonder about the identity of the seemingly nice people who had been so generous with their drugs. As the *Voice* put it, "one night recently, when, to the usual squeal of newcomers, the man-in-the-moon lowered onto Studio 54's scrim and the huge spoon rimmed with sparkling lights swung toward the lunar nose and red bulbs lighted up the eye, one morose and well-established guest snorted: 'That ain't a high. That's an Excedrin headache.'"[15]

Rubell and Schrager's battlefront widened when part of a group of disgruntled Studio rejects—the thousand or so members who had paid $75 to $150 for their privileged access only to discover that they still weren't guaranteed entry, even if the club was half-empty—decided that enough was enough and took their case to the New York City Department of Consumer Affairs. Relishing the prospect of a confrontation with the influential lawyer Roy Cohn, who doubled as a Studio client in his spare time, an attorney for the Department of Consumer Affairs declared, "We will try to negotiate an agreement with Studio 54 whereby they will inform the consumers who've paid for memberships that they have the option for applying for a refund of their money. Our concern is not just the eight citizens who complained to us. We want restitution of the $94,000. If we got eight complaints and the attorney general got 10, there must be more consumers, who have not come forward, who feel cheated."[16]

The spotlight on Studio's misdemeanors intensified when Henry Post

wrote an article for *Esquire* in June that focused on the "sour notes" that were being struck at New York's "hottest disco." Post revealed the seedier side of the Enchanted Garden operation and the shady way in which Rubell and Schrager bypassed their early failure to obtain a liquor license before recounting how the duo mistreated Grace Jones during her appearance at the club on New Year's Eve 1977. She "was treated like a nigger," commented Ron Link, the director for the night. "It was the biggest rip-off ever," added Jones, who didn't get the stage set or the money she was promised.

Post went on to launch a stinging critique of a membership policy that was beginning to give even Carmen D'Alessio pause for thought. "It's embarrassing," she told Post. "Members can't get in. The regular crowd has deteriorated. And many people sent in for memberships and got nothing, their money lost. I have so many people who haven't gotten their cards after they paid for them. And then they can't get in. I mean *big* names."[17] Post surveyed a series of cases in which individuals paid for cards that either failed to materialize or else were subsequently turned away at the door, even if their name was on the list. One was roughed up and a similar kind of abuse was dished out to a special guest and a busboy. This wasn't the kind of press that Rubell liked to nurture.

Mollified by the news that the State Supreme Court was now going to overrule the State Liquor Authority and hand them their long-awaited liquor license, Rubell and Schrager struck a deal with the Department of Consumer Affairs and agreed to refund dissatisfied members to the tune of $94,000, as well as pay the Department of Consumer Affairs $10,000 to cover the cost of its investigation. As the new promotional campaign for the club's own brand of designer jeans declared, "Now everybody can get into Studio 54." Consumer affairs commissioner Bruce Ratner kept a straight face. "Studio 54 has been difficult in dealing with its 'members' whose money helped to make the disco successful," he told *Record World*. "We hope this agreement is an indication that they will be more responsible in the future."[18] *Hope* being the barely operative word.

Yet while the media was beginning to niggle away at Rubell and Schrager, the broader disco phenomenon was now enjoying unprecedented coverage, both in terms of quantity and content. Film had been

---

opposite: Studio 54 dance floor. Photo by Waring Abbott

Studio 54 jeans ad for women. Photo by Gordon Munro

Studio 54 jeans ad for men. Photo by Gordon Munro

well covered by *Saturday Night Fever* and *Thank God It's Friday*, and TV now started to increase its coverage of the dance craze, thanks to talk show hosts Merv Griffin and Dinah Shore plus programs such as *American Bandstand, Midnight Special, Soul Train,* and even *60 Minutes.* By the end of the summer, major advertising agencies Benton & Bowles, J. Walter Thompson, BBD&O, Ted Bates, and McCann Erickson had also started to reference the culture. "There is really nothing new in what we're doing," Roy Eaton, vice president and director of music at Benton & Bowles, told *Billboard.* "We always make the best possible use of current music trends and disco is what is current."[19]

Radio, effectively the last line of resistance, was also beginning to follow, with WBLS still in pole position. "BLS was *the* station, and that was because of Frankie Crocker," says CBS's Vince Pellegrino, who installed a special car radio converter in order to capture the DJ's elusive FM airwaves. "He would blend the sounds of what was going on in New York." Other stations had picked up on the trend. WABC began to play disco music in the autumn of 1974, and in December WPIX-FM introduced a four-hour disco show, "Disco 102," which became a nightly feature in April 1975. Radio, however, remained a rock-dominated format, and it wasn't until August 1978 that disco threatened to get a proper grip on the airwaves when WKTU, an anonymous soft rock station based in New York, made an overnight switch to an all-disco format. The results were astonishing. Having limped along with a one-point-three share of the listening audience, the station rose to an eleven-point-three share, elbowing WABC—and WBLS—out of the way for good measure. News of the coup traveled fast. "When I was in New York, you literally couldn't go anywhere without hearing WKTU," said Ed Boyd, vice president and general manager of KIIS-FM in Los Angeles, which converted to disco in November. "Its impact was that enormous and was a key factor in our decision to make the switch."[20] WKTU-FM was the number-one station in the number-one market, and by the end of the year approximately two hundred radio stations had adopted an all-disco format. Rock's stranglehold on the airwaves was over.

Discotheque owners were even more adroit at profiteering from the dance boom, with moguls such as Michael O'Harro—the owner of Tramp's in Washington and the three-time winner of *Billboard*'s "disco consultant of the year"—realizing that clubs could become design-oriented entities in their own right. O'Harro had started his branding mission in 1977 when he sold two thousand packs of Tramp's cigarettes, and, realizing the potential of the club's name, he subsequently opened a Tramp's boutique and sold a thousand Tramp's necklaces, a thousand Tramp's posters, and twenty thousand Tramp's t-shirts. All of this, it is worth noting, from a tycoon whose founding principle was to open Tramp's as a "disco for people who don't like discos."[21]

By the end of 1978, there were approximately fifteen to twenty thousand discotheques in the United States, a significant proportion of which were opening in restaurant and hotel chains such as Bobby McGee's Conglomerate, the Smuggler's Inn, the Ramada Inn, the Hilton, the Sheraton, the Hyatt Regency, the Holiday Inn, and the Marriott.[22] Most aspired to match the mass-market appeal of the 2001 Club, which, with twenty-four venues up and running and more than a hundred in the pipeline, had established itself as the most prolific disco franchise in the country. "Our complexes are geared like IBM," owner Thomas Jayson told the *New York Times*. "Once you're involved with us, we'll provide you with specifications right down to the macramé wall hangings."[23] Others were more into the warehouse look, taking the spatial contours of the downtown party network into commercial America. "An old garage may be fine," advised Wayne Rosso, an ex–mobile disco DJ who was now director of disco operations for Audio Concepts Inc./Dave Kelsey Sound, a Hollywood-based disco consultancy. "You want to minimize the interior, with as little seating as possible. You want the folks up and circulating. There is a lot of self-service bar activity, and you hit them at the door for admission."[24] Six figures was apparently enough to do the job. "Most of that is for sound and lighting, because that is your attraction. $200,000 is really nice, but you can bring it in for $100,000 to $150,000."[25]

Given the influence of *Saturday Night Fever*, it was only right that hometown Brooklyn should also experience a disco surge. "I was very psyched after I saw *Saturday Night Fever*," says Pucciarelli. "I was already on the way up, and it was clear that everything was going to explode." When the Nite Gallery opened in Bay Ridge in May 1978, the owners hired the native Pucciarelli to play, and within a month the venue was attracting a thousand-strong crowd on a Saturday night. "We were five times larger than 2001," says the DJ, who, with suburbanites assuming an ever-more-central role within the music market, was appointed as Brooklyn's one and only *Billboard* chart reporter. "In terms of size, the Nite Gallery was Manhattan going to Brooklyn."

Yet while clubs were generating an estimated gross annual income of six to eight billion dollars, few of them were top-notch. "There were hundreds of discotheques opening," says Pucciarelli, "and they weren't done properly." Even O'Harro, who had sold more than a thousand copies of his seventy-five dollar *Disco Concepts* manual, concurred. "There are an awful lot of fast buck artists around, and a lot of people with no experience," he told *Los Angeles Times* business reporter Alexander Auerbach. "Arthur was a successful disco in New York that franchised. None of the franchises was successful, and eventually the whole thing killed off the original disco."[26]

Manhattan remained the barometer according to which all other urban dance centers were measured, including Los Angeles, which was hoping that, with Studio One leading the way, it would soon start to rival its East Coast rival in the post–*Saturday Night Fever* dancescape. "With only about eight major clubs catering to the disco tastes of more than five million entertainment seekers in this city, Los Angeles still ranks second to New York, which holds the coveted title of number one disco city in the U.S.," noted Radcliffe Joe in *Billboard*. "However, with new clubs cropping up all over the city, plus the assistance of two major radio stations KISS-FM and KUTE-FM programming disco music, and the growing support of a trends-oriented press, the consensus is that Los Angeles has the potential to possibly pass or at least rival New York as the nation's disco capital."[27]

The San Francisco club scene was also enjoying strong growth. "We didn't take any dives at all during the winter," commented Tom Sanford, owner of the City Disco, the Bay Area's best-known disco, which had showcased acts such as Dee Dee Bridgewater, Grace Jones, Esther Phillips, Silver Convention, and the Village People. "Business is way up Monday through Thursday."[28] The renovation of Dance Your Ass Off (which now included an augmented sound and light system) and the opening of I-Beam (situated in the revitalized Haight-Ashbury area) provided further proof of San Francisco's flourishing nightlife, and the launch of the Trocadero Transfer (the city's first after-hours venue) demonstrated that the expansion wasn't incorrigibly tied to the more commercial aspects of the disco explosion. "The first time I ever went to Trocadero was for a White Party," Gini Spiersch told San Francisco club chronicler David Diebold. "I had been to straight clubs at the time but Trocadero was an entirely new experience. I became a fixture at Trocadero and loved it."[29]

By now the disco rage was international in scope, with Japan one of the most prolific centers. Having mirrored the American wave of growth and decline in the 1960s—when James Brown, the Four Tops, and the Supremes were driving its scene—the Japanese market was now in the throes of discomania, and, while most clubs were relatively small-scale, Osaka's Bottom Line and Shinjuku's Tomorrow both catered to crowds of three thousand plus. America remained the key point of reference: in early 1974 the Bump had spread like wildfire, and the following year Van McCoy's "The Hustle" stayed at the top of the charts for more than twenty weeks. Around the same time, some forty Japanese DJs traveled to the States to study club culture, although they continued the distinctly un-American practice of rapping along to their selections after their return. "The 'rap sessions' of the Japanese deejay is [*sic*] aimed at relaxing what is generally a shy audience," commented *Billboard*.[30]

Europe, too, had established itself as a thriving dance zone—and not just because of the musical designs of Henri Belolo, Cerrone, Alex Costandinos, Michael Kunze, Jacques Morali, and Giorgio Moroder. Important German discotheques included the Trinity, the Blue Bell, and Life 1 in Hamburg, Edith and Why Not? in Munich, and the Biba in Frankfurt. France, the mystical home of the discotheque, hosted approximately 3,500 venues, including the Palace in Paris, which had opened in a 1920s theater in April 1978 and presented a New York DJ once a month. In England, discotheques largely flourished in the form of working-class ballroom chains owned by Mecca and Top Rank, while at the other end of the market a private restaurant club called the Embassy functioned as London's equivalent to Studio 54 (in 1978 the club employed American DJ Greg James, who was hardly setting the States on fire, to show British dancers and DJs the benefits of the most basic mixing techniques).

However, the Soviet Union remained a predictably barren terrain for disco promoters, despite Voice of America's claim that its new hour-long Saturday evening dance program was receiving an unexpectedly positive response, and toward the end of the year Tass journalist Genrikh Borovik published an article in which he argued that American clubs were havens of decadence and loneliness where dancers snorted cocaine and spent the "whole night shaking with the lights and dreaming of fame, success and money." Borovik wasn't reporting from Moscow, but from New York, and his eyewitness account was based on an evening at Studio 54. The lucky entrants, he noted, were stupefied by the distractions of the discotheque, which provided a "nirvana for lonely young people who don't want to have contact with anyone and who couldn't anyway."[31]

In an article for *Esquire*, music critic Albert Goldman came close to echoing Borovik's conclusions. "The one thing that binds all these otherwise dissimilar establishments together is the music and the common atmosphere of overstimulation," he wrote. "If disco is emblematic of where it's all at today, then the stunning profusion of lights, sounds, rhythms, motions, drugs, spectacles, and illusions that comprise the disco ambience must be interpreted as the contemporary formula for pleasure and high times. Examining the formula, one soon sees that its essence is the concentration of extremes. Everything is taken as far as it can be taken; then it is combined with every other extreme to produce the final rape of the human sensorium." Following the Soviet journalist's critique of western egoism, he added, "The real thrust of disco culture is not toward love of another person but toward love of the self, the principal object of desire in this age of closed-circuit, masturbatory, vibrator sex. Outside the entrance to every discotheque should be erected a statue to the presiding deity: Narcissus."[32]

Goldman had done his homework, even if his book on dance culture, which was titled *Disco* and published in 1978, smacked of homophobia and racism. Describing the Sanctuary, Goldman wrote, "Put fifteen hundred gay boys in a private club, feed them every drug in the pharmacopoeia, turn up the music loud, and pour the drinks like soda pop—presto! You've got an orgy." The myth of gay men's irrepressible libido was too powerful to resist. "Every stall was constantly in use as a crib," he added, "the cute little angels on the walls staring down on some of the most outrageous behavior that has ever been clocked in a public place."[33] Just as gay men were posited as being uncontrollable sexual animals, so African Americans only knew how to dance and emit indescribable odors. "When Saturday night would roll around and all the public clubs would shut down, hundreds of boys, all steamed up and ready to romp, would converge on the Loft," Goldman wrote of David Mancuso's parties. "The moment you hit the room, your nostrils were distended by the stench of black sweat."[34]

The banal, fictional, and offensive character of this analysis didn't stop Goldman from drawing a link between the ostensibly distinct ideological tendencies of dance culture. "To the ghetto-inspired pleasure grabbing of the Sixties, the multiple drug abuse, and the off-the-wall screwing have been added all those refinements that come with maturity and money," he argued. "Now every night the big cars with their uniformed chauffeurs stand by the curb for hours while expensively catered suppers are served in lavishly decorated pads in SoHo or the East Seventies."[35] Goldman maintained that the self-indulgence of the disco environment could also be read within the framework of a "displaced quest for certain spiritual values that can only be attained by breaching the barriers of the senses."[36] The goal, however, remained an individualistic one, and Goldman maintained that this was evident in the flow motion of the dance floor. "Looking out on the floor of the modern dance hall, you don't see any of the interpersonal intimacy so glowingly described in the fashion magazines or on the screen during *Saturday Night Fever*," he noted. "The idea that disco has been built on a revival of 'touch dancing' (what a hideously clammy word!) or that it is focused on a step called the Latin Hustle—all this kind of talk is either wishful thinking by instructors at the Arthur Murray schools or just bad women's-page journalism." Independence, Goldman argued, ruled the night. "The truth is that today's hip disco dancer is into the kind of one-man show that John Travolta puts on in the most exciting sequence of *Saturday Night Fever*: a film that speaks the truth despite itself by demonstrating unwittingly how totally fulfilling it is to dance by yourself as opposed to how frustrating and infuriating it is to have to work out something as intimate as the way you dance with some cranky bitch."[37]

Goldman's barely repressed misogyny was far more consistent with the Faces (as they had been imaginatively described by Nik Cohn) than anything that could be seen in *Saturday Night Fever* or, more significantly, American discotheques, which were recognized to have created an important zone of relative female—as well as ethnic and gay—power. Travolta's individual flight, the very scene that Goldman read as being representative of the "true" disco experience, was in fact the very scene that completely misrepresented what was going on—as Pucciarelli notes, *nobody* danced like Travolta, at least not before the release of the RSO film—and, by focusing on Travolta's individualistic display, Goldman misinterpreted the core of the dance experience, which was *communal*, even if it was for the most part nonpartnered. For sure, downtowners were increasingly convinced that, at least within midtown discotheque culture, an ideology of individualism was superseding an earlier core philosophy of community. Capote could posit Studio as an idyllic democracy because the people who had entered the club were the most deserving—the most stylish, the most beautiful, the most interesting, the most moneyed—and the same kind of meritocracy was ostensibly flourishing on dance floors across the country. Dancers, however, didn't get a rush from dancing in isolation: there was no fun to be had if you were the only person in the club. Rather, dancers got high because they were in a room with other dancers and a DJ, and this meant that their experience was simultaneously individual and collective. The pleasure was at its most intense when individual motions came into synergistic sync.

* * *

Disco producers were also sweeping all before them—including Shakespeare. Having produced the Love and Kisses album, Alec Costandinos now assembled a studio band—Alec Costandinos and the Syncophonic Orchestra—and delivered an album-length disco opera titled *Romeo and Juliet* at the beginning of 1978. "I record what I love," he says, "and I loved Shakespeare." *Julius Caesar* wasn't quite right ("not a good album"), and *Hamlet* also didn't fit the bill ("too dark"), but the early modern romance was perfect. "It's a marvelous love story, and the rhyming prologues to acts 1 and 2 have musical flow." As if sampling Shakespeare wasn't risky enough, Costandinos also decided to introduce a vocal remix. "I took the immense liberty of adding a few words of my own," he says. "In general I like making my own mistakes, not other people's." Vince Aletti, for one, didn't mind—he described *Romeo and Juliet* as the producer's "most accomplished and fully-satisfying work" to date—and in April Costandinos continued his prolific run when Love and Kisses came out with its second album, *How Much, How Much I Love You*, as well as the title track for the *Thank God It's Friday* soundtrack.[38] "My next idea was to do *Macbeth*," he says. "When the witches speak—that's a song!" But by the end of April he had another three albums in the pipeline—including a disco medley of songs he had written for European superstar Demis Roussos—and *Macbeth* was saved from the discotheque cauldron.

Meanwhile the hard, pounding beat that had become the hallmark of Casablanca's Gallic production contingent continued to intensify when Jacques Morali released the second Village People album, *Macho Man*, at the beginning of March 1978, and further evidence of Eurodisco's expansion emerged in the same week with the release of *Come Into My Heart* by USA-European Connection, which was recorded in the holy city of Philadelphia and released on the TK subsidiary, Marlin. Composed, arranged, conducted, and coproduced by East European émigré Boris Midney, the LP fell at the more imaginative end of a sound that was becoming increasingly formulaic. Ray Caviano, the newly appointed vice president in charge of national disco promotions at TK, responded by launching a special campaign that aimed to highlight the record's individuality. Noting that TK intended to de-emphasize the use of the word *disco* in the coming months, the executive declared, "Our forte has long been in disco/soul/r&b product, and we want to develop and maintain the flexibility to crossover and establish ourselves in other music markets."[39]

Others were beginning to distance themselves from the d-word more decisively. "Disco has played an important role in the development of my career," commented one-time golden boy Van McCoy. "But I am seeking greater versatility. I do not want to be forever locked into the image of the 'disco kid.'"[40] Norman Harris also wanted to grow up. "In Philly today we're trying to create a slower, mellower sound, somewhere between Marvin Gaye's groove on 'Got to Give It Up' and the high energy sound we have been getting with the Trammps," he told *Billboard*. "Frankly I get tired of hearing the same thing for too long."[41] Michael Gomes joined the

Norman Harris (right), with Bunny Sigler and Tom Moulton. Courtesy of Tom Moulton

growing line of malcontents. " 'Disco' is fast approaching a critical state," he warned. "Unless the Sound continues to vary and change to hold the public attention, 'Disco' may go the way of other trends in modern music: 'Acid Rock,' 'Glitter Rock,' 'Punk Rock,' 'Disco.' "[42] A chance encounter with Francis Grasso provided the *Mixmaster* chronicler with further ammunition. "I had to ask him how he thought the Sound had changed over the years. Had it grown, developed? 'I think it was more interesting then' he told me. 'A record had to stand on its own merit. Now with bass horns and tweeters records get an 'umph' they don't have. I find it kind of nerve racking.' "[43] So did François Kevorkian, the DJ at New York, New York. "The crowd was into all the big hits of the moment, and that was that. I hated having to play this endless series of Cerrone and Alec Costandinos epic, full-length records, although it was better than not having a roof over my head."

Kevorkian could console himself that his high-profile position enabled him to pick up records and proffer opinions in the offices of a range of labels. "While I was at New York, New York I became aware that you could get records from the labels instead of buying them in the store. I started making the rounds, and Prelude was one of the labels I would visit. They would sometimes play things they were working on to get feedback from the DJs, and I would make comments." Having worked with Florence Greenberg at Scepter Records for ten years and then at Chess Records as label president, Marvin Schlachter set up Prelude in 1977. "I started to see this tremendous underground culture taking form, and I thought it offered an interesting way to approach the music business," says the label boss. "I realized that I wouldn't have to compete with the majors because the major companies to all intents and purposes didn't know this world existed." Schlachter made sure that he and his employees went out. "I started looking around to get a sense of what was happening. I approached R&B producers and took them to the clubs. I would say, 'This is what's going on. This is the kind of direction I want to take in terms of the music.'" Up-and-coming producer-arranger Patrick Adams was an early hire, and Kevorkian followed soon after. "We felt that as an extremely talented DJ François was in a position to be the eyes and the ears of the label. He was in a position to remix certain records that we had acquired, and he was also in a position to test play our releases and say, 'This works! This doesn't work! We should do this! We shouldn't do that!' He was a very bright man, and he brought a combination of expertise to the table." Schlachter offered Kevorkian an A&R job. "I really didn't know what A&R meant," remembers the DJ. "I said I'd have to think about it. A week later I was in the studio mixing 'In the Bush.'"

Engineered by Bob Blank, "In the Bush" was the standout track on Musique's first album, *Keep On Jumpin'*, which was released in July 1978. The brainchild of Adams, the disco-funk recording stormed along at 136 beats per minute and featured Christine Wiltshire and Jocelyn Brown's crescendo-style delivery of "Push, push, in the bush/ Push, push, in the bush/ Push, push, in the bush/ Push, push, in the buuuuush." Kevorkian's neat handiwork ensued. "I completely stripped down the intro," he says. "Structurally I added a lot of spice to the middle of the record, I did some effects with delays, and I did some breakdowns. You know, *drama*. For the time it was a pretty cool record." Kevorkian's remix was inserted into the album in place of Adams's original production. "It had this raw energy," says Schlachter. "'In the Bush' became one of the biggest downtown records of the year. Every club played it, and it became a worldwide hit."

Yet while Prelude was going downtown, Salsoul was going straight

François Kevorkian
at Sunshine Sound
Studios. "This is the
place where we all
cut acetates of edits
and medleys." Photo
by Frank Trimarco.
Courtesy of François
Kevorkian

downhill. Ripple's "The Beat Goes On and On," mixed by 12 West resident
Jim Burgess and released at the end of 1977, was a big club hit, but the
release of the Salsoul Orchestra's fifth album, *Up the Yellow Brick Road*,
which included an abysmal "Fiddler on the Roof" medley, and *Saturday
Night Disco Party*, which revolved around a series of Bee Gees "inter-
pretations" by Montana's band, represented a dramatic collapse in judgment. Around the same time, the label decided to drastically reduce its
twelve-inch output, which was allegedly eating into album sales. "As a
result," Kenn Friedman, national director of disco promotions, told *Billboard*, "we are cutting commercial release of this configuration back to
imports which, more often than not, are a one-shot deal."[44] The decision
failed to salvage a terrible run. Double Exposure came out with their third
album in the summer and, with no twelve-inches to distract customers,
sold next to nothing, and the once-mighty Loleatta Holloway suffered a
similar fate when her follow-up album, *Queen of the Night*, flopped in the
charts.

Walter Gibbons restored a degree of respectability to the label more or
less single-handedly. The DJ, who'd become a born-again Christian some
time between the closure of Galaxy 21 at the beginning of 1977 and his
return from a stint at a George Freeman discotheque called the Sanctuary in Seattle, delivered a landmark remix of Love Committee's "Law

and Order" in which instrumental phrases and vocal hooks faded in and out around an elevated, insistent, bongo-driven percussive track. He then produced a perfectly executed blend on *Salsoul Orchestra's Greatest Disco Hits* before he added three minutes of discordant drama to Tom Moulton's smooth mix of "Just As Long As I Got You" by Love Committee. "What he did was incredible, especially the break at the end," says Moulton. "It was sheer genius. He took something I did and brought it to another level. I complimented him, and he was taken aback."

There was, however, no disguising Salsoul's drift into commercial banality—and an unsuccessful commercial banality at that. "We were releasing albums we shouldn't have been releasing because of disco craze," says Carey. "In 1977 we released *ten* albums. In 1978 we released *twenty-seven* albums. They were selling, but there was nothing significant, and we were probably losing money on them. It was our worst year." The Salsoul boss lays part of the blame on Gregory. "He convinced us that we should be releasing more albums. We were also getting ready for a distribution deal with RCA, and we needed a certain number of releases. Chuck said that we couldn't produce everything in-house and that we should go out and sign groups, license imported albums, and give Tom Moulton a label deal. We followed his advice and ended up releasing inferior garbage."

West End, meanwhile, was beginning to climb the ladder of label respectability. Having launched its catalogue with *Emanuelle Nera*, an Italian motion picture import, and *Sessomatto* by Sessomatto, another Italian release that was mixed by Jimmy Stuard shortly before the Everard Baths fire, the label built its reputation around a series of Moulton mixes that included "Mary Hartman, Mary Hartman" by the Dick Lee Sound of Inner City, Jakki's "You Are the Star," and the Michele album *Magic Love*. As Mel Cheren, the joint label head, writes in his autobiography *Keep On Dancin'*, "Although we were still waiting for our first unqualified smash hit, we were up and running, pumping out product, racking up sales, a real record company."[45] West End's first unqualified smash duly arrived in June 1978 with the release of "Hot Shot," which featured Karen Young's feverish vocals alongside a raw blend of Afro-Latin rhythms, jazz, and R&B. "Her scatting is fierce and inspired, hot and sexy in a frankly aggressive way," reported Aletti. "When she screams, the crowd screams."[46] The record notched up sales of eight hundred thousand, and Cheren maintained the momentum by commissioning Walter Gibbons to mix "Doin' the Best That I Can" by Bettye LaVette and the ubiquitous Moulton—who had also mixed Dan Hartman's high-spirited "Instant Replay" for Blue Sky and produced Grace Jones's second album, *Fame*, for Island—to provide a "Mega Mix" of Michele's "Disco Dance."

As it happens, a new disco outfit called Chic, which revolved around guitarist Nile Rodgers and bassist Bernard Edwards, had been led to believe that the Jones assignment was theirs, even though they had begun life as an opportunistic punk outfit. "We figured at that time, what was open to us was punk rock and disco, because those were the two things that were coming in," Rodgers told writer Rick Hollomon. "So, we tried punk rock, because we had always admired rock 'n' roll money." Punk, though, didn't work out. "In order to be big in punk you had to be very risqué and cruel and beat up everybody. We figured that if we were a black group, primarily, we wouldn't last a week. So, we started hanging out at New York discos in order to get a feel for the music."[47] Studio 54 was a particular favorite. "My girlfriend went to the Fashion Institute of Technology and she knew Marc Benecke," Rodgers told Anthony Haden-Guest. "She was the one who would get me in."[48]

Rodgers's queue-jumping credibility was raised when Chic notched up its first disco hit with Tom Savarese's debut mix of "Dance Dance Dance (Yowsah, Yowsah, Yowsah)." "Bert Lockett broke Chic," says Michael Gomes. "'Dance Dance Dance' was going to come out on Buddah, and she got an advance copy from Freddie Taylor, who was doing promotion for the record. Bert was DJing at the *Billboard* music convention, and when she played Chic everybody *flocked* to find out what it was. She told people that Chic hadn't really been signed to Buddah, Atlantic offered them more money, and that was the end of that." Atlantic released the record as their first commercial twelve-inch single—never one to underestimate his own importance, Savarese drew up a contract that guaranteed the size of his name on the cover—and rumors of the Chic-Jones collaboration began to circulate until Edwards and Rodgers went to see their prospective client perform at Studio 54 in the winter of 1977. "It was a big show," said Rodgers, "and we were almost like her guests of honor, because we were really popular."[49]

When the Chic team arrived, however, they were told that their names weren't on the guest list. Cold and dejected, the duo bought some drugs and went back to Rodgers's apartment on Fifty-second Street between Eighth and Ninth. "Bernard and I started jamming, just guitar and bass," Rodgers told Haden-Guest. "We were just yelling obscenities . . . *Fuck*

Chic live at Xenon, June 1978. Photo by Waring Abbott

Studio 54 . . . Fuck 'em . . . Fuck off! . . . Fuck those scumbags . . . Fuck them! . . . And we were laughing. We were entertaining the hell out of ourselves. We had a blast. And finally it hit Bernard. He said, 'Hey, Nile! What you're playing sounds really good.' The lyrics started to evolve: "Fuck Off" was changed to "Freak Off" which was changed to "Freak Out." "Within twenty-five to thirty minutes, we had the biggest hit record of our lives."[50] Moulton went on to produce the Jones album, but Chic now had "Le Freak," which they went on to record at Tony Bongiovi's Power Station studio. Engineered by Bob Clearmountain and underpinned by drummer Tony Thompson's unwavering metronome beat, the song eventually sold six million copies—the best selling single in Atlantic's history.

Steve Rubell and Ian Schrager's discotheque played a more constructive role in generating another of the year's biggest hits, Gloria Gaynor's triumphant torch song "I Will Survive." Having promised that she would never say goodbye, Gaynor had all but disappeared from the music scene, and *Park Avenue Sound*, released in May 1978, provided further evidence of her descent into bland anonymity. "I Will Survive," released a couple of months later as the B-side of "Substitute," a cute pop song, also looked like it would sink without a trace until Richie Kaczor started to play the record at Studio and it became one of his signature anthems. "I mentioned this to Polydor," Kaczor told the *SoHo Weekly News*, "and when the other jocks reported the same reaction, Polydor began to emphasize 'I Will Survive' and look what happened."[51]

Black women had secured an unprecedented presence in the post–rock music market, and other unconventional faces—such as that of Sylvester—were also breaking through. The vocalist had established a niche for his falsetto voice and camp-gay persona in the City Disco in San Francisco, where he performed alongside Izora Rhodes and Martha Wash, and in 1977 he recorded *Sylvester*, which included a cover of Ashford & Simpson's "Over and Over." The twelve-inch became a big record in New York—it was huge at the Loft—and in 1978 Sylvester started to compose songs for a follow-up LP. The collection included "You Make Me Feel (Mighty Real)," a gay affirmation song that made Carl Bean—who had covered Valentino's "I Was Born This Way"—look like he was still in the closet, and when Patrick Cowley, a lightman at the City Disco, heard the song he suggested that the two of them work together. Cowley ended up adding such a dense layer of synthesizers that the result, released in July 1978, was credited with introducing a new sound—as drug-oriented as Giorgio Moroder's work on "I Feel Love" but significantly more upbeat.

Sylvester crossed over into the pop charts, and so did a number of his girlfriends. Evelyn "Champagne" King's "Shame"—which featured Bunny Sigler's rhythm section, Instant Funk, and a mix by David Todd—was released in September 1977 and eventually broke into the charts the following summer after it received strong play in Boston and New York clubs. Linda Clifford's soaring "Runaway Love," released as a seven-inch in April and a Jim Burgess twelve-inch in May 1978, started to scale the Hot 100 in July, thanks in no small part to the vocalist's feisty, improvised rap around the themes of vengeance, fire, and accusation. Further sisterly breakthroughs were logged with strutting superwoman Chaka Khan's "I'm Every Woman," which was produced by Arif Mardin and written by Ashford & Simpson, and Cheryl Lynn's debut, "Got to Be Real." At the same time, established divas continued to control the charts like never before. Donna Summer reached number one with the seventeen-and-a-half-minute "MacArthur Park Suite," even though the song—originally written by Jimmy Webb—included some unlikely lyrics ("Someone left the cake out in the rain/I don't think that I can take it/Cause it took so long to bake it/And I'll never have that recipe again"). Then, toward the end of the year, Philadelphia's finest female trios returned with storming singles: First Choice came out with Tom Moulton's galloping twelve-inch mix of "Hold Your Horses," and the Three Degrees released their new album, *New Dimensions*, which was produced by Moroder and featured the pumping "Giving Up, Giving In."

The vocal force of these and other female performers didn't, however, reflect the power relations of the wider music industry. While Khan worked up a storm, Rita Heyer, the woman behind the woman, was about to be relieved of her responsibilities. It was tough on the promoter, who had single-handedly run the makeshift disco department at Warners, successfully pushing a string of twelve-inch releases by, amongst others, Ashford & Simpson, Linda Clifford, Deodato, Lamont Dozier, Rose Royce, Candi Staton, and Undisputed Truth (A&R impetus came from Tom Draper, previously of RCA and now running the R&B department at Warners). But by the end of November executives from the music giant were letting it be known that the company—and Heyer—had failed to satisfactorily exploit the disco market. "We're in business to make money," an anonymous suit told *Record World*.[52] And nobody was pretending that Heyer, always something of a minor player, knew how to make enough of it.

Warners wanted a disco purist who could also double as an executive, and in TK's twenty-eight-year-old Raymond Francis Caviano they found the perfect chameleon. Caviano had first caught the discotheque bug at the Firehouse, and in April 1977 he became a *Billboard* story when, as national disco promotions director for TK, he declared that gay rather than straight discotheques were responsible for breaking disco singles. Caviano confirmed his flare for attracting the media spotlight in September 1977 when he found himself at the center of a special feature by the *Washington Post* on discotheque culture, and in December 1978 he was made executive director of Warners's revamped disco department. "The story goes that [label owner] Henry Stone permitted Ray to work on a few outside projects, which included 'Rough Diamond' by Madleen Kane, a Warners record," says Brian Chin, a Chinese American graduate from Columbia University who started writing disco reports for *Gaysweek* in mid-1978. "Henry said he had jokingly asked Warners not to go hiring Ray if he allowed him to work on the one record. Of course Warners set about hiring him immediately." Caviano was happy to jump into bed with the giant, even though it had been slow to commit itself to the disco genre. "This deal shows that the executives are stepping out," declared an upbeat Caviano, who was handed a twelve-strong staff, a six-million-dollar budget, and his own customized label, RFC (his initials), as part of the package. "I don't care if you are big or small, in disco, you have to use street tactics."[53]

Caviano was part of a wider employment trend. "This was the first time that any large number of young gay men were hired in the knowledge that they were gay," says Aletti. "I am sure that a lot of them did not fit in very well with their record companies, but they were the best people for their jobs. They worked with these interlocking groups of disc jockeys and became very close." Caviano was also a compelling operator, and when he offered Aletti the opportunity to work as his A&R adjunct in the middle of December the columnist bid *Record World* farewell and handed his four-year-old "Disco File" column to Chin, who had been recommended to Aletti by the editor of *Gaysweek*. "Ray was charismatic, involving, exciting, full of enthusiasm, and dynamic," says Aletti. "He had great ears. He really created TK, and ultimately it was equal to or more important than Salsoul. Salsoul had a powerful identity, whereas TK had a wider variety of sounds."

Having announced his intention to "try to stimulate everybody" at Warners "with a disco sensibility," Caviano made an instantaneous impact when he commissioned Jim Burgess to deliver a twelve-inch remix of Rod Stewart's "Da Ya Think I'm Sexy?"[54] Within a matter of weeks the blond crooner was celebrating the best-selling single of his career, and Caviano wasn't coy when it came to taking credit for the rocker's successful conversion to dance. "We're going to disco-ize the Warner's staff," he told the *New York Times*. "We're going to be aggressive. If there are mindless and repetitious records, they're not going to be ours . . . You can't come into a market as open as this and not feel bullish."[55] The clubification of Stewart snapped the strings of Warners's air-guitar executives. "Ray had a big ego then," says Bobby Shaw, who was hired to work as an East Coast disco promoter. "He was taking all the credit for Rod Stewart's career happening when obviously it was a great record to begin with. The dance mix by Jim Burgess only made it contemporary." Yet while rock's sponsors may have been outmaneuvered in the propaganda war, in truth disco was effectively handing a pair of platform boots to a struggling genre that wasn't about to sacrifice its ideology. Stewart may have been swinging his hips to a different beat, but his message remained unchanged. "Don't worry," he was saying. "I'm still blond, straight, authentic, virile,

Jim Burgess at the
mixing board. Photo
by Waring Abbott

promiscuous, and irresistible. It's just that if you want to come and rub me then you'll have to come to my new site of seduction—the disco."

The simultaneous release of "YMCA" by the Village People demonstrated that disco didn't have to assume rock's gravelly posture in order to be consumed as straight. Jacque Morali's collection of mustachioed musclemen was as gay as any disco lineup could get, and, just in case anyone couldn't read the visual signs, the group's name, song titles, and lyrics referenced institutions and areas long associated with homosexual opportunity: the YMCA, in case you didn't know, was a place where "you can hang out with all the boys." Except that, at least as far as "YMCA" was concerned, the boys themselves weren't terribly interested, with New York's gay discotheques generally shunning the release, just as they had rejected the Village People's last album. " 'Macho Man' did not happen in gay clubs but in straight ones," Friedman—who had left Salsoul for Casablanca earlier in the year—told the *Village Voice*. "The Village People is the first gay-to-straight 'crossover' group, a group with an originally gay image and following that's made it in straight discos." So what did the straight audience make of it? "The funny thing is that straights don't really

The Village People live at Roseland. Photo by Waring Abbott

believe the group is gay. They love 'em in Vegas and in tacky suburban dinner theaters in Midwestern shopping centers. Did straights ever catch on with Paul Lynde? With Liberace? People will protect their identity at all costs, they'll pretend to the last possible minute that it's all an act." [56]

The belief that the Village People were simply dressing up in theatrical drag was not entirely unfounded. Lead singer Willis was heterosexual, and for those who simply didn't get the references, well, Morali and his merry band became increasingly reluctant to set them *straight*. "Everyone finds what he wants in the group," Morali told *Newsweek*. "I am sincerely trying to produce songs to make the gay people more acceptable. But a song can't remake the world. And you can't scare the mass audience too quickly. I don't want to kill my success." [57] Fame had changed the Village People. Having taken off in gay discotheques, they subtly sidelined the risky subject of sexuality as they moved into the spotlight. "I'll tell the gay press I'm gay," said Felipé Rose. "If the straight press asks, we tell them it's none of their business. Or 'none of their fucking business!' depending on how they ask. I don't know why people think we're blatantly gay because it's never been presented that way. The people who live in the rest of the U.S., Middle America, these people still don't know." [58]

Of course the Village People *were* blatantly gay, but Casablanca calculated that straight consumers didn't want to know and were fully capable of kidding themselves that they didn't know—a nimble-footed version of what D. A. Miller calls an "open secret," which is "reminiscent of Freudian disavowal" inasmuch as "we know perfectly well that the secret is known, but nonetheless we must persist, however ineptly, in guarding it."[59] The consequence was a disco group hovering on the edge of the in-out divide, a potentially subversive force that had ultimately organized its own containment. This state of affairs suited the heterosexual center, which happily perpetuated the open secret in order to reinforce its own controlling position—*gayness isn't spreading*—while keeping a punitive eye on an institution that it knew to be gay—*we can see what you're up to so you'd better behave.* "The straights don't see the gay culture, they've only seen what they've made—the styles," declared Friedman, who had test-screened a segment from *Thank God It's Friday* that included a background glimpse of two men dancing together and sniffing amyl nitrate. "I interviewed hundreds of people, showed it to thousands, and as far as I know not one straight person ever saw the men dancing, even after I showed the segment to them two or three times. And yet the gay viewers saw it immediately."[60]

A number of them also saw that disco had changed, perhaps irreversibly. "I would give half my kingdom to the DJ who would play something out of the ordinary," Gomes told Aletti in a "Dialogue Between Two Editors" that was published as a special *Mixmaster* supplement in the summer of 1978. "I want to be shocked. I want to be shocked out of the complacency of just hearing the same thing that I can hear from club A, club B, club C. One night I made a tour of clubs and, I swear, I left one club on one record and made it to the other club on the same record."[61] Writer and ex–habitué of the Tenth Floor Andrew Holleran was also becoming weary of disco's drift into the realm of the predictable. In a damning end-of-year feature for *New York* magazine, he bemoaned the "terrible uniformity of beat and style" that "had come to dominate all disco music" before concluding that "the fast, mechanical, monotonous, shallow stuff that is being produced for a mass market" is "light years away from the old dark disco, which did not *know* it was disco, which was simply a song played in a room where we gathered to dance."[62]

It was as if Holleran was offended by disco's descent (or ascent, if you approved of the transition) into camp. Disco had become artificial, stylized, disengaged and apolitical, emphasizing texture, sensuous surface, and style at the expense of content, all of which made the music entirely consistent with the definition of the term outlined by Susan Sontag in her 1968 essay "Notes on Camp."[63] Sontag had also argued that gay men constituted the "vanguard" of camp, and their frontline position in disco suggested that one day America would have to wake up to the fact that the Village People signified something other than fancy dress fun. The "in" taste of a minority group had been transformed into the dominant, commercialized code without anyone spending too much time thinking about where all of these black divas, macho men, pounding rhythms, and romantic strings had got their break. The moment of realization, however, couldn't be postponed indefinitely.

* * *

The media's intensifying interest in disco had a mixed impact on Manhattan's mixmasters. On the one hand, film and television provided new opportunities for the likes of Bobby DJ (music coordinator for *Thank God It's Friday* and the dance show *Soap Factory*) and Tom Savarese (who appeared on the Tom Snyder show and placed top twenty charts in the *New York Daily News* thanks to the marketing skills of manager Marilyn Green Fisher). On the other hand, radio's conversion meant that record promoters no longer regarded club DJs and record pools as their most important customers. That was certainly the opinion of one-time discotheque champion Billy Smith, now of London Records, who began to argue that the power of the discotheques was in decline and that disco radio was the key medium of the present and the future. "Billy Smith, national disco coordinator at London Records, New York, states that an increasing percentage of disco record buyers are revealing that their purchases are being influenced by airplay on their favorite disco radio stations," reported Lawrence Gray Patterson, "and not necessarily by what they dance to in the clubs."[64] Michael Gomes confirmed the sense of malaise. "At one time the DJ could make or break hits," he told Vince Aletti. "Now the formula is so well known."[65] Nicky Siano concurred. "By the end of the seventies we weren't influential at all. We weren't selling large numbers of records. Radio had regained its control, and club DJs weren't as important anymore."

Many old-school DJs were also failing to land a stable residency in boomtown. Pride and the refusal to play in any old restaurant-disco played its part, although so did the fact that a generation of younger and hungrier disc jockeys were now on the prowl, many of them dedicated readers of an upstate New York periodical called the *Disco Bible* that reviewed records according to their rhythmic pace. These DJs were interested in grouping records not for their lyrical or sonic compatibility but their beat-on-beat mixability—an all-but-irrelevant criterion according to earlier DJs. "It is the only way to ensure a totally smooth music flow," declared publisher Tom Lewis.[66] For others, the *Disco Bible* was the ultimate sacrilegious text. "Older DJs could do phenomenal changes between extreme tempos and it would work because the energy was the same," says Gomes. "But by the end of the seventies they were starting to mix according to this publication that consisted of printed sheets of dot matrix with lists of beats per minute from slow to fast. Bobby DJ called it 'the fall of the vinyl empire.' His generation of DJs couldn't get jobs anymore. A new type of DJ had emerged."

The new guard was more professional and less likely to pass out over the turntables. As Aletti put it in his conversation with Gomes, "The people who are coming up are all kind of aggressive, together kids, in a way, who know what they are doing, who are very straightforward about what they want to do and they are not heavy drug users."[67] That was certainly an accurate description of John "Jellybean" Benitez, who had successfully badgered Aletti for a personalized listing in *Record World* while he was still DJing at the unglamorous La Mariposa in Washington Heights and whose combination of charm and chutzpah had subsequently landed him nights at the Electric Circus, Experiment 4, Fifth Avenue, the Grand Ballroom, Hurrah, the Ice Palace, Les Mouches, New York, New York, Sesame, and Xenon. "I was definitely a little hustler," he says. "I was playing five to seven nights a week, and I was getting one hundred dollars a night." Of the new generation, Gomes thought Jellybean constituted the most likely future DJ legend. "We are wondering if he's gay or not. He's like twenty years old. He's probably the youngest of this whole group. He has a vigorous sound, very energetic and this kid doesn't do a lot of drugs. I'm really surprised at him. For somebody who's only been playing for about a year or more this kid is good."[68]

The displaced DJs included Michael Cappello, whose performance at the Ice Palace 57 on West Fifty-seventh Street in January 1978 reminded New Yorkers what they had been missing—musical gems, a disregard for strict beat-on-beat mixing, and an occasional pause to create maximum excitement. "Keep orchestrating my emotions," cried Gomes.[69] Cappello, however, was looking for a chance to get away, and a few months later he went to work at the Music Palace in Hanover. "The club was based on Studio 54," he says. "Robert DeSilva was involved in setting it up, and after a while he called me over. I just saw it as an opportunity to travel." While Germany possessed one of the most vibrant discotheque networks in Europe, Cappello wasn't impressed. "It wasn't as big as New York. After about eight months I left and went traveling in Italy."

Other high-profile casualties of the changing times included Steve D'Acquisto, Bobby Guttadaro, David Rodriguez, and Tom Savarese, none of whom were able to hold down regular Manhattan residencies, and the onetime Sanctuary deity Francis Grasso was also on the verge of making an undignified exit. "I was bouncing around," he says. "I couldn't find my niche." In part that was because the rise of the twelve-inch had dated Grasso's frantic methods. "There were these nine, ten-minute records, and I was a little resentful. I'm changing the record every two minutes and twelve seconds, and these fucking people are taking a break! It became too easy." The principal problem, however, lay with the evolution of the wider culture. "'Mary had a little lamb' was totally disco. The music was boring, and the crowd all looked the same." Few were interested in paying Grasso the respect he believed he deserved. "I was in a record store, and the fella selling records had a copy of an article by Albert Goldman on the desk behind him. There was a huge photo of me—I was the centerfold! The guy questioned me, and I said, 'Maybe if you turn to page eighty you'll see who I am!' He acted like he didn't recognize me and in my mind I'm going, '*I don't believe this! I'm the reason you're here!*'"

Having lost Studio 54 and the Gallery in quick succession, Siano was also on his way out, although there was still time for a sustained encore at a club called Buttermilk Bottom. "The owner approached me the day we were auctioning off the Gallery sound system," says the DJ. "I did a deal whereby I got 15 percent of the door. Buttermilk Bottom was incredibly successful. I averaged six hundred a week." Robin Lord made up the numbers on just a couple of occasions. "I saw Nicky at Buttermilk Bottom a few times. When I left New York sometime in the early spring of 1978 he was not in good shape. We lost touch for a while after that." Gomes stuck around for a little longer. "I am a tough critic seldom overcome by the siren songs of our local DJs," he wrote in *Mixmaster* in June 1978 "but this Memorial Day Weekend Nicky Siano DJ left me breathless!"[70] Some six months later, however, the chronicler was telling a different story. "He's allowed no visitors, locked in, virtually a prisoner of the very booth he plays in."[71] Siano simply couldn't keep it together. "He did well, briefly," says Gomes who, as Siano's lightman ("There was only one switch!"), had a bird's-eye view of developments. "He became too grand and tried to bring in too many guests. He could still find records, but he didn't have the draw anymore."

Siano was still playing at Buttermilk Bottom when he released "Kiss Me Again" by Dinosaur, a collaborative recording with Arthur Russell. "Arthur used to come to the Gallery," says the DJ. "We used to make fun of him because he danced in a really strange way." It was Russell who made the first move. "He said that we should record something. I had some money from the club and decided to invest. Arthur wrote the song and discussed which musicians we should use. I didn't really know much about recording and went with his recommendations. I started to say things in the studio, but I still took more of a backseat." David Byrne played guitar, Russell played cello, and the record was released on the Warners subsidiary Sire. "Ray Caviano commissioned a remix, and Mike Rosenblatt loved the record, but in the end Ray never really pushed it. I played it reel-to-reel, and it ended up selling some ungodly amount, like two hundred thousand."

Cappello, Rodriguez, and D'Acquisto, meanwhile, kissed their turntables goodbye and scurried along to the Loft, where they received mouth-to-mouth resuscitation. "At one time I tried to hire as many DJs as I possibly could," says David Mancuso. "Michael worked at the door, David helped out in the kitchen, and Steve was employed as somebody who could deal with any situation that I asked him to take care of. He was very good that way. I relied on his eyes and ears." Mancuso and D'Acquisto had been able to rekindle their friendship thanks to the party host's decision to offload the increasingly burdensome New York Record Pool. "The Record Pool was draining David's finances," says Mark Riley, who had started to work for the organization in the middle of 1977, "and he didn't believe that the membership really understood that." Much to their irritation, new applicants had to prove that they were 100 percent kosher. "You had to have this, that, and the other, and *if you didn't have everything* you could *not* become a member," adds Riley. "Guys would be coming in there with these different pieces of paper, and David would keep sending them back saying, 'No, you need something else!' " For their part, members of the Record Pool didn't let Mancuso relax. "There were people that gang-tackled David at the Record Pool. The membership kept hassling him about all sorts of things, and he just got tired of it."

Judy Weinstein, a Loft devotee since 1971, accentuated Mancuso's sense of isolation and frustration—although not immediately. "I lived for Saturday night," she says. "David Mancuso was a messenger. He was the most influential person in my life." Following a recommendation from Vice President Vince Aletti, Weinstein had been employed by the Record Pool to replace the departing Eddie Rivera, and she set about her task with organizational gusto. "Whereas David Mancuso treated the Record Pool like a club house, I had more of a business head," she says. "I organized it better so that he could focus on his parties." Mancuso, however, wasn't sure he liked Weinstein's approach. "Judy wanted everything to revolve around her so that everyone would think that she was the person who could get things done, but the Record Pool was supposed to be of the DJs, by the DJs, for the DJs. We didn't want a manager to take charge. There were simply these methodical procedures that we all had to follow." Little by little, Mancuso began to suspect that Weinstein had her own agenda. "When I came downstairs she would be cold and aloof. It was almost like I was butting into somebody else's business. After a while I stopped feeling comfortable in my own house."

Mancuso eventually concluded that Weinstein was planning to form her own pool. "Her policy was to divide and conquer," he says. "She worked on the weaker people and just took over. Little by little I could tell that some DJs were behaving differently toward me. She was basically organizing her little ducks." In an echo of the Coalition experience, Mancuso convened a meeting and proposed that Weinstein be relieved of her responsibilities, only to be overruled by his own committee. "I said that the Record Pool should leave Prince Street. I figured this would shock them, but it didn't." Aletti, one of Weinstein's defendants *and* an ardent supporter of Mancuso's collectivist principles, watched on as the organization self-destructed. "In the end I felt David was very unfair to her and did pull away from the Pool," he says. "David could be very controlling in an extremely subtle way."

Her position untenable, Weinstein resigned at the end of 1977, and the Pool stopped functioning soon after. "The Record Pool closed somewhere between Thanksgiving and Christmas of that year," says Riley. "I went down there a couple of times thinking I was going to work, and there was nobody in. It just petered out. People still considered themselves members of the New York Record Pool, but for a while it didn't function. There was a question in some people's minds as to whether or not it still existed. Nobody was picking up product by the Christmas of '77. People really felt that David had decided he didn't want to do this any more." Indeed he didn't. "I was like a balloon that had been punctured," says Mancuso. "All the air rushed out of me. After I lost the vote it was like somebody had died, and I stopped answering the phone for a couple of weeks. I said to myself that I couldn't do it anymore, and I went into this very, very depressed state. I wish I could have backed away more gracefully."

That left over two hundred DJs without a pool, with those who didn't want to join Eddie Rivera's IDRC stuck in a particularly nasty rut. Cue David and Joe Itkowitz: two identical twins, two disconsolate DJs. "They went to Judy and said, 'Look, this thing is falling apart. Why don't you start a pool?'" says Riley. Weinstein, who believes that her departure triggered Mancuso's decision to close—"He couldn't deal with me leaving him"—needed something to do. "I lived in this horrible one-room studio on Thompson Street," she says. "I had no money and no job so I had a meeting with my friends, including Mark Riley and Larry Levan. They said, 'David's closed his doors. Why don't you start a new record pool?'"

Weinstein got together with Riley and Hank Williams, found a space on Twenty-second Street, and opened For the Record on 1 February 1978. "I went to all the DJs that I knew with a petition and took it to every record label." It was effectively a solo effort given that Riley and Williams were busy with their day jobs (both worked at BLS). "I got all the best DJs in all the best clubs," says Weinstein. "Richie Rivera, Howard Merritt, Alan Dodd, Jim Burgess, and, of course, Larry Levan. It was a great moment for me." Within a matter of months For the Record had successfully established itself as the most influential record pool in New York, and Weinstein made the most of her experience at the Prince Street Pool, transporting Mancuso's core principles to her own organization. "David had some very strict rules because he wanted to be above and beyond the scrutiny of the record companies," she says. "He wanted to legitimize the organization by making sure that everyone was a serious, working disc jockey and not just taking the records so that they could sell them. In reality, that is where we all learned the trade. His theories were absolutely correct."

Mancuso, for his part, was convinced that he was the victim of an elaborate stitch-up. "It's what Judy wanted," he says. "She had it all planned out." Riley disagrees: "Judy didn't want the New York Record Pool to close, and she really didn't intend to open her own pool. The main reason why we were able to start For the Record was because we had a decent rapport with the record companies. Judy probably was cultivating relationships with the record companies and the DJs, but I don't think she did it with the idea that she was going to start up her own organization. It was just her job." Mancuso, anguished and depressed, saw it differently and briefly attempted to resuscitate the New York Record Pool. "I didn't like the way For the Record was *Judy's organization*," says Mancuso. "The New York Record Pool was 100 percent controlled by the DJs, and if they didn't want me they could have voted me out. That wasn't the case with Judy. She invited people to join *her* pool." The DJs, weighing up the most likely source of vinyl, decided to stay with Weinstein. "David wasn't being very clever," she says. "He had lost the New York Record Pool, and he needed to come to terms with the fact that he couldn't deal with the business anymore."

As the shenanigans around the control of the New York Record Pool unfolded, Mancuso began to rediscover his footing when, having let his contractor talk him into building the Prince Street booth twelve feet above floor level, he decided to return to earth. "I knew I had to get my feet back on the ground," he says. "I liked to be where people are dancing." The reorganization of the space created a new intimacy, and the Prince Street parties settled into a groove. "The Loft on Prince Street was much larger than it had been on Broadway, but it didn't finally change the feel of the event," says Aletti. "There were more people, but it didn't feel less intimate." Kenny Carpenter, ex-lightman from Galaxy 21, confirms the intimate nature of the space. "It was like being at home. Everybody knew everybody. You could cuddle up with David's cat and fall asleep and nobody would disturb you."

The regeneration of the Loft was timed to perfection given that Mancuso's rent had risen more rapidly than any of his trademark balloons. While the party host didn't make any money in the first year at the new venue, by 1978 the profits had started to kick in, with weekly receipts regularly reaching five figures. "I was charging $12.99 and on a *slow* night we would get 950 people," says Mancuso. "The average was 1,500, so I was making all kinds of money." That was just as well given that he was also spending all kinds of money. "Making money is one thing," he notes. "Managing it is another." Talented at the first, disastrous at the second, Mancuso wouldn't think twice about taking ten friends to a top-class restaurant and footing a five-hundred-dollar bill. "We would eat the best food and drink the best booze. I just wanted people to let loose and have a good time." All of which meant that the Loft's bank account was significantly less buoyant than it might have been. "David wasn't really making money at Prince Street," says Penny Grill, who was employed as a cashier at the new venue. "He was just getting by." But that was enough for Mancuso, who continued to throw a free party on New Year's Eve, working at a loss on the busiest night of the year in order to demonstrate that the Loft could give as well as take. "You had to balance big moneymaking days against the not-so-good days," adds Grill. "Money was being made, but it was being spent just as quickly."

It was during this period that Mark Levinson—Mancuso's favorite audiophile—telephoned Michael Kay, the owner of Lyric Hi-Fi, to ask if he could meet the customer who had spent an unprecedented $150,000 on his equipment. The sound designer visited the Loft and quietly observed the unfolding ritual of the party before he approached Mancuso, introduced himself, and gave the host a huge hug. "He thanked me, and I thanked him. He walked gently away and stayed around for a while." What did the engineer-musician think of the Loft? "He loved the whole idea of the party and seeing his work being put to a positive use. It was a very important moment."

Tony Humphries, a black straight music fanatic from Brooklyn who spent his every spare cent at Downstairs Records, was also won over. "David Rodriguez was working at Downstairs," he says. "I'd buy music from him, and he offered to take me to the Loft." The impact was instantaneous. "That was the beginning for me. It totally changed my life. I was a secluded church boy from Brooklyn, and all of a sudden I started leaving my house at three in the morning and returning at twelve in the afternoon. It was the perfect world of partying. Nobody was intimidated, everyone got along. The sound was crystal clear, and the music was so broad in range and tempo. It was fabulous."

David Mancuso

Select Discography (Loft 1977–78)

Keith Barrow, "Turn Me Up"

Crown Heights Affair, "Say a Prayer for Two"

Lamont Dozier, "Going Back to My Roots"

First Choice, "Doctor Love"

Eddy Grant, "Living on the Frontline"

Damon Harris, "It's Music"

Bruce Johnston, "Pipeline"

Eddie Kendricks, "Goin' Up in Smoke"

Idris Muhammad, "Could Heaven Ever Be Like This"

Teddy Pendergrass, "Only You"

Don Ray, "Standing in the Rain"

Rinder & Lewis, "Lust"

Ripple, "The Beat Goes On and On"

Cat Stevens, "Was Dog a Doughnut"

Sylvester, "Over and Over"

A Taste of Honey, "Boogie Oogie Oogie"

Third World, "Now That We Found Love"

THP Orchestra, "Two Hot for Love"

Voyage, *Voyage*

War, "Galaxy"

David Williams, "Come On Down Boogie People"

Lenny Williams, "Choosing You"

Winners, "Get Ready for the Future"

Brooklyn-born dance fanatic David Morales was similarly captivated. "The Loft just opened my brain," he says. "We all used to go there every Saturday. It was religious. It was our church. The whole party atmosphere was incredible. It wasn't a club. It was a family thing. You were going into somebody's living room. There was never any trouble. There were no outcasts. The crowd was very mixed. You could find somebody who was fifty years old partying next to an eighteen-year-old like me. It was just different from going to a commercial club." Mancuso's determination to place music at the center of the party made a huge impression on the young dancer. "He had the finest system. There was no mixer. There was nothing in between to create any noise. He had two decks, and he would play a record from the beginning to the end, even if it was fifteen minutes long. No mixing, no disturbance. The record finished, you'd applaud, on to the next tune. It wasn't about trying to impress with mixing. It was about music." At the Loft, at least, the old school was not yet extinct.

* * *

Work carried on at a punishing rate at the Paradise Garage. "I went in there with Michael Brody, his lover Fred, and Larry Levan," says Nathan Bush. "We had sledgehammers, and we gutted the place ourselves." The owners of Chameleon had put down additional concrete and a parquet floor, all of which had to go. "We broke it up and dumped it outside. I went there quite a few nights a week after work. After a while Michael had construction guys come in to do the job." Brody, meanwhile, maintained the ground floor as a parking lot. "He worked there during the day. I'd come by and we'd go upstairs. Different walls were going up and areas were being created. You could see the space being transformed little by little."

The Paradise Garage officially opened in January 1978 to an ominous seasonal greeting: a snowstorm delayed the delivery of some sound equipment from Kentucky, and as a result the thousand-plus crowd was left standing in line for more than an hour in subzero temperatures. "I remember being there that morning and asking Michael, 'Do you think you'll be able to open tonight?' and his eyes just filled up with tears," says Mel Cheren. "There was a downstairs area where you parked cars, and he could have brought the people in there to keep them out of the real cold but there was so much confusion he didn't think of it. The opening was a complete disaster, and it took Michael a couple of years to win those people back." Others, however, have a less cataclysmic memory of the night. "I remember there was a snowstorm but people *did* come out," says Bush. "Maybe we didn't pass four thousand people through the door that night, but we did have a decent turnout." Michael Gomes, wearing his trademark white cotton suit, surveyed the scene at eight o'clock in the morning and, referencing the presence of Richie Kaczor, David Rodriguez, and Nicky Siano, noted that "there are many familiar faces." Nobody, it seemed, had communicated the severity of the "disaster" to Levan who, according to Mr. Mixmaster, was happily drinking champagne and "playing the part of freaky DJ, sounding like thunder."[72]

The main room did nevertheless require further modifications—the sound needed reinforcement, the space cried out for acoustic treatment, and the floor had to undergo further work—and so Brody went back into the smaller room and held weekly gatherings that were interspersed with official construction parties when the club was ready to temporarily unveil a major structural development on the main floor. "The sound system from Reade Street wasn't really enough," says David DePino. "When they put it in the big room they realized that it didn't sound quite right so they put everything back in the small room and continued the construction work until more speakers were built and the room got treated. They threw parties to raise money for the work and keep the interest going. They didn't want people to think it had closed."

Successful construction parties in April ("Night of the Bats") and June ("Fire down Below") indicated that the strategy had worked. "I remember the first time I saw the main room I was pretty impressed, and when I went back with a friend I was re-impressed," says Danny Krivit. "From the outside it looked like nothing, like a truck garage, and clubs weren't like that then—they always looked like something from the outside. You entered via this ramp that was flanked by these purple runway lights and you could already hear a faint 'bom, bom, bom.' As you walked up the ramp it became louder and as you paid you could hear an occasional scream from the crowd. You just felt the energy that was behind the wall and sure enough when you walked in through this small doorway—small compared to the size of the room—the lights were going and the arms were in the air. I remember all of these tall black men, and I just felt so short. It was *very* high energy, and it was *very* happening."

The vast majority of the opening night crowd had returned some twenty months earlier than Cheren had forecast, which was just as well given that the "Fire down Below" party showcased one of the West End mogul's new signings. "I was at West End, and Mel Cheren told me that there was going to be this club," says Krivit. "He said it was going to be the biggest this and the best that and that West End was going to get priority. He said, 'All of our records are going to get pushed there and this is going to be the place to hear them. They're going to make it—through the Garage!' Everything he said turned out to be absolutely true." Cheren remembers the process well. "Way back in the beginning Larry would get so excited he would put the record right on the turntable." Which is exactly what happened at the "Fire down Below" party, during which Levan crossfaded images of a warehouse blaze and naked porn stars while hammering Karen Young's debut single "Hot Shot" like there was no tomorrow. "'Hot Shot' had a definite Garage sound," says Krivit. "There was a definite feeling there." There was also a definite leg-up for Young and her nascent label. "The Garage and West End," says Cheren, "were a winning combination."

Sound system designer Richard Long was another industry insider who managed to form a profitable alliance with the Garage. Following his run at the SoHo Place, Long had installed systems at clubs such as the Enchanted Garden, 15 Lansdowne Street, Studio 54, and the Warehouse, and, backed by JBL, he also designed a new mixer called the Urei that effectively displaced the Bozak. "The Urei was the result of demands being made by DJs, and Richard was already known for designing his own electronic crossovers and mixers," says Bob Casey, head of Virgo Sound. "The Bozak came from the factory with two phono inputs, two auxiliary inputs, and two microphone inputs. This means that with special conversion cards a DJ could convert an AUX input into a third phono input. But the two mike inputs were monaural, and so they couldn't be used for anything other than microphones. The combinations could only be two phono and two tape inputs or three phono and one tape input, and that was it." The new machine—which David Mancuso maintains was effectively "a distilled version" of the mixer he designed for the Loft—was significantly more flexible. "The Urei 1620 had six inputs, and all of them were stereo," adds Casey. "This meant that by simply adding or changing a few internal cards, a DJ could come up with an infinite number of combinations."

Having become friendly with Michael Brody, Long displaced Alex Rosner just as work was about to begin on the main room. His greatest challenge soon followed: how to build a system that was capable of filling the expansive Garage without compromising the sonic excellence with which his name had become interchangeable. There was a clear need for unprecedented power, but power also risked distortion and so the sound enthusiast set about assembling some of the finest boxes to ever house a speaker. "Sixty percent of a speaker is the box it's playing in," says Casey. "Richard Long was a master carpenter, and his boxes were a work of art. He used the best of birch plywood, and all of the joints were meticulously measured and glued together."

Levan was equally determined to augment force with the quality that had swept him away at the Loft, and, with one eye on Mancuso's notorious Koetsus, he insisted that his consul be equipped with moving coil cartridges. Brody agreed but quickly changed his mind when the DJ decimated five hundred dollars worth of the delicate technology in a single night. The owner delivered an ultimatum: either Levan had to give up the fundamental yet fatal practice of back-cueing or he had to start using some hardier gear. Back-cueing went out of the back door and, in order to continue the practice of mixing, the DJ started to line up incoming records by gently tapping his hand on the side of the Thorens belt-driven T125 turntable, a precarious strategy that was complicated by the technology's tortoise-like pitch control, which made it virtually impossible to keep two records running at the same tempo. "The Thorens weren't designed for DJ use," says Joey Llanos who, having been introduced to the club by fellow drum-and-bugle band player Mark Riley, was quickly hired to work on the security team. "It was an excruciating art form that was never duplicated. Other DJs wanted to grab a record and bang it on, but Larry aimed to recreate David's quality. He was always asking the engineers how the Garage compared with the Loft."

With the sound system in place, a special "Tut, Tut, Tut" party was organized to coincide with the touring Tutenkhamen exhibit and mark the completion of the extended construction phase in September 1978. "You couldn't get near the place," says Mark Riley. "There were 3,500, 4,000 people there." The party was a spectacular affair. "It was like forty dollars a ticket, which was a lot of money at the time," says Bush. "We dressed a lot of people up as Egyptians, and there were mummies hanging from the ceilings. Stirling St. Jacques was carried in as King Tut." When the evening climaxed with a live performance by First Choice, the response of the crowd suggested that the Garage was already generating a significantly more intense atmosphere than its headline-grabbing midtown rivals. "I remember we were at Studio 54 when 'Hold Your Horses' came out," says lead singer Rochelle Fleming. "It was a big publicity show, and Frankie Crocker came in on a white horse. We were so excited but, ohhh, there was *no comparison* between Studio and the Garage!" Studio could be wild, says Fleming, but it was "very subdued" compared to the Garage. "Those people! *Oh my God!* At Studio they were into the show, but at the Paradise Garage they were screaming and sweating and having a ball. It was pure energy coming off the walls. At the Paradise Garage we had our five thousand most dedicated fans, whereas at Studio 54 people generally went there to be seen."

For some the Garage also confirmed that Richard Long, and not Alex

Rosner, had become the premier discotheque soundman. "You got better equipment from Dick Long," says Francis Grasso. "Alex Rosner was well known for using ALTEC Lansing Voice of the Theatre speakers. They would constantly blow, and he made a fortune replacing the horns, which weren't on a fuse system. Rosner's talent was limited." Casey agrees. "Alex Rosner wasn't an innovator. He was a conservative. David Mancuso had to persuade him to do what he wanted to do. When he said that he wanted bass, Alex Rosner went out and bought bass. But Richard Long built bass, and it was far superior. He gave the crowd what it wanted. He put your balls up your ass." That experience wasn't as painful as it might have been. "Michael Brody installed wooden floors and walls that could move with the bass and help sustain the dancers," says DePino. "You could feel the floor moving up and down." Yet there could nevertheless be no distance from this type of sound, which vibrated across the skin and through the bodies of dancers. "The Garage," says François Kevorkian, who was introduced to the gargantuan location by Joey Bonfiglio in September 1977, "was the Loft on steroids." The steroids proved to be popular: when Long started to use the Garage as a workshop-cum-testing-ground, inviting potential clients to hear the system in action, commissions flooded in, and while every space required a different setup, pride of place was always given to Long's custom-built speakers that, in either a generous tribute or a sharp marketing exercise, were dubbed "Levan Horns."

The soundman, however, wasn't without his critics. "I went to the Paradise Garage once, and I could only stay for a few minutes because Larry Levan played so loud," says Rosner. "Anybody who went to the Paradise Garage must have been a masochist because it was so uncomfortable. I walked in there, and I saw people sitting with their legs and arms crossed. Their body language was saying, 'I'm defending myself against this on-slaught of sound.'" Siano was also unsure about the King Street setup. "The Gallery and the Loft sounded like a beefed-up home stereo, but the Garage was too big for that kind of system so Richard built these special speakers. The sound wasn't warm, though. It was almost fake. You could hear the bass and you could hear the midrange and you could hear the highs, but a bunch of frequencies that make the sound warm were missing." Mancuso, too, had his reservations. "The sound was very good—it was up there—but it wasn't all the way. Larry always wanted Klipschorns, and at Reade Street he got them, but at the Garage Richard Long plagiarized the Klipschorn and lost a couple of octaves. He didn't have to do that. The Klipschorns were powerful enough to fill any room." There was also a problem with the volume. "Harry Muntz measured the sound level in the middle of the dance floor, and it was 135 dB. Another ten and you would never hear another sound in your life. Ears can start to bleed at those levels."

Nevertheless the Paradise Garage became the venue where the dance music industry's power brokers, shunned by Mancuso and embraced by Brody, chose to hang out. As Gomes recorded in *Mixmaster* in October 1978,

> After dark, *Pam Todd* is sitting in the DJ booth at the "Garage" on King Street, NYC. Casablanca recording artist, Pattie Brooks, has just come up from the dancefloor where she's showcasing tonight, singing "THE HOUSE WHERE LOVE DIED" (!), to the musical accompaniment of DJ *Larry Levan's* playing of the record. Flashbulbs explode when Casablanca's *Marc Paul Simon*, bearded, flown in from Los Angeles, hugs the President of the "FOR THE RECORD" distribution service to the discotheque disc-jockeys, *Judy Weinstein*, outfitted in basic black. A chorus of the promotion corps steps out of the shadows to applaud the event. The long rectangular DJ booth transformed into a hospitality suite. There's *Kenn Friedman* and *Howard Merrit* [*sic*] from the New York Casablanca office, *Alan Member*, Salsoul Records, *David Todd*, RCA Records, *Jerry Bossa*, Buddah Records, *David Steel*, Polydor Records, *Starr Arnning* and *Roy B*, Prelude Records, on and on, *Vince Aletti*, RECORD WORLD's discotheque editor making visual note of this walking "disco" social register. DJ, *Larry Levan* oblivious to it all, caught up in the effervescence of creation, until *Patrick Jenkins* comes to escort *Pam Todd* away.[73]

Frankie Crocker was another influential operator who enjoyed spending time in Levan's expansive booth. "I probably went to the Garage the first week it opened," says the WBLS DJ, who had lost his job when he was indicted over a payola scandal only to be reinstated after the station's ratings went into freefall. "I went with a date, and that was the only time I stayed downstairs. After that I was always invited into Larry's booth." Crocker would always accept the offer—and not just because the hospitality was so good. "Whatever Larry was playing would go on Frankie's radio show the next day," says Cheren. "Frankie said that BLS became number one because of the Garage." Yet for all of the Garage devotees (and there are many) who witnessed Crocker take a peek over Levan's shoulder, the WBLS maestro maintains that his relationship with the Garage DJ was one of mutual respect. "I wasn't in awe of Larry. I treated him like my friend. It was an exchange. We turned each other onto records." Crocker acknowledges a certain debt. "If people danced I'd find out what the record was, and more often than not I'd play it the next day." Yet he insists that Garage floor-fillers didn't necessarily translate into "secret weapons," and that ultimately it was his taste and sensibility that made WBLS such a success. "I had to take it record by record. Larry had a club to entertain, I had a city."

Crocker claims that if he "went on a record," it could sell an additional 250,000 copies in New York alone, which was more than enough to convince even the least numerate dance music promoter to place him at the top of their DJ hit list and Levan at number two. "Everybody wanted Larry Levan to play their records because if Larry Levan liked the record then Frankie Crocker might play it on the radio," says Warners disco promoter Bobby Shaw. "That was the bottom line." Along with a host of other promoters, Shaw maintains that he was "like this" (crossing his fingers) with the WBLS DJ's musical muse. "I knew my records would get listened to because Larry was a friend of mine. A lot of people could never even get a record to Larry, but he trusted me and he trusted my taste. Sometimes I would take him some records before the club opened. We would listen to them on the system and smoke a joint."

As a result Levan had a clear edge on his contemporaries. "Larry was so far beyond any of us," says Kevorkian. "He would get records six months to a year ahead of time." Keen to ingratiate themselves with Levan, or simply hear their studio work on what was widely considered to be Manhattan's most spectacular sound system, rival DJs also scurried to get their freshly pressed acetates to the King Street DJ. "Prelude didn't really have an in-house promotion person who was into the downtown scene, and I already had an entry point because any member of For the Record could automatically present their card and get in for free," says the New York, New York resident. "I was going to the Garage every weekend so I gave Larry 'In the Bush.' He was very excited. He said how wonderful it was and all of that."

Larry Levan

Select Discography (Paradise Garage 1977–78)

Roy Ayers Ubiquity, "Running Away"

Bionic Boogie, "Risky Changes"

Hamilton Bohannon, "Let's Start the Dance"

Brainstorm, "Lovin' Is Really My Game"

Brenda and the Tabulations, "Let's Go All the Way (Down)"

Peter Brown, "Do Ya Wanna Get Funky with Me"

Bumble Bee Unlimited, "Lady Bug"

Martin Circus, "Disco Circus"

Double Exposure, "My Love Is Free"

Lamont Dozier, "Going Back to My Roots"

Ian Dury, "Hit Me with Your Rhythm Stick"

First Choice, "Doctor Love"

Loleatta Holloway, "Hit and Run"

Loleatta Holloway, "I May Not Be There When You Want Me"

Jimmy "Bo" Horne, "Spank"

Thelma Houston, "I'm Here Again"

Instant Funk, "I Got My Mind Made Up (You Can Get It Girl)"

General Johnson, "Can't Nobody Love Me Like You"

Evelyn "Champagne" King, "Shame"

Gladys Knight & the Pips, "It's a Better Than Good Time"

Kraftwerk, "Trans-Europe Express"

Bettye LaVette, "Doin' the Best That I Can"

Lemon, "A-Freak-A"

Cheryl Lynn, "Star Love"

MFSB, "Love Is the Message"

Idris Muhammad, "Could Heaven Ever Be Like This"

New Birth, "Deeper"

Teddy Pendergrass, "The More I Get, the More I Want"

Teddy Pendergrass, "Only You"

Teddy Pendergrass, "You Can't Hide From Yourself"

Phreek, "Weekend"

Don Ray, "Got to Have Loving"

Don Ray, "Standing in the Rain"

The Rolling Stones, "Miss You"

The Salsoul Orchestra, "Magic Bird of Fire"

Sylvester, "Dance (Disco Heat)"

Sylvester, "You Make Me Feel"

Third World, "Now That We Found Love"

THP Orchestra, "Two Hot for Love"

Andrea True Connection, "What's Your Name, What's Your Number"

Lenny Williams, "Choosing You"

Karen Young, "Hot Shot"

Of course the most effective method of securing unique access to a record like "In the Bush" was to become its producer or remixer, and by the end of 1978 Levan had started to develop such a role. "Tommy Baratta, who works at West End, was my friend," Levan told Steven Harvey. "He used to collect money at the door at Reade Street. One day he said to me 'you want to mix a record?' So I went to this engineer named Billy Kessel, who was my age, which was great, because it wasn't intimidating. There was this song from Sesame Street called 'C Is for Cookie,' and I mixed it, not serious, not getting paid for it or nothing."[74]

Levan's second remix—the altogether more significant "I Got My Mind Made Up" by Instant Funk—arrived a couple of weeks later at the beginning of December 1978. Ken Cayre had signed up Bunny Sigler's band the previous November, and by the summer their first Salsoul album—engineered by Bob Blank, a partial owner of Blank Tapes Studios—was being lined up at the pressing plant. "I knew Larry Levan from the Paradise Garage," says Ken Cayre. "He heard an advance copy of the single and asked me if he could do a remix. I never approached DJs to do a remix—they always had to ask me." Rodriguez played a key role in the commission, encouraging both Cayre and Levan to strike a deal. "Larry did a masterful job and helped to create an immediate buzz," says Cayre. "We released the twelve-inch and the seven-inch simultaneously. The single went to number one on the R&B chart and number twenty on pop."

That didn't stop Sigler from getting into an instant funk when he heard Levan's stripped-down interpretation, all crackling percussion and title chant. "I hated it," he says. "I first heard it in Ken Cayre's office, and I gave it the MFSB response—motherfucker son of a bitch. I wasn't into re-mixes. I'd worked on that song for five months. But Ken Cayre liked it and persuaded me to give it a chance. I wasn't listening with an ear for what worked in the clubs." Sigler changed his mind when he went to the Garage. "It sounded good. I was standing in front of the speaker, and it was then that I could appreciate what Larry Levan had done. *But it was my version that made the money!*"

It was my version that made the money. They might have been Sigler's words, but as far as Mancuso was concerned they could have just as easily come from the mouth of Brody: the Loft sounded good, but it was the Garage that made the money. "The Garage violated the underground," he says. "They called themselves underground, but they weren't." Mancuso was particularly galled by the distortion of his cherished invitation system and the private party ruling that he had won in his battle with the Department of Consumer Affairs. "You walked into the building, and there was a sign up on the wall that said, 'This is a private party by invitation only,' which was exactly the same sign I had on my door. But when you walked a little further you were asked to produce your *membership card*, which you had to *pay for*, so it was a membership club disguised as a private party." This wasn't just a matter of semantics—it was also a matter of economics. "Once you start selling your invitations they're no longer invitations. It's not a gray area. They used this method of getting around the law to put more money in their pocket. Larry told me, 'David, before they put on the *light* they already have $150,000 from the membership fees!' Now to me that's not a private party. They used the word *invitation* and it was a lie."

Mancuso maintains that the Garage was a social club and that Brody should have sought the appropriate legal charter rather than appear as if he was running an extension of the Loft. "If you entered the Garage you would be under the impression that you were going into a similar situation, but you weren't, because the only way you could go in without a membership card, which you had to pay for, was as a guest of someone and *then you paid more money*, which was economic discrimination. What you saw was not what you got. All you got is you had to pay extra." You also had to pay an additional fee when there was a special show. "The artists were willing to play for free as a gesture of thanks to the people who had made them famous, and we didn't charge anything for these shows at the Record Pool. But at the Garage they made you pay to see these groups.

They commercialized everything to the fullest. They went through the loopholes, and they exploited the underground scene."

Even if the Garage was more commercial than the Loft, it still retained many of the core principles of Mancuso's party aesthetic. The crowd was largely built around ethnic and sexual minorities and the music was determinedly non-chart (at least until Crocker got hold of it). Dancers were made to feel at home as soon as they entered the venue by doorman Noel Garcia, and, despite the cavernous quality of his space, Brody managed to create a surprisingly intimate atmosphere. "The Garage was ten times bigger in scale than the Loft or the Gallery," says DePino, "but Larry still talked about the importance of creating a party, not a club." Crucially, the dance remained uncompromisingly central. "There was a sexual undercurrent at the Garage but no one was picking up," says Garage regular Jim Feldman. "Sex was subsumed to the music and was worked out in the dancing. It was like having sex with everyone. It was very unifying." While Brody might have made money, this was hardly his singular aim: he was too much of a perfectionist and too deferential to his DJ's demands to be single-minded about the pursuit of profit. With regard to the membership charge, insiders maintain that the fee simply covered the cost of administering the system and that members also enjoyed compensatory financial privileges, including the right to go to four free parties a year. As with the Loft, once you were inside the food and drink were free.

Despite its sheer size and audibility, the King Street club was also relatively inconspicuous. "Larry ducked the press," says DePino. "Larry was underground. Whenever the radio talked about Larry and the Garage we used to call up and stop it. Whenever anybody came with cameras to do interviews we stopped it. That was the school Larry came from, and that was where he wanted to stay." Brody also avoided publicity at all costs. "When the *Post* reported on page six that five thousand people showed up for First Choice, the IRS called Michael Brody the next day. He didn't want *any* promotion. No shape, way, or form. That was why there was no sign outside the club until the last year or two. People used to walk around in circles looking for it." The mogul's motivations, however, weren't simply financial. "He wanted it to be underground because that was the school we came from, those were the clubs we danced in, and that was the way to control something without getting lawsuits. You could turn somebody away for not being a member if you were underground, but you couldn't turn somebody away from an off-the-street club without being discrimi-

Larry Levan in the booth at the Paradise Garage. Photo by Nick Baratta. Courtesy of West End Records

natory. When it was underground you knew who was coming through your door, and if something went wrong you could call the person up and ask them, 'What happened?' " Even wBLS had to be kept in check. "When Frankie Crocker used to say, 'At the Garage last night . . .' Michael Brody would call and say, '*Please, Frankie, stop talking about us!*' He just didn't want people hearing about it and showing up. He wanted that Loft feeling, only on a larger scale."

Certain tensions were unavoidable. "The atmosphere at the Garage was like an expanded version of the Loft, although it was definitely a little colder," says Vince Aletti. "The doorway was more professional, and the club as a whole was a more obviously commercial venture. With David you really felt like he was throwing a party every week, and that was much less easy to convey in a place as big as the Garage." Sporting so many powerful and prominent music industry connections—dubbed the "disco Mafia" by Mancuso—the Garage was hardly subterranean. "The Paradise Garage was a showplace," says Gomes. "It became the Studio 54 for blacks and Latins." Yet the sheer presence of these movers and shakers (many of whom did most of their moving and shaking off the dance floor) also suggested that the once marginal downtown party network was finally on the verge of contesting the cultural center, and the DJ to whom they were drawn made the most of the industrial scale of the King Street venue in order to take the art of DJing to the next level.

Levan was resolutely eclectic, spanning rock, dub, jazz, R&B, and disco. "The cliché is that Garage music had to be a falsetto or some woman screaming at the top of her lungs along with certain types of keyboards," says Tony Humphries, who thought that the Loft was the ultimate party until he visited King Street. "That's totally wrong. Larry Levan played everything from Herbie Hancock to Mick Jagger to Talking Heads to Sylvester. He would also vary the tempo from 98 bpm to all the way up. If it was danceable, he played it." Ultimately Levan couldn't match the range of music that was being presented at the Loft—playing in his own home and answerable to nobody, Mancuso enjoyed a longer non-peak period and therefore a wider experimental berth—yet he also knew that when everyone was starting to collapse with cramp he could switch into education mode, delivering a mixture of less conventional sounds. "Larry was so in tune with different types of music," says Kevin Hedge, who started to slip into the Garage as an underage dancer in the late seventies. "He was the first guy I heard who played records that you wouldn't consider dance records, and they became dance records." Levan spun records for as long as his dancers would dance. "There would be just ten people on the floor, and Larry would be playing something very serene," says Llanos, who went on to become head of security and would invariably be the last person to leave—sometimes as late as midday. "We would get into fights. I would turn the lights on, and he would turn them off. Then he'd go to Mike Brody and complain."

Eclecticism didn't, however, result in chaotic programming. As Levan told Harvey: "Of all the records you have, maybe five or six of them make sense together. There is actually a message in the dance, the way you feel, the muscles you move, but only certain records have that." Levan provided an example. "Say I was playing songs about music—'I Love Music' by The O'Jays, 'Music' by Al Hudson and the next record is 'Weekend.' That's about getting laid, a whole other thing. If I was dancing and truly into the words and the feeling and it came on it might be a good record but it makes no sense because it doesn't have anything to do with others. So, a slight pause, a sound effect, something else to let you know it's a new paragraph rather than one continuous sentence."[75] As with Mancuso, the mix was secondary. "Larry was capable of mixing as well as anyone, but he often didn't give a shit," says Kevorkian. "He wanted to create an effect on the dance floor, and it didn't matter if the mix was sloppy. He was beyond technical." Beat-mixing perfectionists such as Dan Pucciarelli were also unfazed. "Larry Levan mixed as badly as David Mancuso. He was terrible. But once the record was in he was the best."

That didn't mean Levan was a straightforward crowd-pleaser. If the DJ sensed that his dancers thought they knew what was coming next, he would deliberately clear the floor with a "non-Garage" record—effectively a twist on an old David Rodriguez game. "I loved it when he did that," says Feldman. "Sometimes we left the dance floor. Other times we just stopped dancing, crossed our arms, and stared at him. But Larry would rarely give in. Not only would he leave the record on until the end. He would also start to play it week in, week out, until finally everyone wanted to dance to it." Then again there were also times when Levan (again like Rodriguez) simply wanted to clear the floor for the sake of it. "Sometimes Larry would be in an awful mood," says Jorge La Torre, who had given the DJ his first job. "When he was like that he wasn't very good." Yet Levan also had a knack of breathing new life into songs that were clearing other dance floors. "Lots of times I would hear a record, and I would say, 'I don't care what you say, I'm just not into this record,'" says Krivit. "Then I'd go to the Garage, and I'd hear it, and I'd go, 'I was definitely mistaken. I'm very much into this record. Now I don't care if I hear it on AM radio, I can still hear it the way I heard Larry play it.' The Garage was the only place I got that."

If Levan liked a new record, he would rotate it like no other DJ. That was certainly the case with "Weekend" by Phreek, a studio agglomeration headed by Patrick Adams and featuring Christine Wiltshire on lead vocals. Remixed by the head of disco promotion at Atlantic, Izzy Sanchez, the twelve-inch was only issued as a promo, but Levan loved its disco-funk aesthetic and party-oriented message so much he turned it into one of his ultimate signature tunes, often playing it several times a night, and popular demand led to the record's eventual release in the early eighties (although not before Levan himself had recut the record with Christine Wiltshire under the name Class Action). "He would play a record twenty times," says Judy Weinstein. "I would walk over to Larry if he was playing a record forever and look at my watch and say, 'What time is the next record?' But if you hated it you were going to love it by the time you left. That was the power of Larry. People would leave the Garage and go right to Vinyl Mania on Carmine Street." Situated two blocks away from

King Street, Vinyl Mania was opened by Charlie and Debbie Grappone as a small rock-driven record store in October 1978. "People were coming in on a Saturday morning and asking for the records that Larry Levan had played," says Charlie Grappone. "I thought I knew everything about music, so I was like, 'Who the hell is Larry Levan?'" Garage-heads weren't put off. "They kept coming in even though I wasn't selling what they wanted. I ended up doing more business out of a small box of twelve-inch records than the rest of the store."

The fact that Levan peaked at the Garage led some to argue that the real talent was in fact Richard Long. "The sound system at the Garage was the only reason that Larry Levan was so idolized," says Casey. "As a DJ he was good, not great." Many who thought that Levan *was* great still recognize the advantage of working in such an environment. "Larry controlled a huge club so if he did something special then you heard it in the best possible situation," says Krivit. "If he did something with an a cappella as opposed to some guy somewhere else it was Larry who got the acclaim." As such, the relationship between Long and Levan was finally symbiotic. Just as Long's electronics enabled Levan to become the most revered DJ of his time, so Levan's daring talent invariably drew attention to Long's unparalleled equipment.

Yet, if it was difficult to separate Levan from the system on which he played, that was also because the DJ helped engineer the sound. "I remember times when Larry delayed the opening for an hour or two because he just had to rewire all the speakers," says Krivit. "He was constantly revamping the system." Because the room's acoustics were in a state of constant flux, Levan would also tweak the system as the night progressed, introducing modifications to take account of an additional two thousand bodies on the dance floor, subsequent shifts in humidity levels, and eventual ear fatigue, and this remorseless quest for perfection meant that Long had to re-equalize the system every Friday and Saturday.

Levan also worked the sound system for fun, playing with the equalizer to provide imaginative accents and draw out understated nuances. "You could hear seamless mixing at other clubs," says Manny Lehman, who started dancing at the club in 1978, "but at the Garage the people *experienced the music*, especially when Larry worked the crossover." Accompanying his friend Frankie Knuckles on a trip to the Garage, Bret Wilcox recognized important similarities between the two DJs. "Larry and Frankie both manipulated the sound via the mix and the EQs. I could tell

Larry and Frankie came from the same place." That place was the Gallery, and the result was an unrepeatable reinterpretation of a record that would often appear to be better than the original. "DJs would go and buy a record that they had heard Larry play," says DePino, "and they would end up thinking that they had bought the wrong record because he had worked the sound system so much."

Working the sound system included turning off the music altogether —a Siano trick that Levan took to new levels of theater. "He would stop the music in the middle of the night, and he would put on a little a cappella," says Kevorkian. "The crowd would start to scream, and then he would stop it, and he would wait. I'm not saying he waits ten seconds. He waits five minutes until the entire room is stomping on their feet, and you can feel the entire building vibrate. Then he puts on another little thing, and they scream even more. Then he takes it off, and he just waits. Then, finally, a couple of minutes later, he puts on the new record he's been playing five times a night and the entire room *just explodes*—a thousand people all trying to grab the ceiling at the same time."

While the intimidating scale of the King Street setup combined with the knowingness of the crowd would have reduced most DJs to a quivering shell, Levan thrived in his new habitat. "Larry told me, 'When you play for an audience you've got to have *attitude*,'" says Hippie Torales, a young DJ from New Jersey who started going to the Garage toward the end of 1978. "'You've got to show them who's in charge!'" Indeed Levan's confidence grew in proportion to the size of the crowd. "The more people there were in the room, the better he was," says Kevorkian. "He wasn't a good DJ for forty, but if there was a crowd of a hundred then he was good, and if there was a crowd of a thousand he was extraordinary. The peaks at the Garage were so much more intense than they were at the Loft. Larry was an incredible showman."

However the King Street DJ didn't just manipulate the crowd—he was also closely connected to the mood of the dancers. "I would watch certain people on the dance floor," Levan told Lehman. "Since I always went out dancing, I would use that as my guide. I knew who went out, who used to dance, what songs people liked. That's what I used as an outline of choosing what to play."[76] The DJ's knowledge was encyclopedic. "Larry knew everybody's favorite record," says Judy Russell, who started dancing at the Garage in 1980 and became a key figure within the relatively small coterie of core women dancers thanks to her position behind the counter at Vinyl Mania and her friendship with Levan. "If a group was leaving, Larry would say, 'That's the 'Sentimentally It's You' crowd!' He would put on the record, and they would come rushing back onto the dance floor. It always felt like he was playing the song for you—and he was." The lights—normally operated by Robert DeSilva—became an additional means of communication. "With some of the most memorable records he felt like he had to make this an emotional moment," says Krivit. "He managed to reinvent the lights every time he worked them."

The Garage DJ left nothing to the imagination when he described his main influences. "Nicky Siano, David Mancuso, Steve D'Acquisto and Michael Cappello, David Rodriguez from the Ginza—this is the school of DJs that I come from," he told Harvey. "David Mancuso was always very influential with his music and the mixes. He didn't play records unless they were very serious."[77] Like his mentors, Levan was more interested in the way records could speak to each other than the minutiae of the mix. "He would take you on a voyage with the message," says Krivit. "If you heard a bunch of records about love you knew that he was in that mood." Levan also carried his most important guides to work. "Larry had a specific crate of records that were David records and another that were Nicky records," says Kevorkian. "He had both at his disposal." Larry Levan, AKA David Siano. "He took David's ideas, and he took my ideas, and he took them a step forward," says Siano. "He definitely improved upon it."

Levan's sense of his own importance was also escalating, and the dimensions of his King Street booth revealed all. Whereas Mancuso had finally decided to keep his feet on the ground, Levan opted for a towering nerve center, and while in some respects this was a logistical necessity—how else could the DJ keep his eye on his boundless dance floor—Levan was also a downtown diva who loved the regal authority that his heightened throne conveyed. The booth was also huge—an ocean liner compared to the rubber dinghies that most other DJs worked in—and this meant that Levan could virtually host his own (private) party within a (private) party. The consequences weren't universally welcomed. "The Paradise Garage cultivated the cult of the DJ," says La Torre. "I wasn't fond of this VIP room for Larry's cadre of friends. It became another boring thing about the disco scene. He was the star of the show, and unless you were willing to conform you were unwelcome." Club and DJ had nevertheless come together: the booth became a magnet for attracting both promotional records and invitations to remix records, which in turn helped

David DePino
(front), Judy
Weinstein, and
Joey Llanos.
Courtesy of
David DePino

Levan generate a formidable reputation. "It was at the Paradise Garage that Larry Levan came into his own," acknowledges La Torre. "When he was at the Baths he was just another good DJ, but at the Garage he really blossomed."

Realizing that power requires protection, Brody hired DePino to police the stairway to heaven. "I controlled the booth," says DePino. "That was my job. And if Larry was late I used to put on a record." Levan, however, didn't have to be late in order to forget about his responsibilities. "The DJ booth would hold seventy-five people, and Larry would sometimes get into a conversation with two or three of them. The record would end, and he'd go, 'Oooh!' and run and get another record." The dancers didn't mind. "The crowd learned to respect that with Larry. They were fine with whatever he did. Nobody was there for the mixing. They were there for the whole situation—and it was human." It was left to Weinstein to keep the infectious DJ in check. "I was a disciplinarian figure to a certain extent," she says. "Nobody ever really saw me trashed on the dance floor or falling down stairs because I never really got that involved in drugs.

When I walked into the booth, everybody would stand still because they weren't sure how I would affect Larry's mood, or if I would want the booth cleared for Larry. I was a mother figure, even at the age of twenty-five. I had the power."

The combination of Levan's talent and the sheer scope of the Paradise Garage project provided the DJ with an unprecedented profile, for while there were other big clubs it was only the downtown party network that maintained the DJ as the central attraction. "If Nicky was the first name," says DePino, "then Larry was the first huge name." Yet was Levan as innovative, charismatic, and influential as his teacher-gurus? Aletti didn't think so. "David was better because he had more variety. I loved David's warm-up music—trippy, jazzy stuff that would gradually percolate into more of a beat. Larry was more technically adept, but his range was more limited and a little more commercial." Gomes also thought the Garage DJ fell slightly short. "Larry had it but he didn't have the magic of David and Nicky." Weinstein, however, rated Levan as the best. "Larry was more creative than anybody I have ever heard. He would do things, and you would just wonder where it came from. He was so far beyond everybody else."

Thanks to his ability to switch between a Loft-like dream and a Gallery-style frenzy, Levan developed an unparalleled capacity for surprise, and, by combining Mancuso's sense of environment with Siano's sense of theater, he also introduced a new level of drama into New York's nightworld. "Larry was torn between the Loft and the Gallery," says DePino. "David Mancuso entranced people, whereas Nicky Siano was all about excitement. Larry could do both." Operating in highly competitive conditions, Levan possessed the Darwinian intelligence to absorb, reformulate, and flourish. "Animals that survive are the ones that adapt to different diets, and Larry had the ability to take something and make it his own," says Kevorkian. "He appropriated both David and Nicky. He was our boy wonder. While the rest of us traveled by plane, Larry took the space shuttle."

10. turbulence

Backlash

and Survival

Ray Caviano might have made an immediate impact with his remix of Rod Stewart, but a more important litmus test lay in his ability to sign and develop dedicated disco artists of an equivalent caliber. Early big-money deals included the singles "Here Comes That Sound Again" by Love De-Luxe, which the Warners executive picked up at the MIDEM convention in Cannes at the beginning of 1979, and "Dancer" by Canadian artist Gino Soccio, which reached forty-eight on the pop charts. " 'Dancer' was a very successful record for us," says Vince Aletti, Caviano's right-hand man, "and Gino also had a fairly good follow-up." If confidence was running high, that was partly because major label rival Columbia was lagging behind in the disco stakes. "In an area where one-to-one contact with the disc jockey is the most important thing, the straight record executives were offended by the disc jockey's life style," Caviano told the *New York Times*. "I started by breaking records right out of Fire Island. I didn't see CBS there."[1] Neil Bogart's buoyant label was putting up more of a fight. "Casablanca was our competition," says Joey Carvello, who was Caviano's East Coast promotions director. "We wore jeans, they wore lamé. It was the clash of the titans, but we had the music." The real opposition, however, came from inside Warners. "The rock people hated us," adds Carvello. "They didn't understand the disco mentality. We had a different style of promotion. We drove around in limousines, we stayed in the best hotel suites, and we took the best drugs. We ruled."

Official recognition was heaped onto the disco genre at the twenty-first annual Grammy Awards in February—dance artists swept eight of the fourteen prizes, with the Bee Gees dominating the ceremony—and a spate of articles concluded that disco, having captured the spirit of the seventies, was the music of the moment. *Billboard*, which put on Disco Forum V at the end of the month, maintained the impetus, thanks in no small part to the fact that disco could lay claim to nine of the top ten records in the Hot 100, and the dance industry received a further fillip when CBS, flagging its intention to enter the disco field, hosted a special disco forum party in honor of Bill Wardlow at 12 West (and subsequently secured the best tables at the Forum V dinner awards).

Given that Columbia controlled a roster of dance-oriented artists that included B. T. Express, Dan Hartman, MFSB, Earth, Wind & Fire, the O'Jays, Cheryl Lynn, Teddy Pendergrass, Melba Moore, and Lonnie Liston Smith, its belated entry was strange. "CBS was the IBM of the music business, but it was nowhere in the disco market," says Columbia sales rep Vince Pellegrino. "The company was putting out twelve-inch records with *three-minute versions*. It was *embarrassing*." A conference in July 1977 had revealed the scale of the problem. "They brought in a hundred salesmen from around the country, and there was almost a riot because we were so frustrated about getting beat up by the other companies." In an attempt to defuse the crisis, CBS General Manager Jack Craigo announced that the company would begin to research the disco market. "When I heard him say 'research,' I decided to embark on the project myself," says Pellegrino. "I started to talk to a lot of the accounts, and this became the 'Research Report on Artist Development as It Pertains to Disco-Oriented Product' of May 1978."

Examining disco's consumers and Columbia's competitors, Pellegrino concluded that: (1) disco was a unique market in which buyers wanted long versions that were not available on any album; (2) the twelve-inch should be deployed as a vehicle to expose new artists; and (3) the other majors were way ahead in terms of both marketing techniques and strategic acquisitions. "PolyGram had Casablanca, RSO, Polydor, and Millennium," says Pellegrino. "Capitol had Ariola and United Artists. Atlantic had Westbound Records and Cotillion. And Warner Brothers had Curtom and Whitfield Records." While the report persuaded Columbia to make Pellegrino director of disco marketing in March 1979, the official managerial line was that nothing had changed. "The philosophy of the company remains the same," commented Bruce Lundvall, president of CBS Records. "The orientation of the company is, and always will be, toward the complete development of artists, not the creation of a fabricated disco sound using non-artists."[2]

Pellegrino notched up his first hit with John Luongo's remix of Jackie Moore's "This Time Baby." "I took the acetate to the Paradise Garage and gave it to Larry Levan," says the disco chief. "Larry played it once, Larry played it twice, Larry played it three times. When I saw Frankie Crocker looking over Larry's shoulder, I walked over to him and said, 'Frankie, I'll deliver this to you on Monday.'" Pellegrino kept his word. "Frankie was on between four and eight, so I arrived at about three forty-five, left a copy, and said, 'Please make sure Mr. Crocker gets this.' I started to walk back to the CBS building and gradually it dawned on me that I was singing 'This Time Baby' in my head. It was just going round and round. Then I realized that I was *hearing the song in my ears*. It was on the radio *five minutes after four*. I was floating. I was so excited. I thought they were going to roll out the red carpet for me when I got back in the building!"

Not this time, baby. "Little did I know, but I had walked into my first political battle," says Pellegrino. "The black department went nuts because BLS was a black radio station, and they said, 'Who the fuck is this disco guy? We're trying to get records on that we've been working for a while and your dance guy's going over there screwing up our priorities!'" "This Time Baby" reached number twenty-four on the R&B chart—and Pellegrino refused to get downbeat. "CBS had so many artists that wanted to explore the dance or disco market, from jazz to black to rock." Resistance to the new format remained resolute, however. "I went and asked the A&R director of Pink Floyd to do a remix, and he went fucking crazy. 'You want Pink Floyd, one of the biggest bands in the word, to do a *disco mix*?'"

Dance culture's rise to power received its media consummation on 2 April 1979 when *Newsweek* ran the headline "Disco Takes Over" across a front-page photo of Donna Summer. The genre's apparently irreversible momentum found its embodiment in the subsequent release of "Ain't No Stoppin' Us Now" by McFadden and Whitehead (who had already made a name for themselves by penning hits for the O'Jays and Harold Melvin & the Blue Notes) and "We Are Family" by Sister Sledge (which was masterminded by Chic duo Bernard Edwards and Nile Rodgers). Both records were characterized by an easy and confident optimism, and while this message was intended for the African American community, lyrical references to movement and dance made them available to anyone who was experiencing the transient but nevertheless important collective environment of the dance floor. "We were sent the McFadden and Whitehead by mistake," says For the Record President Judy Weinstein. "I always listened to my records back then, and I thought it was great. I took it to Larry and said, 'Larry, listen to this!' He put it on, and Frankie Crocker was in the room that night. He snatched the record and made it the theme song for BLS."

The feel-good factor couldn't paper over a series of less cheery developments within disco, inc., however, and a number of these setbacks were revolving around radio. On the one hand, programmers were beginning to argue that the length of twelve-inch cuts made disco inappropriate for taped syndication, and, on the other, major and minor music companies alike were noting that disco-oriented radio could eventually supersede club DJs within the sales cycle, all of which promised a future shift to shorter and catchier radio-friendly records that would disconnect disco from its core milieu. The shortsightedness of such an approach was highlighted in May when the latest batch of ratings statistics revealed that the runaway success story of WKTU had ground to an ear-opening halt. "Since December, WKTU-FM has slipped from a 10.9 share in Mediatrend to a 7.4 for April," reported *Billboard*. "Observers are asking if it can hold on to enough audience to repeat the number one position Arbitron performance it won in October/November and January."[3]

Sales were also less spectacular than discophiles had assumed. As Roman Kozak noted in *Billboard* in the middle of May, "Despite the megaplatinum success of 'Saturday Night Fever,' only a handful of disco artists, (Donna Summer, Village People, Chic) sell at the multi platinum LP levels that retailers have come to expect from their top product."[4] Twelve-inch singles were blamed. "Despite the proliferation of disco in radio programming and the burgeoning club scene, the dance movement is not yet translating into massive LP sales, certainly not the kind associated with triple platinum superstars such as Fleetwood Mac, the Bee Gees, Peter Frampton and others who have been credited with boosting business overall by drawing customers into retail outlets," added Kozak. "'The problem with disco LPs is the same problem we had with r&b and soul LPs 10 or 15 years ago,' says one retailer. 'There would be one big hit on an LP and the rest would be filler. Now the kids don't want the filler. Give them a hot disco mixed 12-inch disk with the hit right there and they consider $3 a bargain for it.'"[5]

Looming behind disco's disappointing performance at the cash registers was the slowdown in the American economy in the first quarter of 1979. At the end of the 1970s, a combination of declining industrial productivity, rising inflation, and spiraling structural unemployment prompted Federal Reserve Board Chairman Paul Volcker to declare that, under present economic conditions, "the standard of living for the average American has got to decline," and historian William Chafe notes that "most Americans appeared to accept the verdict."[6] The belated recognition of damaging long-term demographic shifts in the music-buying public—which academic Jon Rieger, warning that *the adventure is about to end*," had forecast as long ago as 1974—added to the sense of foreboding, and by the spring industry executives were beginning to recognize the extent of the economic slowdown.[7] "This industry had always been known as a growth industry of unlimited potential," CBS executive Vernon Slaughter told *Billboard*. "It was always a case of, 'This year we'll do better than last year.' In '74, the recession had some effect on the record industry. That's when they first really started saying, 'Well, maybe we're not recession-proof.' But things got better, and it took '78 and bits of '79 before they finally realized that the record industry was subject to shifts in the ages of population and other economic factors just like everybody else. Before that they thought they were immune to it."[8]

Billboard's May headline—"Disco Rules, But Where Are The Big Disc Sales?"—encapsulated the sense of a wider malaise, questioning disco's profitability while simultaneously implying that the rest of the industry was doing even worse. That was certainly the line taken by Jerry Wexler, who had left Atlantic to become senior vice president at Warners. "Imagine how bad business would be if we didn't have disco," he told the music magazine.[9] A month later Ray Caviano added his voice to the defense. "Record companies staffed exclusively by people who are waiting for disco's death are going to have a hard time adapting to the public's new taste," he argued in an address to the Music and Performing Arts Lodge of the New York B'nai B'rith. "We are not just in the middle of a slump. We are in the middle of a massive change of public taste. The answer to the current sales slump is not a few LPs from the superstars of the mid '70s. It is the development of the new superstars of the 1980s. And most of these superstars will emerge from disco."[10] Disco personalities, Caviano maintained, were just beginning to emerge, and as a result trade was predominantly taking place within the seven- and twelve-inch formats. Donna Summer and Gino Soccio, the executive concluded, were "strong indications of the kind of powerful sales that await us once our stars are built."[11]

In truth Warners had yet to produce a bona fide disco star—Soccio was no Summer—but over at Atlantic executives were beginning to enjoy the dividends of their sustained commitment to dance. As the first major label to sponsor disco, the company had released one of the earliest noncommercial twelve-inch singles, had offered strong support to the record pools, and had skillfully developed a series of dance acts that now included Chic, whose combination of hard-edged drums, prominent bass riff, and shimmering vocals on the tight, smooth, positive, and self-assured "Good Times" appealed not only to America's haves but also to its aspirational have-nots. "More than any other major, Atlantic was truly committed to the dance market," says *Record World* columnist Brian Chin. "The upper echelons were always involved because they had a feel for the way in which records can break out regionally and be worthwhile even if they don't become national smashes. Atlantic felt the incremental sales of those records amounted to something and not nothing." The same couldn't be said for the knowledgeable, enthusiastic yet ultimately erratic Ronnie Coles, whom the upper echelons had decided to offload a year or so earlier. "I lost my job because Larry Yasgar and Ahmet Ertegun wanted me to stop associating with the DJs," says the ex-promoter. "They wanted me to be a yes and no boy, and I wasn't going to kiss ass." The shift in personnel didn't exactly damage the corporation's performance. "The disco department at Atlantic was empowered to sign acts, and Larry Yasgar really knew how to follow up hit singles," says Chin. "He taught us how to maintain a good relationship with the record company bosses. The top of the company was not that far from the street, and they kept with that model for years to come."

"Good Times" was one of a series of strong singles and twelve-inches that broke out in the first half of 1979. First Choice's new album, *Hold Your Horses*, included "Love Thang" and "Double Cross." Taana Gardner's debut single "Work That Body" and Billy Nichols's "Give Your Body Up to the Music" guaranteed West End further rotation in New York's hottest clubs. Casablanca notched up one of its biggest hits to date when it came out with "Bad Girls" by Donna Summer. TK demonstrated that the departure of Caviano hadn't dented its ability to work a catchy dance smash when it persuaded Richie Rivera to deliver a characteristically unconventional mix of "Ring My Bell" by Anita Ward. Earth, Wind & Fire came out with "Boogie Wonderland," which performed strongly in the clubs and the charts. And the release of "Sentimentally It's You" by Theo Vaness and the signing of "Disco Circus" by Martin Circus cemented Prelude's growing reputation.

"Disco Circus," however, also exemplified disco's wider crisis, in which even strong records often struggled to notch up significant sales. "François loved 'Disco Circus,' and it was a good Garage record," says Michael Gomes, who started working for Prelude in 1979. "But you couldn't go into the store and ask for it because there was no hook or lyric. What were you supposed to say to the store assistant? I want the record that goes 'da-da-da-da-da-da-da-da'! Records like 'Disco Circus' sold a limited amount through word-of-mouth and that was it." Disco, it was becoming clear, had not only failed to reverse the emerging recession in the music industry but was also contributing to the economic dip. That was certainly how the horizon looked from the top of Mount Warners, from which Caviano naively bragged to *Newsweek* that "thirty-five per cent of all disco acts are a figment of some producer's imagination."[12] Yet the very facelessness of the label's output combined with the dubious talent of a number of its acts meant that best-selling albums were effectively nonexistent. "A number of the artists that we signed went to number one in the disco charts but didn't have follow-ups," says Aletti. "We tried to find acts that were really going to be able to develop and tour. However, the records that we continued to sign were club hits that had a strong but short life, which also meant that they cost the company a lot of money and didn't end up leading us anywhere."

Halfway through 1979, Caviano was forced to readjust his rose-tinted sunglasses. "The company stopped being so generous with our ability to sign," says Aletti. "As it happens we were actually making them quite a bit of money by promoting things like Rod Stewart. It was just a transitional time for the business." Having told *Newsweek* that the process of taking acetates to New York's hottest clubs was "like Proctor and Gamble pretesting their detergent," Caviano now had to reflect upon the accuracy of his own metaphor, given that fewer and fewer consumers were willing to buy his increasingly antiseptic product.[13] "Warners exploited the disco market," says Chin, "and the spottiness of their surviving catalogue proves it." Bobby Shaw, who was working alongside Caviano in what had literally become the Warners nerve center, confirms the approach. "Warners were just trying to capitalize on what had become fashionable." It is doubtful that the attempt to make the most out of disco was successful. "I'm sure Ray lost money," says Chin. "He had a large staff and no crossover hits whatsoever. He was to have his only gold record, 'A Lover's Holiday' by Change, in 1980. You need way more sales than that to look sexy in the eyes of the guys who run the money faucets. None of the pop hits that had a twelve-inch can really be considered Ray's records."

Columbia's disco department also came under severe pressure. "Nobody wanted to be in the disco ring, and then once it was established everyone wanted to be in, from Andy Williams to Johnny Mathis to Patrick Hernandez to Rodney Franklin to Paul McCartney," says Pellegrino. "It was a monstrous job. CBS never came close to matching the Warners disco department, which had a staff of eighteen. People thought that I didn't want to call them back but I just didn't have the time." The promoter's task didn't exactly become easier when he *did* find the time to catch up on his messages. "My problem was trying to explain to a specific department that certain records weren't going to work," he says. "They would reply, 'You're not going to play God with our music! We want it to be exposed!' I was just trying to say that we didn't need the same version of five thousand records to find out if we have a hit." Everything started to sound the same. "The DJs were looking at us like we didn't know what we were doing. They were getting a hundred records a week, and the market couldn't digest that. In the end I got the feeling that the A&R rockers were loading up the disco department in order to kill it." When satisfactory sales failed to materialize, pop twelve-inches became a high-profile scapegoat following an ill-timed price hike. "We'll watch the situation closely now that 12-inchers are getting closer to the price of an album," Pellegrino told *Billboard* in July. "Are consumers now going to say, 'why not spend $1.50 more and get the entire album?' No one knows the answer to that."[14]

The pressure being heaped on Pellegrino was intensified by CBS's reckless decision to invest millions of dollars in new manufacturing facilities to meet the anticipated huge demand for disco during the winter of 1978–79. Like Warners and the other major labels, Columbia manufactured vast quantities of plastic, only to suffer crushingly disappointing sales that were exacerbated by an anomalous business practice that allowed stores to order and return vinyl on a penalty-free basis. Understanding the risk-free nature of their commitment, the retailers requested huge numbers of records and then sent them back to the manufacturers when they failed to sell. As music industry historian Fredric Dannen notes, "The mistake made by PolyGram—and also CBS and Warners and the other majors—was shipping and logging them as sales, never dreaming that the usual return estimates were way low."[15]

None of this could be disentangled from the broader reality of the recession, and disco, having been cast as the savior of the music industry, was now having to concede that its aesthetic and consumer base made it an inappropriate k/night in shining armor. Being a studio- rather than a star-led phenomenon, the disco production process presented the major labels with an apparently irresolvable conundrum: how to sell faceless music? As journalist Radcliffe Joe noted in the middle of July, "There is growing concern in the discotheque industry, especially among record label people, that the continued dearth of superstars among disco entertainers could result in a longterm [sic] adverse effect on the entire industry."[16] Of all of the producer-concocted groups, only the Village People had joined Donna Summer, the Bee Gees, and Chic in attaining superstar status. The poor return was deemed to be so hazardous that even producers began to warn against the perils of their continued domination. As the British-based producer Biddu told Billboard, "We must begin a search for talented, personable acts which can be groomed for major concert appearances, in order that the concept of disco be proliferated."[17]

Dance music's peculiar functionality raised other problems for the majors. DJs and dancers would home in on a record because it worked, not because it came from an artist or label that they particularly liked, and as a result all sorts of acts failed to build the kind of stable, devoted, unconditional following that the record industry craved. The Bee Gees were a perfect case in point. While tribal loyalties should have prevented DJs from buying into a white straight band with a folk-rock history, "You Should Be Dancing" worked on the dance floor, and that was enough. Yet any sort of loyalty that might have been forged by the release of Saturday Night Fever quickly evaporated when the band recorded the soundtrack for RSO's 1978 movie, Sgt. Pepper's Lonely Hearts. The album didn't work on the dance floor, so DJs and dance consumers didn't buy it.

Part of the sales quandary could also be traced to the nature of the dance floor experience, where the avoidance of the ego-driven performances that characterized best-selling pop and rock recordings enhanced the chances of the DJ and the dance floor reaching a synergistic nirvana. If performers were black, female, and intimately attached to nightworld, then their ability to overcome the double oppression of race and sex through gutsy emotion and bodily expressivity made them an appropriate candidate for the floor, especially if it was gay. But if they were white, male, and primarily interested in stadiums, festivals, and female groupies, then their tried-and-trusted expressions of angst, anger, melancholy, aggression, and arrogance weren't conducive to the club environment. It was the latter group, of course, that had been providing the music industry with its most profitable stars since the late sixties.

Rock and disco were ultimately moving according to different trajectories. As music critic Will Straw notes, rock was no longer motored by the desire to create innovative music. "The sense of a collective, generic progression within rock music had for the most part disappeared," he writes, "and been replaced by an emphasis on the parallel trajectories of individual performer careers."[18] Disco, in contrast, was moving to a beat that was driven by the need to create fresh sounds. "The context within which the currency of a newly-released disco recording was most likely to be judged was that provided by the body of other disco recordings released contemporaneously with it, rather than by the cumulative body of work of its performer."[19] More often than not, innovation was coming from sometimes shy, sometimes dysfunctional, sometimes unsightly DJs and remixers, and this didn't exactly inspire those who were charged with the responsibility of generating tomorrow's disco superstars.

The awkward economics of the disco market was compounded by the rise of the twelve-inch single, which was the ultimate dance music commodity as far as DJs and dancers (the primary consumers of disco) were concerned. That was because forty-fives were far too short to produce the kind of expansive, transcendental flow that was so conducive to the definitive dance floor experience, and albums often contained a mixture of shortened dance and nondance singles that were created for consumption in the home rather than the club. Companies attempted to market disco by supplying record pools with free twelve-inches in the belief that the format would build national hits for forty-fives and albums, but the strategy was finally undermined by the persistent preference on the part of DJs and dancers for the "giant single"—a low-profit format that was considered to be too long for radio play and was widely blamed for undermining the high-profit potential of albums.

The music industry was desperately trying to tread water—even though it was up to its stomach in quicksand. The marketing method of developing new genres to sustain sales was applied to disco as it had been to previous sounds, with top-heavy managerial teams plotting their strategies around potentially lucrative stars and the till-friendly album format in order to create profitable order where there had once been chaos. DJ rations were slashed by record companies when radio belatedly revised its playlist priorities—the fact that disco sounded far better in a club than on the radio was deemed to be unimportant—and disco departments subsequently paid less and less attention to the quality of their output, in part because they believed that anything would sell in the post–*Saturday Night Fever* market. The wider economy, though, was tightening, and audience tastes were diversifying, which suggested that record companies needed to pay more attention to localized, flexible, grassroots sales. Unfortunately, the majors weren't yet ready to adjust. "It became ridiculous," says Coles, who returned to his old job behind the counter at Colony. "They were disco-tizing all these crazy things. It had to end."

* * *

When Chicago rock station WDAI-FM offered Detroit DJ Steve Dahl a job in 1978, he jumped at the opportunity. The honeymoon, however, was brief. A couple of days before Christmas, the station dropped its AOR (album-oriented rock) format in favor of disco, and the new recruit decided that his position was untenable. "I quit because disco really didn't fit the kind of show that I was doing," he says. "I was doing mostly talk, and it was pretty much tailored to my own lifestyle, which didn't really have many intersecting points with the disco thing." Dahl resurfaced in March on WLUP-FM and started to attack the dance phenomenon as if it were freshly laid concrete—easiest to remove before it set hard. "Disco represented superficiality. The whole lifestyle seemed to be based on style over substance." Not that Dahl had always hated the genre. "There was a time when I thought some of it was OK. We used to play stuff from *Saturday Night Fever* on WDAI. When the movie came out it was kind of cool. But then disco achieved critical mass, and I felt that rock music was threatened as a species." Dahl, who knew how to rant like no other talk DJ, began to target dance culture as public enemy number one, and according to the *Village Voice*, "he couldn't help noticing how the phones lit up" whenever he turned the "15-minute lunatic stream-of-consciousness raps" he delivered between songs into "disco-baiting monologues."[20] Realizing that he had "tapped into this anti-disco sentiment that was really out there," Dahl formed the Insane Coho Lips—named after the Coho salmon, which were celebrated in Chicago for having rid Lake Michigan of the lamprey eel, a slithery parasite that had almost succeeded in wiping out the lake's edible fish. WLUP had to hire two additional staff to cope with applications to the self-styled "army" that was, in the words of the organization's literature, "dedicated to the eradication of the dreaded musical disease known as DISCO."

This was no sudden, isolated flash of hatred. Back at the beginning of 1976, music critic John Rockwell had noted a "hardening of rock-critical arteries," and a couple of years later Vince Aletti commented that, for all of its success, *Saturday Night Fever* "may not put an end to DISCO SUCKS buttons."[21] Having settled into the *Record World* chair, Brian Chin also realized he was part of a struggle. " 'Disco sucks' was always there," he says. "There was always anger in the music business." Yet as Tom Moulton notes, radio's rock contingent was the first to bite back. "Radio DJs liked having the power of being able to say, 'If we don't play it it's not a hit.' The clubs brought them down a peg or two, so they were the first ones to put a nail in disco's coffin." By July 1979, that anger was also spewing forth from the likes of Robert Vare in the previously sympathetic *New York Times*. "My question is, how did Western civilization get along for so many years without disco?" he asked. "What in the world did people do for release? Did Socrates formulate concepts of justice, honor and love because he was able to wear a Day-Glo toga and twitch and wriggle until dawn? Can you imagine Leonardo da Vinci cornering Michelangelo at the Florentine branch of Fiorucci and bending his ear for a couple of hours about some new disco's laser beam light show or plastic snow machine? How did Pavlova ever manage to execute an arabesque without affixing glitter to herself and snorting amyl nitrate?" The "poetry" of the Beatles had been replaced by the "monotonous bass-pedal bombardment" of Donna Summer. "By 1984, when we're deaf, dumb and blind from disco, we may all find ourselves dancing to a different drummer."[22]

Rock-oriented radio DJs joined that attack without batting a collective eye at the irony that they were now perceived to be reputable members of the canonical establishment rather than its disruptive antagonist. "Radio guys couldn't wait to drop disco," says Chin. "It was just a personal gut response. They didn't want to own a sound that wasn't male and rock-identified." Dahl became one of disco's most strident critics, and while the Chicago DJ maintains that all he "ever did was make fun of disco music because it was banal" his sense of humor became increasingly vio-

After the explosion: anti-disco rioters at Comiskey Park. Courtesy of Bettman/CORBIS

lent. Two live appearances—in which Dahl sang his single, "Da Ya Think I'm Disco? (Am I Superficial?)," told a round of Village People jokes, and led a fist-waving chorus of "disco sucks"—required police intervention to maintain order, and in the WLUP studio he started playing disco records before "blowing them up" with sound effects. The campaign climaxed on 12 July when the radio jock organized an anti-disco rally at Comiskey Park, home of the Chicago White Sox, which was timed to coincide with a doubleheader against the Detroit Tigers. Fans were told they could pay just ninety-eight cents if they also handed over a slab of unwanted disco vinyl, and forty thousand of them, carrying some forty thousand records, filed through the turnstiles as the first game drew to a close (another thirty thousand were locked outside). Then came the fireworks between games. "Steve Dahl made a big twelve-foot pile with all the records," says disco fan Ralphie Rosario. "He got everyone to chant 'disco sucks,' and then he blew up the records with dynamite." The crowd rioted. "They were losing their minds. The only people who actually enjoyed baseball were rock 'n' rollers. The crowd was made up of middle-class white suburban boys and families with their kids. There were drunken people all over the place. It was Middle America."

Dahl maintains that there was nothing premeditated about his campaign. "It's not like it was some calculated thing on my part. I was like a kid playing with matches. I didn't know what I was doing, and I just tapped into this anti-disco sentiment that was already out there. What's interesting is that it happened in spite of me. All I was doing was horsing around." Yet the Comiskey Park gathering also had its less comic side, echoing as it did the fascist rallies of the 1930s and 1940s, and on this occasion it was Dahl, dressed up in army fatigues and a helmet, who played the role of the charismatic, knowledgeable, and power-hungry conductor. The forty thousand followers, sporting regulation black t-shirts that carried the name of their hero's radio show, embodied the ignorant and inflammable crowd in search of a common cause. Dahl's argument that he was simply "doing a show about my life and it all just clicked" echoed a standard myth of fascism—that the emergent leader instinctively comes to express the will of the masses through a mystical transmission of desire. The public detonation of disco music, which was closely associated with gay men and African Americans, mirrored the fascist-style burnings of jazz, which was tied to African Americans and Jews. And Dahl's acknowledgement that the campaign "worked real well for me" was consistent with fascism's profit motive: "disco sucks" equaled rock 'n' roll bucks.[23]

Yet despite the apparent attractiveness of the clubbing option—fascists only had a choice of one party, whereas dancers could go to as many parties as they liked—the campaign against disco in Chicago continued when WDAI-FM signaled its return to rock with a twenty-four hour looped rendition of Donna Summer's "Last Dance," transforming a song of romantic regret into a grotesque caricature of disco repetition. By midsummer Dahl's campaign was being mimicked all over the country. As the *Village Voice* reported:

> At WLVQ-FM, in Columbus, Ohio, morning man John Fisher put on fatigues and a gas mask, declared himself general of a rock & roll army, torpedoed the Village People's "In the Navy," and sent uncounted hundreds of disco records to the trash compactor between periods at a soccer match. At KGON-FM in Portland, Oregon, morning man Bob Anchetta followed his chain-saw demonstration at the Euphoria Tavern by smashing and burning hundreds more on top of the concession stand at the 104th Street drive-in for a crowd of 900 who chanted "disco sucks" while waiting to see *Animal House*. At WOUR-FM in Utica,

listeners were given three possible means of destruction every morning—for instance, chainsaw, city bus, or wild-animal stampede—and
forced to endure a disco record until someone called in with the means
of destruction that had been chosen for it; then the record would be
bussed to death, say, and the winner would receive a shard along with
a rock record and a little commerative [sic] plaque. At wwww-fm in
Detroit—popularly known as w4—morning man [sic] Jim Johnson and
George Baier set up an antidisco vigilante group they decided ("without thinking too deeply," Baier now admits) to call the Disco Ducks
Klan. They were planning to wear white sheets onstage at a disco that
was switching back to rock when the Comiskey Park riot persuaded
them to cool it. It turned out that on the day it was supposed to have
taken place, they left w4 for another aor station, wrif-fm, where they
now run an organization called dread (Detroit Rockers Engaged in
the Abolition of Disco) and hold on-the-air "electrocutions" of disco-
lovers whose names and phone numbers have been sent in by the dia
(dread Intelligence Agency).[24]

Dahl's argument that the crusade "made a lot of people sit back and
question the disco stuff that was being shoved down their throats" was
suggestive of the way in which "disco sucks" was first and foremost a
homophobic phenomenon.[25] Disco sucks . . . what? Did it suck innocent
listeners into its seductive rhythms? Did it suck the "real" rock music industry dry? Or did it suck cock? "Steve Dahl was one of these Howard
Stern types, talking about all of this stupid shit, downplaying homosexuals, downplaying Jewish people," says Rosario. "The disco era revolved around gays and that was something he took up."

Dahl claims that he was less incensed by disco's gayness than by its
superficiality and artificiality, but his argument holds significantly less
water than Lake Michigan. *Superficial* and *artificial* had, after all, become
derogatory euphemisms for *gay*, and this link was made more explicit
when John Parikhal, a Toronto-based media consultant, carried out attitudinal research on discophobia and reported that his focus groups thought
disco was superficial, boring, repetitive, and short on "balls," and that
homophobia cropped up repeatedly.[26] As cultural critic Walter Hughes
notes, "even the subtler critiques of disco implicitly echo homophobic accounts of a simultaneously emerging urban gay male minority: disco is
'mindless,' 'repetitive,' 'synthetic,' 'technological,' and 'commercial,' just

as the men who dance to it with each other are 'unnatural,' 'trivial,' 'decadent,' 'artificial,' and 'indistinguishable' 'clones.'"[27]

Dahl denies the depiction. "I'm sure I made some gay jokes about the Village People or whatever, but I thought that was fairly obvious. I don't recall the jokes, but there were amusing aspects to all that. I mean if a guy's going to walk around in an Indian getup, then he's asking . . ." That, apparently, wasn't homophobic. "I get the feeling that you want to characterize this as being antigay, and I don't think that's right." Perhaps, but that is only because Dahl's anti-disco movement finally drew on a far more flexible ideology than straightforward homophobia. For sure, gays were far too prominent and had acquired far too much influence, but then so too had blacks and women, and disco as a whole had come to represent excess, extravagance, hedonism, physicality, and expressivity—all of the things that Dahl's constituency felt uneasy about. "In a way I was right with the 'disco sucks' people," says Nicky Siano. "The music had gotten really bad, and a lot of it—although not all of it—was just garbage. But I also remember the anti-disco people being very white, male, and straight. It was like a movement for headbangers. After almost ten years of gay white men and gay black men pretty much owning the scene, heteros wanted to take their power back. Disco was *very threatening* for a lot of men." That included Dahl and his followers. "I think I tapped into young, brotherly, male—and dragged along for the ride, female—angst," says the Chicago talk DJ. "You leave high school, and you realize that things are going to be tougher than you thought, and here's this group of people seemingly making it harder for you to measure up. There was some kind of anger out there, and the anti-disco movement seemed to be a good release for that."

By the end of the seventies, the anger had become national in character, and much of it was related to the poor performance of the economy. Jimmy Carter had narrowly defeated President Ford in 1976, following a campaign in which nearly 70 percent of voters identified economic issues as their basic concern, yet by the end of his term Carter had failed to make a dent in the underlying economic crisis. At the same time anger was being expressed at the way in which sixties social values had in many respects become entrenched in the seventies. Hundreds of thousands of women and African Americans had broken down the traditional barriers that had once kept them "in their place," and while millions failed to benefit from this success story there was nevertheless a clear perception among white male voters that Carter had introduced a series of controversial liberal positions around abortion and affirmative action that were less important to the "average Democratic voter" than the economy.

The loss of faith in the direction of the Democratic Party coincided with the rise of the New Right, a group of conservative voters who coalesced around a series of volatile issues that had become associated with the so-called excesses of the 1960s and the subsequent attack on what conservatives interpreted as the most basic institutions and values of American society—the church, the nation, and the monogamous heterosexual family. This group had begun to articulate its ideas in the late sixties, when it was dubbed the "middle-American" revolt, and the campaign gathered momentum throughout a decade in which the old rules of the Protestant work ethic and abstemiousness were challenged by the new codes of self-fulfillment and pleasure. By the end of the seventies, notes historian William Chafe, "Americans faced a frightening array of prospects—permanent economic stagnation, the presence of an 'underclass' that directly challenged the essence of the American dream, and bitter division over fundamental cultural values."[28] Drawing on this disenchantment, Ronald Reagan's Republican Party recast its political identity. Having been historically identified as the party of sectional interests, it reinvented itself as the representative of the average American, leaving the Democrats—historically the people's party—to represent marginal groups, supposedly at the expense of the nation.

Disco could hardly be disentangled from these developments. African Americans, gays, and women—key players in the countercultural movement of the sixties—were integral to the new culture of the night, and the spreading principles of bodily pleasure, sexual liberation, nonnuclear families, and self-exploration found their most compelling outlet in the arena of the discotheque. When the New Right began to caricature the seventies as stagnant, unproductive, undisciplined, tasteless, wasteful, extravagant, inefficient, morally degenerate, corrupt, and lacking in direction, it was as if they were euphemistically talking about disco. "It wasn't just a dislike of disco that brought everyone together," says Dahl. "It was all of the shared experiences. But disco was probably a catalyst because it was a common thing to rally against." Disco was the perfectly polyvalent symbol of all that was wrong with the outgoing decade, and it also contained potential scapegoats galore.

The left didn't exactly surge to dance culture's defense. If the New

Right believed that disco represented the wrong kind of capitalism, then large swathes of the left maintained that disco simply *was* capitalism, and it was into this hostile terrain that Richard Dyer bravely stepped to justify the party politics of the night, publishing an article entitled "In Defence of Disco" in *Gay Left* in the summer of 1979. "All my life I've liked the wrong music," he wrote. "I never liked Elvis and rock 'n' roll; I always preferred Rosemary Clooney. And since I became a socialist, I've often felt virtually terrorised by the prestige of rock and folk on the left. How could I admit to two Petula Clark LPs in the face of miners' songs from the North East and the Rolling Stones?"[29]

In fact, disco contained many potentially progressive practices, and Dyer was one of the first writers to theorize these credentials, arguing that whereas rock confined "sexuality to the cock" and was thus "indelibly phallo-centric music," disco "restores eroticism to the whole body" thanks to its "willingness to play with rhythm," and it does this "for both sexes."[30] Disco also offered dancers the chance to experience the body as a polymorphous entity that could be reengineered in terms that confounded conservative models of masculinity and femininity. "Its eroticism allows us to rediscover our bodies as part of this experience of materiality and the possibility of change."[31] But for the most part the left distrusted the politics of pleasure, and the overwhelming majority of disco evangelists were more interested in having a good time, producing records, and opening clubs than formulating a coherent response to the public backlash.

* * *

Whereas white suburban rockers viewed disco as being, among other things, irredeemably black, so black urban music aficionados tended to regard the music as being predominantly white. That was certainly the opinion of Nelson George, who outlined his position in an article for the *New York Amsterdam News* in January 1978. While conceding that disco "has definitely put money in the pockets of many Blacks," George maintained that, in the final instance, "disco music has opened up Black stations to penetration by white artists."[32] George's case revolved around a careful analysis of black "crossover" records—"a nice way of saying, caught the fancy of white people"—during the disco boom.[33] According to *Billboard* figures, thirty-six of the top one hundred pop records of 1973 crossed over from black stations; in 1975 the figure was down to twenty-eight; in 1976 the numbers nudged up to thirty; and in 1977 they dropped back to twenty-three. "If these figures are correct," George concluded, "they refute the idea that the disco rage has helped Black performers."[34]

In February 1978 John Rockwell noted that some black groups were responding to the challenge of disco more successfully than others. "For outfits like Parliament-Funkadelic, which has long purveyed jazzish funk instrumentals, the transition has been easy," argued the *New York Times* journalist, citing Parliament's latest release, *Funkentelechy vs. the Placebo Syndrome*, as a case in point. But African American groups rooted in the Philadelphia aesthetic—such as the Trammps, whose latest album, *III*, barely registered on the dance floor and in the charts—were, according to Rockwell, struggling to sell an old sound or switch to a new one. "More traditional groups have had a more complicated task of adjustment."[35] The argument picked up momentum in June when the former *Billboard* soul music editor Ed Ochs warned that while "disco has definitely opened the door" for black music it had also "closed minds to a wide spectrum of black artistry, washing out, some fear, meaningful historical bridges to an entire black music culture."[36] The president of Solar Records, Dick Griffey, added his voice to the chorus of dissent. "From a creative standpoint, it's taken us a step backwards. Disco has caused people to accept less quality material because the beat is so important."[37] African Americans may not have articulated a monolithic rejection of disco, but more and more of them were beginning to doubt the economic and aesthetic advantages of the genre.

Two days after Dahl's "disco demolition" rally, *Billboard* ran an article suggesting that black artists had good reason to be suspicious of disco. "Until recently," the magazine noted, "it was generally assumed that the advent of discomania was the best thing to happen to black music since the invention of the drum. Supporters claimed disco made it easier for black records to crossover into the pop market. But, as witnessed at the recent Black Music Assn. meeting in Philadelphia, many people in the industry are beginning to question disco's affect on black music."[38] Noting that black artists had produced just twenty-one crossover hits in 1978, *Billboard* pointed its glossy finger at the dance market. "The current glut of disco material is obviously hurting the black artist as it is becoming increasingly difficult for an artist to establish an identity with everyone playing to the same audience. Black artists who were once rooted in r&b, jazz, gospel, reggae and even blues are now competing for the same disco dollar."[39] White rockers might have been waging their own backlash against disco, but African Americans were also generating their own *black*lash against the genre.

In his 1963 book *Blues People*, music historian Leroi Jones argued that by the end of the swing era the white-owned music industry had watered down black music to such an extent that it had become indistinguishable from white music and, developing this analysis, George maintained that R&B experienced a similar transition during the seventies. "The same players who performed with such fire on 'Bad Luck' and the anthemic 'I Love Music' made, recording as the Ritchie Family and Salsoul Orchestra, a series of incredibly insipid records, eventually helping drown the Philly sound in clichés."[40] Citing Earth, Wind & Fire and the Commodores, George maintained that soul and funk didn't entirely disappear during this period. "But it should be noted," he added, "that the more successful these bands became, the more mellow and less intense their music got."[41] Only George Clinton and his various ensembles retained a purist aesthetic. "The whole P-Funk concept was a musically amusing way of thumbing one's nose at what Clinton dubbed 'The Placebo Syndrome,' aka funkless black music. Disco, combined with the crossover consciousness of the majors, created music for those who sought mainstream acceptance and didn't want to fight about it."[42]

One solution, of course, was for black music moguls to retain control of their own output, and this was exactly what Sylvia and Joe Robinson, a husband-and-wife team who owned the eight-year-old All Platinum label, hoped to do, despite being knee-deep in a series of lawsuits. Sylvia, a one-time minor pop star in her own right, was at a niece's birthday party at the Harlem International Disco when, as she told George, "All of a sudden I heard these three guys rapping over the microphone. Something hit me—I thought they were fantastic. An inner voice said to me, 'That's a concept.'"[43] A rough approximation of this concept had just made its public breakthrough when Fatback, a struggling funk group from Brooklyn, released "King Tim III (Personality Jock)," which featured a previously marginal DJ called King Tim III and referenced the days when radio rapping jocks infused their shows with rhyming jive. However, it was the three youngsters—named the Sugarhill Gang—who were picked up by the Robinsons to record "Rapper's Delight," a twelve-inch rap that recreated the bass line of Chic's "Good Times" and first entered the *Billboard* chart in October 1979. Appearing on the phoenix-like Sugar Hill Records, the result went top ten in several countries and grossed $3.5 million. The "concept" had moved into the realm of the commercial.

Robinson's account of how she discovered the Sugarhill Gang has been subsequently questioned. "Although nobody knew it at the time," writes rap historian David Toop, "their verses were recycled from groups like The Cold Crush Brothers; they were to Bronx hip hop what The Police were to The Sex Pistols, the difference being that the Bronx originals had yet to find a Malcolm McLaren figure with a stack of confrontational tactics to help them out." Whatever its history, the record was musically less than thrilling. "Ten minutes of Lolleata [*sic*] Holloway, Melba Moore or Bettye LaVette was an emotional epic," adds Toop. "14 minutes 10 seconds of non-stop rhymes from The Sugarhill Gang was more like listening to farming news or stock market reports."[44]

The Sugarhill Gang grew out of a culture that has been traced back to an enduring vernacular tradition that included Muhammad Ali among its more popular practitioners, as well as the mid-seventies Bronx and Harlem block parties, especially those of DJ Kool Herc who, opinion had it, was *disc*onnected from the wider dance scene. "Disco was brand new then and there were a few jocks that had monstrous sound systems but they wouldn't dare play this kind of music," DJ Grandmaster Flash, who was inspired in equal measure by Herc and a mobile jock called Pete DJ Jones, told Toop. "They would never play a record where only two minutes of the song was all it was worth. They wouldn't buy those type of records. The type of mixing that was out then was blending from one record to the next or waiting for the record to go off and wait for the jock to put the needle back on."[45]

Flash's version has subsequently been transformed into the official history of rap versus disco. "It was Herc who saw possibilities of mixing his own formulas through remixing prerecorded sound," writes Houston A. Baker Jr. "His enemy was a dully constructed, other-side-of-town disco-mania that made South and West Bronx hip hoppers ill. Disco was not *dope* in the eyes, ears, and agile bodies of black Bronx teenagers . . . and Queens and Brooklyn felt the same." Baker goes on to form an unspoken alliance with Dahl's homophobic army when he notes that the "club DJs were often gay, and the culture of Eurodisco was populously gay" before concluding, "Hey, some resentment of disco culture and a reassertion of black manhood rights (rites)—no matter who populated discotheques—was a natural thing."[46]

Yet even though disco wasn't "dope," club DJs like Walter Gibbons and John Luongo were developing identical mixing techniques at the same time as Herc, and early rap records drew heavily on the rapping and vamping of the likes of Linda Clifford ("Runaway Love"), Isaac Hayes ("By the Time I Get to Phoenix"), Loleatta Holloway ("Hit and Run"), the Intruders ("I'll Always Love My Mama"), and the Salsoul Orchestra ("Ooh, I Love It [Love Break]"). The mythical rap-disco divide was also crossed by rapping DJs such as Frankie Crocker, Mr. Jive, Jocko, Bert Lockett, Maboya, and DJ Hollywood, and it was Hollywood who was widely credited with breaking rap culture out of Harlem and the Bronx following a high-profile appearance at the Apollo Theatre in 1978 (Flash credits Hollywood with being "one of the greatest solo rappers that ever there was").[47] Moreover, for all of Baker's protests, disco provided the backing track for several early rap recordings. As rap artist Chuck D argues, Gamble and Huff "*invented* disco when disco was the shit and there was no shame, and since rap started on the second half of disco, that makes Gamble and Huff the forefathers of hip-hop."[48]

While Gamble and Huff didn't go down the rap route, New York's established independent dance music labels were happy to dabble. Indeed Mel Cheren claims to have significantly influenced the development of the genre with his very first commission for West End in 1976. "I got Jimmy Stuard to do a mix of 'Sessomatto,' and while we were in the studio he said, 'Mel, I have this little extra piece of tape. Do you mind if I reverse it just for effect?' We put the record out, and it was no great thing, but we would get orders for twenty-five copies from Downstairs, and I would ask them, 'Where's the action coming from?' and they would say, 'Uptown.'" When Cheren went up to the Bronx for a promotion a few years later he was approached by Grandmaster Flash. "He said, 'I've got to get this record! I heard this record! I've got to get it!' He informed me that the record that rappers used before 'Rapper's Delight' was 'Sessomatto,' and they only used the bits where Jimmy Stuard reversed the tape. That was the first scratching sound." Cheren went on to release a couple of rap records on West End and a new label called Fever Records. "They had positive lyrics. My partner said it was a flash in the pan, and I said, 'No, it's going to be another category of music.' I realized that was how kids could express themselves."

Salsoul also began to toy with the rap option, if only because its disco output—aside from a special Walter Gibbons compilation titled *Disco*

Madness and a strong twelve-inch from Candido that included "Jingo" and "Thousand Finger Man"—had reached a new artistic and commercial low. "Ronnie Baker, Norman Harris, and Earl Young weren't working well together," says Ken Cayre. "Norman was hanging around with so many other people that Earl and Ronnie felt distant. They had lost the feeling." Reenter Joe Bataan, who was now exploring the emergent rap scene along with DJ-turned-producer Arthur Baker. "I was living in New York in the summer of 1977, and that was when I met Joe Bataan," says Baker. "He told me that guys in the Bronx and Harlem were talking over records. He took me up to 125th Street to one of the parks in Harlem, and we heard guys rapping over breaks. He said, 'Someone's going to make a million dollars on that!' I said, 'No way!' I thought it was kind of cool, but I didn't think it would make anyone any money." Bataan went away, wrote some lyrics, and then went into the studio with Baker to record "Rap-O Clap-O" for London Records in the summer of 1979. When London went bust, Bataan took the tapes. "I didn't know what was going on at this point," says Baker. "I left New York and went back to Boston. Six months later 'Rap-O Clap-O' came out.'" On Salsoul. The record didn't chart.

Billboard dubbed the "Rapping DJs" a new trend in November, but in truth nobody was looking toward the nascent culture of hip-hop to drag the music industry out of what increasingly looked like a deep and damaging recession.[49] "Inflation is rocking the $4 billion record trade—and the sound of nervous voices is echoing from Manhattan's Sixth Avenue to Sunset Strip in Los Angeles," reported *Newsweek* in August, less than five months after it proclaimed that disco had taken over. "Album prices are soaring, and with a dearth of major hits, sales and profits are both plunging." Escalating costs, increased competition, the rise of home taping, retail overstocking, and internal excesses all added up to the most difficult period that anyone in the industry could remember, and this time there was no "gorilla" (monster hit) to save executive faces. Whereas the Bee Gees had sold fifteen million copies of the *Saturday Night Fever* soundtrack, Donna Summer's *Bad Girls*, the current bestseller, had only reached the three million mark. "There are far fewer recordings 'shipping platinum' (scoring more than a million orders)—only 28 so far this year, compared with 43 in the first half of 1978."[50]

Disco's most rampant hype merchant remained as upbeat as ever. "We can get through this slump," Ray Caviano told *Newsweek*, "because the music ain't never gonna stop."[51] Noting that sales were down and anti-disco sentiment was up, however, Warner Brothers began to reinvest in rock, with the president of the Warners/Elektra/Atlantic Corporation Henry Droz identifying the Eagles, Foreigner, Fleetwood Mac, Rod Stewart, and Led Zeppelin as the artists that would lead the WEA group into the 1980s. "Ray prolonged his life by turning non-disco records into club records," says Vince Aletti. "We were taking things from rock such as the B-52's 'Rock Lobster' and transforming them into huge club hits." The disco category, though, was deemed by insiders to have outlived its usefulness. "The disco department was renamed the dance music department. It was an issue of semantics. All this music was happening, but we couldn't call it disco." Caviano started giving interviews saying, "It's dance music! It's dance music!" while simultaneously blaming the media for disco's decline. "The release of *Saturday Night Fever* compounded that pressure, and soon record label executives were actually beginning to believe that disco was indeed a panacea for all the industry's woes," he told *Billboard* in December 1979. "As a result they were not selective about their releases, but merely put out a glut of product and hoped that at least some of it would be successful."[52]

Casablanca had pursued a similar strategy for much of 1979, and the consequences were the same. While the label notched up hits such as "Bad Girls" and "Hot Stuff" by Donna Summer and the Village People's "In the Navy" as well as cult classics like "Walk the Night" by the Skatt Bros. and Moroder's "E=MC^2," Bogart's finances were out of control. Even though his company was less than five years old, the mogul had two hundred employees on salary and, surpassing CBS, more than a hundred pop acts under contract. "Consider that each signing cost $100,000, or so, *before* promotion," notes music industry analyst Fredric Dannen. "Casablanca began to lose tens of millions a year."[53]

Summer was one of the first to try and jump the sinking ship, although she was more motivated by dreams of artistic expression than sustainable income. " 'I'd like to have as much validity as Streisand and Aretha Franklin," she told *Newsweek*. Having sung blues and rock numbers on her most recent tour, Summer attempted to persuade Bogart to let her introduce non-disco tracks on the *Bad Girls* album, but the label head said he wasn't interested. " 'He saw dollar bills flying out of my pockets when I said I wanted to sing rock 'n' roll. I felt like Marie Antoinette or Joan of Arc—great women of their time who had to deal with ridicule and misunderstanding."[54] Bogart eventually relented—half of the *Bad Girls* tracks were rock-oriented—but the two titans continued to clash, and in February 1980, Summer, claiming that she had been financially defrauded, filed a ten-million-dollar suit against Casablanca.

An increasingly indebted PolyGram, which already owned 50 percent of the West Coast label, simultaneously bought out the rest of the company for fifteen million dollars—"Funkytown" by Lipps Inc. was to be its last monster hit of the disco era—and forced Bogart, the principal stockholder, to leave. The entrepreneur subsequently delivered a keynote speech at the National Association of Recording Merchandisers conference in the spring—"We failed to be realistic, and now something's got to be done"—before spending the bulk of his money on a series of unsuccessful film ventures.[55] Then, in May 1982, he died of lung cancer. Summer, in the meantime, recorded a relatively unsuccessful rock-flavored LP titled *The Wanderer* for her new label, Geffen, in 1980, and PolyGram eventually settled with the singer on condition that she deliver one final album. The title track, "She Works Hard for the Money," released in 1983, dripped with bitterness. PolyGram didn't return to profitability until 1985.

Other mega-acts mimicked Summer's flight from disco. The Bee Gees followed up *Sgt. Pepper's* with the lackluster *Living Eyes*—no hits, dance or otherwise, of any description there—and Chic jumped off the now-derailed disco bandwagon as calculatingly as they had jumped on it in 1977. "Our next single will change direction some," Bernard Edwards told *Billboard*. "We have to; we've decided it's time." Time, that is, to exit. "The public puts you in a category and decides that you're a disco group," argued the bassist, "so obviously if disco dies you have to be concerned. That's why we've worked so hard to get away from that."[56] The band switched to writing "heavier ballads, rock and r&b" and took Sister Sledge with them, alienating dancers and nondancers alike in the process.

The good times weren't over only for Chic. Heads started to rock and roll across the music industry, with disco departments suffering disproportionately, and the final toll, according to music industry commentator R. Serge Denisoff, eventually reached "around 600 victims in one year."[57] In some respects this was simply the old story about people being laid off during a recession, except that there were now two additional twists: the identity of the people who were being laid off and the link between this identity and the process of culpability. "They used disco to try and pull the industry out of recession, and then they blamed disco for failing to achieve this," says Chin. "I didn't notice anyone blaming punk and new wave for the downturn in the music business." The "Disco File" columnist watched on as the world around him unraveled. "They were always watching for the next thing that looked like rock, and that's why I experienced it as such a personal attack. It was about the music, sexuality, race—all of those things. 'Disco sucks' scared the fuck out of me. I thought we were all going to disappear." Not that there was a great deal to cut away. "Disco departments didn't have time to get bloated. At RCA, for example, there were only two people in the disco department and they ended up keeping one guy on to call the DJs." In contrast the renamed dance department at Warner Brothers did get bloated in a very short time and suffered the consequences. "The whole company needed to be downsized. The cuts in the disco department weren't necessarily malicious. It's just that somebody who is gay or black recognizes how easy it is to be let go. It reminded people about who is disposable and who isn't disposable. That's why it was a backlash and not an economic shakeout."

Gomes, however, believes that spiraling expense accounts lay at the root of the cuts. "The people doing club promotion were spending money like you wouldn't believe," he says. "They stayed in the best hotels, they traveled around in a limousine service, they took a large amount of drugs, they had summerhouses on Fire Island, and they took people out to the most expensive restaurants *nightly*." Casablanca was the most obvious culprit. "They were spending money like mad. They had a staff in California, and they had a staff in New York, so they were duplicating two offices. Their overheads were *outrageous*. Then they even bought their own building in New York. In the end the parent company reined them in." Warners came in a close second. "They were spending *huge amounts of money*—and *it wasn't their money! Finally Warners said, 'Let's see what we've made and what we're spending,' and they weren't making what they were spending." Even Prelude, which ran a far tighter budget and was scoring with a higher proportion of records, clamped down. "Our club promotion person had a huge expense account. That person was cut, and the work got passed on to me." Was there an element of lingering racism or latent homophobia? "No, not in the least. It was the wretched excess."

All of this excess might have been overlooked if the math added up, but it didn't. "This industry is geared toward *what sells*," says Gomes. "If disco had been selling in any way, shape, or form they would have sold it. *It stopped selling! People weren't buying it anymore!*" Rock sales had also dropped, although not to the same extent. "You couldn't just cut the rock people because certain areas of rock were still selling. But disco wasn't selling so those people had to go." What's more, radio, and not club, DJs seemed to now be responsible for launching the disco records that did sell. "Diana Ross's 'Love Hangover' really broke through the radio more than the clubs, and after that a lot of club records started breaking through radio," adds Gomes. "The disco department was the easiest to cut because you didn't need to ship records to the clubs."

Record pools were inevitably targeted. RCA was one of the first to announce a radical cutback, and Eddie Rivera's International Disco Record Center was an early victim of the strategic shift when its delivery was slashed from five hundred to fifty copies of each release. CBS and Polydor subsequently announced similar cuts, as did Salsoul, which declared that it was now going to limit its service to "key clubs and key deejays." In August 1979, West End also started to consider substantial cuts. "I'd be less than honest if I said we haven't discussed a cutback," Vice President Ed Kushins told *Billboard*. "But it's the last thing we'd want to do. We have tremendous loyalty among the young kids in record pools and we owe a lot of our success to them. Yet, in an extremely depressed market, we can give away more than we sell."[58]

IDRC representative Dave Peaslee pleaded with the companies to change from within rather than heap the bulk of the blame onto the soft economy. "One of the more viable options," he suggested, "would be the development of a way of selectively previewing and releasing product which is closer to deejay specifications."[59] However, the following month For the Record President Judy Weinstein—whose organization had "felt no ill effects so far"—maintained that the core problem lay not with the glut of inappropriate records but with a general failure to follow through on club play. "A record company will push a record and get disco play," she told *Billboard*. "The people will like it and go to local stores looking for a copy. The disco promotion people will tell the company to ship the record because it's not in the stores. But the company, lacking faith in disco, will overanticipate returns and not ship enough. As a result the record will climb the charts for a while and then suddenly drop for lack of sales." Weinstein wasn't simply pushing her own organization, which, with 125 high-flying members and a waiting list of another 150, had established itself as an elite, streamlined, and powerful unit by the autumn. "A pool in Syracuse can be just as effective in its market as a New York City pool.

But because it is not in a major disco center some companies may stop servicing them." Yet while the bureaucratic and centralized majors were prepared to continue feeding lean and influential organizations such as For the Record, they didn't know how to begin to service nonmetropolitan markets or diversifying niche tastes. "It seems to me that record companies provide certain records for discos, certain records for AOR radio and others for black stations," declared Weinstein, who maintained that rock, funk, and R&B had a place in discos. "It doesn't have to be that structured."[60]

Given its wide-ranging coverage of the music field, *Billboard* remained touchingly devoted to the future of its beloved stepchild. "Disco is far more than a radio format," ran the magazine's editorial of 23 February 1980. "It is far more than a sound. What it really is—and too many of us have lost sight of this fact—is a multibillion dollar industry. It is a facet of the entertainment business that is alive, healthy and thriving, growing stronger with each passing day here in the U.S. and throughout the world." The journal concluded, "If ever there had been a doubt, disco's strength was brought home with full force during last week's International Disco/Dance Forum at the Century Plaza in Los Angeles. There, from all corners of the world, successful club operators, their DJs and their suppliers to this burgeoning industry convened to reaffirm the ever growing strength of the disco phenomenon."[61]

The message at the seventh *Billboard* forum itself was significantly less strident. Craig Kostich, national promotions director at Warners, set the tone when he announced that the cowering music giant would be cutting back on twelve-inch promotional singles, and when disco sympathizers Casablanca and West End followed suit it was clear that the conference organizers had failed to effectively convey their smiley line to participating panelists. An increasingly reproachful atmosphere eventually spread to the DJs, who began to argue among themselves at an apparently innocuous panel titled "Programming Today in the Club" when Chris Hill, the owner of London's Gold Mine, and James Hamilton, a leading British dance music commentator, attacked their American counterparts. "The trouble is you don't sell records in your discos here," Hill told the California conference. "And there are so many ways you can do it. You can do it by talking or by mixing, it doesn't matter. It's purely individual. The point is you just don't do it." Hamilton added his weight to the debate. "This is true," he told the gathering. "The American DJ is to blame for not selling records. That's why disco is dead." *Billboard* reporter and Brooklyn mixmaster Dan Pucciarelli was the first to respond. "We're not there to sell records. Record companies should put us on salary if we did that." Weinstein added her voice to the defense. "The reason disco is dead is because the radio jocks are rock-oriented. Disco deejays are paid by the club owner—and usually not paid enough—not by the record company."[62]

As for the "ever growing strength of the disco phenomenon," that ground to an unceremonious halt at the end of the eighth—and *last*— *Billboard* Disco/Dance Forum, which was held in July, and inbetween times rock began to reassert its brawny authority when it dominated the March Grammys. The release of two films apparently confirmed the pendular swing away from disco. Casablanca's *Can't Stop the Music*, starring a de-gayed Village People—"You can't spend $13 million making a minority movie," bleated producer Alan Carr—was an unmitigated disaster, and the record company subsequently decided that it *could* stop the music when it finally ditched the multicostumed ensemble.[63] Then there was *Urban Cowboy*, which, following the tried-and-true formula of *Saturday Night Fever*, was inspired by a magazine article, sponsored by RSO, and starred John Travolta, but then headed in an entirely different direction when it unflinchingly ditched the suburban disco scene in favor of a plot that revolved around Houston's weekend cowboys. Where there had once been a DJ and a dance floor, there was now a mechanical rodeo bull and a ballroom (although sardonic purists could point to a metaphorical continuity between the rodeo ring and the dance floor at 2001 Odyssey).

Finally, however, the music industry hadn't so much reverted to rock as it had shrunk and fragmented in a way that suggested that no genre would be able to dominate the market in the way that first rock and then disco had ruled in the recent past. What's more, there was no longer an outlet for a simple confrontation between rock and disco because few downtown party freaks seriously mourned the passing of the disco genre. As Prelude and West End, operating in local niche markets, were demonstrating, dance music was beginning to move into a more R&B–oriented groove, and the hollow remnants of disco were bid a distinctly un-fond farewell. " 'Disco sucks' had its place," notes Danny Krivit, who was now DJing at Trude Heller's. "Around *Saturday Night Fever* the major labels said, 'Let's just churn something out,' and it turned into this hype machine that people couldn't take. You would look at the chart and see this garbage and you would just say, *'Death* to this stuff!' It seemed like everywhere you turned there was some kind of meaningless no-talent disco act. Rockers could exploit the fact that disco sucked because there was plenty of sucky disco." Chin, reviewing material for his "Disco File" column, was equally despondent. "I used to get records in the mail, and I thought, 'Shit! What can I say about this?' I was scouring them for something positive to say but they sucked. Costandinos's records—they sucked. Boris Midney's records—they sucked. The Chic album—it was like, 'Oh my God, there's *nothing on here!*' When Gamble and Huff stopped using Earl Young on drums the tracks just got softer—compare 'Bad Luck' to 'I Don't Love You Anymore.' *Everybody* let us down."

Everybody also included Jacques Morali, who worked on the *Can't Stop the Music* disaster and subsequently signed a multirecord production deal with West End that virtually sank the label. As a chastened Cheren later commented, "all he was producing were flops."[64] Giorgio Moroder also disappointed dance enthusiasts, although this had more to do with what he *wasn't* writing. "Call Me" by Blondie contributed to the developing canon of rock dance recordings, and Irene Cara's "Flashdance . . . What a Feeling" gave a commercial shot in the arm to the dance industry in 1983, but Moroder wrote both of these songs for soundtracks, and it was toward Hollywood and not nightworld that the producer now devoted his efforts. Walter Gibbons also went off in a different direction, for, while he produced one of the most important dance records of the 1980s in the form of "Set It Off" by Strafe, his devout religious beliefs led him to sever relations with the music industry and restrict his DJing selections. "I have to let God play the records," he told Steven Harvey in 1983. "I'm just an instrument."[65]

Moulton, too, became an instrument, although he fell under the influence of the ungodly executives at Casablanca and then PolyGram. "My lawyer got me to sign this contract with Casablanca," says Moulton, who mercifully mixed the breathtaking "Love Sensation" by Loleatta Holloway before signing away his soul. "The deal was that I would do three acts a year, plus two artists outside Casablanca. I kept Grace Jones and the Trammps." Moulton released his first record with Casablanca—"Put Yourself in My Place" by TJM on the specially created subsidiary Tom & Jerry—in July 1979, but the agreement turned sour when PolyGram bought out Casablanca and told the remixer-producer that they didn't intend to honor his contract. "I took PolyGram to court, and I won, but in

Grace Jones at Roseland, 31 October 1978. Photo by Waring Abbott

the end I lost because they killed all my enthusiasm for the business. I just wanted to get out of it after that. I didn't return for ten years."

"Disco sucks" might have been a multivalent, complex, and often contradictory phenomenon, but by the end of 1979 there was little doubt that *disco* with a capital *D* was dead—or at least in need of an extremely long rest—inasmuch as nobody was using the term anymore. "*Disco* was obviously overexposed and overused for the mainstream listener of America," says Chin. "That's why nobody cried or protested when it went away. They had quite had their fill." Moulton agrees. "Those records by the Bee Gees were played and played and played and played, and I think people wanted a change. It got to the point that people were so bombarded that they just wanted relief of some kind." A number of insiders believed that the term should be defended against hostile detractors, while others thought that, given its corporate takeover and generic limitations, it should be ditched. Yet both factions agreed that this process of naming—and shaming— didn't have much to do with grassroots dance culture, which was far from comatose. "Everybody said that disco died, but why did all of these clubs still exist, and why were people still going out on the weekend to dance all night?" asks Moulton. "The death of disco! *Jeez, I missed that one!*" Gomes was too busy dancing to go to any funeral. "'Disco sucks' didn't touch us at all. It really didn't faze people. It may have been on the radio and in the media, but how could it touch a community that was not affected by that to begin with? We still went out, and we still had music. *We didn't miss a beat!*"

* * *

In May 1978, Hurrah's (formerly Harrah) started to serve up a mix of punk, new wave, and conventional rock one night a week, and by September the club had shifted to an entirely rock-oriented format, employing two female DJs—Meg Griffin from WNEW and Jane Hamburger from WFIX—to program the music. Then, in November, Stephen Mass opened Mudd on 77 White Street, two blocks below Canal, and served his pierced clients with a similar mix. By the following July *Billboard* journalist Roman Kozak, responding to the multiplication of rock clubs such as Club 57, Heat, the Rocker Room, Rock'n'Roll Queen, Studio 10, and Tomato, was asking, "Is rock'n'roll the future of disco? It may very well be if the mushrooming growth of new rock disco clubs in New York City is any indication."[66]

On the surface, this amounted to a rejection of disco as trenchant as anything dreamed up by Steve Dahl, and when writer Vita Miezitis toured New York's nightclubs in the summer of 1979 in order to research *Night Dancin'*, she was struck by the rampant anti-disco sentiment in these new venues. "Anyone dancing the hustle here would more than likely be bounced out the door, booed and hissed, or stoned and safety-pinned to death," she reported. "The mere mention of disco sends Mudd Club regulars running off, gagging, choking, screaming in agony, squealing and holding their ears."[67] A number of midtown codes were inverted: an external metal chain mockingly replaced the velvet rope, the deliberately ungraceful "Spastic" displaced the Hustle, sexuality was stoned heterosexual rather than flauntingly polymorphous, and clothes were disfiguring rather than figure-hugging. "If the body parts on display at Studio were the cute ass, the exposed nipple, the serrated nostril," notes observer Anthony Haden-Guest, "the Mudd anatomy featured the sunken cheekbone, the unseeing eyeball, the perforated upper arm."[68]

On a more profound level, however, Hurrah's (which was soon referred to as Hurrah) and Mudd (which was soon referred to as the Mudd Club) embodied rock's return to its roots. Rock 'n' roll was born as dance music for record hops and early discotheques, and the emergence of dance-able new wave bands such as Blondie ("Atomic"), Talking Heads ("Take Me to the River"), and the Yellow Magic Orchestra ("Computer Game 'Theme from the Circus'") promised a belated return to the mission of bodily pleasure. While many Hurrah and Mudd Club regulars expressed a profound dislike for disco, their hostility was directed toward the banal, canned, frivolous aspect of the culture—that is to say, precisely the same aspect that downtown dance aficionados were simultaneously disowning in an equal hurry—and these venues remained fundamentally distinct from the Steve Dahl continuum, if only because they were trying to shift dance culture rather than destroy it. "Some lazy journalists were trying to characterize these places as actively fighting disco, but that was just sensationalism," says Barry Walters, who moved to New York in the summer of 1979 and soon started to dance at both Hurrah and the Mudd Club—as well as the Paradise Garage and Better Days. "These clubs were rebelling against the Studio 54/Bee Gees version of disco, and some of the 'disco sucks' crowd did indeed visit them. But their practice of playing underground danceable records, many of them imported from countries where disco was still thriving, actually made them closer to disco's Loft-based roots than Studio 54's pop disco. These places were trendy, progressive, and New York to the core." Michael Gomes, who went to the Mudd Club several times, agrees. "It attracted a white rock audience, but these people wanted to start dancing. People were looking for new music and new sounds, and a lot of what they were playing was innovative and fresh. They played rock, but it was rock with a beat."

Most rock songs, however, were too short for successful club play, and relatively few of them were being made with the dance floor in mind. "I don't know why the record companies don't remix more rock songs for dancing, and then release them as conventional 12-inchers," Mass, proffering a simple solution, told *Billboard* in July 1979. "They could probably make a fortune selling them."[69] Ray Caviano, Vince Pellegrino, and company, having experienced numerous humiliations from in-house rock departments and regular rebukes regarding the pitfalls of the twelve-inch single, could have probably set the Mudd Club owner straight on that one. But by the time the influential Danceteria opened its doors in March 1980, a groundswell of new wave releases had emerged to resolve this particular set of aesthetic contradictions.

Moving into the disco slipstream around the same time that Hurrah was shifting to a rock format, roller skaters also tried to break into dance culture at the tail end of the seventies. Easy Glider, located in the Baldwin Place Mall, opened at the end of 1977, and Skate City, the self-described "original northern Westchester roller disco," followed in March 1978.[70] A year later, Ed Chaplin, head of the Roller Rink Operators of America, estimated that there were five thousand roller rinks offering an average of ten disco sessions a week, and roller disco even survived disco's official dip in July 1979. In November, the High Roller opened on West Fifty-seventh Street—Richard Brezner was the DJ—and in December the Roxy opened its doors on West Eighteenth Street, with the likes of Mick Jagger, Dustin Hoffman, Diana Ross, Francis Ford Coppola, Richard Dreyfus, Billy Joel, Carrie Fisher, Margaux Hemingway, and the Village People donning a pair of opening-night skates. As with the new swathe of rock discos, however, the formula had some teething pains. "You couldn't go too up-tempo," says Francis Grasso, who played at a roller-skating venue called Metropolis before he dropped out of the scene altogether in 1981. "You couldn't get crazy-crazy with the music because people were on *roller skates!*"

Studio 54 also struggled to adapt to the new dance environment, although questions about the long-term viability of the club were being asked some time before the wider turbulence set in. Steve Rubell and Ian Schrager had responded to the opening of Xenon by building a mobile bridge that functioned as a runway on which hoisted artists could land and perform their latest number, and for a while it looked as if the club was about to enjoy a period of stable superiority, even if the revamp had its critics. "After they redecorated it was like, please," says Nicky Siano. "For the first year it was the wonderment of it all, and then it was the commercialism of it all. Studio turned really dark, and the whole feeling was negative." Gomes was also unimpressed. "The only noticeable difference," he commented in *Mixmaster*, "was the improved air-conditioning."[71]

The decisive moment in Studio's downfall arrived when federal agents, armed with a search warrant, descended on the club at 9:30 A.M. on 14 December 1978. Entering the business office at 229 West Fifty-third Street, the representatives of the Internal Revenue Service and the Organized Crime Strike Force confiscated financial records, bucket loads of hoarded cash, and a stash of drugs before arresting Schrager, who was charged with possession of cocaine with "intent to distribute." Rubell's partner was subsequently released on a fifty-thousand-dollar bail, with

Studio lawyer Roy Cohn reassuring the media that everything was in order. "There is no link between Studio 54 and organized, unorganized or disorganized crime," he told the *New York Times*. "There are no hidden interests. They can investigate from here to doomsday, and they will find nothing."[72]

Rubell and Schrager feigned indifference. "There were so many eager assurances of 'business as usual' at Studio 54 last night that they almost drowned out the mind-numbing disco noise," reported the *Daily News* on 15 December. "Owners Ian Schrager, who got busted on a cocaine charge earlier in the day, and Steve Rubell walked around assuring everyone that they were 'confident,' that they 'felt good' and that—'absolutely' —Studio 54 was open." Cohn—along with regulars Bill Blass, Truman Capote, Diane von Furstenberg, Bianca Jagger, and Andy Warhol—was also present, "belittling the drug bust as a 'frameup based on a phony tip,' and declaring that Schrager and Rubell 'are not going to lose a thing— not one night of operation.' "[73] If Studio's supporters are to be believed, it was the biggest crowd of the year.

The informant turned out to be Donald Moon, a discontented Studio employee. According to Moon, the cash and the cash-register tapes were removed from the bar tills in the middle of each night's business. The rest of the night's cash was then collected in eight bank bags, which were bundled into a Heineken beer box. The money was counted, stashed in black plastic bags, and hidden in the ceiling panels of the basement before being split between the co-owners at a rate of thirty to forty thousand dollars a week. Federal agents, who discovered hundreds of thousands of dollars during the raid, appeared to have corroborated Moon's account, but Rubell and Schrager claimed that they had never touched the cash, which had purportedly been set aside to pay outstanding bills and fund renovations. Their defense, however, was unsustainable. The raid yielded evidence "that the defendants evaded taxes through the use of a double set of books," and the U.S. attorney's office subsequently uncovered a safe-deposit box worth nine hundred thousand dollars at the Citibank at 640 Fifth Avenue.[74]

The IRS and the Organized Crime Strike Force, however, were significantly less interested in nailing Rubell and Schrager than in finding evidence of links to the alleged Mafioso loansharking king Sam Jacobson—a nighttime *and* daytime regular at the discotheque—and, when the raid uncovered a five-column accounting sheet headed "Steve Rubell-Sam

Jacobson" that contained weekly dates and dollar amounts ranging from $2,500 to $25,000, the government attempted to persuade the Studio duo to deliver evidence in return for reduced prison sentences. Spurning a genuine lifeline, the moguls refused to cooperate and instead responded by claiming that they had security-sensitive information on the use of narcotics by White House Chief of Staff Hamilton Jordan that they would hand over only if the prosecution dropped its case. Insiders shook their heads in disbelief. "People, especially well-known personalities who frequented the place for relaxation and escapism, may now see the Rubell/Schrager team as being untrustworthy, and may be asking themselves, 'when will they begin ratting on us?'" one industry executive told *Billboard*. Another patron questioned the wisdom of taking on the White House: "If Ham is forced to resign as a result of this scandal, then it's goodbye Studio 54. The Feds will never again leave them alone until they have succeeded in closing their doors."[75]

Holding its ground, the Justice Department announced that it was unwilling to reach a compromise and simply pursued Rubell and Schrager's allegations against Jordan in a separate case. Ironically, the Mob allegations against Studio eventually disintegrated, but the tax evasion charges refused to go away, and in November 1979 the Studio defense collapsed. Rubell and Schrager pleaded guilty to having embezzled $750,000 of the nightclub's 1978 receipts, on which they owed $350,000 in taxes, and ten weeks later U.S. District Judge Richard Owen delivered his guilty verdict. The moguls were sentenced to three and a half years in prison and fined $20,000 each for evading $400,000 in income taxes on cash that was "systematically skimmed" from Studio. Judge Richard Owen criticized the moguls for their "tremendous arrogance." Rubell replied, "I can only say I'm sorry." Later on that night he went to Studio and told friends that he had been treated unjustly. "I'll survive," he declared.[76] The discotheque's liquor license expired on 28 February 1980—Sylvester Stallone is reported to have bought the last legal alcoholic drink—and in March Rubell delivered an enthusiastic rendition of "I Did It My Way" at his farewell party. Rubell and Schrager served the first seven months of their sentence in the Metropolitan Correction Center, after which they were transferred to the Maxwell Air Force Base in Montgomery, Alabama. Their first job was to cut a two-mile stretch of lawn that ran along a chain-link fence, for which they were each issued a pair of scissors. Needless to say, the grass was greener on the other side, and it became even greener when

Jordan was cleared of the allegations that he had consumed cocaine at Studio.

Rubell and Schrager's high-risk combination of illicit finances, bountiful drug consumption, and media saturation was never going to be sustainable in the long term, and when the owners sold out to hotelier and restaurateur Mark Fleischman for a reported five million dollars, the discotheque quickly developed a more sustainable platform.[77] For their part, the duo had taken solace in Fleischman's promise that they could maintain a controlling role in the venue, but there wasn't much that they could do from prison, so Michael Overington was appointed to act on their behalf. One of his first moves was to lease out the club to a series of black promoters, the most successful of whom was Mike Stone. "Richard Long encouraged me to do it," says Stone. "He said, 'Bring the underground to Studio 54!' " Passing over Richie Kaczor, who had departed for the Spanish version of Studio 54 before returning to obscurity on the Jersey Shore bar circuit, Stone hired the novice Kenny Carpenter as his DJ. "I played an underground black sound," says the ex-lightman, "even though my key influences were all white." The white boys — Nicky Siano, Walter Gibbons, and John Monaco — had done a good job. "Kenny created magic for Studio 54," says Stone. "He became a big name, the new Larry Levan." Gomes agrees. "Kenny turned Studio 54 into something new. He was more experimental than Larry, and he attracted a younger type of kid." Not the African American kids, though. "I picked up a Latin and white crowd but the blacks went to the Paradise Garage," says Stone. "They thought that I had gone too commercial, and that I only cared about money and shows."

D'Alessio stayed on. "I didn't own a percentage of the business, which was the smart thing to do," she says. "When Steve and Ian went to jail everyone who had a little percentage of the business went to jail with them, but I was completely free. Steve and Ian introduced me to Mark Fleischman while they were still in jail and I started working with him right away." The new age was less exhilarating than the old one. "It became very commercial under Fleischman. I am not criticizing him — everyone runs a club in the way they want — but it lost a little bit of the glamour because he was keener on making money than investing it." Studio 54, the bête noir of the downtown party network, was being castigated for being too business-oriented now that it was in the provisional hands of Stone — a descendant of the downtown party network.

Yet while Studio, contrary to popular myth, continued to attract huge crowds, plenty of other discotheques suffered in the wake of Rubell and Schrager's fall from grace. In particular, the suburban venues that had emerged in the shadow of Studio's glamorous celebrity image struggled to cope with its symbolic downfall, and the fading memory of *Saturday Night Fever*, combined with the variegated backlash against disco, hardly helped their cash flow. "Clubs opened everywhere after 1977 but they didn't last," says Brooklyn DJ Dan Pucciarelli. "There were only a couple clubs in Brooklyn that had a good sound system and a hardcore DJ working his ass off, and these were the places that survived." The Nite Gallery, where Pucciarelli played, was one of those venues—"The club was like a baby Garage"—and by the end of 1979 the mixmaster had demonstrated his worth. "I asked for a pay raise, the owner refused, and we got into an argument. I said the club's success was due to me, and he said, 'No, it's the other way around.' I left and said that that club would close in three weeks. I was wrong. It took five."

When one of the Nite Gallery owners bought out the club at the beginning of 1980, his first move was to rehire the old resident. Within a month the joint was kicking, which indicated that club owners who were committed to creating a high-quality dance environment could comfortably survive the wider reaction against disco. Pucciarelli, however, now had half an eye on other opportunities. Following a sterling performance behind the decks at a promotional party at the February 1980 *Billboard* Disco Forum, he was asked to guest at a club called the Warehouse in Leeds, England. "All the Brits went crazy because they had never heard anybody mix like me before," he says. "I wasn't Dan Pucciarelli. I was the New York Mixing DJ." He was invited back six months later, and a year after that he returned on a more permanent basis. "There were far fewer jobs in the U.S. in 1982 than there had been in 1978. I never saw that kind of collapse happen in Britain."

Other local discotheques struggled to survive Studio 54's fall from the front pages, the midtown venue having become a heightened reference point for countless dancers from the suburban dance scene, who fantasized about passing through its hallowed door. Then again, many dancers from both the boroughs *and* the city had also tired of Rubell and Schrager's contagious predisposition toward humiliating exclusion. "Studio was part of the reason why people were so soured by the experience," says Siano. "You're talking about maybe a million people being treated really poorly at that door and a lot of them left with a bad taste in their mouth. A number of other clubs started to behave as if they were Studio and a lot of people got turned away as part of the you're-not-good-enough-for-this-club kind of thing." Siano even got a taste of the turn-down treatment himself. "I never had problems getting into Studio, but I had to get my name on the list before I went to Infinity and *who even wanted to go there?* The people at the door didn't know me, and I experienced what it felt like to stand in a queue and be passed over. It was *not* a good feeling." Infinity was forced to close following a blaze at a Valentine's Day party in February 1979—exactly five months before a significantly more popular bonfire in Chicago. "When the radio jocks started scream-ing 'disco's dead!' the people who had been humiliated outside Studio 54 and all of the copycat clubs jumped on the bandwagon."

* * *

Nicky Siano completed his own fall from heroic grace to heroin-space during this period. The drug-dependent DJ walked out of Buttermilk Bot-tom in the summer of 1979, and in August he attempted to reopen the Gallery—Gallery III, in effect—on the site of his original parties. The first night suggested that Siano could still pull in significant numbers, although by this stage nobody knew if the crowd was paying to dance or witness some kind of freak show. In the end it didn't matter. Poor prepara-tion, which included an absent air conditioner and imperfect sound, gave rise to a night of nitpicking. Gomes complained of a heat that surpassed the jungles of South America, David Rodriguez spent the evening whin-ing about a ball of sweat that refused to leave the tip of his nose, and the following week only three hundred revelers showed up—seven hundred down from the opening night. The club closed two months later.

Siano made a brief comeback at Studio, playing for Mike Stone for three months before he was invited to run his own night at the venue. "The parties failed. Not miserably, but they failed. I was drawing six or seven hundred people, and a thousand wasn't enough to fill Studio." Siano struggled on for a couple of months before the bubble finally burst. "I re-member being drugged out for the last night. That was when I realized that I couldn't live like this anymore. I went to my parents' house and they sent me into a drug rehab. I got clean, and then I started working at the Loft." Mancuso's gesture backfired. On one occasion Siano, who was soon using again, walked into the booth, pushed Mancuso aside, and started to play (Freddy Taylor, a close friend of the Loft host, brought the situation under control). Some time later a stoned Siano ran down Prince Street in the nude (this time his parents came to the rescue). But nobody could appease Mancuso when Siano, now as stable as nitroglycerin, stole his treasured guest list. "I got a job to play at the Reggae Lounge on West Broadway, and I called it Gallery IV. That was when I took David's list. I only used the names of people that I knew but it was a totally fucked-up thing to do. David got mad and wouldn't talk to me."

Life was otherwise going swimmingly for Mancuso. In an uncanny echo of the Loft host's philosophy, Rubell had claimed toward the end of 1979, "People come here and it's like their own living room."[78] There were, however, no recorded cases of Loft invitees swapping their weekly ritual on Prince Street for the West Fifty-fourth Street venue. On the contrary, the drift was from midtown to downtown. "The Loft was the first place I could be totally *free*," says Archie Burnett, who was introduced to Mancuso's parties at the beginning of 1980. "I was an outcast at New York, New York, whereas at the Loft there was no gawking." The experience on the floor was also of a different expressive quality. "The dancing was very freestyle. It incorporated gymnastics and the footwork was very jazz-oriented. There were a lot of quick syncopated stabs." Dancers developed their own style. "There was a guy named Smokey who danced to the rhythm rather than the beat. There were a set of twins, Alex and Jean, and they used to scat with their bodies. And there was this guy called Screaming Demon who used to run across the floor and slide." Contact with the ground was the common denominator, and this received its ultimate expression in a move that was dubbed "breaking your back." "You would do a backbend and then twist out on the floor. They would say, '*Break that back!*' It was like a rite of passage that you had to go through. I did it in my first year there." In contrast to his experience at the midtown discotheque, Burnett started to literally treat Mancuso's space as if it were his own home. "I changed my behavior. If some water had been spilled on the floor I would clean it up. If the toilet paper had run out in the bathroom I would replace it. You could leave your bag open—money, keys, anything—and nobody would touch it. It felt like a family and eventually it became that for me."

Mancuso managed to retain the integrity of his space because he consistently prioritized his parties above the pursuit of profit. "I didn't go to see *Saturday Night Fever*," he says. "I didn't think that I was above it.

But the movie commercialized the scene, and I knew that it would hurt us." That didn't stop Mancuso from playing "More Than a Woman" by the Bee Gees. "It was a very sweet song. I would play it next to 'Woman,' although they didn't go together very well." The rigorous integrity of his project meant that he could afford to experiment. "I knew that if it became more commercial this positive statement that I was trying to make would be harder to maintain. I didn't decide to stay in because it was awful outside but because I knew what I wanted to do. Change comes from within."

David Mancuso

Select Discography (Loft 1979)

Ashford & Simpson, "Stay Free"

Atmosfear, "Dancing in Outer Space"

Brass Construction, "Music Makes You Feel Like Dancing"

Candido, "Thousand Finger Man"

Alfredo De La Fe, "My Favorite Things"

Easy Going, "Baby I Love You"

Tamiko Jones, "Can't Live Without Your Love"

Kat Mandu, "Don't Stop, Keep On"

Patti LaBelle, "Music Is My Way of Life"

Nightlife Unlimited, "The Love Is in You (no. 2)"

One Way featuring Al Hudson, "Music"

Pleasure, "Take a Chance"

Risco Connection, "Ain't No Stopping Us Now"

The Salsoul Orchestra, "212 North 12th"

Shalamar, "Right in the Socket"

Bunny Sigler, "By the Way You Dance (I Knew It Was You)"

Slick, "Space Bass"

Troiano, "We All Need Love"

Twennynine featuring Lenny White, "Fancy Dancer"

Fred Wesley, "House Party"

The Whispers, "And the Beat Goes On"

Edgar Winter, "Above and Beyond"

Frankie Knuckles (left), Robert Williams (center), and friend Steve Robinson. Courtesy of
Robert Williams

Over in Chicago, meanwhile, Frankie Knuckles was looking for some
change to come from without. "By the middle of 1978 I was thinking,
'We've got to get some more people around here,'" says the DJ. "I was born
and raised in New York City and was used to a much more diverse mixture
on the dance floor, so I started hanging out at some other clubs and a few
people began to trickle down." Around the same time the predominantly
white gay Carol's Speakeasy offered the Manhattan DJ a weekly spot, and
before long he was playing four nights a week, including Saturdays. "I was
thinking, if this takes off then I can get these people to follow me down
to the Warehouse, too. Eventually they did." In an unlikely twist, college
fraternity boys also began to flock to hear Knuckles. "We rented out the
space on Friday nights, and college fraternities were always having parties
there. Some of the guys started to come by on Saturday night and check
things out. Initially they were appalled but they always came back."

The straight college contingent was reinforced when Jessie Saunders
and Farley "Jackmaster" Funk, two DJs from a mass-advertised party
called the Playground, started to take their student crowd to the Warehouse after their own gatherings wound up for the night at 1:30 A.M., and
it continued to grow when the punk-oriented clique from Medusa's and
the new wavers from the Space Place started to dance at the South Jeffer-

son venue in 1980. "I had a forty-five out called 'Bad Influence' and some-one told me that Frankie had done a mix of it," says Screamin' Rachel, one of the organizers at the Space Place, which was situated two blocks away from the Warehouse. "I went to find out what was going on, and it opened a whole new door to me. It was a cathartic, wild, tribal experience. People were stripping off their clothes and jacking their bodies. It was like being in bed standing up."

Robert Williams was relaxed about the shift in demographics. "At some point in the beginning the Warehouse was a black gay party, but by the late seventies it had become really mixed. People were traveling from all over the Midwest, and I didn't mind *who* was coming as long as they were having a good time." The mogul's decision to convert the previously disused basement into a lounge and refreshment area significantly ex-tended the club's capacity, which now ran across three floors. "We were getting fifteen hundred into the club at any one point, although two to three thousand might pass through the door during any one night." The parties nevertheless managed to retain a level of intimacy that, according to Williams, was second only to the Loft. "Everyone knew everyone at the Warehouse, which wasn't the case with the Paradise Garage. I started to go to the Garage during this period, and I thought it was kind of commer-

The Warehouse dance floor. Courtesy of Robert Williams

cial. You would be in there and you might only know ten people, whereas at the Warehouse it was much more family-oriented. Anyone who was not a regular was nicknamed a visitor or a tourist."

Having given himself five years to get the Warehouse off the ground, Knuckles was able to congratulate himself on completing the job in two. "Everybody was saying, 'Are you going to the house'—the Warehouse—'on the weekend?'" says Knuckles. "The Warehouse became the thing to do for all of these high school kids." Their integration was relatively smooth. "It was a little difficult seeing men dancing together but, then again, there were all sorts," says André Halmon, who first went to the club in 1979. "It was dark in the club and you would lose your sense of time. You could never tell if it was gay or straight. It was very hard to say who was who." The music programmed the dancers to transcend conventional experiences of sexuality. "I was swept away by the music. I already knew people in the industry so I was familiar with some things. But it was also really underground. The music made everybody bisexual." Club kid Byron Stingily agrees. "I always thought it would be strictly gay, but in reality it became a place to break down homophobic barriers. No one really cared about sexuality. Everyone was just into having a good time."

Frankie Knuckles

Select Discography (Warehouse 1977–79)

Ashford & Simpson, "It Seems to Hang On"

Roy Ayers, "Running Away"

Peter Brown, "Do Ya Wanna Get Funky with Me"

Bumble Bee Unlimited, "Love Bug"

Candido, "Thousand Finger Man"

George Duke, "I Want You for Myself"

Ecstasy, Passion & Pain featuring Barbara Roy, "Touch and Go"

First Choice, "Let No Man Put Asunder"

Taana Gardner, "Work That Body"

Jimmy "Bo" Horne, "Spank"

Inner Life featuring Jocelyn Brown, "I'm Caught Up (In a One Night Love Affair)"

Kat Mandu, "The Break"

Chaka Khan, "I'm Every Woman"

Patti LaBelle, "Music Is My Way of Life"

Machine, "There but for the Grace of God Go I"

Sergio Mendes, "I'll Tell You"

MFSB, "Love Is the Message"

Moroder, "$E=MC^2$"

The Originals, "Down to Love Town"

Positive Force, "We Got the Funk"

Diana Ross, "The Boss"

Skatt Bros., "Walk the Night"

Gino Soccio, "Dancer"

Two Man Sound, "Que Tal America"

Knuckles viewed Steve Dahl's disco demolition rally from the comfort of his own front room. "I watched it on television, and I remember it being pretty intense. He just blew up these records and then they said, 'That's the end of disco!' People were telling me, 'I guess you're going to be out of work now!' I said, 'No-ooo!' It didn't affect the Warehouse because the Warehouse wasn't a mainstream discotheque. It was an underground club." Williams was equally unflustered. "You couldn't call the music Frankie played 'disco,'" he says. "If you went to the Warehouse and then to a bar it would be a completely different experience. We were dealing with grassroots music and grassroots people. The Warehouse was completely void of the disco stigma and because of this we bypassed the disco era. As a matter of fact we thought Steve Dahl was *hilarious*." The American judiciary, media, radio, and suburbs might have conspired to write disco's death notice, but the mixed urban crowd kept on dancing, and, in a strange twist of history, the Warehouse took off at the very moment when disco was supposed to have died. "It all kicked in around 1980," says Knuckles. "Enough new people had discovered it and they were turning other people onto it. The Warehouse became the next big thing."

Knuckles began to work some old connections in order to supply his floor with fresh sounds—and stay one step ahead of his Chicago rivals. "I used to fly back to New York City every two or three months. I would do my record shopping on Thursday and Friday and then hang out at the Garage on Saturday." The visits provided him with advanced access to the hottest new vinyl. "There might have been eight killer records that were buzzing on the underground. I would be able to get my hands on all that stuff because everybody would be at the Garage. They were bringing acetates and promos to Larry and they would give them to me as well." Assuming the role of the good godfather, Knuckles also started to reedit existing material on a reel-to-reel in order to feed his kids. "I taught myself how to edit. I would rerecord, reedit, and extend existing records. I would take the break section and make a new intro with it. I would restructure the song in the middle, change the break around a little bit, and up the tempo via the pitch control." Knuckles was driven by a general fall in the output of dance music—especially by the major labels. "It was the only alternative I had. There wasn't enough stuff coming out to keep the dance floor interested, and for the most part what did come out was downtempo. The crowd was still coming to the Warehouse, but I had to give them something to latch onto."

Halmon latched on right away. "It was only when I tried to buy the records that Frankie was playing that I realized I had heard an edit," he says. "Frankie would mix, but editing became his signature. He was really into reconstructing the records. He would cut out the boring parts. It was all reel-to-reel. I remember he did one that started with the opening bars of Sharon Redd's 'Beat the Street,' went into some Sylvester vocals, and then returned to the intense part of 'Beat the Street.' It really got the crowd going." The response of the dancers was accentuated by the paucity of club life in the city. "There were so many venues to chose from in New York," adds Halmon, "but in Chicago we weren't getting anything, so there was a real sense of urgency." Williams, who had once wondered if Chicagoans would be too conservative to adopt Knuckles, was taken aback. "It was a new thing to them and they just went wild. Frankie and I were like, 'Hmmm! Can you *believe* this?' Sometimes he would accidentally take the arm off the record that was playing, and they would go mad because they thought it was a sound effect. We would laugh." Knuckles made the most of the situation. "There was double the energy at the Warehouse. In New York everybody was pretty much educated about the music and the sound. They would give you an air of 'well, we know!' whereas in Chicago everybody's approach was 'it's new, it's great, it's fun, let's make the most of it!' New York had the better sound systems, but the energy and the crowd were definitely better outside New York City, and this was what was going on at the Warehouse. It was the newest thing."

Frankie Knuckles in the DJ booth at the Warehouse. Courtesy of Robert Williams

Knuckles had his critics. "Frankie's mixing skills were atrocious," says Warehouse regular Scott "Smokin'" Silz. "The key to his success was what he played and when he played it. He was also well networked and had the right crowd." Saunders is equally derogatory. "Frankie may have been getting hold of the music before other DJs via his contacts in New York, but he wasn't a consummate technician. His records were good, but they didn't necessarily go together that well. He was more of a myth than anything else. He was just in the right place at the right time." Then again Silz and Saunders can't have been having such a bad time—otherwise why go to the Warehouse every week—and the DJ's huge influence on the Chicago scene was unofficially recognized when his musical selections were given a unique label—house (short for Warehouse) music. Knuckles traces the designation to the turn of the decade. "I was going with a friend of mine to his house on the south side of Chicago, and we left the expressway at the Ninety-fifth Street exit," he says. "We came to this stoplight, and there was a bar on the corner with a sign in the window saying 'We play house music' so I asked, 'What's that?' My friend said, 'All the stuff that you play at the Warehouse!' I said, 'Reeeally?' He said, 'Everybody goes to the Warehouse on the weekends, and these kids are saying that they play the same music as you.' I was like, 'OK.' This was 1980, 1981."

In all likelihood, the *house* label was first coined by the team working at Imports Etc., a record store that opened at the beginning of the eighties and rapidly established itself as Chicago's most influential retail outlet for dance music. "We used to make these little signs for records that were stacked on the wall, and we started to call cuts from the Warehouse 'house records,'" says Bret Wilcox, who had moved from Iowa to Chicago "for the music scene" in 1979 and was now working in the shop. "It was just a marketing tool to sell the twelve-inches that Frankie would play." The idea was a winner. "We would put out all of these records that would come in from New York on Thursday and Friday, and we would take them to the Warehouse on Friday night. Frankie would sometimes listen to a cut while he was mixing, and if he liked something then he would play it. The next morning we would mark them up, and the kids would come in and say, 'Ooh, what was that record that Frankie was playing?'"

Devised by a posse of eager entrepreneur-enthusiasts who wanted to spread "the sound" and make some money in the process, house music had nothing to do with rigid musical formulas, entertainment conglomerates, commercially driven music publications, and generic dance spaces, but instead revolved around a DJ who was always on the lookout for new material in the relatively scarce market of the postdisco era. While there was never a precommodity moment for the house music sold in Imports Etc., this for-sale vinyl was ultimately a diluted version of a far more desirable form of house music that wasn't available—the elaborate reedits that were generated as a tearless response to the music industry's withdrawal from dance. Disco demolition had unwittingly initiated the emergence of house.

New York raised a weary eyebrow. After all, the likes of Walter Gibbons and Richie Kaczor had been reediting for years, and the "Ten Percent" twelve-inch had formally unveiled the technique to the wider public. What's more, DJs had been putting their reedits onto real vinyl for some time now, and Larry Levan spent the best part of 1979 establishing himself as the most exciting new talent in this creative pursuit. Having established a buzz with his reworking of "I Got My Mind Made Up" and Bumble Bee Unlimited's "Lady Bug," the Garage DJ remixed two more Instant Funk tracks—"Bodyshine" and "Slap Slap Lickedy Lap"—and further Salsoul/Gold Mind commissions arrived in the form of Loleatta Holloway's "The Greatest Performance of My Life," "Double Cross" by First Choice, Bunny Sigler's "By the Way You Dance" and "Make It Last

Forever" by Inner Life, Patrick Adams and Greg Carmichael's studio outfit that featured Jocelyn Brown on vocals. "I gave Greg a hard time over 'Make It Last,'" says Brown. "I thought it should have been a duet rather than a solo, but everybody loved it—especially Larry's remix." Mel Cheren persuaded Levan to mix "Give Your Body Up to the Music" by Billy Nichols, as well as Taana Gardner's "When You Touch Me" and "Work That Body" for West End, and Elektra also moved in on the new talent, offering him the opportunity to rework Dee Dee Bridgewater's "Bad for Me." "He played the shit out of all those records," says François Kevorkian, who had announced his intention to quit New York, New York in the spring of 1979 by spinning Blondie's "Heart of Glass"—a favorite of owner John Addison—thirteen times in incensed succession. "They were absolutely major. 'Bad for Me' was a major, major record."

The best in the business believed that the Garage DJ was an outstanding studio talent. "He had the feel," says Tom Moulton. "He would always sacrifice the technical if it meant that he could have the feel, and that's the most important thing in music." He was also more focused on the dance floor than someone like Gibbons. "Walter was an innovator, but he also had an abstract 'I don't give a shit' approach," says Kevorkian. "Walter was a lonely genius and didn't care if anyone danced, whereas Larry would make it for the party. Walter was conceptually the most advanced, but Larry was a little more conscious of what people liked. Whereas Walter was an innovator, Larry made it work. He turned records into hits."

Levan's increasingly prolific presence in the studio also set him apart from other DJs. Gibbons was beginning to run out of commissions and lacked a solid DJing base. Knuckles had yet to release a record, and his move to Chicago made the prospect of this kind of work more remote. Mancuso was a hugely influential spinner, but he had yet to leave his imprint on reproducible vinyl. Savarese had delivered some high-profile mixes but was far from prolific and had also fallen out of the DJing loop. Scott was beginning to produce some tremendous studio work, but he was significantly less productive than Levan and also lacked the Garage DJ's high-profile position from which to present his efforts. And while Siano had started to remix, his catalogue was miniscule in comparison to that of Levan. Even at this early stage of his remixing career the Garage DJ had created such an important canon that even when he wasn't spinning it was more than likely that somewhere else he was being spun.

Larry Levan

Select Discography (Paradise Garage 1979)

Roy Ayers, "Don't Stop the Feeling"

Black Ivory, "Mainline"

Dee Dee Bridgewater, "Bad for Me"

James Brown, "It's Too Funky in Here"

Candido, "Dancin' and Prancin' "

Candido, "Jingo"

Candido, "Thousand Finger Man"

Jean Carn, "Was That All It Was"

Cher, "Take Me Home"

Chicago, "Street Player"

Chantal Curtis, "Get Another Love"

Alfredo De La Fe, "Hot to Trot"

Marianne Faithfull, "Why D'Ya Do It?"

First Choice, "Double Cross"

First Choice, "Love Thang"

Taana Gardner, "When You Touch Me"

Taana Gardner, "Work That Body"

Eddy Grant, "Walking on Sunshine"

Dan Hartman, "Vertigo/Relight My Fire"

Inner Life featuring Jocelyn Brown, "I'm Caught Up (In a One Night Love Affair)"

Inner Life featuring Jocelyn Brown, "Make It Last Forever"

The Jones Girls, "You Gonna Make Me Love Somebody Else"

Fern Kinney, "Groove Me"

Suzi Lane, "Harmony"

Martin Circus, "Disco Circus"

Stephanie Mills, "Put Your Body in It"

Billy Nichols, "Give Your Body Up to the Music"

North End, "Kind of Life (Kind of Love)"

Bruni Pagán, "Fantasy"

Queen Samantha, "Take a Chance"

Diana Ross, "Love Hangover"

Diana Ross, "Once in the Morning"

Rufus & Chaka Khan, "Any Love"

The Salsoul Orchestra, "How High"

Shalamar, "Right in the Socket"

Bunny Sigler, "By the Way You Dance (I Knew It Was You)"

Gino Soccio, "Dancer"

Skyy, "First Time Around"

Donna Summer, "Bad Girls"

Sylvester, "I Need Somebody to Love Tonight"

Sylvester, "Stars"

Talking Heads, "I Zimbra"

Pam Todd and Love Exchange, "Let's Get Together"

Theo Vaness, "Sentimentally It's You"

Levan had crucial supporter-friends in the form of Cheren, who was in awe of the Garage DJ and heavily dependent on his considerable powers of promotion, and Judy Weinstein (For the Record President), who had established herself as probably the most powerful figure in New York nightlife thanks to her virtual monopolization of the New York market in *Billboard* DJ reporters—meaning, of the eleven city DJs who told *Billboard* what they were playing, Weinstein had nine versus Eddie Rivera's two. Two parties cemented and publicized these alliances. In March West End held a special night at the King Street venue, where it officially launched Taana Gardner's debut single, "Work That Body," and also aired "Give Your Body Up to the Music" for the first time. Then, in July, Weinstein held For the Record's first anniversary bash in the cavernous club. "Participating deejays included Larry Levan, Alan Dodd, Wayne Scott, Sharon White and Howard Merritt," reported Barry Lederer, who had taken over Tom Moulton's "Disco Action" column at *Billboard*. "She is totally responsible for the success of the pool which has been in operation for only a short time."[79]

Thanks to her familiarity with just about every emerging dance act and their manager, Weinstein also began to play a central role in organizing live acts at the Garage, and by the middle of 1979 she was helping to engineer twice-monthly performances. "I used to book all the acts at the Garage in those days," she says. "Whenever the record companies had an artist coming through town they would call me up and I would book them for the Garage." According to David DePino, the ad hoc arrangement was soon formalized. "Michael would call and say, 'Judy, do you know how I can get in touch with this person?' and she would give him the information, or somebody would call her and say, 'I want to perform at the Garage,' and she would call Michael. Then she realized she should be getting paid for it so Michael would call her and say, 'Judy, I want to book this person,' and she would get a fee for hooking it up. Then it got to the point where Michael put it in her hands and said, 'Why don't you just do it, Judy?'" The move enabled Brody to entrench the Garage's position within nightworld. Now people didn't just congregate in order to hear Levan— they also flocked to King Street in order to experience the hottest acts in the disco industry. "Everyone wanted to perform there," says Tony Humphries. "If you wanted to be somebody then you had to perform at the Garage because that's where all the real critics were."

The band of critics included a number of converts from Studio 54. "I went to Studio in 1978 before I had even heard of the Garage," says Jim Feldman. "People would spend hours on their clothes. It was all about, 'Aren't I fabulous!' which also meant, 'Aren't I fabulous because I've got money!' I felt like I was at the center of the social scene, and I really got off on that. It wasn't disgusting because it was fun, but I never felt that Studio belonged to me, even though I generally went on Thursday night, which was gay night." What about the Garage? "It was the complete opposite. I immediately felt like I belonged there. It was one of the three places that I considered home. It felt like your best friend was throwing a party. I felt totally comfortable going by myself."

Diane Strafaci also lost interest in the midtown nightspot after visiting King Street. "I was involved in the fashion world so I used to go to Studio 54 for business, but when I found the Garage that was where my heart went," she says. "I was a wife and I was a fag hag, and when I got to the Garage it made me feel like a woman. It made me want to put my high heels on." The adventure soon became an extramarital activity. "My husband Joe liked hanging out in Studio 54 and I would say to him, 'C'mon, let's go to the Garage!' He went a few times but he wasn't into partying like that so we used to go to Studio and when Joe went home I would go to the Garage. After a while Joe stopped going to Studio and I would just head straight to the Garage. You could go alone and walk into the club and feel like you were with 1,500 friends."

By 1979 the Garage had displaced the Loft as the party that almost everyone wanted to copy. The club scene in Newark, New Jersey, embodied this shift, and Loft regular Al Murphy—who had started to hang out at Mancuso's parties before the Love Saves the Day reincarnation— became a key player. In June 1974 Murphy had set up a Loft-style party called Le Jock, where he employed Mancuso's close friend Larry Paterson as the DJ, and when Le Jock was forced to close Murphy started to promote Docks, employing the up-and-coming DJ Hippie Torales to spin behind the wheels of steel. "Docks opened in early 1977 and took off later in the same year," says Torales. "Initially it was 99 percent black and 70 percent gay, although eventually it went 50 percent gay. Docks was very influential." Then, in August 1979, Miles and Bruce Berger opened the Zanzibar and modeled their club not on the Loft but on the Garage. A couple of months later Murphy was hired to promote the club.

The Berger brothers, who owned Newark's Lincoln Motel, had opened their first discotheque in the second half of the seventies. Dubbed Abe's— after President Lincoln—the club did little to challenge Docks as Newark's most popular venue, but the Bergers had the space to expand and, searching for inspiration, began to tour nightworld. "We went to New York, New York and Studio 54," says Miles Berger, "but neither of them were predominantly black." The brothers subsequently found out about the Garage when one of Brody's lighting consultants, Robert Loby of Design Circuits, invited them to tour the King Street showroom. "The Paradise Garage was on a totally different level in terms of size and scope, and the crowd was also black so we figured that if they liked it at the Garage then they'd like it in Newark." Torales remembers Berger's excited report. "He said, 'I've seen the best club ever! I've seen the most beautiful black men kissing!' He loved the atmosphere and wanted to create a club like that in Newark." Richard Long was commissioned to install a sound system, Hippie Torales and Gerald T were hired to DJ, and the Zanzibar—caged tiger, fire-eaters, African decor, and all—opened at the end of August 1979. A crowd of 1,500 filed through the door, danced to Torales's combination of disco with a dash of rock and reggae, and decided that they would come back for more. That translated into a weekly profit of fifteen thousand dollars for the Bergers, who were now the proprietors of Newark's most popular club. "Our crowd was much straighter and we weren't as sophisticated as Manhattan," says Berger, "but basically we were the New Jersey version of the Paradise Garage."

Yet while the Garage had an important black gay contingent, it hardly attracted a uniform crowd to its Friday night parties. For sure, the construction parties were heavily populated by Reade Street regulars, many of whom were black kids, but it also attracted other dancers. "The crowd always felt very mixed," says Vince Aletti, "although as with the Loft it was important that it was more black than white." Echoing the Warehouse, students formed an important constituency. "All of the other clubs were open one night a week—Saturday—but Michael was going for two so he started promoting at the colleges," says DePino. "If you had a college pass you got in half price. That was why the Fridays took off—boom!—immediately." From the vantage point of his concession stand, Nathan Bush witnessed the way these new recruits received a crash course in dance floor etiquette. "They were bringing straight people in on Friday, and they were properly screened. The straight men were almost versed in the manner in which they were expected to behave, especially in terms of not hitting on women, and the straight women just came to party. It was a well-mixed crowd."

Saturdays, in contrast, had been reserved for an exclusively gay crowd, and these nights were much slower to take off. "They planned on Fridays being straight and Saturdays being gay," says DePino. "In the beginning Fridays were successful and Saturdays were wavering. I would go there on a Saturday, and if there were a hundred people in that place it was a lot. Nobody was there. It took forever to build Saturdays." While Brody always knew that it was going to be a difficult party to crack—Saturday, after all, was the most competitive night in clubland—his disappointment at the abysmally low turnout was accentuated by the almost complete absence of white gay dancers. "Michael was shaped by the Stonewall era, and he wanted to create a place for his friends," says Mark Riley. "He knew them and in his heart of hearts that's who he had created his space for."

Brody had ostensibly alienated this group at the blizzard-blighted opening of the club in January 1978. "I ended up apologizing to friends for months afterwards, explaining the problems, promising that they had been corrected, begging them to give the place a second chance," writes Cheren in his autobiography. "I went after key individuals like Mark Rosenfeld, the leader of a very popular crowd of Flamingo boys, who had dragged a huge number of friends to the opening night. But there was nothing I could say to make things right. After that ill-fated night, most of them stuck to Flamingo and didn't return to the Paradise Garage for years, if ever."[80] The West End mogul wasn't about to give up on the dream of attracting what he describes as "A-list guys" to the Garage, however, and he soon advised Brody to divide the club along racial lines in order to achieve this goal. "Michael was desperate to bring back the white boys, and he was always seeking my advice about how to do it . . . I suggested at one point that perhaps the best way was to make the club white one night and black another."[81]

DePino—who was getting the lowdown on Cheren thanks to his friendship with Tommy Baratta, a West End employee who also sold tickets at the Garage—believes that the West End boss was pushing Brody into a corner not of his own choosing. "It was Mel's crowd more than Michael's. Michael was in that crowd when he was lovers with Mel but Michael always had black boyfriends. Mel was a white queen and he was into white clubs. I think he tried to influence Michael into making Saturdays white so he could be more involved." Yet while Brody was undoubtedly attracted to the idea of having a significantly larger white gay contingent at his parties, he was, it appears, finally persuaded to remarket Saturdays as a white gay night by the general failure of the night to take off in its original multiracial gay format. "It was a business thing," says DePino. "Fridays were doing well, but the Garage wasn't working on Saturday so Michael tried to do something else. He just wanted to get the night off the ground. And the only reason why Michael was impatient with Saturdays taking so long to build was because *Larry* wanted a roof deck, *Larry* wanted a movie room, *Larry* wanted a stage, *Larry* wanted this, *Larry* wanted that. Where was the money coming from?" Alternative strategies failed. "Michael organized some special theme parties and they got very crowded, but people generally didn't come back the following week. Then Michael appointed this new manager, Larry Matarese, who used to work at 12 West, and every week Larry Matarese would say, 'Michael, it's empty! Michael, it's still empty! It shouldn't be like this! Let's make it happen! Let's bring in the white kids if the black kids aren't coming!'" Brody apparently succumbed in the nicest possible way. "Michael never tried to stop the blacks from coming, and I don't think he felt he was hurting them because they weren't coming. There were only *three hundred people* turning up on a *Saturday night*! The place was *empty*!"

Matarese, however, came from a predominantly gay white background and, whether Brody realized it or not, his taste—which revolved around corrugated steel and painted banana leaves—hardly helped to promote Saturdays as a multiracial gay night. "All of the white gay clubs had a very cold industrial look," says DePino, "and he slowly started to turn the Garage into this whiteish high-tech club." At the same time Brody asked Bush to alter his preparations. "He said I should make it more upscale so that it would appeal to the white crowd," says Bush. "Sometimes we did little types of hors d'oeuvres that were a little more chic—the kind of thing that the white crowd might have at their own parties—and another time Michael ordered a lot of pastries. We spent a lot more money on a lot less food because it was higher end."

As the whitewashing gathered pace, Levan's residency began to look vulnerable: if Saturday nights weren't working then perhaps this was because Brody had employed a black DJ to play to a white crowd. That was certainly the view taken by Tom Savarese who, having made a name for himself at 12 West and the Sandpiper, was after a new residency. "Tom was supposed to be the first disc jockey at Studio 54," says an insider. "He teamed up with the crew that was trying to open the place before Steve Rubell and Ian Schrager became involved." Then came the Garage, which had the potential to become Manhattan's hottest white gay venue. "A couple of weeks after the Garage opened," continues the informant— who heard the following anecdote "from more than one person," including Brody himself—"he walked up to Michael and said, 'Why don't you get rid of that nigger and let me play here?' He figured that he could do a better job playing to the white gay crowd than Larry. Michael dismissed Tom out of hand. I don't think he even continued the conversation."

Brody, however, soon started to experiment with the idea of hiring a white spinner to alternate with Levan on Saturday nights, and in so doing he realized an earlier objective that had fallen through on the eve of the club's opening. "Michael Brody's original idea was that Larry would play for the straight crowd on Fridays and Mario would play for the gay crowd on Saturdays," says DePino. "Then the two of them broke up before the Garage opened and that whole arrangement fell apart. Larry ended up DJing both nights." Levan, as it happens, wasn't particularly committed to playing Saturdays. "Larry didn't care for the gay crowd. He had never played for them, and the Loft was never gay. The Loft wasn't anything." The Garage, though, had become something, and that something clashed with Levan. "The white queens weren't into Larry's music so Larry Matarese started to bring in white DJs every other week because he knew he couldn't replace Larry just like that." Roy Thode was one of the first to fill the new slot. "Larry and I would show up at about one or two o'clock in the morning and stay for a couple of songs. We would dance where Roy could see us and then we would go up and say hello, just to show that Larry wasn't bothered, even though it was eating him up. Then we would go to the Loft."

The club's strategy was a partial success. "The Flamingo crowd didn't show up because they were too snooty and the Garage was too raw for them," says DePino. "But the S/M–looking white gays from 12 West came in their black straps and leather hats. It was more successful than Larry's Saturday." Black dancers were subtly edged out of the parties. "Larry Matarese would smile at us and say, 'No, we're not turning it white, we're just trying to get a mixture.' But I was another white queen and I knew what he was up to. For a while he tried to kiss Larry's ass because he knew Michael and Mel already agreed with what he wanted to do and the only person standing in his way was Larry. He was like, 'Hi, Larry, honey!' Larry would turn to me and say, 'Thank God you're not like that!' Then he would say, *'Fight her! Fight her! You're both white queens!'*" Brody went along with Matarese, and for a while the black gay faithful effectively disappeared from the dance floor on Saturday nights. "It became so overwhelmed with white people for a couple of weeks that the black dancers vanished. They stood around the edges because they didn't like the music and so you didn't notice them. If you walked across the dance floor you would only see white dancers."

The black contingent was livid. "I don't think Michael was racist in any way, shape, or form, but he knew that the white gay crowd was not comfortable being around a lot of black people," says Riley. "Michael made Friday nights a black night and Saturday nights a white night, and of course the black crowd was furious. They said, 'Wait a minute! We helped build this place and now you're pushing us away!' It was black people who attended the construction parties and basically got the money together for him to finish the interior." The protests were vociferous. "They threw eggs at Michael," says DePino. "They wrote letters which said, 'How dare you? It's a black club with a black DJ who plays black music! You're turning against black people!' They talked to the radio about it. There were death threats in the mail and somebody even shot at Michael in a drive-by incident. It was a whole scandal." Bush was appalled. "That was the beginning of the downfall of the Garage," he says. "The Garage did well again later on, but there was always a strange feeling. It was like the fall of the Roman Empire. You get too greedy, decadence sets in, and you stop giving the type of party you should be giving." Levan was also deeply disappointed. "I know Larry was upset about it," says DePino. "I was like, 'C'mon, Larry! I'm white! You stay with me!' and he replied, 'Please, you're blacker than I am!'" Steve D'Acquisto believed the shift toward a racial divide was deeply regressive. "Suddenly the Garage was like one of those restricted clubs where they won't let Jews in," he says. "I refused to go back when all of that happened." Mancuso was also upset. "We had just come out of the sixties and it was getting all fucked up again. There was only one thing behind it—*money*. It wasn't as if they weren't making money, but they wanted more of it. Larry came from the house parties and he told me he wasn't happy with the situation."

Uncomfortable as they might have been in the face of such opposition, Brody, Cheren, and Matarese were more concerned with the problem of how to eke out a niche in a market that was already mature. The identity of white gay New Yorkers and the discotheque had become so intertwined that they had melded into one, and in 1978 this process was formally and eloquently mythologized by Andrew Holleran in his novel *Dancer from the Dance*. Set in a discotheque called the Twelfth Floor, which was a composite of the Tenth Floor and 12 West, Holleran's book revolved around a narrator named Paul who celebrated the way in which a new gay community had come into being. "The first year contained the thrill of newness, and the thrill of exclusivity—that all these people who might not even know each other, but who knew who each other were, had been brought together in the winter, in this little room, without having done a single thing to bring it about."[82] Kinship found its ultimate expression in a late-night ritual whereby "everyone came together in a single lovely communion" in which they "took off their sweat-soaked T-shirts and screamed because Patty Jo had begun to sing: 'Make me believe in you, show me that love can be true.'"[83] Holleran's dancers discovered a new way of being. "They lived only to bathe in the music, and each other's desire, in a strange democracy whose only ticket of admission was physical beauty—and not even that sometimes. All else was strictly classless: The boy passed out on the sofa from an overdose of Tuinals was a Puerto Rican who washed dishes in the employees' cafeteria at CBS, but the doctor bending over him had treated presidents." The environment was unique. "It was a democracy such as the world—with its rewards and its penalties, its competition, its snobbery—never permits, but which flourished in this little room on the twelfth floor of a factory building on West Thirty-third Street, because its central principle was the most anarchic of all: erotic love."[84]

While Holleran was primarily interested in evoking the utopianism of what he believed to be a bygone era, others continued to enjoy a scene that now included the Cockring. Too tiny to command any enduring attention, the Christopher Street venue nevertheless served up a rotating roster of top-notch DJs that included Phil Alexion, Howard Merritt, Richie Rivera, Wayne Scott, and Roy Thode. "It was really a bar with a postage stamp dance floor," says Brian Chin, who first went to the venue toward the end of 1977. "There was *way* too much high frequency and nothing to absorb it. But it was an all-star lineup and I suspect a lot of records were tested there because the crowd *came to dance* and the DJs could really get a sense of where they could fit it in a set at a bigger, cooler club." At the same time the Cockring also illustrated how some white gay venues managed to retain their racial homogeneity. "Black people would get carded at some places where they didn't want the look of the room to stray too much from the white mustachioed clone. I never got carded at the Cockring and there were usually some black people in the room, but the gay press carried lots of stories about people complaining to local gay activist groups that they were being carded at the door." In this respect the nightspot was fairly typical. "There was generally a problem with carding in the West Village bars, and it surfaced every so often. That didn't happen at a lot of the bigger venues because they were membership clubs, so even if they limited the membership of minorities it still wasn't a *door* problem."

Over at 12 West, meanwhile, Alan Harris had been experiencing a different kind of problem in the form of DJ Jim Burgess. "He was a brilliant technician, but the drama was so extreme and the individual so difficult to work with that a lot of the enjoyment was taken out of the evening," says the 12 West owner. "He had the personality of a *witch*. He sucked the air out of the room. He was just a very difficult human being. The crowd loved his music but hated his personality." Alan Dodd eventually replaced the Infinity-bound Burgess, after which Dodd was in turn replaced by the much-loved and highly talented Robbie Leslie, who had progressed from serving drinks to serving music at the Sandpiper in the autumn of 1977. "I started by offering to play for them off-season when they weren't going to use a DJ anyway," says Leslie. "They didn't pay me, but I was instantly transfixed by the whole atmosphere. The aspect of controlling a dance floor was totally addictive and very, very exciting for a kid." The following year the owners of the Sandpiper hired the nascent mixer to play Mondays through Thursdays, and in 1979 they repeated the offer. "The Sandpiper exhausted its lease at the end of that season," says Leslie. "I played the closing party, which was Halloween. It was called 'Last Dance.' The music at that party was just one hit after another: France Joli, Teri DeSario, Gonzalez—all of the songs that had come out in '78 and '79 stacked back to back to back. You could pull out any one of them and it was a classic." Leslie moved to Manhattan, looked for DJing work in the city, and was offered an audition at 12 West in the autumn. "After my first night there they hired me to play full time." Harris was delighted. "We called Robbie 'Mr. Smooth.' His talents were phenomenal."

Robbie Leslie

Select Discography (12 West 1979)

Ashford & Simpson, "Found a Cure"

Peter Brown, "Love in Our Hearts"

Jean Carn, "Was That All It Was"

Cerrone, "Call Me Tonight"

Sarah Dash, "Sinner Man"

Extensions from (212), "Manhattan Shuffle"

Front Page, "Love Insurance"

Dan Hartman, "Vertigo/Relight My Fire"

Debbie Jacobs, "Don't You Want My Love"

Katmandu, "The Break"

Denis Lepage, "Hot Wax"

Liquid Gold, "My Baby's Baby"

Luis Love, "Manhattan"

Jackie Moore, "This Time Baby"

North End, "Kind of Life (Kind of Love)"

Bonnie Pointer, "Heaven Must Have Sent You"

The Raes, "Don't Turn Around"

Margaret Reynolds, "Keep On Holding On"

Diana Ross, "The Boss"

Barbra Streisand and Donna Summer, "No More Tears (Enough Is Enough)"

Sylvester, "Can't Stop Dancing"

Sylvester, "In My Fantasy (I Want You, I Need You)"

Richard Tee, "First Love"

USA-European Connection, *USA-European Connection*

Theo Vaness, "Sentimentally It's You"

The gay white scene didn't just survive the backlash against disco—
it positively thrived during the late seventies and early eighties. "Frankly,
the gay community on the eastern corridor was partially resentful that
disco was just another one of our discoveries that had been absorbed
and streamlined for straight consumption," says Leslie. "We just thought,
'Here's another fad that the straight world is embracing' and we weren't
really surprised when there was this sudden backlash." Yet the 12 West DJ
didn't sense that the backlash was aimed at gay men. "I really don't think
it was in any way homophobic. I think it was directed at smarmy, creepy
straight men that dressed up, wore jewelry, and knew all the dance steps."
The consequences were uneven. "The gay dance community really didn't
feel like it impacted them, but it was a different story for the DJs because
the production of good music ground to a screeching halt. We weren't
going to be handed great music on a silver platter anymore." Leslie responded by paying more attention to the import market and records like
"Hit and Run Lover" by Carol Jiani, Kelly Marie's "Feels Like I'm in Love,"
"Hot Leather" by the Passengers, Tantra's "Hills of Katmandu," and "If
You Could Read My Mind" by Viola Wills. "These were all right around
the time that American dance music was totally drying up. I was probably
one of the first DJs in a gay club to start playing imports. 'If You Could
Read My Mind' was a *monster* and all the DJs used to line up to borrow my
copy when I wasn't working."

Whatever its true color, the backlash against disco wasn't experienced
as being homophobic within the gay dance population, and as a result the
popular argument that the entrenchment of gay discos at the end of the
seventies constituted a heroic response to an outside attack lacks credibility. A high proportion of gay men—including gay men who had no
interest in discotheque culture, of whom there were many—didn't read
the inside pages of the newspapers on the morning of 13 July 1979 and
accordingly didn't know that anything had happened in Chicago's base-

ball stadium, all of which suggests that the symbolic importance of Steve Dahl's rally has been retrospectively inserted into a narrative of rebellious gay suffering and resistance that hardly describes their night-to-night lives.

One reason why gay clubs went from strength to strength lay on the inside, where growing numbers of dancers were connecting with the elusive unity that had transformed Jorge La Torre from being a party animal into a spiritual pleasure seeker. Writing in *Christopher Street* in June 1978, Barry Laine was one of the first journalists to recognize this ritual process when he noted that "during the dance, the body reaches a point when it goes beyond exhaustion, exceeds its boundaries, and rather than tiring, works harder and produces more." Laine added: "It is the D.J.'s job to help the dancers get to that point. By choosing and mixing the music carefully he makes you want to keep on dancing. He provides rests amid the stimulation, and, working with the lightman, he fires the crowd with successive waves of energy until he delivers the climax, the dance orgasm."[85] By 1979 the peaks had become even more powerful. "At first I was sort of self-conscious about this experience and it was very rare for me to talk about it with anyone else," says La Torre. "But after a while I realized that other people were beginning to experience this, too. We were all looking for the same thing, and when we found it we were able to come together. The whole tribal experience of male bonding became stronger and stronger because more and more people were able to experience this higher source of energy at the same time. As time went on this became the goal of the night. We were all reaching for that one high."

Yet La Torre's favorite club was also being driven by an increasingly high dose of self-absorption. The launch of the first annual "Tetas" (Spanish for "tit") contest—a variation of the female topless dance—in October 1978 confirmed the drive toward vanity and bodily display, with the chest reigning in the new temples of butch, and the following month Nathan Fain noted that Flamingo's members "can barely stand how handsome they are, the first confirmed case of group narcissism on record."[86] Yet in many respects the dance experience, which echoed the ritual practice of the African American church in placing spiritual unity before individual egos, was also radically anti-narcissistic. "I am ordinarily squeamish about touching an alien body," reminisced writer Edmund White, a reluctant visitor to Flamingo. "I loathe crowds. But tonight the drugs and the music and the exhilaration had stripped me of all such scruples. We were packed in so tightly we were forced to slither across each other's wet bodies and arms; I felt my arm moving like a piston in synchrony against a stranger's—and I did not pull away. Freed of my shirt and my touchiness, I surrendered myself to the idea that I was just like everyone else. A body among bodies." White discovered a new sense of liberation by giving up his fragile self. " 'It's real tribal here, isn't it?' my friend shouted in my ear. I nodded."[87]

Fesco's experimental tribalism reached a new intensity at the 1979 Black Party. "I had a carpenter build six of seven stages around the main lounge, and we turned them into jail cells," he says. "Each jail cell had a commode, and they were positioned three or four feet off the floor so they could be seen from across the room. Each cage represented a sin. In one cage I had a man tied to a cross, in another I had a bunch of guys acting as transvestites, in another there was a leather scene going on, and in another we had this huge pig. It was the most expensive act I ever had, and it was the largest pig I have ever seen in New York City! Getting it into the cage was very difficult." Fesco placed a pile of magazines next to the animal, which proceeded to absorb the latest issue of *Architectural Digest* in a more literal manner than anyone had expected. "The pig decided to eat this magazine and I remember someone in the crowd shouted, 'Oh my God, I haven't even *read* that copy yet!' " The handlers ventured to take the pig home at five o'clock in the morning but quickly realized that the club was still far too crowded for such a sensitive operation. "They eventually kept the pig there until eight o'clock in the morning. By that time it had become very agitated, and it ended up running through the place like a bull in a china shop. The rumors were that everyone got the pig doped by feeding it drugs, and people started to call up the next day and say, 'I hear the pig died!' The pig didn't die at all."

Meanwhile, Michael Brody had won many admirers but few regulars from the white gay scene. "The Garage was just incredible," says La Torre. "It was the ultimate mixed tribal experience. They somehow got the recipe right in bringing different people together. It was a great party, but there was only one place to go in the world on Saturday nights and that was Flamingo." Harris was also a fan, although he had his reservations. "Larry's music was phenomenal. He was a great technician and delivered wonderful performances. But his music didn't attract the white gay crowd because he wasn't into that sensual, sexual music that they liked. He was into R&B, and you can only take so much of Evelyn 'Champagne' King."

Three finalists in the Flamingo "Tetas" contest. Courtesy of Michael Fesco

Divine and Andy Warhol, judges of the first annual "Tetas" contest. Courtesy of Michael Fesco

Leslie was more skeptical. "Michael Brody tried to make Saturday nights white gay and it just didn't happen. When you open a club in Manhattan judgment is usually passed in one or two nights, and the white gay verdict was one of indifference. It was NOCD: not our club, dearie." According to Leslie, both the sound system and the DJ were out-of-sync with the taste of the white gay crowd. "The mainstream gay audiences simply didn't appreciate Larry's erratic style—sometimes inspired, sometimes careless, and often flying in the face of club convention—and they never placed their faith in his work."

This resistance helped Levan in his battle to control Saturday nights, and he received an additional boost when his old friend Tee Scott, who was still ensconced at Better Days, made a guest appearance at the Garage. "Better Days was black, black, black, black and gay, gay, gay, gay," says DePino. "Larry and I were always at Better Days. We would go three or four times a week, and Tee was one of the only DJs we would dance to all night." The Forty-ninth Street venue had developed a reputation for being a hardcore black gay club, and Scott drove his dance floor with a combination of earthy dance grooves and gay diva anthems as well as a series of signature remixes on Elektra and Salsoul that included a flawless reworking of "Love Thang" by First Choice. "The funk was undeniable," says Manny Lehman. "Tee Scott rocked." Operating on the same level as his crowd, the DJ was indivisibly part of the party, and his loyal crowd followed his every move. "Better Days was more intense than the Garage or the Loft because it was *entirely* gay and it was only open until three o'clock, so everybody danced really hard," says Kevorkian. "Larry played regularly at Better Days just for the fun of it." Scott, though, remained the main attraction. "Tee's mixes were a little bumpy, but he was a great DJ," says Kenny Carpenter. "He was three hundred pounds, and he would face the wall, tapping his foot. He was like a granddaddy." Brody kept his eye on developments. "Michael always threatened to bring Tee to the Garage when he fought with Larry," says DePino. "That always put Larry in check because if there was anyone Larry respected playing-wise it was Tee. Larry knew that Tee could play as well as he could. The crowd loved Tee."

Scott also loved Levan. "People tried to pit us against each other, but they couldn't," he told Daniel Wang. "Larry was always rebellious and had a way of his own, and when Michael Brody wanted to teach Larry a lesson, there were only so many people who could play at the Garage and get

The Paradise Garage dance floor. Photo by Nick Baratta. Courtesy of West End Records

over. If he threw just anybody in the Garage he'd lose money. So he would ask me if I'd do something, or whatever, and I told him: the only way I'm going to play the Garage is with Larry's blessings—you can't get me to do anything behind his back. If you have a problem with Larry Levan, you have to straighten it out with Larry Levan. Deal with him directly. Don't try to use us."[88]

When Levan went away for a weekend he was happy for Scott to fill his precarious Saturday night slot. "That Saturday was the most crowded it ever was," says DePino. "There were lines wrapped around the corner. It was incredible. Tee turned it out, and everybody came back to see what Larry would do the next week. It was a big night, and I remember Larry played 'It Should Have Been Me' by Yvonne Fair, which was his way of saying that he should have been playing Saturday nights all along. The black kids went crazy. They ran onto the dance floor and just took over. The white kids were standing around the edge saying, 'What's happening?' I cried when he did that." The consecutive impact of Scott and Levan established a new impetus for Saturday nights. "They all came to Tee's night and they all came to Larry's night, so for two weeks in a row it was *packed* and that started a whole momentum. For a couple of weeks the Garage was the talk of the whole black gay world and Saturday nights started from that moment on." The development hurt Better Days, but only briefly. "People realized that the Garage had no liquor, plus it didn't really start until two or three in the morning, so you could go to Better Days at eleven, get your drinks in, and then go on to the Garage," says DePino. "Tee would also come down to the Garage and hang out with us all night."

Despite the success of the Garage, Mancuso's parties remained as popular as ever. "Loft people were Loft people," says DePino. "The Garage never took away from the Loft. Loft people would have killed for David, so forget that." Indeed, Mancuso's main problem was not how to hold onto his dancers but how to satiate their unquenchable thirst so that they would voluntarily leave. "The parties were running until 8 A.M. and they wanted more," he says. "In 1980 I decided to see how long the party would last if I let it run its natural course. It continued until 6 P.M." The extended parties meant that Levan now had somewhere to go once the Garage closed at around 9 A.M. "We would flock to hear David," says Warners dance promoter Bobby Shaw, who was part of Levan's bleary-eyed band. "We all thought David was great and we wanted to do more drugs. We used to stay there until three or four in the afternoon." Penny Grill, who lived on the fifth floor of the building that housed the Loft, remembers the effect of these marathon events. "I used to leave at 5 A.M. and David provided me with my lullaby music. It was amazing to wake up at three in the afternoon and hear the party carrying on."

New recruits to the downtown party network weren't necessarily drawn to the Garage. "Larry was great at what he did, but I didn't dig him personally," says Burnett. "He was very shady, very arrogant. The Garage was more of a pick-up joint, and it was too big. In the Loft I could regress to being a nine-year-old kid, but I didn't feel like I could do that at the Garage." David Morales also favored the Prince Street side of the SoHo divide. "You either went to the Garage or you went to the Loft. I went to the Garage a few times but I was more of a Loft head. The Loft was a lot more mixed and a lot more fun." However, others, such as roller-disco DJ Danny Tenaglia, who had grown up on a diet of Paul Casella before he first went to the Loft in 1978, believed that King Street was paramount. "David

The Paradise Garage team. Photo courtesy Vince Aletti, ©The Estate of Peter Hujar

Mancuso has this theory about not being overwhelmed, but I needed to be overwhelmed, and that was what you got at the Garage. The Loft had a big impact, but the Garage changed my life. Larry really knew how to entertain a crowd. It wasn't just a question of what he played but also how he played." Unable to settle their differences, diehard dancers from both parties pursued their art and rivalry in Washington Square Park on Sunday afternoons. "We would take some balloons and sell them for a dollar so that we could buy batteries for our boom box," says Burnett. "The Garage kids would be on one side, the Loft kids would be on the other, and we would dance to our music. It was like a battle. We would continually try to outdo each other."

There was now a palpable drive within dance culture. Disco was dead—at least as a semantic term, at least for now—but the dance floor practices that preceded the genre were now exceeding it. Urban clubs were thriving, industry insiders were still flocking to hotspots, and twelve-inch remixes were still being commissioned despite recurrent predictions of the format's imminent demise. By the end of the seventies dance culture had become immune to the kind of slump that had hit the discotheque industry at the end of the previous decade. Ethnic groups and gay men—two constituencies that had remained largely outside of sixties discotheque circles—lay at the heart of this revitalized dance population, and these night crawlers, who more often than not partied within definitively mixed environments, weren't about to stop going out just because a handful of radio DJS ran a gimmicky campaign against a pale version of their practices. Dance culture had become a permanent feature of the city nightscape. Love had saved the day.

epilogue

Why write a book about seventies dance culture when decades are little more than mechanistic time frames that rarely contain any cohesive meaning? The answer is that, even if historians agree that the seventies only really became "the seventies" in approximately 1973 or 1974 and probably shifted into the eighties during the first half of 1979, the time-frame really does make sense when it comes to dancing. The unofficial launch of the Loft and the reopening of the Sanctuary at the beginning of 1970 can in retrospect be seen to have marked a decisive turning point in the history of nightworld, and a decade's worth of dancing *symbolically* ended in 1979 when the word *disco* was banished from the everyday vocabulary of the music industry and thousands of discotheques shut up shop. Dance culture, which was so emblematic of the seventies, provided the decade with a decisive beginning and end.

The rise and fall of disco is part of a broader story that is often told about popular culture in which a clandestine underground movement is said to develop a series of innovative practices that are subsequently discovered, exploited, and eventually wrecked by the commercialized mainstream. Indeed the seventies was arguably the key period in which this account became so resonant, for while it is easy to point to various music movements that have made much of their underground credentials in the postdisco era, it is harder to think of any clear-cut examples that preceded this period. Even so, the concept of the "underground"—which initially referred to a handful of unlicensed parties that were organized around a private invite system, a free concession stand, late night opening hours, and an alternative musical agenda—remains a slippery concept. Should it be extended to the series of private parties that charged for both their invite cards *and* admission? Should it include cutting-edge discotheques, even though they were open to the general public? And should it be applied to radical DJs, even if they were generating chart smashes and playing in commercial clubs?

In the end, all sorts of dancers, DJs, label moguls, party hosts, recording artists, and remixers subscribed to the downtown party ethos, and they hung out at private and public venues, talked to local fanzines and national media institutions, scuttled between independent and major record companies, turned anonymous records into huge hits on the pop charts, and even set up the Record Pool to facilitate the spread of music. As such dance culture didn't so much spread according to a simple down-up capillary action from the underground to the mainstream as move in a squiggle of directions: not just up and down but also across and around. Creativity and innovation didn't just emanate from the underground but also from the much broader downtown party network, and, from at least the mid-seventies onward, this popular avant-garde explicitly attempted to change the world (or at least nightworld) into its image.

Pointing to these definitional difficulties, however, is not the same as collapsing the different divisions of the dance scene into an indistinguishable whole. It is now clear, for example, that public discotheques were more vulnerable than private parties to the threat of corrosive commercialism, and a cluster of midtown venues ended up prioritizing celebrities, extravagant interiors, and exclusionary door policies to such an extent that dancing became an adjunct to the evening rather than its primary purpose. Although discologists maintained that some twenty thousand discotheques were up-and-running at the height of the disco boom, the extraordinarily brief lifespan of the vast majority of these venues suggests that they amounted to little more than a disposable fad. Consequently, the seventies didn't so much revolutionize the way in which people experienced the night as establish a cluster of nightspots that would provide the foundation for a more durable transformation in the future.

Downtown venues survived, in part, because they showcased extraordinary DJs. Few, if any, of these insomniac music fanatics were finally bigger than the nightspots in which they played and supposedly prestigious jocks regularly disappeared as soon as they departed from their favorite haunt. The more striking trend, though, is the degree to which these DJs often became synonymous with their dance floors, forming a series of symbiotic partnerships that have since acquired a legendary status. David Mancuso and the Loft formed one such alliance. Francis Grasso and the Sanctuary developed another. Nicky Siano and the Gallery, Frankie Knuckles and the Warehouse, and Tee Scott and Better Days entered into similarly Siamese-like relationships. And Larry Levan and the Paradise Garage became tempestuous yet inseparable lovers.

New York's pioneering mixmasters—a surprisingly high proportion of whom were Italian American—became influential thanks to their ability to program records according to the mood of the dance floor, a radical form of synergistic music-making that their forebears had failed to explore. All DJs began the decade having to hunt out danceable "party music" in a scarce market, and their ability to transform supposedly dead vinyl into best-selling chart hits became a key factor in the emergence of the disco genre. The dance floor's preference for longer and more dramatic pressings culminated in the creation of the twelve-inch single and, in a logical, if (at the time) stunning twist, DJs were invited to mold this new art form. Their subsequent compositions became concentrated imprints of the dance floor dynamic, building and breaking in an unmistakably sexual manner.

Of course, questions of sex, gender, and sexuality were not limited to the contours of vinyl. Contradicting the broad assumption that disco was driven by the gay scene, protagonists of all sexual persuasions talk of an early scene in which resolutely mixed crowds reveled in the novelty of the fluid dance ritual. Self-consciously gay venues didn't emerge as a serious force in Manhattan until the mid-seventies, and when they did they were overwhelmingly white (New York's black gay dance contingent continued to head toward a range of more obviously mixed venues). Women, meanwhile, flourished within nightworld, where the dance floor—if not the more restrictive DJ booth—offered them an important expressive space, and while straight white men managed to develop a sense of balance on the dance floor by the middle of the decade, the rise of a new breed of disco divas guaranteed that there could be no simple return to some of rock's more repressive routines. For all of these movements and contests, however, the dance floor didn't so much reorganize the boundaries of sex as dissolve them into a polymorphous energy that often acquired a distinctly spiritual quality.

Ethnic and racial identities were played out in similarly complex ways. While Italian Americans tended to run (or alternatively finance) the clubs and staff the DJ booths of the early seventies, this ethnic link didn't extend to New York's dance floors (which were definitively mixed) or musical preferences (which were largely black). Indeed, thanks to the fact that recording artists didn't know about the dance-oriented use to which their music was being put, no organic link emerged between the dance floor and the music industry until a cluster of independent label operators sampled the downtown party network and went on to create a new rank of remixers, who were commissioned to reinvent records for this nascent market. The skin color of the first tranche of these new operators happened to be white, but their hearts were unequivocally black, and they accordingly went on to introduce a series of African American musical priorities into their work, creating a new platform from which black artists could cross over from the soul charts to the Hot 100.

As the decade progressed, however, more clearly demarcated racial lines began to emerge. The rise of the white gay discotheque modified downtown's carefree character. Thanks to its rigid pulse, synthesized textures, and notionally alternative birthplace, Eurodisco became a white-identified strand of dance music. And the ongoing growth of the disco market contributed to its increasingly segregated character when entrepreneurs began to build niche markets according to not just sexuality but also ethnic identity—or rather sexuality *and* ethnic identity. Lacking the economic power and social connections that were required to open their own discotheques, gay and straight African American dancers struggled to hold their own in this game of cultural difference, and when Eurodisco started to inundate the pop charts black critics began to ask (in an arguably insular gesture) whether African American artists might not have been better off if disco, which was finally something of a racial chameleon, had never happened in the first place.

Shifting radically between the poles of individualism and communalism, the theme of labor and the economy was played out in equally ambiguous ways. On one level disco culture was the prophetic harbinger of the liberal market reforms of the eighties: DJs began life as a cheap freelance alternative to the entrenched and relatively expensive unionized musicians, and as the economy of the seventies lurched from crisis to crisis the discotheque flourished as a popular site of organized oblivion where, instead of campaigning against their conditions of exploitation, patrons could dance their troubles away. Indeed, the impression that dance culture was actually benefiting from the emergent conditions of the global economy was hardly tempered by the regularity with which clubs were housed in abandoned warehouses. For sure, dancers were focused on an alternative form of "work" in which the only visible product at the end of a ten-hour shift was a sweating body and a smiling face—that was what Taana Gardner was getting at when she recorded "Work That Body"—but these marathon dance sessions didn't exactly challenge the future "work hard, play hard" mantra of eighties capitalism.

Then again, dance culture didn't simply facilitate the forces of free market liberalism but also created the conditions from which they might be imaginatively opposed. DJs challenged the power of the music companies by organizing themselves into a series of record pools that hinted at the collective potential of freelance creative workers. Knowingly or otherwise, these mixers also channeled their labor into the creation of resolutely social, communitarian spaces, for while individualism and inequality could always seep onto the dance floor, clubs where this happened didn't usually stay open for too long. In addition, discotheques became a key site of empowerment for dispossessed groups that included not only multiracial gay men and straight women but also white working class youths. Clubs certainly didn't look like political organizations, but that didn't stop them from functioning as safe havens in which new identities could be cultivated.

Ultimately nightworld highlighted the limits of unfettered commercialism. By the late seventies it had become clear that an inverse relationship existed between a club owner's hunger for profit and the energy on his or her dance floor, and the collapse of the money-driven discotheque industry at the end of the decade demonstrated the way in which such compromises had a habit of backfiring. While the recession undoubtedly contributed to this wave of closures, commercially driven clubs were also the most commercially vulnerable clubs because ultimately nobody felt like they *had* to be part of them. The undiminished popularity of the downtown party network suggests that the closure count would have been less severe if more venues had been run along similar lines, and maybe this would have happened if the Paradise Garage had opened before Studio 54, thereby enabling downtown to seize control of the New York nightscape. Instead midtown became dominant, and less than three years later its descendants formed a layer of disposable skin that was finally shed during the backlash against disco.

In spite of this, the disco decade is almost always remembered through the glittery frame of midtown rather than downtown. Nostalgia films, lurid documentaries, and gratuitous books about Studio 54 have established a near-monopoly over the meaning of disco, with the iconic image of John Travolta's white suit and melodramatic dance posture offering the most enduring alternative snapshot of seventies dance culture. Musically speaking, the era is replayed through the rotation of happy-go-lucky seven-inch anthems on daytime radio, seventies compilations, and tongue-in-cheek cover versions. This form of pop disco didn't finally survive within a nightclub context because it didn't sustain all-night dancing, but that hasn't stopped it from flourishing at school discos for nostalgic adults, office parties for worn-out workers, and karaoke nights for wannabe stars where, iconic and recyclable, the music has become synonymous with drunken fun. Having become an unrivaled source of scapegoats and gripes at the end of the 1970s, disco now functions as an aural reminder of an age of innocence—an age when work was less driven, the mention of drugs didn't produce instant hysteria, and sex was relatively risk-free.

The popularity of this narrative conceals the way in which dance culture survived the much-touted death of disco. That survival is normally traced back to the mid-eighties and the emergence of Chicago house, which revolved around Ron Hardy at the Music Box and Frankie Knuckles at the Power Plant as well as artists such as Sleazy D, Chip E, Steve "Silk" Hurley, Farley "Jackmaster" Funk, Marshall Jefferson, Larry Heard, Jamie Principle, and Jesse Saunders. The more self-consciously futuristic sound of Detroit techno, which was generated by Juan Atkins, Derrick May, and Kevin Saunderson, is rightly seen to have maintained the momentum, while Larry Levan's selections at the Paradise Garage, which inspired the formation of the garage genre, cemented the belief that dance music was as vibrant as ever, even if disco had suffered a humiliating setback. The failure of these genres to match disco's huge impact on the American music market was in some respects alleviated by the revival of the pop-dance megastar from 1983 onward, with Michael Jackson and Madonna the most prominent figures. Jellybean, a seventies DJ who played a key role in Madonna's flight from the dance charts to the Hot 100, had to work overtime to keep up with the number of pop acts that wanted to sport his clubby signature.

There is, however, no need to trace the rebirth of dance culture to the emergence of house, techno, garage, and a string of foot-tapping pop stars because dance culture never actually passed away in the first place. For sure, disco suffered a series of major tremors, even if it soon recovered to exert a heavy influence on house, garage, and even, contrary to popular mythology, techno. Yet in the immediate aftermath of the backlash against disco, dance culture experienced one of its most prolific—if rarely discussed—periods and, while the epilogue might not be the best place to begin to recount this history in its wonderfully rich micro-detail, it is worth pointing out that the idea that urban night owls hung up their dancing shoes at the end of the seventies, or that Studio 54 constituted some sort of "last party," is plain nonsense. Downtowners didn't stop dancing at the end of the decade, and music makers didn't stop recording gravity-defying twelve-inch mixes. The continuities between the close of the seventies and the start of the eighties are far more significant than the disruption of "disco sucks."

Not only did the Loft, the Paradise Garage, the Warehouse, and the Zanzibar reach new heights of intensity and popularity in the postdisco period: a series of other clubs, including Bond's, Danceteria, the Funhouse, and the Saint in New York, and the Music Box and the Power Plant in Chicago, emerged to establish a network of hardcore dance venues that was as potent as anything that had preceded it in the previous decade. If anything the music being played in these venues benefited from the lack of major label input. Free to tap into the still-thriving club scene of hungry DJs and dancers, independents developed a range of new artists, pushed through a fresh stratum of talented young producers and nurtured a diverse range of remixing talents. The dance music of the early eighties was consequently as varied, creative, and dynamic as anything that had appeared during the seventies, with down-tempo funk, up-tempo hip-hop, subterranean dub effects, danceable rock, reinvigorated R&B, and off-the-wall electronic imports all thrown into the studio mix. The media might not have been looking and the tourists might have moved on, but the dance scene of the early eighties—which in many respects echoed the creative chaos of the early seventies—gave the impression that it was, in the words of one of Arthur Baker's most important mixes of the period, "Walking on Sunshine."

The darkest of clouds, however, soon began to cast its shadow over the adrenaline-charged downtown party network. The spread of AIDS, which began to surface at the beginning of the eighties, resulted in the deaths of thousands upon thousands of dance aficionados and contributed to the closure of a number of hugely important venues. Initially referred to as "Saint's disease"—after the white gay club that opened in the autumn of 1980 to such effect that both 12 West and Flamingo closed in rapid succession—the big disease with the little name came close to extinguishing the party fervor, and, with many survivors in no mood to party, dance music's center of gravity began to shift across the Atlantic.[1] Garage, house, and techno hardly dented the American pop charts, but they had a profound impact on the European dance and pop scenes alike, and it wasn't long before American DJs began to make regular and profitable trips to countries such as Britain, Germany, and Italy. The subsequent geographical spread of dance music across clubs, cities, nations, continents, and cyberspace, combined with the expansion of the genre into a myriad of self-generating sounds, mean that only the most dexterous cartographer could hope to map its manic evolution.

At the same time this extraordinary expansion has been matched by a notable desire to unearth the culture's origins and historical lineage. While music doesn't always evolve in polite and respectful patterns, questions of influence are undeniably central for the protagonists of the downtown party network, and recollections of the earliest formation of this culture are punctuated by a longing for a bygone era that has acquired a magical hue. Contemporary dance enthusiasts might find it hard to understand an attachment to a period in which beat-mixing was relatively primitive and rhythms were generated by drummers rather than drum machines, but the sheer newness of dance culture in the seventies, combined with a relatively permissive attitude toward sex and drugs, provided dance floors with an energy and spontaneous pleasure that has become largely unrepeatable in today's more knowing, more cautious, more media-savvy times. Even when protagonists have gone on to enjoy successful DJing and studio careers, there is still a powerful sense that the spontaneous highs of the seventies have gone forever. "Can you say there's a place that makes you feel like the Loft used to make us feel?" asks Frankie Knuckles, popularly known as the godfather of house. "There's no party in the *world* that gives you that now!"

Yet while the world has moved on and the precise contours of the Loft circa 1970 are irreproducible, at the heart of that particular venue lies a simple story: a young man wanted to hold a party, play some good music, dance with his friends, and meet new people. This unassuming goal is as resonant today as it has ever been, and happily it is also one that can also be realized. Controlling entertainment laws, bureaucratic licensing restrictions, elitist dress codes, and discriminatory door policies might stand in the way, but they always did. Nobody, finally, has a monopoly over the night, so while we can look back in admiration at the pivotal parties of the seventies we can also seek out similar venues that are up and running. And if there don't appear to be any then we can begin to organize our own.

Driven by the belief that the music-dance combination can gesture toward the beginnings of an alternative society that is organized around pleasure rather than labor, expressivity rather than uniformity, cooperation rather than competition, tolerance rather than prejudice, and communality rather than individualism, David Mancuso is still listening with his "third ear," selecting records according to the subliminal signals he receives from the dance floor. He no longer plays in his home—bad luck and poor business decisions have made this impossible, at least for now— but he has transformed his misfortune into an opportunity. Forced to come out of his shell in order to survive, Mancuso has begun to accept invitations to travel, and, working with party hosts to make sure that the space, the invites, the sound system, the refreshments, and the decor are as Loft-like as possible, he has been able to "get the message out there in a different format."

While Mancuso's relationship between his home and the world might have moved on, his ultimate goal hasn't changed since he held his landmark Love Saves the Day party in February 1970. "I am always amazed at the way David has managed to remain, through thick and thin, remarkably consistent about what it is he has wanted to do and how it is that he has gone about doing it," says Mark Riley. "Most people would have folded up, counted their money, and moved on. Not David." That he hasn't moved on is testament to the potential power of the party, through which congregants can reach a point of spiritual and joyful unity where egos disappear, where there is no stress, and where life energy is high. The vision is resolutely social—Mancuso can't get "there" before anybody else—which suggests that if the party won't cure the problems of the world it might still be the place where we can begin to imagine a new one. Dancing, mixing, bonding, communicating, working, building, and praying, the night still shimmers with a utopian hope that daylight has yet to deliver.

notes

preface

1 Jim Feldman, "Paradise Enow," *Village Voice*, 14 September 1982.

1. beginnings

1 Barbara Bell, "You Don't Have To Be High," *New York Times*, 28 December 1969.
2 Philip H. Dougherty, "Now the Latest Craze Is 1-2-3, All Fall Down," *New York Times*, 11 February 1965.
3 Sam Zolotow, "Musicians Picket At 3 Discotheques," *New York Times*, 6 March 1965.
4 Hazzard-Gordon, *Jookin'*, 112.
5 Ray Brack, "Phonos Silent As Deejays Play Disks," *Billboard*, 29 May 1965.
6 Nick Biro, "Discotheque: How Is The 'Go-Go' Going?" *Billboard*, 14 August 1965.
7 Aaron Sternfield, "Theque Starts Gotham Listening," *Billboard*, 14 August 1965.
8 Marwick, *Sixties: Cultural Revolution*, 17.
9 Angela Taylor, "Arthur, Once a Hairdo, Is Now a Discotheque: Club's Debut Separates the Ins From the Outs," *New York Times*, 7 May 1965.
10 Louis Calta, "Party to Mark Closing of Arthur Discotheque," *New York Times*, 21 June 1969.
11 Fikentscher, *"You Better Work!"* 101.
12 Charles Grutzner, "Slain Man's Letters Give Impetus to Local and Federal Investigations of After-Hours Clubs Here," *New York Times*, 23 March 1970.
13 Claude Lévi-Strauss, *The Raw and the Cooked* (London: Pimlico, 1997), quoted in Gilbert and Pearson, *Discographies*, 45.
14 Kaiser, *Gay Metropolis*, xii.

15 Lucian Truscott IV, "Gay Power Comes to Sheridan Square," *Village Voice*, 3 July 1969.

16 Duberman, *Stonewall*, 116.

17 "Homosexuals Hold Protest in 'Village' After Raid Nets 167," *New York Times*, 9 March 1970.

18 Sheryl Garratt, *Adventures in Wonderland: A Decade of Club Culture* (London: Headline, 1998), 8; and Matthew Collin and John Godfrey, *Altered State: The Story of Ecstasy Culture and Acid House* (London: Serpent's Tail, 1997), 10–11.

2. consolidation

1 Duberman, *Stonewall*, 161.

2 Garber, "A Spectacle in Color," 319.

3 Marwick, *Sixties: Cultural Revolution*, 490; Nutall, *Bomb Culture*, 175.

4 Nutall, *Bomb Culture*, 173–74.

5 Marwick, *Sixties: Cultural Revolution*, 497.

6 Theodore Roszak, "Youth and the Great Refusal," *Nation*, 25 March 1968.

7 Mercer, *Welcome to the Jungle*, 290.

8 "Let It Bleed," *Rolling Stone*, 21 January 1970.

9 Ellen Willis, "See America First," *New York Review of Books*, 1 January 1970.

10 Albert Goldman, " 'Grab the Money and Run'?" *New York Times*, 1 February 1970.

3. pollination

1 "Court Order Shuts After-Hours Club," *New York Times*, 21 July 1971.

2 Paul Montgomery, "Raids Close 9 After-Hours Bars Linked to Mafia," *New York Times*, 19 July 1971.

3 James M. Markham, "Di Bella, Held in Raids, Called 'Soldier in the Gambino Family,'" *New York Times*, 19 July 1971.

4 "Court Order," *New York Times*.

5 Martin Burden, "Going Out Tonight?" *New York Post*, 18 October 1966.

6 Alfonso A. Narvaez, "City Acts to Let Homosexuals Meet and Work in Cabarets," *New York Times*, 12 October 1971.

7 Jay Levin, "250 Rescued as Blaze Hits a Midtown Hotel," *New York Post*, 24 December 1971.

8 "State Asking Shutdown Of 43d St. Discotheque," *New York Times*, 25 March 1972.

9 Michael Knight, "E. 81st Street Frightened By Drug Scene at Bar," *New York Times*, 12 August 1972.

10 "Residents of East 81st Street Celebrate Closing of Tambourine Bar on the Block," *New York Times*, 18 September 1972.

11 Rosemary Armmia Kent, "Splish, Splash . . . I Was Taken to the Bath," *Women's Wear Daily*, 11 February 1972.

4. recognition

1 "Go Go Discotheque Chain Offers Pay-for-Play to Manufacturers," *Billboard*, 1 May 1965.

2 Tee Scott, interview with Daniel Wang, www.geocities.com/jahsonic/Tee Scott.htm, 14 July 1994.

3 Ibid.

4 Paul Hendrickson, "Discos Are Back, So . . . Bump, Hustle, Bus Stop!" *National Observer*, 30 August 1975.

5 Ibid.

6 "PR Person of the Month: Joe Maimone," *Melting Pot*, 2, 1–2, January–February 1975.

7 Frank Wilson, as told to Harry Weigner, "High Praise," liner notes for *Eddie Kendricks: The Ultimate Collection* (Motown/PolyGram, 1998).

8 Ibid.

9 Radcliffe Joe, "Soul Single Import Stirs Duplicators; Gets $2 to $3," *Billboard*, 19 May 1973.

10 "Atlantic Getting Into The Swing-Frug," *Billboard*, 6 March 1965.

11 Vince Aletti, "Discotheque Rock '72 [*sic*]: Paaaaarty!" *Rolling Stone*, 13 September 1973.

12 Ibid.

13 Ibid.

14 "Discotheques Break Singles," *Billboard*, 6 October 1973.

5. visibility

1 Davis and Willwerth, *Clive*, 144–45.

2 Ibid., 146.

3 Ibid.

4 Harvard University Business School, "A Study of the Soul Music Environment Prepared for Columbia Records Group," quoted in George, *Death of Rhythm & Blues*, 136.

5 Ibid., 137.

6 Nat Freedland, "Col/Philly Cooperation Bolsters Blue Notes' Hit," *Billboard*, 22 December 1973.

7 Murray Schumach, "Broadway Central Hotel Collapses," *New York Times*, 4 August 1973.

8 Robert McG Thomas Jr., "Weekly Parties for Five Hundred Chill Tenants." *New York Times*, 21 May 1974.

9 Robert McG Thomas Jr., "The Loft's Owner Is Told To Vacate." *New York Times*, 2 June 1974.

10 "Untitled," *New York*, 1 July 1974.

11 Ibid.

12 Steven Harvey, "Behind the Groove," *Collusion*, September 1983, reprinted in *DJ Magazine*, 11 March 1993.

13 Scott, interview.

14 Harvey, "Behind the Groove."

15 Ibid.

16 Glenn Fowler, "Planning Unit Asks SoHo-NoHo Discotheque Ban," *New York Times*, 12 August 1974.

17 "Gallery Sets Pace Again!" *Melting Pot*, 1, 5, December 1974.

18 Vince Aletti, "Disco File," *Record World*, 28 December 1974.

19 George, *Death of Rhythm & Blues*, 129.

20 "God Bless Billy Smith," *Melting Pot*, 1, 1, August 1974.

21 Ibid.

22 Is Horowitz, "'Illegit' Disco Tapes Peddled by Jockeys," *Billboard*, 12 October 1974.

23 "Labels Mix Records For Club Scene," *Billboard*, 2 November 1974.

24 "20th and Discos Makes Music $," *Melting Pot*, 1, 5, December 1974.

25 "Disco Play Starts A Hit," *Billboard*, 26 October 1974.

26 "Grapevine . . . New York," *Melting Pot*, 1, 2, September 1974.

27 Tom Moulton, "Discotheque Club Dialog," *Billboard*, 2 November 1974.

28 Tom Moulton, "Disco Action," *Billboard*, 11 January 1975.

29 Vince Aletti, "Disco File," *Record World*, 4 January 1975.

30 Tom Moulton, "Disco Action," *Billboard*, 14 December 1974.

31 Tom Moulton, "Disco Action," *Billboard*, 23 November 1974.

32 Henry Edwards, "Disco Dancers Are Back, and the Kung Fu Has Got Them," *New York Times*, 29 December 1974.

33 Jim Melanson, "Discos Demand Five-Minute Singles," *Billboard*, 14 December 1974.

6. expansion

1 Sanjek, *Pennies from Heaven*, 594.

2 "NADD Members Soon A Must," *Melting Pot*, 2, 1–2, January–February 1975.

3 Tom Moulton, "Disco Action," *Billboard*, 16 November 1974.

4 *Daily Double*, 1, 1, 12th Sun, 1976th Year, 7th Moon.

5 Vince Aletti, "Disco File," *Record World*, 12 July 1975.

6 Richard Szathmary and Lucian K. Truscott IV, "Inside the Disco Boom," *Village Voice*, 21 July 1975.

7 Ibid.

8   Bob Casey, "NADD: One Year Old—Growing Proud and Strong," *Melting Pot*, 2, 6–7, June–July 1975.

9   Richie Kaczor, "Take It From Me," *Melting Pot*, 2, 8, August 1975.

10 Carr and Murray, *David Bowie*, 68.

11 Szathmary and Truscott, "Inside the Disco Boom."

12 "The Envelope Please," *Melting Pot*, 2, 6–7, June–July 1975.

13 Vince Aletti, "Disco File," *Record World*, 5 July 1975.

14 Tom Moulton, "Disco Action," *Billboard*, 28 December 1974.

15 Vince Aletti, "Disco File," *Record World*, 20 September 1975.

16 "Casablanca's Larry Harris Cites Industry $4 Billion Gross," *Billboard*, 1 October 1977.

17 "The Record Industry Sounds A Note Of Joy," *Business Week*, 1 December 1975.

18 Ibid.

19 Ibid.

20 Ken Emerson, "Can Rock Ever Learn To Dance Again?" *New York Times*, 9 November 1975.

21 Cecil Holmes, "The Mayor of Chocolate City," in *Inside the Casbah: The Casablanca Records Story*, liner notes for *The Casablanca Records Story* (PolyGram Records, 1994), 31.

22 Dannen, *Hit Men*, 162–63.

23 Robert L. Weiner, "What's In The News: The New York Scene," *After Dark*, March 1975; Szathmary and Truscott, "Inside the Disco Boom."

24 Weller, "New Wave of Discotheques."

25 Jan Hodenfield, "Cruising the Scene in the Discotheques," *New York Post*, 9 August 1975.

26 Shawn G. Kennedy, "The New Discotheque Scene: 'Like Going to a Big House Party,'" *New York Times*, 3 January 1976.

27 Steven Gaines, "Right This Way Your Table's Waiting . . ." *New York Sunday News*, 13 April 1975.

28 Weller, "New Wave of Discotheques."

29 Marwick, *Sixties: Cultural Revolution*, 7.

30 *Mixmaster*, 27 December 1975.

31 William Safire, "On the Hustle," *New York Times*, 4 August 1975; Vince Aletti, "Disco File," *Record World*, 16 August 1975.

32 Aletti, "Disco File," *Record World*, 16 August 1975.

33 "Disco Dance Party At Garden Likened To Woodstock Idea," *New York Times*, 30 November 1975.

34 Weller, "New Wave of Discotheques."

35 Richie Kaczor, "So This Is Progress," *Melting Pot*, 2, 4, April 1975.

36 Weller, "New Wave of Discotheques."

37 Vince Aletti, "Disco File," *Record World*, 19 April 1975.

38 Haden-Guest, *The Last Party*, 5.

39 Ibid., 6.

40 Ibid.

41 Ibid.

42 "Discomania," *Forbes*, 1 June 1976.

43 Haden-Guest, *The Last Party*, 6.

44 Weller, "New Wave of Discotheques."

45 Marcel Jean, *The History of Surrealist Painting* (New York, Grove Press, 1960), 98, quoted in Dery, *Escape Velocity*, 183.

46 Vince Aletti, "Disco File," *Record World*, 17 May 1975; Szathmary and Truscott, "Inside the Disco Boom."

47 Jan Hodenfield, "Cruising the Scene in the Discotheques," *New York Post*, 9 August 1975.

48 Manny Lehman, "Larry Levan: Exclusive," *Vinyl Maniac*, 1, 9, March 1984.

49 Ibid.

50 *Mixmaster*, 27 December 1975.

51 Vince Aletti, "SoHo vs. Disco," *Village Voice*, 16 June 1975.

52 Ibid.

53 Sheila Weller, "New Wave of Discotheques."

54 Ibid.

7. prominence

1 "What Are We," *Melting Pot*, 2, 1–2, January–February 1975.

2 Jim Melanson, "Product Supply a Key Query At Disco Forum," *Billboard*, 7 February 1976.

3 John Rockwell, "The Pop Life: Disco Forum Disseminates a Craze," *New York Times*, 22 January 1976.

4 Jim Melanson, "Forum: Disco Dandy," *Billboard*, 31 January 1976.

5 Ibid.

6 "14 Awards To 'Most Deserving,'" *Billboard*, 7 February 1976.

7 "Rivera Founds International Disco Record Center," *Discothekin'*, March 1976.

8 Vince Aletti, "Disco File," *Round World*, 10 May 1975 and 5 July 1975.

9 "12-Inch 45s Via Scepter Up Sound Level For Discos," *Billboard*, 14 June 1975.

10 Vince Aletti, "Disco File," *Record World*, 14 June 1975.

11 Tom Moulton, "Disco Action," *Billboard*, 25 October 1975.

12 Toop, *Rap Attack 3*, 60.

13 Ibid.

14 Jim Melanson, "Club DJs Blend Cuts For Cos.' Disco Disks," *Billboard*, 15 May 1976.

15 Rudy Garcia, "12-Inch 45 Disco Disk Sales Brisk," *Billboard*, 19 June 1976.

16 David McGee, " 'Salsoul 12' Discs Mix a Retail Smash," *Record World*, 19 June 1976.

17 Ibid.

18 Garcia, "Disk Sales Brisk."

19 Ibid.

20 Jim Melanson and Tom Moulton, "New Labels Add 12-Inch Singles," *Billboard*, 26 June 1976.

21 Holmstrom, *Punk*, 1998.

22 *Mixmaster*, 14 February 1976.

23 Vince Aletti, "I Won't Dance, Don't Ask Me," *Village Voice*, 26 April 1976.

24 Bob Kirsch, "The Sound Of Music: More Disco, Country Crossovers," *Billboard*, 3 January 1976.

25 Paul Grein, "Is the Disco Scene In a Rut?" *Billboard*, 31 July 1976.

26 Ibid.

27 *Mixmaster*, 10 July 76.

28 Radcliffe Joe, "RCA Exec Knocks Disk," *Billboard*, 31 July 1976.

29 Paul Grein, "Discomania," *Billboard*, 23 October 1976.

30 Vince Aletti, "Disco File," *Record World*, 4 September 1976.

31 Radcliffe Joe, "Disco Music Sounds Undergoing Changes," *Billboard*, 2 October 1976.

32 Ibid.

33 Ibid.

34 Maureen Orth with Betsy Carter and Lisa Whitman, "Get Up And Boogie!" *Newsweek*, 8 November 1976.

35 Vince Aletti, "Disco File," *Record World*, 25 December 1976.

36 Ibid.

37 Alan Hines, "Brooklyn's Mighty Mobile Jocks," *Discothekin'*, June 1976.

38 Nik Cohn, "Another Saturday Night," in *Ball the Wall*, 322 (published as "The Rituals of the New Saturday Night" in *New York*, July 1976).

39 Ibid., 326.

40 Ibid., 327.

41 McCormack, "No Sober Person Dances," 13.

42 Ibid., 14.

43 Michael J. Connor, "A Discotheque DJ Has To Be A Master of Controlled Frenzy," *Wall Street Journal*, 4 May 1976.

44 Orth, Carter, and Whitman, "Get Up and Boogie!"

45 Ibid.

46 Radcliffe Joe, "Deejays As Important As Music They Play," *Billboard*, 23 October 1976.

47 Ibid.

48 Eliot Tiegel, "Defined Profile Of Discotheque Industry Suggested By Keynoter," *Billboard*, 23 October 1976.

49 Orth, Carter, and Whitman, "Get Up and Boogie!"

50 Ibid.

51 Joe, "Deejays Important."

8. ascendancy

1   Vince Aletti, "Disco File," *Record World*, 15 January 1977.

2   David McGee, "Kraftwerk: Chillingly Effective," *Record World*, 19 April 1975.

3   Vince Aletti, "Disco File," *Record World*, 23 April 1977.

4   Sinker, "Electro Kinetik," 101.

5   Vince Aletti, "Disco File," *Record World*, 28 May 1977.

6   Aurora Flores, "Imported Disks Gaining In Clubs," *Billboard*, 3 September 1977.

7   Jean Williams, "Pools Decry Ebb In Record Flow," *Billboard*, 30 April 1977.

8   Ibid.

9   Tom Moulton, "Disco Mix," *Billboard*, 7 May 1977.

10 Ibid.

11 Vince Aletti, "Disco File," *Record World*, 3 September 1977.

12 Paul Grein, "3 Labels Package Hits In Looped Club Sound LP Sets," *Billboard*, 22 October 1977.

13 Steven Gaines, "Disco '77: Chic Sweat," *After Dark*, September 1977.

14 Paul Lamb, "Disco Deejays: The New Record Breakers," *SoHo Weekly News*, 17 May 1979.

15 Gaines, "Disco '77."

16 Haden-Guest, *The Last Party*, 72.

17 Miezitis, *Night Dancin'*, 119–20

18 Ibid., 37 and 40.

19 Radcliffe Joe, "N.Y. Discos Hurt By 'Sam' Deaths," *Billboard*, 13 August 1977.

20 "Casablanca's Larry Harris Cites Industry $4 Billion Gross," *Billboard*, 1 October 1977.

21 Vince Aletti, "Disco File," *Record World*, 11 June 1977.

22 *Billboard*, 18 June 1977.

23 Andrew Kopkind, "Disco's Mixmasters," *Village Voice*, 12 February 1979.

24 Ibid.

25 Harvey, "Behind the Groove."

9. dominance

1   Savage, *England's Dreaming*, 433.

2   Vince Aletti, "Disco Fever Stays More Than Alive," *Village Voice*, 13 February 1978.

3   Ibid.

4   "Saturday Night Fever," *Billboard*, 2 September 1978.

5   Ibid.

6   Aletti, "Disco Fever."

7   *Mixmaster*, 1 July 1978.

8   "Growth Spurs Switch To Disco Forums Bi-Annually," *Billboard*, 1 July 1978.

9   Robert Morgan, "A Landmark Year For the Record Industry," *Record World*, 22 July 1978.

10 Leslie Bennetts, "An 'In' Crowd and Outside Mob Show up for Studio 54's Birthday," *New York Times*, 28 April 1978.

11 "Discothèque Fanatics Mob Latest Addition to Scene," *New York Times*, 9 June 1978.

12 Miezitis, *Night Dancin'*, 36.

13 Dan Dorfman, "The Eccentric Whiz Behind Studio 54," *New York*, 7 November 1977.

14 Nicholas Pileggi and John Kennedy, "Panic Hits Studio 54," *Village Voice*, 12 June 1978.

15 Ibid.

16 Jack Newfield, "Did Steve Rubell Do The Hustle On His Customers?" *Village Voice*, 19 June 1978.

17 Henry Post, "Sour Notes At The Hottest Disco," *Esquire*, 20 June 1978.

18 Marc Kirkeby, "Studio 54 Receives Cabaret License, To Refund 'Membership Fees,'" *Record World*, 8 July 1978.

19 Radcliffe Joe, "Ad Agencies Go Disco To Sell Product," *Billboard*, 19 August 1978.

20 Brown, "Programmers Withhold Judgment," 128.

21 Jesse Kornbluth, "Merchandising Disco For The Masses," *New York Times*, 18 February 1979.

22 Emenheiser, "An Immense Market Emerges," 92.

23 Kornbluth, "Merchandising Disco."

24 Auerbach, "Big Business," 151.

25 Ibid., 152.

26 Ibid., 150.

27 Radcliffe Joe, "The L.A. Scene: Growing, But 2nd to N.Y." *Billboard*, 16 December 1978.

28 Jack McDonough, "Unprecedented Boom Enlivens the Bay Area," *Billboard*, 15 July 1978.

29 Diebold, *Tribal Rites*, 128.

30 Alex Abramoff, "Japanese Discomania Creates Clubs Galore," *Billboard*, 18 December 1976.

31 AP, "Discos Through Russian Eyes," *New York Times*, 8 November 1978.

32 Albert Goldman, "The Disco Style: Love Thyself," *Esquire*, 20 June 1978.

33 Goldman, *Disco*, 117.

34 Ibid., 119.

35 Goldman, "Disco Style."

36 Ibid.

37 Ibid.

38 Vince Aletti, "Disco File," *Record World*, 28 January 1978.

39 Radcliffe Joe, "TK Mart Move," *Billboard*, 18 February 1978.

40 Radcliffe Joe, "McCoy Striving to Blast Image as 'Disco Kid,'" *Billboard*, 10 December 1977.

41 Robert Ford, "The Changing Sound of Records," *Billboard*, 3 September 1977.

42 *Mixmaster*, 20 May 1978.

43 *Mixmaster*, 17 June 1978.

44 Radcliffe Joe, "Salsoul Opens Campaign To Up Awareness Level," *Billboard*, 28 January 1978.

45 Cheren, *Keep On Dancin'*, 179–80.

46 Vince Aletti, "Disco File," *Record World*, 3 June 1978.

47 Hollomon, "Few Label Themselves Disco," 45.

48 Haden-Guest, *The Last Party*, 81.

49 Ibid.

50 Ibid., 83.

51 Lamb, "Disco Deejays."

52 Noe Goldwasser, "RCA & Warners to Bow Disco Depts. as Label Interest Continues to Grow," *Record World*, 25 November 1978.

53 Noe Goldwasser, "Warners Unveils Caviano Label as Disco Fever Builds at Majors," *Record World*, 9 December 1978.

54 Ibid.

55 Kornbluth, "Merchandising Disco."

56 Andrew Kopkind, "The Dialectic of Disco: Gay Music Goes Straight," *Village Voice*, 12 February 1979.

57 Barbara Graustark et al., "Disco Takes Over," *Newsweek*, 2 April 1979.

58 Quoted in Smith, *Seduced and Abandoned*, 22.

59 Miller, *The Novel and the Police*, 207.

60 Kopkind, "Dialectic of Disco."

61 "A Dialogue Between Two Editors: Vince Aletti & Michael Gomes," *Mixmaster*, summer 1978.

62 Andrew Holleran, "Dark Disco: A Lament," *New York*, December 1978.

63 Sontag, "Notes on 'Camp,'" in *Against Interpretation*, 275–92.

64 Patterson, "Changing Or Shrinking With Growth?" 89.

65 "Dialogue Between Two Editors," *Mixmaster*.

66 "N.Y. Deejay Counting Beats Per Minute," *Billboard*, 2 July 1977.

67 "Dialogue Between Two Editors," *Mixmaster*.

68 Ibid.

69 *Mixmaster*, 14 January 1978.

70 *Mixmaster*, 3 June 1978.

71 *Mixmaster*, 13 January 1979.

72 *Mixmaster*, 28 January 1978.

73 *Mixmaster*, 7 October 1978.

74 Harvey, "Behind the Groove."

75 Ibid.

76 Manny Lehman, "Larry Levan: Exclusive," *Vinyl Maniac*, 1, 9, March 1984.

77 Harvey, "Behind the Groove."

10. turbulence

 1 Kornbluth, "Merchandising Disco."

 2 "Record Cos. Expand Involvement In Disco," *Billboard*, 10 March 1979.

 3 Doug Hall, "Disco Stations Leveling Off," *Billboard*, 12 May 1979.

 4 Roman Kozak, "Disco Rules, But Where Are The Big Disk Sales?" *Billboard*, 19 May 1979.

 5 Ibid.

 6 Chafe, *Unfinished Journey*, 449.

 7 Denisoff, *Tarnished Gold*, 106.

 8 George, *Death of Rhythm & Blues*, 167.

 9 Kozak, "Disco Rules."

10 Robert Roth, "Disco To End LP Slump: Caviano," *Billboard*, 16 June 1979.

11 Ibid.

12 Graustark et al., "Disco Takes Over."

13 Ibid.

14 Paul Green, "12-Inch Singles Seen Viable Promotional Tool," *Billboard*, 14 July 1979.

15 Dannen, *Hit Men*, 176.

16 Radcliffe Joe, "Dearth Of Superstars Dims Industry Future," *Billboard*, 14 July 1979.

17 Ibid.

18 Straw, "Popular Music," 172.

19 Ibid., 173.

20 Frank Rose, "Discophobia: Rock & Roll Fights Back," *Village Voice*, 12 November 1979.

21 John Rockwell, "The Pop Life: Disco Forum Disseminates a Craze," *New York Times*, 22 January 1976; Aletti, "Disco Fever."

22 Robert Vare, "Discophobia," *New York Times*, 10 July 1979.

23 Rose, "Discophobia: Rock & Roll Fights Back."

24 Ibid.

25 Ibid.

26 Ibid.

27 Hughes, "In the Empire of the Beat," 147.

28 Chafe, *Unfinished Journey*, 432.

29 Dyer, "In Defence of Disco," 518.

30 Ibid., 523.

31 Ibid., 527.

32 Nelson George, "The Disco Boom and Blacks," *New York Amsterdam News*, 28 January 1978.

33 Ibid.

34 Ibid.

35 John Rockwell, "Records: The Disco Fever Is Spreading," *New York Times*, 26 February 1978.

36 Ed Ochs, "Paradox or Paradise?" *Billboard*, 9 June 1979.

37 Ibid.

38 "Disco Not Proving Panacea For Black Artists," *Billboard*, 14 July 1979.

39 Ibid.

40 George, *Death of Rhythm & Blues*, 154.

41 Ibid., 155.

42 Ibid., 156.

43 Ibid., 190–91.

44 Toop, *Rap Attack 3*, 81.

45 Ibid., 62.

46 Baker, "Hybridity," 198.

47 Toop, *Rap Attack 3*, 70.

48 Liner notes for *The Philly Sound: Kenny Gamble, Leon Huff & the Story of Brotherly Love (1966–1976)* (Sony Music Entertainment, 1997), 32.

49 Radcliffe Joe and Nelson George, "Rapping DJs Set A Trend," *Billboard*, 3 November 1979.

50 Lynn Langway with Janet Huck and David T. Friendly, "The Blues In Vinyl," *Newsweek*, 13 August 1979.

51 Ibid.

52 Radcliffe Joe, "Caviano Hits the Road To 'Crusade' For Disco Life," *Billboard*, 8 December 1979.

53 Dannen, *Hit Men*, 176–77.

54 Graustark et al., "Disco Takes Over."

55 "Neil Bogart's Keynote Highlights," *Billboard*, 5 April 1980.

56 Paul Grein, "New Chic Game Plan: No Disco," *Billboard*, 15 December 1979.

57 Denisoff, *Tarnished Gold*, 110.

58 Radcliffe Joe, "Fewer Promo Disks; Disco Pools Howling," *Billboard*, 4 August 1979.

59 Ibid.

60 Nelson George, "Are Label Cutbacks Overplayed?" *Billboard*, 15 September 1979.

61 *Billboard*, "Disco: What's It All About?" 23 February 1980.

62 "British Tradesters Deploring America's 'Death' Proponents," *Billboard*, 22 March 1980.

63 Smith, *Seduced and Abandoned*, 23.

64 Cheren, *Keep On Dancin'*, 319.

65 Harvey, "Behind the Groove."

66 Roman Kozak, "Rock Disco Pops In N.Y. Houses," *Billboard*, 14 July 1979.

67 Miezitis, *Night Dancin'*, 209.

68 Haden-Guest, *The Last Party*, 101.

69 Kozak, "Rock Disco Pops."

70 Jeanne Clare Feron, "Roller Skating + Disco Dancing = Two Hit Rinks," *New York Times*, 24 December 1978.

71 *Mixmaster*, 23 September 1978.

72 Peter Kihss, "I.R.S. Raids Studio 54; 5 Ounces of Cocaine Seized," *New York Times*, 15 December 1978.

73 Donald Flynn, "Beat Goes On Despite the Bust," *Daily News*, 15 December 1978.

74 Henry Stone, "The Rise and Fall of Studio 54," *New York*, 12 November 1979.

75 Radcliffe Joe, "Studio 54 Operators May Suffer Backlash," *Billboard*, 8 September 1979.

76 Arnold H. Lubasch, "Two Studio 54 Owners Are Given 3 1/2 Years for Evading U.S. Taxes," *New York Times*, 19 January 1980.

77 Joanne Wasserman, "Rubell Cells Out For $5m," *New York Post*, 31 March 1980.

78 Henry Post, "The Rise and Fall of Studio 54," *New York*, 12 November 1979.

79 Barry Lederer, "Disco Mix," *Billboard*, 21 July 1979.

80 Cheren, *Keep On Dancin'*, 207.

81 Ibid., 219.

82 Holleran, *Dancer from the Dance*, 38.

83 Ibid., 39.

84 Ibid., 40–41.

85 Barry Laine, "Disco Dancing: Too Hot for Love," *Christopher Street*, June 1978.

86 "Chests Bared at New York's Flamingo Club," *Billboard*, 17 February 1979; Nathan Fain, "SoHo—Life in the Loading Zone," *After Dark*, November 1978.

87 White, *States Of Desire*, 270–71.

88 Scott, interview.

epilogue

1 Shilts, *And the Band Played On*, 149.

selected
discography

The following discography lists all of the recordings referred to in Love Saves the Day. It provides basic information on the name of the artist, the title of the recording, the name of the label that originally released the recording, and the year in which the recording was first released. Entries are listed in alphabetical order, first according to the name of the artist, and subsequently according to the title of the recording. Albums are highlighted in italics, whereas individual album cuts, seven-inch singles, and twelve-inch singles are written in normal typeface.

Abaco Dream. "Life and Death in G & A." A&M, 1969.
Area Code 615. "Stone Fox Chase." Polydor, 1970.
Ashford & Simpson. "Found a Cure." Warner Bros., 1979.
———."It Seems to Hang On." Warner Bros., 1978.
———. "Over and Over." Warner Bros., 1977.
———. "Stay Free." Warner Bros., 1979.
Atmosfear. "Dancing in Outer Space." Elite, 1979.
Auger, Brian, & the Trinity. "Listen Here." RCA, 1970.
Ayers, Roy, Ubiquity. "Don't Stop the Feeling." Polydor, 1979.
———. "Running Away." Polydor, 1977.
Babe Ruth. "The Mexican." Harvest, 1973.
Barrabas. *Barrabas*. RCA, 1972.
———. "Wild Safari." RCA, 1972.
———. "Woman." RCA, 1972.
Barrow, Keith. "Turn Me Up." Columbia, 1978.
Bataan, Joe. "Aftershower Funk." Mericana, 1973.
———. "Latin Strut." Mericana, 1973.
———. "Rap-O Clap-O." Salsoul, 1979.
———. *Salsoul*. Mericana, 1973.
Bean, Carl. "I Was Born This Way." Motown, 1977.
Beatles. "Here Comes the Sun." Apple, 1969.

Bee Gees. "How Deep Is Your Love." rso, 1977.

————. "Jive Talkin'." rso, 1975.

————. *Living Eyes.* rso, 1981.

————. "More Than a Woman." rso, 1977.

————. "Night Fever." rso, 1977.

————. *Sgt. Pepper's Lonely Hearts.* rso, 1978.

————. "Stayin' Alive." rso, 1977.

————. "You Should Be Dancing." rso, 1976.

Beginning of the End. "Funky Nassau." Alston, 1971.

Bell, Archie, & the Drells. "Dance Your Troubles Away." Philadelphia International, 1975.

————. "Let's Groove." Philadelphia International, 1975.

B-52's. "Rock Lobster." Warner Bros., 1979.

Biddu Orchestra. *Blue Eyed Soul.* Epic, 1975.

Bimbo Jet. "El Bimbo." Scepter, 1975.

Bionic Boogie. "Risky Changes." Polydor, 1977.

Birkin, Jane, and Serge Gainsbourg. "Je T'Aime . . . Moi Non Plus." Antic, 1974.

Black Ivory. "Mainline." Buddah, 1979.

Blackbyrds. "Happy Music." Fantasy, 1975.

————. "Walking in Rhythm." Fantasy, 1974.

Blondie. "Atomic." Chrysalis, 1979.

————. "Call Me." Chrysalis, 1980.

————. "Heart of Glass." Chrysalis, 1978.

Blue Magic. "Magic of the Blue." Atco, 1975.

————. "We're On the Right Track." Atco, 1975.

Bohannon, Hamilton. "Disco Stomp." Dakar, 1975.

————. "Foot Stompin Music." Dakar, 1975.

————. "Let's Start the Dance." Mercury, 1978.

Booker T. & the MGs. "Melting Pot." Stax, 1971.

Bowie, David. *Young Americans.* rca, 1975.

Brainstorm. "Lovin' Is Really My Game." Tabu, 1977.

Brass Construction. *Brass Construction.* United Artists, 1975.

————. "Music Makes You Feel Like Dancing." United Artists, 1979.

Brenda and the Tabulations. "Let's Go All the Way (Down)." Chocolate City, 1977.

Bridgewater, Dee Dee. "Bad for Me." Elektra, 1979.

Brown, Genie. "Can't Stop Talking." Dunhill, 1973.

Brown, James. "Cold Sweat." King, 1967.

————. "Get Up I Feel Like Being a Sex Machine." King, 1970.

————. "Get Up I Feel Like Being Like [sic] a Sex Machine," from *Sex Machine.* King, 1970.

————. "Give It Up or Turnit a Loose," from *Sex Machine.* King, 1970.

————. "It's a New Day." King, 1970.

———. "It's Too Funky in Here." Polydor, 1979.

———. "Mother Popcorn (You Got to Have a Mother for Me)." King, 1969.

Brown, Peter. "Do Ya Wanna Get Funky With Me." TK, 1977.

———. "Love in Our Hearts." TK, 1979.

B. T. Express. "Do It ('Til You're Satisfied)." Scepter, 1974.

———. "Express." Scepter/Roadshow, 1974.

———. "Peace Pipe." Scepter/Roadshow, 1975.

Bumble Bee Unlimited. "Lady Bug." Red Greg, 1978.

———. "Love Bug." Red Greg, 1976.

Byrd, Bobby. "Hot Pants — I'm Coming, Coming, I'm Coming." BrownStone, 1971.

Candido. "Dancin' and Prancin'." Salsoul, 1979.

———. "Jingo." Salsoul, 1979.

———. "Thousand Finger Man." Salsoul, 1979.

Cara, Irene. "Flashdance . . . What a Feeling." Casablanca, 1983.

Carn, Jean. "Was That All It Was." Philadelphia International, 1979.

Cerrone. "Black Is Black." Cotillion, 1977.

———. "Call Me Tonight." Atlantic, 1979.

———. "Love in 'C' Minor." Cotillion, 1977.

———. "Midnight Lady." Cotillion, 1977.

———. *Supernature.* Cotillion, 1977.

———. "Supernature." Cotillion, 1977.

Chakachas. "Jungle Fever." Polydor, 1972.

Change. "A Lover's Holiday." RFC, 1980.

Charo and the Salsoul Orchestra. "Dance a Little Bit Closer." Salsoul, 1977.

Cher. "Take Me Home." Casablanca, 1979.

Chic. "Dance Dance Dance (Yowsah, Yowsah, Yowsah)." Atlantic, 1977.

———. "Good Times." Atlantic, 1979.

———. "Le Freak." Atlantic, 1978.

Chicago. "I'm a Man." Columbia, 1970.

———. "Street Player." Columbia, 1979.

Chocolat. *Kings of Clubs.* Salsoul, 1977.

C. J. & Co. "Devil's Gun." Westbound, 1977.

———. "We've Got Our Own Thing." Westbound, 1977.

Class Action featuring Christine Wiltshire. "Weekend." Sleeping Bag, 1983.

Clifford, Linda. "Runaway Love." Curtom, 1978.

Collins, Lynn. "Think (About It)." People, 1972.

Consumer Rapport. "Ease On Down the Road." Wing & a Prayer, 1975.

Cookie Monster & the Girls. "C Is for Cookie." Sesame Street, 1978.

Costandinos, Alec, and the Syncophonic Orchestra. *Romeo and Juliet.* Casablanca, 1978.

Creative Source. "Who Is He and What Is He to You?" Sussex, 1973.

Crown Heights Affair. "Say a Prayer for Two." De-Lite, 1978.

Curtis, Chantal. "Get Another Love." Key, 1979.

Cymande. "Bra." Janus, 1972.

Dash, Sarah. "Sinner Man." Kirshner, 1978.

Dees, Rick, and His Cast of Idiots. "Disco Duck." RSO, 1976.

De La Fe, Alfredo. "Hot to Trot." Criollo, 1979.

———. "My Favorite Things." Criollo, 1979.

Deodato, Eumir. "Night Cruiser." Warner Bros., 1980.

Dibango, Manu. "Soul Makossa." Atlantic, 1973.

Disco Dub Band. "For the Love of Money." Movers Records, 1976.

Disco Tex & the Sex-O-Lettes. "Get Dancin'." Chelsea, 1974.

Dinosaur. "Kiss Me Again." Sire, 1978.

Doobie Brothers. "Long Train Running." Warner Bros., 1973.

Doors. "Roadhouse Blues." Elektra, 1970.

Double Exposure. "My Love Is Free." Salsoul, 1976.

———. "Ten Percent." Salsoul, 1976.

Douglas, Carl. "Kung Fu Fighting." 20th Century, 1974.

Douglas, Carol. "Doctor's Orders." Midland International, 1974.

———. "Midnight Love Affair." Midland International, 1976.

Downing, Al. "I'll Be Holding On." Chess, 1974.

Downing, Don. "Dream World." Scepter, 1974.

Dozier, Lamont. "Going Back to My Roots." Warner Bros., 1977.

Dr. Buzzard's Original Savannah Band. "Cherchez la Femme." RCA, 1976.

———. *Dr. Buzzard's Original Savannah Band.* RCA, 1976.

———. "I'll Play the Fool." RCA, 1976.

———. "Sour and Sweet." RCA, 1976.

Duke, George. "I Want You for Myself." Epic, 1979.

Dury, Ian. "Hit Me with Your Rhythm Stick." Stiff, 1978.

Dynamic Corvettes. "Funky Music Is the Thing." Abet, 1975.

Earth, Wind & Fire. "Boogie Wonderland." ARC, 1979.

Easy Going. "Baby I Love You." Prism, 1979.

Ecstasy, Passion & Pain. "Ask Me." Roulette, 1974.

Ecstasy, Passion & Pain featuring Barbara Roy. "Touch and Go." Roulette, 1976.

El Coco. "Let's Get It Together." AVI, 1976.

Emotions. "I Don't Wanna Lose Your Love." Columbia, 1976.

Equals. "Black Skinned Blue Eyed Boys." President, 1970.

Executive Suite. "When the Fuel Runs Out." Babylon, 1974.

Extensions from (212). "Manhattan Shuffle." Friends & Co., 1979.

Exuma. "Exuma, the Obeah Man." Mercury, 1969.

Fair, Yvonne. "It Should Have Been Me." Motown, 1975.

Faithfull, Marianne. "Why D'Ya Do It?" Island, 1979.

Fatback. "King Tim III (Personality Jock)." Spring, 1979.

Fidenco, Nico. *Emanuelle Nera.* West End, 1976.

First Choice. "Armed and Extremely Dangerous." Philly Groove, 1973.

———. *Delusions.* Gold Mind, 1977.

———. "Double Cross." Gold Mind, 1979.

———. "Doctor Love." Gold Mind, 1977.

———. "Guilty." Philly Groove, 1974.

———. *Hold Your Horses.* Gold Mind, 1979.

———. "Hold Your Horses." Gold Mind, 1978.

———. "Let No Man Put Asunder." Gold Mind, 1977.

———. "Love and Happiness." Philly Groove, 1973.

———. "Love Thang." Gold Mind, 1979.

———. "Newsy Neighbors." Philly Groove, 1973.

———. "Smarty Pants." Philly Groove, 1973.

———. *So Let Us Entertain You.* Warner Bros., 1976.

———. "The Player." Philly Groove, 1973.

Four Tops. "I Can't Help Myself (Sugar Pie Honey Bunch)." Motown, 1965.

———. "Still Waters." Motown, 1970.

Franklin, Aretha. "Ain't No Way." Atlantic, 1968.

———. "Respect." Atlantic, 1967.

Front Page. "Love Insurance." Panorama, 1979.

Funk Machine. "Funk Machine." TK, 1977.

Gardner, Taana. "When You Touch Me." West End, 1979.

———. "Work That Body." West End, 1979.

Gaye, Marvin. "I Heard It Through the Grapevine." Tamla, 1968.

———. "What's Going On." Tamla, 1971.

Gaynor, Gloria. "Casanova Brown." MGM, 1975.

———. "I Will Survive." Polydor, 1978.

———. "(If You Want It) Do It Yourself." MGM, 1975.

———. "How High the Moon." MGM, 1975.

———. *Never Can Say Goodbye.* MGM, 1975.

———. "Never Can Say Goodbye." MGM, 1974.

———. *Park Avenue Sound.* Polydor, 1978.

———. "Substitute." Polydor, 1978.

Gentry, Bobbie. "Ode to Billie Joe." Capitol, 1967.

Giorgio. *From Here to Eternity.* Casablanca, 1977.

Glass House. "I Can't Be You (You Can't Be Me)." Invictus, 1970.

Grant, Eddy. "Living on the Frontline." Epic, 1978.

———. "Walking on Sunshine." Epic, 1979.

Green, Al. "Let's Stay Together." Hi, 1971.

———. "Love and Happiness." Hi, 1972.

Green, Jesse. "Nice & Slow." Scepter, 1976.

Hammond, Johnny. "Los Conquistadores Chocolatés." Fantasy, 1975.

Harris, Damon. "It's Music." Fantasy/WMOT, 1978.

Hartman, Dan. "Instant Replay." Blue Sky, 1978.

———. "Vertigo/Relight My Fire." Blue Sky, 1979.

Hayes, Isaac. "By the Time I Get to Phoenix." Enterprise, 1969.

———. *Hot Buttered Soul.* Enterprise, 1969.

———. "Theme from Shaft." Enterprise, 1971.

Heart and Soul Orchestra. "Love in C' Minor." Casablanca, 1977.

Hendrix, Jimi. *Band of Gypsys.* Capitol, 1970.

Holloway, Brenda. "Just Look What You've Done." Tamla, 1967.

Holloway, Loleatta. "Dreamin'." Gold Mind, 1976.

———. "The Greatest Performance of My Life." Gold Mind, 1979.

———. "Hit and Run." Gold Mind, 1977.

———. "I May Not Be There When You Want Me (But I'm Right On Time)." Gold Mind, 1978.

———. "Is It Just a Man's Way?" Gold Mind, 1976.

———. *Loleatta.* Gold Mind, 1976.

———. "Love Sensation." Gold Mind, 1980.

———. *Queen of the Night.* Gold Mind, 1978.

———. "We're Getting Stronger (The Longer We Stay Together)." Gold Mind, 1977.

Horne, Jimmy "Bo." "Gimme Some." Alston, 1975.

———. "Spank." Sunshine Sound, 1978.

Houston, Thelma. "Don't Leave Me This Way." Tamla, 1976.

———. "I'm Here Again." Tamla, 1977.

Hues Corporation. "Rock the Boat." RCA, 1973.

———. "Rockin' Soul." RCA, 1974.

Hutch, Willie. "Brother's Gonna Work it Out." Motown, 1973.

———. "Love Power." Motown, 1975.

Inner Life featuring Jocelyn Brown. "I'm Caught Up (In a One Night Love Affair)." Prelude, 1979.

———. "Make It Last Forever." Salsoul, 1979.

Instant Funk. "Bodyshine." Salsoul, 1979.

———. "I Got My Mind Made Up (You Can Get It Girl)." Salsoul, 1978.

———. "Slap Slap Lickedy Lap." Salsoul, 1979.

Intruders. "I'll Always Love My Mama." Philadelphia International, 1973.

———. "(We'll Be) United." Gamble, 1966.

Isley Brothers. "Get Into Something." T-Neck, 1970.

Jackson, Jermaine. "Erucu." Motown, 1975.

Jackson 5. "ABC." Motown, 1970.

Jacobs, Debbie. "Don't You Want My Love." MCA, 1979.

Jakki. "You Are the Star." West End, 1976.

J.B.'s. "Gimme Some More." People, 1972.

Jiani, Carol. "Hit and Run Lover." Unidisc, 1980.

Johnson, General. "Can't Nobody Love Me Like You." Arista, 1978.

Johnston, Bruce. "Pipeline." Columbia, 1977.

Jones, Grace. *Fame*. Island, 1978.

———. "I Need a Man." Beam Junction, 1977.

———. *Portfolio*. Island, 1977.

———. "Sorry." Beam Junction, 1976.

———. "That's the Trouble." Beam Junction, 1976.

Jones, Juggy Murray. "Inside America." Jupiter, 1976.

Jones, Tamiko. "Can't Live Without Your Love." Polydor, 1979.

Jones Girls. "You Gonna Make Me Love Somebody Else." Philadelphia International, 1979.

Joneses. "Love Inflation." Mercury, 1974.

———. "Sugar Pie Guy." Mercury, 1974.

Joseph, Margie. "Prophecy." Cotillion, 1976.

Kane, Madleen. "Rough Diamond." Warner Bros., 1978.

Kat Mandu. "The Break." TK, 1979.

———. "Don't Stop, Keep On." Marlin, 1979.

KC & the Sunshine Band. "Get Down Tonight." TK, 1975.

———. "(Shake, Shake, Shake) Shake Your Booty." TK, 1975.

———. "That's the Way (I Like It)." TK, 1975.

Kelly, Roberta. "Trouble Maker." Oasis, 1976.

Kendricks, Eddie. "Date with the Rain." Tamla, 1972.

———. "Girl You Need a Change of Mind." Tamla, 1972.

———. "Goin' Up in Smoke." Tamla, 1976.

———. "Keep On Truckin'." Tamla, 1973.

———. *People . . . Hold On*. Tamla, 1972.

Khan, Chaka. "I'm Every Woman." Warner Bros., 1978.

King, B.B. "Philadelphia." ABC, 1974.

King, Evelyn "Champagne." "Shame." RCA, 1977.

King, Morgana. "A Taste of Honey." Mainstream, 1964.

King Crimson. *In the Court of the Crimson King*. Atlantic, 1969.

Kinney, Fern. "Groove Me." Malaco, 1979.

Knight, Gladys, & the Pips. "Got Myself a Good Man." Soul, 1969.

———. "I've Got to Use My Imagination." Buddah, 1973.

———. "It's a Better Than Good Time." Buddah, 1978.

———. "It's Time to Go Now." Soul, 1967.

———. "Make Yours a Happy Home." Buddah, 1974.

Kool and the Gang. "Open Sesame." De-Lite, 1976.

Kraftwerk. *Autobahn*. Vertigo, 1974.

———. "Metal on Metal." Capitol, 1977.

———. *Trans-Europe Express*. Capitol, 1977.

———. "Trans-Europe Express." Capitol, 1977.

LaBelle. "Lady Marmalade." Epic, 1974.

———. "Messin' With My Mind." Epic, 1975.

———. *Nightbirds*. Epic, 1974.

———. "What Can I Do for You?" Epic, 1974.

LaBelle, Patti. "Music Is My Way of Life." Epic, 1979.

Lane, Suzi. "Harmony." Elektra, 1979.

LaRue, D. C. "Cathedrals." Pyramid, 1976.

LaSalle, Denise. "Freedom to Express Yourself." ABC, 1977.

LaVette, Bettye. "Doin' the Best That I Can." West End, 1978.

Led Zeppelin. "Immigrant Song." Atlantic, 1970.

———. "Whole Lotta Love." Atlantic, 1969.

Lee, Dick, Sound of Inner City. "Mary Hartman, Mary Hartman." West End, 1976.

Lee, Laura. "(If You Want to Try Love Again) Remember Me." Invictus, 1973.

Lemon. "A-Freak-A." Prelude, 1978.

Lepage, Denis. "Hot Wax." Celsius, n.d.

Lewis, Ramsey. "Sun Goddess." Columbia, 1974.

Lipps Inc. "Funkytown." Casablanca, 1980.

———. "Funkytown (promotional 12")." Casablanca, 1979.

Liquid Gold. "My Baby's Baby." Creole, 1978.

Little Sister. "You're the One." Stone Flower, 1970.

Love, Luis. "Manhattan." [Unreleased.]

Love and Kisses. *How Much, How Much I Love You*. Casablanca, 1978.

———. "I Found Love (Now That I Found You)." Casablanca, 1977.

———. *Love and Kisses*. Casablanca, 1977.

Love Committee. "Just As Long As I Got You." Salsoul, 1978.

———. "Law and Order (Walter Gibbons remix)." Salsoul, 1978.

———. "Law and Order (Tom Moulton mix)." Salsoul, 1978.

Love De-Luxe. "Here Comes That Sound Again." Warner Bros., 1979.

Love Unlimited. "Love's Theme." 20th Century, 1973.

———. *Under the Influence of . . .* 20th Century, 1973.

———. "Walkin' in the Rain With the One I Love." Uni, 1972.

Love Unlimited Orchestra. "Love's Theme." 20th Century, 1973.

———. "My Sweet Summer Suite." 20th Century, 1976.

Lucas, Carrie. "I Gotta Keep Dancin'." Soul Train, 1977.

Lynn, Cheryl. "Got to Be Real." Columbia, 1978.

———. "Star Love." Columbia, 1978.

MacDonald, Ralph. "Calypso Breakdown." Marlin, 1976.

Machine. "There But for the Grace of God Go I." RCA, 1979.

Madonna. "Vogue." Sire, 1990.

Main Ingredient. "Happiness Is Just Around the Bend." RCA, 1974.

Mangione, Chuck, with the Hamilton Philharmonic Orchestra. "Land of Make Believe." Phonogram, 1973.

Marie, Kelly. "Feels Like I'm in Love." Calibre, 1980.

Marketts. "Out of Limits." Warner Bros., 1963.

Martin Circus. "Disco Circus." Prelude, 1979.

Mayfield, Curtis. "Move On Up." Curtom, 1971.

McCoy, Van. "The Hustle." Avco, 1975.

———. "Indian Warpath." H&L, 1976.

———. "Rhythms of the World." H&L, 1976.

———. "Soul Cha Cha." H&L, 1976.

McCrae, George. "Rock Your Baby." TK, 1974.

McFadden and Whitehead. "Ain't No Stoppin' Us Now." Philadelphia International, 1979.

Melvin, Harold, & the Blue Notes. "Bad Luck." Philadelphia International, 1975.

———. "If You Don't Know Me By Now." Philadelphia International, 1972.

———. "The Love I Lost." Philadelphia International, 1973.

———. *To Be True*. Philadelphia International, 1975.

———. "Wake Up Everybody." Philadelphia International, 1975.

Mendes, Sergio. "I'll Tell You." Elektra, 1979.

MFSB. "K-Jee." Philadelphia International, 1975.

———. "Let's Go Disco." Philadelphia International, 1975.

———. "Love Is the Message." Philadelphia International, 1973.

———. "Love Is the Message (Remix)." Philadelphia International, 1977.

———. *TSOP (The Sound of Philadelphia)*. Philadelphia International, 1973.

———. *Universal Love*. Philadelphia International, 1975.

MFSB featuring the Three Degrees. "TSOP (The Sound of Philadelphia)." Philadelphia International, 1973.

Michele. "Disco Dance." West End, 1978.

———. *Magic Love*. West End, 1977.

Mighty Clouds of Joy. "Mighty High." ABC, 1975.

Mills, Stephanie. "Put Your Body In It." 20th Century, 1979.

Modulations. "I Can't Fight Your Love." Buddah, 1974.

Moment of Truth. "Helplessly." Roulette, 1975.

Moore, Jackie. "This Time Baby." Columbia, 1979.

Moroder. "E=MC²." Casablanca, 1979.

Morrison, Dorothy. "Rain." Elektra, 1971.

Morrison, Van. *Astral Weeks*. Warner Bros., 1968.

Muhammad, Idris. "Could Heaven Ever Be Like This." Kudu, 1977.

Murphy, Walter, Band. "A Fifth of Beethoven." Private Stock, 1976.

Musique. "In the Bush." Prelude, 1978.

———. *Keep On Jumpin'* . Prelude, 1978.

New Birth. "Deeper." Warner Bros., 1977.

Nichols, Billy. "Give Your Body Up to the Music." West End, 1979.

Nightlife Unlimited. "The Love Is in You (No. 2)." Unidisc, 1979.

North End. "Kind of Life (Kind of Love)." West End, 1979.

Odyssey. "Native New Yorker." RCA, 1977.

O'Jays. "Back Stabbers." Philadelphia International, 1972.

———. "For the Love of Money." Philadelphia International, 1973.

———. "I Love Music." Philadelphia International, 1975.

———. "Love Train." Philadelphia International, 1972.

———. "Message in Our Music." Philadelphia International, 1976.

Olatunji. "Jin-Go-Lo-Ba (Drums of Passion)." Columbia, 1959.

One Way featuring Al Hudson. "Music." MCA, 1979.

Originals. "Down to Love Town." Motown, 1976.

Osibisa. *Osibisa*. Decca, 1971.

———. "Survival." Decca, 1971.

Osmond Brothers. "One Bad Apple." MGM, 1970.

Ozo. "Anambra." DJM, 1976.

Pagán, Bruni. "Fantasy." Elektra, 1979.

Page, Gene. "Satin Soul." Atlantic, 1974.

Parliament. *Funkentelechy vs. the Placebo Syndrome*. Casablanca, 1977.

Passengers. "Hot Leather." Uniwave, 1980.

Patti Jo. "Make Me Believe in You." Wand, 1973.

———. "Make Me Believe in You." Scepter, 1975.

Pendergrass, Teddy. "I Don't Love You Anymore." Philadelphia International, 1977.

———. "The More I Get, the More I Want." Philadelphia International, 1977.

———. "Only You." Philadelphia International, 1978.

———. "You Can't Hide From Yourself." Philadelphia International, 1977.

Pennington, Barbara. "Twenty-four Hours a Day." United Artists, 1977.

Phillips, Esther. "What a Diff'rence a Day Makes." CTI, 1975.

Phreek. "Weekend." Atlantic, 1978.

Pickett, Wilson. "Don't Knock My Love." Atlantic, 1971.

———. "Don't Let the Green Grass Fool You." Atlantic, 1970.

———. "I'm a Midnight Mover." Atlantic, 1968.

Pleasure. "Take a Chance." Fantasy, 1980.

Pointer, Bonnie. "Heaven Must Have Sent You." Motown, 1979.

Pointer Sisters. "Yes We Can Can." Blue Thumb, 1973.

Positive Force. "We Got the Funk." Turbo, 1979.

Queen Samantha. "Take a Chance." TK, 1979.

Raes. "Don't Turn Around." A&M, 1979.

Rare Earth. "Get Ready." Rare Earth, 1969.

———. "Happy Song." Rare Earth, 1975.

Rawls, Lou. "You'll Never Find Another Love Like Mine." Philadelphia International, 1976.

Ray, Don. "Got to Have Loving." Polydor, 1978.

———. "Standing in the Rain." Polydor, 1978.

Redd, Sharon. "Beat the Street." Prelude, 1982.

Resonance. "Yellow Train." Celebration, 1976.

Reynolds, Margaret. "Keep On Holding On." Sunshine Sound, 1979.

Rinder, Lauren, & W. Michael Lewis. "Lust." AVI, 1977.

Riperton, Minnie. "Stick Together." Epic, 1976.

Ripple. "The Beat Goes On and On." Salsoul, 1977.

Risco Connection. "Ain't No Stopping Us Now." Black Rose Music, 1979.

Ritchie Family. *African Queens.* Marlin, 1977.

———. "African Queens." Marlin, 1977.

———. *Arabian Nights.* Marlin, 1976.

———. "The Best Disco in Town." Marlin, 1976.

———. *Brazil.* 20th Century, 1975.

———. "Brazil." 20th Century, 1975.

Robinson, Vicki Sue. "Turn the Beat Around." RCA, 1976.

Rockin' Horse. "Love Do Me Right." RCA, 1975.

Rolling Stones. "(I Can't Get No) Satisfaction." London, 1965.

———. "Let's Spend the Night Together." London, 1967.

———. "Miss You." Atco, 1978.

Ross, Diana. "Ain't No Mountain High Enough." Motown, 1970.

———. "The Boss." Motown, 1979.

———. "Love Hangover." Motown, 1976.

———. "Once in the Morning." Motown, 1979.

Roussos, Demis. "L.O.V.E. Got a Hold of Me." Phonogram, 1976.

Ruffin, Jimmy. "Tell Me What You Want." Chess, 1974.

Rufus & Chaka Khan. "Any Love." MCA, 1979.

Ryder, Mitch, & the Detroit Wheels. *The Detroit-Memphis Experiment.* Dot, 1969.

Salsoul Orchestra. *Christmas Jollies.* Salsoul, 1976.

———. "Fiddler on the Roof." Salsoul, 1978.

———. "It's Good for the Soul." Salsoul, 1976.

———. "Magic Bird of Fire." Salsoul, 1977.

———. *Magic Journey.* Salsoul, 1977.

———. *Nice 'n' Naasty.* Salsoul, 1976.

———. "Nice 'n' Naasty." Salsoul, 1976.

———. "Nice Vibes." Salsoul, 1975.

———. "Ooh, I Love It (Love Break)." Salsoul, 1975.

———. "Ritzy Mambo." Salsoul, 1976.

———. "Salsoul Hustle." Salsoul, 1975.

———. *Salsoul Orchestra.* Salsoul, 1975.

———. *Salsoul Orchestra's Greatest Disco Hits.* Salsoul, 1978.

———. "Salsoul 2001." Salsoul, 1976.

———. "Salsoul 3001." Salsoul, 1976.

———. *Saturday Night Disco Party*. Salsoul, 1978.

———. "Standing and Waiting on Love." Salsoul, 1976.

———. "212 North 12th." Salsoul, 1979.

———. *Up the Yellow Brick Road*. Salsoul, 1978.

———. "You're Just the Right Size." Salsoul, 1975.

Salsoul Orchestra featuring Cognac. "How High." Salsoul, 1979.

Salsoul Orchestra featuring Loleatta Holloway. "Runaway." Salsoul, 1977.

Sam and Dave. "Hold On! I'm a Coming." Stax, 1966.

Santana. "Jingo." Columbia, 1969.

Scott-Heron, Gil. "The Bottle." Arista, 1976.

Sessomatto. *Sessomatto*. West End, 1976.

Sex Pistols. *Never Mind the Bollocks*. Warner Bros., 1977.

Shalamar. "Right in the Socket." Solar, 1979.

———. "Uptown Festival." Soul Train, 1977.

Shirley & Company. "Shame, Shame, Shame." Vibration, 1974.

Sigler, Bunny. "By the Way You Dance (I Knew It Was You)." Gold Mind, 1979.

Silver Convention. "Fly, Robin, Fly." Midland International, 1975.

———. "Save Me." Midland International, 1975.

Sister Sledge. "Love Don't You Go Through No Changes On Me." Atco, 1974.

———. "We Are Family." Cotillion, 1979.

Skatt Bros. "Walk the Night." Casablanca, 1979.

Skyy. "First Time Around." Salsoul, 1979.

Slick. "Space Bass." Fantasy, 1979.

Smith, Lonnie Liston. "Expansions." Flying Dutchman, 1975.

Soccio, Gino. "Dancer." RFC, 1979.

Sound Experience. "He's Looking Good, and Moving Fast." Buddah, 1975.

South Shore Commission. "Free Man." Wand, 1975.

Spencer, Gloria. "I Got It." Jaywalking, 1971.

Staple Singers. "I'll Take You There." Stax, 1972.

Starr, Edwin. "War." Gordy, 1970.

Staton, Candi. "Run to Me." Warner Bros., 1976.

———. "Young Hearts Run Free." Warner Bros., 1976.

Stevens, Cat. "Was a Dog a Doughnut." A&M, 1977.

Stewart, Rod. "Da Ya Think I'm Sexy?" Warner Bros., 1978.

Strafe. "Set It Off." Jus Born, 1984.

Streisand, Barbra, and Donna Summer. "No More Tears (Enough Is Enough)." Columbia, 1979.

Stylistics. "Hey Girl, Come and Get It." Avco, 1974.

Sugarhill Gang. "Rapper's Delight." Sugar Hill Records, 1979.

Summer, Donna. *A Love Trilogy*. Oasis, 1976.

———. "Autumn Changes." Casablanca, 1976.

———. *Bad Girls*. Casablanca, 1979.

———. "Bad Girls." Casablanca, 1979.

———. *Four Seasons of Love*. Casablanca, 1976.

———. "Hostage." Oasis, 1974.

———. "Hot Stuff." Casablanca, 1979.

———. "I Feel Love." Casablanca, 1977.

———. *I Remember Yesterday*. Casablanca, 1977.

———. "Lady of the Night." Oasis, 1974.

———. "Last Dance." Casablanca, 1978.

———. *Love to Love You Baby*. Oasis, 1975.

———. "Love to Love You Baby." Oasis, 1975.

———. "MacArthur Park Suite." Casablanca, 1978.

———. *Once Upon a Time*. Casablanca, 1977.

———. "She Works Hard for the Money." Mercury, 1983.

———. "Spring Affair." Casablanca, 1976.

———. "Summer Fever." Casablanca, 1976.

———. *The Wanderer*. Geffen, 1980.

Supremes. "Let Yourself Go." Motown, 1976.

———. "Love I Never Knew You Could Feel So Good." Motown, 1976.

———. "Stoned Love." Motown, 1970.

———. "Up the Ladder to the Roof." Motown, 1970.

———. "You're My Driving Wheel." Motown, 1976.

Sylvester. "Can't Stop Dancing." Fantasy, 1979.

———. "Dance (Disco Heat)." Fantasy, 1978.

———. "I Need Somebody to Love Tonight." Fantasy, 1979.

———. "In My Fantasy (I Want You, I Need You)." Fantasy, 1979.

———. "Over and Over." Fantasy, 1977.

———. "Stars." Fantasy, 1979.

———. *Sylvester*. Fantasy, 1977.

———. "You Make Me Feel (Mighty Real)." Fantasy, 1978.

T-Connection. "Do What You Wanna Do." TK, 1977.

Talking Heads. "I Zimbra." Sire, 1979.

———."Take Me to the River." Sire, 1978.

Tantra. "Hills of Katmandu." Philips, 1980.

Taste of Honey. "Boogie Oogie Oogie." Capitol, 1978.

Tavares. "Don't Take Away the Music." Capitol, 1976.

———. "Heaven Must Be Missing an Angel." Capitol, 1976.

———. "It Only Takes a Minute." Capitol, 1975.

Tee, Richard. "First Love." Columbia, 1979.

Temptations. "Happy People." Gordy, 1974.

———. "I Can't Get Next to You." Gordy, 1969.

———. "Law of the Land." Gordy, 1973.

———. "Papa Was a Rolling Stone." Gordy, 1972.

Third World. "Now That We Found Love." Island, 1978.

THP Orchestra. "Two Hot for Love." Butterfly, 1977.

Three Degrees. "Dirty Ol' Man." Philadelphia International, 1973.

———. "Giving Up, Giving In." Ariola, 1978.

———. *New Dimensions*. Ariola, 1978.

Titanic. "Sultana." RCA, 1971.

TJM. "Put Yourself in My Place." Tom & Jerry, 1979.

Todd, Pam, and Love Exchange. "Let's Get Together." Shyrlden, 1979.

Traffic. "Glad." United Artists, 1970.

Trammps. "Body Contact Contract." Atlantic, 1977.

———. "Disco Inferno." Atlantic, 1977.

———. "Disco Party." Atlantic, 1976.

———. "Hooked for Life." Atlantic, 1975.

———. "Love Epidemic." Golden Fleece, 1973.

———. "Starvin'." Atlantic, 1977.

———. "That's Where the Happy People Go." Atlantic, 1976.

———. *III*. Atlantic, 1978.

———. *Where the Happy People Go*. Atlantic, 1976.

———. "Zing Went the Strings of My Heart." Buddah, 1972.

Tribe. "Koke." ABC, 1973.

Troiano. "We All Need Love." Capitol, 1979.

Troubadours du Roi Baudouin. "Missa Luba." Philips, 1969.

True, Andrea, Connection. "More, More, More." Buddah, 1976.

———. "What's Your Name, What's Your Number." Buddah, 1977.

Twennynine featuring Lenny White. "Fancy Dancer." Elektra, 1980.

Two Man Sound. "Que Tal America." Miracle, 1978.

Ultra High Frequency. "We're On the Right Track." Scepter, 1973.

Undisputed Truth. "You + Me = Love." Whitfield, 1976.

Universal Mind. "Something Fishy Going On." Red Coach, 1974.

USA-European Connection. *Come Into My Heart*. Marlin, 1978.

———. *USA-European Connection*. Marlin, 1979.

Valentino. "I Was Born This Way." Gaiee, 1975.

Vaness, Theo. "Sentimentally It's You." Prelude, 1979.

Various. *Cooley High Original Soundtrack*. "2 Pigs and a Hog." Motown, 1975.

———. *Disco Boogie: Super Hits for Non-Stop Dancing*. Salsoul, 1977.

———. *Disco Gold*. Scepter, 1975.

———. *Disco Madness*. Salsoul, 1979.

———. *Philadelphia Classics*. Philadelphia International, 1977.

———. *Saturday Night Fever*. RSO, 1977.

———. *Thank God It's Friday*. Casablanca, 1978.

Village People. "In the Navy." Casablanca, 1979.

———. *Macho Man*. Casablanca, 1978.

———. *Village People*. Casablanca, 1977.

———. "YMCA." Casablanca, 1978.

Vitous, Miroslav. "New York City." Warner Bros., 1976.

Voyage. *Voyage*. Marlin, 1978.

War. "City, Country, City." United Artists, 1972.

———. "Galaxy." MCA, 1978.

———. "Low Rider." United Artists, 1975.

———. "The World Is a Ghetto." United Artists, 1972.

Ward, Anita. "Ring My Bell." TK, 1979.

Warwick, Dionne. "Take It from Me." Warner Bros., 1975.

Wesley, Fred. "House Party." RSO/Curtom, 1980.

Whispers. "And the Beat Goes On." Solar, 1979.

White, Barry. "Honey Please, Can't Ya See." 20th Century, 1973.

———. "I'm Gonna Love You Just a Little More Baby." 20th Century, 1973.

———. "I've Got So Much to Give." 20th Century, 1973.

———. "It's Ecstasy When You Lay Down Next to Me." 20th Century, 1977.

———. "Never, Never Gonna Give Ya Up." 20th Century, 1973.

———. "Standing in the Shadows of Love." 20th Century, 1973.

———. "You're the First, the Last, My Everything." 20th Century, 1974.

Whitney, Marva. "It's My Thing (You Can't Tell Me Who to Sock It to)." King, 1969.

Williams, David. "Come On Down Boogie People." AVI, 1978.

Williams, Lenny. "Choosing You." ABC, 1977.

Wills, Viola. "If You Could Read My Mind." Ariola, 1980.

Winners. "Get Ready for the Future." Ariola, 1978.

Winter, Edgar. "Above and Beyond." Blue Sky, 1979.

Wonder, Stevie. "Another Star." Tamla, 1976.

———. "I Wish." Tamla, 1976.

———. "Signed, Sealed, Delivered I'm Yours." Tamla, 1970.

———. "Sir Duke." Tamla, 1976.

———. *Songs in the Key of Life*. Tamla, 1976.

Wright, Betty. "If You Love Me Like You Say You Love Me." Alston, 1972.

———. "Where Is the Love." Alston, 1975.

Yellow Magic Orchestra. "Computer Game 'Theme from the Circus'." Horizon, 1979.

Young, Karen. "Hot Shot." West End, 1978.

Young, Retta. "My Man Is On His Way." All Platinum, 1977.

Zulema. "Giving Up." Sussex, 1973.

selected bibliography

Altman, Dennis. *Homosexual: Oppression and Liberation*. London: Angus and Robertson, 1972.

Attali, Jacques. *Noise: The Political Economy of Music*. Translated by Brian Massumi. Minneapolis: University of Minnesota Press, 1989.

Auerbach, Alexander. "Big Business Grows Bigger." In *Disco, The Book*, edited by Steve Tolin. New York: Talent & Booking Publishing, 1979.

Baker, Houston A. Jr. "Hybridity, the Rap Race, and Pedagogy for the 1990s." In *Technoculture: Cultural Politics*, vol. 3, edited by Constance Penley and Andrew Ross, 197–209. Minneapolis: University of Minnesota Press, 1991.

Brewster, Bill, and Frank Broughton. *Last Night a DJ Saved My Life: The History of the Disc Jockey*. London: Headline, 1999.

Brown, James. "The Programmers Withhold Judgement." In *Disco, The Book*, edited by Steve Tolin. New York: Talent & Booking Publishing, 1979.

Can't Stop the Music. [Film.] Anchor Bay, 1980, directed by Nancy Walker, screenplay by Bronte Wood and Allan Carr.

Carr, Roy, and Charles Shaar Murray. *David Bowie: An Illustrated Record*. London: Eel Pie Publishing, 1981.

Chafe, William H. *The Unfinished Journey: America Since World War II*. New York: Oxford University Press, 1999.

Cheren, Mel. *Keep On Dancin': My Life and the Paradise Garage*. New York: 24 Hours for Life, 2000.

Cohn, Nik. *Ball the Wall: Nik Cohn in the Age of Rock*. London: Picador, 1989.

Collin, Matthew, with John Godfrey. *Altered State: The Story of Ecstasy Culture and Acid House*. London: Serpent's Tail, 1997.

Crawford, Richard. *America's Musical Life*. New York: Norton, 2001.

Dannen, Frederic. *Hit Men: Power Brokers and Fast Money Inside the Music Business*. New York: Times Books, 1990.

Davis, Clive, with James Willwerth. *Clive: Inside the Record Business*. New York: William Morrow, 1975.

Denisoff, R. Serge. *Tarnished Gold: The Record Industry Revisited*. New Brunswick: Transaction Publishers, 1997.

Dery, Mark. *Escape Velocity: Cyberculture at the End of the Century*. New York: Grove Press, 1996.

Diebold, David. *Tribal Rites: San Francisco's Dance Music Phenomenon 1977–1988*. Northridge, Calif.: Time Warp Publishing, 1988.

Duberman, Martin. *Stonewall*. New York: Plume, 1994.

Duberman, Martin, Martha Vicinus, and George Chauncey Jr., eds. *Hidden From History: Reclaiming the Gay and Lesbian Past*. New York: Meridian, 1990.

Dyer, Richard. "In Defence of Disco." In *The Faber Book of Pop*, edited by Hanif Kureishi and Jon Savage, 518–27. London: Faber and Faber, 1995.

Emenheiser, Daniel A. "An Immense Market Emerges." In *Disco, The Book*, edited by Steve Tolin. New York: Talent & Booking Publishing, 1979.

Fikentscher, Kai. *"You Better Work!" Underground Dance Music in New York City*. Hanover: Wesleyan University Press, 2000.

Frith, Simon. *The Sociology of Rock*. London: Constable, 1978.

Frith, Simon, and Andrew Goodwin, eds. *On Record: Rock, Pop, and the Written Word*. New York: Pantheon Books, 1990.

Garber, Eric. "A Spectacle in Color: The Lesbian and Gay Subculture of Jazz Age Harlem." In *Hidden From History: Reclaiming the Gay and Lesbian Past*, edited by Martin Duberman, Martha Vicinus, and George Chauncey Jr., 318–31. New York: Meridian, 1990.

Garratt, Sheryl. *Adventures in Wonderland: A Decade of Club Culture*. London: Headline, 1998.

George, Nelson. *The Death of Rhythm & Blues*. New York: Plume, 1988.

Gilbert, Jeremy, and Ewan Pearson. *Discographies: Dance Music, Culture and the Politics of Sound*. London: Routledge, 1999.

Gilroy, Paul. *The Black Atlantic: Modernity and Double Consciousness*. Cambridge: Harvard University Press, 1994.

Goldman, Albert. *Disco*. New York: Hawthorn Books, 1978.

Haden-Guest, Anthony. *The Last Party: Studio 54, Disco, and the Culture of the Night*. New York: William Morrow, 1997.

Hazzard-Gordon, Katrina. *Jookin': the Rise of Social Dance Formations in African-American Culture*. Philadelphia: Temple University Press, 1990.

Hemment, Drew. "E Is for Ekstasis." *New Formations* 31 (summer 1996): 23–38.

Holleran, Andrew. *Dancer from the Dance*. New York: Plume, 1986.

Hollomon, Rick. "Few Label Themselves Disco." In *Disco, The Book*, edited by Steve Tolin. New York: Talent & Booking Publishing, 1979.

Holmstrom, John, ed. *Punk: The Original*. New York: Trans-High Publishing, 1996.

Hughes, Walter. "In the Empire of the Beat: Discipline and Disco." In *Microphone*

Fiends: Youth Music & Youth Culture, edited by Andrew Ross and Tricia Rose, 147–57. New York: Routledge, 1994.

Jones, Leroi [Amiri Baraka]. *Blues People: Negro Music in White America*. 1963. Reprint, London: MacGibbon & Kee, 1999.

Kaiser, Charles. *The Gay Metropolis, 1940–1996*. London: Weidenfeld and Nicolson, 1999.

Kempster, Chris, ed. *History of House*. London: Sanctuary, 1996.

Klute. [Film.] Warner Bros., 1971, directed by Alan Pakula, screenplay by Andy Lewis and Dave Lewis.

Kureishi, Hanif, and Jon Savage, eds. *The Faber Book of Pop*. London: Faber and Faber, 1995.

Marwick, Arthur. *The Sixties: Cultural Revolution in Britain, France, Italy, and the United States, c.1958-c.1974*. Oxford: Oxford University Press, 1998.

McCormack, Ed. "No Sober Person Dances." In *Dancing Madness*, edited by Abe Peck. New York: Anchor Books, 1976.

Mercer, Kobena. *Welcome to the Jungle: New Positions in Black Cultural Studies*. New York: Routledge, 1994.

Miller, D. A. *The Novel and the Police*. Berkeley and Los Angeles: University of California Press, 1988.

Miezitis, Vita. *Night Dancin'*. New York: Ballantine Books, 1980.

Neal, Mark Anthony. *What the Music Said: Black Popular Music and Black Public Culture*. London: Routledge, 1999.

Nutall, Jeff. *Bomb Culture*. London: MacGibbon & Kee, 1968.

Ostrow, Steve. "Saturday Night at the Baths: The Inside Story of the World Famous Continental Baths As Told By Its Founder." Unpublished manuscript.

Patterson, Lawrence Gray. "Changing Or Shrinking With Growth?" In *Disco, The Book*, edited by Steve Tolin. New York: Talent & Booking Publishing, 1979.

Peck, Abe, ed. *Dancing Madness*. New York: Anchor Press, 1976.

Penley, Constance, and Andrew Ross, eds. *Technoculture: Cultural Politics*. Minneapolis: University of Minnesota Press, 1991.

Postchardt, Ulf. *DJ-Culture*. Translated by Shaun Whiteside. London: Quartet Books, 1998 (1995).

Reynolds, Simon. *Energy Flash: A Journey Through Rave Music and Dance Culture*. London: Picador, 1998.

Ross, Andrew, and Tricia Rose, eds. *Microphone Fiends: Youth Music and Youth Culture*. London: Routledge, 1994.

Sanjek, Russell. *Pennies from Heaven: The American Popular Music Business in the Twentieth Century*. New York: Da Capo Press, 1996.

Saturday Night Fever. [Film.] Paramount Pictures, 1977, directed by John Badham, screenplay by Norman Wexler.

Savage, Jon. *England's Dreaming: Sex Pistols and Punk Rock*. London: Faber and Faber, 1991.

Shilts, Randy. *And the Band Played On: Politics, People, and the AIDS Epidemic*. New York: St. Martin's Press, 1987.

Sinker, Mark. "Electro Kinetik." In *History of House*, edited by Chris Kempster. London: Sanctuary Publishing, 1996, 93–102.

Smith, Richard. *Seduced and Abandoned: Essays on Gay Men and Popular Music*. London: Cassell, 1995.

Sontag, Susan. *Against Interpretation and Other Essays*. New York: Octagon Books, 1982.

Straw, Will. "The Booth, the Floor and the Wall: Dance Music and the Fear of Falling." *Public 8* (1993): 170–82.

———. "Popular Music As Cultural Commodity: The American Recorded Music Industries, 1976–1985." Ph.D. diss., McGill University, 1990.

Thank God It's Friday. [Film.] Casablanca Filmworks/Motown Productions, 1978, directed by Robert Klane, screenplay by Barry Armyn Bernstein.

Thornton, Sarah. *Club Cultures: Music, Media and Subcultural Capital*. Hanover, New Hampshire: Wesleyan University Press, 1996.

Tolin, Steve, ed. *Disco: The Book*. New York: Talent & Booking Publishing, 1979.

Toop, David. *Rap Attack 3: African Rap to Global Hip Hop*. London: Serpent's Tail, 2000.

Urban Cowboy. [Film.] Paramount Pictures, 1980, directed by James Bridges, screenplay by James Bridges.

White, Edmund. *States Of Desire: Travels in Gay America*. London: Picador, 1986.

index

Disco (music), 115, 116, 151, 167–68, 176–77, 206, 221–27, 284–85, 289, 308, 321–22, 333–34, 363–64, 366–67, 368, 370–71, 372–73, 385–94, 408, 410, 423, 430, 433, 438, 439; aesthetic, 122–23, 221, 224, 225, 289, 333–34, 380, 435; anonymity, 176, 177, 369, 371, 372; beat, 120, 167, 174, 224, 380, 381; black music, 221, 371–72, 376, 378, 380–82, 388, 436; disco beat, 120, 121–22, 174, 327, 381; *Disco Bible*, 334–35; disco divas, 178, 221, 254, 328–29, 371–72, 378, 379, 435; and drugs, 10, 268–69, 289, 328; Eurodisco, 175, 252–57, 306, 321, 436; and gay men, 192–93, 255–56, 259, 328, 329, 331–33, 376, 377–78, 383, 388, 391; independents, 436; opposition to, 221–22, 321–22, 333, 363, 365, 370, 373–82, 383, 385–88, 391–95, 400, 401, 407, 423–24, 438, 439; pop disco, 306, 438; problems with marketing, 209; and rap, 382, 384–85; re-categorized as dance music, 386, 438; rise of, 147–48; studio-driven music, 147, 167, 176, 177, 369, 371; symphonic music, 119, 142, 149, 206. *See also* Remixing; Twelve-inch singles
Discos/discotheques: in the 1960s, xi, 8, 14–17, 316; in the early 1970s, xi, 115–16, 435; in 1973, 115, 116; in 1974, 128, 151; in 1975, 181–85, 202; in 1976, 206, 233, 248; in 1977, 272, 284–85; in 1978, 315–18; in 1979 and after, 400, 430, 433, 434, 437, 439; breaking singles, 116; chains, 185, 248, 315, 316; as an entertainment complex, 248; in France, xi, 58, 183, 317–18; in Germany, 183, 317, 336; hostesses,

90; in Japan, 183, 317; rock discos, 394–95; roller discos, 396; safe havens, 53, 437; *Saturday Night Fever*, 307; in the Soviet Union, 318; and tapes, 41; in the U.K., 183, 318, 400; vulnerability to closure, 316, 400, 434, 437
Discothekin', 206, 207, 211, 228
DJs: African American, 132, 436; automatons, 185; breaking records, 112, 113–116, 142–46, 202, 213, 218, 435; club vs. radio, 155; David's Pot Belly, 115; dealing drugs, 151; as engineers of collage; 112; extended sets, 37, 85–86, 106; flexible workers, 14–15, 128, 248–49, 436; Italian American, 57–58, 69, 132, 435, 436; lack of recognition, 151–52, 156, 157; Latin, 211, 436; mixing, 34, 35–37, 56, 95, 96, 101, 106–8, 112, 134, 214–18, 334–35, 355–56; mobile DJs, 227–28; and professionalism, 207, 234–35, 249; vs. radio DJs, 155; relationship to venues, 434–35; remixing, 213, 214, 218, 220, 263–64, 268–69, 323, 411, 435, 436; storytelling, 56, 106, 355, 359; synergistic music making, xii, 14, 35, 37–39, 72, 108, 301, 358–59, 424, 434–35; tapes, 71–72, 145; with three turntables, 14, 125; women, 91–92, 227, 394. *See also* National Association of Discotheque Disc Jockeys; New York Record Pool; Record pools; Synergistic music making
Docks, 415
Dodd, Alan, 339, 413, 421
Double Exposure, 213, 218–20, 222, 225, 264, 324, 410
Downing, Al, 212
Downing, Don, 145–46

Tim Lawrence (tlawrence1@mac.com; http://www
.timlawrence.info) leads the Music Culture: Theory and
Production degree program at the University of East
London. He has written liner notes for *David Mancuso
Presents the Loft* and *Masters at Work: The Tenth
Anniversary Collection*.

Library of Congress Cataloging-in-Publication Data

Lawrence, Tim.

Love saves the day : a history of American dance music
culture 1970–1979 / Tim Lawrence.

p. cm.

Includes bibliographical references and index.

ISBN 0-8223-3185-3 (cloth : alk. paper)

ISBN 0-8223-3198-5 (pbk. : alk. paper)

1. Dance music—New York (State)—New York—20th
century—History and criticism. 2. Popular music—New
York (State)—New York—1971–1980—History and
criticism. 3. Popular culture—New York (State)—New
York—History—20th century. I. Title.

ML3411.5.L38   2003

306.4'84—dc21   2003010839